112696

B
FOSSE   Gottfried, Martin.

         All his jazz

$24.95

DATE			

112696

ALL HIS JAZZ

BOOKS BY MARTIN GOTTFRIED

All His Jazz: The Life and Death of Bob Fosse
Broadway Musicals
In Person: The Great Entertainers
Jed Harris: The Curse of Genius
Opening Nights
A Theater Divided

BANTAM BOOKS

NEW YORK · TORONTO · LONDON · SYDNEY · AUCKLAND

MARTIN
GOTTFRIED

THE LIFE & DEATH
OF BOB FOSSE

ALL
HIS
Jazz

ALL HIS JAZZ
A Bantam Book / December 1990

Library of Congress Cataloging-in-Publication Data
Gottfried, Martin.
   All his jazz : the life & death of Bob Fosse / Martin Gottfried.
     p.   cm.
   Includes index.
   ISBN 0-553-07038-X
   1. Fosse, Bob, 1927–1987. 2. Choreographers—United States—
Biography. I. Title.
GV1785.F67G68 1990
792.8×2×092—dc20
[B]   90-38650
                                 CIP

Published simultaneously in the United States and Canada

Bantam Books are published by Bantam Books, a division of Bantam Doubleday Dell Publishing Group, Inc. Its trademark, consisting of the words "Bantam Books" and the portrayal of a rooster, is Registered in U.S. Patent and Trademark Office and in other countries. Marca Registrada. Bantam Books, 666 Fifth Avenue, New York, New York 10103.

PRINTED IN THE UNITED STATES OF AMERICA
RRH 0 9 8 7 6 5 4 3 2 1

THIS IS FOR MY FRIENDS.

It is for Michael Alpert, Joan Brandt, Samantha Dean, Cy and Posy Feuer, Clive Hirschhorn, Janice Levin, Dottie Schott, Jerry and Jean Wexler, and my own personal social worker, Stephanie Sacks.

*M*y life is an open pamphlet.
—BOB FOSSE

ACKNOWLEDGMENTS

The writing of a book begins long before the writing of a book begins. This one began with all the Bob Fosse shows on Broadway, seen first as a young theatregoer and then as a professional drama critic. The research continued through a twenty-year acquaintanceship with Fosse, from visits, chance meetings, and strolls to conversations in person and on the telephone. In the same stretch of time, there were conversations and visits with Gwen Verdon, during the time of the marriage as well as through the years of separation.

As the book began to take form, the research also turned formal. Charles Grass was of particular and profound assistance. His memories and memorabilia about the Riff Brothers days provided much of the basis for the story of Fosse's formative years. Rosemary Tirio opened the doors of Chicago, admitting me to the Fosse high school years, his family and friends. My dearest Trudy Ship, who was the assistant editor on several Fosse movies, remembered them in astonishing detail and then became my first reader, editor, and critic.

The actual interviewing of sources—of Fosse's friends, girlfriends, dancers, collaborators, and colleagues—involved hundreds of people over many hundreds of hours. These retentive, articulate, and helpful people provided the memories, facts, and dialogue that are part of this book's foundation, and I am grateful for the time and material they provided so generously and amiably. They include

George Abbott, Richard Adler, Jay Presson Allen, Annette Schroeder Arnold, Jeff Ash, Jane Aurthur, Julian Barry, David Begelman, Nancy Bird, Ralph Burns, Sid Caesar, Elaine Cancilla, Stanley Carlfeldt, Saul Chaplin, Emile Charlap, Carol Wolff Chandler, Chris Chase, Wynn Chayefsky, Alexander H. Cohen, Edward Colton, Betty Comden, Georgia Creighton, Arlene Dahl, Roland DeFosse, Agnes de Mille, Kathryn Doby, Stanley Donen, Richard Dreyfuss, Fred Ebb, Dr. Edward Ettinger, Harvey Evans, John Fernbach, Patricia Ferrier, Cy

Feuer, Melvene Fitzpatrick, Cynthia Fosse, Margaret Fosse, Robert Fryer, Tess Foutris, Bruce Jay Friedman, Rita Gardner, Helen Gallagher, Ben Gazzara, Peter Gennaro, Larry Gelbart, Marion Geweke, Bob Gill, Rosemary Grass, Wolfgang Glattes, Adolph Green, Joel Grey, Buddy Hackett, Albert Hague, Renee Hague, Jay and Fredda Harris, Joseph Harris, Marion Hauser, Alan Heim, Peter Howard, Arnold Hughs, Dr. John Hutchinson, Bernard Jacobs, Page Johnson, Richard Kaliban, John Kander, Elia Kazan, Richard Kiley, Janet Klopfer, Richard Korthaze, Peter Kulok, Peter Larkin, Lionel Larner, Burton Lane, Janet Leigh, Warner Leroy, Viveca Lindfors, John Locke, Jo Loesser, Sidney Lumet, Ethel Martin, George Martin, Marsha Mason, John McMartin, Daniel Melnick, Buzz Miller, James Mitchell, Phyllis Newman, Jennifer Nairn-Smith, Jerry Orbach, Stuart Ostrow, Hermes Pan, Joseph Papp, David Picker, Dr. Jonathan Pincus, Harold Prince, Dr. Stanley Resor, Martin Richards, Jerome Robbins, Eric Roberts, Paul Rosenfield, John Rubinstein, Michael Rupert, Dr. Clifford Sager, Kim St. Leon, Jack Schaffer, Gus Schirmer, Jr., Herbert Schlein, Gerald Schoenfeld, Stephen Schwartz, Ilse Schwarzwald, Betsy Schulberg, Budd Schulberg, Stanley Simmons, Ellen Simon, Vicki Stein, Tony Stevens, Peter Stone, Elaine Stritch, Michel Stuart, Jule Styne, David Tebbetts, Michael Tolan, Miriam Ungerer, Mary Vagos, Tony Walton, Douglas Watt, Patty Watt, Eddie White, Robert Whitehead, John Willis, Albert Wolsky, and Patricia Zipprodt.

Steve Rubin of Bantam Doubleday Dell, and senior editor Fred Klein buoyed my spirits whenever an end seemed not at hand but out of reach. I am also grateful for Lauren Field's literary way with legal advice and to Anne Finlayson for editing my not always legible copy.

Finally and miraculously, I have once again survived the cruel and inhuman editing of Genevieve Young, in that process growing as a writer.

THE BOB RIFF STORY

"*I* never use my name to get anything.
Afraid someone will say, 'Bob who?'"

He showed up in high spirits. That was unusual because, for such a long time, he had worn gloom like an old and cozy sweater, his hands thrust deep in its pockets. He might not even have come to Washington but for the fact that the touring company of *Sweet Charity* had done so poorly in Philadelphia. Now, bad business in Washington might well cause the tour to be aborted altogether.

The day started easily enough. Fosse came to morning rehearsal with Gwen Verdon. They had been separated for fifteen years. Everyone thought that they were divorced, but the truth was that they never had been, and Gwen even signed her name "Mrs. Bob Fosse" on occasion. "A lot of people don't understand our relationship," she would say, "because Bob lives in his house and I live in mine. It's a very strange relationship, but I think it's wonderful." She seemed to think that because they were still married, they were still married.

At least they were best friends and closer than many married couples, but Bob always had girlfriends. Gwen even entertained them. Not everyone was able to understand that either.

The girlfriends were rarely seen at work. Bob's live-in for the past several years, Phoebe Ungerer, wasn't even in Washington. At work, which was the most important place for him, only Gwen was allowed at his side, and even then only for shows and never for movies. Once she accepted that, she willingly became his assistant, teaching steps to the kids in the shows and even shopping for props.

Hadn't she once been Gwen Verdon, the great Broadway dancing star?

Bob was cheerful at rehearsal, and in the afternoon he joked about the notes he was giving because, he said, they really weren't necessary, the show was in wonderful shape. The poor business in Philadelphia baffled him, he told the company, and he repeated what he had so often said before: "If you ever have any problems, call me. My number is in the book," as it was and always had been. Every unemployed actor in New York might be unlisted but not Bob Fosse. "And," he said, "if there is anything I can do to make sure we're a hit, don't worry, I'll do it."

Gwen was on stage, wearing her usual black—black sweater, black pants, just like Bob, who always wore black ("So there's no break in my body line"). *Sweet Charity* had originally been her great starring vehicle, but that was twenty-three years earlier. Now she was teaching her part to others, the steps and gestures and the bits of business that had once been so identified with her. This amazed other actors, who are so vain about their roles, so bitter about aging and about giving way to younger performers. But Gwen Verdon had taught this part to Shirley MacLaine and Juliet Prowse and Ann Reinking and Debbie Allen, and now she was teaching it to Donna McKechnie. Some of the kids had seen her demonstrating the dance steps, and one said, "Even at sixty-two, she's still the best of all."

Fosse was upstairs, rehearsing principals and running scenes. The granny glasses rested on his chest, hanging from a thin chain around his neck. His shoulders were hunched and his knees bent so that his body made a question mark, and he squinted up through the smoke that rose from the cigarette hanging from the corner of his mouth. He turned to his stage manager, Craig Jacobs, and asked, "How much time is left? How much stuff is left to get done?" Jacobs reminded him that he was due downstairs at an orchestra rehearsal, and that Cy Coleman, the show's composer, was there to check sound balances. Bob went downstairs. He and Coleman had been friends for a long time, and they listened to the band. Then Donna McKechnie and Lenora Nemetz, a featured player in the show, sang a number so that Cy and Bob could hear the balances between voices and orchestra.

Because it was opening night, the curtain time was early, and they broke off at the half-hour call, six-thirty. Bob told his secretary, Cathy Nicholas, that he and Gwen were going back to their hotel, the Willard, just down the street, to change for the show. They had separate rooms.

They strolled through the theatre lobby with Coleman and left him under the marquee. Forty-five minutes later the performance began. Craig Jacobs had started worrying even before the curtain rose. Bob had not been pacing the stage as he always had. Then he didn't show up at the intermission, when he would so often pop his head in, backstage, just to ask, "How do you think it's going?" Chet Walker, the dance captain, asked, "If we were as great as Bob said, why didn't he come?" It would have killed Fosse to hear that, and the musicians said that Cy Coleman hadn't been there either. The stage manager Jacobs was sure it was because the decision had been made to close the tour.

In fact, Bob never even made it to the Hotel Willard. As he and Gwen reached the corner of 13th and Pennsylvania Avenue, just down the street from the theatre, he collapsed and fell to the ground. Gwen dropped to her knees and cradled his head in her arms. A crowd gathered, and she urged the people away, assuring everyone that he was fine, which he hardly was. His eyes were half shut, and his complexion was green. She later told Cy Coleman she was sure that Bob was having an epileptic seizure.

Fosse was not having an epileptic seizure. He was having his last heart attack. A man in the gathering crowd identified himself as a doctor and knelt to loosen Bob's shirt and listen for his heartbeat. The doctor began to pound at his heart, but Fosse whispered, "Please stop. You're hurting me. I'm all right. Don't worry about me."

While the doctor ministered to Fosse, Gwen tried to disperse the crowd. She would later say that she hadn't wanted Bob to feel embarrassed by the public display or by the ugliness of lying in the street. She was a profoundly private person, and as if to undo the public event, she would later tell the press that it had all happened in the hotel room.

The ambulance took so long in coming that the fire trucks arrived first. The theatregoers at the opening night of *Sweet Charity* were returning to their seats after intermission while Bob was being sirened to George Washington University Hospital, and there, after an hour and forty-five minutes of emergency room efforts, he was pronounced dead.

At the end of *Sweet Charity*, the curtain fell, and the audience burst into applause. Craig Jacobs, the stage manager, noticed that Joey Harris was backstage. Harris was the show's co-producer, and it was unusual for him to be there. It was even more unusual for Peter Kulok, his general manager, to be there, but now it was all settled in Jacobs's mind. The reason that Fosse hadn't come, or Coleman or Gwen, was the same reason that Harris and Kulok were there. "We're going to have to close."

The company was finishing its bows. Bob had always been strict about curtain calls, never allowing more than two. "Treat curtain calls like a musical number," he would say. "They should be just as crisp." He hated to milk applause. As the curtain came down and stayed down, Kulok said to the stage manager, "You won't believe this in a million years. I have got to talk to the company." Jacobs was positive now that the tour was going to be shut down. "Do you think we should let them change?" Kulok asked. "Or call them right away?" "It'd probably be better to call them right away," the stage manager replied, and he raised his arms for everyone to remain on stage.

The actors and dancers encircled the general manager. The presence of outsiders on stage was always bad news, and talk of closing was already webbing the stage in dark jokes and whispers as the big curtain slowly rose to reveal the empty auditorium. Kulok looked grim as he paused before speaking.

"I have some very bad news for you," he began.

There was nervous shifting and a few wisecracks.

"Bobby passed away."

A hush. Somebody asked, "Bobby who?"

The company hairdresser was named Bobby Abbott, but he was standing right there.

"Bob Fosse," Kulok said. "He had a heart attack when he left rehearsal. Gwen was with him."

One of the girls began to sob.

"He was probably dead when he hit the floor," Kulok said, "so there was no great pain."

In response to a question, Harris replied, "Gwen's fine. She's under sedation."

A dancer's knees buckled, and she sagged. Chet Walker, the dance captain, screamed and fainted dead away. Mascara began to streak down cheeks. Wigs were peeled off, leaving the statuesque girls with damp hair pinned close to their scalps and melting makeup. Donna McKechnie began to tremble. She had first danced for Fosse twenty-five years earlier in *How to Succeed in Business Without Really Trying*. She had just come through the two-year dying of her ex-husband, another director, Michael Bennett. McKechnie sobbed convulsively, first in silence and then hysterically.

Cabaret was the other musical playing in Washington. It was at the Kennedy Center. Fosse's career had been revived when he directed the movie version of the show. He had won the Academy Award for it, and so had Joel Grey, who was again playing the master of ceremonies. On his way to the stage, someone whispered to him that Bob had died. "That's impossible," the actor said, but turning to the company manager he asked, "Is it true?" No answer was answer enough. Plunging ahead, he strolled onstage and into what he called "the wrap up," facing the audience and asking, "Where are your troubles now? Forgotten. I told you so. Here life is beautiful. The girls are beautiful. Even the orchestra is beautiful."

As usual, he took five beats.

Life is a cabaret, old chum
Life is a ca—

He looked around at the empty stage behind him.

Auf wiedershen

He took three beats.

À bientôt

"I saw Bob," he remembered, "out there where the audience was supposed to be." And so he bowed, he bowed to Fosse, and the lights blacked out. Then he fled into the wings, where he collapsed in sobs.

On stage at the National Theatre, Harris, the co-producer, was urging the *Sweet Charity* company to attend the opening night party at the Old Ebbitt Grill just behind the theatre. Getting drunk, he said, would help. Harris also made the arrangements, the next day, to send Bob's body back to New York. Gwen wouldn't allow it to be flown back. She and Bob had a long-standing agreement that they would never fly together because of their daughter Nicole "and," she said, "I'm not going to start now." So after arranging for a hearse to drive the body back to New York from Washington, Joey Harris hired a limousine for Gwen to follow behind on the five-hour journey to New York. At last her love had won out. Their marriage was restored. Bob was hers once again and forever.

He was not merely a healthy child but an almost perfect one, growing up on the not very well-to-do North Side of Chicago, where he had been born on June 23, 1927. And if his parents, like almost everyone else in America's working class, were sweating out the Depression years, at least his father, Cy Fosse, had a job (selling insurance), and there was enough food for Sadie, the five kids, and the two dogs.

Cyril Fosse was a short, slight man with the flushed complexion of a drinker. Physically overshadowed by his wife Sadie, he also lay in the shadow of her personality, for she was not only a large woman but a dynamic one. Cy Fosse might have himself profited from such expansiveness—after all, he was an insurance salesman and could have used the personality—but perhaps that was why he was not a world class insurance salesman.

His pleasures were meek. He took his membership in the Masons seriously, and regularly attended lodge meetings at his Masonic Temple, which was near Irving Park on the other side of Keeler. It was just a stroll from his rented red stone three-story house at 4428 North Paulina Street, a house looking up and down a row of similar houses. Otherwise, family was the focus of his life, and what money he made was spent on family. There was enough—at least there had been in the pre-Depression years— for a car and even a little rented summer cottage in Paw Paw, Michigan.

The house on Paulina was hardly grand, but it was big enough for everyone to have a room of his own. By 1935, that meant four boys— Cyril, Jr., Edward, Donald, and eight-year-old Robert Louis Fosse, who was named, at least he would later claim, for the writer Robert Louis Stevenson—and a daughter Patricia (Patsy). She was two years older than Bobby, but as the baby boy, one whose bouts with double pneumonia had twice scared the family, he was the pampered one.

Cy and Sadie were young at the time, forty-one and thirty-nine. She had been born Sara Alice Stanton, Irish and Catholic, but now they all went to the Methodist Church, and if there was any ethnic identity to the household it was Norwegian. Cy had been born in America, but his parents had come from Norway. Sara had been brought from Ireland in infancy, but his heritage prevailed, and at Christmastime the big tree was hung with paper and wooden Norwegian ornaments; everyone sang Norwegian folk songs and Sadie cooked Cy's favorite Norwegian dish, *rasperboller,* a broth with dumplings, which the children called "rusper-dodgers."

Many a living room is roped off from a family and saved for company but not in this house. Cy, who loved ballroom dancing, would put a record on the phonograph and practice the fox-trot with Sadie. He taught social dancing to his boys, but none of them learned it as well as Cyril, Jr., who followed his father's example in considering the name "Cyril" sissyish and insisted on being called "Buddy." Buddy Fosse would become a regular jitterbugger at the nearby Aragon Ballroom.

That was all right for a boy, learning social dancing from his dad, but as far as Sadie Fosse was concerned, for a girl formal dance school was essential. So when Patsy turned ten, she was enrolled in the Chicago Academy of Theatre Arts. It was a prospect that made her miserable because she was a shy and gangling girl who embarrassed easily. Before the first day of classes she wept so pitifully that eight-year-old Bobby was dispatched to keep her company. As the youngest, and the lowest in the pecking order, he could hardly protest, and it was unlikely that Buddy (twenty), Ed (nineteen), or Don (eighteen) would volunteer since dance school was considered strictly for the girls. So off he trooped with his towering sister. After that first day, Patsy's insistence that Bob continue to accompany her was the accidental turn of events that led to his taking dance classes himself.

In 1935, children's theatrical schools tended to extravagant names, the seedier the place the grander the title. The Chicago Academy of Theatre Arts only amounted to a couple of rooms in a converted apartment above a drugstore at the corner of Ashland and Montrose. Its managing director was Frederic Weaver, a dapper little fellow of forty-eight who inclined to pinstripe suits, red bow ties, vests, and spats. With the added accents of a monocle and a small, waxed mustache, he looked like a threadbare Adolphe Menjou, whom he claimed to have met at least once. But although he spoke with a vaguely British accent (which he attributed to life in Canada) the whole package had in fact come to Chicago from Wade County, Illinois, where Weaver's father was sheriff.

He liked to inform his diminutive charges, with a certain hauteur, that he had attended the Chicago Music College while Flo Ziegfeld had been the director, that he knew Irene Dunne and Gladys Swarthout, and that he had studied music theory with the illegitimate son of Richard Wagner. Frederic Weaver did indeed play the violin and also the piano, at least with two fingers, but his musicianship was never at issue since he did not teach at the Chicago Academy of Theatre Arts. He was the executive director, and he ran the place in the hope of developing child performers whom he might manage in professional situations. In those late days of vaudeville, there was still a market for "moppet acts," as they were called, and so Frederic Weaver was not in this just for the dollar or two an hour he got for shepherding forty or fifty youngsters through the after-school hours; Frederic Weaver was in show business.

Indeed, he loved show business, vaudeville especially, and it was a love that he instilled in little Bobby Fosse from the outset. Always formal, rarely removing his jacket, not even in the brutal heat of a Chicago summer, he would describe his favorite stage acts to the eight-year-old boy, man to man. And he delighted in every detail. "Once you have an act," he would say, "if it's top drawer, then you can do it the rest of your life. Sophie Tucker is doing it with 'Some of These Days,' Jolson did it with 'Toot, Toot, Tootsie,' and now Jimmy Durante is doing it with 'Inka Dinka Doo.' "

Love of vaudeville was the reason why, when Weaver bought the Academy in 1934, he had guided the curriculum away from classical ballet and toward tap, toe, and acrobatic dancing as well as musical instruments, radio announcing, and drama. He organized Peter Pan Productions to sell his school shows as fund-raisers and private entertainments for local organizations and lodges. Considering that his performers were not only unsalaried but were also paying students, he had a good thing going.

Weaver installed Marguerite Comerford as the head of his dance faculty of two. Privately he called her Trixie, but it was an intimacy that was allowed nobody else. It was a pet name used in public only when he was angry with her. She was, as he put it, his common-law wife. Marguerite Comerford's credentials were perhaps not as impressive as Weaver's, but they were probably more authentic. She had been a dancer with the Tiller line, a chorus well established in Chicago vaudeville, and she had assisted with its choreography before electing to make a life with Weaver. So it was Marguerite Comerford who taught Bob Fosse his first dance steps. It was she too who complained almost at once that the eight-year-old would not use his hands properly when he spread his arms. The idea, she repeated until she had to roll her eyes in despair, was for his palms to face either the floor or the ceiling, one or the other. Yet the small, slight, tow-haired boy stubbornly held his hands straight up, Oriental style, so that the palms faced the audience. And not only that. Despite Marguerite Comerford's insistence that he spread the arms wide and keep his fingers together, he resolutely tucked his elbows in and spread his fingers apart. It was really quite brazen, although his manner was disarmingly sweet, and after all he had been involuntarily sent to the Academy in the first place. He was so adamant about these opened fingers that Miss Comerford could only sigh and drop the subject, to pick it up again next class.

Although Fred Weaver was also pushing an accordion duo, the Olson Brothers (Doug and Don) who sang "Ma, He's Making Eyes at Me" and "Oh, Johnny," his efforts at theatrical management had thus far yielded only one viable act, a song and dance trio of nine-year-olds, Artie Miller, Hal Felman, and Charles Grass. Charles's mother Marie, whom he would later describe as "the original stage mother," cheerfully drove him to and from the Academy as well as to whatever engagements Mr. Weaver arranged for the act, which involved the boys performing two popular songs of the day, "The Love Bug Will Get You" and "His Head Tucked Underneath His Arm," in which Charlie Grass played the ghost. The three boys were to perform this routine for the last time in the Academy's 1936 school recital. Shortly afterward, Artie Miller's parents and the family of Hal Felman simultaneously announced the withdrawal of their progeny from artistic training. Fred Weaver did not consider Charlie Grass a solo performer, and there was only one available partner. That was the newcomer, the Fosse boy, but how long would he remain?

Paying for dance lessons was a measure of Cy Fosse's devotion to Sadie, because things were going no better for him than they were for most working-class Americans. Just when the Depression seemed to be easing, he lost his insurance sales job. There was a tense stretch before he found work as a traveling salesman with the Hershey Chocolate Company. That would keep him on the road the whole week, away from his family, and for little pay at that. The rent would absorb most of it, and he couldn't have considered dance lessons of high priority, particularly for Bob. He lost no opportunity to make fun of them.

On June 15, 1937, Patsy Fosse did her last dance at the Chicago Academy of Theatre Arts. It was in the school show, which the always continental Frederic Weaver called *La Folies de l'Academie*. The 1937 edition was subtitled "From Paris to Broadway" and proved all too cruelly that Patsy was not the Fosse headed for Broadway. She was still in the chorus while Bobby, who had made his stage debut at the age of nine in the 1936 show, was already master of ceremonies.

However, Cy Fosse was finding that dance lessons had become an unbearable addition to an already backbreaking budget. Buddy had gotten married and moved his bride into the house. The couple occupied the small apartment on the third floor, and although Sadie loved her daughter-in-law Margaret as her own, it still meant one more at dinner instead of one fewer.

Another strain Cy Fosse must have felt was the birth of a second daughter, Marianne, in 1937. His strain probably didn't compare to Sadie's. A twenty-two-year span of childbearing—six children, this last born when she was forty-one—was taking its toll.

Patsy, having been less than enthusiastic about starting dance lessons, hardly complained about the possibility of stopping them. Bobby, however, was thriving at the Academy, and at lesson time he would hurry out of his room, abandoning his electric trains and tin soldiers in midadventure to trip down the stairs and hurry his sister along. When Cy's financial back finally broke and with tuition arrears of sixty dollars already accumulated, he withdrew both children from the Academy. That was when Fred Weaver came to Bobby's rescue. He offered to place the youngster on scholarship loan, which not only assured uninterrupted lessons but also rescued the endangered vaudeville business, for Weaver promptly teamed the Fosse boy with Charles Grass. In return for the sixty dollars owed in tuition money and all future lessons, Cy Fosse assigned 15 percent of his son's earnings to Weaver until the boy was twenty-one.

Perhaps Cy Fosse resented the need to borrow, or perhaps he felt shame about seeming to be an inadequate father. Perhaps he felt guilty about signing away a piece of a ten-year-old's future. Perhaps that made him feel in some way less of a man himself and perhaps it was why he began to smirk even more about dance school.

Frederic Weaver was only five years older than Cy Fosse, but he could not have been more different. He was of course exotic, but he was also patient and communicative with Bobby. Although he ran a performing school that specialized in dance, he was hardly effeminate. He loved professional sports too, and as Charles Grass remembered, he shared that love with his young student. "Mr. Weaver felt about Bob like somebody does about a favorite child," Charlie remembered. "He had no children of his own, and he was like a second father to Bob."

2

The new black Ford sedan that Marie Grass bought in 1939 would have to last her through the war although she could hardly have known it at the time. The car's original purpose, driving Charles, Hal Felman, and Artie Miller to their occasional engagements, seemed obviated now that the trio had broken up. Soon enough, however, a new act began to take shape. At first the paternal Mr. Weaver called it "The Weaver Brothers," but the final name was "The Riff Brothers (Dancers Extraordinary)."

There was more to that than the usual sham of stage brothers. They really did look alike, Charles and Bob, small and slender and roughly the same height and age, although Bob was a year older, and they were beautiful children. "Bob was better looking," Charles later admitted, "but I was the better dancer."

In dance jargon, a "riff" is a fast tapping of the toe without other body movement. The Riff Brothers were to be a standard dancing double, from riffs to splits, squats, slides, and the traditional challenge routine. Weaver's notion was for the boys to wear formal clothes and be a junior version of the Nicholas Brothers, who were the most famous of all vaudeville tap teams.

Hard and often as Charles and Bob practiced, however, and well as they got on, they were not pals and this was because they knew each other's secret—dance school. They shared in this shame, and so they played it at a distance, "just protecting ourselves," Charles later reflected, from ridicule and "against adverse conditions in the Chicago public schools." To him, "Bob seemed to be very businesslike about the act. I never saw anybody work so hard, but he didn't say much about school or home. We spent most of our time rehearsing." Thus they led a disguised life, "a charade," as Grass put it.

At Ravenswood Grade School, Bob seemed to be just one of the kids, for he acted as if dancing classes simply did not exist. And at home he would come in after an afternoon of rehearsing and, like any other twelve-year-old, grab a couple of cookies and ask one of his brothers how the Chicago Cubs had done. He knew the batting averages of the whole lineup, and he also knew that baseball was a more appropriate interest than dancing.

Patsy was happier now that she wasn't being made to go to the Academy. She pedaled furiously around the living room, riding her bicycle in serious circles. Her determination set the two big Irish wolf-hounds to bounding after her while the boys scrapped on their own. At least Bob and Don scrapped, for Buddy was too married for horseplay, and Edward, the second oldest, had turned so weak with rheumatic fever that he'd had to drop out of high school; in fact he was spending much of his time in a wheelchair.

Buddy's wife Margaret, living upstairs with him, had by now become one of the family. Bob called her Margie to signify their special relationship, for they were pals from the start, even though she must have seemed very grown-up to a ten-year-old. At school too his best friends were girls, like the Schroeder sisters, Annette and Dorothy. More than one Sunday was spent at their house over a brunch of strawberry pancakes, which the three youngsters helped Mrs. Schroeder make.

Through the winter of 1938 and into January, the Riff Brothers rehearsed the new act, after school and usually on weekends. Mr. Weaver designed its running order and chose the music for the general types of numbers he envisioned while Miss Comerford worked out the dances and the specific steps. The structure of the act was going to be simple enough: The boys would first dance as a duo, then each had a solo turn, and then they would rejoin for the finale. It would open suavely with white tie and tails and speed up in the middle with white dinner jackets. As the dancing grew more hectic, even the jackets would go, and the boys would return to the tails at the end for a big finish. They appreciated the bravura of a big finish. It went shamelessly for the applause, and with a "flash" act (one that relied on glitter, whether in costumes, sets, or execution) you could go all out at the end, overwhelming the audience perhaps more with effect than with actual talent. In later years, Fosse would realize just how cheap a trick it was.

For the boys' opening number, Weaver chose "Lilacs in the Rain," a lilting song that would bring them out in a casual way, emphasizing the charm of two boys in grown-up white tie and tails. To this music, as Charles Grass remembered, "We would do two choruses of a moderate, light tap. Then we'd take our bows and leave."

The first solo was Bob's, and the plan was for him to quick-change to surprise the audience with a white dinner jacket and maroon bow tie. At eleven, he was already mastering a machine-gun tap set to "The Stars and Stripes Forever." Weaver said that everyone was war-conscious because of developments in Europe and that patriotic numbers, within reason, usually went over big. The number would go on for a chorus and a half and as the youngster dashed into the wings, the other would trot out in his own white dinner jacket. In contrast to Bob's imitation of a machine gun, Grass's tap-dancing was long-lined, almost balletic. To "The Blue Danube Waltz," he would do a chorus and a half of "Russian floor movements on my toes and then a couple of wings."

The finale was a traditional challenge tap, each boy doing an increasingly difficult step and daring the other to top it. "We would start in stomp time," Grass recalled. "Then we'd take turns doing tap tricks. Bob would do wings. I'd do knee drops and splits in the air. Then Bob would come out again and do pullbacks around the stage. I'd do 'winding the clock,' down on the floor. We'd close with squat wings and final movements with trenches."

Being just kids they had, first of all, mastered the jargon.

That final "challenge" tap involved four routines apiece as each boy answered the other. Bob's double squats had him kicking out and tapping from a crouch, and Charles countered with leaping jump splits that sometimes began with him on his knees and required the kind of energy that only a boy could muster up. Bob might come back with "winding the clock," both hands on the floor while he swung his leg around.

At the end of the challenge tap, the boys would segue into "The Bugle Call Rag," which was their flash finish, done in stomp time (a simple time count kept with the toe—"five, six, seven, eight!"). While one of the boys did a fast and flamboyantly difficult step, the other would stand behind, clapping in rhythm and talking it up, encouraging him, urging the audience to applaud the unbelievable feat. Finally, both of them would finish with trenches, hunched over with their arms swinging, one at a time, between their legs.

Charles insisted, "We weren't the floor-stomping type, like the Berry Brothers or Tip, Tap, and Toe. We aimed for the Paul Draper or Georgie Tapps style." They even got themselves an autographed picture of Georgie Tapps.

It took months of grinding rehearsal before the boys had digested the steps and were dancing together with any kind of precision or flourish. Turns were a particular problem for Bob because he was left-handed, which led him to move instinctively counterclockwise. The right-handed Charles went clockwise. As in everything else, at least at the time, the left-handed were forced to conform to the way the right-handed did things, and so Marguerite Comerford had to remind Bob repeatedly to turn clockwise. He finally got it straight, although the instinct would impose a lifelong problem, as it does for many left-handed dancers and choreographers.

When the act had been reduced to a trim eleven minutes, the Riff Brothers were ready for costumes. Mr. Weaver and Miss Comerford took them to Maxwell Street, where there was a tuxedo rental store that sold secondhand dinner clothes. There they found two full dress suits, a pair of white dinner jackets, and most of the required accessories—dress shirts, suspenders, dickies with wing collars. They ordered professional tap shoes and had the taps loosened so as to make more of a clatter. These were called Max Taps. Mrs. Grass paid for Charles's clothes and Mr. Weaver for Bob's, adding the cost to the loan scholarship. For a finishing touch, Trixie Comerford picked out rhinestone stickpins for the boys to wear in their dickies.

Even as Bob stepped onto the chair in Charles's aunt Catherine's parlor so she could fit the dress suit, Marie Grass, who was sitting and watching, could barely suppress a smile for his earnestness. Catherine repeatedly had to ask the fidgety twelve-year-old to keep still while she pinned the trouser hems and the coat sleeves and then clutched a handful of the waist and seat so as to take them in for his skinny boy's frame.

Bob and Charles took turns on the chair, dutifully lifting their arms, buttoning the white jackets, paying as much attention to details of lapel and of the amount of shirt cuff showing beyond the jacket sleeve as if they were the Nicholas Brothers themselves.

On the day of their first public appearance, they sat down for haircuts, each receiving an extra dose of thick green goo that would dry their pompadours stiff as cardboard. Cy and Sadie didn't make much of it when Bob told them why he would be out late that night, nor did it seem to his sister-in-law Margie that he was especially disappointed by their lackluster response. He certainly didn't encourage anyone to come see him perform, and nobody offered to. For good luck, Margie gave him a set of cuff links and studs. Bob Riff's costume was complete.

His professional debut, paradoxically enough, was to be made as an amateur. The Riff Brothers were to be ringers in an amateur show that was being held in a local theatre, the Oak Theatre. To distinguish such places from traditional (and fast fading) vaudeville theatres, they were called "presentation houses," so as to cover live entertainment as well as a movie. Five acts were presented, instead of vaudeville's traditional eight, between showings of the picture. Friday nights, some offered amateur shows as extra attractions. These shows would be sweetened with beginning professionals like the Riff Brothers. Such acts couldn't be guaranteed first prize, but a certain amount of manipulation was possible in both placement (last was best) and in the way the master of ceremonies held his hand above the act's heads and grinned encouragingly at the audience.

Being minors, Charles and Bob were skirting the law anyhow, and Weaver was not about to press their families about having the boys work on school nights, so the Friday night amateur shows were a good way to break in the act.

The snow was accumulating on a frigid and blustery Chicago night, that February of 1939, as Fred Weaver drove them all to the Oak Theatre in what Charles remembered as "his big black gangster car." Miss Comerford sat beside him while Marie Grass was in the back between the Riff Brothers. The boys were already in their tails. They had the white dinner jackets folded neatly on their laps. Weaver parked the car on Armitage, and they trudged through the snow to Western Avenue, the boys on tiptoe trying not to spoil the dazzling shines on their shoes. The last thing Mr. Weaver said before leaving them at the stage door was that if they won the contest they would split ten dollars in prize money—less, of course, his 10 percent commission. Bob's 15 percent loan scholarship repayment would then be taken out of his share.

Bob and Charles Riff waited backstage for the movie to end. Appropriately, it was *Swing Time*, with Fred Astaire and Ginger Rogers. They watched the musical numbers from backstage, especially Astaire, who was to be Fosse's idea of the world's most beautiful and perfect dancer for the rest of his life. The boys did not, as they watched the fleet and elegant Astaire, talk about their youth or their chances of winning. They did not pace the floor nervously. They did not sham bravado. As Charles recalled, they only tried to reproduce the Astaire choreography, staring up at the giant flat images sidewise and mimicking the fabulous dancer amid the dank steel barrels and the thick dusty curtains in a darkened backstage corner of a Chicago theatre.

When their music started up in the orchestra pit, they rushed onstage in their flapping tails and dazzling shoes. Charles concentrated on Mr. Weaver's first rule: "Never upstage each other." They began tapping side by side. "We knew how to hold out our arms," Charles later said, "to make sure we were in a straight line. And Mr. Weaver had shown us how to use the whole stage for our floor patterns, how to check each other to make sure our feet were together. And how to keep smiling and keep looking into the spotlight."

Now, as they danced, Bob did the toe stands, "because," Charlie remembered, "I wasn't too good at those," and when it was over, they were lined up on stage with the other contestants.

As the audience was being asked to applaud its contestant of choice, Charles turned to Bob on stage and whispered, "Even if we lose, after Rogers and Astaire, not even the Nicholas Brothers would have looked any good." But when it was over, Fred Weaver met them at the stage door and handed them their winners' pay rolled up in a tight little cylinder of dollar bills. Then he took them across the street to Ande's Candy Store for strawberry ice cream sundaes.

The next day, Weaver went over to Fisher's Music and bought the sheet music for some of the songs that he had heard in the Astaire movie. He bought "The Waltz in Swing Time" and, as an alternative opening number for the Riff Brothers, "A Fine Romance." The cost of this music was noted and added to the expense sheets, although, in fairness to Weaver, he had not taken Bob's loan payment from the boy's first earnings. By no means a Fagin, he gave each four and a half dollars to mark their professional debuts. He made it clear to Bob, though, that he would henceforth be businesslike in all dealings, and they shook hands on that.

Businesslike or not, Bob took to calling him Skipper. He did this with an affectionate insouciance, although there might have been a bit of a tweak to it, since Weaver's waxed mustache and continental air hardly called for so breezy a nickname. In later years, such dryness would be typical of Fosse's humor.

Was Weaver becoming a father figure to the boy? Grass was positive that whenever Bob referred to his own father as a "former vaudevillian," it was really Fred Weaver he was talking about. Certainly, young Fosse was spending more time with this man than he was with his father, and he took on a glow whenever Skipper did something paternal like calling a break in rehearsal so that they could sit down at the table in the corner of the studio and listen to a broadcast of a Joe Louis prizefight. "Listening to the fights on the radio," Charlie recalled, "that was a must for Mr. Weaver."

The Riff Brothers played so many amateur shows around town that they were invited to appear on the popular "Morris B. Sachs Amateur Hour," which was broadcast on WGN from the old Sears Building. The notion of a tap-dancing act on the radio, patently absurd, was logical for the time. The studio audience would applaud the dancers while the announcer described what they were doing to the listeners at home.

For "The Morris B. Sachs Amateur Hour," the Riff Brothers performed their regular opening number, "Lilacs in the Rain," and it was enthusiastically received in the studio. They were undone, however, by the next act, a boy who stood on his head beneath a platform and tap-danced on it, *upside down.* Such honesty is touching, for on the radio there needn't have been a platform at all, or, for that matter, a tap dancer. A drummer with wood blocks would have sounded the same, but radio's word was being taken for it, and that was what kept it honest.

The upside-down tap dancer had too much audience appeal, and the Riff Brothers knew it. "All he did," Grass sniffed, "was a few little time steps, nothing intricate," but the audience manipulation that had helped the Riff Brothers to victory in the theatrical amateur shows now helped their gimmicky competitor on the radio. "The announcer went wild," Charles contemptuously recalled, "and the audience naturally responded to him when they were voting and we only got 'honorable mention.'" Years later, Grass relived the memory with a renewed sense of injustice and concluded with a sigh, "He wasn't that great."

The boys got to pick their consolation prizes at Sears. Bob chose a tie clip, and Charles took the Official Boy Scouts Manual.

Despite the considerable time that Bob was now spending on dance practice in the afternoons and vaudeville engagements every weekend, he slipped effortlessly through school, so successfully in fact that he was graduated from Ravenswood Grade School at the top of his class and won an award from the American Legion for academic achievement.

Roald Amundsen Senior High School was located in 1941, as it is now, at 5110 North Damion Street at the corner of Foster. It was not by chance that the school was named for a prominent Norwegian (a South Pole explorer) from turn-of-the-century Chicago. The neighborhood was largely Scandinavian. It was a school joke that if somebody in the hallways called out, "Hey, Swede!" half the kids would turn around, and if he yelled, "Hey, Greek!" the other half would. The reason there were so many Greek students at Amundsen High was that it offered modern Greek as a language study. Students living beyond the school district were given exemption from residence restrictions if they signed up for Greek, and naturally this attracted youngsters from Greek families.

Bob's best friends at school (they all entered Amundsen in February 1941) were George Foutris and Socrates (Socky) Markos, and the three boys were to remain pals until graduation. Bob joined the swim and track teams and was on the football squad for a week until Sadie got wind of it and trundled down to Amundsen in person to yank her slender and beautiful boy out of danger.

He had a certain pride and could be sensitive. He told Grass one day at the studio, in an exceptional confidence, that one of the boys on the track team kept calling him "Foss," and "I don't like it."

"Why not?" Charlie asked.

"Because my name is Fosse."

"Foss is the name of a great war ace [Capt. Joseph J. Foss of the Marines]. Nothing wrong with that."

"Yeah," Bob said grudgingly, "but I like *my* name pronounced Fosse."

He discovered girls and found that it was easy to fall for more than one. There were those who immediately read him as inconstant. Little Mary Vagos, for instance, decided at fourteen that "Bob Fosse was unstable in his relations with women." There would be women much older and more experienced than Mary Vagos who would not put it more succinctly.

He was devoted to one pretty blond in particular, and that was Marion Hauser, a slender girl with shoulder-length hair and a pert sense of humor. The school paper (*The Amundsen Log*) called her "Versatility Plus." The plus could well have referred to her tolerance, for Marion had to accept Bob's flirting with other girls and even his occasional dates with them. Then again, he had not given her his Hi-Y pin, so they weren't exactly going steady. Marion wouldn't always be able to overlook those other girls.

Bob said nothing to George Foutris or Socky Markos about dance school or the Riff Brothers. As Charlie Grass put it, "We did, as they say, lead a double life." To Bob's friends (who later marveled at the completeness of his secrecy) the only hint of dancing was his enthusiasm for acrobatics. Whenever he went to the Foutris house on North Keeler, he would open the front door onto a long hallway that ran the length of the place. He found that hallway irresistible. Without a word he would do cartwheels down the hall, all the way the length of the long corridor, and then he would come back the same way, cartwheeling to the front door. Then, breathless, he would sit down to do his homework with the boys. The cartwheels became his regular entrance at the Foutris house. That was his sunny side, but another side had already begun to emerge.

Like most of us, Bob Fosse was more than one person. In his case, the alter ego was more definitely formed than most, having a different name and leading a distinctly different life. Bob Riff existed in a world that lay utterly apart from Bob Fosse's conventional, moralistic, sturdy, and smiling Midwestern high school life. Bob Riff lived in a world that was something to be ashamed of and something to be kept secret.

The Riff Brothers made prune faces at themselves in the dressing room mirrors, smacking their lipsticked lips and screwing up their noses at the stage makeup of rouged cheeks and eye shadow, blue for the very fair Bob and brown for the somewhat darker Charles. They couldn't wait to scrub it off, "afraid that our school friends would jeer at us," Charlie said, "which they probably would have, and that would have broken our hearts."

An overflow audience of beaming parents and tittering siblings had assembled for the annual show at the Chicago Academy of Theatre Arts. Fred Weaver had squeezed the folding chairs into the studio as if it was a pillow case full of laundry. They craned over and around each other's heads, crowing about this daughter or that sister.

Charles and Bob were by now the established centerpieces of the Academy shows, and Weaver had them costumed in flowing shirts and ballet tights. As they were performing their "Floor Movement and Tap," they became aware of derisive laughter in the little hall. The source of the sniping was a pocket of teenage boys, cowardly cruel in the darkened room. What few remarks the Riff Brothers heard, as they were dancing, were amplified by their own sensitivities, and naturally they took these as aspersions on their masculinity. When they came offstage, Bob said, "After the finale, let's bust them in the nose."

Once the curtain calls were over, they hurried to scrub off the makeup and yank their trousers up over the hated tights. They careened down the stairs and out onto the street. This was something they always knew they would have to come to grips with as artists and as men.

Most of the people emerging from the building recognized the boys and stopped to congratulate them, but Charles and Bob were looking for the hecklers. They never did find them and felt very cheated and frustrated, standing in the street, desperate to thrash the wiseguys, unable to demonstrate their masculinity.

Four days later, the Japanese bombed Pearl Harbor. Two of the Fosse boys enlisted at once, Buddy joining the Seabees and going to the Pacific while Edward, his rheumatic fever outgrown, perhaps overcompensated for his sickly years by enlisting in the Army, going AWOL, stealing a car, and getting caught at it. He would end up joining the paratroopers and jumping into France. He must have been the pride of Cy Fosse. Only Don would wait to be drafted, and he spent the war as a supply sergeant in England. Young Bob stayed at home.

With Marianne now four years old and needing a room of her own, and with Sadie wanting all the wives and children to stay with her while the men were off to war, a bigger place was needed and it was found at 666 Sheridan Road, a fifteen-room stone house with Lake Michigan down the end of the street to serve as the kids' private swimming hole.

Sheridan Road wasn't the grand neighborhood it had once been, but most of the houses on the block were still imposing, still well tended, and they all had neat wire fences and gates with lawns in front and yards in the back. It wasn't elegant, but it was solid, and an empty lot next to the Fosse house gave the kids extra playing room. Besides Bob and Marianne, Edward's wife Dorothy moved in, bringing Ed, Jr., and Donald's Lucille moved in with Donald, Jr. Patsy came back too, since her husband George Lane was also in the service; in fact everyone moved in while Sadie's favorite daughter-in-law, Margaret, moved out. She had found an apartment and wanted to keep it, although she came over every day, pushing her little Cynthia ("Cindy") in a stroller. Sadie could not have been more of a mother to her. "Anytime I went over there," Margaret remembered, "she made me feel as if she had been waiting for me," and Margaret needed company to get past the pain of missing Buddy, whom she loved "as much as God allows a woman to love a man."

The Sheridan Road house was a warm and lively place, filled with the noises of energetic children and their earnest young mothers. One beneficiary of this atmosphere was Sadie's older girl. When the agonizingly shy Patsy was petrified by an invitation to a roller-skating party, her aunt Margaret bought her a pair of skates, and Buddy came home on an Army pass just to spend a day teaching the girl how to use them, right there in the living room. Patsy's big brother and his wife were now acting more like her parents than her parents were. Cy Fosse was drinking too much, perhaps beaten down by money problems and the endless travel for Hershey, and Sadie was bedridden much of the time with a bad heart. As Cy dozed in the easy chair by the radio, Bob would finish off half-drunk glasses of whiskey, and he laughed about that to Charlie Grass. He was also basking in a feathered nest, the favorite (and usually the only) man in a bower of women.

More than ever, then, the Sheridan Road house reflected Sadie Fosse, warm and inviting and protective even in her failing health. The living room seemed so big to the kids that Margaret's daughter Cindy grew up swearing it had four rugs, each nine feet by twelve. At the very least, the room dwarfed the Great Dane who replaced the old Irish wolfhounds. It could have been a fine place for a boy to grow up, but Bob was doing a different sort of growing up in what Charlie Grass called "the other side of our double life." The Riff Brothers were now regulars on such local stages as the Englewood Theatre, the Chicago, the Regal, the Milford, the Portage, the Bertha, and the Oriental. They were booked into these presentation houses at ten dollars apiece for as many as six engagements at each theatre over the year. Mr. Weaver insisted that they refer to the engagements as "dates," and with similar professionalism had their music copied so that they could hand the parts to the pit band maestros, the "professors." When the musicians weren't up to reading these orchestrations, Bob and Charles could make do with standards that everyone knew, like "Nola" or "Dinah."

Weaver also gave them inside tips. For instance, when a musician found an act difficult to deal with, he would mark up its music to alert the musicians in the next theatre—a caricature of a pig with a round rear end and a squiggly tail. Weaver warned the boys that he never wanted to find one of those little pigs in their music.

He found the odd booking for the act too. They once performed on a baseball diamond during the seventh inning stretch of a night game in a semiprofessional league. Another time, a men's club hired a German rathskeller for a dinner, and the Riff Brothers were engaged, only to find the ceilings so low in the underground restaurant, and the stage so high, that they had to eliminate all their leaps, which came to about half the act.

They played American Legion clubs and smokers for such lodges as the Masons, the Moose, and the Eagles. They even played amateur shows in theatres where they'd played amateur shows before, the Belmont, the Admiral, the Harding, the Terminal, and the Commodore. The audiences either changed, forgot, or didn't care. They started playing in small nightclubs, although Chicago ordinances specifically forbade minors from working where liquor was served.

That year, 1942, the famous New York stage director, George Abbott, was in Chicago with the national company of the Broadway musical, *Best Foot Forward*. Choreographed by the new movie star Gene Kelly, it was a college show with several parts for youngsters, and Mr. Weaver wrote to Abbott asking for an audition. "I have a team of boys that it might be to all of our advantages to have you see. The Riff Brothers . . . do a dancing act of good stiff routines. They are good showmen and can read lines."

Abbott's stage manager, Robert Griffith, answered the letter, suggesting that the boys stop by at the Studebaker Theatre for an audition. They didn't get the jobs, but a mere dozen years later, Griffith would be coproducing *The Pajama Game* on Broadway, directed by Mr. Abbott with choreography by the self-same Bob Riff who had auditioned for him at the age of fourteen.

The boys went back to the clubs, the smokers, the amateur shows, and the vaudeville houses. Some nights, when they gave two performances including a late show, Mrs. Grass would drop Bob off in front of his parents' house at daybreak, with the horse-drawn milk wagons clattering up the street. Bob never mentioned any family reaction to such hours, and if Charles's suspicions were correct, there was none.

Then one day, Marguerite Comerford left Fred Weaver. He told the boys that she had gone home to Iowa to take care of her ailing sister, but they found out that she had really gone back to get married. The dapper Mr. Weaver was devastated. He closed the Academy and suggested that the boys take a break. After two months of no word from Skipper, Bob telephoned Charlie to say that he wanted to concentrate on school, that he was "quitting show business because I'm tired of my parents belittling it." But Weaver suddenly reappeared to announce that he had found new quarters at 1961 West Lawrence Avenue, and asked Bob and Charlie to join the faculty. As students began to return, only Charles ever taught dance class, but being on the faculty gave Bob the chance to work out a new number by himself for inclusion in the next school show.

Some time later the boys learned that Marguerite Comerford had suffered a stroke and died. That was when Mr. Weaver started to smoke cigarettes and see new girlfriends, young girls, "girls half his age," Charles recalled. The boys gave him a tin of fancy mustache wax to cheer him up.

Bob started to smoke cigarettes too, Camels, and he resumed work with renewed dedication. Weaver gave the boys the keys to the studio so that they might come whenever they wanted, and Bob would spend hours just practicing hat tricks with a derby: juggling it, flipping it onto his head, rolling it down his arm. When Charlie arrived, they would practice twirling canes or shading their taps. More than merely a manager, Weaver kept the act in check. He stressed the precision of tapping as well as the styling, the movement, and the floor patterns, but especially the precision. He would keep nagging at them, "When you boys are dancing together, your taps should sound like one." Then they would stand side-by-side, facing the mirror, "and every finger had to be just right," Charlie remembered. Bob was absorbing the lesson in his bones.

Homework would be done in the studio too. Charlie might continue working alone while Bob pulled a chair up to the corner table, opened his schoolbag, and took out his assignments. Then he would sit there and write, resting his head on one palm, his elbow propped on the table top.

Summer vacations did not mean a break from rehearsing but rather more of it. Much of the time, Bob was at the studio by himself. Charlie would trot up the two flights of stairs, walk down the long corridor, and open the door, to find his partner working on dance steps in a haze of cigarette smoke. Bob had decided that the machine-gun tap to "The Stars and Stripes Forever" needed a follow-up that was more on the suave side, and he was trying to develop a rhumba tap set to Glenn Miller's "Perfidia." He played the record repeatedly, working out the steps in front of the big mirror, the cigarette dangling from the corner of his mouth. He liked that look. He would stand up close to the mirror and stare at himself with the cigarette drooping from his lip.

When he finally showed the new routine to Mr. Weaver, he was told, "First of all, take that cigarette and smoke it on the back porch." This from the chain-smoking Fred Weaver, and when Bob came back, he and Charles were given the old lecture about the value of a time-proven act. "Once you get it right," Mr. Weaver said yet again, "you can do it for the rest of your life. Look at Sophie Tucker and 'Some of These Days.'" Then he added Jolson and Durante and even Willy, West, and McGinty, who were one of his more obscure favorites, repeating the advice that had been offered thousands of times (but always worth repeating): "You perfect an act, year after year, but you don't change it."

Warming up to the subject and to his teenage audience, the old man ruminated about true greatness in vaudeville. "Pat Rooney," he said, "now there was an act. His hands in his pockets, pulling his pants up and doing the old clog." Weaver's pleasure in the elegance of this act was palpable. "But he loved nobody in vaudeville better than Joe Frisco," Charlie remembered. "Mr. Weaver would tell Bob and me about Frisco over and over again." Frisco was a comedian as well as an eccentric dancer (as they were called), and his trademarks were a derby, a cigar, and a stutter. "He danced the hootchy-kootch," Grass remembered, a sliding, sidewise, slithering kind of shuffle. Many years later, Bob would copy it shame-lessly, and he would have been the first to admit it, if anyone had remembered Joe Frisco as he did.

Weaver did let the boys work on such possible additions to the act as taps with magic tricks (flowers coming out of the sleeve) or a cane dance or a chair dance or a duet done to "Me and My Shadow." Their shadows high behind them, one boy dancing back of the other—they liked that one. But the only change that he ever actually allowed was a song written by Jule Styne and Frank Loesser, "I Don't Want to Walk Without You, Baby," which Bob and Charlie considered much more up-to-date and sophisticated than "Lilacs in the Rain."

Charles especially liked the rare occasions when he was at the studio first. "There was something wonderful," he remembered, "about hearing that door slam downstairs and knowing it was Bob. I'd stop and listen and count his steps coming up the twenty-three stairs. Particularly if he was already wearing his tap shoes. I'd hear the taps all the way up, even doing a little routine up and down the last few steps, because he was always fiddling with a staircase dance like Bojangles Robinson. Then he would click down the hall, and the door would open, and there he'd be, a cigarette hanging from the corner of his mouth, smiling and ready to go to work."

Dances weren't all they worked on. When Weaver had written George Abbott that they "can read lines," it was on the basis of comedy routines that he had worked up for the boys to do in radio announcing class, and later as twin emcees at the Academy's shows. One of the routines brought them on to open a show that had been booked by four Elks Club chapters. The 1943 show was called *Hold Everything! A Streamlined Extravaganza in Two Parts.*

BOB

Ladies and gentlemen . . . let me introduce at this time my friend Charles Grass . . . my friend . . . Charles Grass . . . (looking off stage) Oh, Charlie!

CHARLES

Oh! I've been back there reading the newspaper.

BOB

The newspaper? Why, the newspaper is obsolete. It's only a question of time when the newspaper will be replaced by the radio.

CHARLES

Nonsense. The radio can never replace the newspaper.

BOB

What makes you think that?

CHARLES

Well, you can't swat flies with a radio.

BOB

Well, the radio is a great thing. Think of the broadcasts we get from the war zones. By the way, I understand that Hitler tried to borrow money the other day.

CHARLES

How was that?

BOB

He said to Stalin, "If you give me a Finn, I'll send you a Czech in the morning."

CHARLES

Yes, it's getting so bad over there they say that there won't be any more fishing.

BOB

How do you make that out?

CHARLES

Well, Hitler took all the Poles.

BOB

Well, well.

CHARLES

Yes, and the food is getting so scarce that a woman lived for two weeks on onions alone.

BOB

Well, any woman who lives on onions ought to be alone.

(BLACKOUT)

At the bottom of the program, in the smallest of letters, was a credit that had never before appeared anywhere, in print of any size. The credit read, "Dance Numbers by Bob Fosse." It was his first credit as a choreographer. Perhaps that was why, for the first time, Cy Fosse was in the audience at a dancing school show, watching his son perform. Bob was doing comedy routines, and he was responsible for the choreography. But he was not dancing.

The first group choreography that Bob Fosse ever created came halfway through the first part of this *Streamlined Extravaganza in Two Parts*. It came after the songs of the Three Charmers ("Beauty and Harmony") and a solo dance by Margie McCaskey ("Twists and Turns"). Bob's number was danced by the Glamour Girls to the popular song, "That Old Black Magic" and, as a sign of things to come, it was glitzy and sexy. He had the four teenagers decked out in slinky gowns with props of big, black ostrich feather fans. He would always love props. He had copied this number from one in a movie called *Star Spangled Rhythm*. He went to that movie six times, just to get the dance right and to remember the movements, but the fans were his own addition. The girls dipped, flourishing them, peeking out from behind the feathers to the sinuous blues of the Harold Arlen–Johnny Mercer song. Bob told his father that he had been inspired by Sally Rand, whose fan dances had made such a worldwide sensation. It was almost true. Bob's inspiration had indeed come from a striptease dancer, but not Sally Rand; it came from striptease dancers that he and Charles had actually been working with, for Frederic Weaver was beginning to book the boys into the joints, striptease clubs like the Silver Cloud on Milwaukee Avenue and the Gaiety Village on Western.

Charles and Bob were hardly innocents. They had already been given a fast introduction to the cheaper side of show business, but now they were being treated to true sleaze, and needless to say, they loved it.

Bob had already developed a healthy enthusiasm for striptease dancers and would regularly sneak into Minsky's Burlesque at Lake and Van Buren. It was at Minsky's that he discovered a lower type of comedy act and broader performance values, the pratfalls and slapstick of burlesque routines. He added them to his stock of show business lore. Still, it was one thing to enjoy burlesque, including the striptease dancers, and quite another to work in strip joints, even for such wised-up vaudevillians as the Riff Brothers (Dancers Extraordinary). Despite their bravado the boys were still boys and really rather naive. They were, after all, only sixteen.

The strippers were somewhat older and less naive. On sweltering nights they would lounge naked in the airless dressing rooms, and Charles remembered staring at the G-strings that were only on the table, at the breasts that seemed to be overstuffing the warm rooms. The girls would be amused by the teenage boys' awkwardness, taking time from putting on makeup and pulling on net stockings to urge Charles and Bob onto their laps where they would purr and lick at the boys' ears, hold breasts to their cheeks and nipples to their lips, and fondle them.

One night, all of this fooling around gave Bob an erection just before he was to go onstage. The stripper who caused it roared with laughter. Bob tugged frantically at his jacket, hoping to cover himself as his introductory music began, the cheap drum and the honking saxophone.

Any performance was tough enough before an audience that would invariably lose patience with the Riff Brothers and begin to clap during the act, chanting, "Bring on the girls." To endure, as well, the hoots and catcalls of these gorillas was going to be all but unbearable. No sooner did the boys stride suavely onstage than Bob's bulge was spotted, and afterward he told Charlie it had seemed hours until the wisecracks and laughter subsided, along with his erection.

After each show, the boys would go outside and get into Mrs. Grass's car. She didn't want them to spend time between shows in an unsavory atmosphere. They settled into the warm and woolly upholstery of the Ford's backseat, opening their schoolbooks to do their Latin lessons.

Reflecting, thirty-five years later, on this "strange, schizophrenic childhood," Fosse described it as "a pull between Sunday school and my wicked underground life," a fair enough description of the worlds of Bob Fosse and Bob Riff. "I was a very religious kid," he would say in an interview. "I mean, I did know all the Bible verses, I really believed that there was a God who was there watching me all the time, who knew whether I was thinking the bad thoughts, impure thoughts. I would concentrate on Bible verses if I ever thought about, uh, anything I thought was dirty. I mean, I don't think I masturbated until I was thirty-one . . . and being attracted to pretty women at the same time, it was a struggle, this terrible, terrible struggle, and thrown into these stripper joints when I was so young, the battle that was going on inside of me was just tremendous."

He spent a fair part of his five-year psychoanalysis dealing with this "battle," and came to conclude that he had not been at all well served by these adolescent sexual experiences. "I was really very unhappy and scared," he said. "It left certain impressions on me that weren't too good. I was too young to be exposed to naked ladies." That would seem to have been a singularly valid conclusion, although by the time he was talking to the psychiatrist, a pattern of attraction to older women had long been established, extending from the strippers of his childhood to his wives, every one of whom would be older than he. He would also tend, throughout his life, to disassociate sex with love and identify it, instead, in vulgar terms.

Marion Philbrick was a schoolmarm out of central casting. The dramatics teacher at Amundsen High School was slender, straight-spined, and precise. She even wore her dark hair pulled back in a bun and was called "a spinster lady" by her fellow teachers though she was not yet fifty. As a young woman she had studied ballet but, like Patsy Fosse, modesty had made her painfully unsuited to public performance. She was briefly a script girl for the Keystone Kops movie director, Mack Sennett, but retreated into teaching English and expressing her love of the performing arts through the school drama club. It was there that she found Bob Fosse, and he would be the outlet for her frustrated ambitions. Marion Philbrick would keep his scrapbooks until the day she died.

The highlights of her school year, without a doubt, were her drama club's annual variety shows, one in the fall and the other in the spring. Each would be given three performances, two for the students and an evening gala for the parents. The shows consisted of ten or twelve songs, sketches, and the occasional instrumental solo. Dancers were rare. Nothing seemed to be more embarrassing to high school students than dancing, watching it or doing it. Dance goes to the heart of adolescent cringes, because it deals with ego, confidence, and physical grace—weapons lacking in the teenage arsenal. For the boys in particular, with their masculinity in the making, dancing was a powerful sexual act, one set in homosexual parentheses.

Bob made no attempt to land roles in such dramatic productions as *The Importance of Being Earnest,* which the drama club presented in his freshman year. He managed, however, to let Miss Philbrick know about his dance lessons and even told her that he was working in nightclubs—though in his story the strip joints were wondrously transformed into the elegant Empire Room of the Palmer House. "I don't know how he gets to work in such a fancy place," Miss Philbrick told her best friend. "He must have an in." It was plain to her friend that Marion doted on the boy. She urged him to do a spot in her variety show during his sophomore year, and he agreed. He must have been ready to come out from behind Bob Riff if he felt man enough to dance openly and as himself in front of the kids.

Miss Philbrick watched him practice for hours, having no idea that he would then go to Weaver's studio to work on Riff Brothers routines. Nor could she have known that the machine-gun tap he was repeatedly rehearsing was a number that he had been doing for more than two years on stages all over Chicago.

The school auditorium lights were not yet darkened as he went through one last rehearsal before the first student performance of the variety show. John Rogus, who was in charge of the lighting, worked in the wings clamping the last spotlight in place and jotting down his cues as he watched the slender youngster leap across the stage and slide on his knees toward the footlights. Fosse then stood up, brushed off his pants, tugged at his knee pads, and tried the slide again—and again and yet again. He then walked toward the wings, deep in concentration, to pause, prepare, turn, and dash out once more, to leap and spin and slide. Then he went off to change into costume as the curtains were closed, and the house began to fill.

Teachers led students into the hall. Ceremoniously last to arrive was the school principal, the stern L. Day Perry ("If it can be done well anywhere, it can be done better at Amundsen!"), followed, several appropriate steps behind, by his assistant principal, Harry Fuller. Mr. Fuller was in charge of the lighter school activities, like this variety show.

Backstage, Miss Philbrick made her final checks, as in the pit, the conductor, Forrest Buechtell, raised his baton for the student band to strike up the overture. Rogus cringed in apprehension of a big blat from the band, but with the Buechtell downbeat the boys and girls proved not that bad at all, probably because, as everyone in school knew, the drummer smoked reefers and could give an extra hot beat as a result.

Bob appeared in the wings at the start of the number preceding his own. It was an elaborate production called "Silhouettes," a series of romantic tableaus with backlighting that made the still figures into silhouette compositions. The students would then rearrange themselves and freeze once more, as if to ask for applause that no civilized audience could justifiably withhold. Meantime, Fosse finished his final series of warm-up stretches. He fluffed out his neat blue trousers and the flowing, full-sleeved, white dancing shirt. The stage was cleared. The audience was shushed by the teachers. The curtains were whisked apart and the band launched into the familiar blare of "The Stars and Stripes Forever." The slender boy uncoiled from behind the wings, leaping almost to center stage and into the spotlight. For once he had forsaken the barber's green goo, and now his fine blond hair fluttered and sparkled in the brilliant followspot. The applause that greeted his entrance must have seemed part of a wonderful surge in the auditorium's energy.

His arms swung and spread, following him as he dipped and whirled, and he never looked at his feet except once, in apparent amazement and disbelief, as their tapping seemed to defy mortal limitations. "His grin," John Rugos recalled, "seemed to go from one end of the stage to the other," as Fosse held his outspread fingers to the audience, elbows tucked in tight to his sides. The spotlight followed his moves, and with his machine-gun taps, the students' gasps became audible. When he burst into a final leap that sent him sliding toward the audience on his knees, the applause exploded out of the kids, and he gazed into the spotlight and the darkness and the approval with the held smile and the steady gaze of the seasoned professional. He had made his statement. He had identified himself. He was a dancer.

George Foutris and Socky Markos just couldn't get over it, this pal of theirs, and after the show they made Bob promise that he would do something with them, some kind of trio act.

The next day, Marion Hauser found him no different from the day before the show. She had set out for school, as usual, by picking up Caroline Robinson across the street from her house. They stopped for Annette Schroeder, and then they all strolled over to Paulina to get Bob, three girls in pleated skirts, bobby socks, saddle shoes, and Sloppy Joe sweaters. He, as usual, was waiting for them in front of his house and, also as usual, was wearing a yellow sweater with a vee neck and penny loafers with white sweat socks, and his pants were rolled up to ankle height like Gene Kelly's.

Even after the revelation of his dancing at the variety show Bob never invited Marion to see him dance professionally. "And it seems to me," she later said, "that I knew about it only in the vaguest way. I don't think anybody at school was really aware of what he was doing at night. We just saw him dance in the school shows." Marion did, of course, dance with

Bob at the hops in the gym, "but he didn't like to show off. We would do the jitterbug or the boogie-woogie, like the other kids, and a lot of slow dancing to 'Moonlight Serenade' and 'Adios,' but he would never be flamboyant. He wasn't a show-off. He was really quite shy."

With his senior year about to start, he had found a way to be both shy and outgoing, quiet and sunny. He had hit his social stride, and there was every reason to stick with it because it was certainly working for him. Between classes, strolling along the school corridors, he sliced his way through a sea of friends, waving, joking, and laughing. He had won sports letters for the swimming and track teams. On October 5, 1943, he was elected president of the senior class; he was good with girls and took special pleasure from friendships with boys; in fact when Charlie Grass told him about an act in his school called the Imitators, it gave Bob the idea for a routine: "The Three Musketeers," George Foutris, Socky Markos, and himself. The opportunity was at hand: Senior Hall. This was a meeting every Friday morning, usually reserved for deciding the date and site of the senior prom, scheduling class pictures, or reminding everyone of deposits due on graduation caps and gowns. When there was no such business to be transacted, Senior Hall was used for class shows.

Bob bought a copy of the popular Andrews Sisters record, "Bie Mir Bist Du Schoen (Means That You're Grand)" and played it repeatedly for George and Socky until they were sick of it. He wouldn't say why he was playing the record, but demanded that they pay attention and be serious and learn every word and note of the Sholom Secunda–Sammy Cahn–Saul Chaplin song, precisely as the Andrews Sisters sang it. Then he disclosed his plan: They were going to imitate the record. George would be Maxine Andrews, Socky would be LaVerne, and, being blond, Bob would be Patti. While the record was played they would move their lips—everyone knew what "lip sync" was because it was a common entertainment routine, even on professional stages. It was very popular at the time, and nearly every entertainer started out by doing it, and of course, dressing up in women's clothes would get a sure laugh.

Bob rehearsed the number with the boys for days, the lip movements, the hand gestures, the dance steps, and after he thought they had it just right, he told them they were ready to go to work. George and Socky laughed until they realized he wasn't joking. He drilled them so much that they stopped thinking it was fun, but he clapped them on the backs and told them they were wonderful, and that he was sure they would be perfect after just a couple more runthroughs.

George Foutris took Bob aside during a break and asked him, "How do you keep doing all of this?" "All of what?" Bob asked. "Well," George said, "you get good grades in school, and you go to all the parties, and you go out with Marion, and you're president of the senior class, and you aren't stuck up. You're a two-letter man in swimming and track, and on top of that you're a dancer. That's an awful lot of stuff," he said, "and now you're doing this act with us. How can you do all of that at the same time?"

Fosse thought for a full minute before answering. Finally he said, "You have to learn to compartmentalize, George. No matter what you're doing in life, whatever it is, you have to compartmentalize. Then you can focus in on each area individually. Pay attention to details, that's the key to it, and don't let your mind wander into one area while you're dealing with another. You have got to concentrate on one thing at a time. Really concentrate."

Foutris was impressed, not merely by the advice but by the intensity with which it was given, and he repeated the conversation more than once when Bob became renowned.

The student audience roared when the Three Musketeers barreled out in their Andrews Sisters getups—outrageous wigs, overpainted lips, awesome shoulder pads, and teetering high heels. The boys broadly parodied the gestures and dance steps of the popular singing trio, and the auditorium rocked with spontaneous whistling and stamping, which the teachers excused as appreciation of the arts. Even stern L. Day Perry, the principal, seemed to approve. The number was such a success that the boys were called back for subsequent Senior Hall shows. They changed their name to the Three Fakers and expanded their repertoire to include the Mills Brothers' "Up a Lazy River" and Glenn Miller's "Juke Box Saturday Night." They were even offered a professional New York engagement, though they never found out how serious an offer it was since their parents wouldn't let them consider it.

Of course the act brought a great deal of attention from the girls although that had never been a problem for Bob. He had always been interested in girls as friends, and his sincerity was more successful than any romantic approach could have been. He was at his physical peak, although he could hardly have known it. Below his flashing smile and cleft chin was a body in flawless physical condition. Dancing and track had made his legs powerful and, thanks to the swimming, long muscled rather than knotty. Swimming had also given him broad shoulders, a flat chest, and narrow hips. Nature's skinny freshman frog had turned into a first-class prince. At five feet eight he was not tall, but he was certainly solid, and he weighed more in his senior year (145 pounds) than he ever would again. He definitely had more hair, fine hair that he parted in the center and swept back and upward in stylish twin pompadours.

At dance school he was already a heartthrob. "I was jealous of him," Charlie Grass remembered. "He was handsome, he was blond, he was athletic, and the girls in the studio, well, they just fell all over him." At dance school it was Beth Kellogg and Pat Hogan, and it was the same way at Amundsen High. He seemed to go out with every girl in the class, Mary Vagos and Margaret Whitehill and Mary Farmakis and Melvene Fitzpatrick—much to Marion Hauser's distress. She waited these flings out until Marion Geweke came along.

Trim and pretty, a compact five feet three inches, with curly brown hair, Marion ("Smoochie") Geweke looked enough like Marion Hauser to be her sister, and, as a matter of fact, she was a sister member of the Tri-Hi-Y, the girls' auxiliary of the Hi-Y (the high school affiliate of the YMCA). This made for a sticky situation. Marion Hauser put up with Bob's taking Smoochie to a couple of movies and a hayride, but the limit was his being invited to dinner at the Geweke home. That was serious and with Bob's acceptance of the invitation, the Fosse–Hauser romance was *finis*, making senior year a shambles for both of them. Marion broke their senior prom date and told the reporter for *The Amundsen Log* that she was looking for "*the* date. He should be tall [oh, cruel] and have a medium complexion and be ever so much fun." No matter how much Bob begged her forgiveness, she would not relent.

His pattern for life, then, seemed established in adolescence: He could fall passionately in love, but the feeling would last only a few months and he could not resist others. His brothers had all rushed to get married. Perhaps the war had prompted that. Even Bob's sister, shy Patsy, had hurried into a marriage with George Lane. But for Bob, love seemed to last no longer than the first heat of passion. Much more enduring would be the pain of rejection and loss.

To their pals in the power elite of the senior class, the Hauser–Fosse break was disappointing, because the popular couple was so well matched. Sadie Fosse was already treating Marion like a daughter and, talk about perfect couples, when Bob had been voted the Most Popular Boy in the Class, Marion was voted Best Looking Girl. She was an entertainer too, a singer. She had starred in Miss Philbrick's drama-club production of *Oklahoma!* and had sung in the school Variety Show. She had even won a talent contest singing "Tenderly" on WGN, the very same Morris B. Sachs Amateur Hour on which the Riff Brothers had lost out to the boy who tap-danced upside down. And so Bob and Marion had been a compatible pair. On the other hand, Smoochie Geweke, who did go with him to the senior prom in a pink chiffon gown, disapproved of his dancing and saw no future in their romance. "He had his mind made up about being a performer," she later said, "and it just wasn't the life for me. I knew he would never settle down to a nine-to-five job, and I just wasn't the kind of person who would feel comfortable with a show business type. I'm much more conventional. I'm much more respectable."

That last term at Amundsen High was one of real transition for young Fosse. His mind was made up, not only about being a professional dancer but also about enlisting in the Navy, even though the war in Europe had ended the previous May and was winding down in the Pacific. He spent his last term playing as many dates as possible. He and Charlie were old enough to pass as servicemen, and in borrowed uniforms, they played military shows at Fort Sheridan, at the USO on West Washington, and at the huge and nationally famous Great Lakes Naval Training Center, north of Chicago. There, for the first time, they were given top billing as the closing act. The Riff Brothers also danced for Red Cross shows and war-bond rallies, opening for Buddy Ebsen, William Bendix, and even Ann Corio, although on that occasion the famous stripper merely gave a speech.

While he was at Great Lakes, Bob applied for permission to enlist on a delayed-entry basis, and it was granted. He wanted six months of time out of life to test himself as a professional. He suggested that Charlie, who was a term behind him at Lakeview High, quit school and go on the road with him. "You've got to make a decision, Charlie," he said. "Sign a contract and let's go professional." But not even a stage mother like Marie Grass would allow that, so the boys manfully shook hands and said good-bye.

At eight o'clock on the evening of January 25, 1945, Bob gave the Address of Welcome for his Amundsen High School graduating class, but he had already been graduated, really, and was on his way, leaving Charlie Grass behind to muse for the rest of his life on how different things might have been had he quit high school and remained a Riff Brother. Now, Bob was left to do his act alone.

3

He was ranging as far as Michigan and Missouri for solo engagements, but "after graduation," Bob later recalled, "I had a lot of trouble getting work. That's my life, all glory or I can't get a job." He got some jobs, still as "Bob Riff (Tops in Taps)," at the Cuban Village, for instance, on Wabash Avenue, but the thrill was gone. The waitresses might have been wearing Cuban costumes, but the place was just another strip joint, the same tired band, the same tired jokes, the same gorillas stomping their feet and their glasses for the girls. Moreover, Bob had to face up to the fact that he was too big to be applauded just for being cute and that heavy weekend bookings for a teenage tap dancer and emcee were not enough to support a grown-up of seventeen. He simply was too old to be a kiddie act, and he found himself borrowing food money from Fred Weaver.

He certainly couldn't borrow it from his father. Cy's drinking had gotten worse, and he was spending long stretches in the basement, bottling the gallon jugs of homemade vanilla syrup on which he pasted big white labels that read "My Own Vanilla."

Being a professional dancer who seldom worked put Bob in a limbo. Most of his friends were already in the service, and some had gotten jobs. His first love, Marion Hauser, was waiting out the months until she could begin college, but he didn't fit into any category. He wasn't working, he wasn't in the service, and he wasn't going to college. Even for a golden boy, it wasn't easy starting out in show business, and he might even have been looking forward to the Navy.

In the meantime, he and Marion patched things up. She agreed that the open time they both had, he before the Navy and she before college, was time out of reality, a gift. So, besides indulging in the romance, Marion used it to flirt with her aspirations as a singer. She played a few club dates and joined Bob in his last civilian dancing engagement. Appropriately enough it was a Sailor Show at the Great Lakes Naval

Training Center, where he was about to be mustered in. She sang Irving Berlin's "What'll I Do?" "I wasn't half bad," she recalled. "I had a good voice, but I had absolutely no stage presence."

Boot camp was a long nine weeks at Great Lakes. With his first pass, Seaman Fosse boarded a bus and headed not for home but to visit Marion at Blackburn College in Carlinville, Illinois. He showed up in his spiffy summer whites—tight bell bottoms, a neat jumper, and a sailor hat cocked at the jaunty angle that boys joined the Navy for. As a personality and as a physical type, he couldn't have been more perfect for a sailor suit, and he looked simply smashing, as Marion recalled. Her roommates agreed, the same girls Bob used to walk to Amundsen High with: Caroline Robinson and Annette Schroeder.

The freshly minted Able Seaman Second Class volunteered for assignment to the Great Lakes weekly Sailor Show, *Happy Hour,* and there, for the first time, he danced professionally under his own name. The war had just ended, but Sadie Fosse wasn't taking any chances. More worried than when her youngest boy had joined the football team, she prevailed upon her eldest to protect him. Buddy's many nights spent dancing at the Aragon Ballroom had led to a friendship with a bandleader named Bert Williams (not the great vaudeville entertainer), who was now with Special Services. Williams arranged for Bob's transfer to its Entertainment Branch and so, having never been further from home than St. Louis, he traveled to New York City and reported to the Federal Office Building at 90 Church Street.

The Entertainment Branch's Navy Liaison Unit had five Sailor Shows in various stages of production, rehearsal, or touring. The sailor-related titles were typical of service humor: *Drop the Hook, Full Speed Ahead, Broad on the Beam, Hook, Line, and Sinker,* and *Down the Hatch.* Bob was assigned to *Hook, Line, and Sinker,* because it was about to start rehearsals.

Like everything in the military, show business was treated according to the regulations and set to the jargon. Whether for singers and dancers or for ordinary seamen, orders were cut and personnel were placed on duty rosters, billeted and assigned to tours of duty. Using the gymnasium of a Manhattan YMCA as a rehearsal hall, a director from the permanent staff drilled (rehearsed) the boys for weeks. Then the *Hook, Line, and Sinker* company set out on November 1, 1945, and by the time its Pacific tour ended, three months later, so had the romance with Marion Hauser. She wrote just one letter, and that was to tell Bob that she was being sent to live with her father in California (her parents were divorced) and was being transferred from Blackburn College to Pasadena State Junior College. The purpose was clear, for Marion's mother had never approved of the young hoofer.

He was devastated and opened his broken heart to a new pal, Bill Quillin, who did comedy routines with him in the show. Several months later, when he was back in New York and in rehearsal for a new Sailor Show, he was still in mourning for Marion and still sharing his grief with Quillin, who had wangled an assignment with the same show. They would sit side by side on the Navy dormitory cot, staring at Bob's wallet-worn photograph.

It was April 1946, and shiploads of impatient servicemen remained strewn across the war zones, young men fidgeting through the last dreary months, waiting to go home, frustrated because they had no purpose. Perhaps in the postwar months there was a still greater need than ever to entertain them, particularly those who were marooned on remote Pacific islands.

The Navy had assigned a chief petty officer rather than a commissioned officer to head this new show that Bob was in. It was probably because ranks were being depleted, and this fellow could write, direct, and produce; besides, at twenty-five, he was old enough to seem authoritative to the boys. His name was Joseph Papirosky, and he was a dark, slender, quiet, pipe-smoking, young man from Brooklyn. He had spent the previous year staging variety shows aboard the U.S.S. *Solomon*, a tanker that had been converted into an aircraft carrier. Papirosky had no theatrical aspirations. He was interested in getting into radio broadcasting, but he loved being a master of ceremonies because it gave him the chance to sing. He was crazy about singing.

Asked to command a unit of fifteen performers, he wrote the show himself, basing his outline on the surefire theme of life after the Navy. All he wanted was a vehicle for the individual talents in his unit. It contained a couple of singers, an all-around actor, a comic, an impersonator who could play the girl in the show, an eight man band and two dancers, Fosse and a fellow who, coincidentally enough, was named Roland DeFosse. The show was called *Tough Situation*, or *TS* for short, always good for a laugh, and after a three-week rehearsal it was tried out in a Long Island mental hospital. As one of the musicians remembered, "We figured, if we got laughs there we'd get laughs anywhere."

Papirosky's first sense of Fosse was his heartsickness, his endless staring at the girl in the picture in the wallet and Quillin's patience in listening to repeated renderings of the romantic tragedy. "Outside of that," the chief petty officer recalled, "Bob was a very sunny guy, by far the most personable and interesting in the unit because he was very complex for a kid. No conversation with him was ever trivial so long as you kept off the subject of the girlfriend."

Tough Situation was to play a backbreaking schedule of ninety-six shows in three months on a vaudeville circuit of remote, desolate, bombed-out Pacific bases, from Johnston Atoll near the Hawaiians to the Solomons and Kwajalein, across the Pacific to Guam, Iwo Jima, and Okinawa, ending the tour in Tokyo. The unit had its own twin engine plane, a C-46 that, like most planes of the time, could not fly above the weather. Whenever an ocean storm blew, the lightning and thunder would crash around the bumping, sliding, and lurching aircraft, rattling its quaking passengers. In the dark and bare military cabin, while rain and hailstones pelted the metal skin, the unit's singer, Sherman Cohn, would sing "Strange Music," from the Broadway hit, *Song of Norway.* Cohn had sung with the Los Angeles Philharmonic and had a big tenor.

The tour got off to an unnerving start while playing for the First Marine Division in the Solomon Islands. The boys had finished rehearsing on the temporary outdoor stage, and DeFosse came back to watch the lights being rigged. Bob was still there, at work on his "Fascinatin' Rhythm." It was an hour before show time, and yet while the other fellows were back in the barracks, showering and changing, Bob was still going over his dance. DeFosse told him it looked fine, but Bob said, "Just a couple of more times. Go on back. I'll only be a minute." And just then they heard explosions from beyond the compound. There were cries and whistles from the marines. Everyone seemed to be running somewhere, and Bob asked one of them whether he had been misinformed about the war being over.

"Tell it to the Japs in the hills," the marine said before dashing away. "Come on," Bob said to DeFosse. "Let's see what's going on."

They caught up with one of the search parties and trekked through the darkening forest until it was close to show time. When DeFosse, in his flat Massachusetts accent, suggested they get back for the performance, Bob was too excited. "They won't start without us," he said, "and everybody's probably out here anyway."

There was a rustle and a commotion ahead of them. Hurrying to catch up, they came upon a pair of dead marines, strung up from a tree. Everyone stood aghast. DeFosse recalled with some understatement, "It kind of pulled them up short."

"Jesus Christ," Bob whistled. "They really don't know the war is over."

Then the two young men went back, changed into their costumes of dark slacks and white short-sleeved shirts, and an hour and a half late, gave the opening night performance of *Tough Situation.*

Johnston Atoll was only a fleck of sand afloat in the Pacific, and it seemed to Papirosky that except for the clean white strand of beach and its fringe of palm trees, there wasn't much there except the American airstrip. Even that, he recalled, was skimpy, and the planes regularly overshot it when landing. "The guys stationed on the island had been out about two years," he said, "and that was two years too many. They were looking at the ground, mostly, they were so dazed from isolation, and it was just the hottest place. There were a couple of trees and that was it. It was a very tiny island that could drive anyone nuts."

Fresh from the flight, Fosse stripped off his T-shirt, ran down to the beach, and began to rehearse. The heat was blistering, and Papirosky warned him about staying out in the sun, especially with his fair complexion, but the boy was from the Midwest and had never seen an ocean before. Besides, nothing could beat the sand for knee slides and so, singing his own accompaniment, he fluttered and shuffled, a Fred Astaire in the South Pacific, leaping and kicking up sprays of sand in the dazzling sunlight. "I never saw anyone rehearse harder than he did, alone on that beach," Papirosky would later say.

That night, *Tough Situation* played to an audience of about a hundred sailors seated on the tarmac under the stars. The show's opening number was "New York, New York (A Hell of a Town)" from the Broadway show, *On the Town.* It was a perfect choice, an exciting, real opening number from an exciting, real Broadway show, a show that was about sailors on weekend passes in New York. Bob did his solo dances, and he did a duo with DeFosse, and he did a two-man comedy act with Bill Quillin. Papirosky had loved Fosse's suggestion for a finale, because it gave him a chance to perform himself, and Bob worked out the new number with him and Quillin, teaching them the words, the steps, and the gestures. The trio trotted into the spotlight wearing dresses, wigs, and high-heeled shoes. Drag was surefire with servicemen, and the sailors roared and applauded at the entrance. The music came over the loudspeaker. Papirosky, Quillin, and Fosse flounced and turned, wobbling on their heels, throwing their hips, and patting their wigs, mincing as they lip-synced the words while over the loudspeaker, the Andrews Sisters sang "The Boogie-Woogie Bugle Boy." And so the Three Fakers lived again, the act as successful on Johnston Atoll as it had been at Amundsen High School playing to the same generation of youngsters.

Just as at high school, too, Bob stayed behind after the show to work on a new number.

In the morning, some of the fellows in the show were on the beach early, rushing past the beautiful "cat's eye" shells and into the water, stretching out on the sand before the heat made it unbearable. They laughed like the kids they were, watching the gooney birds fly gracefully toward the beach, swooping down in lovely low arcs toward landings they could never master, crashing clumsily into the sand and reducing the sailors to joyous laughter. Later, as the C-46 droned over the sweeping, sunlit Pacific, Papirosky's nostrils twitched, catching a strange, foul odor, and he scanned his charges in search of an explanation. "What the hell is that disgusting smell?" he finally snarled, and the guys looked up from their V-mail and *The Stars and Stripes*. Papirosky sniffed his way up and down the plane until he came to a powerful concentration of the stench. It was emanating from Bob Fosse's seabag.

The chief petty officer took the pipe out of his mouth and barked at the young seaman, "Open that damned thing up! What the hell have you got in there?" Fosse had a cache of the cat's eye shells that he had collected from the beach. A city boy down to the taps on his shoes, he had no idea that they contained live organisms and that, in the airless heat of a seabag, the creatures had died. Papirosky had collected some of the shells himself, but he knew how to bury them in the sand overnight so that they would die naturally and be cleaned out by morning. The only way to get rid of the stench in the plane, though, was to push the door open, high above the ocean, and toss out Fosse's seabag. It left the boy with nothing except the clothes on his back, but Papirosky assured him that he wouldn't have wanted anything from that bag anyway and that they could pick up new gear at the next base.

As the *Tough Situation* tour passed the halfway point, Bob had become the star of the unit. "He had real thoroughbred quality," Papirosky remembered. Fosse and Quillin remained close as twins. Bob never seemed able to shake his romantic grief, and Quillin didn't appear to tire of hearing about it.

There was something celebratory about Tokyo. It was the first big foreign city that most of the boys had ever visited. Its bomb-cratered streets and the rubble of flattened buildings were unmistakable symbols of America's victory and war's end. It was to be the last stop on the tour, and most of the unit was going home after these five final performances, which at last were going to be given in a real theatre, the Ernie Pyle Theatre, a 2,000-seat auditorium that the Army engineers had put up almost overnight.

Tough Situation was hardly a spectacle, it was barely professional but it was certainly enthusiastic, and so were its audiences. In this auditorium, as on every stage they ever played, Fosse's Andrews Sisters won roaring ovations. But as Papirosky looked back on it, long after he had changed his name to Joseph Papp and become an important New York producer of stage plays, "The most wonderful thing that I remember about those last five shows was Bob on that big stage, ranging from one end to the other for his solo. He danced all over that stage. Gosh, he was an exuberant kid."

On the way home, everyone in the unit was promoted, and in San Francisco Bob was mustered out a seaman first class, who knew where he was going, and it was not back to Chicago. Fred Weaver may have wanted him to teach at the Chicago Academy of Theatre Arts and resuscitate the Riff Brothers, but Bob had no such intention. He was going to New York, to try his luck on Broadway.

First, however, he had personal business to take care of in California. He telephoned Marion Hauser in Pasadena. She invited him to come to the house and meet her father. They even had the day to themselves, but at the end of it, Bob had to accept the fact that the romance was over and with it his youth.

Like many young men arriving broke in New York, he took a room at the YMCA closest to Pennsylvania Station, the Sloane House on West 34th Street, soon to be notorious as "the weirdest 'Y' in the west." As Bob himself later said of it, "You couldn't very well live there without some [gay] experience every couple of days. When gay dancers would come on to me, I would panic and decline by protesting, 'I'm not that kind of boy.' There was a great deal of anxiety attached to it, probably not knowing what I was sexually. When you're young, you're never quite sure. There were many men I found really attractive. I sometimes thought, 'Is there some latent tendency in me I'm unaware of?' But I never found it a big problem for me, never." (He was being particularly sensitive and tactful on the subject, since he was reminiscing in an interview with a gay-oriented magazine, *After Dark*.)

Setting out to make the rounds, he landed a part at his second audition. It was a truly amazing achievement for a youngster who had absolutely no stage experience beyond a Sailor Show and the variety shows at Amundsen High, but rapid achievement was going to be his pattern. He was hired to dance in the national company of *Call Me Mister*, a hit

Broadway musical, a revue built on the same theme of life-after-discharge as *Tough Situation*.

Except for the women in it, everyone in the cast of *Call Me Mister* was supposed to be a veteran. That hardly gave Fosse an edge as almost every actor in town had been in the service, but he had got the part, and it was the dance lead. He didn't have many lines but he would sing and dance the title number and lead the company in the first act finale.

> It's a beautiful day, ain't it?
> So exciting and gay, ain't it?
> There's a beautiful breeze
> In the beautiful trees
> Call me mister!

Rehearsals began October 9, 1946, at the Central Opera House on 57th Street in Manhattan. He was in heady company, although none of them could know it, for in that touring cast of *Call Me Mister*, besides Bob Fosse, were Buddy Hackett, Carl Reiner, Howard Morris, and the notable baritone, William Warfield.

A show's company of actors becomes a family of friends and lovers for a brief, intense time. While it lasts, the love is true, but once the group disbands they might as well have never met—the nomads move on to other shows, other families, other romances and friendships. As Buddy Hackett said about the *Call Me Mister* company, "We were just walk-ons in each other's lives."

At the age of twenty-one, Hackett was a solid baby bull, a chunky athlete with a marshmallow face punched with bright beady eyes and topped with thick black hair. He had a funny little chewy way of talking as if it were a leftover from using cuteness to get him through adolescence, and his round cheeks would get all pursed and munched up whenever he was eager to talk (which was all the time). There was a devilish innocence about him and an inspired humor based on a fascination with incongruity. That was where he loved to ferret out a laugh.

His friendship with Fosse began during rehearsals. The twenty-one-year-old Hackett had surveyed all the girls in the company. There was one who interested him but only one. Her name was Serena Hall, and he thought she was the most beautiful creature he had ever laid eyes on. Then he studied the competition. *Call Me Mister* was largely a comedy show; there weren't many handsome men in it. The only one to worry about, he felt, was the blond dancer, but miraculously Bob Fosse didn't seem to be interested in Serena Hall. "What a classy guy," Hackett thought. "He's leaving her to me."

Hackett and Fosse were night people, and they both loved to laugh. Bob was awed by New York. Hackett, as a Brooklyn boy who looked upon Chicago as farmland, took it upon himself to show the out-of-towner the big town as he knew it. Yet, when Bob was eager to visit a tourist trap, Buddy obliged, and sitting at one such bar past midnight, he listened as Bob enthused about his ambitions.

"What I really want to do some day is make movies. I want to get out of the theatre and go to Hollywood and direct and produce movies."

Get out of the theatre? Bob had just gotten *into* the theatre. Hackett was struck by "the chutzpah of this little shit—who does he think he is?"

However, more curious about this remark was that, to everyone else, Bob spoke only of an ambition to be a star performer. That was Riff speaking. Hackett was hearing from Fosse.

He shouldn't have been so surprised for he had two sides himself, the actor and the comic—the thoughtful, sensitive fellow and the professional comedian who played mischief with whizzing punch lines. That talent was already making him marketable because small nightclubs were prospering. They faced no competition from television, which was still primitive, and there was never enough talent for the floor shows. Clubs paid more than the theatre, and so even after *Call Me Mister* opened in New Haven and began its tour, Hackett would moonlight in local night spots. Bob would often tag along. He loved comedians and felt at home in the subterranea of strip joints, which were usually where young Hackett worked. Bob didn't like to sleep anyway, or just couldn't, and so if Buddy was playing the Rio Cabana in Boston, for instance, he would watch from the bar and then the two of them would stay for the headliner, "Tirza and her Wine Bath." The Rio Cabana was a place where Bob Riff belonged.

Other nights they would party with the rest of the cast. One night, with a group of them drinking in his room, Hackett glanced through the open bathroom door and spotted Fosse standing at the toilet with his trousers and shorts pulled down around his knees, "and he wasn't peeing." Bob was having a go with one of the girls in the cast. The room fell silent as everyone concentrated on this floor show. Bob was too busy to notice. "It was a nimble fuck," Hackett said. "Dancers could do that."

Even after Hackett had more or less settled in with Serena, he couldn't accept being accepted. Once more he tested Fosse. "Look," he said, "I know you like Serena. Who wouldn't? Take her. I'll find somebody else."

"I told you," Bob laughed. "I'm not interested in Serena. I've got my eye on someone."

"Oh, boy," Hackett said with relief. "What a guy wouldn't do for a friend." But Bob really did have his eye on somebody else in the show, and that was Marian Niles, a compact, chain-smoking dancer with dark curly hair and a hilarious sense of humor. Marian Niles had another attraction. She looked astonishingly like Marion Hauser.

She had begun as a child performer and, like the Riff Brothers, had tap-danced on the radio. She had been a regular on "The Horn and Hardart Children's Hour," becoming so popular on the radio program that she was enlisted to read the commercials ("Less work for mother"). She had also worked in nightclubs, but unlike Bob's joints in Chicago, hers had been chic places such as New York's Versailles.

When Bob stopped running around with Hackett to spend his time with Marian Niles, Buddy was ecstatic. "Now I know what a really great guy you are," he said. "You're just going with Marian so you can leave Serena to me." But, as Hackett later recalled, "they were a real couple. Every once in a while, just for a laugh, I'd ask him, 'Are you sure you don't want Serena?' By then it had become a running joke, and we'd both say it together, 'What a guy wouldn't do for a friend!' "

The friendship with Hackett put an adult stamp on a pattern of camaraderie that Fosse had started as a boy with Socky Markos and George Foutris and then continued in the Navy with Bill Quillin. Male friends would always play a major role in his life, and Fosse would be the richer for it.

One day, Marian came to Buddy while *Call Me Mister* was playing Cleveland's Hanna Theatre.

"You've got to speak to Bob," she said.

"About what?" Hackett asked.

"I don't know what's gotten into him."

"What *about*?" Hackett persisted.

"Bobby wants to join the movement."

"*What* movement?"

"I'm really scared, Buddy."

"You're scared of something, Marian, I figured that out," Hackett said. "All I need to know is exactly what."

"Bob is going to become a Communist. He wants to join the Party."

Hackett didn't exactly know what a Communist was. "I was in show business," he said, "and I was twenty-one years old. I knew about clubs and managers. I knew about billing and play dates, but what the hell did I know about politics? And yet somewhere in the dark, dark recesses of my mind, as Marian talked, an old Willie Howard routine emerged. Something about 'Comes the revolution.' That gave me a clue that joining the Communist Party was not such a great idea."

By that time, Hackett had wearied of the most beautiful creature he had ever laid eyes on and had abandoned Serena for a dancer named Nina. After the evening performance, he arranged for Marian to bring Bob to his hotel room for drinks with Nina and him. After a few, he would broach the subject of joining the Communist Party.

"As soon as I brought it up, Bob turned very, very serious," Hackett recalled, "and he talked about injustice and racism, which we all felt very strongly about." The boys talked earnestly, one twenty-one and the other not quite twenty, about international Communism and not being a jerk-off, both of them sipping drinks while Marian and Nina listened in or talked between themselves.

"You don't want to do this," Hackett was saying.

"Oh, yes I do," Bob answered.

He was doing a lot of growing up on that tour. He was seeing things he had never seen and meeting new people. There were bright youngsters in the *Call Me Mister* company, and unconventional ones too. There had even been a wedding ceremony of sorts between two male homosexual actors, and that was surely unconventional. It was a mind-jostling year for this quick and eager young man. He was certainly intense about joining the Party.

"Join the Party?" Hackett was asking. "No, schmuck. You want to do something to help the world, but you don't want to sign your name to the Communist Party. Once you do that, you can't erase it."

They talked into the night. "I was not going to let him out of that hotel room," Hackett later said, "until he agreed with me. I didn't know what the hell I was talking about, but I knew that it would be trouble if he joined the Communist Party, and at five in the morning he finally agreed. I think I tired him out."

The all-night talk in the Cleveland hotel room may have spared Fosse serious trouble a few years later, for in the early 1950s, Congress would be obsessed with uncovering Communists in show business.

The touring production of *Call Me Mister*, having played in Philadelphia, Boston, Buffalo, and Toronto before Cleveland, and Cincinnati afterward, was settled into its Detroit engagement, and Bob was already being anticipated in Chicago as a local hero. The *Sunday Tribune* ran a picture of him with Marian, flying high in their big dance number, and the newspaper printed a feature about him, headlined "Tops in Taps." He was already calling his family and friends to invite them to see the show at the Blackstone Theatre, which was the next stop on the tour.

Every Fosse came of course. Sadie and Cy were there, and Bob's brothers, who had all survived the war. Patsy came, and all the children who were old enough. Socky Markos came and George Foutris with his wife Tess, and the dramatics teacher, Marion Philbrick. (Nearly every woman in Bob's life seemed to be either a Marian, a Marion, or a Marianne.)

Practically the entire January 1945 graduating class of Amundsen High, too, came to see *Call Me Mister* at the Blackstone Theatre during the summer-long engagement, and perhaps the only one who wasn't thrilled was Smoochie Geweke, who still didn't approve of show business. "He went all out to impress us," was her sour observation.

Charlie Grass came with his mother and so, of course, did Frederic Weaver, who had already added *Call Me Mister* to Bob's credits in the Academy's faculty brochure, even though the young man hadn't taught there since he'd joined the Navy.

Marian Niles notwithstanding, Bob used his glamour value to catch up with the old high school girlfriends. Perhaps Marion Geweke wasn't impressed, but there were plenty who were, and after the show he would go out with one or another of them. He also showed Hackett around Chicago, himself now the city slicker. Buddy had just bought a car, a brand-new and extremely hard to get Chevrolet convertible, and Bob guided him to Division Street for a dinner of Chicago style chili, which would remain a Fosse favorite all his life. He had a powerful identification with this city, and he always would.

He also brought most of the *Call Me Mister* company home for dinner at one time or another and didn't mind when Sadie invited the whole family, even the children, to come and meet these exciting show folk. At one such dinner he and Marian Niles unexpectedly announced that they were going to get married.

Inevitably, everyone in the show assumed that she was pregnant. Hackett did. "I never thought Bob wanted to get married," he said. "Marian was two years older, and I think she cried her way into the wedding. Pregnant was the word."

Pregnant or not, Marian Niles appealed to Sadie Fosse, perhaps because, like herself, the girl was an Irish Catholic who was giving up her faith to marry a Fosse. Sadie, who loved giving parties anyway, decided to throw the biggest one of her life to celebrate her glamorous boy's marriage. It would start with a proper ceremony at one of Chicago's fanciest churches, St. Chrysostom's on North Dearborn Avenue. All the family was invited, as well as most of Bob's school pals, even the girlfriends. Marion Hauser had just come back from her year in Pasadena, but Sadie was hardly about to hurt the girl's feelings by inviting her, and none of Marion's friends had the heart to tell her about the wedding.

The haste of a formal affair, on just one week's notice, was not overlooked by the Amundsen set either. Everyone in Chicago seemed to be gossiping about Marian Niles's pregnancy, but that was the least of it to Fred Weaver. Oh, he knew all about that (he said). He even told Charles Grass, several months later, that Marian had gotten herself an abortion, and he knew where too (Indiana). He never gave any source for his information, but there was the plain implication that Bob had confided in him, and perhaps that was so. Many years later, Marian herself admitted to the abortion, but she set the date a year later. "Bob forced me to do it," she would tearfully tell her friends, although, considering her enthusiasm for her career, that was probably exaggerated.

Of direr concern to Frederic Weaver was the effect of these events on his star pupil. He darkly announced to Grass that he was boycotting the wedding. "I'm not going to sit there in church," he said, "and watch a boy with such talent willfully destroy a brilliant career just as it's getting started."

Marian was helped into her billowing white wedding gown by the Fosse women while Bob buttoned himself into a gray cutaway and striped trousers. He had not asked either George Foutris or Socky Markos to be an usher. He was preparing to choose between lives, as if the past were something that could keep him from his future. He made Buddy Hackett an usher and William Warfield.

With Bob standing at the head of the aisle, tugging at his starchy wing collar, Hackett whispered, "What a guy wouldn't do for a friend!" but the old line failed to get a laugh. "He was very, very nervous and not cool at all," Hackett remembered. "That was not a guy who wanted to get married."

Marian, though, couldn't have been cheerier. Always ready to clown, she wore taps on her white wedding pumps and did a little dance step coming down the aisle. Her friends in the cast laughed, they said that was so typical of her, but Hackett said, "That was the trouble with Marian. She wasn't feminine enough for Bob. She was like a great guy."

After the ceremony, everyone in the *Call Me Mister* company (and none of the high school gang) was invited to dinner at the Fosse home. The newlyweds stood on the front porch in the late afternoon May sunshine, greeting the actors and relatives clambering up the front steps.

Inside, Sadie had set out a lavish spread, and although there was a performance to be given that night, Cy presided over a big bar. While the actors laughed and made wisecracks, the nephews and nieces chased each other around the big living room, excited by the crowd and the noise and the strangers and the perception that there was a very special Uncle Bobby in the family.

If the friends of Bobby's youth were excluded from that wedding party, they were invited to a glamorous reception onstage at the Blackstone Theatre after the evening performance. "A stand-up cocktail party," one of them called it. On that stage the world of where he was going stood in clear apposition to the world of where he had been. One of the chorus boys sarcastically remarked, "Who are all these outsiders?" which offended the Amundsen kids within earshot, but it was the last time that most of the old crowd would ever be within earshot, ever be a part of Bob's life, and that was the truth of it.

There was no time for a honeymoon. Between shows, Bob and Marian began to work out routines for a dance act that they decided to put together after the tour was over. Marriage must have seemed like part of show business to them, part of the act. "We were just babies," Marian would recall, and they certainly were, she twenty-two and Bob twenty. "When we were in bed," she said, "we hardly knew what went where."

A few months later, on August 2, 1947, Marion Hauser got married too. She married Bernard Mayer, who had sung "Let's Do It" at Senior Hall and had been called down by Principal Perry because of it, blamed for Cole Porter's racy lyrics.

She was married in the Lutheran Church just down the street from the old Fosse house on Paulina Street, the house where she used to pick Bob up on the way to school. It was a big wedding, "almost three hundred people," Marion recalled, and Bernie wore a white dinner jacket in Chicago's summer heat. Her stepfather had hired a Masonic hall close by for the reception—it was where Cy Fosse went for his lodge meetings and only a stroll from the church. Following at the back of the entire wedding party after the ceremony, Marion held her flowing white skirt high above her heels to keep from stepping on it or dragging it on the sidewalk.

"It was your regular wedding reception," she remembered, "with a band for dancing and everyone noisy and celebrating," but as she laughed and bubbled her way into the Masonic hall, she caught her breath, for just inside the door, waiting for her, was Bob Fosse, who had not been invited. He simply stood there, blond and pale, his arms limply at his sides. He didn't say anything.

Marion was startled. Momentarily disoriented, she couldn't quite understand what was happening, and speechless, she stared at Bob, who looked straight into her eyes. He seemed to her "very, very sad." Then she turned to Bernie, took his arm, and swept into the reception.

The national company of *Call Me Mister* played Los Angeles after the summer, and in November, at the end of the San Francisco engagement, it shut down. "Everybody was waving good-bye," Hackett recalled, "and Bob and I exchanged pictures. Both of our inscriptions were the same. 'What a guy wouldn't do for a friend!' "

The closing of any show is like a death. Worse than death, it means unemployment. Bob and Marian were so inexperienced at life outside show business that, when they got back to New York, they set up house in a hotel room. That was all they knew about living quarters, and theirs was a sorry Broadway hotel just above Times Square. They didn't mean to spend much time there. Mostly, they were in rehearsal halls and dance studios, working on the act and dreaming about dual careers, one on Broadway and the other in elegant nightclubs.

In anticipation of that, Marian changed her stage name to Mary-Ann Niles and, as "Fosse and Niles," they prepared an act that would combine tap, jazz, and ballroom dancing with the occasional song. They intended to be more athletic and breezy than traditional ballroom teams. After all, American social dancing had itself changed from the formally stepped waltz and fox-trot to the improvisatory jitterbug. Star dancers had also become more athletic, Gene Kelly taking the play away from Fred Astaire. The newer and younger dance teams reflected this development, Donald O'Connor and Peggy Ryan in the movies, Marge and Gower Champion in nightclubs. Evening gowns and full-dress suits were replaced with street clothes. To signify this easing of formality, dance acts called themselves adagio teams instead of ballroom dancers, and Fosse and Niles billed themselves as just that, an adagio team.

Creating, rehearsing, and polishing an act can be exhilarating, fueled as it is by hope and expectations, but jobs for the inexperienced are hard to come by, and money was short in the newlyweds' hotel household. Bob regularly wrote to Fred Weaver for $50 loans. Mary-Ann was hardly inclined to the domestic, and they usually ate at Hansen's lunch counter. This drugstore, at Seventh Avenue and 50th Street, was everyone's theatrical meeting place and clearinghouse; it was where gossip and casting talk were exchanged over endless cups of coffee. Bob and Mary-Ann met everyone who was just like them at Hansen's, and of course that made them happy and comfortable.

When the hotel room itself became too much of a luxury, they found a small apartment at Seventh Avenue and 53rd Street. It was cheaper but not cheap enough.

That was a difficult year, 1948. Bob finally had to ask Weaver for a considerable loan. The reason he gave was a need for psychiatric help in dealing with a drug and alcohol problem. That was the story that Weaver repeated to Charles Grass. It might have been true, although at that time drug usage was largely restricted to jazz musicians and a limited underground; it might have been what Bob wrote as an excuse for borrowing money, or the entire story might have been fabricated by a petulant Weaver, but he did lend Bob the money and without strings. The old management contract was not supposed to lapse until Bob was twenty-one, but Weaver released him from it, a measure of his devotion. Whenever Bob could make repayment, he said, would be fine.

At the end of the year, the young couple's luck turned at last. They both landed parts in the national company of another Broadway revue— *Make Mine Manhattan*, starring the great clown, Bert Lahr. It was not exactly progress. Bob didn't have a song, as he'd had in *Call Me Mister*, but they were the lead dancers and were featured in the big ballet. They would doubtless have preferred to stay in New York, where most television shows originated, where they could double on Broadway, and where they could play nightclubs, but they had little choice.

Nor was *Make Mine Manhattan* the cheerful experience that *Call Me Mister* had been. Bob was not as young or as innocent as he'd been just a year earlier. He began to have affairs with girls in the company, making little effort to conceal it from Mary-Ann. She found a way to live with the situation. It was take it or leave it anyway.

When the *Make Mine Manhattan* company arrived in Chicago, the young couple tumbled into the family nest. The sisters-in-law considered Mary-Ann one of themselves, and Sadie had a plain and special affection for the spunky girl. She arranged a huge family reunion, a boisterous picnic, and afterward they all reconvened at Cy and Sadie's. Nobody could dote enough on the celebrated Uncle Bob. He had, for them, a glamour and fame he would himself never believe.

Make Mine Manhattan was just a stopgap for Bob and Mary-Ann. It was not at all what they were after, but it did keep them afloat. When the tour ended, they seemed to be back where they'd started, the new year looming glumly as a repeat of the old. However, 1949 would be better, in the first place because the team was hired for a spot on the immensely popular television program, "Your Show of Shows," and secondly because its star, Sid Caesar, so enjoyed them that they became his opening act when he played the prestigious Empire Room of the Palmer House in Chicago. "It was my moment of glory," Bob remembered, "after playing all those Chicago joints," and so the story that he had told Marion Philbrick, his Amundsen dramatics teacher, about working at the Palmer House rather than the strip joints at last came true.

The engagement must have seemed like a stroke of luck to Mary-Ann. It was the kind of work that they had been aiming toward, and it would give the marriage a real chance, because they were off by themselves in Chicago, with lots of time for reunions with the Fosses. But it didn't work out. She saw more of the family than Bob did. Sid Caesar had brought one of his writers, Mel Brooks, to keep him company, and Bob liked to hang out with them after the show. He didn't telephone his high school girlfriends this time, but like most husbands toward the end of a marriage, if he wasn't out with a girl, then he was out with the boys.

Fosse and Niles continued to do well as an act even if the marriage was foundering. Almost immediately upon their return to New York, they landed a spot in a new revue that was going into rehearsal for Broadway itself, and that was very big news indeed. The show was called *Dance Me a Song* and the stars were the British comedienne Marion Lorne, the comic Wally Cox, and the dancer Joan McCracken. Bob was going to get his first chance as a vaudevillian, playing in a rowdy sketch, and it was just the kind of thing he was writing home to Mr. Weaver about, for Skipper had practically weaned him on the old sketches and routines.

The dance number he was to do with Mary-Ann was an endearing one, the two of them scampering and shuffling through the traditional time steps and breakaways. They would whisper asides with an easy self-mockery and accompany themselves with breathy expletives, "whoosh!" and "pow!" and "tchoo!" and "ta-dah!" And when Mary-Ann sprinkled sand on the floor so that they could do their soft shoe to "Tea for Two," why the breezy couple was said to be just about irresistible. Among the *Dance Me a Song* company, they were considered a real pair of vaudevillians, and James Kirkwood, Jr., who was doing comedy in the show with his partner Lee Goodman, recalled, "We all thought they were a pair of hoydens, a tough and streetwise couple, by far the least sophisticated in the company, while we of course were Broadway smoothies."

Less amusing to Mary-Ann, no doubt, was the unmistakable fact that during the tryouts in Boston, Bob began an affair with Joan Mc-Cracken. Just as with the girlfriends in the *Make Mine Manhattan* company, and, indeed, with Mary-Ann herself during the *Call Me Mister* tour, he was discreet but hardly secretive. He seemed to take sexual freedom as his right, and just as he had openly betrayed Marion Hauser back at Amundsen High, so he would continue throughout his life, which would lead to accusations of coldness and lovelessness. To some it would seem a sadistic pattern, but his lovers were usually dancers, and dancers were trained to live with physical pain. Perhaps that taught them to live with emotional pain as well.

Mary-Ann Niles, however, found it difficult to tolerate the hurt, or to disguise it. She was frankly unhappy. Then things got worse, for as the tryout continued, it became clear that Bob was not merely having a typical road romance with Joan McCracken. He was in love with her.

4

Dance Me a Song was in sorry shape as it stumbled toward an opening night on Broadway. Mary-Ann was in sorrier shape. She could still be funny. She called the show "Dance Me a Bomb," but she didn't have Bob around to amuse with such jokes. She saw him mainly onstage, and so she clowned for the company. Mary-Ann was just beginning that career, clowning for the kids in the cast.

Joan McCracken was funny too. She was also more experienced than Niles, in life and in her career, and she was more ambitious, more serious minded, and certainly more serious about dance. She had joined a neighborhood Philadelphia ballet troupe by the time she was eleven and was dancing with the Philadelphia Ballet before deciding on a Broadway career.

It was in New York that she found her dance niche. Choreographers collect dancers who fit their style. There were George Balanchine dancers, there were Jerome Robbins dancers. Joan McCracken was an Agnes de Mille dancer. Her classical training satisfied de Mille and her body had the right suppleness, her stage personality the right radiance, her moves the right dip and willow bend. She wasn't really beautiful, but there was a glow about her, and she possessed the first quality of dancing, a beat of energy even while standing still. She had straight dark hair, enormous eyes, and a dazzling smile that Agnes de Mille knew would light up a theatre. The choreographer put McCracken into *Oklahoma!* in 1943 and gave her a small piece of business as Sylvia, "the girl who falls down." Agnes de Mille appreciated the dancer's zest, and audiences adored the plucky girl who would stumble and fall and get up again, who would always step or look or kick in the wrong direction. Even one hard-bitten critic who didn't enjoy *Oklahoma!* was forced to admit that the ensemble dancer with the bit part "saved the first act." The sprite (she was only an inch over five feet) tip-toed and sprawled across full-color pages of the country's favorite magazines. She was everyone's prediction for a brilliant future.

Joan McCracken was plucky offstage as well. A diabetic, she once suffered an attack backstage at *Oklahoma!* As she gasped for breath and then stumbled backward on the way to fainting, another dancer, Bambi Lynn, became hysterical. Jerry Whyte, the production stage manager, slapped Lynn across the face and cried, "Get on stage and do your job! I'll take care of her," and with her next cue McCracken was back on stage, comically tripping all over herself as if nothing had happened at all.

Joanie (as everyone seemed to call her) married a dancer in the *Oklahoma!* company, Jack Dunphy, but the marriage didn't survive the war. She went on to a musical comedy career while Dunphy became best known for being Truman Capote's lover and lifetime companion. Such sexual subdivision was common enough in the ambiguous erotic under-web of the dance world, yet it was by no means indicative of sexual anarchy. As a matter of fact, Joan McCracken was something of a prude, but that was certainly no damper on her exuberance. For inexplicable reasons, however, when she was brought to Hollywood, this exuberance was never quite captured on film. Except for the musical *Good News*, she was groomed by MGM to be a dramatic rather than a musical performer, and yet it was *Good News* that made her a star of sorts, at least back in New York as *Dance Me a Song* neared the end of its Boston tryout, late in 1949.

Theatrical revues like this one specialized in the chic and urbane, and *Dance Me a Song* aspired to that with sketches like "If the Lunts Could Read the Phone Book" and another involving Harpo Marx and a mad scientist in what James Kirkwood described as "a sort of Charles Addams horror sketch." The comedian Wally Cox played an idiot savant, Kirkwood was the mad scientist, and Bob Fosse, wearing a blond fright wig and equipped with a squeeze horn, played Harpo Marx. Fred Weaver would have loved that.

How can anyone hold back from a squeeze horn? Fosse couldn't resist the glorious sound, the belching squank of burlesque. He scrambled around stage, swirling his raggedy coat and honking the horn in everyone's face, but he especially enjoyed startling Kirkwood with a squank right behind him. "He would come around behind me," Kirkwood said, "and honk me in the ass, and I'd say, 'Bobby, don't do that. It makes me break up. Please don't do that.' " But of course the more Kirkwood pleaded, the more Fosse honked.

During the Boston tryout, the audiences seemed to share in such fun, although the horseplay probably didn't amuse Mary-Ann. She had started the tour leading the laughing section with her infectious roar. She would follow up her endless jokes with a cackle that even made people laugh on the rare occasion when her punch line failed, but her laughter stopped as Bob's romance with Joan McCracken deepened. On the train ride back from Boston for the Broadway opening, Kirkwood sat beside her, snoozing with a newspaper covering his face. He was abruptly awakened when someone began to take the paper away. The startled Kirkwood grabbed for it, and with the same motion swatted the pest. "It was only then that I saw it was Marlon Brando. He was a great pal of Wally Cox's and had been going around with us to all the tryouts, just to encourage Wally."

Now fully awake, Kirkwood turned to Mary-Ann, who was not laughing about the Brando assault, as she ordinarily would have. Instead she was sobbing. "What's the matter?" Kirkwood asked. Her response was a tear-choked mumble. It didn't make a difference. He knew what the matter was.

Dance Me a Song opened on January 20, 1950, to terrible reviews, and it closed thirty-five performances later. Mary-Ann and Bob were looking for work again. They may no longer have been a personal team but they stayed together for the sake of the baby, "Fosse and Niles," and that team was now professional and respected, if not quite famous. "We were a second-rate Marge and Gower Champion," Bob would later say. Of course the Champions were the top-ranking dance act of their type. Bob would even grin in the middle of a routine and say to the audience, "You've heard of Marge and Gower Champion? Well, we're the runner-ups." Anyone who heard these self-deprecating remarks over a period of time would know them as suspect, would know that there was something worse to them than humorous modesty. But in performance Bob's grin was so sunny that these remarks seemed engaging. Only in later years would the competitiveness and self-doubt lurking behind them become more evident, emerging the way wrinkles do and age spots.

Contemporaries described Fosse and Niles as a class opening act, cheerfully costumed, he in his brown pinstripe suit, she with her dress beaded on top and flared in the skirt. *Dance Me a Song* may have flopped but Broadway lent them prestige. They began to get steady television work and appeared on "The Fifty-Fourth Street Revue" and "The Toni Revue" before being engaged as regulars on the television version of the radio favorite, "Your Hit Parade."

With Eileen Wilson, Snooky Lanson, and Dorothy Collins the singers, and Bob and Mary-Ann as "The Lucky Strike Extra Dancers" (so-called because of the cigarette sponsor), the show was scheduled for a four-week tryout during the summer of 1950. Although they were given secondary billing, Bob and Mary-Ann were particularly important in lending a visual element to the weekly rundown of the country's most popular songs. They would dance in the background while one of the lead singers performed such hits as "I Wanna Be Loved" (number two) and America's favorite song, the week of the premiere, "Hoop De Doo."

The program survived the summer tryout by approximately eight years. For the moment Bob had a steady paycheck, and he was taking steps toward more challenging choreography. He and Mary-Ann had to devise new routines each week, dances for ballads, novelties, and the standards that were titled "Lucky Strike Extras." Sometimes these were ballroom routines, sometimes vaudeville turns, sometimes jazz dancing. In a must-do situation, Fosse was becoming a versatile choreographer with no little assistance from Mary-Ann Niles.

Because "Your Hit Parade" was televised live, the couple could not accept out-of-town bookings, but they were able to moonlight at local hotels such as the prestigious Persian Room of the Waldorf-Astoria. One evening, just before show time, Mary-Ann was noticed scooping handfuls of sand from a floor-standing ashtray and pouring it into her evening bag. She looked lovely in her cocktail dress but a concierge, thinking Niles cuckoo at least, asked exactly what she was doing with the Waldorf's sand. "I need it for the show, honey," she replied, snapping shut the purse and heading for the Persian Room. "We forgot the sand for our soft shoe."

Perhaps the last that was seen of Fosse and Niles, on or off stage, was early in 1951 when they were given a week off to go to Chicago for a guest spot with Dean Martin and Jerry Lewis on another NBC show, "The Colgate Comedy Hour." The show was being televised from Chicago because Martin and Lewis were playing an engagement at the Chez Paree.

If Joan McCracken was not physically there to keep Bob from Mary-Ann, her influence quite easily reached to Chicago. Joan was a woman not only of ingenuity but also of great energy, not at all unlike Sadie Fosse, and she offered Bob sensible advice which he sensibly followed. She was urging him to be a choreographer. "I was very show biz," he said. "All I thought about was nightclubs, and she kept saying, 'You're too good to spend your life in nightclubs.' She lifted me out of all that."

Taking advantage of the opportunity at hand, he persuaded the producer of the Martin and Lewis show to let him choreograph his own number. There was a small ensemble involved, but was it not just a step from working out the dances for Mary-Ann and himself to creating routines for a larger group?

Not surprisingly, since he had idolized Fred Astaire from childhood, Bob decided on a tribute to the great dancer. With Mary-Ann in tights playing Ginger Rogers to his Astaire, and with him in tails and the both of them in top hats, the idea was to dance before a chorus of five boys and five girls. Bob hired the dancers locally, and one of those who came to the audition was Charles Grass.

The Riff Brothers hadn't talked since Bob went off to the Navy. Charles, after his high school graduation, had joined the Ruth Page Chicago Opera Ballet, becoming ballet master and assistant choreographer. Page took him with her to work on a 1948 Broadway show called *Music in My Heart*, which was set to the melodies of Tchaikovsky and starred the rather unlikely trio of Vivienne Segal, Martha Wright, and the comedian Jan Murray. On the way to rehearsal one day, Grass saw Bob walking along Seventh Avenue across the street from Hansen's Drugstore, just behind the Winter Garden Theatre. Fosse was staring at the sidewalk and wearing the same costume he'd always worn in Chicago, corduroys rolled up a few inches and a pullover sweater. He didn't see Charles as he loped past, and Charles, not calling out, was left to wonder "what would have happened if I had? Maybe we could have hooked up again." He thought about that for a moment before adding, "I did beat him to a Broadway credit, didn't I?"

While Grass was in New York that time, he saw a specialist about his leg, which had been bothering him ever since he had suffered a teenage accident at Montrose Beach on Lake Michigan. The orthopedist found the bone potentially cancerous, but after an operation, Charles survived with his leg intact. He retired from active dancing but continued to teach at Fred Weaver's where, three years later, he now heard that Bob was hiring people for the Martin and Lewis show. Bob always got in touch with Skipper when he was in Chicago.

Charlie did not even say hello to Bob at the auditions. He wasn't asking for favors and didn't expect any ("You can't be professional and be sentimental about such things"). Nevertheless, it must have been distracting when Fosse, finally saying something, said tersely, "Remember, we aren't partners anymore." It was hardly a wonder that some considered him chilly.

At the same time, he didn't make Charlie audition, only asking whether he was in shape, whether he could still do knee slides, and how many turns he could do cleanly. Charles was certain that he could handle these demands. At the final selections, Bob nodded at him, and the job was his. Nothing else was said between them during the week of rehearsals, but if it was frigidity, there was a partial explanation. Fosse suffered from shyness of paralyzing proportions. Shyness was becoming in a child. In an adult, it looked like lack of feeling. (The first time he ran into Joseph Papp, his Navy chief who had since become a major New York producer, Papp greeted the old service buddy with warmth. Fosse barely acknowledged their common history. Papp said, "He made it clear that he wasn't interested in reminiscing.")

Yet it was Bob who had put Fred Weaver up to sending Charles over for the television job. He knew all about the leg injury.

Mary-Ann didn't accomplish much in her visits with Margie and Sadie. Both women loved her, but they couldn't save her marriage. She told friends that Bob was slapping her around. By summer they were separated. In show business parlance as well as in the customary sense, he was a single.

The couple that had seemed such "hoydens" to James Kirkwood, so off-the-street, would find somewhat different avenues for themselves, leading to somewhat different destinations. "They changed so much," Kirkwood later said, "that if you put them together after they were in their forties, you could never have imagined them together." Mary-Ann became a renowned Broadway cutup, the driest and quickest backstage wit. She came to spend much of her time with homosexual actors and dancers because of the unthreatening attention they paid and their appreciation of her comedy style, because of the advances she wouldn't have to fend off and the subtext of rejection that she read among them and so sorely shared. Another thirty-five years it would be for Mary-Ann Niles as a working dancer, stage manager, and Broadway character. She would always be known as Bob Fosse's ex-wife.

1951 was going to be a landmark year in Fosse's life. It was not a year for him to do great things, but it was a year that would make great things possible, things greater than dancing. Creating the choreography for the Martin and Lewis television show, for instance, had been one step toward such a future, and enrolling at the American Theatre Wing was another. It was Joan McCracken who pushed him toward that too. "She said I must go to school and I did," Bob said. "It was a terrific time. The GI Bill paid for all of it, acting, diction, singing, ballet, modern dance, choreography." That was the only time he would study dance formally, and it was a brief time, six weeks with Anna Sokolow and ten weeks with José Limon. The foundation for his becoming a choreographer was being laid.

Another decisive event that year was landing the lead in a summer stock production of *Pal Joey*, but it did not lend support toward the same goal. Rather, it furthered the lesser Fosse dream, the smaller goal but the original one, to be a star. It confirmed the continued presence within him of Bob Riff.

Stardom was a limited ambition, but it was all there was for a song and dance man, and it was all that he was capable of dreaming about. However high Bob Fosse was going to climb, an inner self would always yearn to step from behind the saxophone and drums of a sleazy strip joint to gleam in the spotlight of a variety show at Amundsen High, applause cascading for his machine-gun taps as his blond hair sparkled and fluttered and the grunts of the gorillas turned to schoolmate cheers and girlish squeals over his dazzling knee slides on the Broadway stage, his flashing leaps across the movie screen.

So Bob Riff was becoming more sharply defined, evolving as the self that Fosse would always fear was the true one—the cheap performer who knew every corny routine in vaudeville history. Years later Bob Riff would emerge in aspects of his work as a key to his complexity—the Bob Riff who had none of Fosse's popularity but only the anger of his shyness, none of his charm but only his loneliness, none of his imagination and artistry but only his vulgarity as a tap dancer, singer, and emcee. It was Bob Riff who would never be Gene Kelly or even Donald O'Connor, never mind Fred Astaire, Riff who would always be the failed performer, just a hoofer, leaving Bob Fosse as something worse: just an act, a collection of dreary jokes and tired steps, a personal fraud who felt bitter and cheated of stardom, and that was his secret in the dark.

Even though the summer stock production of *Pal Joey* was a modest one, it was quite a stretch for him to play the leading role. He had never, after all, even played a scene on stage. *Call Me Mister* and *Dance Me a Song* had been revues in which he had been entrusted with snatches of dialogue in a few sketches. Beyond his acting classes (he was now at the Neighborhood Playhouse studying with Sanford Meisner), his total dramatic experience amounted to little more than honking a horn at Jim Kirkwood's rear end, and yet here he was, not only playing the title role in a musical comedy but a role that made dramatic demands.

John O'Hara had created the story of *Pal Joey* as a series of fictitious letters published in *The New Yorker.* At the request of Richard Rodgers and Lorenz Hart, O'Hara rewrote the pieces as a musical comedy libretto, retaining the cynical tone of the original letters.

Joey Evans is a second-rate entertainer who doubles as a dancer and master of ceremonies in shabby nightclubs. He abandons his virtuous girlfriend when he meets Vera Simpson, a society matron who is unfettered by conventional sexual mores. Joey persuades Vera to build him a nightclub, Chez Joey, and the scheme nearly works, but in the end, "bewitched, bothered, and bewildered no more," she abandons him to a future of cheap schemes.

Fosse could not have imagined a character more closely related to Bob Riff, his shameful alter ego: *a dancing master of ceremonies in the joints.* "Whenever I get close to the real object," he would say, "I think, 'Whoops, that looks like Tiffany to me. I better get back to the dime store.'" Like that shabby self-image, Joey Evans was also dime store, romancing an older woman. *Pal Joey* was even set in Chicago.

Joey Evans was also the single greatest dancing role in all of Broadway musical comedy. The original 1940 production of *Pal Joey* had made a star of Gene Kelly. Why couldn't the show do the same for Bob Fosse? Then he too could go to Hollywood and become a movie star.

In truth, Gene Kelly had done better than the show. The Broadway audiences of 1940 weren't ready for a heel to be a hero, at least the critics weren't ready. In one of the more frequently quoted and notorious reviews, Brooks Atkinson rhetorically asked in *The New York Times,* "Can you draw sweet water from a foul well?" After that encouragement, ticket buyers treated the show to barely a year's run. Now, ten years later, *Pal Joey* was still lying buried beneath the priggish reviews that had condemned the show, not for lack of quality but for moral turpitude. Several of its songs had become popular, "Bewitched" and "I Could Write a Book," but forgotten were the remainder of its ingratiating and clever melodies, the ingenious lyrics of Lorenz Hart and the unusually adult, cynical, and biting book.

Revivals of musical comedies were not unheard of—there was the occasional *Porgy and Bess* or *Show Boat.* But because Broadway was a commercial theatre, only new models were of real interest to producers and audiences. So it was imaginative of an enterprising young director name Gus Schirmer, Jr., to revive old musicals, in summer stock. He would package small productions and book them onto a circuit of theatres in resort areas, bringing a pianist, the costumes, and a core cast of actors, while the theatre provided the ensemble and scenery.

The summer of 1951, Schirmer planned to tour unpretentious productions of *Brigadoon, One Touch of Venus,* and *The Boys From Syracuse.* A new recording of *Pal Joey* inspired him to add a modest version of that show to his schedule. Since there had been little interest in it after the original production, composer Richard Rodgers consented.

Schirmer hired Bob to play Joey "because I remembered him from *Dance Me a Song* and because his audition was just tremendous." Fosse didn't remember this or any other audition as being "just tremendous." He remembered them only as nerve-racking, stomach wrenching, and thoroughly harrowing experiences ("I used to die. If I had an audition on Wednesday, I'd start throwing up on Saturday night").

Richard Rodgers had cast approval, and he objected that Fosse was "too blond and too slight" for Joey. Like many, he was prone to visualize only the original actor in a role, and of course Gene Kelly, the first Joey, was dark and muscular. Nevertheless, the composer finally approved Fosse, and Schirmer pieced together a ten-week schedule, to play one- or two-week engagements in most of the major summer stock theatres in the Northeast. The little troupe would bounce from Bucks County, Pennsylvania, to Ogunquit, Maine, to Boston and Cape Cod and back to East Hampton, New York, staying at cheap summer hotels or boardinghouses, and nobody would get rich. Carol Bruce, who was playing Vera Simpson, had the fanciest credits and was being paid $500 a week while Bob was given $200, but Bruce rode with everyone on the bus while Bob and Joanie McCracken drove alone through the pretty towns and the road-signed countryside and along the white stretches of beach. Throughout that summer and along those beaches they breezed and sang, and after the show closed on Saturday nights, they would travel on Sundays.

The part of Joey Evans not only calls for flamboyant dance solos but also for the singing of a slew of Rodgers and Hart songs, including "You Mustn't Kick It Around," "Happy Hunting Horn," "Do It the Hard Way," and the show-stopping duet with Mrs. Simpson, "In Our Little Den of Iniquity." Bob did not have a great singing voice, but he certainly could carry a tune, and if it was a gentle song, he could bring a tenderly ingratiating manner to it. Still, his was a small voice.

The summer tour was a wonderful success. Perhaps the Second World War had lifted the country out of the prudishness that had made *Pal Joey* seem offensive in 1940. Audiences loved it, even audiences in traditionally conservative Boston where, while playing the Boston Summer Theatre, one of the local girls said to Bob, "You're going to be famous one day, do you know?" Her name was Jan Solomon. They were strolling through the city's beautiful park, the Common. It was a sunny summer afternoon.

"Do you really think so?" Bob asked.

"Oh, I do," the girl said. "I'm just sure of it."

"It isn't important, you know."

"It isn't important?" the stagestruck girl cried in disbelief. She was herself just a step above apprentice, spending her summer taking any role at all in the little Boston theatre. "Don't tell me you don't want to be a star!" she said incredulously.

"Oh, sure," he replied. "Of course I want to be a star, but what's more important is loving someone who is right for you."

All the girls in the Boston Summer Theatre knew that he was anxious to marry Joan McCracken and was desperate to get a divorce from Mary-Ann Niles.

"The important thing," Bob said, "is loving someone and working at a career that involves something you love to do. If that makes you a star, that's wonderful, but the important thing is doing it."

They were youthful things to say; he was young and probably meant them, but he would never achieve the ability to love one woman exclusively and enduringly nor ever achieve the performing stardom that he was talking so yearningly about.

During the *Pal Joey* engagement at the John Drew Theatre in East Hampton, the Broadway composer Jule (pronounced "Julie") Styne came out to see the show at Gus Schirmer's urging. Schirmer was beginning to translate his little summer success into a bigger Broadway fantasy, and Styne had just started producing as well as writing shows. He was a small man with thick, black-rimmed glasses and red hair, an energetic and ambitious fellow bursting with enthusiasm. He stayed after the performance to visit with Schirmer, Fosse, and Carol Bruce. Strolling with them up the aisle of the elegant John Drew Theatre beneath the green and white stripes of the simulated tent ceiling, they came through the lobby to the small plaza out front. Standing there for a moment, Styne bubbled, "It's a great show, the best I've seen in years."

The three young aspirants lowered their eyelids modestly. They would later tell each other that they were already envisioning their names in lights over Broadway.

"You're a great young director, Schirmer, and you two kids are marvelous."

They all beamed.

"I'm bringing this show to Broadway."

Well, you can just imagine.

"Yes," Styne continued, "its time has finally come. You, Fosse—I'm going to get Harold Lang for your part, and," he continued, smiling at Carol Bruce, "you, young lady—I'm going to bring back Vivienne Segal as Vera, and with a first-class director too, fella," he said to Schirmer. "Abe Burrows, or somebody like that."

Then, leaving the stunned trio standing in front of the white stucco theatre on the warm summer night, Jule Styne waved good-bye, got into his car, and drove back to New York.

In spite of Styne's insensitivity, his ideas were sound. Vivienne Segal and Harold Lang were the stars of the recording that had renewed interest in the show in the first place. Segal had starred as Vera Simpson in the original Broadway production of *Pal Joey*, playing opposite Gene Kelly, and she was a renowned specialist in the shows of Rodgers and Hart, while Lang had just scored a great success in Cole Porter's *Kiss Me, Kate*. With them to top the cast, Styne could and did arrange to bring *Pal Joey* back to Broadway. Spruced up to the first-class level, it opened in January 1952 at the Broadhurst Theatre on West 44th Street to wonderful reviews. Fosse was hired as Lang's understudy, another installment in the thanks-a-lot department.

It was a bitter pill, and the blithe spirit who cartwheeled down the halls, the exuberant sailor who danced across the wide stage in Tokyo, and kicked up the sand on the beach at Johnston Atoll began to fade away. The sunniness of the most popular boy at Amundsen High was overshadowed, the eager performer not eagerly welcomed. Bob borrowed from Joey Evans, playing the role if not on stage then off. Weather permitting he would don the character's costume, his raincoat and fedora, and, as if in a gangster movie, would talk out of the corner of his mouth, from which drooped his perpetual cigarette.

As understudy, he waited for the time when he could be in the spotlight; he whiled away the hours of Harold Lang's show beneath the stage, hanging out with the chorus dancers who lingered there between numbers. Unlike a standby, who must merely be on call, an understudy had to be physically present in the theatre, to go on were Harold Lang to twist an ankle or break a leg—if only he would. But as it turned out, Fosse needn't have come to the Broadhurst Theatre at all, because Harold Lang never missed a show, not for the entire 542-performance run of *Pal Joey*. Bob's chance would have to come, as chances do, from somewhere unexpected.

It came from Neal Hartley, the show's production stage manager. It seems that the stage managers' union had decided to present a one-night benefit for itself, a showcase offering the best young talent on Broadway. The stage manager of every Broadway show was asked to recommend an understudy or chorus member for a revue that would be presented before an audience of show people. Hartley submitted two of the *Pal Joey* chorus dancers, Norma Andrews and Patty Ann Jackson, and when they suggested that Bob choreograph and also dance, Hartley was enthusiastic. Somehow, there were always women to help Fosse along the way.

Talent 52 was to prove the ultimate showcase. The single performance was given in one of Broadway's biggest theatres, the 46th Street. The audience was strictly professional, drawn not only from the theatre but also from radio, television, and Hollywood. The least to be gained from it was a job in an industrial show, or so it seemed to Jim Kirkwood, who would in fact be singing "Ballad to a Buick" within the year. Kirkwood had been in *Dance Me a Song* with Bob and would appear in *Talent 52.* "The most to be gained," he said, "was a Broadway show or even a movie. That talent show was a huge deal."

The dance that Bob created for Norma Andrews and Patty Ann Jackson was plainly a result of Joan McCracken's influence. No mere tap dancer, not even a tap dancer as good as Bob, could have done this. It was a satiric piece about two girls auditioning for important and terrifying choreographers whose identities, Agnes de Mille and Jerome Robbins, became clear through a congenial twitting of their dance mannerisms. The Broadway of the era was accustomed to big, athletic numbers or symbolic dream sequences. In the aftermath of *Oklahoma!* choreographers took themselves very seriously. Dancers swept across the breadth of stages, leaping and lifting. That made Bob's little piece all the more refreshing. It came as tonic to the wise and world-weary audience of showbusiness toughs, an audience that included George Abbott—the formidable Mr. Abbott of the musical comedy world—for Joan McCracken, one of his favorite people, had urged him to come, and he did. She was providing great encouragement and drive, nurturing Bob's growth. And since Mary-Ann had finally given up any hope of a reconciliation and gotten a divorce, Joan and Bob got married, without much fuss and just like that.

They barely bothered setting up house. Joan was terribly serious about theatre and dance, while Bob was terribly serious about his ambitions. But which ambition—the larger choreography from Joan's perspective, or the old Riff star fantasy?

She got a job in a new show. He got something more out of *Talent 52.* Its audience had included a movie talent scout, mythology incarnate. The studios were thriving. There was so much film production that actors were being scouted on the Broadway stage, given screen tests right there in New York, and hired on the spot. MGM was particularly devoted to musical movies, and its scouts were constantly looking for singers or dancers, and so the miracle happened. Bob was offered a screen test and not merely a screen test, but a test for MGM, "Metro," the maker of the best film musicals, home of Gene Kelly, the biggest and most prestigious movie studio of all.

5

"I wanted to succeed Gene Kelly in the movies," Bob said. He had never even gone on in the Broadway production of *Pal Joey,* had never played Kelly's role except in a threadbare summer stock production, and still he imagined himself replacing the dancing star. He was not being boastful. He evidently believed it. "I thought it was a fair bet," Fosse said, "that I *would* succeed him." To make that unmistakable to the people at the New York office of Metro, Bob chose for his screen test still another role associated with Gene Kelly: Harry in William Saroyan's play, *The Time of Your Life.* His logic could not have been simpler. Kelly had made his Broadway debut in 1939 in the play's premiere. That had been the reason he got the lead in *Pal Joey* in the first place.

The part of Harry is a small one, with only two scenes. Saroyan describes the character as "a natural-born hoofer who wants to make people laugh but can't." He is but one of many quaint characters in the sentimental microcosm that the playwright makes of Nick's Pacific Street Saloon, Restaurant, and Entertainment Palace, but it is a flashy part that calls for comedy and dancing, and it carries emotional weight. That was what had drawn attention to Gene Kelly, and it was plainly a comparison that Fosse was after in his screen test.

Harry's first speech in *The Time of Your Life* comes shortly after he has entered the saloon with a tap dance and the announcement that "I do gags and stuff." An eager amateur, he tries desperately to induce the proprietor to hire him as an entertainer, but only improvises a routine that is pitifully unfunny. The monologue is especially challenging for an actor because it has a subtext giving the audience an insight that the character himself lacks. It tells us that Harry is not simply unfunny but that he has dumb, vital nerve. Then, at play's end, he becomes the catalyst for a stirring finale. He is playing cards with Wesley, the bar's boogie-woogie pianist. They hear a harmonica. Wesley looks up from the game and asks:

You hear that?

HARRY

That's something.

WESLEY

That's deep, deep crying. That's crying a long time ago. Some place five thousand miles away.

HARRY

Do you think you can play to that?

WESLEY

I want to sing to that, but I can't sing.

HARRY

You try and play to that. I'll try to dance.

According to Saroyan's stage direction, "Wesley goes to the piano, and after closer listening, he begins to accompany the harmonica solo. Harry goes to the little stage and after a few efforts begins to dance to the song. This keeps up quietly for some time."

The soft shoe builds through a half dozen more lines spoken by others in the bar before rising to a peak of exuberant tap dancing as Harry flashes ever more assuredly and the final curtain descends.

Combined, the two scenes made a wonderful choice for a screen test, "a phenomenal screen test," according to MGM's Saul Chaplin, who had cowritten the "Bie Mir Bist Du Schoen" that the Three Fakers had lip-synced in Amundsen High and who was now to be the musical director for Bob's first movie, *Give a Girl a Break*.

In the America of 1952, a "seven-year contract with MGM" was as common a phrase as "panty girdle" and "Howdy Doody Time." Everyone knew about movie star contracts from the monthly magazines, *Photoplay* and *Silver Screen*, and from the Hedda Hopper and Louella Parsons gossip columns. But for a minor actor, a so-called contract player like Bob Fosse, a seven-year contract was actually a seven-year contract only as long as the studio picked up the annual renewal option. It meant that he would be paid $250 a week, that he would accept whatever picture he was assigned, whatever the role. That was what *being under contract to Metro* meant, and of course Bob leaped at the offer, quitting *Pal Joey*, throwing his toothbrush and shaving gear into a cigar box, and jumping on a plane for, gulp, Hollywood.

He subleased Buddy Hackett's $135-a-month house in West Hollywood while Hackett was back East playing nightclubs. It was a modest but neat and affordable little place, four rooms and a carport just off Sunset Boulevard. He bought himself a red Chevrolet convertible, which he named Baby and drove to the Culver City studio each morning. He was in the movies, and it was going to be one of the most depressing years of his life.

Give a Girl a Break had started out as a major MGM production starring both Gene Kelly and Fred Astaire, as well as Judy Garland and Ann Miller. It gradually lost its stars to either illness or schedule conflicts, finally becoming a minor musical played by the studio's second team, Marge and Gower Champion, Debbie Reynolds, and such newcomers from Broadway as Kurt Kasznar and Fosse. There were residual elements of the big project it had once been, a score by Burton Lane and Ira Gershwin, for instance, direction by Stanley Donen, and musical supervision by Saul Chaplin. The screenwriters, Francis Goodrich and Albert Hackett, were estimable too, although in this instance they had written a slender story involving three unknown actresses competing for a Broadway role that becomes available when the star walks out.

As rehearsals began in September 1952, Donen welcomed Fosse to the movie. He too had seen that almost legendary *Talent 52* stage managers' benefit, and, himself a choreographer, recognized the young hoofer's talent and enthusiastically backed the screen test. But not everyone with *Give a Girl a Break* jumped on Donen's welcome wagon for Bob. The Champions and Debbie Reynolds, having played small parts in previous MGM movies, snobbishly formed a clique and sniffed at the newcomer, who had once derided Fosse and Niles as "second-rate Marge and Gower Champions." Donen, Saul Chaplin, and Fosse were left to become a trio of pals. In fact, Stanley and Saul were to be Bob's only close friends during the lonely, infertile, and frustrating year that lay ahead.

Almost from the start, Donen and Chaplin noticed their young friend's shroud of gloom. He felt uncomfortable in Hollywood, and everything that happened there made it worse. His experiences as an MGM contract player seemed to amount to being an outsider in an insider's world and absorbing a sense that the studio was losing whatever faith in him it once had. He knew nobody and was invited nowhere, and if he concentrated on his career, it too was going nowhere. He was uncomfortable in a movie world that seemed thoroughly superficial and phony to him, and who was he? A tap dancer from the Chicago joints? Bob Fosse from Paulina Street?

Both Donen and Chaplin were known and accepted in Hollywood. Chaplin, a sweet and unpretentious man, was invited to many parties ("only because I would always play the piano") and the warmly intelligent

Donen seemed to know everyone. They were both social creatures, poised and capable and congenial, while Bob's shyness seemed only to turn him further inward as he balanced himself along the social periphery.

One afternoon, though, he boldly pushed his shyness aside to sit down at the Writers Table in the MGM commissary. The table was called that as if the studio expected the writers to eat as a unit. There was also a Directors Table. The directors didn't sit there either, for the same reason—because they were expected to.

The Writers Table had become the regular lunch spot for a group of MGM's younger players, Arlene Dahl, Ricardo Montalban, Jane Powell, Fernando Lamas, Ann Miller, Elizabeth Taylor. Only the beautiful young actress, Pier Angeli, was silent at the animated table, but Bob was electrified by her, and one day he made up his mind to meet her. The others chattered and giggled as he placed himself beside the actress and tried to strike up a conversation, but she was not responsive. He persisted. She remained impassive. He joined the table daily and made daily overtures to her. The others were cordial, but no matter what he said to the dark, slender, exquisite Pier Angeli, whether it was a whispered confidence or a light joke, her response was remote, if not downright unfriendly. "He developed an enormous crush on her," Arlene Dahl recalled, "but she was not turned on by him at all. He was always trying to make her laugh. She thought he was very forward."

Fosse told Donen and Chaplin that he was in love with the actress, and her total lack of interest seemed only to fire his ardor. The others at the table pointed out that she was virtually unavailable, even to someone she *was* attracted to, because, as Arlene Dahl said, "Pier had a very strict mother and practically went chaperoned on most of her dates." It didn't matter; Fosse remained in love.

Since he was married to Joan McCracken, newlywed at that, it did not make much sense, but Joan was conveniently back in New York, rehearsing for a new show. Arlene Dahl thought the obsession with Pier Angeli had something to do with his ambition to be a movie star and the significance of good looks in that respect. At twenty-five he certainly was an attractive young man. He was blond, if ever more thinningly; he had regular and appealing features with bright blue eyes and a flashing smile, and he was slim, yet muscular. But what was that among men who looked like Fernando Lamas and Ricardo Montalban? And what was that to women like Arlene Dahl, Elizabeth Taylor, and Pier Angeli? "He was not happy in his skin at that time," Dahl said. "Bob wished he had been taller and better looking. He hated the way he looked. He really wanted to be someone other than what he was, and he thought his looks were holding him back. And when he talked about losing his hair, it was worst of all. He was afraid it might have something to do with his sexual potency."

One day at the commissary lunch table, he idly said to the group, "Listen, I may be directing all of you one day." There was an awkward silence. Nobody seemed to know how to take this plainly absurd remark. As if to cue them, Bob abruptly burst out laughing, and then everyone joined in. They resumed their chattering, everyone except Arlene Dahl. She fell silent and stared at him, by no means certain that the remark had been idle.

Direct a movie? How could he possibly have imagined such a thing? Where had he drawn the nerve to dream that to Buddy Hackett five years earlier? Where was that dreamer now? "In those early years," Donen recalled, "he never showed any desire to direct, and we were as close as you can get. He wanted to be a performer, that was all." But evidently it wasn't.

"When Bob finally accepted that he would never get Pier Angeli to fall for him," Donen chuckled in his light Southern accent, "he finally gave up and went out with her sister, Marisa Pavan." Pavan was Pier Angeli's twin, but she wasn't the same. As for Angeli, her mother was not quite as rigorous a chaperone as Arlene Dahl thought. As a matter of fact, the actress was in the thick of a steamy love affair with James Dean, and that was her reason for rejecting Bob Fosse.

Donen gave him a good-sized role in *Give a Girl a Break*, almost as big as Gower Champion's, and the two young dancers had several numbers together. Bob was also to dance with Debbie Reynolds, and Donen found him not only cooperative but "the hardest worker I've ever known." Like almost everyone who ever worked with Fosse, Donen was awed by his perfectionism, the tireless repetition until he got something right. If there was any problem, it was a back flip that Donen had decided would be the climax of one of Bob's big numbers, and Fosse was scared to try it.

The young man had not yet discovered his particular dance style "but when he did," Donen said, "it would be delicate and small, with no major physical or athletic moves. He didn't want to do the back flip, but I staged the number doing what *I* knew, not what he did."

A back flip is a backward somersault achieved without touching the ground, "just throwing your feet up in the air," Donen said blithely. It lends the illusion of momentary suspension, the head hovering above the ground, and Donen practiced with Bob for hours, holding an arm behind the small of his back as he flipped.

Finally, the director said, "Okay, we're going to do it for the camera, the whole dance right up to and including the flip." And for the one and only time, with nobody behind him for support, Bob did the flip, and it was perfect. They had it on film, and that is how it appears in the movie.

Donen never did know that Bob flew to New York and spent two days working with Joe Price, an acrobatics teacher, to get the flip right before coming back to do it on camera that one time.

The closing number in *Give a Girl a Break* was called "Applause." Saul Chaplin arranged it with a syncopated, counter-rhythmed handclapping and foot stamping for Bob and Gower Champion and Kurt Kasznar. With Marge Champion standing beside the camera, urging her husband (in vain) to jump higher, Fosse and Champion vied to outleap each other, the two young men destined for Broadway success, each with the radiance of youth, each with his own neuroses. (Champion would always be so distrustful, he would never allow anyone to stand behind him while he was working.)

Give a Girl a Break was Bob's first and best chance at MGM, his biggest speaking part, his greatest dancing opportunity. It did not impress the group of musical-movie producers who informally decided whose career would be pushed and whose not. His manner was sweet but mild, and his dancing was very imitative of Gene Kelly. "He never got the kind of launching that Kelly got," Chaplin recalled, and it might have been just as well. If Bob had been lucky enough to get such support, he could have ended up, as he himself once mused, "a movie dancing star wearing a toupee."

His personal life wasn't cushioning him from the disheartening start, for he was socially isolated, having moved out of Hackett's little house, now that Buddy had returned, and into a one-room studio apartment with a fold-down Murphy bed, located in a rundown section of Culver City. It was all symbolic of his low morale, and as Fred Weaver told Charlie Grass, Bob's monthly letters expressed it repeatedly before concluding with the usual request for a small loan.

At the start of 1953, almost immediately on the heels of *Give a Girl a Break,* he started work on *The Affairs of Dobie Gillis,* a movie destined to achieve a Zenlike oblivion. It was as plain as the hair on his pillow, he was not going to be MGM's next Gene Kelly, despite all of his Kelly-inspired career moves, and perhaps that was why he was making repeated wisecracks about Kelly's dancing. (Comparing him with Astaire, Bob would say, "You can tell which one is the truck driver. All Kelly knows is acrobatics and two or three steps.")

This disparagement of Kelly was also a demonstration of allegiance to Fred Astaire, whom he spent every spare moment watching. Miraculously, while *Give a Girl a Break* was filming on one sound stage, *The Band Wagon* was in production on another just down the alley. Whenever Bob could slip free, he would walk over and hide behind a scenic flat to watch the great dancer rehearse. Saul Chaplin once saw Fosse walking behind Astaire and mimicking the dancer's rhythmic lope, even his swinging arms. Donen noticed Astaire sidestep a nail that was protruding from a board on the ground and abruptly kick it out. Immediately behind, Fosse copied the same skipping maneuver and the kick. When Astaire disappeared around a corner, Fosse remained to rehearse and repeat the sudden sidewise step—skirting the nail and then kicking it—until he got it right.

The movie that would matter the most to him was the one in which he had the smallest role. It was the screen version of the Cole Porter musical, *Kiss Me, Kate,* which went into production almost immediately after *Dobie Gillis*. Fosse's character had a name, Hortensio, but it was never mentioned in the picture and, considering his handful of lines, a name was hardly necessary. He was a bit player, a dancing backup while Kathryn Grayson tossed bouquets, vases, and anything handy into the lens of the 3-D camera.

Fosse's contribution to *Kiss Me, Kate* was to be minimal, but he did ask Hermes Pan, the choreographer, if he might make up his own section of one number. It was a sequence that was to be noticed 3,000 miles away on Broadway, because Joan McCracken would make sure it was. The number was built around a song, "From This Moment On," that Cole Porter had not even written for *Kiss Me, Kate*. It was a reject from *Out of This World* that Chaplin remembered when an extra song was needed toward the end of the movie. The number involved three couples, six unusually gifted dancers, Ann Miller and Tommy Rall, Jeanne Coyne (Gene Kelly's then wife) and Bobby Van, Carol Haney and Bob.

The part of "From This Moment On" that he would stage was his dance with Haney, beginning as she makes a stripper's entrance, leading from the pelvis. Suddenly he flashes in from the wings, feet first, in a long, swooping, startling and dazzling baseball slide that lands him prone on his back at her feet. As he rises, they freeze for three dramatic beats, and at this instant the Bob Fosse style of choreography came into existence. It was born of Carol Haney and sired by the strange and striking choreographer, Jack Cole. For Carol Haney was a Jack Cole disciple.

Jack Cole was one of the most prominent and influential choreographers in Hollywood during the post World War II years. His prominence and influence were peculiar in that their scope was essentially limited to dancers, not extending to other choreographers and the general public.

Cole was a dancer's choreographer; he seemed to work for dancers alone, unaware of outsiders, and among dancers he was already a legend.

Carol Haney had danced for him in the movies and was the lead dancer in his nightclub act, the Jack Cole Dancers, until she quit to become Gene Kelly's assistant at MGM. Apparently she missed performing because she was taking the opportunity offered by *Kiss Me, Kate* to dance briefly on screen, and that was how she came to work with Bob Fosse in "From This Moment On." In the process of working out the number, she introduced him to the dance language of Jack Cole. Fosse did not mimic Cole in his steps, nor did he adopt Haney's own mannerisms wholesale, although as another Jack Cole dancer said, "Jack's dancers not only had abilities but a stylistic sense, and a way of carriage that was unique." But as Fosse was finding his dance self, Cole and Haney had surely led the way.

In "From This Moment On," Carol Haney is wearing an Elizabethan gown while Fosse is in harlequin tights. The music has stopped. They begin snapping their fingers rhythmically, a device that would be repeated on Broadway for the following decades in one or another of the elegant, miniature, quirky, detailed, accented, and syncopated dances that would be identified with Bob Fosse, the "delicate and small dancing" that so pleased Stanley Donen.

As the duet continues, he moves to Haney's side. Both are grinning sunnily as if they know exactly what they had just discovered, and they swivel their shoulders in unison. His knees are slightly bent with an easy tension. He nods with his head, a "let's go" gesture, and they invert their knees and toes, awkward and elfin.

He springs onto the base of a lamppost, swinging out on one arm with Haney beneath him, and again they snap their fingers in time with the big band swing of the music. Off the lamppost, back on the ground, he leads her into a famous Fosse knee slide with arms half outstretched, elbows tucked, wrists limp, hands facing front, and fingers spread, and still he grins; it is infectious and warming. It seems as if they are going to make their exit now, down on one knee and inching along, sidling off, but they abruptly pick up for a big finish, a flash finish, a Riff Brothers finish.

The energy cuts down, leaving them grinning impishly as they slip through small steps, their knees bent, their bodies seemingly relaxed. Bob pushes his hat down over his eyes, and they again edge along on their knees. Then Haney returns to the stripper's bumps that began the dance; suddenly Bob does a complete back flip. Then he and Haney shuffle off, and the whole movie might as well end right there, for nothing in it has approached this number, and nothing can follow it. It is hard to recall a more ingratiating movie dance outside of Astaire, hard not to feel that Fosse is thumbing his nose at Hollywood and saying his not so fond farewell, on camera. The dance practically giggles with relief.

He broke his contract. It was unheard of. Was not Metro the dream of anyone's life? Donen and Chaplin both believed that the studio would have renewed his option, but Fosse apparently felt that his career had stalled, and he certainly had not been happy. He put "Baby," his red convertible, on cement blocks, had its battery and tires removed, and went back to New York and Joan McCracken, just in time for her opening on Broadway in *Me and Juliet*.

They lived in her apartment at 150 West 55th Street, and she, tireless in her dedication to his career, made another telephone call that mattered, a call to George Abbott, who had just directed her in the show. The great master certainly did remember Bob's dance in *Talent 52*, and if Joanie thought her husband was gifted enough to choreograph on Broadway, "her word is good enough for me," he told the producers of his next show, *The Pajama Game*, and so in these vast leaps, in such breathtaking sequence, Bob Fosse was catapulted from being a tap dancer to being an overlooked contract player at MGM to being the choreographer of a Broadway musical.

In Chicago, Marion Hauser, the love of his high school days, had contracted polio. The disease is all but unknown today, thanks to the Salk and Sabin vaccines that were developed in 1953. They were excitedly announced one month too late for Marion. She would be paralyzed from the waist down for the rest of her life.

The fun in musical comedy came of its being the illegitimate off-spring of the legitimate theatre. That gave it the freedom to be antic. It had no history before popping out of an orchestra pit. There wasn't a serious thought in its head. Intellectuals and stage snobs looked down their noses at this bastardized operetta, dismissing it as a product of commerce, and indeed, it was so popular that it might have been con-ceived in a box office. Because of this tainted birthright, the musical's makers, its writers and directors, were never limited by the constraints that could have doused their high spirits. Unencumbered by pretension, not expected to enlighten or ennoble, they were free merely to entertain. That, of course, was the toughest task of all.

Later on, when *Show Boat* and *Oklahoma!* demonstrated that musi-cals could be serious as well as popular, they were still considered a commercial kind of theatre, justified only by a profit statement. The only good show was a hit show; that was the conventional wisdom. An audience might be convinced that it was supposed to enjoy a lofty-minded play because it was being culturally nourished in the process; an audience could be chided for missing the point of something intellectual or abstract. But not the audience for a musical. There, the crowd was the judge, its laughter and cheers had to be won or else the show was given the hook. Such was the point, making entertainment, and even as musical comedy became the much grander *musical theater*, entertainment stayed on to make its demands, like a crusty grandpa who made it possible for everyone to put on airs by founding the family fortune in the first place.

George Abbott was that grandpa. A successful director of drama and farce, he had turned to musical comedy in the 1930s and was equally successful at that. Successful? His record was astounding, and even in 1953 at the age of sixty-six, he was still at his peak. As *The Pajama Game* was being discussed, he was opening two new musicals on Broadway, *Wonderful Town* and *Me and Juliet*, the first with music by Leonard Bernstein, the other by Rodgers and Hammerstein. He was Mr. Broadway Musical, of that there was no doubt.

He was also "Mister Abbott." It was suspected that even his mother called him that, and the respect wasn't a matter of his imposing height (six feet six inches) or even his imperious manner. It was because, like his shows, George Abbott had no nonsense about him. He was in the business of making entertainment, not philosophical statements or art. He was brisk, he was unsentimental, he was unemotional, and if these were shortcomings in the man, they were strengths in the director.

He liked to work with newcomers. Their inexperience assured their freshness, but in the case of *The Pajama Game*, there seemed to be a surfeit of it. The writers of the music and lyrics, Richard Adler and Jerry Ross, were new to Broadway, the playwright had never written a script but only the novel on which this one was based, and even the producers were virginal. In fact, two of them had previously been Mr. Abbott's *stage managers*—Robert Griffith and Harold S. Prince—and they had so little money that they were going to be the stage managers for *The Pajama Game* too. If George Abbott wanted to be in an unquestionably dominant position, he could not have managed it better.

The Pajama Game was drawn from an unlikely source, the novel *Seven and a Half Cents* by Richard Bissell. Set in a pajama factory in Iowa, the story hardly seemed the stuff of musical comedy. In those days, with a death in every Rodgers and Hammerstein show, Broadway considered itself rather open-minded about subjects for musicals, but this show had a subject that was even more unsingable than death: union trouble in a pajama factory. Yet it didn't faze Mr. Abbott and his little row of Broadway chickens. Even when his friend and pet actress, Joan Mc-Cracken, pushed her inexperienced husband into the coop, Abbott remained confident. But if choreographing one number in a stage managers' benefit and playing thirty-five performances in a flop revue were good enough for George Abbott, Bob Fosse's slender credentials made Harold Prince a very nervous young producer. He had never heard of Bob Fosse, which put him in a category that included almost everyone outside of Amundsen High School. Nevertheless, Joan got the entire *Pajama Game* production team to see *Kiss Me, Kate* at the Radio City Music Hall where Bob's big dance number played spectacularly on the mammoth screen. "Perhaps Joanie was right," Prince thought, "and not just biased when she had told Abbott, 'My husband is going to make a terrific choreographer.'" He certainly loved the movie number himself but was that enough of a basis to hire Fosse to stage all the dances for a big Broadway show? Prince's first?

He discussed it with his partners, who agreed that they could not take such a chance. When everyone met later, Prince said, "Look, I think the number is great, but I think we should be protected. We love Joanie. Fosse is a great dancer. The work he did in *Kiss Me, Kate* is wonderful but how do you know he can do a Broadway show? *He's never done one.*"

"I trust Joanie," Abbott insisted, but Prince wanted protection rather than trust and suggested a reasonable alternative. The show already had one creative standby, the composers' publisher, Frank Loesser, who had agreed to help out were Adler and Ross to come up short. Why not, Prince suggested, ask Jerome Robbins to do the same regarding the choreography? After all, Robbins had a history with Abbott dating back to 1943's *On the Town*, and the two men had done many musicals together, including *High Button Shoes* and *Call Me Madam*. Had not Robbins, that very season, helped Abbott with *Wonderful Town*?

The tall, tough director agreed, and when they talked to Robbins, he accepted the arrangement. He would stand by "because of Bob's inexperience" and would help out when there were "things he didn't know that I could come in fast and do." Robbins, himself only thirty-five, was already the most respected choreographer on Broadway, but the billing that he requested was not as a choreographer. It was as codirector. "You know," Prince said to Abbott, "that he's not going to be a codirector, but that's the credit he wants because he wants people to know that he wants to direct."

Abbott replied, "What do I care about the credit? People will know that I did it."

Robbins received a substantial percentage of the show's weekly receipts in exchange for his availability. Fosse, who would not need much help, ended up with a flat salary of one hundred dollars a week. Richard Adler, one of the composers, "was astounded by how little he got. Even we were getting a percentage, and it was our first show too. Bob's must have been the smallest choreographer fee ever paid in the musical theatre." But it didn't make much difference what he was being paid, and Fosse surely knew it. If that was the price of an opportunity like this, then it was the bargain of his life.

Rehearsals for a George Abbott musical were always smooth and orderly, and *The Pajama Game* was no exception. The stars behaved themselves, whether, like John Raitt, they came from Broadway, or were Janis Paige from Hollywood. He played a pajama factory superintendent, and she the union officer he falls in love with. The romantic hinge is obvious—a conflict in job objectives, which is a situation not made in song and dance heaven. The secondary romance sounded like more fun.

From the apeman days of musical comedy, it was common for the central lovers to be seconded by another, funnier pair. *The Pajama Game*, its uncommonly adult and sexy romance notwithstanding, had such a second couple. Eddie Foy, Jr., the veteran vaudevillian, played one half of it as an efficiency expert who is dangerously jealous of his flirtatious girlfriend. Carol Haney, the dancer whom Bob had brought from *Kiss Me, Kate*, demonstrated so infectious a stage personality that Abbott combined her part with that of the girlfriend.

The director tried to ease Bob's choreographic initiation by laying out exactly where he wanted the dances so that the young man could organize his schedule and work at his own pace. The decision to drop the ballet to start the second act, however, was probably based more on Abbott's own inclination than on a lack of faith in Fosse's ability to handle it. "Ballet" was a loosely used word on the Broadway of 1954. It served for any long dance that involved a large group. It could be jazz dancing, it could be acrobatics or toe work, but as long as it lasted more than three minutes and had no singing, it was a ballet. Mr. Abbott put up with such things only because he accepted the audience's current infatuation with them, but he didn't like the idea because his rules for musicals were the same as the rules of farce, where every scene had to advance the story.

Since *The Pajama Game* already had a big, chorus-type number ("Once a Year Day") he told Bob to "forget about the ballet and give me an amateur entertainment that the union can put on at its meeting." Perhaps he recalled Fosse's quirky little dance for *Talent 52*, because he added, "Do something small."

Small? That was Fosse's size, and with instructions no more detailed than that, he turned to the show's songwriters. "We have something that fits into that," Richard Adler told him, "but to be honest, it's just awful. Jerry [Ross] and I did it as an exercise, just to see if we could write a story-related song even if a story was set in a bathroom. Our publisher, Frank Loesser, had just written a big hit that went, 'Bloop, bleep, the faucet's dripping, and I just can't sleep,' so we tried to write one about noisy radiators and steam pipes."

As soon as Fosse heard the song played, he was enthusiastic. He loved sound effects. They accented and highlighted dance moves the way ratchets and drumsticks accented punch lines in the old vaudeville routines. This song was based on the sounds of radiators hissing and steam pipes knocking. Taking it and the rest of his music along with a dance pianist, Bob went into seclusion for "about six weeks," he remembered, "before the dancers came in. I had every dance already worked out by then. I'd worked out every part myself, just to avoid embarrassment."

The "little number" that Abbott requested became the choreographic fugue "Steam Heat." The dancers were Carol Haney, Buzz Miller, and Peter Gennaro (later to be a Broadway choreographer himself). As Fosse started them out in the studio, with the dance already completed in his head, they were posed side by side, their backs to where the audience would be, hats held high above their heads in a freeze. Then they turned, edging sideways toward where the footlights would be. With each raising a shoulder, they toss the hats in unison, catching them simultaneously. The rhythms are jazzy and syncopated, the music starts to build, and then it abruptly shuts down as they dance in silence, except for the sound of their scuffling feet. The three skinny clowns elbow and slide and drop down on their knees and stand up again and then edge along with their elbows tucked and their hands spread in the gesture that would soon be known as "Fosse hands." They become a little machine, clacketing to the sounds of clucking tongues and knocking mouths, with hissing and finger snapping and counter-rhythms of hand clapping and foot stamping. It is like a cuckoo clock gone silly, with ratcheting turns for its three little birds, twitching and jerking, every twitch timed to its own pop and snap with no curled finger, no lifted shoulder, no eyebrow going without a sound accentuation.

Fosse's six weeks of solitary preparation were so thorough, and Carol Haney, Buzz Miller, and Peter Gennaro were so facile, so inspired by the number, that in the rehearsal studio, as Miller remembered, "We just zipped through it." Haney, after dancing with Bob in Kiss Me, Kate, could duplicate a Fosse step even before he finished demonstrating it, and

Miller said, "We were just thick as thieves. Bob would show us what one or the other was supposed to do, or all three, and we'd say, 'uh-huh' or 'mm-hmmm' or 'right!' because we were so zonked out on that number."

The costumes and props for "Steam Heat" were to be as much a part of it as the choreography. The dancers were dressed like English music hall tramps, making for an androgynous and Chaplinesque appearance, with black suits that were tight and skinny—little buttoned-up numbers with pipestem pants that were short enough to show white socks over black shoes (it was Fosse's own look, like his rolled-up trousers, those pipestem pants, short over the shoes and showing white socks). The threesome would also wear white gloves and the hats would be derbies.

Joan McCracken looked on as they worked, saying nothing except during work breaks when she would join in whispered conferences with Bob. Also watching was a slight and earnest young man from the Frank Loesser office. His name was Stuart Ostrow, and he was a musician turned song plugger, already dreaming of becoming a Broadway producer. Ostrow was hopelessly stagestruck and had to be dragged away from rehearsals. He would see Bob Fosse again.

Fosse's preparations had been so thorough that it took only five days to put "Steam Heat" on its feet, along with all the other dances in the show, and on opening night of the tryout in New Haven, the little trio stopped the show. Carol Haney, Buzz Miller, and Peter Gennaro remained in their final freeze, blinking the tears away as the aches of backbreaking, sweaty, exhausting rehearsals and the emotional strain of auditions and rejections were now so overwhelmingly worthwhile.

Was Mr. Abbott thrilled about "Steam Heat" stopping the show? "He was very upset about that," Buzz Miller remembered. "He didn't like numbers to stop the show, and he wanted 'Steam Heat' taken out." Jerome Robbins disagreed. "Look," the would-be director said to Abbott, "the number is just too good. You can't throw it out." But Abbott was annoyed because the show's forward thrust was not only being interrupted; the show was being stopped by three anonymous dancers in a minor entertainment that had nothing to do with the story. "He wanted to keep the action going," Miller said, "that is his forte." But Abbott finally gave in to Robbins, and "Steam Heat" remained in *The Pajama Game*. By the time the tryout reached Boston, "The show was frozen," Harold Prince remembered, "and we were a smash hit. Jerry Robbins came up to iron out a few wrinkles, and he did stage 'There Once Was a Man' in its entirety but that was all, really." The show was ready for Broadway.

Robbins gave Fosse a pair of gold cuff links for luck on opening night, May 13, 1954. They had been Robbins's father's cuff links, and they were to become a ritual opening night gift. Jerry's next show, Bob gave them back to him for an opening night gift, and Bob's next show after that, Jerry gave them to him for good luck.

The ovation for "Steam Heat" burst from the Broadway opening night audience like a fireworks display. Abbott's disapproval of the show-stopper, while admirable in theory, was a refusal to allow an audience its role in the theatrical equation. An audience functions best when caught in the tension of wanting to jump onstage and change the action and being unable to do that. When it can stop a show and restore the characters to their real identities as actors by declaring that everyone is in a theatre and that the actors are on a stage, then the audience has its catharsis. As it brings the show to its knees, begging to be allowed to continue, forced to stop action and acknowledge the cheers, such an audience is elated by its own beneficence, its power, and its role in approving the entertainment and rewarding the players. It has resolved the tension and performs its full part in the event.

That is what the audience did with "Steam Heat" on the opening night of *The Pajama Game*. Carol Haney, Buzz Miller, and Peter Gennaro let the applause flow over them, they let the theatre just rock, and as if shaken from the rafters by this great and rousing audience, one ecstatic review fluttered down upon the other, newspaper clippings from paradise. George Martin, the dance captain from Bob's understudy days at *Pal Joey*, stuck his head in backstage just to give a hug and tell Fosse how great "Steam Heat" was. Bob laughed and said, "That was the easiest one." George couldn't stay for the party; he was going across the street to take Gwen Verdon out for coffee after her performance in *Can-Can*.

Bob's Hollywood pals hadn't forgotten him either. Stanley Donen had come to the out-of-town tryouts to cheer him on, and Saul Chaplin had more than one reason to be at this opening night for, besides Bob, his old pal Carol Haney was in the show. Of all the actors, she had gotten the best reviews, the kind that star careers are made of; she was the discovery of the season, and everyone was predicting a brilliant future for her. Chaplin had a special twit awaiting Fosse, but before he had a chance, Bob admitted it, "I know, don't tell me. I stole your 'Applause' arrangement."

Indeed he had, taking from their MGM movie, *Give a Girl a Break*, the intricate hand clapping and foot stomping that gave such a catchy syncopation to "Steam Heat." Chaplin laughed and said, "You're welcome to it. You're entitled, especially after all that vanilla syrup you gave me" (a reference to the gallon jugs of Cy Fosse's homemade "My Own Vanilla" syrup that Bob gave him for Christmas).

Then Fosse walked off, swallowed into the wonderful engulfing approval, the kisses and envious joy that make a Broadway hit so special, particularly since the kisses and joy are linked to tons of money and more work. Chaplin laughed with his daughter Judy and (though she couldn't know it) her husband-to-be Harold Prince and with Carol Haney.

About "Steam Heat," Jerome Robbins would say, "It isn't surprising that Fosse's style was there at the very start. Either you have a statement to make, and you make it, or you don't. He had a quality that was Bob Fosse's quality and nobody else's."

But nothing in life is really new except French fried ice cream and painless love. Helen Gallagher, the dancer who had worked with Bob in *Pal Joey* and would later replace Carol Haney in *The Pajama Game*, thought he had achieved an original look with "Steam Heat," but she also thought that "the slides and shoulder movements are Jack Cole while the hats and props are Fred Astaire."

Ethel Martin, who had danced in the Cole troupe with both Carol Haney and Buzz Miller of "Steam Heat," felt that "Jack had given us a stylistic sense, a way of tucking under, a way of moving, a way of stance, which Bob had admired and learned. When you had Cole people dancing, like Carol and Buzz, they gave something an unmistakable look. Maybe Bob gave it another point of view, maybe even for the better, but they were using Jack's tools. Because they *were* tools. To have taken those people and put them in 'Steam Heat,' well, with all credit to Bobby, it had to have something from Jack." And Agnes de Mille agreed; in fact "they all stole from Jack Cole," she said. "Jerry Robbins and of course Fosse."

These remarks would not have rankled him. He probably would have agreed.

> I see my style as based on my own physical limitations and I've developed, from them, a style because I've been dancing since I'm nine. So my style is a kind of—I've stolen things from people, I've been influenced by people. I've been forced to dance in a certain way because I tend to turn in more when I'm dancing. I've never been a bravado person so a lot of things I do are very tiny and small. So it's a maze of various influences.

The day after *The Pajama Game* opened, he packed a bag and went to join his wife. *Me and Juliet*, not a success, had just closed in New York, and Joanie had gone with it to play a Chicago engagement. It was time to introduce her to the family.

In New York, the audience for the third performance of *The Pajama Game* included the most important person any actor could play for—a movie producer. The reason Hal Wallis was there was to see Carol Haney, but *she* wasn't there. She was out of the show with a broken ankle. Her friend Buzz Miller believed that "when it came time to get applause or recognition, Carol always hurt herself. She gets these fabulous reviews, with a movie producer coming, and she breaks an ankle. It was built in. We expected it. Only Freud could figure it out."

Some time before, Jerome Robbins, in his vague capacity as codirector, had stopped by at the final auditions for the chorus dancer who would understudy Haney. There was a pretty girl sitting aside, apart from the rest.

"What's the matter with that one?" Robbins asked Fosse.

"She's in the Rodgers and Hammerstein show," Fosse had replied, "and I don't want to take a girl from another show."

"That's ridiculous," Robbins said in his soft and boyish way. "You don't know how long that show's going to last. Let's hear her."

After her reading, Robbins asked to see the girl dance, and then he said, "She's very talented. Listen, they would take someone from you. Go ahead and hire her." There was nothing else to do at that point but sign her as Haney's understudy.

As Hal Wallis took his seat, the stage manager stepped between the curtains, greeted by the traditional groans, for the audience knew that such an appearance meant the announcement of an understudy. "Ladies and gentlemen," the stage manager said, "the management regrets to announce that Miss Carol Haney will not be performing tonight."

The groans turned to outright boos. Carol Haney was the discovery of the year. Some left the theatre, asking for refunds or new tickets. "Miss Haney's role," the stage manager continued, "will be performed by Shirley MacLaine. We hope you enjoy the show."

MacLaine had arrived at the theatre with her resignation in hand. She had been offered a much more attractive job as understudy for Gwen Verdon in *Can-Can*, which was playing at the Shubert Theatre, just across the street. At least Gwen Verdon occasionally missed a performance, and those were big dance numbers. They had made Gwen the biggest discovery until, well, until Carol Haney. As MacLaine arrived at the theatre, she saw Harold Prince backstage and reached into her bag for the resignation letter. She never had a chance to give it to him. After she had been warned by other dancers that Carol Haney would never miss a show, she now learned, in the very first week of the run, that Haney was out for the duration.

The shoes didn't fit. MacLaine had to wear her own sneakers to dance "Steam Heat." Apparently they were good enough. After the show,

Wallis was waiting outside her dressing room, looking just like a Holly-wood producer, "with a face like a suntanned pear," MacLaine remem-bered. When she came out, he simply said, "I'm Hal Wallis, and I'm prepared to offer you a movie contract." He paused. She gaped. After a moment, he added, "In Hollywood."

The Fosses of Chicago quickly forgot about Mary-Ann Niles in the glow of their famous and celebrated young man. Perhaps it seemed to them typical of a Hollywood person to be divorced. Bob's new wife, Joan McCracken, was vivacious, and she was appearing in *Me and Juliet* right there in Chicago. That was exciting too.

He introduced her to the family at a party Sadie gave in the house that she and Cy had just moved into, a smaller place at 721 South Boulevard in suburban Evanston. The kids had grown up and moved out. There was no longer any need for the big Sheridan Road place and Sadie was certainly too ill to take care of it. She rarely got out of bed now, but she got out for the party.

The living room was filled to overflowing, and the kids tried to hush everyone. They had prepared something special. As the stir subsided, the show began with Uncle Bob and Aunt Joan in the seats of honor, alongside Cy and Sadie. It was based on the popular television program, "This Is Your Life." The youngsters mimicked it from first to last, taking Bob from his childhood—with testimony from his brothers and parents and relatives—through dance lessons and school shows and the Navy and all the movies. The kids did impressions of Debbie Reynolds and Ann Miller and especially the sliding along the floor part in "From This Moment On." Then, with great fanfare, they closed "The Big Book of Life" that they had pasted up from old clippings and photographs, and presented it to Bob and Joan just the way the master of ceremonies Ralph Edwards did it on "This Is Your Life." The living room resounded with cheers, whistles, and applause, and afterward, Joan offered to give the kids "one free ballet lesson." She demonstrated the basic positions and taught the French names for them to Bud's daughter Cindy and the oldest of Patsy's four girls. The other Fosse brothers just had sons, and like the fathers the boys were too embarrassed to participate in dance class.

When *Me and Juliet* closed a week later, Bob and Joan flew back to New York and settled into her penthouse apartment in the West Fifties—the apartment that would make Bob a lover of such New York City aeries, though none would ever be quite so original as this. Joan loved the beach, and she had somehow turned a sky-high apartment into a beach house.

One of her friends described it as being "like a windswept tree, it was totally Joan McCracken."

She had filled the place with dollhouses that she'd made, boxes she had painted, collages she had assembled. Strung along the walls were the necklaces and bracelets that she'd rather were seen than stuffed in drawers. When Bob's young nieces came visiting from Chicago, she would take the pretty things down and give them to any little girl who asked.

One afternoon, Buddy Hackett telephoned. He would always drop in like a mystery man. He liked to say he never knew where he would be, or for how long, and it might be years between calls. He invited Bob to lunch at the Friar's Club, and there they sat in unusual silence, drinking their drinks and studying the menu. Bob wasn't smoking for once in his life, because Hackett, even in the days before the surgeon general's warnings, was adamant in his disapproval of cigarettes. He would never sit at a table with anyone who was smoking. (He would later forbid it in nightclubs during his performances.) Hackett was the first to speak. He'd been afraid, he said, that "after *The Pajama Game* you wouldn't be interested in socializing with a nightclub comic like me and, worst of all, I was afraid you would think I was looking for a job in a show." Fosse roared. "I was afraid of the same thing," he said. "I didn't want you to think I wanted something from *you*."

Actually, Buddy did want something from Bob, but it wasn't a part in a show. When they all went to dinner—Joan, Bob, and Buddy, the following night at the Absinthe House—Hackett turned the conversation to Broadway drama. It was a favorite subject of theirs too. Joan and Bob were both studying acting with the famous teacher, Sanford Meisner, at the Neighborhood Playhouse. Their idea of an actor, they said, was Montgomery Clift. They thought he was the best that America had ever produced. Hackett grew pensive. He said that he had written a play. The couple looked up, as if pleased to be confidants. "I named it *Castle in Spain*," Hackett said. "Would you mind reading it, Bob?" As they parted outside the restaurant, he handed over the manila envelope saying, "The main character is Buddy Castle." Bob opened it, removed the manuscript, and riffled through the pages, shaking his head as if wearily anticipating the drudgery of going through this. "What a guy wouldn't do for a friend!" he sighed, and they both laughed and hugged each other good-bye.

The next morning, Bob telephoned to say that he had read *Castle in Spain* and thought it was "wonderful." He urged Buddy to find a producer and even offered to submit it to one he knew. "But I never did do anything with it," Hackett remembered. "I was whored out of the theatre that I loved so much, whored out by Las Vegas. Nobody could pay what they did, so I never did any of the things I'd dreamed about."

Very often, perhaps too often, it takes a lifetime of experience to be an overnight success. Not for Bob Fosse. He was able to succeed deservedly but also quickly and without experience. It could well have been one reason why he would always think his reputation spurious. He could hardly consider his intense discipline to be hard work. The discipline had been drilled into him by Fred Weaver, and by now it was compulsive. Besides, if it was being done only to protect him from being uncovered as a fraud, how could he take credit for it?

In *The Pajama Game*'s morning after, he was certainly established as a Broadway choreographer to be reckoned with. He even won the Tony Award for best choreography on this, his first show. Yet the next job he accepted was a part in a movie, so the Bob Riff in him was still there, eager to be a star, and there was still, too, an unresolved conflict with Hollywood. Since this acting job involved choreography, it was probably easy to rationalize, but it was still a peculiar career decision.

The movie was to be a musical version of the popular Ruth McKinney play, *My Sister Eileen*. Now of course there already was a stage musical based on that play, the current Broadway hit, *Wonderful Town*. But Columbia Pictures owned the movie rights to the play. When negotiations with the show's producer bogged down, the studio simply withdrew and decided to make its own song-and-dance version of *My Sister Eileen*, and so despite the existence of a brilliant score by Leonard Bernstein, Betty Comden, and Adolph Green, another was written to fit the same story, this time by Jule Styne and Leo Robin. There was a certain justice in Bob's working with Styne, who, not that long ago, had turned him down for *Pal Joey* on Broadway. Surely influenced by Jerry—now "Jerome"—Robbins, Bob arranged for his movie credit to be "Robert Fosse."

Janet Leigh was playing the title role of Eileen, the one who gets all the boys, the beautiful sister of the brainy Ruth. Betty Garrett was cast as Ruth, with Jack Lemmon the magazine editor who falls for her. Bob's (or Robert's) supporting role as one of Eileen's devotees was no bigger than he'd had in *Give a Girl a Break*; he still was no leading man, and he had to wear the hairpiece he had always dreaded would be his Hollywood destiny. He'd yank it off every chance he could, replacing it with a hat, which at least wasn't fake. His baldness was the reason that he wore hats, and was doubtless why he put hats on his dancers.

The prospect of making this movie excited Janet Leigh, because she had never done a musical, which was also why it made her nervous. She asked the studio if Fosse could work with her before rehearsals began, "just for me to get sort of seasoned," and he agreed to it. The day after he arrived, he showed up on the sound stage reserved for their rehearsals, at ten o'clock in the morning.

She was afraid he would be contemptuous ("I was Hollywood, he was theatre. I was sure he'd look at me and groan, 'Oh, Christ, what have I got into?' "), but instead he was "almost angelic, sensitive, so gentle and patient."

"Let's just try a few things," he said, putting on a record and easing her into a dancing state of mind. "I needed help with style," she remembered, "but not so much with moving," and after three weeks of work she felt comfortable, and he was beginning to teach her actual steps, for he had been working out the movie's numbers by himself. "When I did something right," she beamed, even thirty years later, "he was so *proud* of me. He really made you feel good."

As filming began, the movie's complex legal background surfaced in the person of a studio attorney who placed himself beside the camera and looked out for similarities to *Wonderful Town*. It was a bizarre way to create. Since the only musical number in the original play was Ruth doing a conga with a group of Brazilian sailors, it was the only song in the movie that resembled anything in the show. The attorney wouldn't even allow musical numbers to be used in the same spots as in *Wonderful Town*, and so, ironically, Fosse had to make a conscious effort to avoid the thinking and work of his two mentors, for it had been Jerome Robbins who worked on the musical staging of *Wonderful Town*, helping the director, George Abbott.

Bob took advantage of the camera to move the dances away from the confinements of a stage, starting one number in front of an apartment house and sending it into a subway station. He took the conga all over the "New York City" that Columbia kept permanently on its back lot. In a duet with Tommy Rall, he graciously allowed his better-trained partner to outshine him in ballet technique but, in compensation, he gave himself his favorite learned trick (perhaps because it was so uncharacteristic of him), a back flip. Inevitably, he drew on "Steam Heat," since, after all, it had just established him with such affirmation. He rehearsed Garrett and Leigh until they were ready to drop, having them endlessly repeat a wriggly, knock-kneed, slithering dance that they did in a gazebo. He kept telling the women, "You have to do this very tight," and he said it so frequently that Betty began to call all the thigh-rubbing choreography, "shaving your hairs."

In the gazebo too, he had his one and only on-screen kiss. It was with

Janet Leigh and was not entirely make-believe. On the set he was no friendlier with her than with anyone else, but when they worked alone, Bob would occasionally take her in his arms and kiss her. She knew that he was married to Joan McCracken, although it struck her as odd that he should be in California for five months of moviemaking without his wife ever appearing. Leigh was herself married to Tony Curtis and had no intention of being unfaithful. "Both Bobby and I knew, even without talking about it," she said, "that an affair would have happened if we let it. There was that much electricity between us."

When filming was finished, he went back to Broadway, the love-hate for Hollywood unresolved. The producers of *The Pajama Game* had bought the rights to Douglas Wallop's best-selling novel, *The Year the Yankees Lost the Pennant*. They wanted Bob to help them make a musical out of it, and it was time for him to meet Gwen Verdon.

6

Gwyneth Evelyn Verdon was born on January 16, 1925, some two and a half years before Bob Fosse, to English parents living in a $12-a-month bungalow in Culver City, California. There was already a son, William. Gwen's father, Joseph Verdon, was a second "best boy" or electrician at MGM. His wife Gertrude was a dancer and a veteran of Denishawn, the modern dance company founded by Ruth St. Denis and Ted Shawn. She now ran a Denishawn dance school in Culver City, and it was there that the toddling Gwyneth took her first dance steps under the instruction of Ernest Belcher, whose daughter would become Marge Champion.

Such pioneers as St. Denis and Shawn had a missionary aura about them and often were as devoted to a philosophy of dance as to dancing itself. Gwen Verdon seems to have been imbued with this devotion even as she embarked upon the unpretentious choreography of the Two Flying D'Arcys, of whom she was one at the age of four. From there it was but a twirl and a curtsy to performing as Baby Alice at six, and three years later she was in a ballet at the huge Hollywood Bowl. By the time Bob Fosse was starting out as one of the Riff Brothers, Gwen Verdon was half of a professional ballroom team, Verdon and Del Velle.

The act was short-lived. She met and fell in love with James O'Farrell Heneghan, a divorced newspaper columnist twice her age, and within a year she was married and the teenage mother of a son, Jimmie.

Leaving dance, she followed her husband into journalism and began reviewing movies and nightclub acts for *The Hollywood Reporter.* Only eighteen years old, she was already an astonishingly beautiful young woman with an ideally proportioned body, the full breasts and muscled swells of a stripper, the physical coordination of an athlete, and a mane of thick red hair scooped into a ponytail.

But in 1949, six years into the marriage, her suppressed devotion to dance reemerged with a spiritual awakening while on a reviewing assignment in a Los Angeles nightclub. She saw her future in the floor show. It featured the Jack Cole Dancers, and as is so often the case, the future that she saw was linked to her past, as if she should have known all the time. For Jack Cole was himself a Denishawn alumnus.

Much as if at a revival meeting, Gwen was born again. She left *The Hollywood Reporter* and James O'Farrell Heneghan too. He had become alcoholic enough to be falling down drunk in the streets, and their son Jimmie would tell a friend that his mother finally wearied of picking his father up and carrying him home. Abandoning this dominating and abusive man, she began life anew as a dancer for the dominating and abusive Jack Cole.

It is not unusual for dancers to consider themselves instruments for a choreographer rather than creative or even interpretive artists, to feel as if they have no steps of their own and exist only to express the choreographer's imagination, to serve his creativity and to challenge him no more than would a brush the painter. It is as if the dancer literally cannot make a move without the choreographer. Gwen Verdon was to be such an instrument for two choreographers in her life. She seemed to know, the moment she saw him onstage in that Los Angeles nightclub, that the first of them would be Jack Cole.

He was a striking figure, a lean and wiry man with chiseled features, high cheekbones, and heavily hooded eyes, all framed by close-cropped dark hair. It was a classical look, almost Grecian, and his body was so taut, so sinewy and muscular that it seemed to be carved from wood, all the more so because he was usually sunbronzed and liked to pose (even dance) nude. More than one of the women who danced for him fell in love with him, drawn by his artistic and personal magnetism, but although he claimed to be bisexual, he had in fact been living with a man named David Gray for many years and was never known to have had any sexual interest in women.

Cole had managed to transplant his Denishawn roots first to movies and then to nightclub floor shows without alienating the world of serious dance. Important critics such as Walter Terry of the New York *Herald-Tribune* admired his work even when the concoction of Oriental, Hindu, and West Indian dance was being done in garish circumstances. Writing about Jack Cole and the Kraft Sisters (the act that preceded the Jack Cole Dancers), Terry said, "The accent is placed upon detailed movements, upon Hindu hand gestures, the slight shift of the neck, the meaningful flutter of eye muscles. . . . Hindu gestures are used, and they are certainly derived from the gesture language of India, but Cole has set them to swingtime.

"He looks Oriental," the critic concluded. "Oriental enough to have been born in the shadow of an Eastern temple," but in fact J. Ewing Cole had been born in New Jersey. After studying at Denishawn, he advanced quickly and became the resident choreographer at Columbia Pictures. The only other studio with such a post was MGM, and even there, at the biggest of all movie studios, Bob Alton did not have his own dancers under contract, as had Cole at Columbia. But perhaps the better word for Cole's dancers is "acolytes."

The Cole contingent was supposed to be available for any picture being made on the lot, and when the dancers weren't needed, which was most of the time, they took classes with the master. "Without a doubt," according to Saul Chaplin, who had been a music director at Columbia before moving to MGM, "they were the most incredible group of dancers ever assembled anywhere."

Not everyone in the dance world shared this view, and a few (Jerome Robbins, for instance) considered Cole something of a joke, but that he created a unique, Eastern variation on jazz dancing, and with it some of the basic Broadway moves, cannot be disputed. *Dance Magazine* dubbed him "the King of Exotica," a campy sobriquet that was not derogatory. Without a doubt he demanded a very high level of precision. Cole in fact practiced a disciplinary fanaticism that, as one of his dancers said, "had us doing pliés from such a crouch we were practically under the floor." So if he had whipped up a polyglot of ethnic dances, it was a strict and arrogant polyglot that had the courage of its excesses and a certain erotic energy reflecting Cole himself and the sexual tension that he created among his dancers. Busby Berkeley might have been more publicized in Hollywood; George Balanchine and Jerome Robbins may have become better known to the public because of their ballet prestige; Broadway choreographers such as Gower Champion, Michael Kidd, and Fosse himself would develop richer theatrical senses and enjoy greater stage success, but to show and nightclub dancers, Jack Cole was the father and guru. He had the nerve to be extravagant. Good taste was not his handicap.

After three years of only sporadic on-camera work at Columbia Pictures, he and the studio began discussing an end to their arrangement. "We don't want to stay here anymore," he was already informing his troupe, who were probably enjoying the steady paychecks. "We want to dance," he told them and so even while they all remained on salary, still on Stage Ten of the Columbia lot, they began preparing the act that would become the "Jack Cole Dancers." At the termination of the contract, he took eight of them into nightclubs: Carol Haney, Anita Beaver, Ruth Godfrey, Ethel Martin, and the boys, George Martin (Ethel's husband), Rob Hamilton, Rod Alexander, and Alex Romero.

It was when Haney quit to become Gene Kelly's assistant that Gwen Verdon dived into the opening. From the outset she was to be not just a member of the troupe but Cole's assistant, his alter ego, his lead dancer, his center of focus, and his model for creation as well as the constant object of his rages.

The first number he created for the act was "Sing, Sing, Sing" based on Benny Goodman's classic recording of the Louis Prima piece for big band. "It was a seven-and-a-half-minute number," Ethel Martin remembered, "and an absolute killer. The way Jack did it, it wasn't 'Sing, Sing, Sing.' It was drive, drive, drive. Even when we were about to open at the Chez Paree in Chicago, we still had never been able to get through it without falling down."

She recalled that "Jack would scream at us—it was just unbelievable, the things he would say—but when dancers see a choreographer they admire, well, it's as close to those evangelists as anything I can think of. You get this group of people who will do *anything*, and Jack had a way of making people do more than they were capable of doing. He took you beyond yourself."

The expression "no pain, no gain," which is usually associated with physical exercise, actually originated among dancers. Many seem to thrive on emotional pain as well, or at least to think that some emotional pain is necessary to artistic growth.

There was no dancer in the group more susceptible to this fire and brimstone than Gwen Verdon. Cole was capable of flying into rages in the middle of the act, while on stage, and when he did, he would shove her good and hard, just to teach everyone else a lesson. After one such occurrence, she was sitting in the dressing room, scrubbing off her makeup when Cole burst in and flew at her in a fury. She faced the barrage of shrieks and insults with the silence of a stoic. The other girls looked away in shame as she kept repeating, "Yes, sir . . . yes, sir . . . yes, sir . . ." When Cole finally left and the room's breath was released, she stood up and took her chair by the top and flung it violently against the wall.

"Why didn't you throw that chair while Jack was here?" one of the girls asked. Gwen didn't answer.

Walter Terry's review of "Sing, Sing, Sing," when it was done in New York, may have justified this kind of humiliation for some dancers. The critic wrote, "It is of course 20th Century American but with the intensity of the dancers, the heavily accented rhythms, the repeated movement figures, the ecstatic leaps followed by the plummetings seem to convey the same magical purpose apparent in many of the tribal dances of Africa."

A year later, Gwen was dancing with Jack on Broadway. The show was called *Alive and Kicking*. Like Fosse and Niles' *Dance Me a Song*, it was a revue, a show made up of songs, dances, and comedy sketches. Television's variety shows, being available free of charge, would soon make such productions obsolete, but for the moment revues were common and popular, and were considered very New York. It was in *Alive and Kicking*, then, that Gwen Verdon made her New York stage debut on January 17, 1950, at the Winter Garden Theatre, three days after Bob Fosse had made his in *Dance Me a Song* at the Royale.

The Cole–Verdon dances were his usual ethnic smorgasbord, and in one of them his costume even included woven anklets that each held a hundred miniature brass bells. "I'm crazy about this Oriental stuff," the King of Exotica told a magazine interviewer as he jingled an ankle. "I've studied with a lot of Indian teachers."

Alive and Kicking was not well received, closing after forty-six performances and just beating out *Dance Me a Song*, which called it quits after thirty-five shows. And so Bob Fosse, Mary-Ann Niles, Joan McCracken, Gwen Verdon, and Jack Cole were all out of work and at personal and career crossroads. But at least Verdon and Cole knew where to turn for work, because they were Hollywood people rather than Broadway. They took the first train back to the movies. Jack already had an offer from Twentieth Century-Fox to become dance director, and he brought Gwen along as his assistant.

This assignment involved no dance troupe. Cole was expected to perform in musical numbers as well as to coach the actors in them. Ultimately, he and Gwen would dance in the Dan Dailey movie, *Meet Me After the Show*, as well as in the Danny Kaye vehicle, *On the Riviera*.

The studio sent them to Paris where Marilyn Monroe was filming *Gentlemen Prefer Blondes*, and Gwen showed the sex symbol how to be sexy while singing, "I'm Just a Little Girl from Little Rock." As another dancer put it, "Nobody was able to satirize sexiness and be sexy at the same time the way Gwen could. She was the one who taught it to Monroe." Ultimately, Marilyn Monroe would sing in the funny and hoarsely whispered and vulnerably sexy way that was Gwen Verdon's idiosyncratic style, the style that would soon make her as beloved a star as there ever was on Broadway.

But stardom was not the Verdon dream. The opposite of Fosse in so many ways, while he yearned to be in the spotlight, she shrank from it, backing off from every opportunity that came her way. She seemed to prefer a handmaiden role, the chief assistant, the woman at the side (or feet) of a man. The man in her professional life was still Jack Cole, who was still dominating and still abusive. Returning from Paris she settled into a routine of watching her little Jimmie grow up, of coaching Betty Grable in *How to Marry a Millionaire*, and of performing with the Jack Cole Dancers in a local nightclub. That was where the New York stage producer Cy Feuer saw her in 1953 and decided that he wanted her for the dance lead in the new Cole Porter musical, *Can-Can*. Feuer and his partner Ernest Martin were the wonder boys of Broadway. They had produced three consecutive hits in five years, *Where's Charley, Guys and Dolls*, and *The Boy Friend*. A role in a Feuer and Martin musical should have seemed the glory dream itself and to almost any other performer it would have, but—according to another Jack Cole dancer working with Gwen—the only reason she accepted the part in *Can-Can* was that Cole had finally gone over the top with his abuse, and if she was to survive with her ego intact she had to get out of there.

Can-Can was a musical comedy set in the Paris of Toulouse-Lautrec. Verdon had the second female lead, the dance lead. In addition to the central "Quadrille" (cancan) number, she had an Apache dance in the first act and a "Garden of Eden" ballet in the second. In these she made no special impression during the out-of-town tryouts, but at the end of the Apache number on the Broadway opening night, the Shubert Theatre rocked with applause. The audience could not be silenced. It demanded her reappearance and would not allow the show to continue otherwise.

Cy Feuer hurried up the spiral staircase of metal steps and knocked on Gwen's dressing room door. He was in his tuxedo. She had already taken off her costume. She was through until the second act and was sitting in a robe at her dressing room table. There was no time for talk, the producer said. She had to go out and take a bow. Otherwise the audience would continue to applaud. He held her door open so that she could hear the tumultuous applause for herself. Waving aside her embarrassment over the robe, he reached out a hand, and she rose to let him guide her out the door and down the spiral steps, through the backstage area and out past the stage manager's desk, past the star of the show (a chanteuse named Lilo), through the wings and into the blinding spotlight and the waves of applause and cheers. This was why they became performers, even the private Gwen Verdon. The audience, the only one who could, declared her a star.

Nonetheless she criticized the show's choreographer, Michael Kidd, for being unartistic. She was a dance esthete, a child of Denishawn, and a product of Jack Cole's fanatical version of it. Indeed, despite the emotional brutalizing that had driven her away from him, instead of capitalizing on her dazzling reviews in *Can-Can* she left the show after barely a year and went back to assisting Cole, left her name in lights on Broadway to go to Paris and help make Jane Russell seem musical and sexy in *Gentlemen Marry Brunettes*. That was where Gwen Verdon was, in Paris, when Robert Griffith, Fred Brisson, and Harold Prince pursued her for *Damn Yankees*. The female lead in their show was to be a dancer, that much had been decided, but of course the role also called for singing and acting. The producers had already been rejected by the movie actress Mitzi Gaynor and the French ballet dancer, Zizi Jeanmaire. Mitzi Gaynor was a movie star, a seasoned actress, a proven singer. Jeanmaire had already starred on Broadway. But Gwen Verdon had not sung a song or had much of a part to speak of in *Can-Can*; in fact she had virtually never spoken a line of dialogue or sung a song in a professional stage production in her entire life. Nevertheless the producers were willing to take a chance on this spectacular new dancing star as the seductive Lola who was the devil's right hand.

She turned them down. She preferred assisting Jack Cole to starring on Broadway. "We persisted and persisted," Prince remembered, "we practically jammed the show down her throat but, damn it, we wanted Gwen and we got her."

Douglas Wallop's novel is a comic variation on the Faust legend, the story of a salesman whose midlife crisis involves fantasies about recapturing his youth and becoming the greatest baseball player of all time. He sells his soul to the devil in exchange for that dream, to lead his beloved but inept Washington Senators to a championship past the hated Yankees. Although Fosse had been a baseball fan since childhood, he did not think much of *Damn Yankees* and would later say so, but it was, after all, only his second Broadway assignment, and after the success of *The Pajama Game* he could hardly reject an offer to work again with the same producers, the same composers, the same Mr. Abbott. And yet no sooner had the producers signed Gwen Verdon as their star than Bob announced that he wasn't at all certain about being able to work with her. "I have to meet her first," he told Prince. "I have to get to know her. I'm not sure we can get along," and why not? He had, after all, already choreographed exactly one Broadway show.

It was Gwen who should have been concerned, and in fact she was "very leery of Bobby," according to Prince. Considering her scorn for choreographer Michael Kidd and her Denishawn background and her adulation for Jack Cole, there was every reason to anticipate her snubbing Fosse, the self-described "Broadway hoofer." For what was dancing to him? Squat wings and time steps in strip joints? Dancing on the radio? Something his father disapproved of, that he couldn't tell his friends about? Gwen danced for the love of it, perhaps even the pain of it, the physical discipline of it, possibly even a sensuality inherent in it. Bob danced because he was good at it, and because he got to meet a lot of pretty girls. He knew the nightclub world for sleaze and was fond of it for the sleaze of it, but he knew it for sleaze. Gwen may have been a worshipper at the shrine, but Bob would stub his cigarette out on the altar and quiet the gorillas with a split.

The producers of *Damn Yankees* arranged for Gwen Verdon to meet Bob Fosse in a dance studio near Lincoln Square, on Broadway at 64th Street, and the men sat down apprehensively to watch the mating of choreographer and star. A few simple steps were tried out in the dusty sunlight of the big rehearsal room with its empty floor. Bob's sidewise shuffles and slinky maneuvers evidently had an immediate appeal for Gwen. It was as if she already had the moves in her body. As Bob's dance assistant on this show, Pat Ferrier, would say:

> A dancer is always creating a persona with the body. It's like sculpting in space. That's how you express yourself—with your body. And as you do it you see yourself doing it . . . in a strange way. You work so long training your body and developing the control of it in front of mirrors that you have a mind's eye that says, "Oh, that feels good. I know it looks good."

Gwen's childhood problems with rickets and a hernia in addition to corrective shoes prescribed for her outward-turned feet led her to stand easily pigeon-toed and knock-kneed, a stance that Bob had already made central to his dance vocabulary on the way from *Kiss Me, Kate* to *The Pajama Game*. And she had an additional appeal for him. Gwen was sexy in her black tights, "hot when I met her," Bob said. "Her in the leotard, I will never forget that. That alabaster skin, the bantam rooster walk."

They continued their dancing in the rehearsal studio as the producers sat in the room's wooden chairs, earthbound outsiders in this place for dancers. Both Bob and Gwen were smoking. She would even mock him, dangling a cigarette from the corner of her mouth as they stood together, side by side, knees and ankles locked. When they were done, Gwen told the producers of *Damn Yankees* that she was willing to work with Fosse, and he told them he was willing to work with Verdon. They scheduled rehearsals. There was no Jerome Robbins this time to serve as insurance. Abbott would still direct the singers in their singing of the songs (musical staging) but whenever there were dance steps in the midst of a number, for instance the vaudeville during "(You Gotta Have) Heart," Bob would do it.

Gwen was not yet the full star. A Broadway star is billed above the title, that is the official rule. Abbott minimized her dialogue, but she took easily to her scenes, projecting a disarming, comic vulnerability. It mixed cozily with her stunning body, "a body that never quit," as cocomposer Richard Adler described it. He tailored her showpiece to that combination of sex and humor, the seduction tango, "Whatever Lola Wants, Lola Gets."

The dance that Gwen and Bob worked out to accompany this song was a joking version of the bump and grind routines that he was all too familiar with from his strip joint adolescence. Gwen was also a burlesque aficionado. She took to the lusty gyrations and to Bob as well. She was already transferring her dependency from Cole, transferring a corresponding maternalism along with it. She gave all the credit for "Lola" to Bob, saying that he had "choreographed everything . . . the flirtatious quality, the accent, miniscule things like that—where you push your hair back, when you breathe, when you blink your eyes and when you just move your little finger."

The little things in the dance certainly did look like Fosse. The big things, however, looked like Verdon, the strides and turns. There is hardly any way of separating their contributions but the number seems more a Verdon creation than one by Fosse.

He had asked Janet Leigh to call if she got to New York, and when she did, he invited her to watch his dance auditions. Perhaps, in some ingenuous way, he was eager to impress her.

"This is the hardest part of the whole thing for me," he whispered, as she took a seat beside him in the 46th Street Theatre. It was an early audition, and there were many dancers because he liked to give lots of people the feeling that they had a chance, however slim the chance might be. One of his assistants was on stage, demonstrating the combination of steps that he wanted to see. Bob turned to Janet. "I can cope with the problems of putting a show together," he said, "and I can even deal with the producers, who can sometimes give me a terrible time. But *this*— having to choose a handful of them out of hundreds—it just breaks my heart."

He looked up to watch one of the girls go through her steps and then he turned to Leigh and whispered, "Terrible . . . this one just doesn't have it."

There is nothing easy about creating a musical. The likelihood of so many creative people meshing, compromising egos, settling on the same vision, simply *getting along*, would seem to dash all hope of collaboration and even when, somehow, a successful musical comes out of it, the success isn't always satisfying. Mr. Abbott might have believed that the only good show is a hit show, but success can turn sour when a show is popular yet not very good. Sooner or later, most of the creators of *Damn Yankees* would apologize for it, and even the pragmatic Abbott would dismiss it as minor. Naturally Mary-Ann Niles scoffed too. "Wouldn't you know," she cackled, "that Bob would do a *baseball* show?"

But *Damn Yankees* was a necessary education for him. Abbott believed in getting things done and getting them done fast. He wanted a baseball dance number, and Bob had to set it to "Shoeless Joe from Hannibal, Mo," which inexplicably was written in country hoedown style. Various do-si-do's and clicking heels were inevitable with such music, but Fosse ingeniously introduced dance variations on such baseball movements as fielding stabs, kicked spikes, swinging bats, and slides into bases. Yet another dance number, "Two Lost Souls," was set in a nightclub. These were the kind of big Broadway production numbers that he was learning to do while on the job, and then would spend a career avoiding, but contempt counts for nothing if you are incapable of doing what you are contemptuous of.

As the company prepared for the New Haven tryout, there was one dance that worried Prince, and it came at a crucial point: at the end of the first act. It was essential that the audience stroll up the aisle at intermission feeling good about the show and eager to return, but as Prince watched the final rehearsal in New York, he was convinced that this number would send the theatregoers out in sheer bewilderment. It was set at a party given for the Senators baseball team by the hero's fan club. Bob had the team playing musical chairs. One of the players, a character modeled on Yogi Berra, was leading the game, standing on a chair, wearing a gorilla suit with a Yankee uniform on top of it. He was terrorizing the other players, and as they danced around the chair, he looked out at the audience and spoke as if a master of revels or, as Prince said, "a compère." The producer added, "I know the whole thing sounds strange, but it *was* strange. It was a gorilla number, really."

Fosse worked on it for days and was still at it the night before the departure for New Haven, but, it seemed to Prince, "It just got stranger, and Bobby was growing very upset. He wanted desperately for it to work."

There were to be three previews in New Haven, and as Prince stood at the back of the theatre waiting for the first of them to start and for the show to be given its maiden performance, he saw the creative team nodding nervous good lucks at each other. Everyone was there but Fosse. The explanation for his absence was soon evident. He was onstage. He had put himself into the Yogi Berra part in that troublesome number. "He even read the lines," Prince recalled with enduring amazement and bewilderment. "He played the gorilla in the Yankee uniform, leading the team in a game of musical chairs."

Afterward, Prince returned to his room in the Taft Hotel, bringing along some of the people working on the show, to hash the preview over. He opened a bottle of Scotch and poured drinks all around. Then they began going over each other's notes. There were few serious concerns. The preview had gone well, the show seemed solid, the audience had been enthusiastic, "But I have to tell you fellows," Prince said, "I really think the musical chairs number is just terrible, and I'm tired of waiting for Bobby to give up on it."

Before anyone could respond, the room telephone rang, and Prince answered it. "Hal," the voice said. "This is Bob Fosse." He always introduced himself with his full name, even in person and to someone he knew. It was, he would say, in case the other person didn't remember who he was.

"Where are you?" Prince asked.

"I'm on the other side of the wall, in the room next door, that's where I am, you son of a bitch. Why don't you have the courage to tell me these things to my face?"

"I'll be right over," Prince said, and hanging up, he left the group in his room, went out, and knocked on Fosse's door. Bob opened it glaring. Joan McCracken was sitting on the bed, "looking very apprehensive," Prince recalled, "and Bob's eyes were just murderous."

Fosse remained standing and staring icily at Prince, who sat down in one of the armchairs, smiled at McCracken, and tried to speak as calmly as he could. He thought that anything he had said to the men in his room could have been said in front of Fosse and that there was nothing to hide.

"Bobby," he began, "you asked me why I didn't tell you. It's simple. This was just a preview. I was waiting until opening night here."

Bob didn't move. His expression was one of hatred. Prince continued as if he didn't notice, hoping that a calm tone would defuse the anger. He peered anxiously at Bob, spoke in a reasonable way so that everything he said might seem reasonable. They were about the same age, twenty-seven, a couple of successful young men in the theatre, but Prince was a middle-class Jewish businessman while Fosse was a Midwestern, Scandinavian, Methodist vaudevillian. Prince was college-educated, socially deft, smooth in the sophisticated milieu of Broadway while Bob was uncomfortable among facile people and defensive about being uneducated.

When Prince realized that Fosse was not going to reply, he continued: "Okay, I was having a drink in my own room and I was expressing myself. Is there supposed to be something wrong in that? If I have to apologize to you for being in the room next door so that you could hear what I was saying, fine, I apologize for being in the room next door. But I have no obligation not to say what I think. I am the producer and besides," he paused, "I'm right."

Everything might have been getting better until Prince said he was right. Then Bob's color changed, from ice white to livid crimson, and the anger crunched through. He became venomous and abusive. Joan Mc-Cracken burst into the first opening. "Bobby! Hal's telling you the truth, he's telling you what he feels. He's just being honest."

Fosse hardly let her finish. He couldn't begin to tell Prince how little he thought of him. Who were the people who made shows? Not the money men. What did money men know about show making?

"Leave him alone, Bobby!" McCracken implored, but the room quivered with his rage, his pain and confusion. Remembering the scene, Prince said, "I would always say after that, 'Don't talk in hotel rooms. We all live next door to each other.' "

Even after *Damn Yankees* opened in New Haven, Fosse held on to his gorilla number, still struggling to make the piece work. "That was very characteristic of Bobby, to be that stubborn," Prince said.

George Abbott finally got him to replace the strange dance by suggesting an alternative. It was the same suggestion that had prompted "Steam Heat," a proposal that Bob cook up something small and funny, something that a baseball hero's fan club might present as an entertainment. This was a pitiful contrivance, but fixing and patching was Abbott's specialty, and when a show of his had a problem, he had no qualms about solving it with an irrelevant distraction. Bob would learn how to repair shows from the old master, but a difference would lie between them, and it would be their attitudes toward their own talent.

Abbott fixed from necessity, and in that circumstance he was pragmatic, not looking for greatness but for utility. His axiom was Broadway's "If it works, it works," and he needed no organic resolution of the trouble. But Fosse regretted his inability to originate and seemed ashamed of his facility in the theatrical repair shop. "I wish I could come up with ideas," he said to a friend, "but I'm not an idea man." Then, with contempt for the show business he had mastered and despised, he added, "I can take shit and make it look good."

Fixing troublesome shows was not the only thing that Fosse learned from Abbott. His whole life he had difficulty expressing feelings and convincing people that he actually had any. Nobody was as unemotional as Mr. Abbott. "Now George Abbott," Bob once said, "*he's* cold," and then he added, "but there's something nice about that because he's also very straight.

"Cold but straight."

In response to Abbott's suggestion of a small entertainment, Fosse came up with a duet based on the mambo, the grunting South American dance that was the rage in 1955. Adler and Ross hurried off a song that was as minimal as Bob's dancing. The melody was mum, restricted to a six-note span. The lyric was hardly literate.

> Who's got the pain when they do the mambo?
> Who's got the pain when they go "Ugh!"

But the Latin rhythm had a good, jittery hitch to it, making the song irresistible for dancing, and the grunt worked like one of Fosse's favored cowbells on a percussionist's kit. He and Gwen figured out the number in the studio. They were spending hours there together, growing very close while working. When they had the number finished, they summoned her dance partner in the piece, Eddie Phillips, who watched and learned it. Phillips was "a rubber-legged vaudevillian," as one of his fellow dancers put it, and he had no trouble following the steps of a fellow hoofer like Fosse, but for all the whimsy of "Who's Got the Pain?" it looked a lot easier than it was. Like Bob it was loose only on the outside.

The number was less startling than "Steam Heat," but it had a similar economy, a similar sense of mischief, even a similar androgyny. The two dancers wore tight black pants, bright Caribbean tops, and the little hats that, after two shows, had already become a Fosse trademark, and they wriggled their shoulders and waddled like Charlie Chaplin and even leaned against each other, back to back, with their legs skittering out from under them. The dance was good fun, another show stopper, and Harold Prince was pleased, naturally, but he couldn't shake the memory of the number it replaced, the gorilla in the Yankee uniform, and he couldn't forget the scene in the hotel room. "It was strange," the producer said. "That was a very strange thing."

Considering the solid reviews in New York, *Damn Yankees* should have been more of a hit than it was. Broadway smarties had been wagging their fingers from the outset, dredging up ancient Broadway conventions about the unpopularity of sports on stage. Perhaps they were right. Certainly of no help was an advertising campaign that featured Gwen Verdon, the brand-new star, in a baseball uniform. As pictured, she was adorable and she was funny, she was everybody's mischief maker, but she wasn't anyone's pinup, and funny women never sold tickets, not Martha Raye, not Nancy Kelly, not even Bea Lillie.

When the producers met with the advertising people to deal with the problem, they decided to change the marketing approach and emphasize Gwen's sexiness. After all, "Whatever Lola Wants" was becoming a national hit, and though it was a funny number in the show, it was sexy on Sarah Vaughan's record. Gwen was taken out of the baseball uniform and put into underwear in the advertisement, and business rose dramatically.

So did her assertiveness. She knew exactly what it meant to sell tickets. Her name may not yet have been above the title, but she was definitely a star, aware of her prerogatives and her power, and although she was never rude or demanding, she began to exercise her rights.

She was also allied with her choreographer to the power of two. Jack Cole might (and did) shriek that she was debasing her talent, even destroying it by playing roles like Lola, but Gwen seemed to believe that when she met Bob Fosse, she had found the choreographer made for her in dance heaven and, as she so confidently put it, "I do think I dance Bob Fosse better than any other dancer."

So, she was in love.

When Joan McCracken learned of the affair, she got one barb in ("Sometimes the artificial can be very attractive, Bobby") and then he was gone. "She was crushed, she never really recovered," said her friend, dancer Buzz Miller. There is never a good time to be abandoned but this was a bad time. Although Joan was only thirty-three, she had already developed heart disease, and very much like Sadie Fosse, she had been told by doctors that she could live with it only if she did not exert herself. That had been when Sadie took to bed for much of the time, but Joan was too young and energetic for that. The bad heart did, however, put an end to her dancing days.

With Bob's departure, she returned to the beaches she loved so much, abandoning for months the Manhattan aerie that she had made into an ocean house in the sky. She had a real ocean house looking out on the silent wintry strands of Fire Island. Later, when she was better able to cope, the pert and sparkling dancer would drag herself back to New York and resume the acting classes she had begun with Sanford Meisner. Being unable to dance did not mean being unable to perform, and she had already begun to act in esoteric plays by Bertolt Brecht (*Galileo*) and Jean Cocteau (*The Infernal Machine*), but for the moment she had to deal with desertion, and she dealt with it by walking the beaches while Gwen flashed across the big stage of the 46th Street Theatre in *Damn Yankees*, and Bob went to Hollywood to work on the movie of *The Pajama Game*.

His old friend Stanley Donen, who always had such great faith in him, was waiting in welcome. Donen was directing the picture, but that didn't cheer Bob. He was returning to the scene of rejection, returning triumphant and yet still in doubt of himself, still sure that his success had been fraudulent. "I had to work twice as hard as everyone else," he would say, "to be half as good."

Donen could only shake his head with pity when Fosse said things like that. "Bob never lacked for confidence while on the job, but before or afterward, he insisted that he was a failure."

The movie was not going to be a simple matter of photographing the stage dances. In many respects, *The Pajama Game* movie is a rare transcription of a Broadway show, with many of the original cast, but Fosse was set on exploring the movie potential of dance. Two years earlier, in 1954, Donen had himself expanded film choreography when he directed *Seven Brides for Seven Brothers*. In collaboration with choreographer Michael Kidd, he had worked out a series of rousingly athletic dances that were filmed out of doors. Bob borrowed that outdoors notion when he rechoreographed the exuberant "Once a Year Day." He asked for the number to be shot in Griffith Park in Los Angeles and patiently prepared with Donen, learning about camera setups, lenses, and angles. He designed his choreography for the park's landscaping and topography, to send his ensemble scampering across the rolling hills and between the trees while the camera pulled back to shoot from unusually great distances. But he returned to New York as soon as his dances were done. He had another show to do, *Bells Are Ringing* for Jerome Robbins, who had finally become a director.

"It was my first or second time as a director," Robbins said, "and I wanted to do a good job so I asked Bob to come in and help." They were billed as cochoreographers but Robbins eventually left little for Fosse to do, for he loathed collaboration, and *Bells Are Ringing* was light on dance anyhow. It had a wonderful star in Judy Holliday, but she was a comedienne, not a dancer. Bob did come up with a catchy little number, "Mu Cha Cha," but as a takeoff on a South American dance, it was an obvious clone of "Who's Got the Pain?" and *Bells Are Ringing* was a minor Fosse credit.

He almost immediately reversed direction and returned to California to work on the movie of *Damn Yankees*, and this time it would be for the duration because Gwen was re-creating Lola in the picture, and in Jimmie she had a thirteen-year-old son to visit as well as her parents.

Hollywood may have been the badlands to Bob, but it was home to her. They rented a house in Malibu, and he took his red convertible "Baby" out of storage, off the concrete blocks, and had its battery charged and its tires inflated and put back on.

His friend Stanley Donen, who was codirecting the movie with George Abbott, immediately noticed Bob's depression, the same depression he'd been sunk in while filming *The Pajama Game*, the same depression that had clung to him during the year with MGM. "He was always discouraged," Donen remembered. "About everything. He was a depressed, worried person. Life was difficult for him," and it seemed to Donen that Gwen was capitalizing on that. "He was always thinking that the world was somehow against him, and she fed those fears, and here I liked him better, I suppose, than any man I've ever been friendly with."

Harold Prince had already learned about Bob's fear of betrayal in that New Haven hotel room. Now Donen was running into it. "Bobby would eavesdrop," he said. "He would think people were saying things to get rid of him."

Gwen usually came to the set, whether or not the shooting involved her. This was not necessarily the behavior of a dominating personality. Gwen had grown up on movie lots, and much of her professional experience had been as a movie coach. But Bob also had his own assistant, the tall, brainy, and beautiful Patricia (Pat) Ferrier, who had worked with him in the Broadway company of *Damn Yankees*. Each morning he would drive in with Gwen on the Santa Monica Freeway, pick Pat up, and then they would wind through Topanga Canyon in the open red car on the way to the Warner Brothers lot in Burbank.

When it came time to film "Who's Got the Pain?" the three of them appeared on the set with not only Gwen in costume but Bob too, much as he had shown up in the gorilla suit in New Haven. He announced to Donen and Abbott that *he* was going to dance the number with Gwen. It was his performing compulsion at work again, but unlike the strange New Haven scene, this was no aggravated insistence on a disapproved number. Nor was there, this time, any Harold Prince to wonder about his performing. Many years later, Mr. Abbott impassively remembered that he hadn't really cared whether Fosse did the dance or didn't.

Stanley Donen was delighted about it. He had first known Bob as a dancer, had first believed in him as a performer (and still did). In fact he allowed Fosse complete autonomy in directing all the dance sequences. Bob didn't know the moviemaking jargon but, polite as a schoolboy, he would explain to the cinematographer what effects he wanted. "This is what I mean," he would whisper, and ask, "Could you give it to me?"

In his own dancing, he was as great a perfectionist as he was with others. About to begin filming "Who's Got the Pain?" he turned to Pat Ferrier and said, over his shoulder, "Watch us closely. If my leg is higher, or Gwen's is lower, even by half an inch, or we aren't exactly together—exactly together—stop us! Don't even let them keep shooting!" The finished number proved to be a rare and flawless record of Gwen Verdon and Bob Fosse dancing together at their peak.

When the movie was done, Bob and Gwen came back to New York where Joan McCracken, like Mary-Ann Niles before her, clung to the technicality of marriage after all evidence of it had disappeared. Now there was neither hope nor sense in further delaying the divorce. Delay only prolonged the pain that she was wrapping around herself in the icy winter wind, walking the beaches of Fire Island until friends feared for her sanity.

But a divorce hadn't been necessary. Bob and Gwen were in no great hurry to be married. They were already more married, more of a team, better friends than most couples and, besides, they had yet another show to do. Another show produced by Brisson, Griffith, and Prince, another one directed by George Abbott, but this was hardly just another musical comedy. Set among Swedish Americans in waterfront Manhattan, it was about the reunion of an old sea captain with a daughter who, unknown to him, had become a prostitute. The grim story was not just like Eugene O'Neill; it *was* Eugene O'Neill. This was to be a Broadway musical based on *Anna Christie*. If Bob was tiring of lightweight musical comedies, he could not have found a heavier alternative, and if the basis of *New Girl in Town* was an odd one for Broadway, in the bargain the show was going to have little dancing despite the presence of New York's reigning dance star.

The mere announcement of Gwen Verdon's name by now stimulated excitement, investor interest, and inquiries from theatre party brokers. *Damn Yankees* had made her a very big attraction. Bob Fosse was not nearly as well known, and yet there seemed no jealousy or competition between them. Gwen was a dancer with her own choreographer, and he was a choreographer with his own star instrument. In show business he was as celebrated as she. He already had three hit shows, he'd won another Tony Award for choreographing *Damn Yankees*, and just that year, *My Sister Eileen* was being released. With this, his fourth musical, his credit was being expanded to include musical staging as well as choreography; thus he was mastering the direction of songs—the movements of the actors singing them, and more important than that, he was learning how to stitch the musical moments smoothly into a show's dramatic fabric.

He gave a party for the kids in the dance chorus, an evening for them to meet each other and launch rehearsals. It was in his one-bedroom apartment on Manhattan's West Side, and as the dancers hovered around Gwen, drinking wine and munching pretzels, she talked about Jack Cole. She told outrageous Cole stories, funny Cole stories, inspiring Cole stories, laughing about his rages and his genius while the dancers listened raptly. One of them recalled, "As Gwen talked about all of those wonderful Jack Cole numbers from the movies, we were enthralled, and Bob seemed enthralled too. That was probably the strangest kind of relationship, Gwen and Cole. She seemed to be in love with him, or whatever kind of love that could be. It had to be bizarre for Bob, coming into Gwen's life and having her be so strongly influenced by Jack Cole."

Bob had brought Pat Ferrier back with him from California to begin preproduction choreography on *New Girl in Town*. In the past he had done this work with Joan or Gwen. Now, Gwen was busy with acting classes. Just as Joan had urged him to study acting, and just as he had followed her into Sanford Meisner's classes, so he now urged Gwen to study with the celebrated teacher in preparation for this, her first real acting challenge.

"She had no trouble with ordinary musical comedy and dialogue at all," Bob would later say. "I mean, how to be cute and deliver a joke, that came kind of naturally. But," he went on, "I thought, well, this is an O'Neill, and this is going to demand a little more than how to read a joke, so I thought it would be very beneficial to her to spend some time with Sandy Meisner. She took classes, and he coached her privately, and it was very, very helpful."

Although he was talking like a director, he was not one yet. Mr. Abbott was directing *New Girl in Town*, but Bob was thinking about it, that is clear. "George Abbott is the kind of director," he said, "that requires almost immediate results. He does not want to go into anything at all. He wants it, he hears it, and that's the way he thinks it should be. And it's very good, it's a different kind of direction, so I thought she needed another influence so that she could also give Abbott what he wanted, not quite as quickly as he wanted but able to give it and then fill it in underneath. Sandy Meisner could give her that."

Because *New Girl in Town* was to have so little dancing, Fosse worked with Pat Ferrier on walks, on ways of standing, "maybe clumps of movement," she said, "or a series of steps." In the studio, as the steps developed, they began to couple and multiply. He developed a sequence portraying Anna Christie's dream of her past life in a whorehouse. By the time actual rehearsals got under way, he told Abbott that he had come up with a ballet.

To say that Abbott was startled would be an understatement, but the director withheld judgment until he saw it on stage at the New Haven tryout. That was when the trouble began. The whorehouse ballet was built around a great staircase that led to the bedrooms upstairs. On the floor, the prostitutes would dance with the customers, "in and around a group of chairs," as Pat Ferrier remembered, "with the girls in a series of lifts with the men. And the men carried us upstairs. We were wearing garter belts, that was all everyone seemed to notice, and," she continued, "all of us were writhing pretty sexily."

Another dancer in the ballet, young Harvey Evans, remembered Gwen being carried up the stairs in one of these lifts, "carried over John Aristedes' shoulder." Evans was playing "the shy young kid brought to the whorehouse, naive and dumb, teased by Gwen." Bob had found Evans as a seventeen-year-old in the *Damn Yankees* road company, and he used to grin while watching the youngster rehearse. Evans was still naive enough to be dazzled. It wasn't so long ago that he had asked Gwen for her autograph. He thought Fosse was laughing at him until someone told him that Bob said Evans reminded him of himself in *Call Me Mister.* "After that," Evans said, "he gave me all the shy bits."

When John Aristedes carried Gwen up the stairs in *New Girl in Town,* Evans remembered, "It was as if he was taking her to bed. I mean, that was the point. And she was wearing a very brief costume, a sort of corset, and her breast would occasionally pop out."

As far as Harold Prince was concerned, "the ballet was revolting. It was a scatological dance that didn't belong in the show, a lot of girls lying on their backs with Japanese fans in their toes . . . it was crotch dancing." Evans disagreed. "It was terrific dance theatre," he said, "better than the show."

Following the New Haven reviews, the local police came after *New Girl in Town,* and during dance rehearsal, they padlocked the stage door. The dancers were told that "the City of New Haven would not let the show go on if the ballet stayed in, it was so dirty." If that particular threat had in fact been made it was never consummated. Still, by the time the show arrived in Boston, the ballet dispute was critical, with Abbott and Prince on one side, Fosse and Verdon on the other. The mediocrity of the show didn't help matters. Abbott had himself written the script, and it was a workaday affair. The undistinguished songs were by a newcomer, Bob Merrill, and they lay at quite some distance from the score that Leonard Bernstein had just written for *West Side Story,* which that February of 1957 was just starting tryouts of its own. *West Side Story* very likely weighed on Bob's mind as a reminder of the strides Jerome Robbins was taking toward a new kind of dance theatre, and its producer was the very same Harold Prince who had complained about the gorilla dance and was now giving Bob such difficulty with this whorehouse ballet. Why wasn't Prince respecting *his* work? Wasn't Fosse as good as Robbins?

Then there were egos. Although Gwen was the star and the show was her vehicle, the movie actress Thelma Ritter was in it too, and Ritter was getting most of the attention from the press. The reason was not obscure. She was playing a funny role while Gwen was the tragic heroine, not very appealing except in opera; moreover, she was taking this dramatic assignment very seriously. Before each performance, she would stand near a backstage wall, eyebrows scrunched and forehead furrowed, thoughts turned inward, not doing a dancer's warm-up stretches but developing her mood and character. Comedy is easier for an audience to enjoy, "musical comedy" was still the generic term for musicals, and Thelma Ritter's audiences were having what little fun the show was providing. One Boston rehearsal, Gwen exploded.

It had been a trying day. There had been trouble with the lighting designer, and the company had been onstage with technical rehearsals for more than five hours, repeating scenes and waiting while lights were set and adjusted. The tension over the whorehouse ballet had been building for weeks, and it was at a peak. As Abbott described it, "We argued that dream ballets were overused, that the ballet glamorized the bordello, and finally that the audiences hated it. Fosse and Gwen replied that it was high art, that they didn't care what the audience liked, and that people had thrown fruit at Stravinsky."

Then Jack Cole arrived. Perhaps Gwen had invited him to provide moral support. Cole was the sexual-dance master. In 1950, he and his troupe (including Gwen) had been thrown out of Ciro's, the Los Angeles nightclub, because of a whorehouse ballet (Cole had argued that the patrons wouldn't be offended because they wouldn't know what it was about anyway). Three years later, he created another whorehouse dance for the flop musical, *Carnival in Flanders*, and he would still be doing it in 1965 with a model of taste and elegance, the whip and rape dance in *Man of La Mancha*. Now, through Gwen, he was influencing Bob to do much the same sort of thing.

Young dancer Harvey Evans, standing by chance at a window in his Boston hotel room, glanced down toward the street. Bob and Jack were strolling along with Gwen between them, and everyone's arms around everyone's shoulders. Cole, who had complained about Fosse ruining Gwen's career, suddenly approved.

After Cole's visit, Fosse went to Abbott and said that he had decided on a substitute ballet. When the director saw it, "it was the same old peep show," and he ordered Bob to cut the ballet altogether and work on something else. Pat Ferrier remembered the dancers being upset "by all those voices raised in Boston," but Harold Prince felt, "the truth of the matter was that the dance didn't belong in the whole goddamned show in the first place. Certainly not with Anna Christie dancing. It made no sense that this shy, completely disoriented creature would dance at a party in such a place."

As the show's turmoil and critical disapproval increased, so did its dancing. Prince realized that Gwen wanted *New Girl in Town* to prove that she could sing and act as well as dance, but he also knew that she would accept the need to save the show. "With it not working in Boston," he recalled, "suddenly dancing was going to be the means to make it into a hit." The question was whether she would submit to the extra dancing while accepting the veto of Bob's whorehouse ballet.

While the argument continued, the rest of the show was revised. In the afternoons there would be rehearsals of dramatic scenes. Since these involved Gwen, she could not rehearse with the dancers. At night the show was being performed. Only after that was there time for her to work on new numbers, "and she'd kill herself," according to Ethel Martin, who was also dancing in the show. "Gwen would rehearse all day long, she'd go on and do the performance, and afterward she'd change and go and rehearse until three or four in the morning."

But Mr. Abbott was not going to allow that whorehouse ballet, and Harold Prince was standing firm beside him. Abbott would tell Fosse to work on a waltz number, "but if I happened to drop into his rehearsals," the director remembered, "I would find him flogging away at that same damn ballet. It was like a disease—I couldn't eradicate it."

Bob had always been deferential to Abbott, but when he was ordered either to edit the whorehouse ballet or eliminate it entirely, "he felt an enraged sense of impotence," Pat Ferrier remembered. "He needed full control." As for Gwen, as the ultimate stoic, she internalized her anger, taking sick and staying in her hotel room for three days. "We couldn't work on the show," Ferrier said, "because that ballet made her sick—the problem with George Abbott and Harold Prince made her sick."

Bob reworked the ballet, and that was the end of not only the problem but any further professional association with Prince and Abbott. *New Girl in Town* opened in New York on May 14, 1957, and, according to Prince, "it got the reviews it deserved, which were not very good. But it was a hit and paid off."

Afterward, without informing either Abbott or Prince, Bob came back to work with the dancers, restoring the whorehouse ballet almost entirely. Artistic frustration was apparently unbearable to him.

It would be difficult to separate Gwen and Bob's working relationship from their personal connection. In many ways, the working relationship *was* the personal connection, because it captured the essentials of their attraction, it reflected their needs, and it was so physical in its representation of their characters. One of Bob's dancers said, "We always talked about wanting to watch them make love because they were so hot. They were exciting together, just standing there in the flesh, but especially when they worked." Pausing to savor the memory, he continued, "They were never lovey-dovey, kiss-kiss, but whenever they were together in a dancing situation, in rehearsal or in the studio, there was an awful lot of sexuality."

It was difficult for them to stop working. It was as if once they stopped working together, they would stop being together. They did become part of a show business social network. They liked to give parties, and they liked going to parties. Their careers were blossoming, the worlds around the theatre were beckoning, and one of those satellite worlds was the Seventh Avenue garment industry, which considered itself in some way allied with show business. At one such party for someone else's opening night, Bob was approached by a curly-haired, chubby-cheeked young man named Herbert Schlein, who stuck out his hand and said, "I think you're something else."

Fosse stared at him blankly.

"Did you hear what I said?"

"I'm sorry," Bob said, only now focusing. "Would you mind repeating that? What's your name?"

"My name is Herbert Schlein, and I think you're one of a kind."

Seemingly dumbstruck, Fosse again gazed at Schlein as if weighing the import of what had just been said. Finally he grinned and said, "Well, I think *you're* something else, just coming up and saying that. I guess I was distracted. This makes me nervous," he said, indicating the party, "waiting for the reviews, even for someone else's show. Tell me," he continued after a pause, "are you 'one of a kind' at what *you* do?"

Rather than admit to selling children's and infants' wear, the young man said that he was an expert cook, which he was, and probably an expert eater, for he was considerably overweight, but he changed the subject, believing himself too unimportant to discuss.

"What are you working on now?"

"I'm getting ready to do another show with Gwen," Fosse answered. "I hope you'll come and see it."

"I see all of your shows," Schlein replied.

"But I want you to be my guest. I think it was very nice of you to come over and say what you said. Because I think you meant it."

"I did mean it," Schlein said.

"Have you ever met Gwen Verdon?"

"Look," Schlein said, "I just happened to see you, and I wanted to tell you that I admired you. It was very nice meeting you. I believe in brief encounters."

As he was starting away, Bob caught him by the arm. "Just a minute," he said. "Did you see that movie? *Brief Encounter*?" Schlein nodded.

"Do I remind you of Trevor Howard?"

"No, you remind me of Bob Fosse."

"Thanks," Bob grinned. "I'd like to talk to you again, sometime."

"Well, I just wanted to meet you," Schlein said, this time succeeding in pulling away. "I'm a very shy person."

The new show Bob had mentioned to Herb Schlein was to be a musical murder mystery set in turn-of-the-century London against a background of music halls and wax museums. It had been written for Bea Lillie, but when the great British comedienne proved unavailable, Gwen was invited to come and hear the songs. They had been composed by a tall and fortyish German intellectual named Albert Hague who had but one Broadway credit, the hit *Plain and Fancy* (many years later he would be nationally known for playing a music teacher in the television series, *Fame*). Hague's lyricist was Dorothy Fields, a member of a great theatrical family. Her father was half of Weber and Fields, the old vaudeville team, and her brother Herbert was an established librettist. She had written the lyrics for such songs as "A Fine Romance," "The Way You Look Tonight," and "I Can't Give You Anything But Love."

Auditioning the show for Gwen, Hague recalled, "She brought with her a skinny young man who we knew only as a choreographer, and we also knew was her boyfriend." Everyone sat down and lighted cigarettes— everyone smoked at the time—and Dorothy Fields began by summarizing the show's story. She was a sophisticated woman, tall, dark haired, a lover of wide-brimmed hats. In the vernacular of the period, she looked "smart." Hoping to appeal to the British in Gwyneth Verdon, she began by pointing out that Gwen would play a turn-of-the-century Cockney. Describing the show elsewhere, Dorothy characterized this girl as "wistful and shy Essie Whimple" who creates figures for a London wax museum that is operated by her two aunts.

"Now Essie is a visionary," Miss Fields continued. "Let's say she has visions. In one of these she sees the face of the strangler who has been terrorizing London. But her favorite and most persistent vision is of a strong, smiling man . . . an American in a strong man act at the Odeon, a second-rate London music hall."

The plot allowed for a show-within-the-show at the music hall, "a number called 'The Uncle Sam Rag,'" Miss Fields said, and there was also a dream ballet with Essie watching her adored strong man at the Odeon and imagining herself a music hall star. The rest of the show was threat, chase, and romance.

At the Verdon audition, Albert Hague, conservatory-trained, extremely accomplished as a pianist, played thirteen of the songs, heartily singing them with Miss Fields, and when they were finished, they tensely awaited the reaction. Were Gwen to do the show, the financing would be easy, and the production could proceed immediately. She was money in the bank.

"I love it," money in the bank said, "and I want to do it, but only on one condition." She looked at the producers, Robert Fryer and Lawrence Carr, and then nodded toward Bob. "This guy is going to be the director."

The silence was tight. Fosse was a choreographer of achievement but having only recently learned how to stage a song, was he now to learn how to direct *with their show*? While everyone sat dumbstruck, Bob said with a slight smile, "I like the songs too. Only a couple of them need to be changed."

The producers had little choice, even though, Robert Fryer recalled, "Rewriting the show from a Bea Lillie vehicle to one for Gwen Verdon was no small task." Moreover, such shaping was a director's job to be done with the librettist, who in this case was two people, David Shaw and Sidney Sheldon (soon to be a novelist of some success). But "as soon as work began," Fryer said, "I was convinced that Bob had the two traits essential for a director—the ability to communicate with people and an overview of what a show should be."

Gwen was so much the star of *Redhead* that the show was actually named for her, but even still, nobody wanted her to have a perfunctory leading man. Richard Kiley, a superior actor as well as a fine baritone, was approved even before he came through the door, and so rehearsals began. At the studio, first day, Bob ran into Jerry Robbins, who asked him how he felt about directing his first show. "Throwing up every morning?" That was likely. Bob was inevitably sandwiched between the heavy dancing load and directing the dramatic scenes. He delegated as much of the dancing as he could to the assistant choreographer, Donald McKayle, and while the dancers were working elsewhere, he would stand midway in the theatre with his arms crossed, squinting through the cigarette smoke. For a moment he would close his eyes, imagining what he wanted, before strolling down the aisle to lean against the orchestra pit rail, describing his thought. Sometimes he would even step up on that rail, stretching a leg across the pit to the stage, balancing himself precariously as he spoke softly to the company.

Among the first lessons that he learned about directing a musical was the importance of smooth segues in and out of musical numbers. As Kiley said, "One of the toughest things in the world for an actor in a musical is to justify stopping in the midst of a scene and starting to sing." To help the logic, Fosse would sneak the music under the dialogue, minutes before the actor was to sing. This underscoring would establish the musical convention, and then Bob encouraged Kiley to speak rather than sing the first line of his song, making the transition from dialogue to lyrics all the smoother.

One afternoon, in the midst of rehearsal, Kiley stopped in mid-speech to disagree on an acting point. Bob was not accustomed to a performer with an opinion. Dancers were not permitted to have opinions. He was starting to grow testy when Gwen popped her head in.

"What's the problem?" she asked.

"Hey!" Kiley said. "Out! This has nothing to do with you. You may be the star of the show, but this isn't any of your business. I'm talking to the director."

Richard Kiley was hardly one to take orders from a director's girl-friend even if she was Gwen Verdon. (She was nastier with coauthor Sidney Sheldon. The two got on so badly that, when giving interviews, she would omit his name, crediting David Shaw with the authorship.) "Kiley was very imposing," Albert Hague remembered, "and neither Gwen nor Bob would dare abuse him." In fact after Kiley snapped at her she popped her head right back out of the rehearsal.

But rehearsal had lighter moments too. Bob got it into his head one day that Kiley's receding hairline was not right for the leading man. Hair was something he was very conscious of. "Let's go down and look at some wigs," he said.

"Bobby wanted me to look like one of those guys on a Greek coin," Kiley recalled with a laugh, and when they got to the wigmaker, the director asked for a full head wig. "It was one of those naked Greek statue things," Kiley said. "Well, try it on," Bob said, already grinning because there are few things in life funnier than toupees. Looking it over seriously, Bob asked his leading man to turn around. He crossed his arms and pondered and peered, settling comfortably into this little comedy routine, and at last he said, "Jesus, you look like Tony Bennett." That was when they both laughed until the tears rolled down their cheeks.

As for Albert Hague's relationship with Fosse, "It was very difficult to talk music with him," the composer said, "because he didn't know music. He literally couldn't count beats. Mind you, he wasn't alone. George Abbott and Josh Logan couldn't count beats either, and George Kaufman once told me, 'Music is a very expensive and unnecessary element in the musical theatre.'" Fosse was hardly unmusical. Rather, he was ashamed of his musical illiteracy, at least consistent in his low self-esteem.

As was his standard practice now, he arrived at rehearsal with the choreography already in his head. He strode into the studio, greeted his ensemble of sixteen dancers, and proceeded to teach them every part of every number. He might say, "Try it again," and "again," and "again," and yet "again," but if he sounded sarcastic or cutting, it was usually because somebody wasn't coming through, not dancing up to potential. "Then," one of his dancers said, "he could be nasty." Soon enough, his patience started to go under the pressure of both directing and choreographing. Even after a number was finished and even after the tryout tour had begun and even after everyone agreed that the dancing was the best thing in *Redhead*, precision perfect, even then he continued to rehearse the dancers, all afternoon and often after a performance. "Everything was finished and right," one of them, Harvey Evans, recalled, "but we kept working and working. We were ready to get hepatitis, to drop," and a lack of sleep was only making Bob testier. He was so tense that he had to take a sleeping pill, sometimes two, to get to sleep, but sleeping pill sleep never seems to provide rest, and the amphetamines that he was taking to wake him up were providing a false, nervous energy. They also eliminated what little appetite he had. He was very edgy.

Finally, Lawrence Carr, one of the producers, said, "You have got to give the dancers a break or they're going to die here." Only then did Fosse rest them, and it was just for an evening.

"We understood," Evans said. "After all, this was his first directing, and he was a little crazed about it." Doubtless, Fosse was also aware of the new criterion for Broadway dance that Jerome Robbins had just established with *West Side Story*. Mere numbers were no longer enough. A choreographer-director was expected to make dance an integral part of the whole.

Richard Kiley had a complaint of his own as the tryout began in Philadelphia, but instead of speaking to Bob about it, he decided to rewrite a scene himself. He had done it before and was hardly insecure about writing although it is the kind of thing that drives librettists crazy. When his rewrite was finished, he brought the pages to Bob and said, "Why not try it this way?"

The next day, Bob handed the scene back. "I'll tell you, Dick," he said, "I read it, and it's interesting, but I really don't think the scene needs it."

"Okay," Kiley said equably. "I can accept that."

Even though *Redhead* was doing very well, with good reviews and good business, the strain was showing on Gwen. Buzz Miller, a lead dancer, said, "She was a little tough on the rest of the dancers. She'd criticize the chorus behind her. They couldn't figure out how she saw them."

She also started missing performances. One of the dancers said, "No wonder she's tired, she's keeping track of the whole cast." Being both the star and the girlfriend, she felt responsible for the show and for Bob's welfare, but she wasn't the only tired one; Bob's inner turmoil merely bubbled to the surface in different ways. When the company moved to Washington, D.C., Hague arranged to have the sheet music of his score duplicated so that he could give it to everyone as Christmas presents. It was a lovely idea, and as he handed an autographed set to Bob, he said, "Merry Christmas," only to receive a scowl in response. The director seemed to take the gift as a reference to his musical ignorance. "What are you giving it to me for?" he snapped. "You know I can't read music."

The pressure on Gwen was growing too. She would occasionally ask to skip a song, purely out of fatigue. When it became a regular occurrence, the dancers took to wearily whispering, " 'I'll Try' is out," or, "It's in tonight." Such changes forced quick thinking on the parts of the stage manager, the actors, and the musicians since dialogue had to be altered and song cues dropped in order to accommodate any change. After Gwen dropped *seven songs* from one performance, it was no longer trivial, and the composer objected vehemently, only to be asked by the producer, "Do you want to complain to the Dramatists Guild and close the show?" This was the threat that was regularly leveled at authors who protested unconsulted changes in their work. They are protected, but naturally they back down, preferring anything to an end of the production.

As the tryout tour drew to a close, Gwen had the orchestrations for her songs transposed so that, depending on how she felt, she could sing numbers either a key higher or a key lower. By the time *Redhead* came to Broadway, she was staying in the lower key, which was easier for her to sing, except on special occasions such as an Actors Fund benefit, when the theatre was filled with professionals.

Redhead was a fine success. New York's opening nighters seemed to fall in love with her all over again. Bob had managed, through the device of the British music hall, to bring a Chaplin quality to his dances, and that meant the Fosse canes and Fosse bowler hats and bowlegged, sidewise Fosse movements. Chaplin's physical antics derived from the eccentric dancing of British music hall, and in that Bob found a quirky kindred spirit. He enjoyed, too, the violation of period, he found tension and surprise in that, and he felt free to do it because of the basic unreality of musical theatre. So he dressed his dancers in black leotards and stylized costumes that were hardly appropriate to the show's 1907 setting, and he was right, it worked. *Redhead* was his fifth consecutive hit; he would win yet another Tony Award for it, and still he would not feel that he was given quite enough credit for the success. His feeling was partly justifiable. The show certainly was received as a Gwen Verdon vehicle, she was taken as the reason for its existence. Whatever was wrong with it was the director's fault.

Composer Albert Hague was as aware as anyone of how much the success was Fosse's doing. "It was everything," he said. "Bobby alone took that thin book and made it into a hit show." He was demonstrating the traits necessary for success in any field: the ability to perceive the presence of an opportunity, the inclination to capitalize on it, the sense of how to exploit it, and the talent to bring it off.

So he had become a leader, a director, and he had turned his choreographic perfectionism to serve all of his work. It did not cease with the opening night performance. After the third performance, he stopped by at Richard Kiley's dressing room. His clouds had parted, and he was calm. "You know what?" he said. "We're going to rehearse tomorrow. I'm going to put in that scene change you wanted."

Kiley looked up in annoyance. "Oh, Bobby, come on," he said. "The show is open, we're a big hit. It's a long trip for me to come in. We've been working so hard. I'm exhausted."

"Well," Bob said, no longer in such a great mood, "I want to do it."

"Well, I wrote it and I *don't* want to do it," Kiley said, "and I'm not going to do it."

"You're usurping my authority," Bob replied.

"I'm just telling you," Kiley said firmly, "I'm not going to do that rewrite. We're in. The show works. And I'm tired. I want to be with my family, and I'm not coming in to rehearse."

Fosse stalked out of the dressing room. Kiley picked up the telephone and called his agent, and said that he couldn't psychologically afford to be upset because he was exhausted from the tryouts and the pressure of opening on Broadway. "Either this is resolved," he said, "or I'm putting in my notice because I'm not playing that scene, *period*."

Bob never mentioned it again.

□   □

Early in 1960, at the conclusion of the Broadway run, the *Redhead* national company played a Chicago engagement to warm up for an extended booking in California. Gwen would be able to meet Bob's family and then visit with her own. There was something very rewarding about playing a Broadway show away from Broadway. Audiences have personalities, and there are other sensibilities, other moods in other cities. Most actors enjoyed the road, and it was on the road that Gwen and Bob decided to do something about having a baby. She was thirty-five (he was thirty-two), and while the expression "biological clock" had not yet come into fashion, the concept had no trouble existing untitled. Her childbearing years were running out.

Bob had no qualms about having an illegitimate child, but Gwen may have been more of a traditionalist. She could also have given lessons in privacy to a hermit crab, for even though they were in Chicago, with his family at hand, they decided to get married in secrecy. On April 2, they took out a license, and the next day the couple drove to suburban Oak Park and found a justice of the peace on North Maple Avenue. There, in the living room of Gilbert Volk, J.P., Gwyneth Heneghan (she'd never changed her married name) and Robert Louis Fosse were wed. Bob's family was only a forty-five-minute drive away in Evanston, and yet none of them was told, and none of them was there.

It is difficult to imagine what reason Gwen might have had for such extreme secretiveness and what made her require such psychological protection, but she certainly took privacy to unusual lengths. The only indication of any chink in this armor was a girlishly whispered backstage outburst to Pat Ferrier: "We got married! But don't tell anyone! Don't tell anyone!" It wasn't until October that the marriage became public, and perhaps even then it was only because Sadie Fosse was dying.

On December 19, at the age of sixty-six, Sadie succumbed to heart disease, and Bob tearfully told Stephen Silverman of the New York *Post*, "You see, I loved my mother. I think there would have been nothing better than to have had an affair with her. I think everyone ought to have an affair with his mother."

7

The Broadway of 1960 was a thriving center of commercial theatre, doing what had made Broadway *Broadway*, a lot of good show business with an occasional artistic highlight. Laurence Olivier and Anthony Quinn were starring in the Jean Anouilh play, *Becket* and for the fun of it, were alternating in their roles of Thomas Becket and King Henry II. Melvyn Douglas could be seen in Gore Vidal's biting political comedy, *The Best Man*, while Anne Bancroft was starring in *The Miracle Worker* and Angela Lansbury was playing a cockney in *A Taste of Honey*. The two great dames of the musical stage were in formidable vehicles made in their images, the girl scout Mary Martin in *The Sound of Music* and the lowdown Ethel Merman in *Gypsy*. Richard Kiley had returned to drama in an adaptation of Allen Drury's best-seller, *Advise and Consent*. Musical theatregoers could choose among *La Plume de Ma Tante*, *The Unsinkable Molly Brown*, *West Side Story*, *Fiorello*, *Irma La Douce*, and *Bye, Bye, Birdie*. The more soberminded could see Paddy Chayefsky's *The Tenth Man*, Tennessee Williams' *Period of Adjustment*, or Lillian Hellman's *Toys in the Attic*. Two of the country's brainiest comedians were appearing in *An Evening with Mike Nichols and Elaine May*, and *My Fair Lady* continued its great success while New York awaited its apparent heir, *Camelot*, with two great stars, Julie Andrews and Richard Burton.

Even with such a stir and to-do, there was room for criticism, but Broadway's main failing, the lack of classical and adventurous theatre, was not its fault. Such theatre was the responsibility of an institution, a theatre that didn't have to pay its own way by selling tickets but was instead, like a symphony orchestra or a museum, subsidized by contributors and the government. Just such a theatre was being readied to fill precisely that need, and Broadway people were being appointed to direct and manage it. This was to be the Repertory Theatre of Lincoln Center. The artistic director was Elia Kazan, who then bestrode Broadway as the director of Tennessee Williams, Arthur Miller, and William Inge. The managing director at Lincoln Center was Robert Whitehead, perhaps New York's most serious-minded producer.

Whitehead was impressed with Bob Fosse's shows, stimulated by his talent, and charmed by his personality. He nurtured a chance meeting into an acquaintanceship, hoping to find a drama for him to direct at Lincoln Center even though Fosse had never staged a play in his life (and never would). But like so many drama-centered theatre lovers, Whitehead was a secret enthusiast of musicals, and talk of doing a play at Lincoln Center inevitably turned to plans for Whitehead producing a musical that Fosse would direct on Broadway.

Robert Whitehead was a tall, slender, handsome gentleman who came to New York from prestigious Canadian social circles. Intelligent, civilized, gracious, and gentile, he was inevitably described as "patrician" in the generally Jewish world of Broadway. Bob Whitehead looked as if he had spent every minute of his urbane life in a pinstriped suit somewhere near a chapel.

Whitehead had a reputation for producing prestigious dramas. He had made his debut presenting Judith Anderson in Robinson Jeffers' adaptation of *Medea*; he had produced Carson McCullers' *A Member of the Wedding* as well as the Gertrude Stein–Virgil Thomson opera, *Four Saints in Three Acts*. He presented such playwrights as T. S. Eliot, Terrence Rattigan, and Jean Anouilh. He was preparing Robert Bolt's *A Man for All Seasons* to be produced in 1961. Only two years older than Fosse, he carried culture casually on his flawlessly tailored shoulders, and their conversations must have seemed heady stuff to the ex-hoofer from Chicago who had never gone past high school.

The idea that Fosse and Whitehead came up with, and about which they quickly grew excited, was a musical version of the Jean Giradoux play, *The Madwoman of Chaillot*, to star the celebrated Lynn Fontanne in the title role, with her equally celebrated husband Alfred Lunt as the Rag Picker. On the Broadway of those years, anything was conceivable and was usually produced. Had not Fosse only recently worked on a musical version of Eugene O'Neill's *Anna Christie*? Had not its composer, Bob Merrill, just made another hit musical (*Take Me Along*) out of yet another O'Neill play (*Ah! Wilderness*)? Why not inveigle the Lunts to do a musical *Madwoman*? Whitehead and Fosse excitedly decided to visit the pair of reigning theatrical monarchs and sell them on the song and dance.

It was not across town. Alfred Lunt and Lynn Fontanne had abandoned the Times Square hurly-burly for America's heartland. They lived on a farm in southern Wisconsin. Genesee Depot was little more than a postmark, but it was there the thespians dwelled, close to the earth and far from New York.

The Lunts were friends of Bob Whitehead's. He had produced their last vehicle, *The Visit*, by the Swiss playwright, Friedrich Durrenmatt. It had been the best kind of success, profitable as well as prestigious, and so when Whitehead telephoned to ask whether he might visit and bring Fosse to discuss a theatre idea, they were not only pleased; they insisted on an overnight stay.

The two men flew to Chicago and rented a car for the drive to Wisconsin. This was the kind of boys' night out that Fosse always enjoyed, and they had plenty of time to talk. They developed, discarded, and evolved several concepts for the artistic, entertaining musical they were hoping to make. Whitehead conceded that the idea was risky, but he thought that with Alfred Lunt and Lynn Fontanne it just might be commercially feasible. Without them, of course, it was impossible.

Whitehead's scheme was to snare the prized couple by luring Alfred with the chance to direct a Broadway musical. Lunt already fancied himself a director of plays, and Whitehead was sure the actor would leap at the chance to do a musical, for although it was still fashionable for theatre intellectuals to look down on musical comedy, almost every actor yearned to do one. Whitehead assured Fosse that ultimately Lunt would need help, and if George Abbott had allowed Jerry Robbins to be billed as codirector of *The Pajama Game*, then Fosse could certainly allow this. The prestige of an association with the Lunts was worth it, and Bob agreed.

After dinner, with the dishes cleared and the coffee served, the four of them sat at the long table in the farmhouse kitchen. Lynn pushed her cup and saucer out of the way, opened a deck of playing cards, and dealt herself a hand of solitaire. Whitehead and Fosse watched her play while they listened raptly as Alfred talked on and on about his pea patch. Finally, Whitehead raised the subject of Broadway.

It was silent except for the pendulum clock's ticking. Lynn scanned her row of cards.

Whitehead described the idea, he outlined the show. Fosse filled in the picture with descriptions of dances and musical staging. Lunt said he very much liked the idea. Lynn slowly turned over one of her cards.

"You would be just sensational as the Rag Picker," Whitehead said, and Alfred seemed to agree. He beamed. Without looking up from her game, in fact still turning her packets of three, Lynn paused with cards in midair. "Don't you think," she asked, "the play is a bit abstract?"

The Lunts were accustomed to naturalistic drama. *The Madwoman of Chaillot* was not an absurdist play, but there were cartoon elements to it, and the characters certainly were outlandish. The main point to be stressed, Whitehead said, was that it was a modern-day classic written by a great French dramatist.

The conversation turned to the extent of its musicalization. Whitehead was smoothly evasive, assuring the actors that "just how far the show will go with music and dance, we'll all work out together. Either it will be a play with songs or a full-out musical."

Bob gave them an idea of the kind of choreography he had in mind, musical movement, he said, rather than conventional numbers. In Whitehead's recollection, "Nobody could have been more charming than he was that evening." The only question was whether they had managed to sell Miss Fontanne on the show, for Whitehead was convinced that the ultimate decision was hers.

The three men looked at her. Her eyes were on the cards, and she tentatively reached to move one, playing her solitaire scene for all it was worth. At last she said, "It really isn't my sort of thing," and moved the card. Lunt looked up from his coffee cup, but he couldn't catch her eye. She was having her moment. He was eager to do the musical, that was plain, but the producer knew that when Lynn Fontanne said it really wasn't her sort of thing, the project was dead.

Robert Whitehead, for all his urbanity, was just as prone to madcap theatrical notions as his less refined, gunslinging colleagues. It had been a wonderfully loony notion, the Lunts in a Giraudoux musical, a notion created with zest, pursued with enthusiasm, and even shot down with zaniness. This was precisely what had once made Broadway fun but, alas, that Broadway was fast disappearing. There ultimately would be a musical made of *The Madwoman of Chaillot* but it would star Angela Lansbury, which was much more conventional casting. (It failed.)

Whitehead, on the trip back to New York, turned to Fosse and said, "I'm really sorry. I just had the feeling that maybe I could pull this off," but Bob wasn't morose. He already had another idea. He was an admirer of Preston Sturgis movies, and there was one in particular, *Hail, The Conquering Hero*, that he felt would make a strong, serious-minded, entertaining musical. Whitehead went for the idea; he bought the rights to the movie, and Bob bought a hat to wear at rehearsal and a whistle to hang around his neck. They assembled a creative team, the music to be composed by Morris ("Moose") Charlap, the lyrics by Norman Gimbel. For the script, Bob suggested Larry Gelbart, who had no Broadway credits but who had already cowritten a Stephen Sondheim show, the not yet produced A *Funny Thing Happened on the Way to the Forum.*

The Conquering Hero, as the show was to be called, followed the general outline of the satiric Sturgis movie about Woodrow Truesmith, an Army reject who comes back to his hometown during the Second World War and is mistaken for a military hero. Its appeal for Fosse seemed to lie in the antihero. He set his sights on Donald O'Connor to play this central character, but O'Connor was not available, and so Fosse walked into the Palace Theatre one sunny Sunday afternoon during the summer of 1960 and sat down to do what he hated most in the theatre—audition actors. He so identified with these earnest and vulnerable performers, he so understood the pain of rejection, that he would have chosen to hire every last one of them rather than to refuse any. His gentleness during this process was such that actors wrote him thank-you notes for rejections.

On this particular day, young James Kirkwood, Jr., was reading for the part of Truesmith. The comedian had worked with Bob in *Dance Me a Song* ten years earlier. Tall, slender, and good looking, he heard his name called and walked nervously from the wings, bravely flashing his big, beaming grin. Bob was sitting some seven or eight rows back in the theatre. Kirkwood didn't recognize the others out there; they were the authors and the producer. He nodded, and as he did, Bob rose from his seat and came down front.

"Nervous?"

"No," said Kirkwood, full of baloney. "I'm just fine. I never knew you were going to turn into Bob Fosse."

Bob grinned. "Neither did I," he said.

Kirkwood wasn't trying to delay the audition or ingratiate himself with the director. He really was amazed that the vaudvillian of *Dance Me a Song,* the street kid who had been married to Mary-Ann Niles, had somehow been transformed into a Broadway choreographer and director.

"But did you have any idea," he asked, "back then, of wanting to direct?"

"Oh, yeah," Bob said. "Didn't you know that?"

"No, it never occurred to me," Kirkwood replied. "I thought you were a real great tap dancer. I thought that was what you were going to do. I never thought I'd be asking you for a *job.*"

"So how about auditioning?"

Bob turned and went back to his seat. Kirkwood walked upstage and began his song. He was not a singer. Singing was not his strength. All he wanted was not to be thrown out before he had a chance to read.

"That was just fine," Bob said from his seat. "Have you prepared the speech?"

Kirkwood nodded. He had been told that he would be expected to read the play's climactic speech. He read it, and when he was through, he peered into the darkness. There were more people in the theatre than when he had started: design people, investors. Bob got up and walked down the aisle once more, this time all the way to the orchestra pit. He leaned against the brass rail and looked upward.

"Jimmy," he said. "Come here a second."

Kirkwood walked down to the footlights. Bob motioned him to come still closer. The actor knelt.

"This time," Bob whispered, "when you read the speech, don't sell it. You know? Trust the character."

It had been heard from actors before. "Bob directed you at an audition," one said, "as if you were at acting class. Like you think directors are going to do. Usually, at auditions, they're very brusque, they just say, 'Okay, go over there and say the speech.' But Fosse gives you help. 'Now when you do it again,' he says, 'do this or try that or pull this out.' He gives you something to go on."

Kirkwood stood up and started back to his spot. Then he turned as Bob was headed back up the aisle.

"Bobby!" he called in a stage whisper.

Fosse stopped in his tracks and turned. "Yeah?"

"Come here for a second."

Fosse walked back down the aisle and into the pit. "Yeah?"

"What the fuck do you know about directing anyway?"

Bob laughed out loud. They both did.

Kirkwood did not get the role of Woodrow Truesmith. It was given to Tom Poston, a humorist and actor who had developed a certain popularity on a Sunday night television show. Bob wasn't pleased with Poston, considering him not a leading man but a supporting actor and a nonmusical one at that, but Whitehead felt he would be a box office attraction.

When auditioning the dancers, Fosse naturally inclined to people he had already worked with, hiring Pat Ferrier, of course, and Buzz Miller from *Pajama Game* and John Aristedes from *New Girl in Town*. He even remembered Dick Korthaze, one of the backup dancers on the Martin and Lewis television show he had done with Mary-Ann back in Chicago, ten years earlier. But he also hired newcomers. His taste in females tended to tall, sinuous beauties reminiscent of strippers and certainly more luscious than the usual Broadway dancer. He was the rare heterosexual choreographer, and it showed in the women he hired (and the men too—he preferred "character dancers," a euphemism for ones who were not pretty boys).

At auditions, when asking for demonstrations, Bob had, as Pat Ferrier put it, "a limited dance vocabulary." Where a ballet-trained choreographer might start with a sequence of arabesques, entrechats, and pirouettes, Bob would begin by asking for moves and shuffles and lots of jumps. He wouldn't bother at all with long, lyrical movements. "That's what he lacked," Ferrier said. "It was astounding that he went as far as he did with such limited training."

With the dance ensemble hired, rehearsals for *The Conquering Hero* began at the New Amsterdam Theatre on 42nd Street, just off Times Square. It was a historic house, once a Broadway showplace, the home of the Ziegfeld Follies, now shabby and woebegone and part of a row of pornographic movie houses. Its elegant second theatre on the top was being used only for rehearsals such as these, and it was there that the first day of work on the show was scheduled. Next to the downstairs lobby, just under the marquee advertising *The Nude in the White Convertible*, Fosse came in from the crisp of early autumn to wait in the grimy vestibule for the elevator to take him upstairs. There was a fedora on his head, a whistle strung around his neck, and waiting, too, was one of his dancers, a nervous young woman named Georgia Creighton. It was her first Broadway show. She would have preferred that Mr. Fosse were not there to notice her.

The tiny elevator came, the door squeaked open, they both got inside, and it creaked upward. At the stop its door ground sidewise, and they both stepped out, finding themselves in a noisy room filled with women who were playing bingo.

"I don't think this is the place, folks," Bob said, and he rang for the elevator again, this time finding the old theatre and the old stage with the old runway intact, cutting down the middle of the old auditorium with its cobwebbed rows of ancient and broken seats, the crooked teeth in the decrepit grin of an abandoned funhouse. It was cold and dusty in there, and he apologized to the company for the conditions. Then he introduced everyone to everyone, starting with the dog in the cast, who, being a prop (or property), was called "Props."

Dance rehearsal started before script readings. Bob had new ideas that he wanted to explore, "innovative ideas," Pat Ferrier remembered. "He wanted one dance done not to music but to chants and the spoken word, and he had worked up some things with magic that later ended up in *Pippin*."

A week later, as book rehearsal began, there was a bad omen. An actress was about to be replaced. Everyone knew it except her. While she was working in one room, her replacement was learning the role in another. Actors are an insecure lot; it is in the nature of their sporadic work, and that incident did not make for a general ease. It was also clear from the outset that Bob was not thrilled with Tom Poston. It was Poston who was reading from the script when Larry Gelbart finally appeared. A family emergency had delayed the playwright's arrival. Now he was hearing Poston read lines that were not in his original script. They were the narration for a war ballet illustrating a story that Truesmith fabricates when he is asked to describe his military adventures.

When Gelbart inquired about the authorship of this dialogue, Bob said, "You were off fucking around somewhere." He didn't take his eyes away from the actors, he didn't turn to look at Gelbart, but he added, "*Somebody* had to make the changes." It was implicit in that remark that *he* had written the dialogue.

"Okay," Gelbart said, suppressing his anger. "Well, now that I'm back I'd like to do it myself. I see what you want. I see what you need. Now let me put it into my own words. I'd like to do that."

In the tension of the moment, as Bob sat at the table on stage, with the actors and the metal folding chairs all around, his face went dead white. A gurgling noise came up from his stomach into his throat, a rasping, gargling sound. In the face of this display, Gelbart joked, "A simple 'No' would have been sufficient," but the words went to ice on his lips as Bob took a deep, guttural breath, tipped over backward in his chair and fell sprawling to the floor, striking the back of his head against the hard wood. He thrashed his limbs, whipping his arms, kicking his legs, rolling his eyeballs upward into his head, and he frothed at the mouth in the throes of a full epileptic seizure. "The only time I've ever seen a grand mal seizure," actor John McMartin remembered, "and let me tell you, I don't ever want to see one again."

The company was paralyzed. Gwen sprang from a side chair, having been sitting and watching. In an instant she was next to Bob, and with the calm of a professional nurse, plainly having seen this happen before, she turned him on his side and covered him with her sweater. Softly, she shooed the crowd away. She gave one of the dancers the telephone number of Bob's doctor. The chilled and dusty old theatre was much too quiet. The director of a show is its father, and everyone depends on him, trusting safety to him, but with the director stricken helpless on the floor, who is to feel secure? The actors were dismissed for the day.

The reason Gwen had turned Bob on his side was so he would not choke on his froth. Commonly referred to as "foaming at the mouth," it is actually gastric material that is being forced up by the intense stomach contractions that are being suffered during the seizure. It is the violence of these involuntary muscular movements that makes a grand mal seizure so frightening and, for that matter, so dangerous to the epileptic. In itself the attack is not harmful, but the thrashing about can result in broken bones, even a fractured spine in the opinion of Dr. Jonathan Pincus, chairman of the Department of Neurology at Georgetown University Hospital in Washington and a leading authority on epilepsy. As for the notion of putting a pencil or tongue depressor in an epileptic's mouth, Dr. Pincus says that while the victim of a seizure may bite his tongue, he is in no danger of swallowing it.

Fosse had for many years been taking the common seizure suppressant, Dilantin. Joan McCracken had told a friend that "Bob hasn't had a seizure for ages," and she credited the Dilantin with that, but this medication is not always effective and can be defeated by, among other things, a lack of sleep. Too, Dr. Pincus is convinced that "epileptics tend to have seizures at times of emotional stress."

Fosse's doctor arrived at the theatre and injected him with a sedative. Gwen, meantime, took Philburn Friedman aside. He was Bob's production stage manager and she showed him exactly what to do should there be a recurrence in her absence (the epilepsy may well have been one reason why Gwen was almost always at Bob's side during rehearsals). Although this was his first and only public seizure, her calm and knowing manner suggested a familiarity with the problem. Fosse himself once attributed his epilepsy to a head injury suffered in a fall from a horse after his foot had been caught in the stirrup, and he had been dragged some distance. Epilepsy can be developed through just such a head injury or else through inheritance. Perhaps this story of a riding accident was true, although nobody ever saw him on a horse. However, since hereditary epilepsy is usually outgrown, and since he never suffered a known seizure again, it seems likelier that his was actually a genetic epilepsy.

The day after the seizure, Gelbart arrived for a script conference at the Fosse apartment on Central Park West. He was greeted by a German shepherd named Charlie, a cat named Tiger, and a very subdued Gwen Verdon. It was dusk, and while he waited, Gelbart browsed through Bob's collection of books on Charlie Chaplin. There, the writer thought, was Bob's model, a skinny little vaudevillian with a bowler hat and a cane, the star performer who had become a writer, a director, and even his own producer.

Bob semimaterialized, wraithlike, wan, weak, and drawn in a thin chenille bathrobe and slippers. As Gelbart remembered, "He looked even smaller and more vulnerable than he usually was."

The Camel hanging from the corner of his mouth was the only healthy looking thing about him. In a shaky voice he asked Gelbart if he would like to go outside on the terrace and see the American astronauts. Their space capsule was in twinkling orbit. They walked through the French doors, and as they stood high above Central Park, peering at the sky, Bob told Gelbart, "What a wonderful writer" he was. After a pause he added, "But I don't intend to ever work with you again."

Considering that their disagreement had set off an epileptic seizure, nobody could blame him, although the actual reason for the remark was probably a growing reluctance to collaborate with anyone at all. He was beginning to have, and have confidence in, his own theatrical visions.

As the *Conquering Hero* company concluded rehearsals before leaving for the first tryout engagement in New Haven, its skin was pulling taut. While Bob was directing scenes, Gwen ran many of the dance rehearsals, and she could be testy. "You're not doing that full out," she once complained. "You do it for Bobby, why don't you do it for me?" Like Bob, she would not allow "marking"—walking through a number that had already been finished. They had to do everything full out at all times.

Nor did all the dancers appreciate Gwen's criticisms ("You've got too much eye makeup on") or her assuming an authoritative role. She was not, after all, this show's choreographer. Once, when she attempted to give notes, a dancer said, "Thank you very much, Gwen, but I think Bob's my choreographer."

Directing the dramatic scenes, Fosse made it clear that *The Conquering Hero* was going to be a brainy musical. "I've done *Damn Yankees* already," he told the company, "and I'm not going to do any more numbers just for the sake of applause." The show, he said, was going to make serious comments on war, politics, and sociology. Some of that struck Gelbart as ingenuous. "Bobby was getting ideas for the first time," he said, "ideas that had been around a long time. For instance, he discovered Momism about twenty-five years after Philip Wylie, and he kept pushing intellectual and political points that I thought were passé, but he was very enamored of them because they were new to him, so a lot of the friction was from trying to accommodate stuff you didn't believe in."

Probably emblematic of all the trouble was the twelve-minute "war ballet." Here was Bob's choreographic statement. With Poston at stageside, fantasizing about his heroism, the dancers were to portray him mowing down the enemy in the Guadalcanal jungles. The boy dancers played the marines, the girls the Japanese. Whitehead fretted about this, and Fosse thought the producer was upset because he thought the marines were coming across as effeminate. This developed into a quarrel over the ballet's taste, a dispute not dissimilar to the one over the whorehouse ballet in *New Girl in Town*. The war ballet, Whitehead felt, "was strangely unpleasant." He didn't at all like the way the male dancers were dressed. The only thing that production stage manager Philburn Friedman would say was that "Bobby had a way of looking at things that, for 1961, was, well, very advanced."

Still another troublesome spot was Truesmith's campaign speech at show's end, when he is running for mayor. Bob was trying to make a point about political double-talk, having the candidate spout nonsense while the chorus chants a vocal counterpoint. There was some grumbling about the confusion as well as its theatrical effectiveness, but what are tryouts for, if not for trying out? Bob had learned about fixing and doctoring from the best, from Mr. Abbott. Every show of his, so far, had been a hit. As *The Conquering Hero* headed out of town, its future might well have been rosy too. However, not many thought so.

Before the New Haven premiere, Bob began keeping his producer at arm's length. Whitehead felt, "Bob wanted to do it all himself," and he wasn't the only one to feel alienated by Fosse's drive for artistic control. When the composer, the gentle Moose Charlap, complained about a musical tempo, Bob snapped, "Why don't *you* take the baton?" and when Whitehead asked him to take it easy on his collaborators, Fosse replied, "I'm not here to win a popularity contest, I'm here to come up with a hit show."

"Well, it had better be a hit when we open here," Whitehead retorted, "because there's going to be a rebellion on your hands."

It was considerably less than a hit in New Haven. "It was a shambles," Whitehead said, and it was not being helped by the increasingly hostile atmosphere. Poston was suffering the most because Fosse was not concealing his dislike of the performance. To be sure, the actor (who had health problems at home in addition to friction with his director) was not giving what anyone considered a heavyweight performance at the Shubert Theatre in New Haven. One evening, after a show, Gelbart dryly said to him, "Well, tonight you seemed unusually understated."

"There's a certain part of the audience," Poston explained, "that expects me to do lines a certain way," which was presumably a reference to his deadpan comedy style on television. "I don't want to do it the way they expect it," he said. He paused a moment, considering the whole picture.

"And there's another part of the audience that *knows* I don't want to do it that way . . . and are expecting the *switch* . . . so I don't want to do it that way either."

Gelbart eyed him sideways.

"So I found a third way to do it," Poston concluded.

As this first phase of the tryout ended, and the company prepared to move on to the National Theatre in Washington, D.C., Whitehead sat down with Gelbart at a bar in their New Haven hotel and tried to relax after the tension of the first few weeks. The producer brought up a more cheerful subject.

"I wonder what the Israelis are going to do with Adolf Eichmann," he said, "after the trial is over."

Gelbart didn't hesitate: "They ought to send him out of town with a musical." The line became instant Broadway lore. It also momentarily defused Whitehead's nerves. "The air around that New Haven tryout was just charged," he remembered, and on the way out of the bar, he said to Gelbart, "Maybe we need a little more of that humor in the show."

However, there was nothing funny awaiting them in Washington. As *The Conquering Hero* company prepared for its engagement at the National Theatre, Bob seemed sadistic with Poston. He would blow his whistle in the middle of the actor's speeches, asking for repeats. Whitehead felt that some of the dances were "terrific, really," but he was still extremely unhappy about the war ballet. "Bob was somehow trying to make it Chaplinesque," Whitehead said, which for him was the only way to describe one of the favorite Fosse moves, the elflike, bowlegged walk with out-turned feet. "To me," he said, "it was just unpleasant and unfunny."

With the inevitably negative reviews and the approach of the Broadway deadline, Fosse began to seem irrational. When Whitehead came to Gelbart's aid and defended some lines that Bob was cutting, saying they were "delicate and charming," Fosse icily responded, "Jesus Christ, if that's your taste, God help Lincoln." At that moment, onstage, Bob was glaring so hard that, it seemed to one actor, John McMartin, he might pop a vein in his forehead, and McMartin had a sickening feeling in the pit of his stomach that another epileptic seizure was imminent.

Gwen evidently thought so too, because she marched on stage, snatched Bob by the arm, and propelled him off. This time the actors just stared silently at one another.

Tom Poston finally asked Whitehead for relief. "I can't make it with him," the actor pleaded, and the producer promised that he would speak with Fosse, but they were unable to make civil conversation. Even Bob's usual darlings, the dancers, were finding him difficult. To one of them,

"He seemed kind of overwhelmed . . . it was as if some kind of scramble was going on, he was very off center."

Finally, he did not want to go to rehearsal at all. "He was really climbing the walls," Gwen told one of his closest friends. He was late one morning, she said, and while the company awaited him at the theatre, back in the Jefferson Hotel, "Bob went around clutching a cheap Mexican statue of Jesus, screaming, 'Why don't you help me?' " She was now taking him to rehearsal herself every day. "He was scared to leave the room," she said. "I had to get him out with a chair, like Clyde Beatty."

Whitehead knew that something had to be done before the enterprise exploded. The authors were complaining about being "humiliated"; there was an atmosphere, Whitehead said, "of serious craziness." Finally, Bob brought the situation to a head himself. At one day's production meeting, he announced that he was unhappy with Poston and that, "Despite my own best efforts, I am not optimistic about getting the performance that I'd like to get from Tom. I think we ought to replace him right now."

"Replace Poston?" Whitehead gasped.

"Right away," Bob replied.

"But with who?" asked Gelbart.

"He's got an understudy," Bob said. "Let's go with Bob Kaliban."

"That's impossible," Whitehead said. "He won't sell a ticket."

"Okay then," Bob said evenly, not really pushing the Kaliban suggestion. "I have another idea for you. Why don't I replace him myself?"

"You?" It was a choral response.

"Sure," Bob said, and he proposed that he audition for them that very night, right after the show. He rubbed his hands. "You just gotta see this," he said.

As Gelbart remembered, "After the show we all slipped back into the theatre, Whitehead, Charlap, Gimbel, and myself. We sat there and waited." The door opened at the back of the auditorium. Gwen slipped in and took a seat in the last row, far behind the uncomfortable cluster. Then the stage lighting went on, and Fosse walked out. He had his hands stuck deep in his trouser pockets, his elbows tucked, his shoulders hunched. It was the question-mark stance. Gelbart, who didn't know that Bob had ever played *Pal Joey*, whispered, "He's doing *Pal Joey*."

Fosse started with a speech of Woodrow Truesmith's and then had Bob Kaliban, the understudy, come out and read a scene with him. "He was totally wrong for the part," Whitehead recalled. "Truesmith was supposed to be an absolute innocent, and not only that, the character was a Main Street, U.S.A., type of dumbbell. I could understand why Bob always wanted to play *Pal Joey*. Joey wasn't a bad part for him. But not Woodrow Truesmith."

As Bob continued his audition, Gwen roared in the back row, she laughed as loud as she could, "which only made it worse," Gelbart said, "because it wasn't funny, and he wasn't funny, and she was selling so hard."

To Whitehead, "it was a folie à deux, absolute madness, and Gwen almost seemed to be feeding it." Finally, Bob sang one of Truesmith's songs and did a dance. "I suppose," Gelbart said, "that it was one of the most uncomfortable moments in my life."

The situation was awkward to say the least. Somebody was going to have to tell the director of the show that he wasn't good enough to be in it, and Whitehead also knew that with Fosse's attitude toward Poston, he could hardly continue as the director. As Gelbart said, "If in fact you don't have any faith in the leading man, how are you going to turn around and start directing him again tomorrow?"

The producer went backstage with the news. "Look, Bobby," he said straight out. "I don't think you should play the lead, and I don't think you should go on with the show. I think I have to try and make some sense out of this, and the only way I will is if I get somebody I can work with."

Whitehead needed to say no more but Bob did.

"There's two things I'd like, before I go."

"What's that?"

"First, I want to clean up some of the dancing tomorrow morning."

"Okay."

"And then I would like to have the company alone. To say good-bye."

The cast was held back after the next day's matinee. Phil Friedman, as production stage manager, herded them on stage. They gravitated to stage left because Mr. Whitehead was standing there. Actors never liked stage meetings with a producer. The stage was their place, not his, and he never had good news. Friedman asked for quiet but he didn't have to. It was quiet already and Whitehead was brief. "Bob wants to say a few words to you all," he said, and then he walked into the wings as Fosse came out with Gwen. She was wearing a mink coat that almost came down to her ankles and, underneath, her usual black pants and black sweater. She looked somber as she sat on a stool and smoothed back her lustrous red hair.

Bob was wearing a trench coat, a tan raincoat all closed up, and belted with the collar turned up. He had a matching rain hat on, a fedora. It was pulled down over one eye. The other eye was squinting through the smoke that curled upward from the cigarette dangling from the left corner of his mouth.

He was in his *Pal Joey* costume.

He pulled up a folding wooden chair, turned it around, and sat down, straddling it with his arms resting on the back. "I have to talk to you," he began. He would later describe this as the worst moment in his life. "This show of ours . . . the producer wants it one way . . . and I want it another."

As he recalled the scene himself, he told the company, "I got the show together, I hired all the actors, the ideas for the sets and costumes were mine, and *then*, the first thing that goes wrong, they fire me."

One of the actors remembered him telling them, "I should have produced it myself. I wanted to give this show a twist, an edge. I wanted it like a cartoon and a spoof but forget about that with this producer. He wants it so apple pie," he sneered.

He had been tilting back on the chair, and now he gently brought its legs to rest. "I'll tell you one thing I've learned," he said to the rising chorus of sniffs. "They'll never take a show away from me again."

Then, to the incidental music of protests and applause, he rose and, with Gwen taking his arm, strolled to stage left, pausing only to turn, say, "Good-bye," drop his cigarette on the floor, stub it out with a twist of his toe, tug the fedora brim a bit further down over his face, and disappear into the shadows.

Bob Fosse knew how to make an exit.

MIDLIFE
CRISIS

"*I* was so cold. No one called me. No one wanted anything to do with me."

8

Hoping to save *The Conquering Hero*, Robert Whitehead hired a new
director, Albert Marre, and a ballet choreographer, Todd Bolender. There
was not enough money to delay the New York opening by more than a
week while Bolender tinkered with the number that had come to symbolize all of Whitehead's headaches, the war ballet. When Bob heard about
the changes, he became enraged and set out to do something about it.

Now Bob Fosse was a man with a refined sense of justice, a sensitivity to it as acute as a child's. It made no difference to him that his name
had been taken off the program for *The Conquering Hero*; he wanted his
ballet restored to its original state, and he pursued this through the
American Arbitration Association. His attorney settled the dispute for
twenty-six cents in damages, which was all that Fosse had asked for.
When he was awarded the judgment, he framed the check but dismissed
the attorney for agreeing to the settlement without the ballet being entirely
restored even though that was hardly practicable.

The show was to open at the ANTA Theatre on West 52nd Street on
January 16, 1961, and Broadway was always busy in those weeks after the
holidays. The city was still festive and the shows were not yet the stars;
the stars were still stars, like Lucille Ball who was about to open in
Wildcat, Phil Silvers in *Do Re Mi*, Carol Channing in *Show Girl*. These
oversize performers were not outdazzled by Tom Poston, and *The Conquering Hero* did not arrive in New York a surprise winner. The only pause
it gave the critics was where to assign the blame, for it had arrived
disowned. No choreographer or director was named on the program.

The day the show was to close after eight performances, Harold
Prince bought two tickets for the matinee and went to see it with his
producing partner, Robert Griffith. It was common for producers to keep
up with the shows, even the flops, and they took their seats in the last row
of the orchestra, just on the aisle. As the performance ended, with the
curtain rising and falling, and the cast taking bows, Fosse got up from his

seat and started out. Even at this late, indeed final date, he was checking to see what had become of his show. Coming upon the coproducers of
The Pajama Game, Damn Yankees, and *New Girl in Town* at the rear of
the theatre, he stopped abruptly, leaned down, and grabbed Griffith by the
collar and tie, pulling him half out of the seat.

"What the fuck are you doing here? Did you come to gloat?"

After staring nose to nose at the dumbfounded man, Fosse released
his grip and disappeared into the crowd of departing theatregoers. Griffith
started up from his seat. Prince clamped him by the arm and pulled him
back down.

"Don't follow him."

"I have to," Griffith said. "We're friends. What kind of thing is that to
say?"

He got up and walked out, and Prince followed. In the lobby, Bobby
Griffith was huddled with Fosse. Prince strode the few steps apprehensively, shuddering as he conjured up the memory of the scene in the New
Haven hotel room after the gorilla ballet, but there was no scene. Fosse
and Griffith were smiling, embracing, making up, and Gwen had her
arms around both men. But it wouldn't be so easy for her just to hug Bob
through the crisis. "I was in trouble after that arbitration," Bob later
remembered. "I sat around holding my head."

What saved him from this depression, what he found to rescue him
from the head holding, seems inevitable in hindsight. It was a chance to
star in a revival of *Pal Joey*, playing the role that he seemed to think was his
destiny. It was not to be on Broadway, but it was close enough, a revival at
the New York City Center of Music and Drama, a cavernous theatre on
West 55th Street. Hiring him had been the idea of Gus Schirmer, Jr., who
had directed Bob in the summer stock tour of the show ten years earlier.
Schirmer even found Carol Bruce to play Vera Simpson again, and
though he was offering Bob the same salary as everyone else in the cast (the
Actors Equity minimum of $137 a week, which was less than he had paid
Bob in 1952), this was hardly being done for the money.

What *was* it being done for? Schirmer would state it succinctly: "In
his heart of hearts, more than anything else in the world, Bob wanted to
be a performer."

The City Center was an ember remaining from the days of burning
cultural proletarianism. In exchange for an extraordinary number of seats
with poor sight lines, it offered low-cost entertainment for working-class
highbrows: ballet, opera, and revivals of former Broadway hits, dramas as
well as musicals. But Broadway's dedication to new shows had corrupted
New York's audiences. There was such a stigma attached to anything old

(even Shakespeare's plays were deprecated as "revivals") that the lowest of prices could not lure significant audiences. Who wanted, needed, or saw any sense in a *Guys and Dolls* or a *Glass Menagerie* when something new was always available? "Classic" was a euphemism for yesterday's milk.

The City Center's revivals, then, were the high-minded but seedy stepchildren of the New York theatre. Money was so limited that the choices of shows depended on what scenery was available. The performers, however, were always first rate. Then as today, talent was the theatre's most abundant (and wasted) resource.

Gus Schirmer, star struck despite his family prestige (his father was the music publisher), did not know what ego problems to expect from the Bobby Fosse who was now famous on Broadway but, he said, "Bob never stuck his nose into anything but his own part and what he was doing and what affected him. Even though he was by then a big star in his own right, he treated me with enormous deference and respect."

Not really wanting that much deference and respect, Schirmer offered Fosse creative freedom, hoping for at least a dance, but Bob considerately left the choreography to the choreographer, Ralph Beaumont.

He and the show were well received, though not so ecstatically as to warrant a transfer to a Broadway theatre for a regular run. The ten-day engagement was extended by two weeks, and naturally, the theatre community turned out in great numbers. Had he been able to grasp the truth of it—that these audiences were coming to see Bob Fosse the choreographer rather than Bob Fosse the dancing star—he would have known that the recognition he so coveted was already his. Even Harold Lang came to see him, the man Bob had understudied, the man who had never missed a performance. He came with Helen Gallagher, the wonderful dancer who had taught Bob the *Pal Joey* steps when he first got the understudy's job.

Actors are jealous of their roles, and Harold Lang was no exception, but he was not ungenerous. As Gallagher pointed out, "Bob's dancing was so different from Harold's . . . there wasn't any reason for him to be negative." Lang was athletic and acrobatic, with lots of leaping, very much in the Gene Kelly manner, while Fosse worked with attitudes. As Gallagher put it, "He did more body language with Joey. He was very Fred Astaire, looking over his shoulder with his body in profile."

Why did Bob Fosse fail to become the star performer of his dreams? It was not for a lack of dancing ability. Was it because he was only a passable actor or singer? How good an actor or singer was Gene Kelly? Even Kelly's dancing was not the explanation of his stardom. There were better dancers but their names ring down the halls of anonymity. What Kelly had was a communicable charm, personal electricity, the "star quality" so indescribable, and unmistakable, and that was what Bob lacked. He had a thin stage presence, a stage absence, so to speak. The subtle details of his psyche could not be highlighted like his body isolations, with white gloves, finger snaps, and percussive sounds.

Still, he was starring on the New York stage, and it was cathartic for him. *The Conquering Hero* may have shot him into the black tunnel of self-doubt, bringing him his first dismissal and his first flop, but *Pal Joey* pulled him through. He had instinctively sought out the emotional help he needed, being in the spotlight on stage. When it was over, perhaps he would be able to wrap up his youthful performing ambitions in nostalgia, pack them away, and get on with his career. But it would not be that simple. He would still be addicted to performing, still have star fantasies, and that urge would lead him down some strange byways. Bob Riff remained within, the tops in taps.

The real performer in the family, Gwen Verdon, wasn't going on-stage at all. After *Redhead* had played in Los Angeles, and after she had disclosed their marriage, she announced her professional retirement. Presumably her reason was that she wanted a child. As a thirty-six-year-old dancer, she wouldn't need a doctor to tell her that it might help her to conceive were she less physically active (the doctors would come later).

But when Gwen's old friend from *Can-Can*, its producer Cy Feuer, contacted her about work for Bob, she knew what to prescribe for her husband, and that was choreographing again, as soon as possible.

If Robert Whitehead was a patrician producer, the irresistible word for Cy Feuer was "feisty." He was a man with a barreling energy, a little guy with red hair and freckles, always on his toes like a prizefighter, canny and yet quite unlike the usual Broadway operator. In fact Feuer was a musician by training. He had begun as a cornet player in the presentation houses of last-stand vaudeville (and early Fosse), stepping out of those orchestra pits to work in Hollywood as a director of music at Republic Pictures. There he met the songwriter, Frank Loesser. They teamed up to try Broadway, Feuer producing with his partner, Ernest Martin, and Loesser writing the music and lyrics. Their first show was *Where's Charley?* and the next was *Guys and Dolls*. Feuer and Martin went on to produce a string of hits, including *The Boy Friend*, *Can-Can*, and *Silk Stockings*.

Feuer and Fosse were friends on sight. Fosse was thirty-four, Feuer fifty, and the older man's tough manner appealed to him. Cy Feuer's affectionate bark fit in with a creed that Fosse was developing, a creed of absolutely no bullshit. The producer, too, could not abide pomposity or pretension in the theatre. He knew what professionalism was, he had worked with Frank Loesser and Cole Porter. It was tough enough to put on a show, to "get a laugh," he would say, "and bring on the tootsies," without laying claims to "artistic baloney." If *Guys and Dolls* achieved greatness, it did so without hanging out a sign to that effect. This was a philosophy similar to George Abbott's but on a more stylish level. In short, *Guys and Dolls* was good enough for Cy Feuer.

It was good enough for Bob Fosse too. He thought it was "the greatest American musical of all time" and felt that it had forced the Broadway musical theatre to grow up. "Frank Loesser was the forerunner of today's musical comedy," Bob said. "He established reason, sanity, and the anti-hero." That was something Fosse had fixed on, the antihero, whether in the form of a yokel like Woodrow Truesmith in *The Conquering Hero* or a pretend-tough like *Pal Joey* Evans. The new Frank Loesser show was about an antihero too, an ambitious, gleeful young backstabber in corporate politics. Fosse liked that, and Feuer liked Fosse.

If there was anyone Fosse could respect, who could be tough but still offer approval and affection, it seemed to be Cy Feuer. If there was anyone who might understand him, who was good at show business and loved it but was wise to it, that man seemed to be Cy Feuer. Indeed, Cy Feuer might well have appeared to be the father figure to Bob that Cy Fosse had never been, and the similarity of names was positively spooky.

The problem that Feuer and Martin were having with *How to Succeed in Business Without Really Trying* lay with the choreographer, a young man who had been hired on the basis of a wonderful dance, a satire of television choreography, that he had staged for an industrial show. But as *How To Succeed* was trying out in Philadelphia, three weeks away from Broadway, only a single dance was satisfactory, "The Pirate Dance," and it was a virtual duplicate of that television satire. As Feuer put it in his forthright way, "I had hired a guy who could only do one number."

Fosse sympathized, but he also sympathized with the young chore-ographer. "He's just a kid," Bob said. "I don't want to take over. Leave his name on it. I'll pretend I'm supervising him," and so Bob was credited with "Musical Staging."

He enjoyed the songwriter Frank Loesser, who was an older rascal, as unphony as Feuer. Loesser was a big city boy and a big-time success; he was educated without acting lofty, and he shared Bob's regular-guy sports interests as well as his aversion to bullshit. He was also playful and enthusiastic. When Frank Loesser got excited, he actually jumped up and down with both feet.

Bob's arrival in Philadelphia was preceded by his reputation. He was one of the biggest choreographers, one of the best, one of the most successful, and one of the best prepared. He came with his wife, the fabulous star Gwen Verdon, who was prepared to act as his dance assistant. "The dancers were amazed," Feuer remembered. "Gwen was practically Bob's 'gofer.' She even went shopping for costumes and props."

While tryout performances continued, Bob started work on "Coffee Break," danced after the song about caffeine addiction was sung by a gulpingly hypertense Charles Nelson Reilly. Fosse's only request was for privacy, and while he worked late at night after the show, Loesser paced the corridor outside the locked rehearsal room. When an assistant stage manager arrived with sandwiches and the information that the composer was peeping through the keyhole, Bob resumed work, seemingly indifferent, only to snatch open the door without warning. Loesser was surprised on his knees, crouching at the door. "You son of a bitch," he griped, rising stiffly and brushing his trousers. "I've been writing since you were a kid. Who the hell are you to tell me I can't watch the goddamn number being rehearsed?"

"Come on in," Fosse said, grinning as he held the door open. The now blushing giant of the songwriting world shuffled meekly into the room and looked shamefacedly from the dancers to the rehearsal pianist to Gwen. He plugged his hands into his jacket pockets, and as if surprised to find anything there, said, "Oh! Here are some cuff links I had made for you." Fosse was just tickled by that. "They were gold," he remembered, "and monogrammed—and beautiful. Now what are you going to do with a man like that?"

If Bob was enjoying Cy Feuer and Frank Loesser, the work with the company was not quite so easy. He had not hired these dancers, and except for several by chance, they were not his people. More than one noticed a chip on his shoulder, fallout, no doubt, from the *Conquering Hero* debacle. It was not so much his perfectionism, the "again" and "again" and "again" of it. They could respect that. It was his withering meanness when he was not satisfied. He stopped one rehearsal after a string of repetitions and, from halfway back in the theatre, began calling out the name of each dancer in a weary tone. He seemed to know how painfully embarrassing the simple public announcement of a name could be. After each name he would say, with palpable disgust, "You are so stupid."

After a time, one of the dancers spoke up. "If we're so stupid," she said, "it's because we are being led by a stupid man."

Sitting alone in the vast space of empty seats, Fosse stared at the stage of silent dancers.

"Take five minutes," he finally said, and when the dancers came back, he apologized.

With "Coffee Break" finished, he began making a dance out of a song that had as yet defied choreography. "A Secretary Is Not a Toy" had been written as a lilting waltz to be sung by Rudy Vallee, who was playing the president of World Wide Wickets in this satire of corporate politics. As a waltz the number was not going anywhere, and one night after the show, they hashed it over, Loesser and Feuer and Martin and their director, Abe Burrows. Fosse squinted around the edges of the discussion, and while the others were trading ever unlikelier ideas, Feuer heard him say, almost to himself, "I'm thinking of a giant soft shoe." It was a phrase that lingered, and at one o'clock in the morning, as they walked down the hotel corridor to their rooms after the meeting, Feuer asked Fosse, "What did you mean by that? 'A giant soft shoe?' "

"I don't know what I meant, but I think I have an idea."

"What's that?"

"Let me think about it," Bob said.

In the morning, he telephoned Feuer. "Listen," he said. "About 'Secretary.' There's something I'd like to work out, but I need a space and I need time. I'm going to screw around with it, but I don't want Frank to know."

There was a Masonic Temple across the street from the Shubert Theatre in Philadelphia, and it was often used for overflow rehearsal. To make sure that Loesser didn't find out what was going on, Feuer arranged for the place to be used at night, while *How to Succeed* was being played. The composer never missed a performance, and while Loesser was at the theatre, Bob worked on the number with Gwen and the dance pianist. After two days, he called Feuer aside in the theatre lobby and said, "Okay, tonight, right after the show starts, come on over. *Alone.* I want to show you something."

The "something" was a dance set to a radical change in the meter of "A Secretary Is Not a Toy." Bob had made a giant soft shoe out of it, all right. He had transformed the waltz's three-four time into the four-four rhythms of his beloved "Tea for Two," the ultimate soft shoe.

It was daring for another reason too. As Feuer recalled, "Not only was the guy nervy enough to change Frank's meter but none of the principals were to be in the dance. It was going to be just the chorus, the whole world of this Wickets company singing about the foibles of the secretary and doing all kinds of moves and lines and entrances. A *giant soft shoe.*"

After Gwen and Bob performed it for him, Feuer got so excited he dashed across the street to the theatre where, in his words, "I collared

Frank and said, 'Listen, I want you to come over and see something, but I don't want you to say anything, you hear? Not a word. Just watch."

When the two men returned to the Masonic Temple, Bob and Gwen were leaning against the piano, talking to the pianist. Bob's ashtray was filled to overflowing, and as he stubbed out yet another cigarette, he whispered to Feuer, "Frank's going to kill me for fucking with his rhythm."

Feuer smiled and turned to Loesser. "Now I don't want to hear a goddamn word from you till they're finished showing this thing. I mean it, Frank. Not a word." The increasingly suspicious Loesser sat down on a wooden folding chair pushed up against the wall, with Feuer beside him. Bob and Gwen walked out of the room to prepare their entrance. The dance pianist started the syncopated rhythm that was quite a distance from the original Loesser waltz. The composer turned toward Feuer and glared.

"Just shut up and watch," the producer barked. Bob and Gwen danced in, identical in tight black pants, she wearing a heavy, white, ribbed wool sweater and he in a loose white shirt, with sweat socks and sneakers for the both of them. There, gliding and swooping lightly in their sneakers, not tapping but using the balls of their feet, the sides, the heels, sliding and scraping and scuffling as in all soft shoe, they did all of the dance, all the parts of all the dancers, pert and edgy, and when they were through, they stopped and waited nervously for Loesser's reaction.

"Jesus Christ!" he yelped. "How the hell can you use that miserable lyric with this thing? I'm going to have to write the whole goddamned lyric again," and he marched out to the piano they kept in the men's room and worked it out to Bob's metric invention.

> A secretary is not a toy, not a toy
> No my boy
> To fondle and dandle
> And playfully handle
> In search of some puerile joy

How to Succeed in Business Without Really Trying opened in New York on October 14, 1961, to truly tremendous reviews and became the longest-running musical in Frank Loesser's career. Returning to the stage in *Pal Joey* had certainly had a salutory effect on Bob, and success was even better. In contrast to his erratic behavior during *The Conquering Hero*, he was now just sailing along.

A few weeks later, Joan McCracken died at thirty-six. He had not seen her while she was ill. He did not want to visit anyone who was ill. He could handle life; it was death he didn't want to be reminded of.

Some years later, when asked about Joan McCracken, he said, "She was unique, a very direct kind of person . . . a lovely, lovely person," and, Gwen added, "Bob can have half a million in the bank, all the Tonys, Oscars, and Emmys one human can amass in a lifetime, and all he lives with is the fact that Joan McCracken died so young on him."

This was a striking slip of the tongue, for Joan McCracken certainly did not "die on him." He had long since been gone by the time that she died, in fact he was already married to Gwen. Yet in some fashion McCracken *had* "died on him," only it was years earlier, when heart disease ended her dancing days, and she had died as a dancer. A dancer who cannot dance is of no use to a choreographer and is a spectre of future death to another dancer. Perhaps Gwen was expressing guilt, or was giving vent to her own fears of being too old to dance, but nevertheless, had Joan McCracken heard this expression of sympathy, she would surely have awarded Gwen Verdon the championship in the give-me-a-break competition.

At her funeral, Agnes de Mille remembered a coffin with an open lid. "Joan's mother bent over and kissed her most tenderly. Sweetly." Then de Mille stepped forward for a last look at her favorite dancer. "She was like a star in that coffin."

Agnes de Mille lived in a private residential community called Merriewold Park. The group of houses was nestled in the woods of the Catskill Mountains, not far from the village of Monticello. After returning from Joan's funeral, de Mille stopped by to visit George Abbott in his neighboring house. With his giant lanky frame folded into a rattan chair like a grasshopper, the seventy-four-year-old director asked about the funeral. Although Joan was one of his favorite performers as well as one of his daughter's best friends, he had not attended. He was an emotional iceman and peering up at Agnes de Mille from a corner of his eye, he asked, "Was Bob Fosse there?"

"I don't think so," she replied, standing at the door of the screened porch. Abbott made no further comment. Neither of the icemen had come.

Bob, when asked about Joan, remembered her as being "quite a bit older than I was when we were married. I think she was about ten years older." She was only five years older, and he claimed that she had misled him about her age, but dancers have a special reason for delaying age. To a dancer, age itself is death.

Age was the significant factor in Bob's and Gwen's life as they now concentrated all their energies on having a child. There was nothing physically wrong with her, nothing the doctors could find. It had been twenty years since she had given birth to Jimmie but that seemed to be no reason for her present inability to conceive.

Like so many couples at that time, when sophisticated fertilization techniques had not yet been developed, Bob and Gwen made the rounds of pregnancy specialists, taking the tests, checking the days and hours, keeping the charts of her temperature, scheduling lovemaking. None of it worked, and inevitably the inquiry turned to him and "those embarrassing things," he remembered, "of taking your sperm out of a tube and having it tested. You carry it down in a bottle and the guy says, 'I don't know. They're awfully slow, kid. You better take a rest.' They said I was tired and needed a vacation," he sighed, but finally, "We were told we couldn't have a child, that it was one of those things . . . and so we started investigating adoption, and of course . . . Gwen was immediately pregnant."

He would recall it as "my best moment. I mean, I've been involved with lots of abortions," he said, "and was running away from being a father . . . I finally decided that I was as grown-up as I'd ever be. Then, when it looked like it wasn't going to happen, she was pregnant. So it was kind of very happy."

Joan Simon was also pregnant (with her second child). The wife of the playwright, Neil Simon, she had spent most of her marriage in show business, but her husband's show business had been the show business of comedians, of Catskill Mountains resorts, nightclubs, and television, not the theatre, for Simon had been a writer of comedy material. He had only one play behind him, *Come Blow Your Horn*, when he was asked to write the musical, *Little Me*. But the star was going to be Sid Caesar, and Simon had been part of the legendary team of writers on Caesar's television program, "Your Show of Shows"—a team that had included Woody Allen, Mel Brooks, Larry Gelbart, and Carl Reiner.

Feuer and Martin, who were producing *Little Me*, wanted no one but Fosse as its choreographer; however, Feuer wanted to direct the show himself while Bob had intended to work only as a choreographer-director. Once again, it was a matter of credit, and Bob agreed to do the show as a codirector. They went to work.

The songs were being written by Cy Coleman and Carolyn Leigh, a new team with but one show (*Wildcat*) behind them, but a brightly talented pair. The show must have looked like fun to Fosse, based as it was on the notion of Sid Caesar playing eight different men in the life of a promiscuous movie star. There were very few people who did not find Caesar hilarious. At times, the makers of *Little Me* would be among them.

He was a quirky, absentminded man, sometimes difficult and occasionally violent, a particular distraction in view of his size and his hobby, which was weightlifting. He announced that he intended to sing as little as possible and that he felt encumbered by the requirement of following a script. He either cleared his throat on punch lines or forgot them entirely. Otherwise he was perfect.

Caesar, who barely remembered Bob from "Your Show of Shows," did not slight him when making demands. He was not a dancer, he declared, and did not intend to become one. Bob promised easy steps, and the promise was kept. "I didn't do any knee slides or cartwheels," Caesar would later say victoriously.

The auditions for Bob Fosse dancers had become a set routine, a series of steps known along Broadway as the Fosse Combinations. Usually danced to thirty-two measures of "Tea for Two," this was a set of moves and poses and gestures as well as dance setups. They ranged from finger snapping to sudden sidewise slides and undulating pelvic thrusts. As a concession to actual dance there were also elevations and jumps, a bit of ballet and jazz movement. As dancer Dick Korthaze described these combinations, they were an audition program "that showed style, rhythm and whether you had any ballet training. What Bob wanted in his dancers was the ability to isolate, to move one part and that part alone, to bend a wrist or crook an elbow or swivel an ankle or move the shoulder without moving the rest."

Of course every Broadway choreographer had an audition program, designed to eliminate efficiently all but those dancers best suited to his style. Michael Kidd, for instance, asked for duck walks because he was inclined to comedy in his dances. Gower Champion was a no-nonsense auditioner who wanted elevations and leaps, lots of running and jetés and high kicks. "Bob would not only give us the steps and the gestures," Korthaze said, "but also the emotion, the *idea*, to go with them, in terms of the building number. So it wouldn't just be a step for a step's sake. He wanted us to be actors, to have something going on inside rather than just the footwork . . . he couldn't stand all that flashy business, *selling* everything to the audience with a big smile and energy going, and you're doing all these fabulous steps. God, how he hated that stuff!"

As Bob returned to a seat beside Cy Feuer, after having whispered encouragement to a shaky auditioner, he turned to the producer and said, "Do you know what I would like better than anything else right now?"

"Yeah?" Feuer asked.

"I'd like to be up there auditioning . . . and getting the job."

Being a musical comedy with a comedian star, *Little Me* was not going to be a heavy dancing show, but Bob did have one big number in mind, a dance for the snooty rich children. This was to become "The Rich Kids' Rag," an elegant comedy piece for dancers dressed as youngsters, the girls in party dresses and hair bows, the boys buttoned up in suits with knickers, all of the costumes in pastels with white knee socks and gloves. The hands in those gloves regularly faced the audiences with the fingers splayed. The gesture that Marguerite Comerford had so rigorously and vainly sought to drum out of the ten-year-old Bob Fosse at the Chicago Academy of Theatre Arts was now his trademark.

As usual, by the time Bob went to work with his dancers he had the choreography largely finished in his head although this piece was different in that it was set to original dance music, composed by the dance pianist and conductor, Fred Werner (most theatre dance music is a pastiche of melodies from the score). Bob had asked Werner to come up with four different ragtime themes, and then he assigned each to a different group of his dancers. He improvised dialogue that would be spoken by the individual dancers to rhythmic underscoring, blending the number into the spoken part of the show. Thus it was not so much a "dance" as a rhythmic, musical scene. And so, one of the snooty, spoiled, and bratty kids begins "The Rich Kids Rag" in syncopated style, "We (music under) are the wealthy children (ping) from the right side (plunk) of the tracks."

"That's right," another of them says (twang). "We're rich."

"She's right."

Yet another of these fancy twerps adds (pop), "We are here to celebrate Noble Eggleston's sixteenth birthday" (pleep).

"Hey!" a final one says, coming up with a bright idea. "Let's do our favorite fun dance, 'The Rich Kids' Rag.'"

"Oh boy!" is the final dry remark as the vaudeville ragtime opens at full tilt, "a Mickey Mouse ragtime" as the dance captain John Sharpe put it, and after Ralph Burns orchestrated it with the full array of favorite Fosse percussion sounds, whistles and ratchets and bass drums, the four-minute dance came to full funny bloom, a prancing minuet of snobbish rich kids with their noses in the air and their backs arched, wriggling with their knees turned in, on tiptoe. As Sharpe put it, "Everything in the piece derived its look, its feel, its style from that particular configuration of the body, that knock-kneed, pigeon-toed posture."

A full week of dance rehearsals, eight hours a day, was put into this one brief number, making "The Rich Kids Rag" one of Bob Fosse's most perfect creations. If there was any choreography of his that could have been transferred, intact, to the repertory of a dance company, it was this, and in a real way it was a sign of Bob's fine new friendship with Neil Simon for it seemed inspired by the playwright's unique sense of humor, translating that humor into movement.

While this was being worked out at the Variety Arts rehearsal studios on 46th Street, production meetings were being held in a suite that the producers had taken in the Edison Hotel, a block away on West 47th Street. It must have seemed as if all the useful work was being done in the studios while the headaches arrived at the hotel. At one afternoon meeting, Sid Caesar announced that he was not going to sing more than three songs. It was a simple enough matter to him, and he couldn't understand why anyone was surprised. "I am playing eight characters, gentlemen," he said to Cy Feuer, Ernest Martin, Neil Simon, Cy Coleman, and Bob Fosse, before turning to Carolyn Leigh and adding, with a quick grin, "and lady." They all nodded sympathetically. He continued his pronouncements. "You've got four or five choruses of this song, 'Real Live Girl.' One chorus is enough for me."

Carolyn Leigh's eyes welled up. She was in love with words, especially her own, but not simply as a matter of conceit. Her confidence was too shaky for that. She loved her lyrics because of the thought that went into their precision, the wordplay and elegance of phrasing. They were herself at her best.

"Lyrics tie me down too much," Caesar said. "Lyrics for sure you have to sing the same thing every night. I have an aversion to lyrics."

Feuer suggested, "Why don't we get on with the rest of the show?"

"Okay," Caesar agreed, only to continue: "Now there are two scenes that aren't working. Everything is great except those two scenes."

"Well, that's a relief," Coleman whispered to Fosse.

"Don't worry," Feuer said, "we'll fix them out of town."

"No," Caesar replied, "we won't fix them out of town, because there's going to be enough craziness out of town. So let's fix it now."

"Sid," Ernie Martin said, "we can't fix it now."

"Why's that?"

"Because we're going out of town in a few days," Feuer said.

"Doc," Caesar said. (The playwright's nickname was "Doc" because he frequently fixed or "doctored" troubled shows.) Simon looked up, his face a serious setting for eyes that saw humor everywhere and in everything.

"Yeah, Sid?"

"Will it take you more than a couple of days to write two scenes?" Turning to the rest of the room, Caesar said, "On 'Show of Shows' he would write five scenes a day because he had to. Look, fixing it out of town means mayhem out of town. I know that. I've been there. Why not fix it now while we have the time because when you're doing a show in Philadelphia you want to relax afterward. And," he added, now italicizing every word, "you don't want to start getting lines, learning new lines, do this, do that. Do you understand what I mean?"

They understood what he meant. Cy Coleman called it "muscle in the hotel room."

Caesar concluded, "So let's do it now."

Sid Caesar could (and would) rip bathroom sinks out of hotel bathroom walls. There was not a peep. Finally, Feuer said, "You can't ask Doc to do that. After all—"

"Doc," Caesar interrupted. "Can you do it?"

"We did it on 'Show of Shows,'" Simon said dryly, "so why can't we do it now?"

He knew perfectly well why not. He hardly needed to tell everyone else that a Broadway musical wasn't a weekly television show. It was more ambitious, and it was supposed to be better. "Your Show of Shows" was televised live, Saturday evenings. After the broadcast everyone had Sunday off and then the next week's script had to be written by Wednesday, with a staff of eight writers brainstorming. The show would be put on its feet on Thursday, the next day would be technical rehearsals, and on Saturday they would go on the air. Must-do meant can-do, but it also meant make-do. Everyone knew that except Caesar, or else Caesar didn't want to know it. As he'd said, he didn't want to start getting lines, learning new lines, do this, do that.

As *Little Me* was rehearsed in Philadelphia's Erlanger Theatre, the situation with Caesar remained maddening, all the more because he was so funny. He was funny even while sabotaging some of Simon's best material. Pauses were built into performances to allow for audience laughter, but if there isn't laughter because of a mangled punch line, a pause becomes a vacancy. When Caesar was approached, very carefully, about the jokes, he said, "Okay, now you listen to me. Doing a show eight times a week, you can become mechanical and I don't want to get that way . . . so even though I understand that the lines have to be the same every night, they don't have to be *exactly* the same."

The star wasn't the only eccentric in the group. One evening after a dress rehearsal, Carolyn Leigh came steaming down the aisle of the Erlanger Theatre. She was an extremely overweight woman in her thirties (the weight would ultimately do her in), very bright and very gifted but very highly strung and very neurotic, and she was very upset about an unauthorized change in her lyrics for the song, "Lafayette, We Are Here." It was the opening number of the second act, and the lyrics had been abbreviated for that run-through only. Everything was being tried to fix the number. It was the most troublesome in the show.

They had all watched the performance in the empty Erlanger. Now they were pulled down the aisle in Carolyn's downdraft, and as she glared through her thick eyeglasses, yawing like a Thanksgiving Day balloon, she visited her rage upon the cowering pack, there beside the orchestra pit.

They hushed and soothed her, Coleman and Fosse and Feuer and Simon. It was, they explained, just another try at saving the number, but Carolyn would not be mollified. "I know my rights," she wailed, her eyes brimming over with tears. "I'm a member of the Dramatists Guild."

"So what do you want to do?" asked Feuer.

"Close the show?" Coleman asked.

"I'm protected," she insisted, marching back up the aisle. "I'm protected by my contract, and that's the *law!*" and with that she disappeared through the theatre's back doors.

With calm restored, everyone sat down in the front rows and reviewed the performance. The shortened lyric had not made the number any better:

> We're the belles of '17
> Each and every one a queen

Nobody was happy with "Lafayette, We Are Here," Fosse least of all. Whatever the humor intended, it was a big, traditional, second act opening with lots of kicking and squealing cancan girls, a great deal of noise but no energy, and it would surely start the second act to six hands clapping. Improvements were discussed halfheartedly, for their minds had gone dry from rehashing. Finally, Feuer turned to a couple sitting just behind the group, listening attentively.

"You're objective," he said to them. "You see a lot of the shows here, managing the Erlanger. Do *you* think the number is salvageable?"

"I'm sorry," the man said, "but we don't manage the theatre."

"You don't?" Ernie Martin said.

"Then what are you doing here?" Cy Coleman asked.

"We came to buy some tickets," the woman said, "and when we saw all of you sitting down, we thought we would stay to watch you work."

"It's very interesting," her escort said.

"Thanks," said Simon.

"And we think the show is just wonderful," the woman concluded.

As the couple started to leave, the rear doors of the theatre opened, and Carolyn Leigh plowed through with a policeman in tow.

"There they are," she cried triumphantly, pointing to her collaborators. "I want you to arrest all of them! They broke the law."

"All of them?" the policeman asked.

"All of them," she repeated. "Feuer and Martin, these miserable producers, and this guy with the glasses, Simon, and the little guy, Fosse, over there." She paused and glared at her composer, Cy Coleman. He gazed back meltingly. "Him," she said, "him you can leave to me."

When she was finally convinced that her Dramatists Guild protection did not require an officer of the law for enforcement, she released her grip on the policeman. Feuer promised the man that there would be two passes left for him at the box office for the first preview.

None of this was disturbing to Fosse, who was probably more at ease in the making of this show than he had ever been before, or would be afterward. Pregnancy was known for having a healthy effect, but usually on the woman. Gwen was happy to be sure, she was rosy, billowing and bumping around rehearsals like a great happy whale, arm in arm with her new friend, Joan Simon, Doc's wife, who was also whalishly pregnant. But Bob and Doc, especially Bob, were cheerfully afloat too.

He was on stage with Swen Swenson, the lead dancer, to work on Swenson's solo, "I've Got Your Number." The dancer stood some ten feet behind him, slightly to the side, so as to be able to see and follow Bob's steps. Like a couple of gliding ice skaters or Bob's old shadow routine, they turned and stepped in tandem while Fred Werner, the dance pianist, played for them. As he played the music for "I've Got Your Number," Gwen looked on from stageside, her hands in the classic pregnancy position, bracing her back at the waist, but she was also grinning like a mother as Bob danced smoothly and silently, except for his light thumps on the floor.

The number was about sex, it was a seduction dance, Bob's vision of himself as a sex object. Without question it was made for him, from the hands hooked in the vest armholes to the derby pushed down over his brow to cover the balding dome.

He turned his hips sideways and worked from profile, slithering and sliding, a gliding and undulating lure. One of the other dancers, John Sharpe, watching from the wings, saw it as "a wonderful way of taking off your tie and making it look as if you've got all your clothes off."

Swenson finished the dance behind Fosse but it was difficult for anyone who was standing there and watching to keep his eyes on Swen Swenson when Bob Fosse was doing the dance in his own sinewy way, and when he was finished, he smiled very broadly and so did they all.

Meantime, the band had been setting up in the pit. Ralph Burns had just brought over his finished orchestrations. One of a musical's most exciting moments was imminent: when the cast first hears the score played by the full orchestra, after weeks of hearing it performed by the rehearsal pianist. And when the band lighted into the overture, with the brass blazing and the crisp thump of the drums and the surging drive of Cy Coleman's Broadway music, the theatre was filled with exhilaration, for everyone knew in that thrilling moment that they were doing the most exciting and wonderful thing that it was possible on this earth to do.

Fosse was not quite that carried away, not when he heard the music for "Lafayette, We Are Here." "This just plain stinks," he told Burns. "You'll have to redo it." The orchestrator was stunned. It was the first time he had ever worked with Fosse. He was a young man with a lofty reputation among tough jazz and commercial musicians, and it was the only time anyone had ever complained about his work. He was also a highly strung fellow. "I went out," he said, "and got drunk for two or three days after Bobby said that to me."

Burns later realized that the dissatisfaction was not about his orchestrations but with the dance itself. As previews began, Bob said that "Lafayette, We Are Here" was never going to work. He already had an idea for replacing it. Caesar, true to his word, had refused to sing more than one chorus of "Real Live Girl." As he put it, "If they liked it so much, they could have someone else sing it," and that was exactly what Bob decided to do, since the pretty little waltz was now just a modest throwaway in the first act. Always up for a soft shoe, and with a tip of his hat to "A Secretary Is Not a Toy," he would make another ensemble piece out of "Real Live Girl."

When he invited Neil Simon, Cy Coleman, Carolyn Leigh, Cy Feuer, and Ernie Martin to see what he had prepared, they found nobody in the rehearsal room except, as Simon recalled, "a pianist, Bob, and a few props. And Bob proceeded to do the new version of the song as fourteen soldiers would be doing it. He sang and danced not as one person but as fourteen, making them all so vivid and clear and different you didn't know which guy you liked best."

It still had to be taught to the dancers; the dance music had to be orchestrated; only an audience could decide whether it was any good. Bob told Ralph Burns that he wanted the orchestration delicate, a musical counterpart of sand sprinkled on the stage for a soft shoe. What he wanted the audience to hear were musical accents. "It's an old nightclub trick," Burns recalled with a chuckle. "You underline every gesture, you hit everything. Bob was queer for percussion sounds, and the musicians always had a lot of fun getting the right sound for him, a wood block for this move or that kick; a rim shot or choke cymbal" (the one that looks like two facing saucers clapping up and down).

The day "Real Live Girl" was being put into the show as a second act opening number, Bob at last had something to worry about, to pace the lobby about. The Erlanger Theatre in Philadelphia has an unusually long lobby. It runs the full length of the auditorium's *side*, instead of being at the rear. He paced up and down that long, long lobby as the performance began. Gwen sat on a bench, keeping him company, and they waited through the hour-and-ten-minute first act until intermission. The audience finally spilled out, chattering and lively. *Little Me* was a good show, and Sid Caesar was a popular star. It would be only minutes before they went back for the second act and "Real Live Girl."

The lobby grew foggy with smoke, and Bob contributed his share. As the doors were shut behind the last returning theatregoers, Emil Charlap appeared, his arms spilling over with music. Charlap was the copyist who wrote out the parts for each musician after Burns finished the orchestrations. This was no emergency, just a new version of one number, but he would have to wait with Bob and Gwen until the performance was over, before he could bring the music down to show the conductor. Charlap lighted a cigarette and said, "I'm the only guy who smokes as much as you do."

"No, Emil," Bob said. "If you want to smoke as much as I do, you've got to smoke with two hands."

Fosse was himself smoking with two hands, pushing one butt into the sand of the floor ashtray while he inhaled a fresh cigarette. Then, holding it behind his back, he would open a door and crack a peek into the darkened theatre to see how his new number was going.

> Nothing can beat
> Getting swept off your feet
> By a real, live girl

As the whispery chorus sang the sweet and easy tune with Carolyn's delicious lyrics that Caesar wouldn't sing, the number built casually. Fosse was using his full bag of tricks: Underneath the staccato singing, there was whistling and knee and thigh slaps, and most definitely finger snaps.

> I'll take the flowering hat
> And the towering heel
> And the squeal
> Of a real, live girl

He closed the lobby door gently, drew deeply on his cigarette, and resumed pacing the long lobby. Charlap exchanged sympathetic smiles with Gwen. Just the day before she had called out from the window of her limousine, offering him a lift to the theatre. He was new to show business, and she was the famous Broadway star, Gwen Verdon, and not snooty at all. It had thrilled him.

Bob couldn't resist another peek to see how his little masterpiece was going. He tiptoed back to one of the doors and opened it a peep. The finger snapping had turned syncopated. Much as he disliked lyrics so complicated they distracted his dancers, he could hardly have objected to Carolyn Leigh's delicious wit.

> Don't be a holdout for Helen of Troy
> I am a healthy American boy
> I'd rather gape
> At the dear little shape
> Of the stern and the keel
> Of a full-time vocational
> Full operational—

A pause was arranged just there, after the doughboys welled up in full choral harmony. Abruptly, they dropped to a whisper and drew it out

> G-i-r-lllll

With that and the orchestral "button," the plunk to tell the audience the number was over, the applause poured out through and between and under the row of shut doors, filling the lobby with its great wonder, the reward for all the work and worry. The cheers and whistles spread through and swelled the place, rushing down the walls and bubbling along the floor, and it was the nearest thing there was to whatever being a hit really meant: approval and confirmation and love outright.

Bob turned and beamed at Gwen. Then he raised his arms way above his head and did cartwheels all the way down to the end of the long lobby. When he reached that wall, he turned around and did cartwheels all the way back to where he had started. They were as exuberant as a boy's, celebratory and openhearted. "Real Live Girl" *worked*. "Working" meant productive and successful, and there was such a joy over that that he did another string of cartwheels, just for good measure. He did them clear down to the other end of the lobby.

9

Some minutes into the second act of *Little Me*, not long after "Real Live Girl," the long separated lovers, Belle Poitrine and Noble Eggleston, meet by chance aboard an ocean liner. "Oh, Noble," cries Belle, "isn't there *some* way we can go on seeing each other?" "What's the matter with you?" Noble (Sid Caesar) tuts. "Do you want to go sneaking around back alleys . . . checking into cheap hotels . . . lying to our family and friends? Is that what you want?" A chastised Belle replies, "Of course not." "Well," Noble concludes, "it was only a suggestion."

If there can be such a thing as a guaranteed laugh, this was it, but on the Broadway opening night of *Little Me*, November 17, 1962, Caesar read the punch line as "It was only a congestion," and, standing at the back of the Lunt-Fontanne Theatre, Cy Feuer and Cy Coleman and Neil Simon and Ernie Martin and Carolyn Leigh and Bob Fosse were aghast in the silence of the baffled audience.

Caesar managed to clear his throat in the midst of three other punch lines, that opening night, and Simon remembered turning toward Coleman. "Cy looked at me, and then we both looked at Bob, who very simply put his arms down at his sides, closed his eyes, and fell backward, every part of his body hitting the floor simultaneously."

Despite such problems, despite, even, a newspaper strike that threatened to keep the show a secret, *Little Me* was a success, and Bob had to be pleased. Everything seemed to be going his way, and he brought Gwen home to Chicago for Christmas to show her off to the family.

His father was not well. Heart disease was beginning to ravage the family, and there was no denying that it was lurking in Bob's genes. He knew it himself and said so. He told his brother Buddy that he was sure he would not live to be old. Everyone in the family begged him to stop smoking, even his sister Patsy, who smoked as much as he did, four packs a day. At least, Bob said, he had switched to Parliaments because they had filters. It hardly sounded responsible, and at that he was lying. He hadn't switched to Parliaments at all. As soon as he was out of sight, he would go back to Camels, as if it really made any difference, at four packs a day, whether they were Camels or Parliaments. He was like an alcoholic with a hidden bottle, but as his sister-in-law Margie said, "The Fosses always did have a knack for putting their heads in the sand."

He talked to Buddy and Eddie and Don and Patsy about what to name his expected child. He wanted a link with the family. "Listen," he said to Buddy, who was considered the Fosse historian. "If it's a boy, if we have a son, I'd like to give him a real masculine name, a wonderful strong name." The family historian began with the immediate relatives. "There's Uncle Emil," he said, who was married to Sadie's sister Flo, "and, on Dad's side, Uncle Erwin . . ."

Their father was not speaking to his brother Erwin. They hadn't seen each other for years.

"There's Uncle Richard," Buddy continued. Dick Fosse had died of cancer at thirty. He was the one Bob had liked best. Dick used to tell his nephew about long ago attempts to persuade Cy to join him as a singer in a vaudeville act, but when Bob asked his father about it, the old man dismissed singing as effeminate.

And then, Buddy said, "There's Uncle Nicholas."

"That's it!" Bob exclaimed. "Nick! It's so unphony!"

He telephoned Frederic Weaver to pay a visit. He hadn't seen Skipper since he'd paid off all the loans. Now he found that there was no more Chicago Academy of Theatre Arts. The old man had run it as long as his energy and physical stamina would allow. Now he was living on Social Security checks.

Weaver sniffed with disdain at any hint of charity, and so Bob asked the seventy-five-year-old father of his career whether he might be interested in operating a "Bob Fosse School of Dance." There wasn't a great deal of money available, Bob said, but perhaps the school could get rolling with a $10,000 start. The impresario, seated in his wheelchair beside his prize protégé, said he would think about it.

Once again the nieces and nephews had prepared a show for their glamorous uncle. In the bargain, it must have been thrilling to have the movie and Broadway star, Gwen Verdon, there in the house on South Boulevard in Evanston. The "This Is Your Life" they had done for Joan McCracken was hardly good enough. They put on a special Christmas revue, drawing a curtain across the middle of the living room and yanking it open to great ta-dahs, doing numbers from *The Pajama Game*, *Damn Yankees*, and *How to Succeed in Business Without Really Trying*. Buddy's daughter Cindy brought a girlfriend over to be her partner dancing "Who's

Got the Pain?" and they played the record while performing both Bob's and Gwen's parts in costumes copied from the *Damn Yankees* movie. Cindy was going to do the number in the Variety Show at Amundsen High. Marion Philbrick was still the dramatics teacher. When she had spotted the name "Cynthia Fosse" on her Drama Club roster, she launched into a history of her celebrated student, and she seldom let Cindy pass without providing another installment in the Bob Fosse story. Cindy knew that she would get an A from Miss Philbrick, but she also knew that in exchange for it she would have to master "Who's Got the Pain?" and do it for "a teacher who had probably seen *Damn Yankees* about a hundred times." Before Bob and Gwen left, they coached her in every detail of the number, a fair enough treat for a seventeen-year-old.

On March 24, 1963, Gwen gave birth, and Nicholas turned out to be a little girl. Her name was changed to Nicole. Years later, when Bob had writer friends and wanted to sound literary, he would say that he had got the name from *Tender Is the Night*. Dorothy Fields, the lyricist of *Redhead*, came up with the middle name. Because Gwen and Bob had wanted a child for so long and had tried so hard and had given up all hope, she suggested "Providence" and so it was. Nicole Providence Fosse was to be the darling of Bob's life.

How to Succeed in Business Without Really Trying was in its second year at the 46th Street Theatre. An uncharacteristically joyous Fosse stopped by to visit backstage and announce the birth of his daughter and even hand out cigars. One of the dancers said that she had never seen him express such feeling, "or show that much vulnerability. After that," she said, "his cleanup rehearsals became easy and fun."

Cleanup rehearsals are held periodically to keep a long-running show in crisp condition. Some directors and choreographers are responsible about this and come back regularly while others leave it to their dance captains and stage managers. Fosse was particularly rigorous about doing it himself and would frequently stop by unannounced to see one of his shows. At *How to Succeed*, the company that had once been fearful of these visits now welcomed them.

Little Me did not yet need such cleanup rehearsals, being only a few months old, but it was playing diagonally opposite at the Lunt-Fontanne Theatre, and Bob liked to stop by and visit with his dancers during intermission. The day of Nicole's birth he strolled across the street and walked up the theatre's alley to its stage door. As he passed out the cigars and the good news, he told the boys and girls about "a marvelous new idea I have for a show. I'm going to start it off by pushing a lady into the orchestra pit."

It sounded like a funny Fosse image conjured up for the sake of a laugh but it was the staging notion that would lie at the center of the new musical. In fact, that would be exactly how *Sweet Charity* began.

Two weeks later, on April 10, 1963, Cy Fosse died of heart disease at the age of sixty-nine and was buried alongside Sadie in Memorial Park cemetery, Skokie. Bob managed to get even with the man who was so macho that even singing was too effeminate for him. "In the coffin," he told a friend, "my father was finally wearing lipstick, and I thought, 'Well, you finally got your wish.' "

Two months later, he was back on stage as *Pal Joey*. The connection that he seemed to make between security crises, an inability to express emotion, and being a performer was being played out like a textbook case of the child in the man. Bob even found a dancer in the *Pal Joey* chorus to team up with him and re-create the "Me and My Shadow" routine from the Riff Brothers days, one fellow doing the same steps just behind the other, their shadows projected behind them. He reset the dancing duplicates to Richard Rodgers' music and interpolated the number into Joey Evans' act.

Gustav Schirmer, Jr., was again directing the Rodgers and Hart musical in still another revival at the New York City Center and "this time around," he said, "it was a much classier production." Bob took a more assertive interest in the show, persuading Schirmer to replace Carol Bruce with the beautiful Swedish actress, Viveca Lindfors. He choreographed Joey's big song and dance, "You Mustn't Kick It Around." He got Ralph Burns to reorchestrate it, paying the cost himself. With typical formality, he asked Schirmer's permission to borrow a piece of his own "Coffee Break" choreography from *How to Succeed in Business Without Really Trying*. "It's going to be the same exit," he warned the delighted Schirmer, "except I'm adding white gloves for the girls." Although famous for his derbies, Bob doted as well on white gloves, having used them in both *Redhead* and *Little Me*. They were the visual equivalents of finger snaps and drum shots. Nobody could miss a hand with outspread fingers when it was gloved in white.

The theatre world turned out to see Fosse dance, perhaps in even greater numbers than for the last *Pal Joey*, now that he had two more hits behind him. "They were always accusing him of being a lightweight performer," Schirmer said, "but he was awfully good in this part." What the director liked best about Fosse's performance was its heterosexuality. "Joey is straight," Schirmer said, "he's a womanizer, and he's open about that. When a gay dancer plays him, you sense something fake. The part fit

Bobby like a glove because he had the same antibullshit flair as Joey did, and talk about cocksmen . . ."

Once again, Fosse was finding the ladies irresistible and, as he himself said, "That's reason enough to be in this business. Just look at them," and even though he would later say, "I was perpetually unfaithful," he was probably just getting rolling in 1963, three years into his marriage. Anyone who wants to find the time can find the time, but Gwen was with him at home and at work, and to some in the *Pal Joey* company at that time, she seemed to be all women to him, mother and mistress, best friend and dance assistant. She was at rehearsals, and she was backstage, a great Broadway star but a modest one. Indeed, both of them were unpushy. When orchestra rehearsal ran late one night, and there was time to work on only one number, Bob told Schirmer that he would forgo his own rehearsal time so that the ingenue, Rita Gardner, could work on her song, "I Could Write a Book."

The young actress was touched by this generosity and said so as she introduced Bob to her husband at the opening night party. Her husband was the playwright Herb Gardner, author of A *Thousand Clowns*. One day he would be among Bob's closest friends.

Gwen was eager to return to the stage, and there were a number of possibilities. Her choice was a musical version of the 1926 Maurine Dallas Watkins play, *Chicago*, which had been made into the popular movie, *Roxie Hart*. But Bob had become a foreign-film enthusiast, and he thought that either Mario Monicelli's *Big Deal on Madonna Street* or Federico Fellini's *Nights of Cabiria* would make a good musical. He thought the latter in particular had a leading role that suited Gwen (the role that began with a shove into the orchestra pit). Another possibility was suggested by *Redhead's* producer, Robert Fryer, a musicalization of the popular Truman Capote novella, *Breakfast at Tiffany's*.

Maurine Watkins was retired and living in Florida, and she was very opposed to a musical version of her play. A born-again Christian, she did not think that *Chicago*, her account of murderesses in 1920s vaudeville, was a fit subject for musical comedy. *Nights of Cabiria* seemed the likelier project, and Bob was contemplating it as half of a double bill of one-act musicals. He had decided that he wanted to write it himself, to avoid the pains of collaborating with writers. He had worked on the script of *Redhead*, and he believed that he could do it. He had persuaded Elaine May to write the other half of the show, but the comedienne was taking her time about it. When Fryer went ahead and paid $25,000 for an option on *Breakfast at Tiffany's*, it became the going project. Fryer persuaded Fosse to accept an experienced collaborator on the script, and Bob left with playwright Hugh Wheeler for six working weeks on the island of Jamaica.

While they were there, Fryer received a telephone call from the celebrated literary agent, Audrey Wood, who represented Truman Capote.

"I'm terribly sorry," Miss Wood said, "but we have a real problem with Truman and your option on *Breakfast at Tiffany's*."

"What's the problem?" Fryer inquired.

"Well, it's rather delicate," she said. "You see, Truman thinks that Gwen Verdon is too old for the part."

Capote's heroine, Holly Golightly, was supposed to be twenty. Gwen was nearing forty and about to become a grandmother (her son Jimmie had followed her example and married young).

"Does Capote realize," Fryer said with some heat, "that Fosse and Wheeler have been working on this script for almost two months?"

"I'm terribly sorry, Mr. Fryer," the agent said. "I can sympathize with you, and with them, but I can't do anything about it. I'll return your payment. That's the way it's going to have to be."

The producer became less diplomatic. "It's not going to *have to be*," he said, "without going to court. For Christ's sake, Audrey, what good is a contract?"

"Please," she said. "I'm not disagreeing with you. I'm only following Truman's instructions."

"Well, I have an idea," Fryer said. "Why don't you both come down to *look* at Gwen. I promise you, if Capote sees her—she is a stunning woman—he'll certainly find out that she is not old looking."

When Fosse returned from Jamaica, Fryer had second thoughts about this notion. He told Bob the script was fine. "Nothing else worries me about it," he said pregnantly.

"What do you mean?" Bob asked, and so Fryer recounted the Capote situation, pointing out his conflicted feelings about putting Gwen up for inspection. Just the subject of age, he said, was bound to agitate her, and the idea of sitting still for an appraisal would humiliate anyone. "On the other hand," he said, "I can't think of any other way to save the project."

After talking it over with Gwen, Bob told Fryer to "have Capote come up to our place."

"You're sure, now?"

"There's nothing to worry about. Gwen looks great, and musicals aren't that realistic." But after Capote stopped by with Audrey Wood for breakfast at the Fosses', the agent called Fryer to say, "She's too old. Truman told me he thinks Gwen is just too old to play Holly Golightly. We will return your option money," and Wood did just that. (A couple of years later, Capote approved the thirty-year-old Mary Tyler Moore to play Holly Golightly in a musical version of his book. The show closed during New York previews.)

Fryer then suggested adapting Christopher Isherwood's *Berlin Stories*, but after reading the book that would ultimately serve as a basis for *Cabaret*, Bob told him, "We don't quite see it as a musical." The producer finally turned his attention to *Nights of Cabiria*, which he agreed to do with Bob and Gwen, and in the meantime, while the rights to Fellini's film were pursued, Bob agreed to direct and choreograph a musical about the *Ziegfeld Follies* star, Fanny Brice. The show was called *Funny Girl*, the star was Barbra Streisand, and Fosse introduced himself to its composer, Jule Styne, as if they had never met even though they had worked together on both *My Sister Eileen* and *Bells Are Ringing*.

"My name," Bob actually said, "is Bob Fosse," and no matter how long Styne knew him, that would be the introduction—in a Broadway of instant familiarity, the full name. "We worked together for quite a while," the composer said, "and Bob made some tremendous contributions that we kept in the show. One idea he had, which I'm sorry we didn't keep, I thought was revolutionary." This was a notion for staging the song, "Who Are You Now?" It was a ballad, a slow song. Slow songs are the bane of choreographers, seemingly unstageable, for apparently the singer can only stand at center stage and sing. With a sluggish rhythm there is nothing to move to. Fosse once not so humorously joked to Cy Coleman, "If you must write a ballad for that spot, could you put it in a fast tempo?"

His idea for staging "Who Are You Now?" was for Fanny Brice's unreliable husband, Nicky Arnstein, to be on stage behind her, and while she is singing her slow song, he is at a gambling table, rolling the dice, surrounded by bettors, sycophants, and girlfriends. This mimed scene would support the song, providing a dramatic subtext; it would make for musical drama and *movement*. Styne was right, the idea is ingenious.

When the composer played another slow song called "People," Fosse mulled it over and hummed it to himself and asked the composer to play it once more and mulled it over some more, and finally he said, "Well, Jule, it's a beautiful song, no doubt about it. It's a very beautiful song." He paused. "But I'm afraid we can't use it."

"What do you mean, 'We can't use it?' " Styne asked, stunned, for he knew just how beautiful "People" was.

"Well, it just doesn't make any dramatic sense," Fosse said, "for Fanny to sing this song."

"Why the hell not?"

"Listen to the words," the director said reasonably, as if the words were really his reason for scuttling this extremely slow song.

"What's wrong with them? They're great words."

"Yes," Fosse said. "Bob Merrill wrote beautiful words for it, but what do they say? They talk about 'people who need people.' Fanny Brice isn't a person who needs people."

"She isn't?" Styne asked, only to recover his hard-boiled senses and snap, "What do you mean, she doesn't need people?"

"Well, she's a great star of the *Follies*," Bob said, "and she's surrounded by people—people on stage and people backstage. Then she has a family, she has a mother, and she has neighbors; she has all kinds of people at home. So she doesn't need people there either. She doesn't need people anywhere, Jule, that's why the song doesn't make any dramatic sense. And that's why there's no point in her singing this song," he concluded hopefully.

Styne's eyes narrowed. He liked Fosse, he respected Fosse, he thought Fosse was doing great work on *Funny Girl*, but Fosse didn't know about songs while Styne was feeling very on top of things, still on a high after the brilliant *Gypsy*. "Listen, kid," the little songwriter said in icy and measured tones. He brought his dialogue down to one step above a whisper. "I'll tell you what the point of singing this song is. Do you want to know—would you like to know what the reason is for Barbra Streisand to sing 'People?' "

"Yeah," Bob said, biting and loving it. "What's the reason?"

"The reason she is singing this song," Styne said calmly before raising his voice to a roof shaking shout: "IS BECAUSE THIS SONG IS GOING TO BE FUCKING NUMBER ONE ON THE HIT PARADE! THAT IS WHY SHE IS SINGING THE FUCKING SONG!"

Bob loved it. He had to laugh. He loved the horse sense of it. Frank Loesser and Cy Feuer would have loved it too. He waited three beats before replying to Styne, timing his response as if waiting for an audience's laughter to subside.

"Okay, Jule," he finally said. "Now I understand."

And he did, too.

Funny Girl was ultimately directed by Jerome Robbins, who also wanted to cut "People," and probably for the same reason. Styne had to sign a written agreement stipulating that if "People" did not stop the show at every performance before *Funny Girl* opened on Broadway, he would agree to its being dropped.

It never missed.

The reason Fosse did not direct the show was that Styne talked too much. One day he passed along a piece of gossip about their producer, Ray Stark, who was a Hollywood person rather than a Broadway person, which probably made the man seem even less trustworthy to Bob than producers in general. Stark was producing *Funny Girl* because his wife was Fanny Brice's daughter. Styne told Fosse that Stark was not convinced of his abilities as a director and had been asking around for second opinions. Stark, he said, had even called Cy Feuer. "He asked Cy whether you were any good," the composer said. "It looks to me as if we have a producer who doesn't have a whole lot of faith in you."

Without even trying to verify the story, Bob quit the show. According to Feuer, Stark had never even asked about Fosse, but Bob had a quick emotional trigger. Anyhow, he was making a great deal of money from royalties on long-running shows and had another offer, and all of those things would make anyone feel good and safe and wanted and happy unless he was completely depressed, which Fosse wasn't yet.

His other offer was merely a Frank Loesser show. The composer, as his wife Jo said, "had fallen crazy for Bob after *How to Succeed* and just had to do a show with him."

Ex-Lover was to be an elaborate, expensive ($450,000) production set in the White Russia of 1787 and involving, if one can imagine, Potemkin, Catherine the Great, and John Paul Jones. It was based on the play *Once There Was a Russian*, which had opened on Broadway February 18, 1961, and closed the same night.

Historical plays were seldom Broadway favorites, musicals especially, although there were exceptions, *The King and I*, for instance, or *Camelot*. Broadway taste in musicals inclined to the flashy, the bright, and the contemporary, and so did the Fosse style of choreography, which, with its vaudevillian roots, hardly seemed suited to czarist Russia, not to mention a show with trap doors, lightning, and fake horses. But what is optimism, if not the start of rehearsals?

Rehearsals for *Ex-Lover*—whose title quickly became *Pleasures and Palaces*—began early in 1965, and Bob had an awesome assignment, directing and choreographing a show with a cast of fifty and a warehouse-ful of scenery. In dance terms alone, he had an ensemble of fourteen (it would be the last Fosse show to have separate dancing and singing choruses—Broadway economics would soon end that luxury). His chief dance assistant, of course, was Gwen. She left Nicole at home with the Brazilian nanny. This was a bold step for the hovering mama, but she did hover over Bob as well.

The stars of *Pleasures and Palaces* were Phyllis Newman, whom Bob had met when she'd been Judy Holliday's understudy in *Bells Are Ringing*, and John McMartin, of the late and unlamented *The Conquering Hero*. Considering the superstructure on which Fosse and his star players were roosting—the army of performers, the endless costumes, the requirement for major "traffic management," as Broadway people called the movement of scenery and actors on and off stage—for all that, he seemed calm as rehearsals got under way in New York. That was how Phyllis Newman remembered it.

She knew he was worried about her performance. "I just wasn't giving him what he wanted. I'm not very fast in developing a character," she later said, "and I couldn't find the way to tell him, 'Don't worry.' " But Fosse stayed with her, and when he began staging her musical numbers, "Well," she said, "that was just like heaven. I got what he had to say, in *shorthand*. It was that kind of instant communication."

The itinerary for the show was going to be unusual, with but one tryout, a long one of six weeks in Detroit, which was farther afield than producers liked to go, the wisdom being that the closer a city was to New York, the closer the mentality of its audiences to Broadway audiences and, therefore, the more reliable the reactions. Performances of *Pleasures and Palaces* began at the Fisher Theatre in Detroit on March 10, 1965, with the official opening the following night, and of course it was a gala and excited audience for they had already, that season, seen the premiere of one Broadway hit (*Fiddler on the Roof*) and with a Frank Loesser show, naturally, they anticipated another. As the rustling of programs subsided and with the putting away of bulky winter coats and furs, and the hushing of whispers, the conductor, Fred Werner, strode into the orchestra pit to the ritual applause. He poised his baton above his head, and with his downbeat, the overture began.

At its conclusion the curtain whooshed upward. Fosse had set the opening of the show in absolute darkness. The audience was given a moment to tense for a surprise, as an audience does in the dark. Then, instead of hearing the music as expected, it heard the stamping of boots, an army of them. They were marching boots, boots stamping in parade time, and momentarily they were joined by syncopated claps. A different, brighter foot stamping entered into the counterpoint, and then finger snaps were added to the pulsating march rhythm. At last, a drumbeat joined in, snares and a big bass drum, building the rhythm, escalating the volume, a musical round made of a march beat, and only then did the lights go up, revealing a stage ensemble resplendent in red and gold Russian military uniforms. The dancers, fourteen strong, were in Fosse drill formation, and the orchestra abruptly opened into full brass, and the audience burst into applause. Well, what else could it do?

After that, it was all downhill.

Gwen worked on the dances by day while Bob rehearsed script revisions, and at night she watched performances from the back of the theatre alongside Frank Loesser. Phyllis Newman was getting her laughs, but her material and her songs were curiously American and contemporary in this St. Petersburg of 1767. The show was schizoid, simultaneously historic and satiric, and "the experience was grim," she remembered, "and Bob was grim."

Loesser was grim too, but he was surviving with black humor. Bob was having a tougher time. "He kept getting smaller and smaller," Newman said.

Yet he worked. With the tryout entering its last week, he pushed on while the producers (one of whom was Loesser) determined whether to continue to Broadway or close in Detroit. As if oblivious to that, Fosse spent afternoons rehearsing a new dance number. The show, he decided, was too humorless. He was adding a satiric dance for the Czarina's court, to be put in on Thursday, but on Tuesday the notice was posted for a closing in four days, and of course all further rehearsals were canceled. The dancers voted to continue working anyway, without pay. They were, most of them, Fosse people, dancers from *Damn Yankees, New Girl in Town, Redhead*, and the rest, and as one of them, Kathryn Doby, remembered, "We felt, if Bob has been working so hard, let him have his rehearsal and finish his number." They even offered to contribute the cost of orchestrations just so the new dance could be put in for the last four performances. It moved Fosse visibly, a rare thing as he stood and blinked in his now standard dark costume, the sleeves of his black shirt rolled up to the elbow, his black pants made dashing, tucked into high black boots with a cuff at the top. So they worked on the new dance for its own sake, and for his sake and for their own.

On the last day of the work, he sat them down on the stage floor and told them how sorry he was for disappointing them all. It was a farewell speech rich in contrast to the bitter and confused "farewell to the troops" he had paid the *Conquering Hero* company. Of course in this case he had been neither dismissed nor disapproved of. Frank Loesser knew that it was the material that was to blame, not the director, but still, Bob apologized to these favorites of his, his family of dancers. "I'm sorry," he concluded, "sorry I couldn't do better for such talented people."

They sat and looked at him, loving him, and they would not leave the stage. After a moment of stillness, a few rose the way dancers do, without using their hands, effortlessly and exempt from gravity. They started to move. The rehearsal pianist began to improvise. A couple of the people who had been in *Redhead* reconstructed bits and pieces of "The Pickpocket Tango." The pianist followed them, he picked up on what they were doing. Several dancers who had been in *How to Succeed in Business Without Really Trying* stood up and dovetailed into the giant soft shoe, "A Secretary Is Not a Toy." The rehearsal pianist knew that one too and knew what was happening; he was fluent with that dance music. "We were doing a Fosse retrospective," Kathy Doby said, "out of love and warmth," and they were doing it sealed off, by themselves, for themselves. She herself stood and began to dance "The Rich Kids' Rag" for that was where she had first worked for Bob, dancing in the national company of *Little Me.*

Then, strong and confident and sensual, two of the girls slithered into the whorehouse ballet from *New Girl in Town*, the troubled number, the original version, and two boys stood to carry them in the great arching lifts that had made magnificently sensual creatures of the women, and when they reached a climax in it, a great bunch of the others eased into the pained and proud memory, the war ballet from *The Conquering Hero.*

Everyone up now, they finished with their new dance for *Pleasures and Palaces*, the number that no audience would ever see.

He never told them, and they could not have known that he had offered to invest $75,000 of his own money to keep the show running (Loesser wouldn't hear of it). For someone so contemptuous of artistic pretensions, for someone so committed to the commercial stage, for someone so accepting of the hit philosophy, Bob Fosse was a true theatre lover and, even more than that, a lover of *the people in the theatre.* The theatre of these dancers was what mattered to him. The noncreative people, those who thought the theatre was about money, they were the enemy.

That night, seated morosely at a restaurant table, John McMartin asked Fosse what he would be doing next.

"A couple of one-act musicals. I'm going to get together with Elaine May. She'll write an original and I'm going to write the other one myself. It's based on the Fellini movie, *Nights of Cabiria*. In fact, Jack," he said, managing a smile, "there's something in it for you."

"You're kidding," a blushing McMartin said. John McMartin, tall, slim, pale, and boyish, very Minnesota and very bashful, with prematurely gray hair and watery blue eyes, would blush at the change of a traffic light. "This is the second bomb I've been in with you," he said. "Between *Conquering Hero* and this, I thought you'd be sure I was bringing you bad luck."

"That's funny," Bob replied. "I was afraid to mention the new show to you because I thought you felt the same way about me."

McMartin had long since forgotten that exchange when he ran into Fosse a few months later on Broadway at 64th Street. Almost as far as one could see, Lincoln Square was being transformed into Lincoln Center for the Performing Arts. White theatre buildings were rising all around, making the place look like an architect's model, as if there should be little cardboard trees with stick figures on the sidewalks and toy cars in the streets.

"That show I mentioned to you in Detroit," Bob said, "I'm starting to put it together. Come in and read for it. There aren't any songs for you, but there's a nice scene."

The "nice scene" was one of two that Neil Simon had written after Bob had asked his opinion of the script and then for his help in fixing it. There was no longer an Elaine May one-act musical to go with it. *Nights of Cabiria* was now the full-length *Sweet Charity*, and Simon had done more than add two big scenes and a few jokes; he had shined and polished the manuscript, he'd rewritten it, and in exchange for that he demanded exclusive credit. He was not about to be a coauthor and had the clout to back that up, for he had become the most popular playwright on Broadway, with *Barefoot in the Park* still running and now *The Odd Couple* the most tremendous of hits. Bob was his friend but friendship had nothing to do with it.

The importance of theatrical billing and the negotiations involved with it can seem foolish to people outside show business but billing is a ritualization of credit, and credit is essential to justice and ego. Many people consider such concerns unworthy of adults. In show business, where the childlike is legitimized, credit is not only talked about but hammered out with the intensity of a business transaction.

Neil Simon was a compulsive worker, an edgy and restless fellow. He might express his nervousness with comic outbursts and could be as funny as a professional comedian. Or else he might reveal his agitation by abruptly elbowing his way out of a crowded elevator, crying, "Let me out of here!" It was this claustrophobia, in fact, that inspired his introductory elevator scene for Charity and her love interest, Oscar Linquist, in *Sweet*

Charity. When Doc Simon caught cold, he might not merely take to bed; he had been known to fly to Arizona to cure the cold. Fortunately, nature had provided him with a productive outlet for these tensions. Writing was his relief, and it was a happy therapy for it had made him a success and a fortune. However, one play a year was not nearly enough work to expend all that nervous energy. He burned the rest of it fixing shows that were trying out in Washington, Philadelphia, or Boston. That was Doctor Simon.

In the case of *Sweet Charity*, his doctoring had come earlier than usual and at the request of the author himself, and so it was not aggressive for Simon to take over the entire writing of this libretto. He had nothing else to do anyway. His next play, *The Star Spangled Girl*, was already written.

Fosse would later say he always felt that he had done the major work on the *Sweet Charity* script and had been shoved out, but he accepted this situation as paying his dues. It was the second installment. (The first had been losing out to Harold Lang when *Pal Joey* went to Broadway.) Meantime, one could do worse than direct a musical written by Neil Simon.

And so Fosse's writing aspirations, which were becoming ever dearer to him, were also becoming more difficult to realize. He had already written this basic script and had even invented a pseudonym to go with it, "Bill Lewis," but neither Fosse nor Bill Lewis was going to have an author's credit on *Sweet Charity* even though the idea of making a musical out of *Nights of Cabiria* had been his, and all of the groundwork, and all of the original adapting. Even now, much of his dialogue remained but the credit line was going to read, "Book by Neil Simon," and that was that.

10

If Fosse's first attempt at writing ended painfully, it also proved how sturdy he could be, for he was able to deal with the pain, accept the disappointing turn of events, and still work on *Sweet Charity* and work productively and well with Neil Simon. He would not forget but he would forgive.

The first draft of *Sweet Charity* must have demonstrated to him that he could, in some fashion, write, which was important because the act of writing was itself a metaphor for a creative Fosse, not the crafty and flashy fixer but a Fosse who could express himself and had something to express: an artist.

He decided to find a place of his own to do this writing work, a place away from Gwen's noisy menage at 91 Central Park West with Hermocinda, the omnipresent Brazilian nanny, and toddling Nicole, always pushing her nose up to the door of Bob's den and asking, "Have you finished work yet, Daddy?"

He found and took office space on the eleventh floor of 850 Seventh Avenue, between West 54th and 55th streets. The solidly built old building catered to a theatrical clientele who appreciated the informal nature of offices that were converted apartments rather than business cells.

The place that Bob rented was but a single room, a studio apartment, and he arrived there early each morning for he still did not sleep very well. Once there, however, he had little to do. He hung a framed publicity picture from his first City Center revival of *Pal Joey*. In the corner of the frame was a strip clipped from the show's advertisement. ("The best of all Joeys, including Gene Kelly."—John Chapman, *Daily News*.) He put up a wall of framed posters, *Pajama Game*, *Damn Yankees*, *New Girl in Town*, *Redhead*, *How to Succeed in Business Without Really Trying*, and *Little Me*. All the hits, none of the flops.

What to do next? He could reread the script of *Sweet Charity*, with its Neil Simon byline, and he could even make notes on it but to what purpose? There are few writers who appreciate criticism, especially of a work in progress, and Simon was obviously not among them. Bob could also write in the office, that was a possibility, and he even had a writing project at hand, for along with *Nights of Cabiria* he had taken an option on the other Italian movie that interested him, *Big Deal on Madonna Street*, but he did not write that script. As a choreographer and director, he was accustomed to working among people, on concrete projects for an immediate audience. It was something else to cope with the solitude and abstractness of writing.

Rather than be alone, he visited the office next door. Lionel Larner was an elegant young British theatrical agent, and his office was a lively place. Larner was himself an ebullient and sociable fellow, and Bob knew many of the actor clients. He was especially fond of Larry Blyden, who had once been married to Carol Haney. Blyden was smart, he was funny, and at forty he was a contemporary, just two years older. They both had been stunned by Carol's death some months earlier.

She had died in Las Vegas—Carol Haney, once of Jack Cole and later of *Kiss Me, Kate*, central to "Steam Heat" and celebrated in *The Pajama Game*. She had been a hard luck girl to the end. Gwen Verdon had succeeded her among the Jack Cole Dancers, to be discovered by Cy Feuer and create a sensation in *Can-Can*. Shirley MacLaine had become a movie star by stepping in as her understudy the night a Hollywood producer came scouting. Now a diabetic, Haney had no business drinking, but she was a classic self-destructor, a trait perhaps related to the traditional dancer masochism. "Every time before the big performance, she would hurt herself in some ridiculous way," Buzz Miller had said. "It was some sort of self-punishment that she did."

When she came down with pneumonia, her system couldn't resist it, weakened as it was by diabetes and alcoholism. She died at thirty-nine in the midst of playing a nightclub engagement.

Fosse came upon Larry Blyden in Lionel Larner's office as the actor was being buoyed by the agent's news of a part in a Broadway show. While they were all slapping backs, the playwright Paddy Chayefsky blew through the door at full tilt. He had the big corner office at the other end of the eleventh floor.

Chayefsky was a sturdy man of forty-two, compact and burly in the bulky way of a schoolyard athlete, with thick dark hair and a bent nose that could pass for a streetfighter's. He was a grown-up with one foot in the boys' clubs of his city youth, a street snob who would not allow the loss of his nostalgia. He was an intellectual competitor, always spoiling for a political argument or a philosophical argument, or any exchange over any issue, changing sides for the fun of the fray. A liberal, he was annoyed by liberals; a proud Jew, he wouldn't let anyone call him a "Jewish writer." In short, the life of the mind was a participant sport for Paddy Chayefsky.

He was a successful writer, the most celebrated graduate of television's "slice of life" school of naturalism. Several of his television plays had been made into movies, and one of them, Marty, had lifted him into celebrity when it won the 1955 Academy Award for Best Picture. He had since written several hit Broadway dramas, including The Middle of the Night, The Tenth Man, and Gideon. At the moment he was, without question, a considerable figure in the theatrical world but he was at the peak of what would prove a transient stage reputation. The truth was that Paddy Chayefsky's plays had little artistic weight, that his naturalism was going out of style, and that he would never again have a Broadway success.

It didn't matter. His career was well timed, when declining on one front then rising on another, and perhaps some of that was a reflection of the personal vitality that had so salutary an effect on other men. For in a remarkable way, Chayefsky was revered by an army of friends that ranged beyond show business and across the worlds of literature, journalism, and politics. Even men more cultured than he, better educated and more artistic, simply idolized him. Talented as he was, his greatest gift was his personality. Wherever his career led, into television, the theatre, or the movies, the swelling fraternity gathered around him. Movie stars (Peter Falk) went to basketball games with him, presidential advisers (Arthur Schlesinger) went for walks with him, the executives of major newspapers (A. M. Rosenthal, executive editor of The New York Times) asked his political opinions. Paddy Chayefsky was one of the most popular and beloved men in the power and celebrity orbit of his time.

Yet for all the stereotyped masculinity of his style, the Friday night poker games in the office, the sports events—basketball and baseball games, prizefights—the regular workouts at the Business Men's Club gym, the hanging out with the guys, for all this formula maleness, he had little interest in women. He had few woman friends and no girlfriends. He lived with his wife Susan and their son Danny on Central Park West near 81st Street. The unit might have seemed a typical upper middle class, successful New York Jewish family but it was not. Paddy was seldom at home. He was always out with the boys, and he often stayed out until dawn. Friends saw less and less of Susan Sackler Chayefsky, and she grew reclusive while Paddy took to making the late night rounds of New York's nightclubs with his friend, the gossip columnist Leonard Lyons. When asked about this odd marriage, he evaded the question with a sad joke, "I won't get divorced. I learned when I was very young that I cannot sleep unless I know I'm annoying somebody."

Most of his friends suffered or enjoyed and talked about their urgent and constant lust. They were on the cusp of middle age and on schedule for potency worries, sexual second breaths, and perhaps some seeking out of rejuvenation. But when the talk turned to women and sex, Chayefsky's mind appeared to run in neutral, poised to bring up the subject of Israel or the Kennedy assassination or Vietnam or at least Muhammad Ali or the New York Mets or the Knicks. Finally, his friends stopped talking about women when he was around.

He maintained, or at least affected, the mannerisms of the Bronx streets he'd grown up on and the inverted snobbery of the highly academic but proletarian City College of New York from which he had been graduated. "No phony bullshit for me," he would say, facetiously redundant, enjoying street slang's implied hard-core honesty, and the whole package won Bob Fosse's heart. This gruffly cultured, baggy suited, shoulder swinging Jewish intellectual with warmth and an atheistic rabbinical wisdom and a paternalism beyond his years came rushing at the slender, Nordic, emotionally withdrawn, midwestern choreographer with something approaching kismet as Paddy Chayefsky barged into Lionel Larner's office to "borrow the Xerox machine."

Here was a writer, a man of the mind to admire and learn from. Bob was defensive about his lack of formal education and had been impressed with dramatists ever since classes at the American Theatre Wing. Now that he was himself trying to write, playwrights probably impressed him all the more, especially as contrasted with the low glitter of musical comedy. He doubtless agreed with Chayefsky's assessment of musicals as pure show business for he never had any problem seeing himself and his work as but a front, a flash act like the Riff Brothers.

There was an irony in this, for Chayefsky's scorn of musical comedy was that of a spurned lover. Fifteen years earlier he had volunteered himself to Cy Feuer as a lyricist for *Guys and Dolls*, unaware that Frank Loesser wrote his own lyrics. Chayefsky had even written a musical of his own, the book and lyrics for a show called *No T.O. for Love*, and it had been produced in London in 1954. He had written it while convalescing in an Army hospital in England. In short, if Fosse yearned to write, Chayefsky wanted to dance.

His time in the Army had provided him with the nickname "Paddy." It went back to the military unit on the Bronx campus of Fordham University, where he had been assigned in 1944, fresh from basic training, to brush up on his German and become an interpreter with the occupation forces. At one morning formation early that spring, Chayefsky's unit commander asked the platoon of draftees, "Will all Jewish personnel who wish to be excused for the Passover holiday please step forward?" Private Chayefsky did so, and his name was duly registered.

Some weeks later, with Easter imminent, the same unit commander brought up the subject of Good Friday. "Will all Catholic personnel," he asked, "who wish to be excused for Good Friday please step forward?" Once more, Chayefsky took the step.

"Listen, Chayefsky," the captain said. "Didn't you ask a couple of weeks ago to be excused for the Jewish holidays?"

"Yes, sir, I did," Chayefsky said.

"Then how come you're doing the same thing now for Good Friday?"

"I observe both holidays, sir," Chayefsky replied. "My father is Jewish, and my mother is Catholic."

The captain walked over, tweaked what Chayefsky himself described as "my Jewish nose," and said, in an Irish brogue, "And I suppose now your first name would be Paddy?"

It stuck. It stuck so tight that few people beyond his immediate family knew that his real name was Sidney. In the great and warm friendship that lay ahead, Bob would occasionally call Paddy "Sidney," the real name becoming the private nickname.

As Chayefsky burst into Lionel Larner's office, the agent was saying to Larry Blyden, "I'll take you to lunch to celebrate. Just name it. We can go to one of those 'La' places—La Caravelle or La Cote Basque."

"Lionel!" Chayefsky cried. "He wants Jew food!" Larner, for all his Savile Row swank, enjoyed Chayefsky's puncturing of pretensions. "Blyden wants to eat downstairs!" the playwright roared. "Don't you, Blyden?"

"Downstairs" was the Carnegie Delicatessen, next door at 854 Seventh Avenue. It was a kosher-style delicatessen restaurant typical of the hundreds that had once warmed the city's Jewish neighborhoods when boys wore corduroy knickers and played stickball in the streets. The Carnegie was one of the few such restaurants remaining in the city, a nostalgic reminder of a Jewish childhood in New York. It had become a meeting place for the boys who had grown up to be comedians and movie producers, trading jokes across the pastrami sandwiches and pickle bowls.

Larry Blyden went off to one of the "La" restaurants with Larner that day, but not long afterward he stood outside Fosse's door as Chayefsky bellowed, "Fosse! Let's eat!" and the three of them went downstairs to plunge through the line on the sidewalk, Chayefsky imperiously leading the way, his arm waving like a student with the right answer.

Some know the maître d' at Maxim's in Paris, some can get a table at

Spago in Los Angeles, some have connections at Le Cirque in New York. Paddy Chayefsky had clout with Herb Schlein, the seating host at the Carnegie Delicatessen, and so, it turned out, did Bob Fosse.

"Bob Fosse! This is indeed an honor," the host boomed, grinning broadly. Schlein treasured his show business contacts. He would bring news of them home to his mother Ethel in Elizabeth, New Jersey. "Hello, Mr. Chayefsky. How are you, Mr. Blyden?" He relished the names as morsels of glamour. "This way, gentlemen," he said, and with a pleased arrogance befitting a top ranked restaurant in the Michelin Guide, the short, stocky, thirtyish, shirtsleeved, and much too openhearted kosher delicatessen maître d' led the way through the tables overflowing with potato salad and chicken soup, past the towering and quivering sandwiches, to a small, formica-topped table in the rear, set against a mirrored wall. Seating the threesome he swept linen napkins before them, linen rather than the paper napkins that served the hoi polloi in the crowded and noisy room. "Linen," Schlein announced, had anyone not noticed, or not known what it was, and, he added, "A waiter will be with you shortly, gentlemen. I remain a great admirer of yours, Mr. Fosse."

The grandiloquent host, having introduced himself to Bob at a garment industry party some five years earlier, had subsequently written a congratulatory note on the occasion of the opening night of *Redhead*. In appreciation Bob sent him opening night tickets for both *Little Me* and *How to Succeed in Business Without Really Trying*. Without a doubt, Fosse saved a tenderness for the overlooked; for all the auditioners who never got the jobs. He apparently remembered Schlein although they had only met once in an entirely different context. Bob smiled as if he comprehended how a children's clothing salesman could have become a table host at the Carnegie Delicatessen, and then he turned to his new friends. Chayefsky was saying, "Don't look now but there's Mansfield, and he's coming our way."

"Irving Mansfield?" Blyden asked.

"I'm leaving," Bob said. "I don't want to see that son of a bitch."

When Irving Mansfield had been the executive producer of Sid Caesar's "Your Show of Shows," he had refused to pay Fosse and Niles the $1,100 a week that Bob had told his agent to ask for. They had settled for $900, but Bob didn't think there should have been any settlement because he had only asked for what he believed he and Mary-Ann deserved. He hadn't spoken to Mansfield since.

With a whisper to Schlein, Chayefsky kept the television producer from their table. Fosse had held this grudge for fifteen years, and was not letting go of it now. "And I don't want to see that son of a bitch Steiner either," Chayefsky said, mocking Bob's anger in the hope of demonstrating its foolishness. Leo Steiner was one of the Carnegie Delicatessen's owners. "Don't let him pick up our checks," Paddy said dryly to Schlein, who thereafter would protect Fosse's privacy as jealously as he did Chayefsky's.

Then, much to Paddy's amusement, Bob ordered an extremely Methodist chopped liver sandwich on white bread with butter. It didn't matter. He only finished the beer anyhow.

Ralph Burns, the orchestrator, gave Bob a new toy, a "drum machine." It was a small, primitive electronic sound synthesizer that was designed to reproduce drumbeats in rhythms labeled "swing time," "fox-trot," and "rhumba." Burns knew that although Bob was crazy for music, whether Satie or Mahler, Dixieland jazz or rock 'n' roll, when he worked by himself in the dance studio he was interested only in a beat. This taste for rhythm was a logical extension of tap-dancing, which of course makes a human a percussion instrument. Bob's rim shots (the stick rapped against a drum's metal rim), his love of cymbals, ratchets, finger snaps, and other sound effects, followed naturally.

With the drum machine under one arm and a sheaf of records under the other, Fosse would take a taxi to the Variety Arts rehearsal studios, across the street from the 46th Street Theatre where *How to Succeed in Business Without Really Trying* had finally closed after playing an amazing 1,417 performances. That was how, and where, work on *Sweet Charity* began, often before dawn, Fosse dancing while the luckier slept.

His legend spread among the theatre's gypsies, its itinerant dancers, and the story was true. "Fergy" Ferguson, the owner of Variety Arts, had given Bob a key to the place so that he might let himself in to work whenever he wanted. It amazed Broadway's dancers that this famous and powerful choreographer-director could be as emotionally involved with dancing as they were, but it was really no different from the days when Frederic Weaver had given Bob a key to the Chicago Academy of Theatrical Arts. He had worked there in the ghostly hours too.

Sometimes he would wake Gwen in the middle of the night and drag her along with him, bringing her down to the Variety Arts rehearsal studio. Barely awake, shaking her head to clear it, she would help demonstrate and work out the steps he had dreamed up in bed in the middle of the night.

Perhaps Bob slept better in the summer house they bought in Amagansett. There was no rehearsal studio to go to (though he would find a way to work there too). Amagansett was near the eastern tip of Long Island, a ten-minute drive from East Hampton. Their house was just a walk through the sandy scrub to the Atlantic Ocean beach that Gwen looked so good on, looking better in a bikini than a forty-year-old mother (or anyone else) had a right to.

That house was her first substantial investment. Bob said, "I never thought I would have this kind of money in my life. It's just pouring in." When he talked about how he and Gwen pooled their now considerable earnings, he joked, "I pay the bills and she buys the houses," but it wasn't just houses. Gwen had a mind for business, and she engaged in money dealings with enthusiasm, seriousness, and success. The house in Amagansett was only the first in a series of profitable sales and resales in real estate in an area primed to blossom into one of the most expensive resort communities in the country.

She liked to socialize there, to go to parties and give them with beer, corn on the cob, and filet mignon cooked on the charcoal grill. Bob protested his shyness but he certainly could be sociable; as soon as guests started arriving he would start the Ping-Pong tournament, cheating openly and enthusiastically. Doc Simon and his wife Joan were in Amagansett too, just up the street, and the two couples were close. Even their youngsters became best friends, the Fosses' Nicole and the Simons' younger girl, Nancy. They had been born just weeks apart, as in fact were Doc and Bob. ("I always look up to you, Bob," Simon would sometimes say, "and want to be just like you when I get to be your age.")

The men were surviving the hard feelings engendered by the Sweet Charity credit crisis; Doc was the first "best" friend of Bob's adult life. Like many men, Fosse had stopped having male friends with the onset of adult responsibilities, career, and family. Beginning with Neil, he would enjoy many rich and rewarding camaraderies and at summer's end, when work on the show began, "Bob didn't do anything or go anywhere relating to Sweet Charity without Doc," according to the coproducer, Robert Fryer. "While he trusted me, he still had the actor's mentality with producers. He stayed on his side of the line, but he asked Neil's opinion of everything."

Simon had pared the Sweet Charity script down to a series of efficient scenes, almost sketches, which linked the Cy Coleman–Dorothy Fields musical numbers. The only scenes of any duration were the two that he had written at the outset. The first was set in the apartment of an Italian movie star who hides Charity Hope Valentine in his closet where she spends the night rather than anger his unexpectedly arriving girlfriend. This serves to establish her as a sad but lovable victim, an eternal survivor in an eternally cruel world. The other big scene takes place in an elevator and introduces Charity to the claustrophobic Oscar, starting their romance and showing her maternal side with someone as vulnerable as she. Oscar, in fact, is the only neurotic leading man in Broadway musical comedy, and that is all too evidently a Neil Simon contribution.

Bob's original image remained, Charity being shoved into the Central Park pond—the orchestra pit—by a purse-snatching date.

"Charity" is Bob's name for Cabiria, the meek and victimized prostitute of the 1957 film, *Nights of Cabiria* (*Le Notti di Cabiria*), which Federico Fellini wrote with Tullio Pinnelli and Ennio Flaiano. While she has been transformed into a dance hall hostess as a concession to period morality, there remains a vague implication of after-hours prostitution. Certainly, the hinge of the slender plot turns on the new boyfriend's discovery of her sexual history. As Fosse said, "No matter how much he loves Charity, this guy cannot deal with the fact that she does what she does."

By making her a taxi dancer (as the dime-a-dance hostesses were often called), he more than moved the little tale from the harsh streets of Fellini's Rome to the bright lights of Broadway; he transposed it to the milieu that would be central to all his subsequent work: the seamy side of show business, the sleazy joints of his theatrical birth.

Sweet Charity, then, is not quite the lighthearted entertainment it seems. The colorful look of the show, the style of its music, and the energy of its dances suggest a musical comedy, but the facts of the story are at odds with that, for the heroine is a victimized innocent and the man she loves is "an emotional pacifist," as Fosse once described himself, afraid to feel. John McMartin, who landed the offered role, like Bob was a reedy and shy Midwesterner. In preparing to play the part he went to see *Nights of Cabiria* and was surprised to find the character rather different from the Oscar in Neil Simon's script. "He was much darker in the movie," McMartin recalled. "He was venal."

That character was now divided between the rat who snatches Charity's purse and dunks her to start the show and the neurotic Oscar who abandons her to end it. Between the two is the Fosse presence, part Riff, who has (or shows) no feelings and uses women, and part Bobby Fosse of Amundsen High, the innocent in the whorehouse. Nor is it farfetched to liken Charity's cohostesses to the strippers of Bob's youth. The Fan-Dango Ballroom is a fair stand-in for the cheap joints where he danced in 1943 Chicago, and the Norwegian Fosse even gave Oscar a Scandinavian name (Linquist).

Perhaps the show reveals a Bob Fosse beginning to accept both sides of himself, the tap dancer and the class president, the hedonist and the artist, the heartless man and the vulnerable one, selfish and generous, and perhaps both sides were necessary to success, drive, and talent. It does seem as if, at just this time, the door was opening to a self-acceptance and self-knowledge that would enable him to bloom as an artist and go on to create his best work.

Excepting McMartin, the casting of *Sweet Charity* was largely choreographic, for there was going to be a great deal of dancing in this show. It was a Gwen Verdon musical, after all. The adored star was returning to Broadway after a five-year absence, and audiences wanted to see her dance. She was punishing herself into shape for that. At forty-one it was getting tough.

With the start of autumn and the crisp excitement of a new Broadway season, Bob emerged from his dawn work at the studio prepared for the week of dance rehearsals that would precede work with the entire company. He was poised to become a powerful and celebrated director. He might have been dismissed from *The Conquering Hero. Pleasures and Palaces* had certainly been an out-of-town flop. But his record in New York was unblemished and unparalleled. He had brought seven musicals to Broadway, and every single one of them had been a hit. He had won the Tony Award for the choreography of *The Pajama Game, Damn Yankees,* and *Redhead.* Now that Jerome Robbins had quit the theatre, frustrated by the compromises of collaboration, and with George Abbott no longer at his peak, he was primed to be peerless. His only real competition was Gower Champion. Cy Feuer considered him "the most brilliant stage person I ever worked with."

The musical number that launches *Sweet Charity* is a unique ensemble piece called "Hey, Big Spender," and it introduces the working conditions and the working girls at the Fan-Dango Ballroom, as the taxi dancers vie with each other for the approaching customer much as a group of prostitutes might. Set to a burlesque beat, its "dancing" is really an insinuating series of moves, poses, and stances, a writhing of women who are at once alluring and threatening. They are erotic in their undulation, their limbs are serpentine, and their urgent approaches are the lusty invitations of streetwalkers. As one of the girls, Helen Gallagher, herself a dancing star and Gwen's understudy, said, "It was as close as the show got to saying we were hookers."

With Gwen acting as dance assistant, since this number allowed her a rare break, Bob began work on "Hey, Big Spender" by teaching the girls the song:

> The minute you walked down the street
> I could tell you were a man of distinction
> A real big spender . . .

Then, as one of the dancers, Elaine Cancilla, put it, "the magic started." With the number already in his head, Fosse lined up the ten girls facing what would be the audience. They were in a holding area, penned behind a ballet barre that was a railing in the dance hall. "He put chairs in front of us before we had the barre to work with. He pushed us, like puppets, into these broken doll positions." Staring insolently into where the audience would be, lower lips quivering and pouting, eyelashes drooping, the "broken dolls" thrust their hips back to lock them and bent their legs inward at the knees and toes. Using stop action, or visual or musical accents, he would direct the audience's eyes. As Kathryn Doby said, "He could move the littlest part of the body, and everyone would see it." One of the girls' legs was curled over the top of the barre that they were lined up behind, and another actually straddled it. Every possible limb seemed bent at every possible joint.

As Fosse had used rhythmic dialogue in "The Rich Kids' Rag," so he did again with "Hey, Big Spender," interpolating it in a counterpoint.

> "What do you say to a—?"
> "Hey, how's about a—?"
> "I can give you some—"
> "Are you ready for some—?"   "Laughs?"
> "How would you like a little—?"   "Fun?"
>   "Good time?"

He had developed an affection for these trades—strippers, whores—and their language, a result of Bob Riff's life along the seedy side of show business, and he used the suggestive come-ons for two purposes. First, they added humor to the earthiness, which helped make "Hey, Big Spender" the most successful of his sexy numbers because it didn't take itself seriously, sexually, the way the whorehouse ballet had in *New Girl in Town*. Secondly, the rhythmic dialogue blended the musical number into the play.

In this use of all music theatre forces—dialogue, song, and dance—"Hey, Big Spender" exploits musical staging so completely that most audiences would probably describe it as a dance number rather than a song, not because it is a dance but because it gives the impression of dance. Like "The Rich Kids' Rag" it was not strictly dance or song, but musical theatre.

Another number that was designed to give Gwen a rest was squeezed into the show as a nightclub visit, with the disregard for motivation that Bob learned at George Abbott's feet. In an era of serious changes in the musical theatre, an era of *West Side Story, Fiddler on the Roof,* and *Cabaret,* such devices would make *Sweet Charity* seem lightweight despite its essential darkness and the ingenuity of its musical staging. Yet this nightclub sequence involved a dance that would prove as enduring as any ever created for Broadway, "The Rich Man's Frug."

Like "Who's Got the Pain?" and "Mu Cha Cha," it came out of Fosse's affection for popular dances. The title's reference to "Rich Kids' Rag" is based on a similar mockery of fancy people in the *Little Me* number, but that is the only connection between the two. "Frug" shows a maturing of Fosse's theatrical sense of dance, a willingness to depart from traditional regimentation in which every dancer does the same step. This dance is an exploration of visual dissonance. Everyone seems to be going in a different direction, leaning and tilting, angular and arch. The dance opens and closes like an exotic flower. As one of his dancers said, "Bob was becoming more about style than steps."

Preparing for the first runthrough, the girls slithered into Irene Sharaff's glittery dresses and the silk stockings with the hand-sewn beads. The dancers chuckled over the costume designer's fretting. "Don't do anything rough in these," Sharaff pleaded. *Rough?* The number was exhausting, even for dancers as young and as brilliantly conditioned as these. "Thousands of dollars they cost," Sharaff kept whispering as the girls wriggled into the delicate dresses.

Bob and Gwen sat in the empty theatre anticipating their first costumed sight of "The Rich Man's Frug." A dance, of course, is a look as well as steps. Its effect would be complete with the costumes.

The number started with the electrified disco beat of a "Rocksachord," the first electric keyboard to be heard on Broadway. The ensemble inched out in typical Fosse profile, cigarette holders and noses in the air, and with the first sudden thrusts, the first bumping jerks, the first knee bends, the costumes were in trouble. "Hold it! Hold it!" Fosse yelled, standing up in his seat and blowing his whistle. It was only halfway through the dance. "But by then," Elaine Cancilla remembered, "we looked as if we had all gone through a war. Jackets were torn, sleeves were down, backs were ripped open, and those gorgeous stockings were shredded."

"Break!" Fosse yelled. "Get out of those costumes!" He turned to Gwen beside him and said, "Find Sharaff." He turned and looked for his writers. "Doc! Cy! Dorothy!" They all headed for a meeting with the producers.

The costumes had to be scrapped no matter what they had cost. Gwen was the one with the solution. She herself had been dancing in a little black dress that looked like (and in fact was) a slip. With the dancers sent out for lunch, she showed the seamstresses how to whip up similar black shifts, suggesting that each be individualized by a slit up the side, or a design on the skirt, or with some differentiating trim. When rehearsals were resumed an hour later, "The Rich Man's Frug" had a new and more practical set of costumes.

It wasn't the only costume crisis. In Gwen's first scene in the Fan-Dango Ballroom dressing room, one of the girls was given a robe sewn with big and colorful patches. Like the "Frug" dresses, it was handmade with sequins and beads, and as Helen Gallagher said, "It was upstaging everybody." The first time the girl wore the robe on stage, she got no more than two steps past the wings before Bob shouted, "Out!"

Nearly half of Irene Sharaff's stunning and expensive costumes were ultimately discarded, and Gallagher said, "the other half were sprayed down with paint. The seamstresses were weeping. They had slaved over those clothes, they were gorgeous, but they had made it a show about costumes."

The ensemble dances notwithstanding, *Sweet Charity* was, first of all, a vehicle for Gwen Verdon and took its cue from her unique combination of sexuality and humor. That was spelled out in the picture of her that advertised the show, the same pose in which she appeared as the curtain rose. It was a stance that had her peering over a shoulder with a come-hither look of impure innocence. One hand rests casually on a jaunty fanny. One knee is locked, the other playfully bent, the foot resting back on a high heel with the toe up in the air. The picture and the pose represent the culmination of Fosse minimalism; it is a concentration of details, the holding of all isolated positions and movements in a single pose. It is precise down to the curling of a pinky on the hand that Gwen has placed on her thigh. This is dance in stopped action.

The show's first extended scene is interrupted by "If My Friends Could See Me Now" in which she dances with a top hat that seems to do everything short of singing the song. She has only two offstage breaks between this number and the second act's "I'm a Brass Band," which is just as flamboyant and draining. The show, in fact, was so much of a Verdon workout that as it shipped out to Detroit for the start of tryouts, the authors expressed concern that *Sweet Charity* would not only begin with Gwen Verdon but would also end when she left, as *Redhead* had.

The Fisher Theatre in Detroit did not bring back happy memories, being the site of *Pleasures and Palaces*, but *Sweet Charity* was looking fine, and Bob was relaxed, even having fun directing Gwen and John McMartin in a hotel bathtub with the shower curtains drawn to capture the oppressive feeling that the claustrophobic Oscar felt in an elevator. But there were tense moments too, as when Gwen (probably Bob) decided that she did not want to sing two slow songs in the show. The composer, Cy Coleman, had faith in his own brilliance, and it was justifiable, albeit coupled with an eagerness to convert the world to that faith. Coleman knew all about Fosse's limited enthusiasm for slow songs, but it was Gwen who was saying, "I have a small voice, Cy. I can only do one of these songs, either 'Where Am I Going?' or 'Poor Everybody Else,' but not both."

"You can have your pick," Bob said magnanimously to Coleman.

The composer grew exercised as the discussion heated up. Then Bob cut it short. "We're dropping one of them," he snapped, "and if you don't like it, you can go back to New York, and we'll pick which one ourselves."

"Hey, pal," Coleman said. "I'm the composer and the music is my department. Check it out with the Dramatists Guild."

Fosse looked at his friend for a long time before he responded. "Don't forget, Cy," he said quietly. "I've got Gwen."

Coleman turned and walked away and "Poor Everybody Else" was dropped, later to turn up in Coleman's *Seesaw*, but that was as bad as things ever got in Detroit.

As the show moved to Philadelphia for its final test, Bob invited some of his writer friends to come see it, but with Neil Simon as the author none of them was likely to suggest so much as a moved comma. They were more like a cheering section. Gwen brought Nicole and the nanny Hermocinda. Paddy Chayefsky came, and he brought Bob and Jane Aurthur, old friends of his and new ones of Bob's.

Robert Alan Aurthur was, like Paddy, a graduate of television's early dramatic era, its so-called golden age. Like Chayefsky, he had sought out the greater prestige of the theatre, but he was making his success (and money) as a producer and writer of movies. To his credit, as far as Fosse was concerned, Bob Aurthur refused to move to Los Angeles.

He was a solid and cuddly fellow, not dissimilar in appearance to Paddy, athletic and willing to smile a dazzling smile, and he had a great head of hair, curly and always wet-looking.

Everyone was basking in the glow of *Sweet Charity*'s out-of-town success. Fosse was especially proud of a staging joke he had devised for Gwen, having her light up a cigarette in the Italian actor's closet and then, fearing discovery, blowing the smoke into a clear plastic garment bag and zipping it shut. The bit of business always got a laugh, and Fosse probably appreciated the laugh more than most others because it was a vaudevillian joke, based on a prop and the visual impact of smoke in the bag.

Something else happened in that scene that was not so funny. A feather boa was hanging in the closet, and as Gwen breathed (through her mouth, as dancers tend to) she inhaled one of the feathers. Soon she began to complain of respiratory trouble, and after a few days she was wheezing. Still she played every performance and coached the dancers for hours afterward. "This line should be a little longer," she would say. "Put your arms a little higher, a little longer," as "The Rich Man's Frug" was rehearsed yet again. Then, she would awake early the next morning to tend to Nicole.

Until she found it difficult to breathe.

"I feel something in my throat," she said ominously.

The duck feather from the boa was wrapped around her vocal chords. She kept performing in the show until her voice grew so raspy and her discomfort so intense that she had to go into the hospital. Understudies usually aren't rehearsed until a show opens in New York, and so one performance had to be canceled while Helen Gallagher was run through the part. She played Charity for a week in Philadelphia but understudies ought to be sold in pharmacies, because they are cures for almost anything that ails the actor they are substituting for. In fact the only thing better for a star's health than an understudy is a Broadway opening night.

On the snowy January 29, 1966, that *Sweet Charity* opened at the Palace Theatre, Gwen was fully recovered and in dazzling form. Again and again, the glamorous first-nighters rose to their feet, applauding mightily as she stopped the show with her exhilarating dances, her irresistible demands for compassion, even her endearingly hoarse singing. After the last of the curtain calls, the big crowd clogged the aisles with elitist clubbiness about having been first to see New York's newest hit. Among those energized first-nighters, warmed against the winter cold by their exclusive involvement in this glittery event, was Herb Schlein, table host of the Carnegie Delicatessen. Once again, Bob had sent him tickets for a premiere, and this time, for the first time, Schlein had brought his mother, in part to prove that he actually did know Bob Fosse. Bob was smiling at him even now, as Herb and his mother were being shoved along by the crowd, through the auditorium doors and out into the lobby.

There, Ethel Schlein was telling her son that she wanted to meet Gwen Verdon.

"Opening night," Herb said exasperatedly. "You can't bother these people."

Somehow, through the din and the crowd and the shouting in his ear, Bob heard that, and he said, "Mrs. Schlein, would you like to meet my wife?"

"Oh!" she cried. "I'd love to meet her, but I know it's a very important night for you."

"It's an important night for your son too," he said, and the way he spoke assured Schlein that his friend Bob Fosse grasped the importance of this moment, that he understood and took pity. "He knew that I had a yen for this type of life," Schlein said. "The opening night of *Sweet Charity* was the first time that anyone in the show business world would meet one on one with my mother, informally, and let her know that I'm not nuts, I'm not crazy, I'm not off the wall, and I'm not that completely living in a fantasy.

"I did live in a fantasy," he admitted, "but I have met these people and some I have cultivated—nice relationships with. So I must have some qualities."

Fosse took mother and son by their elbows and steered them through a side door and down a corridor leading backstage to Gwen's dressing room. He led them past producers and theatre owners and investors and the boisterous opening nighters. Tapping at Gwen's dressing room door, Fosse said, "It's me," and ushered in the two Schleins.

"You're a favorite of mine," Ethel said.

"That's very nice of you to say," Gwen replied, smiling.

"You're my favorite dancer," the woman continued. "The best."

Then, at Herb's insistence, they left, but not until they were home in Elizabeth, New Jersey, did he finally say, "Look," his anger as constant as his pain. "I won't argue with you. You put me through hell in my life but somehow or other I need you, I'm dependent on you, and this is unhealthy. I can't seem to find my niche in life, and every time I lose a job or run out of money, I wouldn't dare go to anyone else."

"I wouldn't *want* you to go to anyone else," his mother replied. "You don't *need* to go to anyone else."

"But," the thirty-four-year-old Schlein continued, "I want to live to come to a time when I don't have to come to you, and I can stand on my own two feet and be independent of everyone and be in complete control of my life."

He was able to repeat all of this to Fosse, who had the patience and the compassion to listen, who invited such confessions, created such conversations; Fosse seemed to be more comfortable with those in pain than with the strong—more at ease in soul-baring conversations than in the thick of a noisy opening night party such as the one he was being swept through while Schlein was pleading for his independence from his mother.

As the critics' reviews arrived or were reported, the success of *Sweet Charity* seemed assured. By no means was there unqualified approval, but there were only raves for the great and beloved dancing star who had returned to reclaim Broadway. Gwen's reviews were enough to guarantee a long run. The show would be produced across the country, and ultimately many different dancers would play Charity Hope Valentine, so the authors' fears were unwarranted. This musical would most certainly have a life of its own, and yet it would be Gwen Verdon who would forever be identified with it, hers on which every performance would be modeled for she and Bob had added the creation of a star character, the creation of a performer style, to the usual ingredients of musical comedy.

But he wasn't getting credit for that, and the reviews angered him. Years later, he admitted to a friend that he had been bitter about the credit Gwen had been given while he was blamed for the show's shortcomings. "Whose performance do you think she gave anyhow?" he said. "Do they think a performance comes out of the air? She didn't make it up. A performance has to be directed. It has to be created."

He insisted that he was not angry with Gwen about that. She deserved her praise, he said, and had she been asked, she undoubtedly would have given him much of the credit for her performance, he said. But the critics treated the show as if it was her show, a Gwen Verdon show.

Sweet Charity was to run some six hundred performances on Broadway. The little family was on its way to financial security but not to family security. One Saturday, deep into the run, Gwen called Bob Aurthur. She had just finished a matinee performance, but she was distraught.

"Take it easy," Bob Aurthur said, "and tell me what the problem is."

"Bobby called," she quaked. "He told me he's having chest pains."

"Oh, shit," the writer said. "Can he get himself to a doctor?"

"I don't know. When I called home just now after the matinee, there was no answer. Nobody else was there, and I'm stuck here at the theatre." Her voice shook with even more than its normal quaver. "And," she said, "I've got another show to do in a couple of hours."

"Well, what can I do from here?" Aurthur asked. He was a hundred miles away in East Hampton.

"I don't have my book," Gwen said. "Could you give me Paddy's number? I'm very, very nervous."

He found the number for her, and the next morning he finally reached Fosse himself.

"Jesus Christ, are you okay?"

"Of course I'm okay," Bob said. "Why shouldn't I be?"

"You went to a doctor?"

"No. I have no reason to see a doctor."

"But what about the chest pains? Gwen said you were having chest pains."

"Oh, that," Bob said with a laugh. "There weren't any chest pains— but I hear that Gwen gave one hell of a performance last night."

12

Bob's professional representation was CMA, Creative Management Associates. The agency and its clients were part of the dust that had cleared after the Justice Department broke up MCA (Music Corporation of America) in 1962. When that giant talent agency was forced to choose between producing television shows and representing the people who directed and acted in them, its management chose production. The choice had hardly been difficult as the television shows were by far the greater source of revenue. Beyond television, however, loomed the company's true target.

Whatever the movies meant to the public, whether they were entertainment, glamour, or even national mythology, to the executives at MCA, the movies meant the big time in American show business, and exactly one month before shedding the talent business, the company acquired Universal Pictures. Its agents, meantime, had dispersed and regrouped, taking their clients with them to second-generation agencies. Freddie Fields and David Begelman, for instance, started CMA, bringing with them such clients as Judy Garland, Barbra Streisand, and Bob Fosse.

Agency is a fascinating notion. It is the acting of one person in the place of another, the acting of one person *for* another. While the client has the actual creative ability, he is encouraged to become dependent on the calculation, the ambition, and the grand design of the agent to exploit that ability. This provides the agent with a purpose, and the artist sometimes becomes a ward, even a commodity. In that case, he is referred to simply as "the talent."

It would be unfair as well as inaccurate to characterize all agents as manipulative, parasitic, or predatory. Their function of career and financial management is a necessary one, and most creative people prefer to pay professionals to perform it, as one would pay an attorney or an accountant. Yet agents are inevitably cast as villains because they seem to be paid for what the artists do.

In a way they play Archbishops of Canterbury to their royalty in a realm where the state religion is deal making. The brilliance of the agent's maneuvering is his creativity, the deal is his work of art, and in 1967 nobody was taking the art of agency more seriously than the agents themselves. So it was not by chance that this, the largest of the agencies spawned by MCA, was called Creative Management Associates. In the end, the MCA men who worked there (and at the other new agencies) would come to dominate Hollywood, running the movie studios. As in *The Invasion of the Body Snatchers*, then, the representation would come to control the thing itself.

Since the time of *Call Me Mister*, Bob's agent at MCA had been Maurice LePugh, a man who was, as his name might suggest, of the old school. He was essentially a negotiator of contracts for Fosse the actor and then Fosse the choreographer and director. But now that *Sweet Charity* was attracting movie interest, the Fosse career was being taken out of LePugh's hands, and he was being "looked after" (as a more suave generation of agents would put it) by higher-ups. So it was that the film rights to the Gwen Verdon musical were sold to CMA's former self, MCA-Universal Pictures, with an eye toward furthering Fosse's career.

The artistry of the deal lay in the provision that he would direct the picture. That was creative management, and thus it would come to pass, as Bob had vowed to Buddy Hackett in 1947 and as he had forewarned Arlene Dahl and Fernando Lamas and Pier Angeli and Ricardo Montalban around the Writers Table in the MGM commissary in 1952, he was going to be a movie director. As Daniel Melnick said, "*Sweet Charity* was about coming back as a conqueror."

Melnick, who would become head of MGM and later produce Bob's movie, *All That Jazz*, remembered him as a 1952 contract player who "had done all those parts that Donald O'Connor didn't do. Now," Melnick said, "after Bobby had made his success on Broadway, he wanted to make it in the world that he thought was the big league."

The movies were indeed the big leagues of show business. Broadway was only Broadway to Broadway. Fosse had told Buddy Hackett that he considered the stage "just a step along the way to directing movies." The great Elia Kazan had long since abandoned the theatre to direct films. It seems fair to hypothesize that Fosse's emotional and professional impulses were setting him in the same direction.

The *Sweet Charity* deal done, Bob took Nicole to summer in Amagansett while Gwen was playing her eight shows a week at the Palace. The little girl was four years old, the age of perfection, and she made his heart swoon. Too, the house at the beach was more fun all the time. Just as in his adolescence, for a shy person Fosse was very good at friends. He was finding that writers were his type, or at least he wanted to be their type. He spent lots of time with Bob Aurthur and befriended another pal of Paddy Chayefsky's, the playwright Herb Gardner. Old friends like Doc Simon, Cy Feuer, Frank Loesser, and Cy Coleman were still in the general neighborhood. Simon had sold his house up the road but his new place was in nearby East Hampton, and Bob frequently drove over to visit Neil and Joan, bringing Nicole along to play with the kids. He especially liked to watch 'them dance, and he told nine-year-old Ellen Simon it was useful to him as a choreographer "because what children do comes so naturally."

One afternoon, he put on a record in the Simons' living room and said to Ellen and the two four-year-olds, her sister Nancy and his own Nicole, "Just dance to this, dance any way you like, kids. I'm going to copy whatever you do. Whatever movement you do, I'm going to imitate."

It wasn't show music that he put on, but rock and roll. Fosse knew his youngsters, and Ellen, who had already taken to dancing, started to boogie.

"He loved it when I did that," she remembered many years later, "and he copied me, and it was just thrilling, I remember that, because even though I was a kid I still knew it was Bob Fosse."

The former Simon house in Amagansett had been bought by Sam Cohn, an agent at CMA and a man whom Bob was going to enjoy, but then he was enjoying almost everyone and everything, even sports. He had seldom been seen at athletics; dancing was exercise enough. But suddenly he was slamming around Sam Cohn's Ping-Pong table or water skiing with Bob Aurthur, taking turns steering the boat. Why, nobody had even seen Fosse in a bathing suit since swim team at Amundsen High, but then this summer of 1967 was vigorous and vital, and he was finding women and his sexuality too heady not to enjoy. He was rushing toward forty and had been married for six years. Beautiful young women, actresses and dancers, were excited by his fame and power, and it was an era of exhilarating sexual liberation, of pleasure seemingly for the taking. Gwen was busy with the show, and as Fosse would later say, "Whenever we were working together, it was great. It was when work was over that things started to go bad."

Well, work was over, he had girlfriends, and acquaintances were willing to bet that Gwen knew.

He spent the winter tending to the industry that a hit Broadway musical can become, directing secondary productions of *Sweet Charity* and romancing their leading ladies. And then he went to California to begin work on the movie version. His unwillingness or inability to resist sexual temptation was putting a real strain on the marriage. He told a friend, "When I started wanting to work away, that changed things. Ah," he paused and shrugged his shoulders, "it's too complicated."

In his less than beloved Los Angeles, he went to work with Peter Stone, who had been assigned to write the screenplay of *Sweet Charity.* He looked at all the Federico Fellini movies with his old friend Stanley Donen. He scouted locations with Robert Surtees, the cinematographer who would be working with him. And he hung out with his new water-skiing friend, Bob Aurthur, who had also gone west, to write and direct a remake of the thriller classic *Odd Man Out,* to be called *The Lost Man* and to star Sidney Poitier. That, too, was being made at MCA-Universal Pictures.

As 1968 began, MCA was building a new headquarters in North Hollywood, a complex to be centered on and symbolized by the so-called Black Tower, a dark glass skyscraper rising incongruously and ominously from the Southern California hills. As yet, however, the old Universal remained in its original offices, sound stages, and back lots. "Not only did it look like the old days," Stone remembered, "but it was the last of the studios to stick with the star system, and so it really felt like the old days."

Each morning, he would bring his script to Bob's office, which was half of a bungalow. Most of the directors, writers, and stars were given such cottages, two offices with a common porch, set back on secluded stretches of lawn, shaded by palm trees, and spaced comfortably along winding lanes. To complete this idyllic picture, squirrels scampered across the lawns as if stocked there like bass in a lake. The studio provided electric carts to transport the actors, directors, and writers from these bungalows to the sound stages, and on any given morning, the many contract people at Universal could be seen on star parade—Marlon Brando, Paul Newman, Anthony Perkins, Tony Curtis, Alfred Hitchcock, and the superstars of the studio, Rock Hudson and Doris Day—all perched on their little electric carts, gliding in commonplace celebrity along the curving lanes beneath the palm trees, breezily shooing squirrels from their paths as if they were in a Walt Disney cartoon.

Peter Stone was a tall, bespectacled, curly haired, extremely funny fellow in his thirties, and he was wise to the ways of Hollywood. He had grown up there, the son of a movie producer, and he was very confident of himself, for professional as well as genealogic reasons. In 1964 he had won an Academy Award for writing *Father Goose,* and in Hollywood an Oscar was a license for two years' worth of confidence at least. Stone was fascinated with the notion of taking a show that had been based on a movie and turning it back into a movie, but remaking a Federico Fellini movie from a Broadway musical into a musical movie set in New York City was something that gave him pause. "The realism of a movie is overwhelming," he told Fosse. "You can't have real people standing in the middle of a real street in New York, singing and dancing. That's over. And you can't pretend that a bunch of hookers are dance-hall hostesses. Besides, there aren't any more dance halls."

Actually, there still was one operating in Times Square, the ironically named Maiden Lane Dance Hall. Bob had done some of his research there, and furthermore, he pointed out to Stone, the movie of *West Side Story* had actors singing and dancing in the streets of New York, and "it worked there, didn't it?" There was no arguing with that. *West Side Story* was an immensely successful film.

While *Sweet Charity* would look as if it were being sung and danced in the streets of New York, in fact little of it would be photographed there. Even the real bridge from which Shirley MacLaine was shoved into a real pond at the movie's outset was not a Central Park bridge but a California bridge over a California pond in a California park.

MacLaine. She was going to play Charity in the movie. It must have come as a nightmare to Gwen Verdon, who had been Charity Hope Valentine on the stage and in the advertisements and on the posters, who was Charity in character and dance style and certainly in the Broadway audience's mind, who had been the model for Charity, whose every move and mannerism had lovingly been grafted onto the character. "Bob had made a musical," Stone said, "that was actually based on his wife's form," and his wife was not going to play her.

Was she not star enough for Universal Pictures? Was she too old? She was only seven years older than the thirty-three-year-old MacLaine (all right, nine), but how old was Charity supposed to be anyhow? She was not a twenty-year-old Holly Golightly.

Bob said that when the studio linked its purchase of *Sweet Charity* to Shirley MacLaine, "I went to Gwen, and I said, 'How do you feel about it?' And she said, 'Fine, please do it. It's your movie and your property. You instigated it, you should see it through to the ultimate of what you can do with it.'" But that sounded suspiciously like his words in her mouth. More likely, *he* thought it was his property, because "Gwen was incredibly disappointed," according to Kathryn Doby, who would dance in the movie and later become Bob's chief assistant. "She should have played that part."

When the Broadway show closed, Gwen packed up her daughter and her pride and joined her husband. They found a rentable house in

Westwood, away from Beverly Hills and closer to the ocean they loved so much, and they enrolled Nicole in a kindergarten.

Bob had already whipped Shirley MacLaine into the shape of her life. He had been flogging at her in a studio for weeks before Gwen came. MacLaine hadn't danced seriously since the fateful night she had stepped in for Carol Haney in *The Pajama Game*. Now she was in prime condition, and perhaps inevitably Gwen began coming to help out. As if she were coaching Marilyn Monroe or Jane Russell in how to sing and dance, she coached Shirley MacLaine in how to sing and dance like Gwen Verdon.

"I don't know how she did it," Kathy Doby said. "To come here and actually work with her." To Ralph Burns, who was again writing the orchestrations, "She was made of iron."

One evening, when Pat Ferrier and her husband, Richard Kiley, came to the house for dinner and, Pat remembered, "There was an awful lot of rum being poured," Gwen expressed her fears about growing older. It was a moment of exceptional candor, but if she was frank with anyone, it was with Pat Ferrier, who had danced with her in *Damn Yankees* and *Redhead*. Now, she gloomily admitted, neither age nor death terrified her as much as her dancing coming to an end. It must have seemed ironic that not long ago she had voluntarily retired to help conceive Nicole. Now the biological clock was again running out on her, only this time for dancing. Perhaps Ethel Martin, who had been in the Jack Cole troupe with her, put it most eloquently. "When dancers get to that point in life," she said, "where they can't dance or shouldn't, very many are at a total loss. Because that thrill is gone—that high, it's indescribable, this wonderful feeling of performing and making it happen and being onstage and getting your blood going. People don't realize what a hold it has on you."

Now Gwen had to let go. She was passing her peak as Bob was reaching his.

Although he had written the first draft of *Sweet Charity*, its revision by Neil Simon had apparently disengaged him from the script, and he gave Peter Stone freedom in transposing it to the screen. In the meantime, he played with Bob Aurthur. On days when Gwen stayed back, the two men would give each other lifts to the studio. As they pulled up to one or the other's bungalow, they would speculate on a Hollywood future where they would have their own Bob and Bob Building with their own Bob and Bob Parking Lot, a lot with just two parking spaces, as compared with the studio lots that had hierarchies of reserved spaces for executives and stars, arranged in elaborate pecking orders. The only problem with the Bob and

Bob Parking Lot, they laughed, was which one of them would get the more prestigious parking space.

Jane Aurthur described her husband as "a born fan." Bob Aurthur was so taken with Fosse that he even copied the costume, going to Universal every day in black jeans and a black shirt. Most days they would have lunch together in the pretty Sun Room, which was the studio commissary. Fosse often brought a girlfriend, and Aurthur was amused by the comparative seduction styles of Bob and Sidney Poitier, whom he was directing in *The Lost Man*. The handsome actor had a gambit that he seemed to use with every girl he went out with. At some point during lunch or dinner, Poitier would reach across the table, take the girl's hand, look deeply into her eyes, and whisper hoarsely, "You know . . . you really are very lovely." He would say it in a lower and hoarser voice with every succeeding date and would appear serious about it even when other people were at the table, like the Aurthurs. Bob's wife Jane said, "After watching Sidney do the same thing," and she lowered her voice an octave, " 'You know, you really are very lovely'—with four different girls on four consecutive nights—I had to leave the table to keep from bursting into laughter."

Fosse's approach was subtler. He never made an outright overture. Rather, his approach was to act like a girlfriend. He might say, "Maybe you should try your hair another way. Let's see how it looks pulled back. Come on, show me." He became their confidant.

As if to make up for imposing Shirley MacLaine on him, Universal left the rest of the casting to Bob. He kept his Broadway leading man, John McMartin. He drew his dancers from New York regulars, the Bob Fosse Greek Chorus, some were beginning to call them. Among them were Suzanne Charney, Kathy Doby, Ben Vereen, and Lee Roy Reams. Studio executives made occasional suggestions. Diana Ross, for instance, was proposed to play the one black girl among the dance hostesses (Bob hired Paula Kelly), and Rita Moreno was pushed for Charity's best friend (Bob took Chita Rivera). Fosse himself thought up the notion of hiring Sammy Davis, Jr., to appear in a cameo role singing "The Rhythm of Life," and since Peter Stone knew the entertainer, he was assigned to sell him on the part. Stone flew to Las Vegas in Davis's private jet and came back with the deal, not even having to spend the night.

On the first day of filming, it was customary for a studio's publicity department to invite the press on the set. At this promotional event for *Sweet Charity*, there was a heavy turnout of reporters and photographers, and as Bob was posing with Shirley MacLaine, demonstrating dance steps for the popping flashbulbs, Gwen was recognized among the onlookers and asked if she would also pose with the star of the movie. Thus, and only by chance, did it emerge that Gwen Verdon was coaching Shirley Mac-Laine in how to play the role that she had created and lost. There was a great deal of newspaper coverage on this angle, and there were pictures of Gwen and Shirley MacLaine throughout the movie-oriented Los Angeles press. It was wonderful publicity, although Gwen probably loved it less than some.

It was seven months, writing, casting, rehearsing, and making the movie, and certain details of the finished film make for interesting foot-notes. A lengthy courtship sequence between Charity and Oscar is a rare expression of sentiment by Fosse. This sequence is accompanied by music he specifically asked Ralph Burns to derive from Erik Satie's "Gym-nopédie's No. 1." Burns shamelessly paraphrased the exquisite piece, even mimicking Claude Debussy's orchestration, and Fosse used it to accom-pany Charity and Oscar through a series of idyllic and romantic reveries.

Elsewhere in the movie and again at Bob's request, Burns imitated the then-popular style of Herb Alpert and the Tijuana Brass. Fosse was so taken with this catchy sound that he enthused to Peter Stone about a mariachi stage musical based on the movie, *Big Deal on Madonna Street*. He had for years been interested in musicalizing this picture for Broad-way. Stone's reaction was terse and canny. "A bunch of bungling Italian crooks is funny," he said, "but make them Mexican, and it's sad."

Perhaps saddest and most telling is the end of *Sweet Charity*, when Oscar deserts Charity at the marriage license bureau. "Don't you see?" he cries. "I would destroy you." "It's okay," she replies, "I'm not doing much of anything anyhow," but there is no staying him. "Oh, God, forgive me," he groans, and dashes down the corridor where he mournfully repeats, "Please forgive me."

This was not in the Broadway show. This is Fosse, wretched in his inability to feel or at least to express feeling; this is Fosse regretting the pain he inflicts, agonizing over his repeated failures to sustain relation-ships, asking forgiveness for the abandonment that inevitably awaits Gwen, his Charity.

Universal was not happy with his gloomy ending, and Fosse agreed to film an alternate. He would always be uniquely practical among the artistic film directors, on the one hand difficult and even obstinate, yet never taking the obvious, idealistic stand, being too good a student of George Abbott for that. He prevailed in keeping his original ending in the released version of *Sweet Charity* and met little resistance because the studio executives were wallowing in optimism. Making their expectations even rosier were the advance reviews from the "trades," *Variety* and *The Hollywood Reporter*. Universal was anticipating a major payoff on its unusually large ($10 million) investment. Bob had gone over the budget by $3 million, it was true, but Universal tended toward expensive pictures, and considering the general euphoria, nobody was worried about a few million dollars.

Except Bob. He was worried about the whole movie. He had months to wait before its release, and that was making him even more anxious, as he told the personable top executive at the CMA office. As a matter of fact, Bob said, "You're the only guy in this place I can talk to. The others are too Los Angeles for me."

"Well, I live in New York," the fellow said, "and I work out of the CMA office in New York." His name was David Begelman, and he was a dark, robust, sophisticated man of considerable intelligence. His interest in show business was positively erudite. He was knowing about high-powered, international show business, and yet, as Fosse was delightedly learning, he was equally knowledgeable about vaudeville and nightclubs. Bob never got over his Frederic Weaver education. He enjoyed nothing more than remembering old acts and routines, and David Begelman could even talk about the old act of Fosse and Niles with the wisdom of someone who knew fifty such acts. He could describe them all, their music, their routines, their costumes, and he did this with a benign and easy charm.

"It's perfectly normal for you to be worried about your movie," he told Fosse. "It's your beautiful baby, and now the rest of the world is going to pass judgment on it. They're going to look at it this way and that, and say it's big or it's little or it's fat or it's skinny. . . ."

"I know all that," Bob said, "but it doesn't make me any less worried."

"Get to work on something else," Begelman suggested, and by the time the conversation was finished, he and Bob had arrived at an agreement. "I became the responsible agent," he said, "and I looked after him."

Begelman found a property that interested Fosse, a thriller novel called *Burnt Offerings* written by Robert Marasco, who had recently written a successful Broadway thriller, *Child's Play*. Bob started work on the script, but he was much too edgy to concentrate thoroughly, and by the time he found himself at the New York premiere of *Sweet Charity*, he was so agitated that he couldn't sit still to watch. He got up and left the Rivoli Theatre, asking Richard and Pat Kiley to look after Gwen. He sought out the comforting glare of Times Square, walking off his nerves along the garish few blocks to the Maiden Lane Dance Hall at 47th Street on the west side of Broadway. He trotted up the flight of stairs and pushed through the glass doors. The dance floor was harsh in its bare wood, the decor whorehouse red. The dance hostesses approached him as if he were a customer. They didn't know who Bob Fosse was; they certainly didn't remember him from his research visits. That had been almost three years earlier, and most of the girls were different anyhow.

They weren't as beautiful as the girls in "Hey, Big Spender." They were certainly cruder. They surely weren't as good dancers, but they were good at what they did, dancing all slithered up and hanging on a man's bones with their hips and thighs and knees pushing through thin dresses.

He said he hadn't come to dance. He only wanted their good luck wishes for his movie and gave each of them a twenty dollar bill just for that. It wasn't enough.

The reviews were not good, and everything said about *Sweet Charity* seemed to be based on its opening sequence, for Bob had cinematographer Bob Surtees zooming in and out of Griffith Park as if the camera had been on a telescoping roller coaster, and that was just for a start. The dark story and the spectacular musical numbers faded into the background, upstaged by the fledgling director's movie pyrotechnics. He played among the photographic devices, swooping from long shots to close-ups, twisting in and out of focus, dallying with freeze frames and slow motion, shooting in shadows and in silence. Surtees seemed to go along with his every whim. The cinematographer had just finished work on *The Arrangement* for another Broadway director, the most prestigious of all, Elia Kazan. Perhaps he had an extra case of the awestruck and did not give Fosse the feedback that might have profited a newcomer. Instead, the striking and considerable qualities of *Sweet Charity*, many of them creative and soon to be exploited by Fosse in *Cabaret*, were lost in the flash of camerawork. A destined master was at work; that much is plain when one looks at the picture from the perspective of Fosse's later work. But without the perspective, it is easy to miss the potential, for the indulgences are blatant and often naive. "When I finished it," Bob said, "I thought it was very, very good." But, he added, in something of an understatement, "I guess I had too many cinematic tricks in it. I was trying to be kind of flashy. That's a pitfall on your first film."

"I don't know what went wrong," he went on to say. "The trade papers predicted it would be the biggest moneymaker of all time. Suddenly *Time* magazine whacked it, *Newsweek* whacked it. It just didn't do well . . . and Universal oversold it."

The movie wasn't a disaster. As Peter Stone said in mock Hollywoodese, "It may have been a flop, but it wasn't a *flopflop*. Let's say that compared to what Universal expected, it was a disappointment."

The studio, in fact, became frantic and replaced Bob's ending with the happier alternate. In that version, Oscar goes home after fleeing the marriage bureau, only to become claustrophobic and go out into Central Park where he sees Charity about to leap (he thinks) into the pond. He saves her life, and as John McMartin described it, "They walk off into the sunset."

In addition, or subtraction, the studio edited some fifteen minutes out of the two-hour-and-twenty-minute movie. "They're in business," Bob said reasonably, "you can't blame them. The only thing is, they didn't call me. If they'd said, 'We want to take some of it out, we'd like to have your ideas,' I could have taken twenty minutes out." He would have, too, and it probably wouldn't have made any difference. Universal only half-heartedly distributed the revised version anyway.

According to David Begelman, "The failure of *Sweet Charity* caused a rift at the highest echelons of MCA. There was a group of people who thought the company just didn't know how to make movies. They had been making a lot of money in television, but they had been trucking along for seven or eight years without any success or distinction in feature films."

Between 1966 and 1968, MCA grossed nearly $225 million from its Decca Records subsidiary and television production. Yet the company still faced an $80 million debt, because its film division, Universal Pictures, produced such box office disasters as *Thoroughly Modern Millie, The Loves of Isadora*, and now this.

"To a lot of people," Begelman said, "*Sweet Charity* seemed final proof that they should get the hell out of the movie business." And so while this very gifted and very insecure first-time director thought that he had merely made less than a hit with his debut movie, he had unknowingly stirred up a major crisis at MCA-Universal. He was going to suffer for it, suffer more than such a striking first effort deserved. As Begelman said, "The rift it caused at MCA was so serious that it almost changed the management of the company at the very top. To this day," he said, "there are certain scars that will never clear even though some of those players are now dead . . . Bobby just made the best picture he knew how, but there was this whole scenario in the background."

MCA probably would have quit the movie business too, Begelman speculated, had it not been for *Airport*, which was already finished. "It was the kind of picture which, given their frame of mind, would never have been made, but they had already made it, and it hit a home run. And that started Universal being a prime presence."

Airport would help Universal but not Fosse. Everything had been going so well, and suddenly, he said, "I got so cold." The way he said it was itself enough to evoke a shudder. *So cold.* He would say it with a hollow whistle, with his shoulders hunched and his eyes sunken. "No one called me," he said, a one-man echo chamber. "No one wanted anything to do with me."

Begelman didn't think it was quite that bad. "You don't kill a career," he said. "You just put it on retard. You put it on hold. You slow it down. I think it put Bobby back on a time schedule, and the problem with that is you don't see an end to it."

Someone as depression-prone as Bob Fosse does not easily handle a confirmation of his most dreaded nightmares. To him, the situation seemed dire. Begelman, like many good agents, could play psychoanalyst to his clients with great perception and sensitivity. "As an ambitious filmmaker," he said, "Bob didn't see how he could ever get to his destination. He was afraid that somehow he had been 'found out.' The worst fears and inner demons went to work. In his darkest moments, at night, all alone, he probably thought, 'I'll never work again.' "

Bob told his friends that was exactly how he felt.

13

It did not usually rain so hard in New York City during the summer but Bob was probably glad to be back no matter what the weather. Paddy Chayefsky greeted him like a little boy who had gone too long without anyone to play with, and his first suggestion was that Bob join him as co-fire warden of the eleventh floor in their office building. No recruitment speech was necessary; Fosse signed up at once. Lionel Larner, in suite 1101 next door to Bob, only hoped that there would never be a fire.

Then it was down to the Carnegie Delicatessen for lunch, as if Paddy had been the one deprived of pastrami sandwiches. He was in so much of a rush that he didn't bother with a raincoat or an umbrella, standing outside Bob's door and roaring his traditional, "Fosse! Let's eat!" By the time they reached the lobby and saw the downpour, it was too much trouble to go back for wet weather gear. The Carnegie, after all, was only a few steps away, and Chayefsky suggested they make a dash for it.

Pushing through the building's front door, he started to run only to take a sloshing slide and flop on his backside, splattering himself in a puddle. He lay sprawled on the wet sidewalk, stunned and shaken, the rain splashing his startled face, and Fosse rushed after him and, struggling to express concern in some way, stood over his friend and laughed and applauded in the downpour.

"That was fantastic, Paddy!" he cried. "It was the greatest fall I ever saw in my life! Do it again!"

In vaudeville a pratfall isn't a real fall, and that is why it can be funny, even lovable, but a real one like Paddy's can hurt. Bob's real fall, the real hurt, was yet to come, for the failure of the *Sweet Charity* movie was only the beginning. He was on schedule for a midlife crisis. He had just passed the forty-year mark and was trying for forty-one.

His birthday fell just eleven days short of Neil Simon's, which came on the Fourth of July. "I always look up to you," Doc would grin on such occasions, or if it was Bob's birthday, he would stand up and give his pal a seat, saying, "It's okay, I understand. The legs are the first to go." The bitchy side of Fosse would rise up defensively to reply, "In the first eleven days of my life, Doc, before you were born, I had more girls than you would ever have in all your life." And it was almost true, that was what was almost funny about it.

After Paddy's flop on the sidewalk and Bob's in Hollywood, the summer stretched into a winter that was seemingly without end. He was dead in the movie business, not working and not being asked to.

It was different in the theatre business. Those offers were coming in all the time, but Fosse was not interested in them, because they were not movie offers. They were offers to direct musicals. "The other guys," David Begelman said, "were going from show to show, fellows like Gower Champion and George Abbott." Even Harold Prince, the producer who shared so much history with Bob, had become a successful director with such hit musicals as *She Loves Me* and *Cabaret*. "But Bob didn't want to do that, one musical after another," his agent said. "If he was going to do theatre, it would have to be something of his own invention."

Despite a conviction, then, that he was a nonentity in the movie business, he was still Bob Fosse on Broadway. Yet Begelman understood that a hole had been blown in the Fosse ego and that it was going to have to be filled in Hollywood, not on Broadway. For Bob had made an emotional, a professional, and a public commitment to moviemaking. If he quit now, he would be crawling back to the stage in defeat.

"It's a real comment on show business," he would tell an interviewer in response to a question about *Sweet Charity*. "I was offered about forty-three movies after the smash reviews in *Variety* and *The Hollywood Reporter*, but after business went down, nobody would talk to me. You've heard that story before, but I can testify to it."

He misdiagnosed the disease he was carrying. It was not merely the lackluster box office showing of his movie that had damaged his reputation; he had nearly destroyed Universal Pictures. That was his stigma.

Fosse shook his head. "Only one guy said, 'It was great, and now I want you to do a movie for me.'" The guy was Lawrence Turman, who had produced *The Graduate* and who was now agreeable to producing *Burnt Offerings*. Bob's friend, director Stanley Donen, thought it was a bad idea. "Don't do it!" he pleaded. "It's no damned good. Why are you doing it?"

"I've got to do something," Bob said quietly. "I need the work."

He spent three months preparing *Burnt Offerings*, working out a budget and scouting locations with the designer Tony Walton, but the project ultimately fizzled, and he began sliding into a depression. After nearly a year as a movie director, a year begun on a dizzying crest, he was taking a swan dive into limbo.

Begelman sought out an associate at CMA, Sam Cohn. Already friendly with Fosse, Cohn was a short, ruddy, sandy-haired package of some forty years, a fellow whose sharp blue eyes pierced his glasses with a dangerous brilliance. Not at all dapper like David Begelman, he had a look of his own creation. He invariably wore collegiate sweaters and open-collared shirts, even to fancy restaurants or the theatre. Cohn was so inventive a nonconformist that he snipped off the status-significant gold stirrups from his Gucci loafers, which had already made him a legend in circles that cared about such things, but although his style and his tousled hair made him seem casual, his brains and a commitment to his clients were making him the wicked whiz of all agentry.

"Sam was a good soldier," David Begelman said, "and when I told him I wanted something for Bob Fosse, something that would excite him, he put his shoulder to the wheel."

Cohn represented a young playwright named Steve Tesich who had written a screenplay that was being, as they said, "shopped around," offered and rejected. It was called *The Eagle of Naptown* because it was set in Indianapolis, a city known to the locals as Naptown the way Chicago was once called Chi and San Francisco Frisco. Using the metaphor of bicycle racing, Tesich's story dealt warmly and humorously with an adolescent's coming of age, and both Fosse and Begelman were excited about it. They met regularly to work out a production budget, and Begelman felt Fosse was emerging from his gloom into a more productive state of mind. When the two of them finished their research, organizing, and financial planning, they had the picture whittled down to an $800,000 budget, which Begelman considered "amazing." He took the figures and the script to David Picker, the then president of United Artists, "and I did the best pitch I could" but Picker turned the project down, and that, Begelman said, "was almost as crushing to Bob as *Sweet Charity*." (In 1978, *The Eagle of Naptown* was finally and successfully produced under the title *Breaking Away*. Cohn was still Tesich's agent. He had stuck doggedly with the screenplay for ten years.)

Gwen and Bob were living on savings. "They never had any dough," Begelman said, "not enough to have any independence. But they came from the Broadway gypsy tradition, so they didn't need much money, just enough to get by."

They had their friends, but when you are out of work, successful friends can be depressing, especially when they are as successful as were

Harold Prince and Doc Simon. Gwen stayed home the memorable evening that Bob spent with them. There were strains at home, and he would later recall these as the years of "a bad marriage."

It was meant to be dinner for six, Neil and Joan Simon, Hal and Judy Prince, Bob and Gwen. Prince and Fosse weren't exactly pals, but they were amiable despite the stresses and distresses of the past. Now Prince was a director as well as a producer and thus was not strictly a money person. He had also married Judy Chaplin, the daughter of Bob's old friend at MGM, Saul Chaplin. Judy was a beautiful young woman, clever and show-wise, a gifted pianist, and a longtime Fosse fan. Bob was not about to sacrifice his affection for her, not even for the sake of a grudge stretching back to *Damn Yankees* and *New Girl in Town*. He rang the doorbell at the Simon town house on East 62nd Street, and when the door was opened, he strolled into Judy's big waiting hug, and Neil's and Joan's. There were the perfunctory "How's Gwen?" and "Hope Gwen's feeling better," but polite company did not ask, and so it was just five for dinner. Afterward they all moved into the living room for coffee, and they sat and talked. Prince was on his way to winning more Tony Awards than any other director on Broadway. Simon was already the most popular (and richest) playwright in the history of the theatre. Fosse, sitting cross-legged on the floor, was probably convinced he had never deserved to be a success, wasn't one now, and never would be one again.

Ordinarily, they would have talked show business. Lawyers talk about cases, surgeons talk about operations, and theatre people talk about shows. But having a summer house had become a way of life too, and that was especially topical now that the Princes had bought one in, of all places, Majorca. It was a house high atop a hill. It had a swimming pool and a spectacular view of the island, with the glittering Mediterranean beyond. It was far away, and yet it wasn't, since most of their friends went to Europe for work or summer vacations. They were already inviting people to stay with them for a week or two next summer.

Neil and Joan said they were themselves leaving East Hampton, at least for the summer of 1971, to give Majorca a try. They had found a house to rent "and, Bobby, maybe you and Gwen can come and visit." The offer went unanswered, and the subject was dropped in favor of shop talk, show talk. Prince had just come back from Germany where he had been directing his first movie, *Something for Everyone*, starring Angela Lansbury, and he was about to go into rehearsal with a new Stephen Sondheim show. That was why he wasn't doing the movie of *Cabaret*, he said.

"The movie of *Cabaret*?" Bob asked, rising from the dead.

Prince had produced and directed *Cabaret* on Broadway. "Bob," he remembered, "was very enthusiastic about it. Now he wanted to know exactly and in detail how we had achieved all of our production effects."

"Who's producing it?" Bob asked nonchalantly.

Prince smoothed his beard. The goatee was new to him. It made him look less like a businessman and more artistic, which befit a producer turned director. He was a charter member of what would become Broadway's Beard Mafia. Jerome Robbins had started it. Stephen Sondheim would follow Prince into the club, and then Fosse himself, but right now the cleft in Bob's chin was still there, to see and rub.

"Allied Artists and ABC Pictures," Prince replied. "They're cofinancing it."

"But who's the producer? Who's the guy?" He was only slightly desperate.

"It's Cy Feuer," Prince said, God's messenger.

The next day Bob called Cy for lunch. "It may have been for lunch," Feuer remembered, "and it may have been in a restaurant, but Fosse was much too excited to eat."

The business lunch ritual usually doesn't call for the subject to be brought up until somewhere between coffee and the check, but Bob was talking about the movie as they hit the table.

"What about *Cabaret*?"

"What about it?"

"You're producing it, aren't you?"

"That's right," his old friend said, and Feuer went on to say that several major decisions had already been made. Jay Presson Allen was writing the screenplay, and Liza Minnelli was going to play Sally Bowles, the young British singer in the German club. The Broadway show had been written for Minnelli but Prince had rejected her as too American for the role. She had since been nominated for an Academy Award for *The Sterile Cuckoo*. "I went to see her sing at the Olympia Theatre in Paris," Feuer said, "and, boy, she was fantastic."

Joel Grey, too, had already been hired and was to repeat his stage performance.

"And the director?" Fosse asked, with a calmness bordering on mania. "What about the director?"

"That was Fosse," Feuer remembered with a laugh. "He always came out swinging."

"I've got to do it," Bob said to his friend. "It's my last shot. I can't get arrested in Hollywood."

"I don't have to tell you what I think of your work," Feuer said.

"Well, I hear you're seeing everyone."

"I have to."

The chief executives at Allied Artists (Manny Wolf) and ABC Pictures (Marty Baum) were urging Feuer to talk to the biggest names in directing. They liked Joseph Mankiewicz. Gene Kelly wanted to do it.

"We go back such a long way, Cy—"

"Look, I have to see the other guys," Feuer said. "After I see them, I can go in and tell the studio, 'Okay, I've seen everyone you've suggested, and I want Fosse.' "

"Yeah?" Bob asked, desperate for reassurance.

"*My* mind is made up," Feuer said, "but if I refuse to see those guys, I'll seem unreasonable. I'll get you the job. Don't worry."

Hah.

Feuer still had some selling to do. Baum acknowledged that Fosse might be wonderful, but everything about *Sweet Charity* worried him, from photographic excesses to cost overrun. The picture had gone $3 million over its $7 million budget. The entire budget for *Cabaret* was $3 million, "a tight collar," the tough-talking Feuer called it. In fact the film was being made at Bavaria Studio in Munich not only for atmospheric reasons but economic ones.

"It's my job to keep him in line," he said about Fosse's spending.

"This is a serious story," Baum said. "Can he direct?"

"Here's my bet," Feuer said. "If the book is directed ten percent less and all the musical numbers work, then you have a shot. But if the book is directed a hundred percent and all the numbers are lousy, then you'll have a flop. If we protect the numbers, we'll get by on the book, and there is nobody better on musical numbers than Bob Fosse."

Fosse got the job, and a scared Fosse it was. "But I'm always scared when I start something," he told his friend Bob Aurthur, "until that moment comes when it all turns around, and then I'm in control."

Work began in New York with script meetings between Bob and the screenwriter, Jay Presson Allen. Their chemistry was bad from the start. Miss Allen found Fosse "so depressed that it took two hours just to get him into a frame of mind for work." He was unhappy with her script. He had asked Paddy and Doc and Bob Aurthur to read it, and (he said) they all thought it was unsatisfactory. Feuer agreed that some rewriting was necessary, but Allen was very much in demand and already had another movie assignment.

When Bob flew to Los Angeles to meet the brass and settle on the cinematographer, there still was no screenwriter. He was anxious to work with cameraman Robert Surtees again but Feuer and the executives disapproved. In the second place, they were hoping for a European cameraman and crew to take advantage of lower union costs, but first of all, Surtees seemed to symbolize everything that had gone wrong with *Sweet Charity*—the zooming, the freeze framing, the overshooting, the overspending. "Fosse had the guy hypnotized," Feuer said.

They finally agreed on Jay Presson Allen's script being rewritten by Hugh Wheeler, who had worked with Bob on the aborted *Breakfast at Tiffany's*. *Cabaret* was based on John van Druten's play, *I Am a Camera*, and Christopher Isherwood's *Berlin Stories*, which Bob had once rejected as unlikely material for a musical. Now he was reading those self-same stories, Feuer said, "until that book was falling apart." The decision was already made to drop the Broadway show's subplot about a Jewish green-grocer's romance with Sally Bowles's rooming house landlady. Bob suggested replacing it with Isherwood material about a wealthy Jewish girl and a suitor who has been passing for gentile. He agreed that the Isherwood figure should be openly bisexual (on the stage he was heterosexual) and enthusiastically supported Feuer's notion of dropping all musical numbers that were not "justified," that is, keeping only the songs that were sung where songs would be sung in real life. This mainly meant entertainment in the cabaret. For Bob, it was a lesson learned from *Sweet Charity*, whose musical numbers in the streets had seemed stagey, the success of *West Side Story* notwithstanding. Musical logic was going to be taken so seriously in *Cabaret* that had the movie been wall-to-wall with song and dance, it still would not have seemed to be a musical. Even the numbers in the cabaret would be more than entertainments. They would (and this was a fascinating notion of Fosse's) relate to the dramatic action. For instance, Sally Bowles might be in a laundry when she flirts with a rich German. He is driven off in a limousine. After the camera has lingered lovingly on the automobile, the movie cuts to the cabaret where Joel Grey and Liza Minnelli barrel through "The Money Song." In this same fashion, either a scene would be followed by a musical number that related to it, or the number would be done and then a relevant stretch of the story would follow. The only song that would be sung outside the cabaret was "Tomorrow the World Belongs to Me," a Nazi anthem spontaneously performed by the public in a beer garden (it would be the only musical number Fosse regretted).

While John Kander, the composer, and the lyricist Fred Ebb wrote numbers to replace the plot songs that were being deleted, Hugh Wheeler went to work on the script. Michael York was hired to play opposite Minnelli. "She didn't think he was right," Fosse remembered. " 'Liza,' I said, 'I've looked at a lot of people, I've auditioned and tested them all, and in my opinion, Michael is the best possible choice.' She said all right but she didn't seem very enthusiastic."

There were smaller parts that remained uncast, and Feuer and Fosse left for Germany to audition actors as well as to hire dancers, engage designers, and scout locations. The cinematography issue was still unsettled. ("Cinematographer" and "cameraman" are interchangeable terms but neither of them refers to the man who actually operates the camera. Reasonably enough, that person is called the "camera operator." The cinematographer or cameraman is the one who lights the set and works with the director to decide on the camera angles and lenses.) Bob and Cy went over the cinematographer issue yet again during the flight overseas. Feuer said, "Let's look at all the guys, wherever we have to go, from Geoffrey Unsworth in England to Sven Nykvist in Stockholm," who, the producer later would say, "was only Ingmar Bergman's cameraman."

"Okay," Bob said, "as long as you keep an open mind about Surtees."

"It's open," Feuer said, "as long as you know I don't want the guy."

They checked into Munich's best hotel, Vier Jahreszeiten (Four Seasons), and as Feuer unpacked, he worried not about the cinematographer but about Bob's ability to direct the dramatic portions of *Cabaret* ("What had he directed before? A couple of silly musical comedies?"). The next morning they plunged into the wealthy and elegant city. Germany's postwar economic recovery was at a peak, and Munich reflected that as much as any city in the country. Its sidewalks and stores were crowded with shoppers anticipating St. Nicholas Day, the German children's holiday that comes two weeks before Christmas. The streets were jammed with white Mercedes-Benz taxis, and the city's legendary rathskellers were crowded and boisterous.

In the Hotel Vier Jahreszeiten, the restaurant was hushed, and its fireplace crackled as Bob and Cy sat down, one wintry Saturday afternoon, to interview a potential scenic designer. The man spoke no English, and so they had arranged for an interpreter to join them at lunch. Her name was Ilse Schwarzwald, and she was a secretary with the local production company working on *Cabaret*. This was her weekend time, but the notion of meeting Bob Fosse was exciting to her. When she entered the hotel restaurant she looked straight at him and he at her. "And it was one of those eyes across the room things," she said. "It was like magic."

Less like magic was the conversation between Fosse and Feuer that evening as they went upstairs to their rooms after a full day of interviews and a dinner of discussing them. Whatever they talked about, whether it was the set designers, actors, or locations, their conversation seemed to return to cinematographers and Bob was taking a stand on Surtees.

"Fuck that," Feuer thought as they strolled down the hallway from the elevator. "My job," he would say, "was to bring this picture in within the budget. Liza was getting $100,000, and Joel was only getting $35,000. Jesus Christ, Fosse himself was getting just $75,000, and Surtees and his crew would have gone $50,000 over anyone else we found in Europe."

The issue remained unresolved as they bade each other good night that midnight. Or at least that was how Feuer perceived it, for as Fosse recalled, "Cy had promised that he would at least try to get Surtees." Minutes later, Feuer's telephone rang—Marty Baum was calling from ABC Pictures in Los Angeles.

"What's happening?" the executive asked.

"We're still talking about cameramen."

"Forget about the cameraman," Baum said. "I'm having other problems."

"What other problems?"

"Second thoughts," the executive said. "This may just be a forecast of headaches to come. We can get out of it now. If we made a mistake, let's pay him off."

"Let me tell you something, Marty," Feuer said. "When I first suggested Fosse, it was because I was interested in the musical staging. I didn't know whether this guy could direct his ass. But the way he's been auditioning these actors, the guy's a born director."

"But what about the cameraman?"

"I'll tell you right now," Feuer said, "I don't want Surtees, and we're not going to have Surtees."

The Hotel Vier Jahreszeiten was the finest hotel in Munich. It was a reconstructed prewar building, its walls thick enough for a vault, thick enough for protection against radiation. But they posed no great obstacle when it came to human paranoia. However he did it, using a glass tumbler or even a doctor's stethoscope, Bob Fosse was eavesdropping from his room next door, just as he had listened in on Hal Prince in New Haven after the tryout of *Damn Yankees*. He now heard Cy Feuer's telephone conversation with Marty Baum in Los Angeles, and he later told Bob Aurthur, "It was a terrifying experience. Cy had promised me he'd fight for the cameraman I wanted, but now I heard him say, 'No, no, I won't let Fosse have him.' It was a nightmare. I sat an hour listening to this. I've never felt so deceived."

He telephoned Gwen in New York, and after telling her what he'd overheard, he asked what she thought about it. Their family economy was as shaky as his career. She said that whatever he decided was fine with her, leaving him to grapple with the problem through the night.

The morning must have seemed a week away as the agonized Fosse strove feverishly to be clear minded ("I needed the job," he told Aurthur, "I needed the money"). If to confront Feuer, when? How? What to say to the man who had been so much a part of his life, so much a part of his good career, so much a part of this job which had seemed to be his salvation? "I realized," Bob dramatically concluded to Aurthur, "that our whole relationship had been a deception."

Fosse was forty-four. Feuer was going to turn sixty in a few weeks. Fosse knocked on his friend's door at eight o'clock in the morning. When Feuer opened it, the friendship was over forever. Bob's red eyes stared out from their dark and hollowed-out sockets as he said, "You no good son of a bitch. Last night I heard your whole conversation with Baum through the wall."

The producer was dumbfounded and, as Bob recalled, "white faced."

"You never thought I could direct this movie, did you?" he hissed. "You hired me only for the fucking choreography. You never intended to give me Surtees."

"I never said I was going to give you Surtees."

"That's a goddamned lie!" Fosse snarled. "Now I know you for what you are. You're a two-faced shit!"

"Listen, prick," Feuer shot back. "You don't know what was going on at the other end of that conversation. The guy wants to fire you, and I can just pick up the phone right now and do it. But I'm not going to do that, because I want to make this picture, you stupid son of a bitch."

Bob stared at him, sick with aggravation.

"I'm sorry you heard the conversation," the fired-up Feuer continued, the tendons stretching on his neck as he jutted toward Fosse, standing on his toes (neither of them was very tall). "That phone call was supposed to be private."

They raged and cursed at each other in the corridor of the German hotel, Fosse railing in his stale overnight clothes, while the bathrobed Feuer alternately took and returned the vituperation, neither of them wanting to send the movie up in smoke. Finally the producer said, "Okay, Bob, what do you want to do?"

This was the part that Fosse had been rehearsing since dawn. "If you want me out," he said carefully, "you're going to have to fire me." It was a neat ploy, an honorable way of not quitting. In a better humor he would have laughed about it. He waited several beats—he wasn't a director for nothing—while Feuer dealt with a similar conflict between emotion and need ("I wanted him on this picture very badly because I didn't know how to do it without him—how to stage those musical numbers"). The older man looked into the younger one's eyes, two sets of tough and cool blue eyes, smart and stubborn, the eyes of gifted, ambitious, egotistical men. Were there psychological resonances in this exchange? Cy Feuer, Cy Fosse, and Feuer had his own sons, he was himself a tough father.

The two of them stood in steamy silence in their version of a movie shootout until Fosse turned and walked away, down the hall, and into his room.

"After that phone call," he would later say, "I couldn't look at Cy or talk to him. I couldn't help it."

That wasn't entirely true. There were necessary communications between a director and his producer, but they would be curt. The two men would even have to travel together for the picture, here to scout a location or there to audition an actor, but through it all, Bob was frigid. He would remain angry with Cy Feuer for the rest of his life. Geoffrey Unsworth was hired as the cinematographer, and Feuer stayed away as much as he could, away from rehearsals and away from the set. It was uncomfortable and sad.

From the magic of eyes across the dining room, Bob and Ilse Schwarzwald progressed to earthier matters. She had been born in Munich, gone to school there, and was now thirty-one years old and divorced. As a child she had been struck by flying shrapnel during an air raid. A faint but discernible scar on her right cheek betrayed the accident, lending distinction to her good looks. She was five feet four inches tall, she had long straight brown hair, and she bore a striking resemblance to Gwen Verdon, who was on her way over with Nicole, coming to work with Bob whether or not he appreciated her help at this particular time. She probably would have been better off not coming.

It was a good time, Bob decided, to solve a convenient tax problem. He was about to incur a German obligation if he stayed much longer without leaving the country to work elsewhere, however briefly. Engaging the British cameraman, Geoffrey Unsworth, suddenly had its advantages. Bob could justify a visit to London as a working trip, he could have a romantic excursion with Ilse, and at the same time he could escape the German tax liability, not to mention Gwen's arrival. The couple flew to England from Munich on a long and sexy weekend, "and," Ilse laughed in recollection, "I went gambling for the first time in my life." But it wasn't all in London casinos. "Oh no," she chuckled in her deep voice, "it was terribly romantic."

Bob already had two dance aides, Kathy Doby, who was now his chief assistant, and John Sharpe, who went back with him to *Little Me*, but of course they were both deferential to Gwen when she arrived. With Bob's return from London, the little Fosse family settled into the Hotel Residenz in that cold German February, moving in with the company of actors and dancers who had descended on the town of Schwabing on the outskirts of Munich.

The Hotel Residenz was not the liveliest place for the likes of Liza Minnelli, Joel Grey, Michael York, Gwen Verdon, or Bob Fosse, but they created a communal atmosphere, and late-night card games were soon under way. There was little else to do in Schwabing, and there had to be some way to unwind after the Fosse style of rehearsal, all day long and exhaustive. There was going to be six weeks of work on scenes and musical numbers while the sets for the Kit Kat Klub and Sally Bowles's rooming house were being built.

On the first day of rehearsal, Bob took Joel Grey aside and said, "We're starting on 'Two Ladies.' " Of course Grey had sung the song in the show, but "everything was totally different," the actor was to remember. "It was like beginning again for me. Even the makeup was changed."

Bob said, "I was wondering whether you could do this acrobatic trick—?"

The actor eyed him incredulously. The Master of Ceremonies he played was a chalk-faced androgyne. Such a character hardly called for acrobatics.

"What trick?"

"Here," Bob said. "Let me show you."

As he began, John Sharpe called out, "Wait a second! Let me spot you!" (To "spot" is to brace.)

"No! No!" Bob cried, and without pause or support he did a back flip the way he had done it in *Give a Girl a Break, Kiss Me, Kate*, and *My Sister Eileen*. Those back flips had been difficult fifteen or twenty years earlier when Bob had been in his twenties. This time his feet flew up in the air, and he seemed to hang suspended above the ground for just one breath. Then he fell flat on his face.

"It was horrifying," Grey recalled. "His face was swollen for days. He kept smoking too. It looked bizarre, a cigarette hanging out of the corner of that puffy face."

It was surely different from the face that Grey had seen on the Bob

Fosse who had once done those flips with such young innocence—the Fosse he had first met in 1948 when they were fidgety youngsters who knew everything about show business, hanging out at Hansen's Drugstore near Times Square. "I used to look up to him then too," Grey remembered, "because he and Mary-Ann Niles were a going dance team, and the rest of us were out of work. I would watch their act at the Latin Casino. She was very antic, and he was a handsome, boyish vaudevillian."

Where had that handsome young vaudevillian gone? And how did it happen that he was metamorphosing into this moviemaker who so confidently announced he was making "the first adult musical"—this director so fascinated with Grey's weird character? "I think he secretly loved that character," the actor said. "He called me Mister Porno."

On Broadway, Joel Grey had cut an unreal figure playing this Master of Ceremonies, a character who was somehow both lascivious and asexual. "But in the movie," he said, "the character had to be dealt with as more literal than symbolic because he was now in close-up." He discussed the role with Fosse, "where he slept, what he did, where he lived, what his politics were, where he ate, who he lived with, what the girls in the Kit Kat Klub had to do for him to get their jobs, what their auditions were like. We even developed a relationship between him and Sally. It was expressed in shorthand, an exchange of glances between Liza and me, or just pursed lips. It was enough. It didn't matter whether he had actually slept with her.

"Bob and I shared a past in vaudeville and nightclubs," Grey said. "I used to go where my father [Mickey Katz] worked as a singer. I saw plenty of sleaze. I tried to remember all the cheap and vulgar acts. Hal Prince had encouraged that when we first created the character, and now it continued."

Sleaze was part of Fosse's strip-joint childhood; it was Bob Riff's point of departure, and Fosse was becoming artist enough to extrapolate from that. He was starting to perceive in lowlife show business a metaphor for all existence as being tainted and vulgar. He seemed to be concluding that life was innocence corrupted, the strip joint extruded to its slimy essence, that in life as on stage, flash succeeded rather than quality. His childhood education in vaudeville, the lore learned from Frederic Weaver, was now to be etched in acid. In *Cabaret*, "The Money Song," for instance, would be performed by Minnelli and Grey as if it were a vaudeville turn done in a moral abyss, a jolly evil.

Fosse told Ralph Burns that he wanted the all-girl band in this 1931 Berlin café to sound as bad as he remembered cheap bands sounding in the seedy clubs he used to work in. "So," the orchestrator said, "we hired musicians [ten actually played for the eight on screen] from the German

The Riff Brothers, 1940, on the "Morris B. Sachs Amateur Hour," WGN Radio, Chicago. Charles Grass (left), age 12 and Bob Fosse, 13. *(Courtesy of Charles Grass)*

The Riff Brothers, 1943, Bob (left) at 16 and Charles Grass a year younger. "We hated this picture," Grass recalled, "because our pants were too short and too baggy." *(Courtesy of Charles Grass)*

Jack Cole.
(Courtesy of the Museum of the City of New York)

The Fosse family in 1945. (Back row from left)
Edward, Sadie, Bob, and Cy; (middle row from left)
Bud, Patricia, Donald, with little Marianne.
(Courtesy of Margaret Fosse)

Right: Bob Fosse and Mary-Ann Niles, 1952.
(Courtesy of Donald Saddler)

U.S. Navy, April, 1946. Special Services Sailor Show No. 3A, "Tough Situation." Newly promoted Seaman First Class Fosse (holding clarinet) at 19, kneeling in front of pipe-smoking Chief Petty Officer Joseph Papirosky, himself destined for stage success as New York producer Joe Papp. *(Courtesy of Arnold Hughes)*

"Give a Girl a Break," the first picture at MGM for Fosse (left), dancing with Gower Champion (center) and Kurt Kasznar, 1952.
(© 1953 by Loewe's Inc. Renewed 1981 Metro-Goldwyn-Mayer Film Co.)

Above: Gwen Verdon and Bob Fosse dance "Who's Got the Pain?" in the *Damn Yankees* movie, 1958.
(© 1958 Warner Bros., Inc.)

"Steam Heat," as danced in the movie, *The Pajama Game*. Eddie Phillips (left), Carol Haney, and Buzz Miller. *(© 1957 Warner Bros., Inc.)*

The controversial gorilla number that was cut from *Damn Yankees* during the New Haven tryout. *(Billy Rose Theater Collection)*

Fosse and Verdon happily at work on
New Girl in Town, 1957. *(Courtesy of
Patricia Ferrier Kiley)*

Below: Gwen Verdon sits by unhappily
while George Abbott rehearses Thelma
Ritter in *New Girl in Town*, 1957.
(Billy Rose Theater Collection)

A weary Fosse rehearses Tom Poston in the tryout of *The Conquering Hero*, 1960. *(Courtesy of Patricia Ferrier Kiley)*

Gwen Verdon, *Redhead*, 1959. *(Billy Rose Theater Collection)*

Nicole Providence Fosse.
(Courtesy of Patricia Ferrier Kiley)

Above: "Hey, Big Spender," *Sweet Charity.*
(Copyright © 1988 by Martha Swope)

Right: Fosse brings his white gloves to the
N.Y. City Center revival of *Pal Joey*, 1963.
(Courtesy of Patricia Ferrier Kiley)

Fosse rehearses Janet Leigh for *My Sister
Eileen*. *(Courtesy of Columbia Pictures. Copyright
© 1955, renewed 1983 by Columbia Pictures
Industries, Inc. All Rights Reserved.)*

Top: Fosse rehearses Shirley MacLaine during a publicity session for the movie, *Sweet Charity.* *(Copyright © by Universal Pictures, a Division of Universal City Studios, Inc. Courtesy of MCA Publishing Rights, a Division of MCA Inc.)*

Liza Minnelli in the movie *Cabaret*.
(Photograph from Cabaret *courtesy of Capital Cities/ABC Video Enterprises, Inc. Copyright 1972 ABC Pictures Corp. and Allied Artists Picture Corp.)*

Below: "The Manson Trio" with Ben Vereen in *Pippin*, 1972. *(Copyright © 1972 by Martha Swope)*

The *Dancin'* poster, one of the most commercially effective in Broadway history, was assembled by the designer Bob Gill. It was made up of a man and a woman, but when Fosse re-created the making of that poster in *All That Jazz*, he showed it as a man and two women, and used it to lead into a reference to sexual threesomes. *(Courtesy of Bob Gill)*

As Eddie White looks on, Fosse shows Paddy Chayefsky the time step at a party for Herb Gardner's movie, *The Good-bye People*. *(Courtesy of Eddie White)*

Dustin Hoffman in *Lenny*, 1974. *(© 1974 United Artists Corporation. All Rights Reserved.)*

Fosse as The Snake in *The Little Prince*, 1974. *(Courtesy of Paramount Pictures. THE LITTLE PRINCE Copyright © 1974 by Stanley Donen Films, Inc. and Paramount Pictures Corporation. All Rights Reserved.)*

Roy Scheider as Joe Gideon in
All That Jazz, and his role model.
*(Courtesy of Columbia Pictures. Copyright
© 1979 by Columbia Pictures Industries,
Inc. All Rights Reserved.)*

Eric Roberts as Paul Snider in *Star 80*. *(Copyright © 1983 by The Ladd Company.
All Rights Reserved.)*

Ann Reinking dances with Nicole Fosse's alter ego,
"Michelle," played by Erzsebet Foldi, in *All That Jazz*.
(Courtesy of Columbia Pictures. Copyright © 1979 by Columbia Pictures
Industries, Inc. All Rights Reserved.)

Bob and Gwen, 1980, East Hampton, New York. (*Courtesy of Eva Rubinstein*)

union's third class, the class 'C,' but they were too bad to be bad so we got Class 'B' musicians, who cost maybe five dollars an hour more. They were too awful also. So we got Class 'A' musicians and told them to play like bad musicians. That was *too* terrible. Finally we said, 'Play it good,' and then it sounded bad the right way."

By this time, Bob's romance with Ilse had become more than a location fling. He told her that the only reason he was still married to Gwen was his daughter. "My priorities," he said, "are Nicole and my work." After a long pause he mercifully added, "And then you—maybe." Then he would go back to the Hotel Residenz and his wife.

By chance, Nicole had the same birthday as Joel Grey's daughter Jennifer (later to star in the movie, *Dirty Dancing*), and a joint birthday party was planned. In anticipation, Bob showed the two almost eight-year-olds how to perform "The Money Song." Liza had already taught the girls the words.

Gwen enjoyed Liza Minnelli. She did not seem to envy the way Liza was being transformed by Bob into a spectacular dancer. It was *Cabaret* that was going to deliver Liza to the general public. "Right before our eyes," Kathy Doby said, "she was becoming a star," and that was part of the mystique on the set. In fact Minnelli's emerging star quality was more interesting to the cast and crew than Bob Fosse's love life.

The behind-the-scenes affair was common knowledge on the set. There were awkward moments when Gwen innocently chatted with Ilse, but otherwise the subject was of little scandal. Romances on location were as old as movies themselves, and this was a worldly group, hardly surprised by an unfaithful husband, Bob Fosse especially. He had already slept with several women on the picture, and there were whispers about threesomes in bed. Too, Bob wasn't the only cheater in this little romance. The man Ilse was living with wrote a tattletale letter to Gwen.

"She was angry, no?"

"No," Bob told Ilse after it had been read to him in the hotel room. "She wasn't angry." Gwen Verdon seldom demonstrated anger. "She was just sarcastic."

"And the letter? What was in the letter?"

"He warned me about your expensive tastes," Bob said. "He wrote my wife to warn me about your expensive tastes." It was worth a grin and a disbelieving shake of the head.

"I'm a princess, is that what he said?" Ilse laughed. "And you always thought I was just—"

"A kraut," Bob filled in. "He said I didn't know what financial headaches I was taking on with you."

They both laughed about that, but even after the letter their affair continued, and Gwen stayed on, coming to the set, working with the dancers, shopping for costumes, and even sewing them. "Bob was very unhappy with our costume designer," Cy Feuer said. "She couldn't quite get the sleazy look that he and Gwen knew so well." And so while Bob danced around with Ilse, Gwen went poking through secondhand stores and flea markets for costumes. That was how she found most of Minnelli's clothes for the movie, including a spectacular dress with a beaded centerpiece that Liza would wear while singing the title song. And she also worked on Liza's personal style. It was Gwen who thought up the green nail polish, and it was Gwen who created the painted-on style of Minnelli's hair.

Perhaps Gwen was hoping, as had Mary-Ann Niles and Joan Mc-Cracken before her, that Bob would come to his senses. Many wives harbor such hopes; that isn't unusual. But not many wives stay to watch their husbands continuing the affairs, and not many work "as an assistant," Feuer said, "or maybe even a kind of slave." That seemed excessive, eerie, and perhaps even masochistic, but this was a Gwen Verdon who had let Jack Cole shriek abuse without giving him the satisfaction of her pain. It was a Gwen Verdon who had thrown a chair against a wall only after he had left the room. The only sign now of any grief was a serious loss of weight that grew worrisome as rehearsals neared a conclusion. She began to drink a great deal of beer. She said that it might help her regain the weight, but it didn't help.

Some of the actors and crew did talk, now, about feeling awkward and bad for her, although they claimed that the situation wasn't hurting the work process. There are actors who actually find emotional turmoil stimulating. They seem to think that life exists in order to motivate acting performances, but even Gwen Verdon had her limits. As Bob and Ilse became more comfortable with each other, as their romance emerged into plain view, Kathy Doby said, "Gwen left in heat," flying back to New York with Nicole.

And filming began, with Bob working "as if his career was on the line," Joel Grey remembered. "He was intent on proving himself a director of drama as opposed to musicals."

The intensity of his perfectionism deepened as mistakes were now preserved on film, to be projected and magnified at the morning "rushes" or "dailies," the screenings of the quickly processed, unedited film footage from the previous day's shooting. "As soon as we started seeing those dailies," Grey said, "we all knew that we were involved with something special." There was a sure feeling throughout the company that *Cabaret* was an extraordinary thing in the making. "And," Grey said, "we were lucky to have Geoff Unsworth as the cameraman because he had exactly the same vision as Bob." Even Fosse conceded that Unsworth "turned out great," although he felt compelled to add, "He was still my third choice."

In California, the studio executives shuddered at the sight that was so impressing the actors. They equated the filtered look of *Cabaret* with the look of *Sweet Charity* and the overspending and failure of *Sweet Charity*. Fosse later told Bob Aurthur, "After the fourth day of shooting, I got an enraged call from them. 'What are you doing? It's so smoky and foggy in the nightclub. If you use one more filter we'll consider it an act of insubordination.'" He laughed. "Can you believe that?"

"Did you stop using filters?" Aurthur asked.

"Hell, no, but we had a game on the set. For my continued 'insubordination,' the cast and crew would line up and strip me of my viewer."

Feuer said that whenever he suggested the filtered effects, while beautiful, could be overdone, Fosse would make plain his contempt for know-nothing money people. "But," the producer added, "he did back away from the constant filtering, and the picture was better for it."

The particular and recurring image in this eerie, exquisitely grotesque cabaret was one of immobile German faces, the faces of burghers vacantly observing contortionists, transvestites, even whippings, as if they were entertainment. In fact, the stage show of the cabaret was not evil; the evil lay in the audience's unresponsive, insensitive, soulless, impassive faces. The only gleeful responses that Fosse allowed the audience were in response to female mud wrestlers. It was hardly necessary to point out further the parallel between these observers and the Germany of 1931, sitting still for the Nazi show.

Fosse was in the process of making the best movie version ever of a Broadway musical, and yet it was so different from the stage *Cabaret*, so transcended the original, that it became a new thing and hardly a movie version of the show at all.

The rule of realism was the key to the picture. As with the songs, there were no dances where there would not have been dances in real life. This is the reason why the *Cabaret* movie does not seem to be a "musical." Thus, while it has considerable musical staging, there is little choreography other than an occasional (and abortive) entrance of chorus girls to start a floor show. Moreover, the stage on the set was only ten by fourteen feet, which was the size it would actually have been in such a club, and Fosse said, "It does not 'grow,'" by which he meant that the stage does not, through movie magic, expand to accommodate a host of dancers or sets or production effects. "I never used more than six girls," he said, "and I had to work within those restrictions. I tried to make the dances look not as if they were done by me, Bob Fosse, but by some guy who is down and out. You think, 'Oh I can't really have them do *that*. That's so embarrassing; it's so bad, so cheap.' But you think, 'But if I were the kind of guy who works with cheap cabarets and clubs, what else would I do?' So I worked from that."

To do those cheap dances perfectly, he drilled the dancers to the ground. For instance, Liza Minnelli was to sing "Mein Herr" while perched on a chair with one leg in a squat and the other extended flat out. It was a position that not only looked difficult, it looked painful. The viewer's sense of the pain would lend the number tension. "Behind Liza," dance assistant John Sharpe said, "one of the German dancers had difficulty in rehearsal, tapping on the beat. She would tap on the offbeat. She was draped on a chair, her head near the floor with her finger tapping on the chair leg, and try as I might, on the day of the shoot I couldn't get into position to see her finger tapping, but what I could see looked all right to me."

At the rushes the next day, Sharpe cringed at the sight of her tapping on the offbeat.

"John Sharpe!" cried a warning voice from the front row of the screening room. The dance assistant well knew that voice and its glacial edge. "Did you see that?" Sharpe understood exactly what "that" was, and the entire number had to be rephotographed.

Fosse was similarly exact when directing dramatic scenes. Joel Grey was coached until he spoke his few German lines with an absolute Berlin accent; Fosse, rehearsing with Liza for a whole afternoon, glared at her as she walked off the set one evening at quitting time.

"Where are you going?" he called out. "Come here! I want to talk to you about this right now."

She stopped and turned to face him. "No, Bobby," she said. "We'll talk about it tomorrow."

"Right now!" he said. "I want to see you in my office, and we're going to talk about it."

"No, we won't," she said. "If I go in there now, you're going to say things that you'll be sorry for tomorrow, and you'll be sending me flowers. I'm going home. We'll talk about it tomorrow."

She disappeared, past the set, off the sound stage, out of the studio. The next morning, as Minnelli remembered, she and Bob calmly talked about the previous day's problem. "You don't have to play to somebody else's script," she said about the incident. "I learned about leaving the room."

There were some who said that *Cabaret* lyricist Fred Ebb had "invented" Liza Minnelli. It was he who wrote her material, he who directed her act. John Kander, the composer of the songs, said, "Fred was Liza's Pygmalion," but if so, then Bob was finishing the creation, providing her with gestures, moves, and a personal style. "He created a physical line for her," Joel Grey said, and that was what she was now growing into. "On the set," Kathy Doby said, "you could feel her electricity." As Minnelli sang her big song, leaning over the stage, reaching into the audience with her waggling fingers

Come to the cabaret

she had become a master entertainer, and she was sophisticated enough now to appreciate Michael York. "Oh, Bobby!" she cried, "was I wrong! He's sensational, that mysterious personality, and that terrific face, that broken nose."

York was indeed the better actor. He had classical technique, he had no accent like Minnelli's, and he was a real repertory actor. What he lacked was passion, and on screen it is passion that counts, while technique is usually laid bare in the first close-up, and York's was. On the other hand, despite Minnelli's lack of acting discipline and despite her seemingly top-of-the-head performance, she radiates a warmth, a humanity, and a sexuality that make her character leap out from the screen while York works across it from a distance.

Joel Grey understood that "Bob wanted the book life of the movie to be as vibrant and magical as the musical numbers." It is difficult to think of another movie as painterly as *Cabaret*, except for John Huston's *Moulin Rouge*, which Fosse admitted to having been influenced by in terms of color and composition. *Moulin Rouge* also showed the way to a fresh filming of dance. Common wisdom, Fosse said, was to photograph a dancer's full figure, but Huston demonstrated that breaking up the body and photographing it in segments, in close-up, could make for very different, choreographically effective sights. Still, his own favorite moment in *Cabaret* was to be purely pictorial, an image of Liza Minnelli surrounded by a sea of candles while she talks hopefully of having a baby.

As the winter freeze began to thaw, the picture wound down. Soon there would be a packing up and going home while the director and crew moved out for final location work. Bob was still postponing the viciously anti-Semitic duet that Joel Grey was supposed to sing with a female gorilla, "If You Could See Her Through My Eyes (She Wouldn't Be Jewish at All)." The song was to be played in a soft-shoe rhythm not unlike "Tea for Two," and the gorilla was to be dressed in a pink veiled hat and a flower-covered ballet tutu, partnered by Joel Grey in a straw boater hat. The little duet was to draw its acid from being modeled on a classic vaudeville turn, and it was not at all unlike a Fosse and Niles routine. At first, the dance assistant John Sharpe was to dance the gorilla part, but it wasn't looking right. Fosse felt that somehow this gorilla (who would never be unmasked during the number) had to seem feminine in her movements. Finally Louise Quick, who was one of the two American dancers in the film (Kathy Doby being the other), got inside the suit, but there was still no head for it. Bob had rejected a long series of gorilla heads that had been brought in from costume shops, secondhand dealers, and toy stores. None came close to an image he had in his mind.

He telephoned Gwen in New York and asked if she could find a gorilla head for him. He told her precisely what he was looking for. That she agreed to do it did not surprise Joel Grey. "I always accepted Bob's relationship with Gwen as being extremely unique," he said.

Within a week she returned to the scene of her humiliation, reappearing on the set with an enormous and rather unusual gorilla head in her arms. For one thing, it had a ring through its nose and, for another, "This gorilla head," Grey said with enduring astonishment, "it looked like—well, if Gwen were a gorilla, that was what she would have looked like. It was very much her kind of stage persona. It had elements . . . I mean . . . Gwen is beautiful, but if she had been born a gorilla—"

14

One of Hamburg's most popular tourist attractions, certainly the most infamous, is the Reeperbahn. The red light district is notorious for open-air prostitution marts and such erotic distractions as the female mud wrestling that Fosse adapted to his Kit Kat Klub of 1931 Berlin. Rolf Zehetbauer, the *Cabaret* set designer, was showing Bob these sights, much as Buddy Hackett had once shown the country mouse around New York. Ilse stayed behind at the hotel. She had declined Bob's invitation to join them.

Inevitably, the two men went to one of the sex clubs that offered live pornographic shows. They were seated at a table in a half-filled room. On stage a nude couple was moving listlessly through the sex act. The male member was not performing, so to speak. He was getting through the floor show as best he could, and the audience was no more responsive than his partner. Its applause was perfunctory.

Fosse and Zehetbauer rose from their table and walked to the *Toiletten*, a route that took them past the dressing, or undressing, room. "The club manager was yelling at the guy," Bob later remembered. "He was saying, 'You told me you could do it every night!' "

Recalling the experience, Fosse shook his head and laughed compassionately. "This guy was like anyone else who lost a part. He kept telling the manager, 'I'm sorry, I'm sorry. I don't know what's the matter with me.'

"It was so sad."

They were in Hamburg to film a scene at the railway station in nearby Lübeck. They had already been to Eutin where there was a beautiful castle that served in the movie for the home of Sally's bisexual aristocrat lover.

When Bob and Ilse went on to Berlin to finish the location photography, a letter from Gwen was waiting. She loved Bob, of that there was no question, but they had to separate, she wrote, because he had been cheating on her from virtually the moment they met.

Trying to explain himself, he told a friend, "Perhaps I did all that screwing around because I was thrown into a situation constantly with beautiful women . . . but I always made it clear that I was married and that the affair was not to lead to anything big."

Most married men say something similar when they screw around, and most men probably mean it when they say it, as if frivolous intentions somehow excuse the screwing around. "After Gwen's letter," Bob said, "I dived into the relationship with Ilse." He made it sound as if it was practically his wife's fault.

They "wrapped" in Munich, moviemaker jargon for finishing photography. Bob could go home now but, Ilse said, "He didn't want to go back to New York because Gwen had kicked him out, and he had no home." He met with the insurance men, the people who had furnished the *Cabaret* "completion bond," the guarantee of money to finish a movie even if it meant bringing in a new director. The bond could be invoked when the original director exceeded his budget or the time limit. The *Cabaret* budget had apparently been exceeded, or at least Feuer told Bob, "This is it, there's nothing left." The insurance men were there to find out just how serious the situation was.

"How Bob hated money people," Ilse said, hardly the first to notice. "Especially these portly and very stern men from England," but after they looked at a rough version of the picture, they were so impressed that they said he could even add the "run by's" he wanted, the pedestrians and cars moving past the camera to establish period and location. The budget had truly been restrictive, "a tight collar."

In celebration and relief, he flew away with Ilse for a week in Spain, but their first stretch of actual, noncheating freedom was not much fun. Reality set in like a bad fit, and it only exacerbated the usual directorial postpartum depression. He took all of this out on Ilse, using her choice of a less than elegant hotel in Madrid as an excuse for a week of foul moods. His temper alternated with depressions that only deepened with guilt feelings about Nicole. Finally, he informed Ilse that he had telephoned Gwen in New York and that they had decided to reconcile, or at least to try to. He was flying straight to Majorca to rendezvous and give the marriage another try in the warm green neutral waters of the Mediterranean. He was accepting Doc and Joan Simon's invitation to come and visit, and it must have seemed the most perfect and romantic place for a couple to make up. The weather was balmy, the island was lush, the beaches were smooth and white and protected, and the Simons were as trustworthy as family yet as diplomatic as friends. Moreover, Hal and Judy Prince were just beyond, on an interior mountaintop, and socializing would keep the pressure off the reconciliation. Bob and Gwen wouldn't have to talk about *it* every moment they were there.

They didn't even have to stick to the Simons. One evening they met Hal and Judy for drinks in Palma before going back to the Prince house for dinner. The capital city was intimate and picturesque with its winding alleyways, whitewashed stucco, and tropical scents, and the Simons probably appreciated the evening to themselves. It is never easy, entertaining a troubled couple.

The older Simon daughter, fourteen-year-old Ellen, loved to dance. She got the love from her mother, who would occasionally perform at parties. The youngster had fantasies of becoming a dancer-choreographer herself, and she took Bob and Gwen's absence as an opportunity to work out a piece that she hoped to perform on their last night on the island. It would be a farewell gesture, and it was probably an exciting prospect. Her father was a famous playwright, but he had merely written *Sweet Charity* whereas Gwen had been the star and Bob the dance master.

After a week together, though, the Fosses were back where they had started, and by the last night the reconciliation was a shambles. A disintegrating couple can be explosive, never more so than when they are trying to make up; there is too much ego and rejection in the mix. Nevertheless, perhaps even in hope that her little program would lighten the atmosphere, Ellen Simon put on her costume, laced up her toe shoes, and danced for the sullen guests while Neil and Joan radiated parental pride.

When the girl was finished, the proud Simons turned to Gwen and Bob. "Well?" must have been crayoned across their hopeful, suntanned faces.

Bob's reaction was terse. "Another choreographer," he said.

Even Gwen, who was usually diplomatic, seemed unable to step into the awful breach. Perhaps all the fighting had momentarily punched the kindness out of her. Ellen was not upset ("I thought they were just grown-ups arguing"), but her parents were not disposed to forgive. After a mean silence Neil icily said, "Get out of here."

Bob and Gwen packed up and left. They spent their last night on the island in a hotel in Palma. Then he went back to Ilse, and Gwen went back to Nicole. In Hollywood, the thirty-nine-year-old Pier Angeli was found unconscious and unrevivable following an overdose of barbiturates. In Chicago, Frederic Weaver was dead at eighty-four. He never had responded to the offer of money for a Fosse School of Dance.

When Ilse received Bob's cable asking her to meet him in London, she sagged with relief. Anywhere would have been perfect, but the reunion would be especially appropriate at the scene of their earlier rendezvous, when he had been cheating and guilt-free. Alas, London was not the same. Ilse found him depressed, which was getting to be his normal state. He told her nothing of what had happened in Majorca except that the reconciliation had not worked out, and it seemed to Ilse that he had been hoping it would.

He could avoid New York no longer. *Cabaret* was waiting to be edited, and that was going to be a six-month job. He had not seen Nicole for months, not since she had sung "The Money Song" with Jennifer Grey at her eighth birthday party in Munich. He went back to Germany, filmed his run by's, and then brought Ilse to America, checking into the Hyde Park Hotel on East 77th Street near Park Avenue in Manhattan.

He went to the editing (or "cutting") room each day, leaving Ilse alone at the hotel. She had few friends in New York and wasn't accustomed to a life of idleness and solitude. He warned her that New York was dangerous and told her not to leave the general area of the hotel and under no circumstances to ride on the subway. She was also forbidden to answer the telephone. "He was afraid," she said, "that Nicole might call and get a shock." And so she spent her time window-shopping and visiting the art galleries on upper Madison Avenue, or walking the echoing halls of the Metropolitan Museum of Art. The only friends she had were the two American dancers she had met during the making of *Cabaret*, Kathy Doby and Louise Quick. Kathy had married Wolfgang Glattes, the German assistant director on the movie, and he made Ilse feel at home, but Bob didn't take her to the theatre or to any parties, and the only friends he introduced her to were Paddy and Herb. It was her first time in New York, and "I was wide eyes," she remembered, but she was in love, and she was unhappy.

Bob visited Nicole regularly at the old apartment on Central Park West, but that only seemed to sadden him. He told Ilse that he was betraying his daughter and that seeing her sporadically only made him miss her more. Guilt was nagging at him and making him testy while she felt useless. She missed her friends and family, and she was worried about her visa, which was about to expire. "I felt like a terrible alien," she recalled, and probably would have decided to return to Munich herself had not Bob beat her to the punch and suggested it.

At last a show interested him. "I had been away from Broadway for five years," he said. "I missed it." *Cabaret* had made the difference, getting the movie under his belt. It would not be released until early in 1972, but it was not going to be another *Sweet Charity*. He was almost positive.

The name of the show was *The Adventures of Pippin*, and it had been sent to him by Stuart Ostrow who, so many years ago, had sat star struck, staring at Bob rehearsing *The Pajama Game* and *Damn Yankees*. Stuart Ostrow was now a producer, a very independent-minded and successful one. After two years, his prizewinning *1776* was still running at the 46th Street Theatre. He had always dreamed of doing a musical with Bob Fosse. *The Adventures of Pippin*, he hoped, would be that musical. Bob had read it, he had listened to Stephen Schwartz's songs, and he was interested in the project.

Even were that to work out, however, it would have to work out later, because he had decided to go ahead with a Liza Minnelli television special, a one-hour "concert for television."

Fred Ebb, the *Cabaret* lyricist who created her nightclub act, said, "We wanted the television show to be an elongated version of it." The "we" was show-biz for a star and the creative team that packaged the act. In the past that team included John Kander but had essentially been Fred Ebb— Ebb who wrote the dialogue, staged the movement, chose the songs and organized them, wrote the special material to Kander's melodies, and supervised the orchestrations and costumes. An hour on television, how-ever, required a director more experienced than someone who staged a nightclub act. "We went to Bob," Ebb said, "because everyone in the business admired his stylishness." The lyricist knew that Fosse was de-pressed about being unwanted in Hollywood. "But to tell the truth," he said, "there was never any aura of failure about him other than that which he created himself." Ebb understood that Fosse had just created some-thing spectacular in *Cabaret*, in the process taking Liza Minnelli to a singular level, but as yet the only ones who knew that were those few who had seen very rough cuts of the movie.

With so full a work year ahead, it should have been a relatively cheerful, relatively secure Bob Fosse who was strolling south down Mad-ison Avenue toward the CMA offices at 56th Street. He was still at the Hyde Park Hotel, but now that he was in New York for the duration, more permanent quarters had to be found. At the agency, David Begelman was at a slightly more advanced stage of marital transition. He had been separated from his wife Lee for almost a year. In the course of a long talk with Bob he said, "I need to change more of my life than I have. I'm going to move to the coast."

"But you're such a New York person," Bob said.

"I don't have the attitude about L.A. that you do," the cofounder of the agency said, "and I want to do more with movies."

"Then who's going to be my agent?"

"I'll continue to look after you out there," Begelman said, speaking as a priest-therapist. "But Sam Cohn will be looking after you in New York." As the agent put it, "He already knew Sam and liked him, so there was no trauma for Bobby in that."

Fosse's concerns were more down to earth, and he promptly asked, "What kind of apartment do you have?"

"Nothing special," Begelman replied. "Two bedrooms in a new building on 58th between Fifth and Sixth. The twenty-sixth floor, a nice view."

"I need a place to live."

"Well, it isn't special, but it's serviceable," Begelman said. "Take it. I'm leaving everything except my clothes and some pictures." He had used the agency's decorator. The apartment looked like an interior design exhibit for the anonymous bachelor, yellow chairs and glass tables. Now Bob was the anonymous bachelor in apartment 26B at 58 West 58th Street, paying a rent of $430 a month. He was single again at forty-four.

Never a materialist, never interested in opulent homes or expensive cars, he made this apartment his own with touches that might have come from a young dancer, a gypsy. He brought in mementos from past shows and mounted them on the walls, most notably a blinking neon sign from *Sweet Charity*. He placed an old theatrical wardrobe trunk in front of the sofa, to be used as a coffee table. It was a trunk that every Broadway dancer either knew or had heard about, a trunk that usually materialized at Fosse's first day of dance rehearsal. Inside was his collection of props: hats of every description—derbies, straw boaters, top hats, fedoras. There were canes and walking sticks, feather boas and capes. It would come to be known as Bob Fosse's Magic Trunk, part of Broadway lore.

He and Ilse had been staying in touch. The letters and telephone calls were lobbing back and forth across the Atlantic, hers pleading, his refusing, until at last he capitulated to her urgency, and she flew back, moving into the Begelman apartment with him. And when he went to California to finish *Cabaret*, he took her along. There was a month of sound balancing ahead and such details as the color corrections of the final print and the main and end credits. By that time, some twenty minutes had been cut from the picture, but since he had included footage that he expected to delete, there were few painful excisions. He continued to deal with Cy Feuer in the icy way that would never thaw, but the general feeling about the movie was good. Then again, so had been the feeling around *Sweet Charity*.

While he was in Los Angeles, he contacted John Rubinstein about possibly acting in *Pippin* (to which the title had been reduced). The young actor had auditioned for *Cabaret* a year earlier. He had even been given a screen test when Michael York's availability had been in question. Bob remembered the earnest young man whom he had teased about a hippie pony tail. It was easy to remember John because he was unusually charming and smart, and his wife Judi West had danced with Bob in one of the *Pal Joey* revivals.

As Rubinstein showed the director into his living room, he wondered why so important and powerful a man had come to *his* house for an audition. He was unable to imagine a successful man this unimpressed with himself. While he read the lead role, Bob read all the other parts in the show, and, Rubinstein remembered, "He read them rather flatly. He was concentrating on watching me, not on being an actor." Then he closed the script and looked into Rubinstein's eyes. "Well?" he asked. "What did you think of it?"

The young actor could not believe what he heard himself saying. "I'm not crazy about it," he said. "But I do like that song, 'Corner of the Sky.' "

"Yeah," Bob said. " 'Corner of the Sky' is a real nice song."

Struggling to repair the gaffe, Rubinstein said, "It could be effective on stage—I mean the song and the whole show."

"We're going to do a lot of work on it," Fosse said.

Some years later, the actor wondered "that I could have had such chutzpah as to criticize a script that represented a starring role on Broadway when I was almost completely inexperienced. But Bob gave me the feeling that he was grounded in a certain kind of reality—a total lack of bullshit that made you feel completely comfortable."

Fosse was also making it clear to Rubinstein that he was himself aware of the script's shortcomings "and so I didn't have to shine him on," the actor said, using the old theatrical expression. "It wouldn't hurt my chances if I was honest," and he was right.

"I want you to come to New York," Bob said, "and I want you to audition for the writers and the producer."

Rubinstein agreed rather quickly.

Ilse and Bob were not having quite so dreamy a time of it as they got back to New York. "I do love you," he would tell her, "but I love a lot of people." He was having fleeting affairs with other women, and she knew it because he told her about them. He reminded her that he had been married to Gwen for ten years "and I'm enjoying my freedom now, after a bad marriage. I *need* that feeling of freedom now. This is getting too limiting . . . too restrictive." He was not going to let himself be tied into an exclusive situation again. "You should try marriage one day," he told one of those fleeting affairs, "just for the experience . . . though I think it's shitty."

Late one Sunday morning in February 1972, the *Pippin* team gathered in the Majestic Theatre on West 44th Street for John Rubinstein's audition. The producer, Stuart Ostrow, was there with the librettist, Roger Hirson, and the composer-lyricist, Stephen Schwartz. They sat behind Bob in the middle of the house as the actor walked tentatively onto the stage where Cary Grant had once performed under the name of Archie Leach, where Richard Burton had sung to Julie Andrews in *Camelot*, where *Carousel* and *South Pacific* had first been seen. The Majestic Theatre had its own association for Bob. It was where the original Broadway production of *Call Me Mister* was playing when he had auditioned for the national company, fresh from the Navy. It was where Joan McCracken had danced her last dance on Broadway.

Rubinstein smiled bravely at his judges. He nodded toward Bob and began to sing the same songs he'd sung in California. Stephen Schwartz asked if he knew "Corner of the Sky" from the *Pippin* score.

"I don't know the words," Rubinstein said, clearing his throat.

Schwartz had a gentle and friendly manner. "Sing it in the pit, John," he said. "The lyric is on the piano."

Rubinstein walked to the lip of the stage. Breathing deeply to still his nerves, he slid down into the orchestra pit and, standing behind the pianist, sang the song.

"Very nice, John," Bob said when he was finished. "Now read us a scene."

Rubinstein read a speech that was handed to him. He was asked to read another and then a third. Finally he stood at center stage as his fate was decided in the remote gloom of the theatre. He waited in the stage light. At last Bob strolled down the aisle. The actor walked to the edge of the stage and squatted. Bob leaned against the stage and whispered, "If you want it, this role is yours."

Oh, for Christ's sake, Rubinstein thought before managing to speak. "Well," he said, "I want it."

"Why don't you work out in a gym?" Bob suggested, still whispering. "You're a little skinny."

The actor could hardly pay attention. "I very much noticed though, how much pleasure Fosse took in doing this," he remembered years later. "He wanted that for himself, giving me the news. He did not want me to leave, for him to tell the casting person and that guy to call my agent, and the agent would get the fun of calling me on the phone and hearing me say, 'Oh, boy!' *He* wanted to see that. I liked that. It made me love him. I thought, I would want that too. If I was some big director, and I was going to give some kid a big chance, I would want to tell him."

Rubinstein took a taxi from the theatre directly to John F. Kennedy Airport for the flight back to California. He didn't want to leave his wife alone any longer than necessary as she was due to give birth. Arriving early in the evening, he went directly to the Los Angeles Music Center where Judi had gone for a concert. As he took the seat beside her in the concert hall, he leaned over, kissed her on the cheek, and whispered, "I got the part."

Movies are released a little bit at a time, like kites, and are first chanced on friendly breezes. One of the first showings of *Cabaret* was given in a private screening room in New York before a specially invited audience, intimates of the makers and actors. Naturally, Liza brought her father, the celebrated director Vincente Minnelli, whose movie musicals included *Meet Me in St. Louis* and *An American in Paris*. Minnelli had been a king at MGM when Fosse had been a cipher.

Bob sat in the last row of the screening room, on the edge of his seat, his eyes darting and hopping along the audience for the least hint of boredom or disapproval. At last his movie's surreal coda passed across the screen with a dissonant replaying of the title song and a series of reprised images. Then Joel Grey looked into the audience of the cabaret and the audience for the movie.

Auf wiedersehen

He paused.

À bientôt

He bowed. Then he slipped through a curtain, leaving only darkness and a drum roll and a twisted mirror for the cabaret audience to view itself and be viewed in. The credits began to crawl while the screening room stayed silent. There was no applause. The lights came on. Fosse remained in his seat. Still there was silence until one person rose. It was Vincente Min-nelli. Overcoat in hand he turned and walked slowly up the aisle. He looked neither ahead nor to the sides but at the floor, his eyes downcast. As he came to the last row he looked up and saw Fosse. He stopped and took Bob's hand. "I have just seen the perfect movie," he said and left.

Fosse and Ebb had agreed to make the Minnelli television show in three mediums so that it would be a theatre event as captured cinemat-ically for presentation on television. Bob was going to structure it around the kind of musical staging—the dance/song—that he had refined in *Cabaret*, a blend of gesture, body picture, and musical number. Liza's songs, which were solos in the nightclub act, would become intimate ensemble pieces, and if her staged movement became so active that it was full-out dancing, then her singing would be prerecorded.

His first decision had been to use film rather than videotape. He could control film more precisely, he could edit it more easily, and the images were technically superior. The show was to be performed in a Broadway theatre before an invitational audience. There would be no pauses for camera setups, but eight cameras would shoot simultaneously, one in each wing, one in each aisle, two at the back of the orchestra, one at the back of the balcony, and one in the lobby. After a single dress rehearsal, the performance would be given on May 31, 1972, at the Lyceum Theatre, leaving three months for editing and postproduction work before the late September air date. But before all that, a magical thing happened. With the release of *Cabaret*, Bob Fosse was reborn. The movie fit at least one definition of genius: It was different from anything that anyone had done before. Its unity of vision and materials, its realistic use of musical numbers, its easy strength, the consistency and startling originality of its style were plain and evident marks of a master. Bob Fosse had been a superlative choreographer, and he had been a thoroughly professional director of musical shows, but *Cabaret* presented him in a much more creative and dominating role. He had become a major director of motion pictures and a candidate for greatness. Who could possibly have predicted such a thing? His movie's reception was stunning in every respect. It was acclaimed by the reviewers, and it was a box office sensation. It would ultimately be one of the year's most profitable movies, and no Fosse film would ever do better. In London, Stanley Kubrick pronounced it "the best movie I think I have ever seen."

As work on the Minnelli television show began, it was apparent that this was a musical Fosse beyond "Steam Heat," "The Rich Kids' Rag," and *Sweet Charity*. As the *Cabaret* composer, John Kander, said, "He had Liza singing numbers that she had been singing for a long time, but the songs were suddenly staged in ways that made my eyes bug." Stuart Ostrow thought, "He was running on white heat. He had finished *Cabaret*, was working on 'Liza,' and we had *Pippin* coming up. He was just white hot."

There was the same boldness to his work on the television show that had been evident in *Cabaret*, the same strong stroke. His artistic muscle was now flexed in spareness and certainty. On occasion he would trade in dance but warily, as a painter might deal with a primary color. Minnelli herself was his basic material. He created with her and on her. He gave her gestures that physicalized her singing; he found the persona within her, a self she could play in public. And if he was no longer a dancer, then she would dance for him, she would have his edge, his slinky curl, she would wear his derby, she would tuck his cane under her arm, she was now the centerpiece for the flash.

As a "concert for television," "Liza with a 'Z' " was going to involve one star, ten dancers, a series of musical numbers, and virtually no dialogue. It was chamber musical theatre, so lucid that it dared the observer to spot the tricks. The order of musical numbers was decided, then repeatedly revised and reordered. Eventually the show would start with a title song and then move on to the Billie Holiday classic, "God Bless the Child," the soulful "Son of a Preacher Man," the special material "Ring Dem Bells," and an old favorite, "Bye, Bye, Blackbird."

Songs with "bye, bye" appealed to the sardonic and morbid Fosse. "Bye, Bye, Blackbird" seemed to capture his nature—the irony of this farewell with a lilt, the darkness of its theme and, too, its dark central image. There was also an appealing minimalism in its musical span for, like "Who's Got the Pain?" in *Damn Yankees*, "Bye, Bye, Blackbird" extends over an unusually narrow range of notes. Like Fosse, then, it is contained and tight, and the words themselves are without mercy

> No one here
> Can love or understand me
> Oh what hard luck stories
> They all hand me

To prepare the number, Fosse wrote detailed work sheets before teaching the piece to his assistants. There have been various attempts, Laban Notation most notably, to record dance steps. None has really worked. Each choreographer finds some system of his own. Fosse's was on graph paper. For this number he scrawled "Birds" at the top of the page and then defined his musical bar (or measure) as four counts, citing as an example the first line of this song. The words "pack up all my" are numbered one to four, as are "care and woe" (three beats cover the last two words). He begins his dance outline with eight counts for the introduction. At this point the lights have come up, and the dancers are frozen. "On third bar," he scribbles, "dancers' heads move up (girls) or down (boys) with snaps."

Finger snaps, inevitably.

The next dozen bars of orchestra music are numbered on the graph paper, next to each number a notation, "Boys—knee changes," for instance, or, "all stop and two finger snaps," or "center girls start original snap combination."

Fosse sometimes indicates dancers by name, for instance, "Barbara circles, Loretta and Candy snap to sides."

With the start of singing he marks his musical bars with the song's words, matching each line against a description of movement. Thus, "make my bed and light the light" (which is eight beats) is marked, "all move to stage left," while "I'll be home late tonight" is noted as "they all stop on 'late.'" The work sheet concludes, "Blackbird, bye, bye" as the "dancers wave and sing bye."

Blackbirds evoked birdlike black costumes. Black (against a brilliantly colored cyclorama) was to be the dominating shade in the Minnelli television show. Black was Fosse's favored shade, but he was as finicky about colors and costumes as he was about finger snapping, and his dependency on amphetamines was only intensifying such obsessions. They could lead to sudden sharp outbursts of temper. "Dexedrine," he said, "makes you care about the color of a hair bow," and Fosse's concern for such details could wreak havoc on others.

"Ring Dem Bells" was the lone number in the show to be prerecorded. It was too hectic for Liza to sing and dance at the same time. Bob kept on top of the recording session as ruthlessly as he attended to performance and costume. As Minnelli was preparing to sing the number, he was particularly aware of the percussionist. "With Bob," the copyist-turned-music-producer Emil Charlap said, "if any dancer pointed somewhere, there was a woodblock, if he touched his head it was the bell of a cymbal, if he did a split it was a ratchet."

Fosse's interest in sound accents was even more particular than that. What Fred Weaver had taught him from vaudeville was now refined. If Charlap provided a woodblock, Bob would want to hear how it sounded when it was hit on the side, or with a soft mallet or a hard one. Inevitably, all this focus on noises made the percussionist nervous, and Herb Harris was a nervous percussionist already. "He was notorious for being clumsy and easily rattled," Charlap chuckled. As a result, he tried too hard. "Every time a sound was asked for," Charlap remembered, "Harris would reach for the instrument and knock something else to the floor. He just kept crashing into things."

As this routine was playing itself out, the musicians were calling each other's attention to the hapless percussionist (who was actually the top man with the New York Philharmonic). As the laughter spread, Fosse grew uneasy.

"What the hell are you all laughing about?" he snapped, annoyed that it might be him.

At that moment the percussionist fell into the whole setup of drums, sending everything tumbling and banging and crashing to the floor. Charlap and the rest collapsed in gales of laughter, and Bob, at last realizing what the joke was, laughed too.

Intense as rehearsals were, and with a show that was entirely musical, the repetition was endless, even Fosse had to take time off because the union insisted on it. One radiant Saturday afternoon half into May, Buddy Hackett telephoned, appearing with his usual unexpectedness.

"I'm inviting you to a very special dinner."

"With who?" Bob asked.

"Never mind with who," Hackett said. "All my friends, that's who."

"Okay," Bob said, "but I don't have a date."

"So? Somebody's bound to break up."

"Where?" Bob asked. "Where's the restaurant?"

"We're meeting at Vincent's Clam Bar," Hackett said. "It's on Mott Street. Vincent's Clam Bar on Mott Street at six o'clock."

Bob still didn't know who was coming. With Hackett it could as easily be a group of doctors as nightclub comedians, because medicine was his hobby. He was one of those people who really wanted to hear about symptoms when they asked how you were feeling. The group that convened at Vincent's Clam Bar, however, was neither comic nor medical. The first face Bob spotted was Paddy Chayefsky, who plainly knew everyone in the entire world. At the table, too, were Doc and Joan Simon. Neil stood up and shook hands with Bob and gave him a hug. Joan turned toward him in her seat as he leaned down to kiss her. They let it go as if Majorca had never happened.

Buddy's wife Sherry was there, and Vidal Sassoon, slender and dark-haired and bright-eyed. There was also a beautiful girl sitting between two men. ("They all live together," Hackett told a fascinated Fosse, who preferred his threesomes heterosexual in his favor.) "I don't know who does what to which," Buddy said. More beautiful still was the movie star

Ava Gardner, whose date was the disc jockey William B. Williams. It was quite a group.

Menus were not distributed. No orders were taken. Hackett had arranged everything in advance, and great platters were brought out, heavy with a warm Italian antipasto of calamari and shrimp in a special hot sauce. Hackett warned everyone to eat slowly and not overdo the bread, because a full evening of food lay ahead, but there was also a lot of working it off for this was going to be what he called a "walking dinner." Only the first course was to be eaten at Vincent's Clam Bar. Then they all crossed the street to the Italian Civic Club for a wine break before the whole group chattered its way over to Mulberry Street. They must have been a sight, these glowingly successful people on safari in the narrow lanes of Little Italy, led by bushbeater Buddy Hackett with a beautiful movie star in tow. Hackett waved his way to the Luna Restaurant, and the whole party moved in for the pasta course, sitting down with a now familiar heartiness.

"I didn't know you knew Doc," Bob said.

"I was friendly with Doc before he was Doc," Hackett said. "I bought material from him when he was seventeen years old, writing jokes with his brother Danny. They spent a week with me at the Nevele Country Club in Ellenville."

"That's a million dollars worth of material," Bob said.

"Yeah? Well I only paid twenty-two hundred dollars for it, but I'll give you an idea of the special sense of humor that Neil Simon had," Hackett said, "even before he started writing plays. He wrote a joke for me about a guy who walks into a doctor's office, and as he comes through the door, the receptionist gets up from her desk and walks over to him. She says, 'You'd better sit down, Mr. Greenberg, because we have some pretty serious news for you.'

" 'What's that?' the guy asks. 'Did my tests come back?'

" 'They came back,' the nurse tells him, 'and you have a malignancy. Mr. Greenberg, you have terminal cancer.'

" 'Oh my God,' the man says, and he collapses into a chair in shock when the doctor comes out of his inner office. He says to the nurse, 'That's Mr. Greenberg over there, isn't it? You'd better send him in ahead of everyone else, because I have something terrible to tell him.'

" 'Do you mean about the tests, doctor?'

" 'Yeah,' the doctor says. 'I'm afraid so.'

" 'Well, I already told him about the terminal cancer,' the nurse says.

"The doctor looks at her, he stares at her, and then he stamps his foot and he says, *'I wanted to tell him.'* "

As Bob laughed, Hackett said, "Now that's the Neil Simon sense of humor, and he didn't even get paid the twenty-two hundred. The agent took it and gave him and Danny six hundred."

After pasta at the Luna Restaurant, they walked over to Broome Street for veal scallopini at the Grotta Azzura.

Hackett would not let the evening be rushed. He provided his guests with time for digestion, making regular stops in the back rooms of tavernas along the way, where they would watch card and bocci games and drink more wine.

In each restaurant he was greeted by the owner and would introduce his guests. Ava Gardner was attracting almost as much attention as he, but Hackett had the kind of celebrity that comes in this life only after seventy-seven appearances on "The Johnny Carson Show." Hardly bashful, he ambled through each restaurant, greeting the customers, exchanging small talk, listening patiently to jokes, and even singing to youngsters. He was so relaxed in public, so accessible and genuine, so at ease with strangers that he provided his companions with a shared sense of recognition and public ease. He made them all act like relaxed and beloved stars.

It was almost midnight when the ebullient group pulled up or rolled up or trundled into the inevitable last stop, the famous Ferrara's on Grand Street for a dessert of cannoli and cappucino. There, as at every waystation along the six-hour route, Hackett was awaited and treated with extravagant hospitality. His tables were organized and reserved, the special desserts were waiting, the coffee steaming and freshly brewed, and of course there were never any checks (to be seen).

At evening's end, with all of them stuffed and aching from laughter, for few people in life are funnier than Neil Simon and Buddy Hackett, they bade each other cheerful good nights and waved for taxis and shouted last jokes, and it was wonderful to be famous and in show business.

The afternoon of the filming of "Liza with a 'Z'," Fred Ebb arrived at the Lyceum Theatre while everyone else was still at lunch break. One of the craftiest and cleverest of Broadway lyric writers, he was also one of the most nervous. He unzipped his leather jacket and sat down in one of the theatre seats to wait for rehearsal. After some moments, a man came down the aisle with the hats for the dancers to wear in the number "Ring Dem Bells."

When the man handed him the package and presented him with a bill for $450, Ebb considered the price rather high. They were, after all, only hats, "airline stewardess hats," he remembered. He also thought that someone else should be asked to pay for them, but nobody else was there, and he knew how important details could be for Bob Fosse, especially *hats*. And he knew, too, how angry Bob Fosse would become were the hats not there for the show.

But miraculously the production supervisor, Kenneth Utt, materialized on stage, and when he learned what the problem was, he told Ebb to calm down. The panic, however, was on. Ebb's hairspring anxieties seemed painfully, perfectly matched to Fosse's perfectionism. The two of them were a vaudeville team playing on each other's problems. "I was pale with fright," Ebb remembered. "If Bobby didn't have his stewardess caps, well, that was just the kind of thing that could set him off."

Utt refused to pay the fellow the $450. "This guy is holding us up for them," he told the paralyzed lyricist. And as Ebb sat in the fully lighted theatre while Utt argued with the hat man, he wondered whether "I might have to go out in the street and beg for the money." But the production supervisor finally settled the negotiation. "That guy knew a pigeon when he saw one," the lyricist concluded.

It was raining that night. The cameras were rolling in the dressing rooms and in the lobby of the theatre. They captured the backstage tension and the audience anticipation, the stir of a special night at the theatre. This invited audience had an extra edge. A ticket was a certificate of success, an assurance of importance. Spiffed up in black tie, they were cast as the perfect Broadway audience and were doubtless eager to play the role.

Paddy was seated in the second row on the left side of the theatre, behind Stuart and Annie Ostrow, and beside them was the socialite publicist Earl Blackwell. On the other side of the theatre was the songwriter Harold Arlen in his thick-lensed, rose-tinted glasses. Arlen had written "Over the Rainbow" for Liza's mother, Judy Garland. He was an old family friend.

Next to Arlen was Kurt Weill's widow, Lotte Lenya, who had been in the Broadway production of *Cabaret*, and behind her was one of Liza's stepfathers, Sid Luft. Scattered through the theatre were Cliff Robertson and his wife Dina Merrill, Frank Yablans and Otto Preminger from Hollywood, Fred Silverman and Roone Arledge of television.

Elsewhere in the Lyceum Theatre that May 31, 1972, were Cy Coleman, Tony Bennett, Senator Jacob Javits, Richard Avedon, and the designer Halston. The hot new choreographer Michael Bennett was there too. John Kander and Fred Ebb had four tickets apiece, and Fred gave two of his to Chita Rivera. The only notable absentee was Ilse Schwarzwald. After a particularly nasty siege of quarrels, Bob had told her, "I think it's better if we're not in the same city."

The orchestra struck up this night's overture. It was a "hot audience," Stu Ostrow said, "and Fosse was enough of a showman to know that he had to keep that audience hot, and so he set out to make this as much a stage show as a television show."

The cheers and applause were obediently brief as Liza flashed on-stage in a white pants suit. She was fresh to stardom, or superstardom as the same thing had come to be called. *Cabaret* was being shown across America, all over the world, and Minnelli personified the movie. She was the latest news, she was on the covers of *Time*, *Newsweek*, and *Life*, she symbolized young success, and still, as Judy Garland's daughter, she had an association for older audiences.

Fosse's cameras photographed her from the knees, from below the stage and at shoulder level, from the back of the theatre, from the balconies, from the wings. He would ultimately photograph the show not only from eight angles, but from four more cameras when brief stretches had to be refilmed a week later because of lighting mistakes and camera failures.

The Robert Randolph setting surged to bold rectangles of solid color behind Minnelli and the squad of dancers. She changed costume with speed, out of the white pants and into a brief scarlet beaded dress that left her long legs bare to the hip. For "Ring Dem Bells" Bob spread the dancers stagewide in an expansiveness unusual for him. Then "Bye, Bye Black-bird" came sly and writhing with its finger snaps and derbies and Bob Fosse lookalikes, two skinny fellows in black pants and boots with cigarettes dangling from their lips.

There has been the occasional movie director who was also a chore-ographer (Stanley Donen, Gene Kelly, Herbert Ross), but Bob Fosse would appear to be the only one who succeeded absolutely in blending the two disciplines. This show, "Liza with a 'Z,' " may well be the best dance film ever made.

15

Two ladies
Two ladies
And I'm the only man
        —song from *Cabaret*

The summer of 1972 began the second marriage of Bob Fosse and Gwen Verdon, this one based on friendship, on parenthood, and on love for their child, on professional collaboration, on mutual respect, on their friends' need to sentimentalize a celebrated show business couple, on separate living quarters, and on sexual freedom for Bob. It would take some time for Gwen to grow accustomed to this novel arrangement. She was a regular pioneer.

Apparently she had spoken to nobody about the yearlong crisis that had conceived the new arrangement, and she didn't yet speak to anyone about the peculiar relationship that was now evolving.

She had little work and began to express interest in nonmusicals. She involved herself in the activities of the social psychologist Karen Horney. She talked about starting an employment office for out-of-work dancers. She could well sympathize with them.

She urged Bob to come to the beach house for weekends, and he was willing. Editing the television show was going to be an exhausting job. The house represented a way of life that he loved, and it gave him his friends, it restored Nicole to him, at least for a few days at a stretch, which was all the time he could spare anyway.

There certainly was something bizarre about the summer weekends with Gwen. She seemed to treat them as if they were denials of the rest of the week. "She's lining up all these social things for me," he complained to a lover in the city, "lunches and barbecue dinners, but maybe it's better this way. We don't have much to talk about anymore except when it comes to Nicole." She would play the hostess from the charcoal grill, the

Broadway star with a cookout apron over her jeans, stepping out of a magazine story about famous folks at home. Yet, he also played his part in this little game of pretend family, acting the role of a weekend husband and father who, like so many men out there, joined his family at the beach after a week of work in the city. The main difference between him and many of them was that he made no secret of his girlfriends in the city.

There was also a growing circle of male writer friends. Sam Cohn introduced him to E. L. Doctorow and Peter Maas, two clients who were Hamptonites, and on such occasions Bob would take Bob Aurthur aside and ask what they had written, jotting down the titles and whispering, "Must read it."

Surely, they too enjoyed Bob and Gwen at the beach. It was fun to be with so glamorous a couple.

In New York, Bob received a letter from Ilse asking why there couldn't be two kinds of love in his life, that of a father for his daughter, that of a man for a woman? She yearned to be with him. She denied that she was jealous of Nicole. She admitted that the frustration of trying to understand his attitude was, more than anything, sad.

Doc and Joan Simon sometimes seemed to spend more time on their East Hampton tennis court than they did inside the house. They entertained each other at play and treated their matches earnestly, even when nobody else was watching. In 1972 people were still fussy about tennis fashion and played the game in its uniform whites, a badge of country club class. Joan liked to wear these brief, yet oddly prim white tennis dresses, and she had the trim athletic figure to carry them off. Looking (and being) small next to her six-foot husband, she was a compact and well-conditioned woman of thirty-eight with a flashing grin and thick, dark hair. It dropped in bangs across her forehead.

Neil, owlish in his glasses and writerly, also played in tennis whites even when it was just the two of them on their home court, both suntanned; they looked sturdy and fit, a handsome couple. Then one day during a match Joan fractured her arm. She hadn't fallen down, and she hadn't struck it against anything. It just broke. It was what doctors call a "spontaneous fracture."

Herb Gardner had grown so attached to Paddy and Bob that he took an office on their eleventh floor at 850 Seventh Avenue, just to be near them. He was too tall and bulky, really, for someone so sensitive, and it often seemed as if he was embarrassed about that. He was big all right and burly, a curly-haired bear with an unlikely combination of sentimentality and wit. He had been nicknamed "Whimsy" in the partnership that he, Paddy, and Bob joked about (the serious-minded Paddy being called "Boredom" and Fosse, of course, "Flash"). It was typical of Gardner's charm that, even now, he could be sentimental and witty—while in the tenth year of a spirit-draining dry spell that would have worn down a man of lesser hope.

Fresh out of Antioch College, he had been a wonder boy, the cartoonist of "The Nebbishes," which was syndicated in sixty-one newspapers. He quit cartooning to become a playwright, and his first play, A *Thousand Clowns*, was one of the biggest Broadway hits of 1962, when he was twenty-seven years old. Since then he'd had nothing. His last play, *The Goodbye People*, ran a dismal seven performances in 1968 after being roasted by the critics. Yet Gardner was ever the optimist, a rare one in a cynical world, and in that lay partial explanation of his bad fortune for his work reflected his optimism, and a cynical world reacted to it with jeers.

He didn't spend as much time at the office as his friends did, perhaps because his private life, lived with the actress Marlo Thomas, was more cheerful than theirs. On the days that Herb did come to the office, it would be three for luncheon at the Carnegie Delicatessen—and an unlikely combination they were, two emotional Jews and one dancing gentile with his heart on hold.

Gardner, Chayefsky, and Fosse looked forward to, enjoyed, and spent so much time at the Carnegie that it sometimes seemed as if their offices were there while it was on the eleventh floor that they took occasional work breaks. "We tried to help each other," Gardner would remember. "We tried to have serious talks, mainly kvetching about who we were working with, but mostly we just hung out and laughed."

"I don't know about you guys," Bob said after one long lunch and a stroll, "but it's four o'clock . . . I gotta get back to work."

"Fosse," Chayefsky chided, "you forgot. You have no work. You're finished in the business."

"Oh," Bob deadpanned. "That's right, I forgot."

In fact, Paddy Chayefsky had himself recently survived a career crisis during the same period as Bob's. He had not even been able to get a Broadway production for his 1968 play, *The Latent Heterosexual*. That led him to abandon the theatre. A brilliant survivor, his Academy Award for 1971's screenplay, *The Hospital*, not only established him as a film writer but gave him such reputation that he could work in New York (he despised Los Angeles almost as much as Bob did).

Bob, of course, was just soaring. Not only was *Cabaret* a commercial and artistic triumph and not only was "Liza with a 'Z' " finished and almost ready for broadcast and not only was he about to start work on *Pippin*, but Sam Cohn had just completed negotiations for his next movie. Life was in exhilarating condition, which was exhausting.

The ostensible energy generator, Dexedrine, made that certain. The drug had become a steadier diet than food. It was an appetite depressant anyway, which meant less weight on this already slender frame and little sleep, because of the amphetamine stimulation. The long and anxious nights, which the Dexedrine either exacerbated or actually caused, led to predawn telephone calls desperately pleading for company, but there were always dancers eager to please Bob Fosse. He had started to inform new lovers that if they were not interested in threesomes—two girls and himself—they need not apply, but at two in the morning, he couldn't always be so particular. A number of unadventurous, uncompliant girlfriends found this ultimatum to be just a bluff. He would settle for them alone.

One afternoon, Herb and Paddy took the usual postlunch stroll up West 57th Street without him. He stayed behind at the Carnegie Delicatessen to have his first production meeting with Patricia Zipprodt, who was to be the costume designer for *Pippin*. Herb Schlein had given him his preferred table at the rear of the restaurant, and now the shortsleeved maître d' walked over, limping slightly from the gout that was starting to bother him. In Schlein's white, soft, and heavy arms was a ribboned box. Inside was Venetian crystal.

"Happy birthday, Bob. It's your forty-fifth, isn't it?"

"That's right." June 23, 1972. "How did you know?"

"If Bob Fosse isn't in *Who's Who*, who is?"

But Pat Zipprodt waved from the front of the restaurant and strolled toward the table, and that was the end of that.

There was no mistaking Patricia Zipprodt for anything but a costume designer, because everything that she wore was so carefully mismatched. She was a bohemian with style, and it was a style suited to her intelligence, her scholarliness, her cheerful gossip and warmth. Patricia Zipprodt was tall and dark, a vivacious woman in her thirties with a shock of thick black hair, and she was one of Broadway's premier designers. She sat down and asked Herb for a cup of tea. He said that he would send a waiter over. Herb Schlein did not wait on tables.

Patricia and Bob had worked together before (on the *Sweet Charity* movie), but that didn't seem to make it any easier for him to plunge into conversation with her. When the waiter arrived, he ordered two cups of tea. They remained silent until it was served. Then they took turns spooning in the sugar and sat and stirred. Still, neither spoke. Pat knew that costumes were a tough subject for Bob. He had difficulty visualizing them. He could not even "read" sketches very well. Designers of scenery, too, often had to wait until their work was finished before he made his decisions. He knew what he thought only when he saw the thing, although when he saw the thing, he certainly knew what he thought. On occasion a sketch would strike him just right like a slap on the forehead, but it was not to be counted on, and they sat there, stirring their teas.

"Well, Mr. Fosse," she finally ventured, "how do you think we should approach this show, *Pippin?*"

He looked into his cup of tea for a while over that one.

"I think," he finally said, "it should be magical."

"Wonderful," the designer said with a broad smile. She stirred her tea. She sipped at it. Then she said, after an extra pause, "Besides magical—?"

Bob sipped his tea. Then he stirred it.

"I'd like it to be"—and he paused to find just the right word— "anachronistic."

Zipprodt looked up from her cup. She had no idea what he was talking about.

"Anachronistic, you say. That's very good." After a moment she said, "Look, why don't I go home and make some rough sketches?"

That seemed to relieve him tremendously. He said sketches were a great idea.

Sitting at her drawing board, surrounded by costumes from plays and operas with drawings pinned to the walls and art reference books tumbling out of the cases, piled on the floor, she aligned a stack of fresh drawing paper. She arranged her newly sharpened pencils in a neat row. Then she thought, "I don't know what on earth he *means* by those words, 'magical' and 'anachronistic.'"

It wasn't only in the area of costumes that Bob was tentative about *Pippin*. He told a friend, "I'm scared. I don't know the show at all. Here it is, the start of summer, we're going into rehearsal next month, and I'm still auditioning. God, I'm exhausted."

Patricia Zipprodt picked up the telephone and dialed his number. "Tell me, what do you mean when you say 'magical and anachronistic?'"

There was a silence at the other end until he finally replied, "Well—I mean Jesus Christ in tennis shorts."

"And he couldn't have given me more," she recalled. "That was a wonderfully rich image. It gave me a whole slant. He was after the unexpected." But it was not to come that easily. The opening stage directions of Roger Hirson's script were, "Enter the strolling players of an indeterminate period." Her response to that was incredulity. "Well, son of a gun," she said, "how can you have an 'indeterminate period?' Once you put on a pair of shoes you're someplace in time." Nevertheless she started to sketch, and thus began the departure from the authors' original intent.

The departure from the authors was taking a different turn at chorus auditions. Fosse seemed to be hiring the ensemble without regard to singing ability. He was interested only in the dancing, and in the girls' looks, and this was understandably distracting to the composer, Stephen Schwartz. One of the auditioning dancers, Jennifer Nairn-Smith, remembered trying to think of the Beatles as she strained to carry a tune. "I was no singer," she said. "I was a ballet dancer."

Indeed she was, having come to Broadway from the New York City Ballet. As a dancer who had been trained by George Balanchine, she considered herself a cut above the average Broadway gypsy, but there were other ballet-trained dancers at the *Pippin* auditions, most especially Ann Reinking, who had danced with the San Francisco Ballet.

A large and mixed group, then, they milled about the stage, finally working themselves into rough formation as they started to dance the Fosse Combinations. The pianist played louder, and Nairn-Smith remembered, "Everyone was panting, trying to learn the thing."

Bob's combinations sent them through leaps, slides, spins, and slithers. He needed only five boys and five girls, but Kathy Doby and Ben Vereen already had their jobs. Bob kept eliminating, reducing the large group while the pianist played for the great thumping mass, and it seemed to Jenn (as her friends sometimes called her) that he had already found the girls he needed. "He put me on the side, and I was sure I didn't have a job because I couldn't do all those back bumps and the grinds and all that stuff. That wasn't what Balanchine had taught us."

She was tall for a dancer, nearly five feet ten inches, and at thirty she was too old, although she said she looked twenty-two. She had long, dark, thick brown hair and unusually full breasts for a dancer. As anyone could see, Jennifer Nairn-Smith was a stunning creature. She had come to New York from Australia and had no natural, cultural, or learned feel for show (or "jazz") dancing. "Ballet dancers are always up on our toes," she said. "We're on pointe and we're taught to elevate all the time, to rise, so we can hardly even bend our knees. I'd never studied jazz dancing in my life," she said, but Jennifer Nairn-Smith wanted to be on Broadway, and she had the long legs that Bob wanted. "Not just long legs," she proudly pointed out, "but a long thigh bone."

She left the theatre with some slight remaining hope, not yet having been eliminated, and in the evening Bob called, but it was not about the show. He was asking her to dinner. She declined—she had a boyfriend, and Bob seemed to accept that. The next day, however, he called again to repeat the invitation, and since her agent had told her that she had been asked back for a second audition, she decided that this time she had better accept for dinner.

But "tell me," she said forthrightly on the telephone, "is this what I have to do to get the job?" It was better, she thought, "to just be awful and blunt about it." Fosse took offense. What kind of man did she think he was? She thought, "Oh, God, I'm going to lose this job," so she apologized for the remark.

At dinner he was interested in her childhood in Sidney and in her growing up in Queensland. She talked about dancing for Balanchine and "how he taught us to feel superior." Bob said that he was sorry he had never studied classical ballet. "I admire Jerry Robbins more than anyone," he said. "I wish I could do that. I've thought about taking classes, and the Joffrey company asked me to do a ballet, but I've never done anything longer than four or five minutes. I don't think I could sustain it."

At ten o'clock she said that she had to get home because, smiling, she had a dance callback the next morning.

"You can come up for a nightcap, can't you?"

"You mean to your place?" she asked unnecessarily.

"Well, it's just across the street."

That was when she "knew that I'd been set up," but she agreed to the nightcap anyway, and as they walked into the apartment, he chatted idly about a piece of company gossip. Then he poured the cognac and reached for her. When she resisted and pulled away, the scene became unpleasant. "He picked me up and shoved me against the wall," she remembered. "I was bigger than he was, but dancers are strong. I kicked him in the groin," she said and then laughed, adding, "not very well."

Then she fled, yanking the front door open and shouting, "For a job I have to do this?" and was gone.

At the auditions he didn't seem to remember the night before. She danced in the group, she danced for a grueling eight hours, and when it was over, she had the job.

Most Broadway dance rehearsals had moved eight blocks uptown since the Variety Arts studios on 46th Street had burned down. The same owner, "Fergy" Ferguson, ran the new place, Broadway Arts, at 1755 Broadway, near 54th Street, upstairs over a car dealer. "New" was something of a euphemism. The creaky elevator, scarred pianos, and dusty, sun-streaked rehearsal rooms were all soaked in show business lore, and everyone who used the place was grateful that there was nothing new about it.

To begin, Bob and Kathy Doby worked alone, trying a series of walks and moves. When they hit upon something that Fosse liked, Kathy would jot it down on a pad of long yellow legal paper, not unlike his notes for "Liza with a 'Z,' " with phrases like "turned-in" or "knee in" or "knee out." It was an improvised stenographic system.

Dance rehearsals began a week before script work. The five women were magnificent and voluptuous. As Ann Reinking said, "Fosse women are differently beautiful—sort of sexy and not quite real." (She also thought that Bob himself "on first sight looked very nifty.") Fosse allowed the same sexuality for the men. Those who were gay he allowed to act gay. This was a break with general practice, where choreographers tried to make their male dancers look and act like cops. "When I first started choreographing," he said, "if I thought someone was camping on stage, or indicating they were gay, soft, or effeminate, I would stop it and make them all be macho." Now he decided to stop doing that. "It was the first time I never said, 'Don't be so minty,' and I found that I got better performances."

Even among these beautiful women, Jennifer Nairn-Smith was stunning, and it sometimes seemed as if Bob was being cruel to her precisely because of it, as if to strip her of the intimidating and protective armor of her beauty to make her vulnerable. But Jennifer hardly needed any disarmament to be vulnerable. Her analysis of his nastiness was that he was intimidated by her classical training. Kathy Doby felt that Bob was being cruel because "Jennifer was not picking up on his style as well as she should have." Ben Vereen told her, "They're just trying to take away your sexuality," and Ann Reinking wasn't sympathetic at all. She considered Jennifer the victim type. "Every company has its victim," she would later say. "With Bob you knew right away," and she watched the harsh treatment develop "real cruel and slow."

Being alone made Jenn feel even more vulnerable. Kathy Doby had a new husband. Ann Reinking had a husband too—Jennifer called him Mickey Mouseketeer because, she said, "he seemed so young and innocent." But after Annie got the job, he went back to Seattle. He had at least for a while provided his wife with some emotional support. Jennifer's boyfriend, on the other hand, was too self-centered and emotional to help her.

Bob's telephone calls were continuing nightly. She repeatedly declined his invitations. "But," she said, "it made me so nervous. I'm a ballet dancer, and you do what a choreographer says. You could drag me around the floor. I had no self-esteem. I was a victim. Balanchine used to say in his Russian accent, 'You know, there's plenty of fresh flowers in the [dance] school,' so we were scared all the time of losing everything."

When Bob assigned her to carry the American flag in one of the numbers, she broke down. "I was from the ballet," she said, "and here I was carrying a flag and doing bumps." She fled the stage in the middle of rehearsal and was sobbing in the wings when the producer, Stuart Ostrow, came to comfort her. "He explained the overview of the show," she said. "I hadn't been able to see how it all fit into Bob's conception. All I could see was that the other girls had harder and more complicated things to do while I was carrying a flag.

"That was the turning point," she said. "That's when I said to myself, 'Oh, you'd better go to bed with him,' and the truth was, I would have been better off if I had done it from the top."

She had another problem. Her boyfriend, a sometime actor and a would-be writer, was prone to jealous rages. He had not, in the past, spared her the occasional slapping around. "I don't know why I always run into these evil guys," Jennifer said.

As the actors' rehearsals began, composer-lyricist Stephen Schwartz's problems were escalating. Like others before him, he was not handling youthful success with style. *Godspell* remained an international bonanza, and one of his songs from it, "Day by Day," was a big hit. Fame and money, he would later acknowledge, had made him bratty. Bob told an interviewer, "Stephen is only twenty-five years old . . . and sometimes he's only twelve. But he's a very talented person, and I like this score very much," which was baloney.

Truth was, as *Pippin's* designer Tony Walton recalled, "None of us could understand why Bob even wanted to do the show—or could imagine how it could amount to anything." Kathy Doby said, "Schwartz wanted it done exactly as he had written it in college, which was too long for Fosse and certainly too fey. It was even more primitive than *Godspell*," she said. "It was simpler and sillier," but Bob must have seen possibilities in it. Otherwise, as he himself said, "Why wait for *The New York Times* critic to decide your life? Movies are the art form of our generation."

There was something about Broadway, then, that was attracting him. "It's been five years since I've been there," he said, "and I've missed it a great deal," but he'd forgotten about the aggravation of collaborating.

Herb Schlein turned forty-one on August 10, and Bob gave him a birthday present from Mark Cross, the fancy leather goods store. It was a dark blue leather purse, a man's clutch bag. Perhaps Bob wanted to demonstrate that he was respectful and not condescending, that he would get Schlein the same kind of expensive gift that he would buy for one of his friends, although it is hard to imagine him giving a dark blue leather Mark Cross clutch bag to Neil Simon, Paddy Chayefsky, or Herb Gardner.

An overwhelmed Schlein immediately emptied his wallet into the new bag, he added the week's pay that he had just received, and walked two blocks north to the First National City Bank to make his regular deposit. The clutch bag was, he thought, terrifically handsome, and he was very proud of it, thrilled that it had come from Bob Fosse, "the only human being that I did have a little bit of friendship with. A *little* bit. And who was never mean to me."

After he filled out the savings account slip, he turned to get the cash and that was when he found, alas, that the bag was gone. He pulled away from the counter in shock. He looked on the floor and turned to search behind him. The purse was nowhere to be seen. He stayed on the spot for some minutes, rooted by disbelief, perhaps waiting for the bag to reappear. He spoke imploringly with the bank guards and with the bank manager. He reported the theft to the secretary who handled the lost and found property. She showed him several key cases in her desk drawer as proof that some items were actually lost and found, but he knew that his clutch bag was stolen and gone forever while the business of the bank carried on, heartless and oblivious to his grief.

The *Pippin* production team was in the theatre as the actors rehearsed their scenes. Besides Fosse and Schwartz there were the librettist Roger Hirson, the producer Stuart Ostrow, the set designer Tony Walton, the lighting director Jules Fisher, the costume designer Patricia Zipprodt, and Schwartz's wife, Carol. It was unusual for an outsider to be allowed into rehearsal at so early a date, but Carol Schwartz was an actress. She had been in Ostrow's production of *1776*, and she was considered part of the family.

She arrived in the theatre, this particular day, up to her chin in packages. They had just bought a house in Connecticut, and she had been shopping for housewares. Stephen was oblivious to that as he glared at the stage where the dancers were writhing. He was not only a composer and a lyricist but a man of the theatre. As Tony Walton said, "Stephen himself had directed *Pippin* when it was produced in college, and he had strong feelings about how it should be done." Bob was not overwhelmingly interested in those feelings.

Abruptly—nobody seemed to have sensed it coming—Schwartz said loudly, "I'm getting out of here."

Bob stared hard at the actor on stage. He didn't say anything. He just scratched and rubbed at his chin and at the beard he was growing. The composer rose and edged along the row of seats, into the aisle. The actors watched speechlessly, anxiously from the stage. Carol gathered her boxes and followed her husband in a show of support, arms full and packages tumbling. Patricia Zipprodt came to help but was urged away. Stephen did not go out through the rear doors of the theatre but instead decided to make a statement by stalking down the aisle and up the small flight of stairs that had been pushed against the side of the stage. Carol followed with her packages. They trooped across, one behind the other, past the actors, before disappearing into the wings.

Stuart Ostrow was not alarmed. Collaborator quarrels were not surprising; they were only surprising this early in the game. Perhaps he was placing more faith in his director than he was in the authors, but that was only reasonable since Fosse was the one with all the experience. Ostrow was in fact placing a great deal of faith in him, and when Bob learned that the show was budgeted at $750,000, he was aghast. Only the year before, Hal Prince had set a record for the most expensive show in Broadway history with the $700,000 *Follies*, and all of that money had been lost. Yet, aghast or not, when Bob learned that Stuart had raised only $500,000 of the budget, he took it as a personal affront. "Don't worry," the producer said. "With you doing it we'll get the money." But Fosse would remember that bitterly. "It was a little bringdown for me to find out that nobody would invest in me. Maybe they didn't think I was any good."

The truth simply was that Ostrow was having difficulty raising money for *Pippin* because it was an expensive show written by a young man with a solitary off-Broadway success, because *Follies* had recently lost a great deal of money and investors were leery of big musicals; because he was an independent producer who had always been a maverick and never had major backing by the theatre owners. The money shortfall had nothing to do with doubts about Bob, but there was no convincing him of that.

Drugs were not allaying Bob's fears and suspicions. He liked to smirk about "the Doc Simon crowd, trying to be so young and with-it, announcing after dinner, 'Okay, everyone, we're all going to turn on.' " He was right. The times had made smoking marijuana a middle-class and middle-aged recreation, but he smoked marijuana too, and he had learned about amyl nitrate "poppers" from the gay dancers who favored them. These were pressurized ampoules that released powerful fumes upon being snapped (or popped) open. They were available only by prescription and were designed to stimulate the heart in case of a strong arrhythmia, a skipping beat. Gays were not the only ones to appreciate the fact that, in racing the heart, these fumes also created an intense sexual aura. It was a stimulant for all sexual persuasions, perhaps, but a violent stimulation of the heart was not the most advisable of joyrides for someone whose family had a history of heart disease. As usual, Fosse could not deny himself the pleasure.

Then, too, he had graduated from Dexedrine to Dexamil, a narcotic cocktail that conveniently added a dose of the tranquilizer Miltown to the amphetamine Dexedrine so as to calm one down after being sped up. The middle-class after-dinner marijuana crowd, then, was in knee pants in Bob's world of better living through chemistry.

Simultaneously with *Pippin* rehearsals, he was editing "Liza with a 'Z'." David Breatherton, who had done a superlative job cutting *Cabaret*, was not working on "Liza." Breatherton had won an Academy Award for editing *Cabaret*, but he had made a mistake in his acceptance speech— he had remembered to thank God, but he had forgotten to thank Bob Fosse. The movie director Sidney Lumet, an East Hampton friend, recommended Alan Heim for the editing job. Heim was the Fosse type, a Jew with the wit and wisdom of the New York City streets. Looking no-nonsense, a working person with crumpled clothes and a bushy mustache, he was short and smart, and could be respectful without being subservient. He showed up for an interview at the Broadway Arts studios where Bob was rehearsing with Minnelli. "It was my first time in a rehearsal studio," Heim remembered, "and it was pretty exciting to be in a room with Liza Minnelli and Bob Fosse." The only question Bob asked was, "Are you a musician?" Heim wasn't, he couldn't read music. He didn't know why the film editor of the Liza Minnelli television special needed to read music, and Fosse looked annoyed, but he hired Alan Heim, who would be his only film editor from then on.

The cutting room for "Liza with a 'Z' " was on the tenth floor at 1600 Broadway. It was a smallish, bare-boned room with long tables for the splicers and the Moviolas, the machinery of editing. It might as well have been windowless for all the city grime on the panes. There was one deep leather armchair and several straight wooden chairs. It was a work room, and Heim worked there all day until Bob would arrive after *Pippin* rehearsals, heralding himself with a cigarette cough all the way from the elevator.

Editing is as essential to moviemaking as the writing, the acting, the photography. It is where choices are made, which performance, which scene, which angle, which take. Performances can be made or destroyed in the cutting room, the rhythms and attitude of the movie can be set there. Nothing in Bob Fosse's background could have prepared him for this kind of work, but film editing was something that he took to naturally and learned quickly. Perhaps it drew on the same instinct for rhythm and timing as dancing.

The film editor, while often a creative figure, is less a collaborator than a lieutenant. In fact, while moviemaking does not offer a director absolute power, the right of final cut that Fosse won after *Cabaret*, and which he demanded for every subsequent movie, was as close to autonomy as any director could come. For Fosse, this must have stood in happy contrast to the theatre's frustrating compromises, and the editing room was the place where that power was exercised.

At *Pippin*, Bob was ready to show some of his dances. He invited Tony Walton and Jules Fisher, the scenic and lighting designers, to come into the rehearsal studio and see what he had done. "It wasn't even set to Stephen Schwartz's music," Walton recalled. "It was set to 'Down by the Riverside,' " he said, "somehow blended with [the Fosse favorite] Erik Satie's "Gymnopédies No. 1," and as the dance ended, "Jules and I sat there in amazement," the designer remembered. "We looked at each other as if to say, 'He's going to turn this into something!' "

When, as a courtesy, Bob showed the same number to Schwartz, he made certain that the dance pianist had replaced "Down by the Riverside" with melodies from songs from the show. The orchestrator Ralph Burns came in to watch, eager to get a head start on the dance music. Bob watched with the usual cigarette dangling from his lip, but oddly it was now on the right side of his mouth instead of the left. The reason for the switch was that a blister had developed on his lip when he had absent-mindedly let a cigarette burn too close to his mouth.

Watching the dancers finish, he said, "Okay, that's it. That's the opening number."

"Well," Schwartz said. "It isn't exactly what I had pictured."

Everyone gaped. The young composer continued headlong. "I thought," he said, "it would be more like the kind of thing that Jerry Robbins did in *West Side Story*."

It must have been almost funny. Fosse's rage, the seething contempt for this arrogant beginner, the simmering disgust with the college boy who hadn't exactly pictured it this way, must have boiled through the hoofer's wiry body. Unbelievably now, Schwartz actually rose from his chair to demonstrate the kind of dancing that he had expected.

"Bobby looked at me," Ralph Burns said, "and I looked back at him, and it was all over with Stephen Schwartz."

□ □

In the original script of *Pippin*, a company of strolling players arrives in a field singing:

> Join us
> Leave your fields to flower
> Join us
> Leave your cheese to sour

but setting the scene in an actual field as the troupe arrives with its wagon of props was too literal a notion for Bob Fosse. These traveling players were going to arrive on stage in a real theatre—"*this* theatre," Walton said, "where they are playing on this night with this audience." Bob was feeling liberated from realism after his moviemaking experience. *Cabaret* had been strengthened by the restriction to realism. There had been no arbitrary songs to violate the close-up truth of film and remind the audience that it was watching a musical movie. Instead, the audience was actually *reminded* of the cabaret's reality by the numbers, for they were what in fact would have been on the stage of a German nightclub of the period. However, in the theatre, arbitrary musical numbers are acceptable, because the audience walks in prepared to believe anything on that stage—prepared, as the saying goes, to suspend its disbelief.

As Fosse said, "I don't think there is any such thing as a realistic musical. As soon as people start singing to each other, you've already gone beyond 'realism' in the usual sense. The singing and dancing lift the show into a different realm." In short, as he had capitalized on absolute truthfulness for *Cabaret*, he was going to capitalize on fantasy and imagination and magic in *Pippin*.

Patricia Zipprodt was struggling to deal with this freedom and escape the usual requirements for historical accuracy in designing costumes. She had already put Charlemagne the King "in his medieval tunic and a huge cape. He was all fourteenth century." In coping with Fastrada, his wife and Pippin's wicked stepmother, "I didn't know where she was," the designer said, and then, "at one of those big, tough, noisy New York cocktail parties, I saw a woman, and she was working the whole room, and I thought, 'I've got to get out of her territory.' The next morning I said to myself, 'That woman was Fastrada.'"

Patricia sketched quickly, giving her character a choker necklace and a silver lamé dress. Studying her handiwork, she added a fringe to the hem and flashy shoes, "and after the this and the that," she said, "she was absolutely totally modern in the very tough sense of the word." Polishing the drawing and touching it up with colors, she brought it to Fosse and said, "Bobby, I'm going to show you something that's totally off the wall."

When she handed it over, he said, "Well, that's it. That's the whole show. That's what the show is."

"You see," she said in recollection, "that's what 'anachronism' was all about. This woman in her cocktail dress being married to, you know, Charlemagne. That's Fastrada. That's what Bobby meant by Jesus Christ in tennis shorts."

He also liked the dancers' own costumes, the way they dressed for rehearsal in their ratty sweaters and woolen leg warmers. He sat alongside Stu Ostrow, their backs against the mirrored wall of the dance studio, and watched. The floor was taped to indicate the shape and dimensions of the theatre stage and, Zipprodt said, "The dancers were flying by, watching themselves in the mirror, sweaty, with holes in their clothes and runs in their leotards, the hair wet on their necks." The clothes weren't pretty, but they were awfully sexy, and these "stunning women," the designer remembered, "were close enough for Stuart and Bobby to touch."

Such spectacular dancing was taking *Pippin* away from what John Rubinstein called "a very sincere little piece that wore its heart way out on its sleeve. Bob's purpose was to make sure that no bullshit could possibly creep in," which was ironic because Rubinstein had first feared that Bob liked the script *too* much. ("What am I going to do," he'd asked himself, "if he thinks this is a masterpiece?") Now the question was whether Bob knew when to stop the show business.

As the company prepared to leave for the tryout in Washington, D.C., and Kennedy Center, the composer and the director were barely speaking to each other, and Bob was rewriting Roger Hirson's script at will. By the time they arrived in Washington, D.C., Ann Reinking was his number one girlfriend. She was beautiful, she was a brilliant dancer, and she was a charming, sophisticated young woman. At twenty-three she was Bob's youngest so far, just half his age. Her long, dark, straight hair was set far back on her temples, which accented the breadth of her brow and her enormous eyes, lending her face a flatness and width reminiscent of Joan McCracken. Those huge eyes had an intelligent sensuality that almost concealed her vulnerability, but without a doubt her most striking asset was her legs. Ann Reinking was not a tall person, but she had the legs of one, and those legs would cross and lift, fold and extend like wondrous antennae. They were the last word in legs.

Going with Bob Fosse, she left her innocence behind and her husband too. "He probably was weeping back in Seattle," said Bob's other lover, Jennifer Nairn-Smith, "where people are true blue and have good hearts." John Rubinstein was also struck by this contrast, Ann "coming from a wholesome world into some *Cabaret*-ish world with him," but as Jennifer said, "It was that era. Everyone was experimenting."

Fosse was staying at the Watergate Hotel near Kennedy Center. The performers were put up in the Howard Johnson Motor Inn across the way. There was so much backstage gossip about Bobby's busy sex life that Jennifer took to wearing the same dress every day as a disguise. "It was a wonderful long shabby dress that hid my body," she said, and she wore it all the time, "so that the kids in the show wouldn't know whether I'd been in the hotel or over at the Watergate with Bobby. The gay guys would gossip backstage about whether Annie or I had slept in our rooms."

Lovers or not, his abuse of Jennifer at rehearsal seemed only to grow more intense. "She was gorgeous," Bob's assistant Kathy Doby said, "and he was a little infatuated with her, but there were five of us in that group [of dancers], and she was the weakest in his style. Bob knew he could make her better, and that's why he pushed her. He sometimes got pretty rough, but it was worth it," Doby said.

In a dawn telephone call to New York, he told yet another lover, "I'm practically living with two women here. My private life is so complicated that I'll never dig my way out," and then Ilse arrived for a visit from Germany. It was a bedroom farce.

Influenced by *Cabaret* and "Liza with a 'Z,'" *Pippin* was moving rather than dancing. "Musicals are more of a piece now," Bob said, "not scenes directed by one man and dance numbers staged by another. The ideal is to make the movement consistent throughout, make the actors' movements blend with the dance movements." That was precisely what he was doing, and no director on Broadway was doing it better.

The day before dress rehearsal, there still was no closing number. Everyone had been asking Bob when he was going to do it, and he kept answering, "Wait till we get to Washington. I'll do it before dress rehearsal." Well now they were in Washington on the day before dress rehearsal, and there was still no closing number. Bob walked on stage and gathered his dancers. "By now they were like a basketball team," Ralph Burns said. "Everyone knew where everyone was and where they were moving and what they would do next. They seemed to know what he wanted before he said it." A calm Fosse strolled from one dancer to the next. "You do your step there," he would whisper, and "you're on the other side" and, it seemed to Burns, "everyone sensed what was coming. In two hours it was done, and Bob handed me a cassette of the piano music that had been worked out and he said, 'Okay, Ralph, here's your finale.' "

Patricia Zipprodt thought the dress rehearsal was going well from the costume point of view too, and so she was startled when Bob and Stuart approached her during a break and said that they were disappointed in what she had done for the girls.

"What's the problem, fellas?"

"They aren't sexy," Ostrow said, rubbing his beard. He had just started to grow one too.

"Who isn't sexy? Everything about this show is sexy," she said.

"The things on the girls," Bob said. "They're just not sexy."

The producer nodded in absolute agreement.

"Aren't sexy?" Patricia cried. "Those leather and macramé things? They're practically illegal! I can't go any further, guys. The girls won't put up with it."

Neither Bob nor Stuart could explain why they found the costumes unsexy, and Zipprodt was truly puzzled. "I guess as a woman," she later said, "I just didn't know what they had in their minds." But since the director and the producer were asking her to redesign the costumes for the number, she had no choice but to do so. She decided on "a trashy approach, designing Fredericks of Hollywood stuff," complete with rising suns on the crotches and hands painted on the bras. "It was horrendous," she laughed, "but I thought, what the hell?"

When she showed the designs to Ostrow, he was delighted. "Oh! I knew you could do it!" But Bob stared at them and then smiled in recognition of a fellow sly. "You really know how to design a bad costume when you want to, don't you?" he said, and later Patricia realized that "what had stayed in their minds had been the sensuality of the girls dancing in the rehearsal studio, when they were hot and sweaty in their torn sweaters and leotards, six inches away from the guys' noses."

The leather and macramé costumes stayed.

The friction between Bob and Stephen Schwartz had become more than merely abrasive. Rubinstein felt that "Stephen was genuinely concerned that his work was being turned into a vaudeville show. Bobby was just as genuinely concerned that this sentimental thing was going to have no guts. I thought they both were right."

Whenever Schwartz found Fosse changing any of the written materials, in the script or the songs, he would assert his rights under the Dramatists' Guild contract. There would be no changes, he declared. One day he added, with the entire company as his audience, "Anyhow, that will never work. Listen," he said, turning to Fosse and speaking directly to his face, "I'm the guy who has the hit in 'Day by Day' [the song from *Godspell*]. I'm the one who's selling the records."

Bob blew the whistle that was always strung around his neck. "Okay, everyone," he called. "Take a break."

"I'm getting out of here," Schwartz said yet again, and Bob in chilly and measured tones replied, "You can get out, and you can stay out," and he barred Schwartz from all further rehearsals.

Then, as previews began, Fosse received a murder threat from Jennifer's boyfriend, who had been sitting at the bar in Joe Allen restaurant, the theatrical restaurant in New York, when he heard the gossip about the sexual merry-go-round at the *Pippin* tryout. Jennifer had painful knowledge of his violence. If he was calling up and threatening to kill Bob, she said, then there was a chance he might come to Washington to try just that. At Kennedy Center the evening of the threatened murder, there were private police in front of the theatre and, Jennifer said, "all those limousines in a circle around the stage entrance. It was very dramatic, with all those black-clothed cops," she said, and it was virtually impossible for anyone to get through, although Herb Gardner and Marlo Thomas did manage to go backstage for a visit. As Bob was whisking Jennifer into one of the cars to head for the airport, he said, "You love all this, don't you?" It wasn't exactly true. She did think it was funny, and so did many of the actors, but Stu Ostrow didn't think the threat was amusing, and Bob certainly didn't think so. It was Saturday night, and there wouldn't be another performance of *Pippin* until Monday. Bob and Jenn had been advised to get out of Washington for safety's sake, and so they went back to New York, but the boyfriend had never come to Washington. He had telephoned the threat from New York, and he stayed in New York. He never attempted to assault Fosse, but he did get hold of Jennifer, and when he did "he tried to stop me from dancing in the show by beating me up." She went back to Washington anyhow.

As the world premiere approached, Bob learned that Ostrow had never raised the $250,000 he had said was lacking. In fact, Stuart had not even raised the basic $500,000. He was $120,000 short of even that, but he was sure he would have the money within the week. He was going to get it, he admitted, by mortgaging his home.

"His own money!" Bob said with wonder. "Do you know the guts of the guy? He never put any pressure on me. He kept saying, 'That's okay, we've got it, everything's fine.' That's some big man, let me tell you," and although there was and would continue to be a parade of producers whom

Bob either came to hate or hated from the outset, he would never change his mind about Stuart Ostrow. "He's the producer I feel most affection for. He's probably the best producer I've ever worked with."

The "probably" was necessary. He could go only so far.

"Liza with a 'Z' " was broadcast to tremendous ratings and critical acclaim, which by now seemed only to be expected of a Fosse production. Meantime work on *Pippin* continued during the Washington previews. Bob used the lockout of Stephen Schwartz to make the show absolutely his own. "We're going to fix this where it's sentimental," he told the company, "and get some pizzazz into it." To Fosse, "pizzazz" was the glitter that blinds. Flash could pass for heart, that was the showman's way, and he recast *Pippin* in his own image. "He would demonstrate how I should stand," Rubinstein said, "with his elbows tucked in and his fists curled under his chin and his knees bent. Bobby wanted the Pippin character to be the purest, most essential, and vulnerable side of him. He was going to allow himself to be reflected in the play and in the portrayal of Pippin."

Rubinstein resisted, eager to "flesh out the character with humor, but Bob wouldn't let me. I was supposed to be only naive and pure."

On the other hand, Ben Vereen, in black satin shirt and pants, wearing spats and a boater hat, portrayed the black Fosse, flash incarnate. As the Leading Player he was a vaudevillian translation of the *Cabaret* emcee, Mr. Porno, as Fosse used to say. Vereen's every sliding step was Fosse's, his swiveling hips, his hunched shoulders, his tilted hat. Here was the song and dance man raised to diabolic archetype.

The way Bob described the plot to the company, "The troupe would go from town to town doing this play about Pippin and Charlemagne, and they would get a young guy to play Pippin, and by the end of the play they will have depressed him so much that he'll kill himself. He'll set himself on fire."

As Rubinstein interpreted that, the Leading Player's proposition was, " 'You may die but what a way to go!' It would be Pippin's moment of stardom and won't it be great?" Nor does it seem farfetched to suggest that in this battle between Pippin and the Leading Player, Fosse was setting into conflict the two sides of his own nature, tempting the suicide of the "good" side for the survival of the "evil." This was the murder-by-show-business of Bobby Fosse by Bob Riff.

Playing an innocent brought to the slaughter was making John Rubinstein very unhappy, and his wife Judi was so annoyed that "she cut me dead at the first preview. She came backstage," he remembered, "and didn't say a word to me. She just went to the bathroom." But Fosse remained assuring. "Don't worry, John, you're coming off great," he would say. "You're nervous."

Rubinstein was too intelligent to be patronized. "I'm not nervous!" he snapped. "And I'm not talking about me. I'm talking about the play!"

Bothering him most was the end of it. Ben Vereen, as the Leading Player, is luring Pippin toward the fiery suicide. The young man is tempted but refuses. He returns to his wife and their son and "the domestic life that he has so much distaste for, with none of the glory and dreams that he wanted." This comes so close to Bob's own attitude toward a wife and home that he cast a Gwen Verdon lookalike as Fastrada, Pippin's evil stepmother. He put a red wig on Leland Palmer and so closely modeled her on Gwen that Jennifer Nairn-Smith felt, "He was really kicking her in the pants. Everyone thought so."

Gwen's presence could be felt anyhow. She was still, as the girls in the show called her, the Wife (Chayefsky called her the Empress). Some would even say she was a role model for Bob's girlfriends. There were rumors that, like a ghost, she had actually come to Washington. "The omnipresent Gwen," Jennifer said. "She was like the shadow over everything."

In the show, when Pippin refuses to commit suicide, the Leading Player ("the devil defeated," as Rubinstein said) angrily strips the youth of his theatrical trappings. Standing in simple undergarments, lone and forlorn, he is asked by his wife if he feels betrayed. He replies that he doesn't. He only feels "trapped."

That always got a laugh. As Rubinstein saw it, the laugh was based, like all good laughs, on truth. "After the heavy philosophizing, this guy is facing the reality of a wife and a kid. It wasn't just a yuck joke. It was meaningful."

He would wait out the laugh and then add, "But happy, which isn't too bad for the end of a musical comedy," and he would hold up his wife and son's hands as the curtain fell. It made him feel satisfied. It was a good ending, he felt. "It let all the married people in the audience off the hook, and after all the glitter and the showtime, the nugget of the show remained."

But after getting past the Washington critics ("A rare, welcome original"—Richard Coe, the Washington *Post*; "A razzle dazzle show of magic and wonderment," David Richards, the *Evening Star*), Fosse replaced the script's Middle Ages imagery of falcons and flasks with what Rubinstein called "the asshole jokes, the fuck jokes, the bullshit jokes, taking out what sentimental qualities remained." Then, only days before the company packed up and returned to New York for the Broadway premiere, Bob altered the final lines, cutting the phrase, "but happy."

"You can't do that!" the actor cried.

"I'm afraid of Clive fucking Barnes [the critic for *The New York Times*]. He's going to call me sentimental and, God damn it, I'm not!"

"Who cares what you are?" Rubinstein pleaded. "I'm talking about a play. I'm playing this guy all night long. I know who I am at the end. I know who the audience is thinking about. They've got to be left off the hook. If you take 'but happy' out, you leave the thing a tragedy."

"You're an actor," Fosse said. "*Play* the 'but happy.' "

"Can't be done," Rubinstein retorted. "It'll ruin it."

"Sorry," his director said, and he walked away, and so the final line of *Pippin* became, "Trapped, which isn't bad for the end of a musical comedy."

"And," Rubinstein would later say, "the New York critics went 'Fuck you' for that."

The critics' chance was to come after the opening night, October 23, 1972, at the Imperial Theatre. As New York previews started, Jennifer was back in her one-bedroom penthouse apartment on the upper West Side, although Bob summoned her soon enough. He had moved to a larger apartment in his building, three floors higher, the 31st floor. When Jennifer arrived, Ann Reinking was already there and waiting to greet her. "She showed me around the place as if she had decorated it herself," Jennifer remembered, "especially the bedroom. It was beautiful, all white."

Reinking had her own place too. "We both did," Jennifer said, "and we went back and forth. He would call us when he wanted us."

Pippin began with smoke and darkness and a row of spotlights shooting upward from the stage floor through a track or grating. The effect was of a "curtain of light," as the designers call it. Ben Vereen stepped through that light to appear and then slipped back into the blackness and the stage fog.

Dramatic as the effect was, the smoke and fog didn't always leave when they were supposed to. They sometimes stayed to wreak havoc with John Rubinstein's voice as he sang "Corner of the Sky" in the next scene. It all depended on the amount of smoke and the temperature in the theatre and the level of air-conditioning. The flecks of powder that floated through the stage smoke were capable, at times, of lodging themselves in the actor's throat.

"Please let's use less smoke," he had begged Bob in Washington. "I don't have a big singing voice as it is," and the smoke was cut back. It seemed to Rubinstein that the audience still responded to the magic and the disappearing Vereen in the opening number, but when the final Broadway previews began—the critics' previews—Bob and Stuart stopped by at his dressing room. "For the next three performances," Fosse said, "we're going to put the heavy smoke back."

"But what about my singing?" Rubinstein pleaded.

"You can sing through it," Ostrow said. "It really makes a difference on that effect."

"You're a great performer," Bob said, and Stuart added, "You're a trouper." Bob piled it on. "You aren't a prima donna," he said. It was what Rubinstein called "the old show biz bullshit," but he caved in.

"Okay, okay," he said wearily, later to muse, "So with all the critics listening to me make my Broadway debut, I had no voice."

16

As an opening night present, Stephen Schwartz gave John Rubinstein a framed first page of the song, "A Corner of the Sky." He inscribed his thanks for John's help during a difficult time. When the actor returned to his dressing room after the show, he found that Fosse had taken a brown makeup pencil and scrawled on the framed glass, "How nice!" and Ostrow had added, "Just send back the cash!"

Despite this backdrop of conflict, the opening in fog and magic launched *Pippin* with the stylishness of *Cabaret* and the bravura of "Liza with a 'Z.'" The dense stage smoke at the outset made "Magic to Do" especially exciting, and if it bothered Rubinstein, his singing didn't betray it. The white gloves of the satanic Ben Vereen and his troupe of players pierced the rays of light flashing through the grating in the stage floor, and as the hands passed through the vertical beams, seemingly afloat in the air, the theatre erupted into cheers.

Vereen, his role now expanded to star size, wickedly announced that his little troupe was going to present "our most magical tale," and he made a devilish song and dance man as he ran through the old vaudeville vocabulary of magic tricks, a handkerchief plucked from the air, a palm bursting into flame.

Fastrada and Charlemagne were a fanciful couple, she a gaudy and lusty matron ("I'm just an ordinary housewife and mother") who looked like Gwen Verdon and the King sounding as if Bob Fosse had written his lines ("Sometimes I wonder whether the fornication I'm getting is worth the fornication I'm getting"). Vereen—who had himself grown a beard—inched out with his partners, the "Charles Manson Trio," (that was how Fosse had begun to refer to these showfolk). The number, in the long run, would receive the show's mightiest applause. It was the dance that Bob would film for the *Pippin* television commercial, the first television commercial ever to be made for a Broadway show. Some of the immense success that awaited this show was going to be credited to that commercial. When audiences saw the number on stage, they would recognize it and cheer. They cheered the commercial.

This number presented the essential choreographic Fosse. Bob was seldom doing outright dance anymore, but when he did do it, he was like a composer who, at the height of his powers, could say more with a string quartet than he used to with a symphony orchestra. Tony Walton once wondered to a Manson Trio dancer, "That must be a treat to do," and the dancer replied, "It's the hardest thing I ever had to do in my life. Every movement is against itself. Your body is moving one way, and you're pulling it the other way. Every time you're opening your hands, he wants your fingers to stretch way beyond where it's comfortable although you must never show it in your face. The audience will feel it, the tension working against this appearance of great ease, and that will draw them in."

With macabre satisfaction, Vereen introduces Pippin to the lusty pleasures of "sex presented pastorally," stressing that double entendre lest anyone missed it. Rubinstein peered through a giant prop keyhole to watch two dancers embracing, arousing each other, groping and petting each other. Voyeurism is an ingredient of any ménage à trois, and Rubinstein was watching two women (Kathy Doby and Jennifer Nairn-Smith) at sex. Discovering him, they take him to bed in a decidedly explicit and nearly pornographic sequence, and there can be no mistaking its reference. Fosse has put his love life on stage, succumbing to an urge to confess, to reveal, to expose himself. It is as if the drive to perform is a need for self-exposure.

Broadway opening night audiences are composed of friends of the producer, of the authors, of the actors, investors and show folk. Critics seldom attend opening nights anymore, preferring the calm and advance time of previews. A show is actually open by the opening night, but the official premiere has become a ritual for theatre people, a night for celebration and gala. Tickets are seldom available to the general public.

Pippin's opening night invitations went out to Herb Schlein and Bob's brother Buddy, to Hal and Judy Prince and their best friends, Stephen Sondheim, Jerry Orbach and his wife Marta. None of them could discuss the show during the intermission, because there was no intermission. That had been Paddy's idea, lest anyone managed to understand the plot, he said, and wanted to leave. *Pippin*, then, was a two-hour flash act, designed to dazzle its way past skeptical audiences, but Hal Prince was not dazzled. At show's end he steamed up the aisle alongside a likewise angry Sondheim. Prince was fuming that Fosse had stolen the curtain of light that he said he had conceived for *Cabaret*. He could still remember Bob sitting on the floor in Doc Simon's living room, asking for detailed explanations of how the show's various production effects had been achieved. Sondheim was unhappy because he was usually unhappy. He and Prince were still smarting over *Follies,* a master creation that had been churlishly received with critical equivocation and inadequate ticket sales. To Orbach there was a striking similarity between Ben Vereen's Leading Player and Joel Grey's Master of Ceremonies in *Cabaret,* but, it seems fair to speculate, what was really bothering these friends was the acclaim that Fosse was enjoying for the movie *Cabaret* after Hal Prince had done so much to create the original show, not to mention his curtain of light.

In fact, Orbach said, "We were fucking furious, we wanted to kill Fosse." But the actor later realized that nobody ever invented anything, "everyone on Broadway was interlocked in a community of ideas," and, as both Tony Walton and Jules Fisher pointed out, the "curtain of light" had been used long before either Prince or Fosse had tripped over it. But as Sondheim wryly admitted later, "It isn't enough for us to succeed. Our friends have to fail too."

After the opening night performance, after the bows and the cheers and the great wonderful whoops and roars, after the curtain's rise and fall and the visitors coming backstage to take a dip in the excitement and after the *there's no business like show business* of it all, Ann Reinking sponged off her makeup and changed into a gray pinstriped jacket, matching pants, and a shirt and tie. It was a chic and offbeat outfit for the big party that was just a walk away, through the chill of the autumn night, to the ballroom of the Hotel Piccadilly. By the time she got there, the party was going full tilt, "one of those star-studded things," Stuart Ostrow recalled. Herb Schlein was standing in the crowd watching Shirley MacLaine disco on the dance floor when Bob arrived, and naturally a great hurrah swept across the big room as all energies converged on him, seeking a piece of his ego and perhaps one bit of his just-this-second success. He sailed atop the enthusiasm with a shy grin on his skinny face, a grin that Paddy called "bullshit shy," but perhaps it wasn't outright fraud. As John Rubinstein said, "People take this business so seriously—or themselves in it so seriously. But Bob never lost his sense of humor about it all." And perhaps this "bullshit shy" grin contained a hint of amusement.

A choreographer has a certain walk about him. He is a dancer with authority, never more so than when he is also a director fresh from a smash hit on Broadway. Bob shook hands and grinned his thank-you's for compliments he probably couldn't hear. He was handsome with his beard neatly trimmed, even with his rapidly thinning hair. Instead of the black velvet dinner jacket that he usually wore on formal occasions, he was dressed in a gray pinstriped suit. It was the same as Ann Reinking's. Jennifer Nairn-Smith was wearing one too. The three of them had come to the opening night party in matching clothes. They had gone shopping together in Bloomingdale's and "bought these really trendy suits," Jennifer said, "stylishly mannish for Annie and me. It really was a hoot." And it certainly was a special kind of fashion statement.

The reviews were not all raves. As John Rubinstein had feared, many "went fuck you . . . that it was a show about Fosse's brilliant direction, costumes, lighting, Ben Vereen and razzle dazzle and the rest was shit. The music and lyrics were shit and the character of Pippin was negligible." But the reviews that mattered were the ones from New York's daily newspapers; they were the reviews that sold tickets, and they were rave reviews. For once in his shows, the success was all his. "Fosse's brilliantly creative staging of *Pippin*," Douglas Watt wrote in the *Daily News*, "has been responsible for the season's first big musical success . . . it is unmistakably and triumphantly the director's show." In the New York *Post*, Richard Watts wrote that Pippin is "the most brilliantly staged and produced musical imaginable." The newspaper that mattered most in commercial terms was the *New York Times*, and while its critic, Clive Barnes, had his quarrels with the show, he had none with Fosse. He too gave the director credit for making "considerably more out of something comparatively little. Fosse," Barnes added, "is fantastic."

Pippin was a hit then, and Bob Fosse was the reason why. He was one of Broadway's greatest fixers, by his own admission better at repairing shows than conceiving them, but what was "fixing"? For Fosse, saving a show and making it work was not a matter of organic resolution. It was a matter of flimflam, and *Pippin* was indeed blown past the audience in a rush of noise, lighting, beads, and feathers. The audience was gullible, and this was a flash act. "Watch the rabbit," Bob would say, "not my hands."

Pippin was his ultimate flimflam, the repair job that totally obscured the authors' original intentions and, to top it off, trampled on a message of virtue and principle. Left underfoot were the innocence of Pippin, of Stephen Schwartz, and Robert Louis Fosse. The show was Bob Riff triumphant.

When on occasion Bob would admit to a fear of being revealed as a fraud, it may have sounded like ordinary artistic insecurity, but there was sense in it. Being revealed is having one's trick disclosed, one's act. In vaudeville, as Fred Weaver had drilled young Bobby Fosse from the outset, "Once you have an act, you can do it for the rest of your life." Nothing was so sacred, the act was the performer's life, and the corollary was implicit. Without the act, all was lost.

When *Pippin* was produced in Australia and Mexico, Stephen Schwartz insisted on restoring the original script and concept. Those productions were not successes, but they pleased him and gave him some small satisfaction that the show had survived after Fosse had sent it up in flames in exchange for success. But for what did a Mexican or Australian production count? Broadway was all that mattered to a musical, and on Broadway Fosse had proved that an audience could be fooled every time by the beads and feathers, the drum raps, the flames in the hand, "the old razzle dazzle," as he came to call it. This was the creed by which he would live the rest of his life, rising from depression to a doomed joy as he poised for the drop into pleasure, "the final affirmation of life," as he wrote in the *Pippin* script—"death."

Death was his fancy, a devil's dare as he chain-smoked, drank to drunk, partied with pills and poppers, didn't eat and didn't sleep, and sought after every woman in sight, unable to resist pleasure if his life depended on it. If death was going to be the price for ultimate license, then he was willing to pay that price. He would rather go down in flames than settle for the mundane.

On a more practical level, *Pippin* was positioned for a four-and-a-half-year run on Broadway. It would ultimately earn three and a half million dollars, and Stuart Ostrow no longer had to worry about losing his house. He could even afford to eat at Wally's.

Wally's was a steak house on West 49th Street between Broadway and Eighth Avenue. It wasn't a theatre restaurant in the sense that Sardi's was, with caricatures of old stars and old producers; nor was Wally's a theatre restaurant the way Joe Allen was, with its young working actors being served by young out-of-work actors. Wally's was a steak house for heavy hitters. David Begelman ate there and Sam Cohn, which was how Bob came to the place. When he wasn't at Trader Vic's with dates or at Elaine's with his writer friends, he would often have dinner at Wally's with David or Sam, or with Stu Ostrow or Herb and Paddy. On such occasions he generally came alone. He seldom made plans with women when he made plans with men. It wasn't until past midnight that he put out the emergency calls, the middle-of-the-night alarms.

He started playing the Truth Game at Wally's. Nobody remembered exactly how it began, but it was usually after a couple of margaritas, which was what Bob mainly had for dinner. On one particular night he sat at Wally's with Sam Cohn, Jane and Bob Aurthur, David and Nessa Picker, Herb Gardner and Marlo Thomas. Picker was producing Bob's next picture, *Lenny*. It was going to be the first Fosse drama.

While the others were sawing at their steaks and buttering their baked potatoes, he announced that it was time to play Truth. It was a party game that was going around, so they all knew what it was; in fact some at the table considered themselves too sophisticated for such things. Was Geography next?

Fosse used his sly charm to rope in the city slickers and began with the question, "What would you say if it was the last day of your life? Remember, you have to be honest. You'll be tested."

It seemed harmless enough, until he refused to let anyone off with a simple answer. That was when one answer led to another question, until Bob would focus in on his subject "and finally," Jane Aurthur said, "it could get awful." One occasional player, the director Sidney Lumet, described it as "always having an edge to it. It was pretty rough." It was a relentless asking of personal questions on painful subjects, a technique that Bob was going to use in *Lenny*.

The movie about the controversial comedian, Lenny Bruce, was to be based on the Broadway play whose author, Julian Barry, was already simmering over rumors that Gardner or Chayefsky was going to write the screenplay. He decided to call Fosse himself, and not much later, it was an angry Julian Barry who stalked through the door for the appointment on the eleventh floor at 850 Seventh Avenue. "In this business," he would later observe, "you're always auditioning. I wrote this play, and now I had to come in and audition."

The first thing Bob said was, "You're probably somewhat pissed off that you had to come in and audition for this job."

"That's right," the startled writer stammered. He was a friendly looking fellow on the messy authorly model. Writers work alone, they don't have to make an appearance. Julian Barry was fortyish and fighting a weight problem.

"Let me tell you," Bob said gently, "why I might be somewhat hesitant about using you for this picture." His voice was high in pitch and uninflected, but it was so quiet, so warm, so thoroughly reasonable that Barry could only sit down like a good boy. This manner of speaking, which had been too light for Fosse the actor, was proving to be a powerful whisper for Fosse the director.

"You've been working on these materials for three or four years now," Bob said. "You're very conversant with them. You know what works and what doesn't work. I *don't* know what works and what doesn't work. For me to come into this now, I have to go all the way back to the research and listen to Lenny Bruce records and tapes, read the interviews that you did for your research."

Before Barry could interrupt, Fosse continued in this wise and gentle vein. "I have to be innocent," he said, "and make mistakes and stumble and fall on my ass a little bit. My question is, are you so jaded that you couldn't go back to the beginning and do that with me?"

Julian Barry considered that "a very smart question." It was also an example, he later realized, of how seductive Bob could be.

"To be honest with you," the writer replied, "I don't know whether I can do that."

"Are you going to say things," Bob continued, "like, 'There's no point in trying that because I tried it and it doesn't work'?"

"I don't know," Barry said. "I have to think about it."

They were interrupted by a ringing of the telephone. Fosse answered and covered the mouthpiece, whispering, "It's Frank Sinatra."

He listened and smiled and made agreeable noises and interpolated an occasional "thank you" before responding. "Well," he said, "I'd like very much to do that, but I understand you don't rehearse." He paused and listened before concluding. "Look, if you don't rehearse, I just can't do it. I'm sorry."

Hanging up, he told Barry that Sinatra had seen "Liza with a 'Z' " and wanted him to direct a television special. "It was flattering," Bob said, "but I won't do anything with anyone who won't rehearse."

Abruptly, "Fosse!" was heard beyond the door. It was pushed open. "Let's eat!" roared the loudspeaker.

"Come in, Paddy. I want you to meet Julian Barry."

"We can meet downstairs," Chayefsky said, and so they started down the corridor. Waiting for the elevator, Bob said, "Do you know what made me want to do *Lenny*?" Chayefsky was being uncharacteristically silent. "That monologue about Jackie Kennedy hauling ass."

This distressed the playwright. For Barry, Lenny Bruce's use of the outrageous for humor, as imagining the president's widow a prostitute, was not important. He was more interested in the humanity of Lenny Bruce, his relationship with his wife, the beautiful stripper Honey. But Julian Barry had just met Bob Fosse and could not have known what he really saw in the story of Lenny Bruce, a wiry little emcee in strip joints, a performer beleaguered and destroyed by accusations of vulgarity, a man whose seemingly cruel approach to love was redeemed by his feelings for his daughter. There was plenty that Bob Fosse saw in *Lenny* beyond "hauling ass" jokes.

"What have you been working on?" he asked Julian Barry as the elevator started down.

"A musical."

"No kidding."

"Yes. With Jack Cole."

"No *kidding*."

"But I don't know," Julian said. "Some of his ideas sound crazy to me."

"Listen," Bob said. "If Jack has an idea, any idea, be smart and go for it." He turned to Paddy, who remained silent, and said, "That's the only guy I was ever afraid of. Jack Cole."

As they strolled into the Carnegie Delicatessen, Herb Schlein was already waving them in, past the crowd waiting for tables. They elbowed through with their heads down as if they were movie stars avoiding photographers and autograph hounds. Barry was impressed to be part of such a power entourage, even in a Jewish delicatessen. They eased to the head of the line and were led to a table at the back of the long room. The linen napkins were set out by a Herb Schlein who was very pleased to meet Julian Barry. He pronounced *Lenny* a masterpiece.

"What are you doing now?" Julian asked Paddy. "I thought *Hospital* was a great picture."

"Thanks," Chayefsky said.

"Paddy didn't like the play," Fosse said.

"Which play?"

"*Your* play. He didn't like *Lenny*."

"So the critics weren't crazy after all," Julian said, trying to ease the situation.

"I *hated* the play," Chayefsky said, looking down at his plate and then across the table into the playwright's eyes, and these were small tables.

"Okay," Barry said.

"It's bad for the Jews," Chayefsky said. "It's derogatory. I don't like that kind of language, that kind of life. I especially don't like it when Jews do that on Broadway."

He was serious.

"Shit," Bob said suddenly, looking toward the door and getting up. "That newspaper guy is after me. I've got to get out of here," and he was gone, slipping through the swinging door that led downstairs to the men's room.

"Well, besides hating my play, what are you doing?"

"Another screenplay," Chayefsky said. "About the Arab–Israeli war."

"The Six Day War?"

"Yeah."

"But you didn't like my play."

"No. I thought it was helpful to the anti-Semitic."

When Fosse got back, he said, "This is crazy. You work your whole life to become famous, and then you spend your life in men's rooms hiding from people."

After lunch, standing on Seventh Avenue in front of the office building, Bob said to Julian, "Here's what I think. I'm going away for a few weeks to do a cameo in a movie. There's a couple of scenes I know I'm going to use in *Lenny*. If you don't mind, why don't you write them, and I'll have a look when I get back."

"I think that's just fine," the playwright said, and they parted.

The Little Prince was finally going to be filmed after many announced and many canceled productions. The allegorical fantasy by Antoine de St. Exupéry had become a minor classic. Now it was going to be set to music by Frederick Loewe with lyrics by Alan Jay Lerner, who had also written the screenplay. Stanley Donen was going to direct it, and his heart was set on Bob playing and dancing the role of the Snake, but Bob had asked, "Who wants to see an aging choreographer dance?" and Alan Jay Lerner agreed. He told Donen that he wanted a girl to play the Snake, and he didn't want Richard Kiley, who was playing the aviator-hero, to play the aviator-hero. He wanted Frank Sinatra to play the aviator-hero, and he didn't want Gene Wilder in the movie at all. "Lerner was really a son of a bitch," said the ordinarily mild Donen.

Fosse didn't much like Alan Jay Lerner either. They had once begun work on a show (*On a Clear Day You Can See Forever*) that was partly set in the seventeenth century, and the lyricist insisted on explaining the style of the period to a presumably ignorant Fosse. "I'm going to get you this guy," Lerner said, "and he can show you how to move these characters the way they move in Restoration comedy."

"It's okay, Alan," Bob had said. "I know how to do that. I've seen plays." But Lerner insisted on bringing in the expert.

"That's it?" Bob asked after the demonstration.

"That's it," Lerner replied.

"Okay," Bob said. "Thank you." And he never forgot or forgave it. Now he was adamant about not doing the cameo. "I kept discouraging Stanley," he said. "I was too old, I couldn't dance anymore. I kept recommending other people, and he'd talk to those people, and he'd come back to me."

"But Bob never gave up on being a performer," Donen remembered, "and I was counting on that." He flew to New York with a tape recording of the music and said, "I just want to play your song for you. At least listen to it," and the lyric certainly had an appeal.

If you would like to cure the fever called life
Get some relief from all the struggle and strife
The grandest medicine that I can propose
Is under your nose
A snake in the grass
One sting and you can say goodbye
To all your friends
One sting and you'll be singing
As your spirit ascends
All's well that ends

Lerner might have been a difficult man, but he was a wonderful lyricist. Bob had never been a great lover of lyrics. As a choreographer he found that they distracted a performer's attention from dancing or moving and distracted an audience's attention from the performer. "Bob liked simple lyrics," Donen said and he did too. "Complicated ones get in the way of staging." These were complicated lyrics all right, but Bob couldn't help admiring them. "And don't forget," Donen added, "we're going to do this movie in the desert, and you can direct your own sequence." He paused to smile. "You can even wear a bowler hat and spats."

"Boy, you sure know how to appeal to a guy," Bob grinned. "Play the song again," and they both stared at the little cassette machine as the tape played. After a second hearing, Bob shook his head.

"I don't think so, Stanley."

"Why not?"

"I think I've done my last tango."

Several weeks later, when Bob ran into Richard Kiley on 57th Street, he still felt that way.

"Stanley Donen tells me he wants you to play the Snake in *The Little Prince*."

"That's right. Some say the part is perfect for me."

"I told him I thought it was a wonderful idea," Kiley said, "but he said you weren't sure about it."

"Oh, I'm sure about it," Bob said. "I'm not going to do it."

"Nobody can visualize anyone but you," Kiley said.

The only person who could possibly have changed Bob's mind was his daughter, and she said, "Do it, Daddy. I want to see you in the movies."

"That was why he finally agreed," Donen said. "He did it for peanuts. He did it because Nicole wanted to see him dance on the screen."

Fosse put it this way: "I'm getting fat and rich. Maybe I'd better get into a studio and teach myself some humility and also take off five or six pounds. It might be good to know how an actor feels again. It's been a long time since I did it, and I must always remember how it is to be in front of the camera or onstage."

It had also been a long time since he'd performed. Perhaps he was fearful of being reminded of his love for it. He had been a performer since the age of nine and had wanted, first of all, to be a star. Now he was busy rationalizing the decision to play the Snake. "Sitting out front," he said, "a director tends to say, 'Well, why the hell can't they do that? It's so simple.' You forget all the emotions and problems that go into it. Doing this'll be good for me."

Thinking back on the hectic year past and the work ahead, he could well joke, "At least it's something to keep me busy."

It didn't hurt that Kiley was going to star in the movie. If, as a couple, Gwen and Bob had made any friends, it was Dick and Pat Ferrier Kiley. Was it not Pat whom alone Gwen had told about their marriage while on the road with *Redhead*? Now Pat could be Bob's assistant once again, and the prospect of catch-up with the Kileys in Tunisia, of all places, must have been appealing. So he went to work, as usual first in the studio. He had to take his cigarette-smoking, liquor- and wine-drinking, speeded-up and tranquilized, sleep-deprived forty-five-year-old body and slam it into dancing condition. When he was ready, when he had created in the rehearsal studio the dance that he was going to do in the desert, he called Herb Gardner and invited him to come take a look.

"It was early evening," Gardner remembered, "just me and Bobby."

"Okay," Fosse said, putting on a derby and inserting a cassette in the tape player. "It's not much, but here's what I've got so far."

"Then," Gardner recalled with lasting awe, "he proceeded to dance." The recollection says as much about Gardner's love for Fosse as it does of the event itself. "There followed one of the most—and I choose the word carefully—*dazzling* seven or eight minutes of my life. The dance ended with Bobby doing what for a teenager would still be an incredible fifteen-foot slide along the raised barre on two arched feet and one guiding hand."

"It's not very good," Bob said to the goggle-eyed Gardner, "but maybe I can fix it."

He was busy with more than this. Once again a heartsick Ilse came over from Germany. With Ann and Jennifer in *Pippin*, he still invited Ilse to stay with him in the apartment. It would not disturb the other arrangements in his life. The freedom to see other women was always a precondition of his romances.

No sooner had Ilse moved in, however, than she had to leave. This time it was not because of her usual problem with visas; this time she had to go home for a minor operation to remove an ovarian cyst. Since Bob was about to leave for Tunisia anyway, he suggested that they meet for a vacation after her operation, and they decided on Madeira, the isolated Portuguese island off the coast of North Africa. It was a striking locale, almost Scandinavian in the cold and bleakness of January, but they had not come for the sun. They bundled up and walked along the island's rocky shores and poked through the quiet little village. Bob brought research about Lenny Bruce—interviews that Julian Barry had conducted for the play, tape recordings of Bruce's comedy routines, and while he worked on these, he asked Ilse to read Barry's play, *Lenny*, and write a report about its movie possibilities.

He was using his reading glasses most of the time now. The granny glasses would go on and off as he read and talked, the glasses strung on a thin chain around his neck. Ilse glanced up to look at him from time to time as she read the play. She was enjoying this very much, and when she handed over her notes, Bob read them with grinning murmurs of appreciation. "You're a great assistant," he told her. "Maybe you can read all the scripts I get and write up reports." She thought it was a wonderful idea. Then he flew to Tunisia to meet another woman who was coming in from New York.

The village of Nefta sits at the edge of the Sahara Desert, not far from the Algerian border. The Nefta Palace was a small hotel, but it was the best in town. Bob had called ahead to make certain he got the room immediately next door to Stanley Donen's. One never knew.

The date was waiting when he arrived, a passing romance. "I give my relationships two weeks now," he was starting to say. "Sometimes I bring it in ahead of schedule." It was a glib remark and only partly true. He would inform each new lover that there was no possibility of a serious romantic development, nor any chance of his fidelity. Some would accept it, some for just a brief time; some he simply tired of, and some remained friends for many years, some as lovers and some not. The Nefta girl was one of the transients, a run-by in his life. She sat beside him in the hotel restaurant with Lerner, Donen, and the Kileys. Abruptly Bob was so overcome by a fit of coughing that the cigarette nearly fell from his lips.

"You've just got to cut down on your smoking, Bobby," Pat Kiley said.

"Listen, Patty," Bob responded in a tough guy accent, the cigarette bobbing once more from the corner of his mouth. "I smoke too much, I drink too much," he winked at his date and added, "I do everything too much. It's just"—and he paused to snap his fingers—"the way I am."

Kiley didn't think that was funny and said, "Bobby, do you want Sam to play it again?" He thought that Fosse "had really invented himself. He liked to play the burned-out star. He wanted us all to think he was born behind an ash can, began tapping, someone said to him, 'Hey, kid, here's a nickel!' and out came Fred Astaire."

The reason for such self-invention, Kiley thought, was a fear of having one's sham revealed. "Basically, what we do in show business is fun. It's not like money that you have to earn. We grew up in a man's world where people went out and did something, worked at it, got paid for it, and that was it. All of us had fathers and uncles and grandfathers, who we saw slaving away at jobs they loathed because they had to do it—to feed the family. So this business of following the muse and having fun in life—to Americans is a fairly new game, I think. To Bobby that wasn't man's work. Man's work was shoveling coal."

But "following the muse" as Kiley put it wasn't always fun for Fosse. Moodiness always seemed to come at the end of a project. "He had to start on something new," Kiley remembered, "before the old one ended. He would not allow himself to be out on that limb, having it cut out from under him."

The reason, Bob once said, was that "if it failed, my pain would be so great that I couldn't deal with it."

Kiley understood. "You always want another ice floe you can step onto," he said. And speaking of a Norwegian hoofer like Fosse, that was well put.

In preparation for the snake sequence, Bob went into the desert to scout locations with Pat Ferrier, settling on a small area where there was a tree that he could slither down and two dunes that were close enough and high enough for him to leap between. He kicked through the area to get a sense of the footing, which was soft, shifty, and treacherous. He set and moved two large sheets of plywood. Then, playing the music cassette on a big, battery-operated portable, he demonstrated a portion of his dance for Pat, and she practiced it alongside him. When she had it right, he let her do it alone so that he could watch and decide which camera angles and lenses he wanted. Then he would teach her another section of the dance and continue in the same way to the end. On the day of actual photography, he arrived early with the technicians to supervise the lighting and camera setups. Then he went into the trailer to change into costume, a body-hugging version of his basic black. The trousers were tight, stretchable jersey, and the fitted silk shirt had a ruffled front trimmed with white edging. He wore black leather gloves and aviator goggles, and the promised derby had a snakeskin hatband to match his snakeskin spats. As he left the trailer, closing the door behind him, he was startled to find the crew waiting for him, a group of Englishmen lined up in a row and applauding.

Cabaret, one of them grandly announced, had just been nominated for nine Academy Awards including Best Picture and Best Director, but it wasn't just the Academy Award that Bob had been nominated for. He was also up for the top prize on Broadway, the Tony Award, and that was two nominations, Best Director and Best Choreographer for *Pippin*.

He was hardly a sure winner of any of the prizes. At the Academy, *Cabaret* was up against the formidably successful and admired *The Godfather*. On Broadway, *Pippin* was competing with *A Little Night Music* and its director, Hal Prince. But Bob had already won something. He was the only director ever to have been nominated for a Tony Award and an Academy Award in the same year. To top that, he was also nominated for a third major award, television's Emmy for "Liza with a 'Z.'" That prize was due for presentation in April.

America's show business awards are regularly derided, perhaps with some justification, as being overly commercial and inherently illogical for trying to compare the incomparable, yet they do reward the entertainer in the most appropriate way, providing the attention and applause that lured him into the spotlight in the first place. Upon the announcement of Bob's various nominations, an award watch began in the national press. A drama had been created. Unfortunately, he now had to win everything; for anything less than a sweep of all three awards would be considered a disappointment.

Fortunately, Nefta, Tunisia, was some distance from all this. With the Sahara Desert stretching into infinity, tuxedos and television lights had to seem remote. And so they went to work filming the snake dance in the cold and the wind. "That made it hard to stay steady," Pat Kiley remembered. "The sand was blowing up, and Bob wasn't dancing on a solid surface."

Dick Kiley added, "They were kind of dangerous things that Bobby was doing. He was jumping between those high dunes."

"It was freezing," Pat said, "in that skinny black shirt."

The cold wind notwithstanding, Fosse insisted on repeating the sequence. When everyone applauded, he would say, "Now let's try it again." The long number was photographed in segments until each was perfected. Then he came to the big finish when he went flying toward the camera and slid on his knees on the sand, just as he had done on the beach of Johnston Atoll as a teenage sailor, sliding toward the audience as he had done in the variety show at Amundsen High School. The sheets of plywood were concealed beneath the sand so that he could land on them and slide toward the camera.

"After he hit the sand with his knees," Kiley remembered, "they must have been bleeding, he did it so many times on the plywood. It was a sensational shot."

When the scene was finished, when Bob was satisfied with it, and when everyone was at the dinner table in the hotel, toasting his assorted nominations, he changed the subject by prankishly needling Alan Jay Lerner about the lyrics for "Snake in the Grass."

"You know, Alan," he began, "there's one lyric that just bothers the hell out of me."

Lerner looked up in disbelief. He was justifiably proud of his craftsmanship.

"It's incomplete," Bob said. "It just sounds strange."

The lyricist went for the bait. "No! Where? What do you mean?"

"Well, where it goes, 'goodbye to all your friends, one sting and you'll be singing—"

"Well, that's fine," Lerner said. "I don't see where—?"

"No, no, Alan. It's still coming. 'One sting and you'll be singing, as your spirit ascends, All's well that ends—"

"Yes?"

"Ends what? Isn't something missing?" Bob asked mischievously. "All's well that ends— I think we should cut that last line."

He watched Lerner turn a sickly white. Only then did he burst into laughter.

"He knew," Kiley said, "that it was the best line in the whole god-damned song."

"Oh God," Lerner said, "I walked right into that one."

Bob looked at the rushes of his snake dance. He pieced together the best takes from the various sections, and decided that it was "pretty good. Not great but okay." Then he returned to New York and *Lenny*. He gave Julian Barry the writing assignment after reading the test scenes, and from winter's end to the spring of 1973, the writer wrote. He lived in Westport,

Connecticut, and each morning he would come to Manhattan, to Bob's office, where they would sit on the sofa and read the scenes aloud, playing the various roles and talking them out. Then Barry would drive home, "and I would rewrite everything and come in the next morning, and we'd read the scenes all over again."

He found these sessions exhilarating but draining. "You were always being judged," he felt. "You had to be at your best. It would be exhausting. Bobby always made you think so hard. It was a relief not to have to see him. When you sat in a room with him, you'd have the urge to confess to anything terrible you had ever done." But Barry came to realize that Bob's intensity had some chemical assistance, and it came from a leather attaché case. "He had it with him all the time," said Julian who, having had his own experiences with Dexamil, was ruefully familiar with it. "I would get Bobby about two hours after he had showered and shaved and used his eyedrops and taken his Dexamil. He was really into it then, he loved it."

"Dexamil," Barry said, "is great for the first sixty days, but then you have to keep increasing the dosage, or you can crash and go into a terrible depression." That was funny. Depression was now Fosse's natural state. Where could he crash to?

"He was still in the romantic period with it," Barry said, "so he would be a hundred percent more verbal than he had to be, overflowing with ideas. He couldn't stop talking. I'd tell him, 'Bob, it's just the Dexamil. You really don't mean everything you're saying.' He was so charged up."

Although it further shrank what little appetite Fosse had, he would jump when they broke for lunch, and then they would join Gardner or Chayefsky at the Carnegie. Bob would eat a corner of his sandwich and leave the rest. For a while, the two of them, Bob and Julian, switched loyalties to a restaurant several blocks north on Seventh Avenue. The place was trying to change its image and had hired girls who, Bob and Julian agreed, were "hot looking." They abandoned the Carnegie for the hot-looking waitresses. One afternoon as they set out for a stroll to the new place, Herb Schlein looked out from inside the Carnegie Delicatessen plate-glass window and saw Bob walking by. His expression was forlorn. "It was," Julian remembered, "as if he was saying, 'Where have you guys been going?'"

"Herb looks as if we're destroying him," he said to Bob.

"Well, I hope he doesn't find out where we're going," Fosse replied, "because he's going to start wearing brassieres to get us back into the Carnegie."

□ □

The Tony Awards and the Academy Awards came within three days of each other that year, the Tonys first on March 22, 1973. The show was televised from the Imperial Theatre, where *Pippin* was playing. As Bob arrived, the crowd was pressing against the police barricades outside, hungry to see the arriving celebrities. He slipped through the onlookers unrecognized and ducked under one of the wooden barriers, and at that moment he heard an ominous noise, the sound of his pants splitting. He hurried backstage to find a seamstress and then stood and waited in his underwear while the seam was repaired. He got to his seat just in time to be one of the first winners, taking the prize for choreography. His closest competitor had been an old and not-so-good friend at MGM, Gower Champion, whose musical *Sugar* was not a hit. Accepting the award, a silver medal mounted on a wood base, Fosse looked healthy but weary. He smiled and lied, "The cast made *Pippin* the happiest experience I've ever had in the theatre." Then he joked his thanks to Stuart Ostrow, "who even contributed a few of the less effective dance steps in the show."

Winning this prize made no difference. Were he to win the Tony for choreography but not for directing, it would have meant the end of his triple bid. His competition in the directors category was formidable. *A Little Night Music* was not the smash hit that *Pippin* was, but the Hal Prince–Stephen Sondheim shows always had prestige, and if prestige was good for anything, it was good for awards. Fosse seemed truly surprised when Diahann Carroll announced, with a shriek of joy, that he had won the award for Best Director of a Musical.

"I confess," Bob later said, "I thought I had a shot at the choreographer, which is why I had that little joke [about Ostrow's dances] prepared." As for the director prize, though, he said, "I had a loser's good sportsmanship type speech I was going to give to the winner at the ball later."

In accepting he said, "Thank you to all the marvelous people who helped with the show. They couldn't have done it without me." That was charming, it was relaxed and nice. Even Paddy thought so. "The real shy you came out," the arbiter of honesty said, "not that bullshit shy. I've seen you do the bullshit shy too, but the real shy you was up there."

Three days later and three thousand miles west, he was back in a tuxedo for the Academy Awards in Los Angeles, "full of tranquilizers," he said, "and ready for failure." Besides the nominations for Best Picture and Best Director, *Cabaret* was in the running for Best Actress (Liza) and Best Supporting Actor (Joel Grey) as well as assorted technical awards, and

Geoffrey Unsworth was already strolling toward the stage to collect his Oscar for cinematography. That was decreed by fate, considering the bitter history with Cy Feuer over the cameraman.

Now they all sat in a row, Cy and Bob as well as Liza and Joel, not needing side aisles to make the acceptance run because there was a crosswise aisle in front of them. Feuer's wife Posy, a pert and twinkling woman, sat between the two former friends, keeping them from picking up the old arguments, which they probably would have done right there in the Dorothy Chandler Pavilion, calling each other a prick and a son of a bitch on national television.

Each went around armed with those arguments, brandishing them whenever the other's name came up, but Bob chatted warmly with Posy Feuer now, as fond of her as ever. Still, "It was a double tension," Joel Grey said. "I was nervous about my own chances, and I was nervous knowing about Cy and Bob not burying the hatchet." He was certain, too, that Al Pacino was going to beat him out as the best supporting actor for *The Godfather.* Francis Ford Coppola had won the Directors Guild Award for the movie, and that prize invariably pointed the way to the director's Oscar since the same people voted for both prizes. Feuer was convinced that it would lead to *The Godfather* winning Best Picture and sweeping most of the other awards, but instead Grey was announced as the winner for Best Supporting Actor, and Liza kicked his chair and said, "Don't let anyone tell you that this isn't a terrific thrill." As Joel trotted toward the stage for his statuette, it was *Cabaret* that seemed to be doing the sweeping, and then Bob was being announced as Best Director.

The audience gasped audibly. Coppola had been considered a sure winner. Fosse dashed up and over and grabbed his Oscar and grinned into the Hollywood community that had meant so much to him and given him such unhappiness.

"My legs were like cooked spaghetti," he later said. "I was thinking, 'What am I going to say? I should be bright. How am I going to look on TV? I wonder if Nicole is watching? Don't make an ass of yourself. Show enough emotion but don't slobber.'"

What he actually said was, "You're letting me stand up here because Coppola hasn't shown up yet." Then he thanked Gwen, describing her as "a dear friend of mine." He added, "And I'd like to mention Cy Feuer, the producer, with whom I've had a few differences of opinion. But at a time like this you have affection for everybody." If he had to say something mean-spirited, he had at least found a way to say it in an oblique way. Feuer himself was so caught up in the *Cabaret* landslide that he wasn't even offended. He was too busy thinking up his own acceptance speech for Best Picture.

Posy congratulated Bob as he slid back into his seat while Rock Hudson was already naming the nominees for Best Actress and declaring Liza the winner. Hudson annoyed her when he said, "In a horse race, bloodlines count, and Liza's got the bloodlines." She disliked suggestions that her mother had anything to do with her success. "Thank you for giving *me* this award," she said with a smile, and added, "You've made *me* very happy."

The Godfather finally won a prize, Marlon Brando as Best Actor, but he didn't come to get it. Instead, a diminutive woman in Indian costume strode to the stage and reflexively extended her hand as Liv Ullman handed over the Oscar. Then she pushed aside the statuette.

"My name," the young woman announced, "is Sacheen Littlefeather. I'm Apache . . . and I'm representing Marlon Brando who very regrettably cannot accept this very generous award. And the reason for this is the treatment of American Indians today by the film industry."

The remarks were received with scattered applause and a chorus of boos. The show proceeded as if that had been a musical number, and after *Cabaret* swept eight awards, *The Godfather* was declared the year's best picture. Cy Feuer, who by then had formulated his entire acceptance speech, swallowed it while Clint Eastwood was telling the producer of *The Godfather*, "I don't know if I should present this award on behalf of all the cowboys shot in John Ford westerns over the years."

As soon as Bob could find a telephone in the backstage chaos, he called Nicole. It was late for his ten-year-old, but he knew that she had stayed up to watch the show.

"Hiya," the Best Director of 1972 said to his kid.

"Hiya."

"How are ya?"

"Nice," she said. He waited for his daughter's thrilled reaction to her dad winning the Academy Award on national television. A few days earlier she had seen him win a Tony, yet somehow the Oscars were the most fabled of all prizes. But the only thing she said was "Nice."

"Well," he said, "how's your new bicycle?"

She asked whether he wanted to talk to Mom.

"Gee," he said to Gwen, "I gotta tell you, I gotta be honest with you, I'm so disappointed. I thought Nicole would say something to me, you know, it was like I knew she was watching me. I thought she'd at least say something about my beard or my baldness. But she hardly said anything."

"You should've been here," Gwen replied. "When you won it, she screamed so loud she said, 'I broke something in my throat! I broke something in my throat!' "

"But on the phone," Bob would remember, "she's so cool to me." He shook his head and smiled at the joke on himself, smiled at the vulnerability in a parent's love for a child.

With the two biggest show business prizes under his belt, he told an interviewer, "Nothing is equal to what I have now. Before, when I had various moments of success, I was always afraid it was going to go away. I could never enjoy it because I was always afraid something would go wrong." Soon enough he would tell friends that the Tony and Academy awards made him feel "terrific for six days. Then, after seven, I thought, it's all false. They made me feel I fooled everybody."

It isn't called depression for nothing.

THE
BIG
FINISH

"*I* read my horoscope every day. I think to myself, 'What am I? Maybe they'll tell me in the *Daily News* today.' "

17

Jennifer Nairn-Smith decided that she'd had enough. "I didn't want to be the second person. When Bobby talked to you, he would give you a hundred percent attention, but whenever I would go to talk with him, there was Annie, right there, and I couldn't squeeze in. Some people can be available for any threeway," Jenn said. "They can sit back and follow him like a puppy and be humiliated, but not me."

Actually, Ann was having her own difficulties with Fosse. She told Bob Aurthur that her psychoanalyst was afraid of the kind of person he was. The doctor thought that Bob's obsession with death and sex was unhealthy for Ann.

Jennifer had different needs. She spent some time thinking of the right words to say and then pulled open a lipstick to scrawl them on the mirror over the bedroom bureau:

> To whom it may concern
> A threeway to nowhere
> I'm out!

Usually, when a girl was upset, Bob would be friendly and reasonable, but this time he was quick on the trigger. When he saw Jennifer's lipsticked farewell, he called her up and was so abusive that years later she was still suppressing the memory of his rage and unwilling even to repeat what he had said. For somebody who seemed to have it all, for someone who was at the moment sitting on top of the Academy Award and the Tony Award (the Emmy would be but icing on the cake now), he was grim and explosive.

While the prizes had been dropping from the tree, Bob gave Chris Chase an interview for *The New York Times*. He liked and trusted Chris because she wasn't a reporter, she was an actress who wrote; as a matter of fact, many (fourteen) years earlier, she had even auditioned for him.

Chris Chase was a compact, attractive blond, very smart, and when she had shown up to sing for Fosse in 1959, he'd climbed onstage and crouched beside her, peering up and whispering advice. He was so young, so blond, so sweet, and so not New York. "Those blazing blue eyes of his," she remembered. "They stared up at you, giving energy, as if he was just hoping you would be great-great-great."

But when she broke her back in a car accident and wasn't able to run around onstage anymore, she became a writer.

He was in a pensive mood for the *Times* interview and told her many personal things, some of which did not appear in the eventual article, either because he asked her to keep them off the record or because she chose to. For instance he told her, "My mommy was strong," sounding childish, "and my father remarried," which was untrue.

But he also could be amazingly confidential for publication. For instance he told her, "I used to be terribly interested in and near-experimental with suicide. I've come awfully close sometimes. Just out of drunkenness and not knowing how many pills I've swallowed. I forget. I get so drunk I think, 'Did I take a sleeping pill?' I don't know, pop a couple, and pretty soon you're in trouble. I'm fascinated by that thin line that makes a person jump. I think it's a flirtation, you know, and a flirtation can go only so far. It's like flirting with a girl. It's like you flirt so many times, sooner or later you have to go through with it; you can carry on a flirtation just so long, and then ultimately you say, Well, this is it. But since Nicole, I could never commit suicide."

He looked up from the interview, momentarily distracted by something he heard. "These new buildings," he said. "They drop mail down the chute. You can hear it." It was a non sequitur. Chase jotted it down.

He said, "I alternate between these terrible states of thinking I'm a fraud and this raging ego; it's just incredible. Part of your ego is you don't relate to other people who say they feel the same thing. Part of you says, 'They don't know what I'm feeling, I'm feeling something special.' It's almost embarrassing you, that they feel the same thing. But if *they* feel that guilt, then I don't want to feel it."

A few weeks later he checked into the Payne Whitney Psychiatric Clinic. He said it was on account of a "terrible depression." It was the end of May, and he had just won the Emmy Award for "Liza with a 'Z.'"

Bob Fosse will probably always be the only director ever to win the top prizes in the movies, the theatre, and television in a single year. He was the first and likely will be the last even to be *nominated* for all three prizes in the same year. He could not have been more successful or more richly rewarded, and it was then—after an amazing, unprecedented sweep of the top prizes in his field—*then* that he broke down under overwhelming depression. Hopelessness and gloom of that kind is irrational of course. Nothing can assuage such grief.

Payne Whitney is not really a clinic but a private hospital, one of the top psychiatric facilities in the country. The 108-bed institution is a division of New York Hospital and part of the Cornell Medical Center on East 68th Street and the East River in Manhattan. It is no more expensive than other private psychiatric hospitals, but it does have a reputation for being a celebrity crisis center.

"The women in the clinic," Bob said, "the nurses and volunteers, they were all so agreeable and attractive that I wanted to scream. All they would ask was, 'Are you depressed? Are you depressed?' And I'd scream at them, '*I don't know!*' "

Bob told his doctors, "It's been bad for me. Like I know I don't really want to be with anybody, and I've got people worried about me. I don't want anyone to worry, and I don't want to stay here, but I think it's dangerous that I'm staying alone. That's what I'm afraid of, going that little step too far."

His psychiatrist, Dr. Clifford Sager, was a specialist in family therapy, and Bob had probably first started to see him about his marital problems. Sager's analysis of his real problem, arrived at years later, was that "Bob's central conflict was based on his intense wish to be a performer."

The facts of Fosse's life seemed to corroborate that theory. He had been on the stage from the age of nine until he was twenty-six. Even after establishing himself as a choreographer, he had attempted to step back into the spotlight in such strange and strained circumstances as the gorilla number in *Damn Yankees*, the repeated appearances in *Pal Joey*, and the chilling tryout for *The Conquering Hero*. This need to perform had been suppressed throughout his marriage to Gwen, when she was the star in the family, but after their separation, he got another taste of performing in *The Little Prince*. Apparently the need to be a star persisted, whatever being a star represented.

Fosse must have been a tough subject for psychological therapy, so alienated was he from his feelings. What was plain, however, was that despite his achievements and recognition, he was tremendously unhappy—unhappy beyond any rational cheer. The needs that had driven him onstage were not being satisfied. He had said it to Chris Chase:

A lot of people have turned and looked at me on the street and I like it. I really like it. I was like, "Well, gee, this is what I've been working for, people to turn around and smile at me. I've never had the kind of public attention others get."

He came to realize in therapy how much rage toward Gwen he had been suppressing. He expressed it now during his breakdown. "He suddenly allowed a lot of this submerged rage to emerge," Tony Walton said. The soft-spoken designer was one friend whom Bob trusted and confided in. Walton was a warm and focused person, someone who made conversations count. "The anger Bob felt toward Gwen," he said in his gentle British accent, "was violent. During much of their joint professional career, whenever they did a show together, Gwen was very much the critics' darling, and if there was any blame to be placed, Bob was always the recipient even though *who knew* how much of her performance was his creation?

"I don't think he could ever be angry with her," Walton added, "but something had to suffer if the overall production wasn't perfect. They were such an integral part of each other's work [but] he tended to be the one who got whacked."

Bob never complained about Gwen getting the credit while he took the blame. If he was angry about it, he never let off the steam. Whatever resentment he harbored was kept to himself while his wife was being showered with accolades, love, and attention. *Her* fingers were spread, *her* elbows tucked, *her* hair sparkled in the spotlight, *she* was taking the bows, *she* was beaming into the audience, bathing in the applause and the cheers.

So Fosse might have been relieved when he'd gone to Hollywood to work on the movie of *Sweet Charity*, leaving Gwen behind on Broadway. He might even have been grimly pleased that Shirley MacLaine had gotten the starring role. If so, his satisfaction was short-lived, because the same thing happened all over again. According to Tony Walton, "After he worked with Shirley MacLaine for several weeks, getting her back into shape, the press was interested in Gwen. Shirley was a chorus dancer [never a star dancer] and his work with her was apparently very intensive. He put a lot of himself into it, but on the first day of shooting Gwen was there, and everyone wanted to see *her* teach MacLaine a few steps."

The designer pondered the irony of it. A short, sturdy, sweet-faced man, he had come to Broadway from England as the young set designer of *The Boy Friend*, which Cy Feuer and Ernest Martin had produced on Broadway in 1954. Walton had married the new star of that show, nineteen-year-old Julie Andrews. Twenty years later, and long after a painful divorce, he was one of the top designers in both the theatre and the movies. He was intelligent, thoughtful, and articulate. He loved both Gwen and Bob and mourned their earnest, painful relationship. "It hurt Bob terribly," he remembered, that after his weeks of drilling MacLaine, "the press had Shirley learning this role from Gwen. It may have been partially true, but in this crisis of depression that Bob was now suffering, these past injustices were being magnified."

But even while Fosse was disinterring his buried anger, he was ashamed, Walton said, "that he could let such small things bother him."

After seventy-two hours at Payne Whitney, Bob signed himself out. "I know I'm a closed-off person," he would say, "but there's nothing I can really do about it. I don't think I can change. I just can't."

Just a few weeks after his weekend at the clinic, he turned up in his home town to receive an honorary degree from Columbia College Chicago (not to be confused with New York's Columbia University), a liberal arts college specializing in the performing arts. Any academic degree would have seemed improbable to this unlettered hoofer whose field of authority ranged from time steps to hat tricks. According to lyric writer Fred Ebb, "Bob always thought of himself as uneducated. It bothered him a great deal. He constantly referred to his lack of education. He could be intimidated by big words." Or as Bob himself said, "Everything I know I learned from 'Hollywood Squares.' "

Now the big words were in his honor, proclaimed against an academic backdrop which, for the graduation ceremony, was the auditorium of Prudential Plaza in downtown Chicago. Bob had of course invited his family to watch him perform in cap and gown. There were no college graduates among the Fosses, and it surely was a title to savor: Honorary Doctor of Arts.

While another honoree, Harrison Salisbury of The New York Times, was delivering his acceptance remarks, Bob turned to his favorite sister-in-law, Margaret, and asked her, "What in the world am I going to say when I get up there?"

She kissed him on the cheek, whispering, "Just tell them, 'Now that I've won every award in sight I'm going to try for Miss America,' " and that was exactly what he said after the royal ribbon of the honorary doctorate was draped around his neck and he was pronounced "Master Artist of Dance, Theatre, and Music. Singularly distinguished in film, theatre, and television." When the laughter of the students and the faculty

subsided, he added, "But I don't think I'm going to make it." Fosse knew
how to milk a laugh even when the house was academic.

"I was mortified," Margie remembered.

Joan Simon had terminal cancer. The earliest symptom had been
her broken arm the previous summer. A spontaneous fracture is a common symptom of spreading bone cancer. For most of that year she stayed
in the house on East 62nd Street, at home with Neil and the girls. Only a
few friends knew, and they were asked to keep it secret.

She died at thirty-nine, in the summer of 1973, and Bob looked
drained at the funeral, unable to console Doc Simon, who was slipping
into a depression of his own and developing a duodenal ulcer in the
process. The playwright had been trying to distract himself during his
wife's ordeal by writing an uncharacteristic play called *The Good Doctor*.
Patently identifying with Anton Chekhov, he based it on several short
stories by the Russian master, who had been a doctor-turned-playwright.
Doc Simon, of course, was a physician of another sort, but there were
none of any kind who knew how to help his wife. When she died, he
disowned his nickname, preferring afterward to be called Neil.

Although Bob said that he wanted to concentrate the remainder of
his career on moviemaking, he had not ruled Broadway out entirely, and
now he agreed to return for Gwen's sake. Going back to work together
surely had layers of meaning for both of them. Their relationship had
always been best at work. Bob had to have wondered whether doing
Chicago meant going back to her in some way. Perhaps Gwen was hoping
that it meant exactly that.

She had herself bought the rights to the Maurine Watkins play
Chicago. The author had died, and her estate now agreed to what she had
always opposed. Fred Ebb (who was going to write the lyrics and collaborate with Fosse on the script) said, "Everyone thought Bob was doing the
show out of guilt over the separation, Gwen's career, and money for her."
Bob thought so too. He told Stanley Donen, "I'm doing this for Gwen.
Otherwise I wouldn't do it."

What was his guilt? For cheating on her? Not reconciling? Outlast-
ing her in show business? He had in effect stepped over her body to reach
his own success. As long as she had been the star, his role had been
supportive, secondary, the power behind her throne where no spotlight
could reach. Her eclipse had made it possible for him to step out into
that star spot, or so it seemed. Moreover, it was particularly as a movie
director that his success was completely his own. Returning to the theatre,

with Gwen on the stage, he would resume the role of making her look good.

These psychological ramifications aside, simply as a work schedule, the burden must have been crushing. He had been working without rest since the start of *Cabaret* and even now was preparing to cast the movie *Lenny*. And he was surely still shaky from the breakdown.

It was one of those parties that, in the narrow perspective of show business, included everybody because theatre people were there and movie people were there. If a party included press lords, real estate barons, merchant princes, Nobel Prize winners in peace and science, and two or three Supreme Court justices, but nobody in show business, it would mean that "nobody" was there.

Bob Fosse was there, as were John Rubinstein and Dustin Hoffman. Fosse drew Rubinstein into a corner of the noisy room and asked, "Do you know Dustin?"

"He's right over there," John said.

"Yeah, I know. I want you to talk him into playing Lenny."

Rubinstein laughed. "I don't *know* him, Bob. I just know that's him over there."

"I want you to tell him," Fosse continued as if he hadn't heard, "I'm a good director, and I'm fun to work with."

"I don't *know* Dustin Hoffman."

"Go ahead," Bob said. "It'll be okay."

The poised and amiable Rubinstein shook his head and made his way over to Hoffman. When he introduced himself, the conversation immediately turned, as it so often did, to his father, the great concert pianist Arthur Rubinstein. Hoffman talked about his own piano playing and his youthful dream of becoming a concert pianist.

"When I was a kid," he told John, "I was forced to listen to one pianist's records over and over, and that was your father."

Rubinstein talked about his own piano playing. He was eager, he told Hoffman, to have two careers, one as an actor and another as a composer. Finally he came to the point.

"Look, Bob Fosse asked me to tell you he's a good director. And he is. He *is* fun to work with, and he's terribly smart. I know they're talking to you about doing the picture. Do the picture."

Hoffman said nothing in response. He just looked at John. Bob had personally brought him a first draft of the *Lenny* screenplay, and he didn't particularly like it. Julian Barry thought, "Bob never wanted to use a star with a lot of clout. He was very competitive with his leading players." But the need for a box office attraction was going to be a determining factor. This movie, with a main character who ultimately overdoses on heroin, was not going to be held over in Disneyland.

Rawness of subject matter, in fact, was the argument Fosse successfully used to film *Lenny* in black and white. That was an important victory. It would strengthen the impression of a documentary movie. The television networks wanted their pictures in color, but there obviously was never going to be a television sale of *Lenny*. The studios made sanitized versions of their movies for the networks' sake, but trying to clean up an obscenity-filled picture about drugs and sex was obviously futile.

Proceeding with production by no means demonstrated that Bob was free of the demons that had chased him into Payne Whitney. For a time he was medicated with lithium, the drug designed to control manic-depressive mood swings, the uncontrollable ups and the murderous downs. That, however, was not the nature of his problem. If only he'd had the ups. When he quit the lithium treatments, he said it was because he found the moderate moods boring and missed the old depressions.

Paddy Chayefsky recommended another line of therapy. While researching the novel *Altered States*, he had come across a radical psychiatrist. Always a polemicist, Chayefsky's argument in this book concerned the threat of mood-altering drugs. Inferentially castigating the fashion for hallucinogens, it was to be a Jekyll and Hyde tale about a research physician who is undone by brain chemistry experiments conducted, unfortunately, upon himself. The doctor whom Paddy had met and, with typical inconsistency, was now recommending to Fosse was Richard Ariola, a man Bob Aurthur and Tony Walton also knew. "Ariola was a psychiatrist," Walton said, "who practiced 'rational chemical therapy,' based on how the body's chemical balances cause depressions and associated troubles."

Walton considered Ariola dangerous, "somebody who had pushed the boundaries too far." In fact, Dr. Richard Ariola had left the psychiatric department of St. Vincent's Hospital in shadowy circumstances, after having been a respected physician on the staff. All that the chief of that department, Dr. Joseph English, would say about the departure was that "an accident had left him unable to carry out his responsibilities."

Tony Walton said, "After that, Ariola had to practice psychiatry in more eccentric ways."

"This is going to change your life," the slender, bespectacled psychiatrist said, holding out a vial of pills. Bob liked the man. Perhaps it was because of the dramatic turn his life had taken, a respectable and even distinguished medical career being destroyed by an obsession with a radical and perhaps hedonistic (since it was drug-related) notion. Perhaps there was a trace of the *Pippin* syndrome about it, going down in flames for a flash finish.

Bob would occasionally pay midnight visits to Ariola's current office, a dingy room on the lower East Side ("a very scary environment," as Tony Walton described it). On occasion Bob would even bring girlfriends along. "The only thing," Ariola told Fosse about the pills, "is you can't drink if you're taking this stuff, and you can't mix it with any other substance." Then he said something so frightening that Bob repeated it to both Walton and Aurthur: "Now you have the power to kill yourself. Take one drink with these pills, and you're dead. Your head will explode."

Fosse, who was not out of his mind, backed off. "That's like putting a loaded pistol in my hands," he said, and he returned to Dexedrine.

But Ariola continued to experiment. One weekend he went off with a girlfriend. Bob had sent over a gift, a case of Bushmill's Irish whiskey, of all things. Now he considered it a stupid thing to have done, and when Ariola didn't call to acknowledge it and didn't answer the telephone, he went down to see what had happened.

Ariola was dead. "He had accidentally killed himself with the drug," Walton said.

Fosse—having fallen apart from a depression that no medication, legal, illegal, experimental, or even bizarre seemed able to lift him out of, being seriously underweight and seriously overworked, wracked by hacking coughs from his four-pack-a-day cigarette habit, using amyl nitrate poppers in addition to the Dexedrine and Seconal in his ever-present attaché case, dining on double margaritas, virtually living with Ann Reinking but making love to as many others as the nights allowed— Fosse, in this shape, began to work on the script of the new musical *Chicago* during the afternoons while polishing *Lenny* in the mornings.

"You're five minutes late," he said when Bob Aurthur arrived one afternoon for a lunch date. "I thought you forgot." He didn't even let his friend take off the raincoat, instead jumping up and leading the way to the door. "I want to put Chita Rivera with Gwen in *Chicago*," he said. "They could be dynamite together. To tell the truth I'm not too crazy about the original material, but we're going to do number after number. What I want to do is put on a show, a really terrific show!"

It wasn't egoism or thoughtlessness that kept him from asking about his friend's work. It was the soreness of the subject. Bob Aurthur wasn't doing much. It was his turn for a career crisis, and it had been his turn for too long.

Bob Aurthur's movie at Universal in the good old laughing days of the Bob and Bob Building had failed just as *Sweet Charity* had. Both men had gone under after that, but Bob Aurthur had not yet resurfaced. Fosse, however, would not abandon a friend whose career was in trouble, although the crisis did seem to have changed Aurthur's attitude. He was worried, nervous, defensive, and obsequious. He was being sycophantic with Bob, and that was bad shape to be in. "Lunch with Fosse," he wrote in *Esquire*, where he had a monthly column called "Hanging Out."

> Heavy rain, Seventh Avenue is a river as I run south from the 57th Street bus stop . . . nothing will stop me. This year's Mr. Amazing, winner of practically every 1972 award known to man in three media . . . I will swim raging urban torrents if necessary to see a man I respect and care about as much as anyone.

Fosse was not one to be contemptuous of the needy, and he never took comfort from a friend's travails as so many do, in and out of show business. He lived with (and spoke of) the memory when he was "so cold, no one called me. No one wanted anything to do with me." Bob Aurthur was a friend of his on this rainy day too.

When he got back to the office, Fred Ebb was waiting, poised to start writing *Chicago*. Although Ebb had worked with Fosse on "Liza with a 'Z,' " he didn't know what to expect in terms of coauthorship. He did not know how much of a writer Bob actually was. Too, "I was in total awe," he admitted. Fosse was a good talker. He had already told Ebb and his partner, composer John Kander, "You have got to feel free to say anything. If you don't say the dumb things, then all of the good things won't come out." The words sounded fine, but they didn't mean much. How were Fred and Bob going to write the script together? Ebb found out. "My primary contribution to this show," Bob said, "will happen when we're in rehearsal. That's when I think of lines, that's when I think of business, that's when I think of throwing out whole scenes or redoing them or reconceiving them in terms of movement."

In other words, Ebb was going to have to go home and write the whole script by himself, which probably made him even more nervous than he normally was. For although he was a professional lyricist, he had never written the book of a musical.

Then Bob boarded a plane and flew to England to prepare the London company of *Pippin* for an October 30, 1973, premiere at Her Majesty's Theatre. At the opening night party, Stephen Schwartz approached him. The young composer smiled and extended a conciliatory hand, but Fosse would not respond. He turned away and resumed his conversation with Stuart Ostrow.

The show, badly received, closed after eighty-five performances.

When Dustin Hoffman agreed to star in *Lenny*, production plans were begun. While Bob was casting the movie, Julian Barry polished the script. Rehearsals were scheduled to run through November and December, and then filming was to start in Miami in January 1974. Julian and Bob were already arranging to fly there to scout locations as they sat down for lunch with Paddy. The hot waitresses at the newfound restaurant had lost out, inevitably, to the cold cuts at the Carnegie Delicatessen. To Herb Schlein's relief, Bob was back ordering his pastrami on white bread with mayonnaise and not eating it.

Chayefsky was disconsolate. While working on *Altered States*, he had been looking forward to the production of his screenplay about the Arab–Israeli War of 1967. Now, this movie plan was wrecked when Israel was attacked by the Arabs on Yom Kippur. The second war made Chayefsky's screenplay outdated. He was as staunch a Zionist as there was in America, but if he was happy about the Israelis' stunning victory, he didn't act it. He only had greater reason to hate the Arabs, and the anger simmered and glowed around him like the garlic from the pickles in the bowl on the table.

"Hey, Paddy!" a voice boomed.

Herb Schlein had been trying to intercept the man, but hadn't been able to move quickly enough. It was difficult for him to move quickly because of his weight and because of his worsening gout. Bob and Julian looked up as Paddy turned to see who was calling him. The man arrived, squeezing his shoulder, pounding his back. "I'm really sorry to hear about your last movie," he said.

"My last movie?" Chayefsky asked. "My last movie was *Hospital*. What are you talking about?"

"I don't mean that one," the man said. "I mean your *last* one. The one that nobody wants to make."

"You see what a rotten fucking business this is?" Chayefsky said when the show business sadist was finally got rid of. "Your last movie isn't your last movie. It's your last screenplay that nobody wants to produce."

Dustin Hoffman lived with his then wife, the ballet dancer Ann Byrne, in a modest apartment on West 55th Street. They'd had to move out of a Greenwich Village brownstone when it had been demolished by a bomb set off in the basement workshop of a young political activist and ungifted munitions maker. Hoffman now lived next door to a pal of Chayefsky's, an actor named Eddie White. Paddy would frequently stop by to see White, sometimes unexpectedly. Paddy's wife had become so reclusive she virtually never left home. His reaction was to leave as often as possible.

White was a barrel-chested fellow who looked like a former prizefighter, which in fact he was ("thirty-one bouts as a flyweight in the amateurs, and I won thirty of them. The other was a draw."). Besides acting, he managed the show business careers of such ex-boxers as Sandy Saddler and Rocky Graziano. With his tight curly hair, twinkling eyes, and fair skin, he looked very Irish for a Jew.

Eddie White was concerned about the way that Dustin Hoffman would portray Lenny Bruce. The comedian had been a pal of White's, and although he was aware of the drug addiction, he had known a different side of Bruce. "The guys who hung around his place during the drug days, like Keefe Brasselle and Murray Hamilton, they wouldn't even let me in when I rang the doorbell. If I'd've been smart, I would have broken in and dragged him out of there. Lenny was a different kind of guy with me, a sweet guy," and White kept reminding Fosse and Hoffman of that. "Don't play Lenny as just a drug addict," he pleaded with Hoffman next door. "That was only one side of him."

The actor listened patiently and sympathetically. He was a disciplined technician and believed in research. He was spending a month of nights watching comics perform in small clubs. In his first play, while a twenty-three-year-old, he had convincingly played a middle-aged Russian clerk and had only grown as an artist since. There was no question but that he was tremendously gifted.

With work on *Lenny* about to begin, Fosse was in conflict with him already. David Picker, the movie's executive producer, described them as "two perfectionists pestering each other," but Julian Barry put it less delicately. "Bob didn't have a rough time with Dustin," he said, "but Dustin had a rough time with Bob." Fosse could dish it out, but he wouldn't let anyone give it back. "Dustin took a lot of crap," the writer said. "I think that afterwards a lot of other directors paid for it."

The "crap" that Hoffman had to take from Fosse began early, as the movie went into rehearsal in New York. With Valerie Perrine playing Bruce's wife and Jan Miner as his mother, they were going to spend the first month of the six-week rehearsal period working on the script as if it were a play. Bob seemed to be tense and dark even as they began to work on the first nonmusical of his career.

"Hey, Bob," Hoffman said late one morning at the start of rehearsal. "I worked something out last night."

"Yeah? What's that, Dustin?" Fosse asked, the glasses hanging from the chain around his neck and the cigarette drooping from the corner of his mouth. He stared intently at the actor as Julian Barry looked on. ("Fosse talked so quietly during this phase," the writer said, "that he would draw you in until you tripped and fell." It was a ploy favored by many directors, from Jed Harris to Elia Kazan.)

"I worked out a walk," Hoffman said.

"Oh?" Fosse replied tartly. "I hope not."

"Why?"

"Because the last four parts I've seen you play," Bob said, "have all degenerated into a 'walk.' "

The rehearsal studio fell silent. Valerie Perrine and Jan Miner averted their eyes.

"It was a deadly silence," Julian Barry remembered. "I could see Dustin's mind cracking and falling like glass, and him thinking, 'I'm not taking this crap off anybody ever again.' "

The actor glared, and Fosse looked back with his cool blue Nordic eyes, the smoke curling heartlessly from his cigarette. Then the actor waggled a finger at the director in a rabbinical way.

"Limited gains, Bob, limited gains," he said, "talking to me that way."

Lenny wasn't set in Miami, but it was going to be filmed there because there were houses that looked like Los Angeles, nightclubs that looked like strip joints in Chicago or smart clubs in Manhattan, exteriors that resembled Hawaii, and a courtroom that could be New York's, almost. That was one of Bob's complaints about the tight budget, using a modern Miami courtroom for New York's, which were more imposing, but filming all in one place would be economically wise for a production that had roughly a $2 million budget, of which Hoffman was getting half.

It was going to be a grueling schedule, sixteen weeks of six-day weeks. As Bob and Julian walked toward their hotel rooms, the first day on location, Fosse stopped abruptly, and setting his attaché case on the floor, he put an ear to the door of Dustin Hoffman's room.

"What are you doing?" Barry asked.

"I learned a long time ago," Fosse said, "during shows out of town, that listening at people's hotel-room doors is one of the most useful things

294 THE BIG FINISH

that you can do. You hear them talking on the phone, and you find out exactly what they think of you and the work you're doing, and it saves you a great deal of time and effort."

Barry looked quizzically at Fosse. He was not certain how to take this.

"Whenever you get out of town," Bob advised, "always listen at people's hotel doors."

The writer decided that Fosse was joking.

The plot of *Lenny* is straightforward enough. Lenny Bruce, born Leonard Alfred Schneider, is a young and not very special or good comedian doing corny jokes and Jimmy Durante impressions in cheap nightclubs. The raucous audience is tamed only by the bleating saxophone that signals the stripper, Hot Honey Harlow, a full-bodied pornographic fantasy who makes him swoon with love.

Bruce is a bright but uneducated innocent. His playful contrariness and increasingly free language begin to upset nightclub owners as well as show business professionals and ultimately the authorities. After he marries Honey, her involvement with hard drugs, brought on by morphine administered after an automobile accident, leads her to a heroin habit that wrecks the marriage. Bruce goes on to win considerable success as a radical social satirist, and he becomes a favorite of intellectuals and sophisticates, but censorship problems and then drug arrests destroy his career. He dies naked on a bathroom floor of an overdose of heroin.

During the New York rehearsals, an unseen interviewer was worked into the script. The device allowed Bruce's wife, his mother, and his agent to speak directly to the camera, lending another element of the documentary. Fosse decided to conduct these interviews himself, and his is the voice on the soundtrack. "Interviewing in the movie," said David Picker, the executive producer, "may well have come out of Bobby's love of performing." It may also have come out of his fondness for the Truth Game. Some of his questions were extemporaneous and drew improvised responses from the actors. Just as at Wally's playing the game, when Fosse was after a particular response, he could be quietly cruel. Julian Barry said, "He would do anything he had to do to get the response he wanted. He would hand you a telegram and tell you your mother died." The shaken sobs of Valerie Perrine, for instance, were the result of Bob's relentless questioning about her boyfriend's recent death. After the effect was achieved, his questions were deleted from the soundtrack.

The reason Fosse wanted Perrine to cry was to help create a Lenny Bruce who was emotionally perverse, or at least inconsistent when urging his wife to join him in a threesome with another woman. Although Honey is loath to do this, he convinces her by relating it to her love for him and to her sureness of his love for her. The photography of the bedroom scene is perhaps the most dramatic and striking in a film of extraordinary visual power. The cinematographer was a Surtees, but it was not Robert Surtees. The *Sweet Charity* cameraman was unavailable, and so Fosse hired his son Bruce, also a cameraman and, to judge by *Lenny*, a brilliant one. There are certain reminders in this work of the imagery, light, and shadow of *Citizen Kane* and suggestions, too, of Ingmar Bergman in the tight close-ups against a hum of silence. One could do worse than be influenced by Orson Welles and Ingmar Bergman.

In this sexual scene, the women approach one another in silence while Bruce looks on from an emotional distance. The faces are expressionless, and yet their eyes seem all-admitting. The second woman is sexually concentrated but not passionate. Bruce's wife is shamed, her glances beseeching her husband for mercy and rescue, or at least for approval and love, but he is a frigid observer. For a time he even seems fully clothed, although Fosse does not let the audience know for certain since Hoffman is not shown below the neck. The women are nude, however, and the photography of their bodies is sculptural and moonscaped with light brilliantly edging the curves of their flesh. The shadows lend substance, the light allows no escape.

Bruce finally enters the sexual picture, kissing one woman and then the other, but these are not the faces of lovers. They are clear-eyed and unaroused faces, perhaps even faces of grief. It is one of the longest and most powerful and painfully beautiful sequences in the film.

In the next scene Honey weeps in disgrace and disgust while Bruce condemns her for having done what he has urged her to do.

"Jesus Christ," she cries. "You were the one who talked me into these freak scenes."

"I didn't have to do much talking, did I?" he says icily. "You didn't tell me you were going to like it so much."

There is no factual basis for Lenny Bruce being involved in sexual threesomes. There is no record of Bruce's wife having experimented with that while they were together, and there is no mention of such erotica in either the play *Lenny* or the Albert Goldman biography, *Ladies and Gentlemen—Lenny Bruce!* on which it was partly based. The scene in the movie was conceived by Bob and Julian "and," the writer remembered, "once we came up with it, Bob threw himself into it enthusiastically."

There are reminders of Bob's own life in other scenes. Early sequences in strip joints with cheap comedians, shabby audiences, and the juvenile Lenny Bruce as master of ceremonies suggest the life of young Bob Fosse in the sleazy Chicago clubs of his youth. Neither this nor the sexual threesomes means that *Lenny* is the story of Bob Fosse. It is too strong and too original a work to be merely that, too powerful in its feeling, too vital in its rhythms and filmic nature. But like the work of any artist, it is an expression of the self and an exploitation of the self.

Another aspect of *Lenny* that seems to relate to Fosse's own life is the treatment of the judges in later scenes that deal with Bruce's legal problems. Here the young comedian pleads first for his career and later for his life, seeming much like a son begging forgiveness from an unfeeling father. In casting the judges, Fosse chose actors who communicated deceptive tenderness, making the courtroom scenes in *Lenny* especially sorrowful as the beleaguered comedian pleads in vain for a chance to work and, obliquely, for the judges' love.

One afternoon as a break was called, Bob hurried to the elevators in the hall outside the Miami courtroom. He stopped one of the extras who had been locally hired. She was dashing for an appointment, although she was not supposed to leave the set.

"Excuse me," he said. "Would you come with me for a moment?"

"I did a 'who, me?' take," the extra would remember, certain that she was due for a reprimand, if not outright dismissal. Her name was Kim St. Leon, she had long, straight blond hair, she was extremely good-looking, five foot six with a willowy dancer's body, and she was nineteen years old.

I'm in trouble, she thought. He knows I should be back in the courtroom. She also suspected that he might be attracted to her, because men usually were. The previous day, Bob had come up as she sat on a barstool in another scene. He had gripped her waist with both hands to nudge the stool several inches to the side, and as he did it, he said, "I came over on purpose so I could touch you," and so Kim St. Leon waited to hear exactly what Mr. Fosse wanted.

He wanted to have dinner with her "and he put a lot of pressure on me to date him," which she agreed to do "because I was scared not to." He was, after all, Bob Fosse, twenty-seven years older than she, "and when he talks," she said, "he doesn't come across as being just out to nail you."

Kim was a Florida girl; she had grown up and still lived outside Miami, and she had acting aspirations. She had just broken up with a boy who was considerably closer to her own age, and when she went out to dinner with Bob for the first time, she remembered, "He made me cry the first night, telling him my life story. He was able to pinpoint my unhappiness. It was one of those numbers he was doing on me. He knew what buttons to push. He was a director, and because he was a director he knew what to ask and what to say."

She became Bob's lover. She didn't see their age difference as being significant. "He was never an old man," she said. "He was more of a kid than I was." When Bob would fret about his rapidly disappearing hair, she would razz him about it. "Oh poor me," she would mock. "You know you're cute. You've got all the women in the world. Go fuck yourself."

She was having more success with Fosse the man than with Fosse the director. Every scene that she played as an extra was cut out of the movie. She came to the set each day and, having little to do, "hung out, mainly with Lenny Bruce's daughter." At seventeen, Kitty Bruce was just two years younger, "and we spent a lot of time together." Then Kim would see Bob late at night, after he watched the day's rushes.

Sometimes he would come to her place and cook a late dinner for them. "He made the best potato skins in the world," she said. "They came out so crispy and perfect, and he said it was because of the sea salt and the safflower oil." She tried to cook for him too, "which at nineteen I was scared to death to do." Then they would sit and talk, and Bob would reminisce about the days when he had been a contract player at MGM and in love with Pier Angeli. "He thought she was particularly beautiful," Kim remembered, "and he was really crazy about her.

"But she never thought of him as a real suitor," Kim said. "He talked about her a lot." But he didn't talk about Pier Angeli's suicide.

It was a Fosse made young by this girl, a Fosse very different from the cynical friend of Chayefsky and certainly different from the dark and testy director on the *Lenny* set. There, his relationship with Dustin Hoffman had further deteriorated since the "limited gains" episode. There was always something about Hoffman to bother him. Bob wasn't happy with the actor's sexual projection. "Dustin wasn't sexy when Bob wanted him to be sexy," Julian remembered, "and he said 'man' too much."

"Every other word out of his mouth," Fosse said, " 'man,' 'man,' 'man.' "

Yet he remained respectful of Hoffman. He could hardly complain about perfectionism when he might himself spend half a day re-photographing a single moment for the sake of a perfectly raised eyebrow. "Without perfection it's mediocre," he would say, and he respected the same quality in others. When Hoffman asked to redo a lengthy comedy monologue, Fosse agreed instantly, even though he considered the previous take excellent and would have to assemble an entire nightclub audience and crew to do the scene again.

298 □ THE BIG FINISH

Bob's primary worry was the picture's motion. As Julian Barry pointed out, "This was a movie about a mouth. No movie ever talked as much as *Lenny* did. Bobby's job was to keep it a moving picture."

He had a fundamental rule about movement in a movie. It was as if he had transposed dance into screen terms. "We're dealing with moving pictures," he told Barry. "If you're not moving the camera, then you must be moving something through that frame, because moving pictures are what movies are all about." As yet, the problem of the moving picture in *Lenny* was not solved.

Hoffman's focus was not on pictures but on acting, on dialogue and character, on dramatic relationships and emotional power. Fosse, however, had a film event on his mind, and "he had a special vision that he wanted to get on the screen," according to Alan Heim, the editor of *Lenny*. A film editor is usually thought of as someone working on the materials after the photography is completed, but the editor's work actually begins while the movie is being photographed. He confers with the director at each day's screening of rushes so that the final effect being sought is pursued during current filming and not at the end when it is too late. "There was a whole look to this movie," Heim said, "and Bob made you reach inside of yourself to help him get it. The look that Fosse wanted," Heim said, "was a grainy look, a newsreel documentary look," but the process was stressful, and Fosse's darkness of spirit only made it worse. "He was almost always unhappy with the dailies," the editor said. After the two of them looked at the footage, "Bob would drive me back to the hotel in silence," Heim said, "and there was a black cloud around him." Dustin Hoffman used a more rigid image to describe Fosse. "He doesn't enjoy. He's a fucking vise out there," the actor said.

The producer of *Lenny* was trying to lighten Bob up. David Picker was utterly in his thrall. This was one money man who would not give Fosse trouble. Picker was more than devoted. He worshipped. Picker would stop by for his director at the hotel each morning. Bob would cough his way down the hall ("He was my alarm clock," Hoffman said). The producer would drive him to the set, arriving a half hour before the crew. "He would just sit there quietly," Picker said, "until everyone came. It was an extraordinary experience, because Bobby on a craft level was such an extraordinary man. Bobby's brilliance and his demand for the best that anyone could give was just something you didn't see. Bobby," he repeated, "was just brilliant."

Picker had been the president of United Artists when Julian Barry's play had first been bought. He quit that position to produce his own pictures for the studio, and this was the first. Fosse had been given creative control, which was remarkable considering that it was only his third movie, but of course he had just won the Academy Award, and at the time Hollywood was on a honeymoon with directors, riding the wave of the auteur phenomenon. Julian Barry liked to refer to Fosse as "this auteur tap dancer."

When filming came to an end, Bob persuaded Kim to come to New York and get an apartment of her own. "I wanted to study acting," she said, "and Bobby encouraged it." He suggested a teacher and even gave her a reference, and when she arrived, he introduced her to Ann Reinking. "Isn't she beautiful?" he whispered, giving Kim a teasing nudge.

"He put pressure on me to join a threesome," she said, adding that she always resisted. "That was part of his excitement. The woman's form for him was such a turn-on. And he liked going over the edge. He liked being different. Being in bed with two women, most men want to do that, but Bob didn't just fantasize. He did it."

That was a time of transition, the spring of 1974. Jack Cole died. Gwen had long since outgrown his tirades and Bob his intimidations, but Cole was not forgotten. He was in their every step, emotional as well as choreographic.

Other people in Fosse's life were facing up to realities and changing with them. Neil Simon's *The Good Doctor* was not a hit, but writing the play had been a catharsis, and he married one of its cast members, the beautiful, smart, and gifted Marsha Mason. He began writing *Chapter Two*, a play about new starts.

Herb Gardner had a girlfriend in a play too, Marlo Thomas. When his comedy, *Thieves*, ran into trouble out of town, she stepped in. *Thieves* was not well received on Broadway, but it did run nine months, long enough to give its eternally optimistic author reason to think that his professional travails might at last be coming to an end.

With Bob's encouragement, Ann Reinking left the *Pippin* company, where she was in the chorus. In March she would be opening on Broadway in an "Andrews Sisters musical" called *Over Here*. Some thought she might be the next Gwen Verdon.

Whatever was motivating Bob to do the backbreaking and simply unwanted *Chicago* for Gwen, he had to find out just how much the years had taken out of her dancing. They decided to accept an invitation for her to perform on an Ed Sullivan television special, to dance "Who's Got the Pain?" with Harvey Evans, the Fosse veteran. Bob rehearsed the pair in the old *Damn Yankees* number, and it went so well that she agreed to play a summer revival of the show. When the tall and handsome Jerry Lanning was engaged as leading man, the company went to Chicago to rehearse for a March opening. The Arie Crown Theatre was inaugurating a revival policy, and *Damn Yankees* had never played Bob's hometown.

At rehearsal, Gwen invited Lanning and Harvey Evans to dinner. When the dancer was unable to make it, the amiable leading man came alone, and thus began the first and only extended love affair of Gwen Verdon's life after Bob. For several years, she and Lanning would live together, on and off.

The tour had an auspicious start. "She's forty-nine now," William Leonard unkindly reminded the world in his *Chicago Tribune* review before adding, "Indeed, still every inch the seductress . . . and she was worth the wait." In fact, Gwen was overweight, and of course could not dance Lola the way she had at thirty, but there was time for her to get into shape. After a three-month tour the show was scheduled to end up in suburban New York by midsummer. Rehearsals of *Chicago* were set to start in the fall.

As *Damn Yankees* was winding down at the Westbury Music Tent, Bob would drive past the theatre along the Long Island Expressway on the way to a house he had rented in Quogue. It was a modern gray-shingled beach house encircling a swimming pool, just a walk from the ocean. Bob had bought himself an enormous black Lincoln Mark II to get there, the first car he had owned since "Baby," the little red convertible he used to drive to the MGM lot. A big black Lincoln didn't seem his style, but as the editor Alan Heim pointed out, "He didn't buy it because he was into cars. He bought it because he was into black."

Quogue is on the south shore of Long Island, stretching it a bit to be included in "The Hamptons." It has the advantage of being some twenty miles closer to New York City than East Hampton, where Gwen had bought a bigger place with more land after selling the old house in Amagansett. The new house wasn't near the ocean but set back from Spring Close Road, more private, and more of a country house with trees and lawns instead of sand and brush. The sign out front read "Verdon–Fosse."

Now she was adding a swimming pool to it. Bob used to be welcome, but she was virtually living with Lanning that summer. One evening she brought him to a party that the Aurthurs gave, and there was Bob with Ann Reinking. The writer Nora Ephron, who had herself come with ex-husband Dan Greenburg, surveyed the scene—nobody seemed to be with the proper spouse—and she said to Jane Aurthur, "Look what's in this room." At the moment, Ann Reinking's arms were wrapped around Fosse. "Now this is what I call an East Hampton party," Ephron said.

The relationship between Bob and Gwen, however, was not simply a matter of sophistication. He said he preferred Quogue to East Hampton because "it isn't as show biz," but nothing on this earth had ever been too show business for Bob Fosse. More likely he wanted a certain distance between his house, his girlfriends, and his wife. He didn't appreciate Gwen having an affair with Jerry Lanning and said so. He admitted that the attitude was inconsistent with his own demands for freedom, but said it was just the way he was. He wouldn't let Ann or Kim see other men either. He could intimidate them into accepting a double standard, but Gwen was another matter at the moment.

Late one night in New York the two of them, Ann Reinking and Kim St. Leon, showed up at the cutting room. Bob had invited them to come see some of *Lenny*. The scene that he had Alan Heim bring out was the sexual sequence between Lenny Bruce and the two women. Bob plopped into the deep leather armchair while Heim's assistant, Trudy Ship, set up the big reel of film on the Moviola. This was a self-contained projection system, like a little television set. The assistant editor stepped back to turn off the lights and let the girls have the screen to themselves.

Bob's cigarette glowed in the dark and Alan Heim and his assistant watched silently while Ann and Kim, young and lovely women with their straight hair and long muscular legs, stood side to side, their arms crossed, their faces aglow in the reflected light of the images. In the dark they watched Valerie Perrine tell the unseen interviewer—surely they recog-

nized Bob's voice—about Lenny urging her to have sex with another
woman and him. They looked on as Bruce watched the two women kiss
each other while he kept his physical and emotional distance, only at last
joining the silent orgy, even then more as a voyeur than a participant. Ann
and Kim stared as, unreasonably and perversely, Lenny Bruce turned
against his wife, and they watched Valerie Perrine collapse under the
onslaught of his snarling cruelty.

"You were the one who talked me into these freak scenes."
"I didn't have to do much talking, did I?"

They stood there, Ann Reinking and Kim St. Leon, in the dark in
the cutting room, and their eyes filled until they overflowed, and the tears
streamed down their cheeks.

The editing of *Lenny* was a second making of the picture, for it was at
that stage that Bob decided to create a visual tempo and choreography
through quick intercutting back and forth through time and place. The
film's rhythm and thrust was created by this visual percussion, the movie's
jitterbug. As Heim said, "You knew every moment where you were, but
you never knew how you got there."

This was Fosse making the picture. This was what was meant by
"creative control." The writer Julian Barry was not a part of it. The
executive producer David Picker was not a part of it. Nobody from United
Artists was looking over his shoulder, and it was not work of someone else's
origination that the great Broadway repairer Bob Fosse was now going to
bamboozle past an audience.

He was going to use Lenny Bruce's monologues as if they were
musical numbers. Like the songs in *Cabaret*, they would occur as they
had in reality, on the nightclub floor, but they would also continue in
voice-over, so that the comedy material was juxtaposed against its sources
in Bruce's real life, commenting on or reflecting the events that immediately preceded or ensued. When Bruce is in the sex scene with the two
women, for instance, he is heard in voice-over and then seen on the
nightclub floor doing now double-edged material about lesbians ("That's
what Will Rogers said once, 'I never met a dyke I didn't like. . . . If you
notice, comics will do endless fag jokes but never dyke jokes. You know
why? Because dykes will only punch the shit out of you.")

Bob was in a foul mood during the editing. When Alison Heim gave
birth, he said meanly to Alan, "You were a better editor before you had a
kid." Heim would notice people stopping by to visit and, seeing Fosse,
leave. At first the mercurial nature of these moods baffled the editor, but

one evening Bob went to the bathroom and left his attaché case on the table, its lid open. Alan Heim was as nosy as anybody else. When he saw the packages of Dexedrine and Seconol in the briefcase, he realized what was causing Fosse's extremes of mood. He realized, too, that the case had been intentionally left open, that Bob was trying to explain himself. After that, Alan thought of the briefcase as "the drugstore."

Despite the moods, work was progressing with a sense of excitement and rightness. The editor said, "Interweaving and intercutting *Lenny* instead of discrete sections was giving this picture a rhythm and life and time fragmentation." Other directors had employed fast cutting, particularly Richard Lester, who had done the Beatles' *A Hard Day's Night* in such a fashion. However, Fosse was creating more than organized chaos, more than a visual counterpart to musical rhythm; he was creating a sense of Lenny Bruce's careening life, his hurtling, ricocheting mind, and the drugged skewing of its logic.

The sexual threesome was one of two barbituratelike sequences, dreamy and languid in long and brooding contrast to the film's otherwise amphetamine pace. The second languorous scene was of Bruce in a heroin daze, naked beneath a trench coat, taking a nightclub floor toward the end of his life. It happens after the long harassment he had been enduring at the hands of the law. Driven out of work, he is a show business pariah, obsessed with his own martyrdom. Instead of doing what he does, instead of being funny, he harangues his audiences with accounts of his persecution and details of his legal problems. Even his fans desert him.

The tragic monologue was photographed in one long uninterrupted scene. It was shot from a high angle, "looking down on the stage," producer David Picker said, "as if you were sitting at a table looking at the floor show. That was called the 'master shot.' Normally, when you're doing a scene you shoot the master and then you shoot the coverage," Picker said. "In other words, you shoot the scene from one angle, and then you come in and do your close-ups, your over-the-shoulders, whatever you're going to use to intercut to make the scene. The master shot may not even end up being the dominant shot in the scene, but it is the shot in which all the scene's information is included from one angle."

This nightclub monologue, this mad scene, was Dustin Hoffman's toughest, coming at the end of Lenny Bruce's rope. The actor stayed awake for forty-eight hours to look haggard. "He wanted to walk out on that stage absolutely exhausted," Picker said, "and out of his mind." Since Fosse had suggested the possibility of using just the master shot for the whole monologue, Hoffman's performance had to be all but flawless and the photography perfect. "There couldn't be a camera problem," Picker said, "though Dustin could slip a line, because Bruce is deteriorating in the scene."

In fact Fosse ultimately did use only the master shot, never cutting away for the whole five minutes. This risking of keeping an audience's attention without a variety of camera angles was quite daring. (It was also convenient, since some of the exposed film in the close-up cameras was ruined when it was carried from the air-conditioned nightclub into the Miami heat.) The monologue is the only scene in *Lenny* that allows Dustin Hoffman a sustained build and development. While he communicates humor and passion and pain elsewhere in the movie, the full range of his technique was to be regularly defeated by the constant intercutting. That was what would make him angry about the editing. On the other hand, Alan Heim says, "Dustin Hoffman is an actor who has an inordinate need to be liked in performance. Whenever we went into the cutting room, we found that he was always trying to pull back from the cruelty, from Lenny Bruce's cutting edge. We found in editing that by fragmenting the script, tying in the comedy routines with the relating drama, we were able to give Hoffman's performance that edge." Perhaps Heim and Fosse thought so, but evidently Hoffman disagreed, and yet he was able, later, to admit gamely, "Bob's the only director I've ever worked with who ever beat me. He's the only one I ever met more obsessive than I."

Kim St. Leon had been staying at Bob's apartment so regularly that she felt comfortable answering his telephone. She even referred her home calls to his number. One that came in was from an actor with whom she had been working on a scene in acting class. When Bob saw Kim's scribbled message with the fellow's name and telephone number, he became enraged.

"You can't do that."

"It's just acting class."

"I know it's ridiculous," Bob said, "but I can't allow it."

"Every time I answer this phone," she said, "it's some girlfriend," and the truth, as Kim admitted, was that "I wasn't supposed to go out with anyone else and didn't want to even though he made it clear that he was seeing other women." But this was different. She really was just working on an acting scene.

"I don't care," Bob said. "I don't want to see any more names. I don't want you mentioning anyone."

"But, Bob—I was only rehearsing a *scene* with this guy. You said I should go to acting classes in the first place."

"I know it doesn't make any sense. *Just cut it out!*"

Ann Reinking had also slammed into this unreasonable jealousy and told Bob Aurthur that she felt "real rage" about Bob's double standard, having other lovers but denying her the same privilege. "I don't really understand some of his behavior. He inflicts pain on other people [that] he's not willing to assume himself." Perhaps she tried to understand too much. "I have respect for another's right to live his own life," she concluded on the subject of Bob's double standard.

Now as Kim dealt with the same double standard, sitting on the sofa with her heart thumping, she shared Ann's rage but not her compliance and felt she was more mature at nineteen than Fosse was at forty-seven. This isn't the guy I know, she thought. He is neurotic, and with that she said, "That's about the most unfair thing I've ever heard. You're being silly, Bob."

"Look," he finally said, "if you can't go by the rules, then I guess we can't see each other."

"Well, I guess we can't then," she said, and she got up and walked out the door.

After mornings in the editing room, Bob spent the afternoons working on *Chicago*. It was set in the thirties during an era when vaudeville promoters were in love with "freak acts"—prizefighters, bank robbers, and most especially convicted murderesses whose victims were cheating lovers. On stage these nonperformers might sing or dance, but they were there primarily to be gawked at. Audiences flocked to do that.

Fosse and Ebb decided to reset the Maurine Dallas Watkins play on a vaudeville stage so that all the musical numbers would be "justified," as in the *Cabaret* movie. These would be the traditional variety acts raised to archetype: ventriloquists, female impersonators, tramp clowns, or as Bob told an interviewer, "a Bert Williams type number, a Helen Morgan type number, an Eddie Cantor type number." It was home territory, Fred Weaver territory. Within the styles of these routines, the lyrics would relate to the story. Between the songs, in sketchlike scenes, the plot would unfold—the arrest and trial of Roxie Hart for shooting her boyfriend, her defense by the lawyer Billy Flynn, her friendship with another murderess, Velma Kelly, her trial and conviction, and finally her debut on the vaudeville stage. With Gwen as Roxie, Jerry Orbach was cast as Flynn and Chita Rivera as Velma.

All the while that *Lenny* was being shot in Florida, Ebb had been writing a first draft of *Chicago* "and it was basically funny," his partner John Kander recalled. "Sunny funny." When Bob read it, he edited the manuscript, circling and underlining sections, scribbling along the margins. Then Fred would rewrite, and they would meet and play out the scenes and talk, much as Julian and Bob had done with *Lenny*. John Kander sat in on some of these early script meetings, "and it was just laughing," he remembered. "It was fun. We were putting the show together stone by stone." Apparently, as Julian Barry had been entranced by Bob in this situation, so were Kander and Ebb.

"Well, what if the guy slaps her here?" Bob might say, or, "What if the guy turns out to be a cop?" and Fred would go home and give it a try, and in that way they collaborated.

When Jules Fisher saw Tony Walton at the first production meeting, he hurried over, and the two friends embraced warmly. They hadn't seen each other since Jules had lighted and Tony designed *Pippin*. Bob snickered about the display of affection. "He would not like it if people hugged him," Fisher said, "but I think he wanted them to."

Fosse made it clear to Walton that he wanted a set so dominating there would be little room for Gwen to dance. "I don't want her to have to dance flat out," he said, and he wanted to leave no space for the audience to expect it, or for anyone else to show her up. As far as he was concerned, "She's still the greatest star on Broadway."

Too, for the first time he didn't want a show to be pretty. "I don't care if it accidentally turns out to be beautiful," Bob said, "but don't go for pretty. I want it to be tough," he said. "Up to then," Walton said, "all of his shows had stylish and attractive moments. Now he wanted strength." The designer came up with one set that he was sure Fosse would love, and he built a model of it. "It was a giant top hat," he said. "The onstage band would be on top of it. The brim curved so irregularly that it would give the audience a different view whenever the hat revolved a quarter turn. The action would be played on that brim," Walton continued, "some of it ramps and other flat areas."

He sneaked the model into Bob's house in Quogue and then went home to nearby Sag Harbor to wait for the delighted reaction. When the telephone call came, Bob said, "It's a very striking set, Tony. I'd love to see a show done on a set like that. But I'd sure hate to have to try and stage it myself." That sent Walton back to his drawing board, and it was getting late, already October, and rehearsals were scheduled to start in a few weeks.

In the editing room, *Lenny* was taking shape. Sometimes Chayefsky would stop by and visit with Heim. "You're the only editor I ever met," he said, "who's funnier than I am."

"That's a dubious compliment," Alan replied, "but I'll take it." He was becoming one of the most highly prized (and paid) film editors in New York, and Chayefsky hired him to cut *Network*, a screenplay he had just finished and which he was going to coproduce.

Bob had little interest in this chitchat. He sat slumped in the deep leather armchair, rubbing his outstretched left arm, flexing the fingers, and opening and clenching his fist. Heim had seen him do that before. He assumed Bob was trying to restore circulation in a hand that had fallen asleep.

"Hey, Bobby," he said cheerfully, "I always wondered why you wore black all the time."

Fosse squinted up. How could anyone not know why he wore black?

"It's a much better line," he said with some fatigue. "You look better when you're wearing black. It thins you out," as if he needed thinning. "It gives you a dramatic silhouette. There's no break in color, and you make a nice straight line on the page."

Heim liked that, "a nice straight line on the page." He was glad that *Lenny* was almost finished because Bob obviously needed a rest. The house in Quogue was supposed to offer respite from New York, but instead Bob was bringing New York to Quogue. He was giving a party for the *Pippin* company. The rest of his world was invited too. Even Paddy came.

Kim St. Leon drove out early, with Bob and Nicole. The two girls romped on the lawn, doing cartwheels. "Bob had business meetings," Kim remembered, "while we were playing like kids." She was more a contemporary of Nicole's than of Bob's. "I didn't get much of a chance to do that kind of thing in New York," she said. "I was a scared little girl."

She liked to drive the big Lincoln, and Bob let her ferry him around although her style at the wheel could be alarming. "I liked to peel off," she said—shoot out from a standstill so that the tires screeched. "You should drive more carefully," Bob said. "You're a regular hot-rodder," and he certainly sounded a few years older than she.

When Kim slowed down at a cross street, Bob asked quietly, "How about us starting up again?" They had just been friends since his jealousy episode.

"I don't think so, Bobby," Kim replied, leaning over to give him a peck on the cheek.

Ann Reinking came to the *Pippin* outing, and so did Jennifer Nairn-Smith, along with the rest of the cast. Because of the show's Tuesday through Saturday schedule, the party couldn't start until Sunday, but then Bob had them stay—the whole day. In the afternoon he arranged sports events and dominated the croquet court with Paddy, who was a brazen cheater at this quintessentially correct game. In the evening there was social dancing around the piano and outside on the pool deck. Bob graciously danced with the wives. "It's amazing," Alison Heim said afterward. "When you dance with him, it's as if you are the only person in the world."

At the height of the night, in the thick of the crowd, Bob and Ben Vereen broke into what Kim called "a showboat dance number." The crowd backed against the living room walls to watch as the two spectacular dancers improvised a soft shoe routine and then worked it into a flamboyant, high-stepping piece.

As John Rubinstein was leaving, Bob took him aside and said, "I've just put together a rough cut of *Lenny*. Would you come and see it and tell me what you think?" A "rough cut" wouldn't have opening titles or a musical soundtrack, and there would be a certain lack of final polish, but it would be the movie. Of course he would come, Rubinstein said; he was flattered to have been asked.

Gwen was already in the screening room when he arrived. David Picker was there too and Sam Cohn. When the lights came up at the end, they all told Bob how wonderful *Lenny* was. Rubinstein said, "I loved it and I thought Hoffman was tremendous," but late that night Bob called to ask what he *really* thought. The actor repeated that he loved it except, he said, perhaps one scene bothered him.

"Oh?"

"It's one of your off-camera interviews," the actor said.

"What's that?"

"Well, your voice can be very seductive, to men as well as to women. You can melt anyone with that soft sweet voice of yours and the focus of your eyes."

"It gets results," Fosse said.

"Sure," Rubinstein said, "but when you're talking to Valerie Perrine, well, you can see in her face that she's dealing with an off-camera Bob Fosse. You're someone who's hotter than hot; you just won every prize on earth, and here she is in your next picture, only she's supposed to be a drug addict, a widow—this was after Bruce died, right?"

"Right?" Fosse warily repeated.

"We don't know who she's talking to, a psychiatrist, a journalist, but the guy asking these questions should not be such a big part of her life. I don't buy it, the way she's looking at the camera answering these questions. Her relationship with you is wrong. You're too important to her."

John Rubinstein was an acutely sensitive man. "She's *auditioning* for you, Bobby," he finally said, "and that's wrong."

Now he worried about the silence at the other end of the telephone call.

"I think you're dead wrong," Bob finally said.

"What do you mean?"

"Valerie did everything I told her to do. Exactly."

"Great," Rubinstein said, "but maybe"—he just couldn't leave it alone—"maybe with a couple of cuts, just of her bursting into smiles and being sort of teasy and flattered by your attention—otherwise her performance is so good. Like Dustin. He's wonderful."

Another mistake.

"Oh, Dustin was a pain in the ass," Fosse snapped. "He fucked me all the time. He didn't like this, and he wouldn't do what I said, and he argued."

"You know, Bob," John said. "I felt kind of that way with *Pippin*. You wanted me to do a very innocent, very vulnerable, very—*you* kind of thing. Which I did. But I fought you on it, because I thought you were robbing me of my credibility with the audience. Part of the reason I think I'm doing a good job now is because I think I've found the sincerity, the real line in *Pippin*, so that he's doing all your stuff, but he's still real, not coy."

He held his breath, playing back what he had just said.

"I think," he resumed recklessly, "Valerie is doing too much of that."

Another pause at four in the morning. Fosse was slowly coming out from the emotional folds and swirls of his Nordic mist.

"So you're telling me," Fosse said, "that you think I ruined your performance, and I've hurt you. You're taking everything I've given you and throwing it back in my face."

"*No*," Rubinstein hurried. "I'm saying that as a director you sometimes lose sight of the person in the character. It won't work except when it's a cartoon character, like Joel Grey's or Ben Vereen's."

He waited for a response. There was only white noise. "The person the audience identifies with," he continued, "is the real person. Dustin made that guy really live. Maybe he had to disagree with you once in a while to do it. Good as Valerie was, she did too much to please you, the way I did, aping you in *Pippin*."

He heard the withdrawal through the telephone. "I love you," he said, trying to bribe Bob back, "for helping me with everything in the show. I love you anyway, Bob, but it's true."

Maybe it was but Bob didn't talk to him, "not for a very long time," Rubinstein said.

□   □

Not uncommonly, movie directors are depressed at the end of the job. They often fall sick. It was difficult to tell whether the gaunt, concave, and violently coughing Fosse could withstand illness, but it was not surprising that in his depressed state he found a book about death as the basis for his next movie. It was a novel called *Ending* by Hilma Wolitzer. Stuart Ostrow had bought the rights, eager to move into film producing. Bob agreed that it would make a good, serious little picture, and he persuaded Stuart to hire Bob Aurthur to write it. Aurthur needed the work.

Jane Aurthur remembered, "It was not happily" that Paramount Pictures bought the project, but Fosse was hot, and Sam Cohn had become what the press called a "superagent." Thus the deal was done, and Aurthur proceeded with the screenplay while Bob headed toward *Chicago*.

Its producer was the veteran Robert Fryer in association with the newcomers James Cresson and Martin Richards. The era of the lone Broadway producer was over. The cost of a show had grown too great for one person to arrange, and so the solitary entrepreneur was vanishing. No longer would lone desperadoes barrel through the countryside, flourishing their theatrical brainstorms like sabers as they headed for the Great White Way, raising money from gullible, stagestruck investors, those "butter and egg men" of yore. Financing would now have to be painstakingly assembled, and money alone could make anyone a producer. There was no need to have survived the spiel and boffola of the carnival midway, and it was sad for the theatre, marking the demise of creative producers and spelling the end of a certain fun and flamboyance. To Fosse this only made it easier to be contemptuous of the producers, because now they had no greasepaint connection whatever.

Economics had also generated a new, businesslike cold-bloodedness. In the past, any mention of a stage person's health would have been superstitiously hushed out of the theatre. Now the producers were taking out a million-dollar insurance policy on Fosse. Notwithstanding his morbidness or living style, he had never been seriously ill. He seldom suffered even traditional winter colds. He was healthy despite the blistering pace of his work and the beating his body was taking from his life. Associate producer Marty Richards had heard of stars being insured but never a director. "This gave me a strange foreboding," he said, and because of such superstition the existence of the policy was kept from Fosse until the last minute—and wisely too in view of the mantle of gloom that he now pulled around his shoulders just for comfort.

As auditions began, John Kander found himself in the same situation that had so aggravated Stephen Schwartz during *Pippin*—confronting Bob's disregard for singing voices. "There were times," Kander recalled, "when he was casting the girls, that he would be if not impatient, well, he'd just make it the least important thing." At script meetings, Fosse's contribution was in terms of production concept. "We still had to figure out," Kander said, "which scenes we would use and how the style would emerge." Fosse took the creative lead in that respect which, of course, was authorship as much as the writing of dialogue.

"What scene are you working on?" he asked Ebb at one of these meetings.

"The trial."

"Well, why don't you do—remember those old things in burlesque? With the judge and the girl, and they hit the guy with the bladder every time he says something?"

"Yeah?"

"Do it in that style."

It was Harpo Marx and Fosse's squank horn and Minsky's Burlesque in boyhood Chicago, the real Chicago.

"I think I can stage it that way."

That was how the show was finding itself, and as Kander said, "You talk so much that by the end of the talking, you're all doing the same show."

Meantime, Bob and Gwen were beginning to work out the dances at the Broadway Arts rehearsal studios. There were other assistants, Kathy Doby foremost among them, but Gwen was Bob's dancing alter ego, and their relationship was paradoxically becoming more coherent as well as more bewildering. They were finding a way to be mutually respectful, a way to be a couple of professionals who were extremely concerned about each other's work and welfare, a way to be married and not. Some evenings Nicole would even stop by to watch the end of rehearsals, and then the three of them would go out to a Chinese restaurant like a regular family. It was fine as long as Bob could go home to his own place, and as long as Gwen did not take it personally.

The first public screening of *Lenny*, the first view allowed outsiders, was going to be a special showing for an audience of studio executives and employees. It was scheduled at the Sutton Theatre in Manhattan, and Bob called Julian Barry to remind him of it. The call did not come on the writer's best day. His wife had gone away to think things over. "Our marriage was in the toilet," he remembered. She was with friends in Georgia, leaving him alone in the house in Westport, "where I was having a complete breakdown," he said. He had still not seen *Lenny* and at this point did not much care whether he ever would.

"Julian? It's Bob."

"Yeah? Hi."

"I know you probably feel bad—"

No kidding.

"—because you haven't heard from me and I haven't let you see anything, but now I have a cut of the movie that I really like. I've deliberately kept you away from it, because I wanted to get a completely objective opinion from you about it."

Baloney, but it didn't matter to Julian.

"Please," Fosse said, "come to a screening at the Sutton Theatre."

Barry said he would, and when the day arrived, he was looking forward to it; the distraction might even cheer him. *Lenny* was a major movie by a major director with a major star, and he had the screenwriting credit. He showered, shaved, and dressed. He was fine right up until he went outside to check the mailbox and found a letter that his wife had written from Georgia. She had fallen in love, she wrote. She was not coming back at all, and he fell to his knees in the cool autumn morning grass beside the mailbox. He stretched out on the ground and wept.

That morning he drove to New York in a daze, unaware of the road, his speed, the time, or even the reason that he was driving. He had one concrete thought for most of this drive, and that was of the need to buy a pair of sunglasses as soon as he parked the car.

"Well? What did you think?"

It was Fosse standing in the aisle and looking down at the writer of *Lenny*, who was sitting in the Sutton movie theatre wearing a pair of sunglasses. The lights were up, and the audience was filing out. Julian did not remember a single frame of the picture. He had been sobbing from first to last. He looked up.

"Hi, Bob."

"Well?"

"Well, what?"

"How did you like it?"

"I don't know," Julian said.

"What don't you know?"

"Bob, I don't remember it. I don't remember the movie."

"What do you mean, you 'don't remember it'?"

"I know, I just saw it, but I don't remember it."

"Why not?" Fosse asked in exasperation. "Don't you have an opinion?"

"No," Julian said.

"Why not?"

The writer reached into his jacket pocket and pulled out the envelope with the letter. "My wife just left me," he said, as a wail started up from his throat. "She just wrote telling me about this other guy—" The rising sob choked off his speech.

Fosse slapped the letter out of his hand, and Barry watched it flutter toward the carpeted aisle of the theatre.

"I don't give a shit about your wife!" Bob cried. "I want to know what you think of our movie! The hell with your fucking wife!"

He stormed up the aisle, and later Barry wryly decided, "That actually straightened me out for a few days."

But to Sam Cohn, Fosse "looked like a man who was very ill."

Lenny was all but finished. Minor sound editing remained and last-minute tinkering, but Bob was free to concentrate on *Chicago*, and the dancing had already begun, as usual a week before general rehearsals. First thing, he met with Peter Howard at Broadway Arts. The dance pianist would improvise the music as the dances were created, drawing the melodies from John Kander's score. Bob explained the concept of the show—"a musical vaudeville"—and described the set, which was a large cylinder that contained an elevator through which the characters in the story would often make entrances and exits. The orchestra was going to have the tinny sound of a jazz-age Chicago band, and it was going to play on a platform atop the cylinder.

Peter played the Kander and Ebb songs through, first in one dance style and then another, altering his arrangements until Bob found something that appealed, or made a suggestion ("Let's turn this one into a ragtime," "Do that like 'Me and My Shadow.'")

Graciela Daniele was one of the dancers whom Bob had personally invited to join the show. Hardly a Broadway gypsy, she was a classically trained dancer who had already worked as an assistant to the choreographer Michael Bennett, and Bob had been particularly courtly with her ("Would you mind coming to an invited audition?" he had said on the telephone). At thirty-four she was not young but considering the ages of Gwen Verdon (nearing fifty) and Chita Rivera (forty-one) in the leading roles, she was an appropriate age to play one of the other murderesses in the show. There was to be no chorus or ensemble. All the dancers had speaking parts. Graciela was not an actress, but Bob assured her that she had to speak only one line and that was "Not guilty."

At least it was her only line in English. She would be playing a Hungarian murderess and was going to be phonetically coached by Kathy Doby (who *was* Hungarian) in the rest of her dialogue. She was happy about more dialogue. Dancers love to act the way actors love to dance. It was also a treat to work with Bob Fosse, Gwen Verdon, and Chita Rivera, and so Graciela was uncommonly excited the day she arrived at Broadway Arts for the start of rehearsals. "Gwen was already there and Chita and all those wonderful dancers. It was like being in the company of the crème de la crème."

Bob greeted them all by name and said, "There's a box of props over there. Take anything you want." It was his legendary Magic Trunk, filled with canes and hats and feather boas, and Graciela Daniele thought, "How amusing, it's like children dressing up for a party." She took a hat with a feather on it and grabbed a garter, slipping it over her leotard thigh.

"Okay," Bob said, "now spread out wherever you like."

Graciela went where downstage right (or the audience's left) would have been "because that's where I like to be."

"Now," he said, "we're going to be working with old dances, like the shimmy and the black bottom and the Charleston." It had been a while since he had done pure choreography. No longer working it out in advance, he seemed to be enjoying this improvisation with the dancers.

Kathy Doby demonstrated the various popular dances, and when she was finished he said, "Pick one of them, whichever you like, and make your entrance doing it."

"Are you all right?" Kathy asked Bob as they walked off to the side.

"Fine—why?"

She nodded toward his arm. He was rubbing his left forearm.

"Oh, just circulation or something. Okay, ladies," he said, "I don't want to see anyone doing the same dance," and so it began.

The final sound mixing for *Lenny* was being done in a studio on West 54th Street, and Bob didn't arrive until early evening, straight from Broadway Arts. He made his usual coughing entrance and dropped into the big old armchair. Alan Heim ran only the last few reels of the movie, which was all that they had been polishing. Bob wasn't saying much. He watched the screen from the distance. "The picture was basically finished," Heim remembered. After a few minutes Bob started to push himself out of the chair. He meant to walk the several blocks to Roosevelt Hospital to visit Ann Reinking, who had hurt her back when a dancer dropped her on stage in *Over Here*, but instead of getting up and out of the chair, he just sat there.

Heim walked the few steps over. "Bob looked old," the editor recalled, "very old and very fragile." He extended a hand, and Fosse grasped it, pulling himself out of the deep chair. Heim took him by the elbow and guided him to the elevator, went down with him to the street, and hailed a cab. Bob was thin against the cool evening, and as he glanced toward Alan from a corner of the taxi seat, he hugged himself. The editor shut the door, went home to his wife, and said to her, "Bob is looking pretty terrible."

Monday morning, the cast of *Chicago* met for the first day of script rehearsal. It was a conscious day of birth, a time of optimism and hope for everyone but Fosse. "I have to kick myself into rehearsal," he told Cohn. "The thought of doing one more time step, one more irrelevant musical is unbearable." But besides getting Gwen one more musical to star in, he had also got her an investor's share in the show, and that was a double payment on his guilt premium.

They sat with scripts on their laps, Gwen and Chita Rivera and Jerry Orbach and Barney Martin, who was playing Gwen's betrayed husband. Bob and Fred Ebb and John Kander also had scripts and so did the design team, Tony Walton, Jules Fisher, and Patricia Zipprodt, and the producers, Fryer, Cresson, and Richards. Bob's production stage manager, Philburn Friedman, was ready to begin marking up the most important script of all, the one that would ultimately become the "prompt book"— the script to run the show by, with notes for all the lighting and scenery and sound cues, the script which would list every prop, every safety pin, and rubber band that was needed on- or backstage. The prompt book would sit on the stage manager's desk in the wings, the lectern from which every performance would be conducted.

Phil Friedman was also in charge of rehearsal, organizing work schedules, attending to details and logistics. For something so seemingly haphazard as a stage show, the daily running of operations is really quite organized, or at least it can be when an efficient production stage manager provides the eye in the center of the artistic hurricane. Friedman was considered an ideal production stage manager. He had been with Bob for fifteen years and with Cy Feuer before that. A mild, reasonable man, he had the perfect personality for the job, being almost compulsively organized and without artistic ego. Better still, Philburn Friedman idolized Bob Fosse with a devotion that approached the maternal.

After the first day's read-through, Bob asked Phil to schedule the singers and dancers on the next morning, with the actors coming in after lunch. When he arrived, however, he told Friedman that he felt ill. "I feel like a truck is on my chest," he said. "Call Dr. Leder and make an appointment for me. Maybe I can see him during the lunch break."

Friedman made the appointment with Harold Leder, Bob's personal physician, for two o'clock. Meantime the singers and dancers were beginning to straggle in with their dance bags, theatrical and sexy in rehearsal tights. Halfway through the morning's work, Bob was seated on a wooden folding chair, watching the girls dance and fiddling with a stick doll from Tony Walton's model of the set. The number ended, and one of the dancers stopped to tell him that she had never before been involved with such exciting choreography. Bob smiled. "It isn't easy for a guy from burlesque," he said. He had dropped the doll and looked down for it. The head had broken off.

He rose and walked over to Joseph Harris, the show's general manager. They had known each other since *Call Me Mister.* "Joey," he whispered. "I don't think I'm going to be able to continue this morning."

"What's wrong?"

"I don't know," Fosse said, putting a hand to his chest. "I just feel terrible." He turned to Phil Friedman. "If I'm late coming back," he said, "when Gwen and Chita get here, have Stanley work on 'Jazz' with them." The "Stanley" was Stanley Lebowsky, the show's conductor and musical director, and "Jazz" was the opening number, "All That Jazz."

Leaving his assistants with the dancers, Bob asked Harris to come with him. Producer Bob Fryer tagged along. The three of them took a taxi to New York Hospital. The last time Bob had checked into the Payne Whitney clinic, but on this occasion Harris asked the cabdriver to take them to the Emergency Room on East 70th Street. Bob did not ask why they were going there instead of to Dr. Leder's office. In fact the doctor had suggested it after Phil Friedman had described Bob's chest pains.

The taxi pulled up in front of the row of doors under the big red Emergency Room sign, and Bob stepped through the chilly air into the institutional heat of the bare and efficient hospital. Leder was waiting and led the way to an eight-by-ten-foot examining room. The speed wasn't privileged. Nobody with chest pains is kept waiting in an Emergency Room.

The doctor asked Bob to take off his shirt and sit up on the metal examining table and its paper sheet. He was pale and thin, but with the muscle tone of a lifelong athlete. While Leder was listening to his heart and lungs through the stethoscope, Bob described the crunching pain he had felt before and was feeling now. Leder asked a nurse to page Dr. Ettinger.

Edwin Ettinger was an internist/cardiologist on the hospital staff, and Leder had already made certain that he would be there. When Ettinger took the call, Leder picked up the telephone and said, "Bob Fosse is in the Emergency Room, and I would like you to come down and take a look at him." It sounded as if Ettinger was supposed to know who Bob Fosse was, but the cardiologist had never heard of him.

Bob glanced toward Joey Harris and said, with quiet seriousness, "The show is over." Then he gestured vigorously in the direction of his attaché case—the drugstore he had brought along. "Throw it away," he whispered. At the first opportunity, Harris snatched the case. Later he would spirit it out of there.

When Dr. Ettinger stepped into the examination room, he nodded at both Harris and Fryer and suggested they step outside while he looked at the patient. He asked Bob how he felt, and the crushing chest pain was described yet again, a description that the cardiologist had heard only too often (although another frequent description was more psychological, "a feeling of impending doom." Fosse said nothing about that).

"You ought to come into the hospital," Ettinger suggested almost casually as Dr. Leder watched him moving the stethoscope's chest piece across Bob's narrow breast. It was hardly a command.

"It's not a great time, Doctor," Bob said. Ettinger was preparing to give him an electrocardiogram (EKG) test, attaching the machine to Fosse's chest with wires leading to small, cold metal electrodes that were pressed to the flesh, sticking there with creamy white salt paste. As he applied the mild electric current and watched the needles jiggling on the moving graph paper, Ettinger said, "It's never a great time, Mr. Fosse, but I'm afraid"—and he glanced toward Dr. Leder—"this man is going to have a heart attack."

19

Phil Friedman was not unduly alarmed when Bob didn't return by the end
of the lunch break. "An hour and a half," he figured, "it's hard to get to a
doctor and back in that time," and so he went ahead with the afternoon's
work. He told the musical director Stanley Lebowsky that Bob wanted
Gwen and Chita to begin learning "All That Jazz" and assigned the three
of them to one of the rehearsal rooms. Lebowsky probably approached the
task with limited enthusiasm, because he didn't think that Bob liked the
song.

Soon, all three studios were thumping and echoing with the sweaty
stomps and full-throated bursts of a show at the start. When the dancers
and actors hurried through the corridors on their way to the coffee maker
or the candy machines or the bathrooms, they would pass Friedman and
ask where Fosse was. "Gwen asked me maybe a dozen times," the stage
manager remembered, and he told her the same thing he told everyone
else: "Bobby had an appointment."

Quite mysteriously, Cy Coleman began calling from Los Angeles,
first asking for Fosse and then insisting on talking to him. Finally,
Coleman demanded that Friedman tell him where Bobby was, as if he
sensed that something was going wrong or had gone wrong already.

At four-thirty, Joey Harris telephoned from New York Hospital.
"We're at the Emergency Room," he told Friedman. "Don't say anything
to the company. Just get Gwen over here."

That was when Phil began to tremble. He opened the door to the
studio where Gwen and Chita were standing at the piano and said, "I'm
sorry, Gwen, could you come out a minute?" Friedman was a gentle man,
which gave his bulk a curious vulnerability, and when she stepped outside, he whispered, "The company isn't supposed to know anything"
before giving her the message. She sat down on a wooden chair and
calmly took off her dance shoes. "She really went through this like an
actress," he remembered. She walked into the ladies room to change into

street clothes, and if he hadn't known what she was doing, he would not have guessed "because she didn't go frantic."

At the hospital, Dr. Ettinger, his six-feet-three-inches exaggerated by a long white laboratory coat, was speaking in his best bedside manner. "A heart attack," he confidently recited to the pale, trembling, sweaty Fosse, "is an acute myocardial infarction. It occurs when the arteries are clogged. Once it begins, there is a progression of damage within the heart. You can watch this progression over a period of days. Your heart," he said, "has probably already suffered a certain amount of muscle loss. You're feeling pain, shortness of breath, and palpitations."

Fosse stared.

"The pain you're suffering, Mr. Fosse, is caused by an acute reduction of blood flow to your heart muscle."

Young as Edward Ettinger was (about thirty-seven), he was probably reassuring in his foursquare knowledgeability. His sobriety may have been un-show business, but nobody wants a glitzy cardiologist. "What I'm suggesting," he said, "is a couple of tests before we decide to do anything."

Bob really had little choice, and still he protested. "Everyone is depending on me," he insisted, and with that he started up from the examining table. Ettinger and Leder glanced in alarm at the electrocardiograph machine as the needle shot upward. Seeing it too, Bob cried, "You guys are giving me a heart attack!"

"He was angry that he was being told he was sick," Ettinger later said. "This is not an uncommon reaction when people are confronted by information they don't want to hear," but Bob's protests meant little, and he probably knew it. He was whisked away to the eleventh floor, the Intensive Care Unit.

The company showed up at Broadway Arts the following morning, but the producers knew that they were going to have to postpone the show whether Bob stayed in the hospital or not. They called everyone together. Phil Friedman had already said that Bob was ill, and now Fryer explained exactly how ill that was. Gwen told the shocked actors, "Don't worry, it's okay, he's going to be fine," and Fryer added, "We'll be in touch. We'll try and get you jobs, and keep you together."

Herb Gardner was backstage at the Broadhurst Theatre where *Thieves* was still struggling for an audience when an assistant stage manager told him that Bob was in the hospital after having had a heart attack. Gardner hurried to a telephone to call Paddy, who hadn't heard about it either.

Kim St. Leon was in acting class. Her teacher, Michael Shurtleff, gave her the news. She screamed and ran out of the room, but she had nowhere to go because the only visitors allowed in the ICU were the immediate family. Not even Vicki Stein, Bob's personal secretary, was permitted to see him. When she brought his robe and toilet articles, she had to leave them at the nurse's station. Vicki was told that he was comfortable, but he wasn't. The first telephone call that he made was to Ann Reinking, who was still at Roosevelt Hospital with her back injury, and he told her that the pain was terrible.

When Gwen arrived, he uncertainly promised "I'll be all right," and after Nicole came, the mother repeated the words to the daughter as if to hear them one more time for herself. "He'll be all right," she told Nicole. "It'll just be a few weeks. The doctors said they'll hold him for some tests, just to put him on the machine and see what happens." An electronic heart monitor was now Bob's full-time partner.

"I'll get through it," he smiled, "and get the show on."

Nicole looked at her dad in bewilderment. Gwen had been vague when the twelve-year-old had asked what was wrong. She imagined it had something to do with epilepsy.

At Broadway Arts, Phil Friedman gloomily packed away his *Chicago* materials. He did not consider it likely that this show was going to be back in rehearsal anytime soon, and it certainly wouldn't take much for Bob to quit on it altogether. Other directors and choreographers were already making discreet inquiries about whether their help was needed. "Anyway, Bob was only doing it for Gwen," the stage manager said along with everyone else. But look what it had done to him in return.

The truth was that this devastating blow to his idol's immortality had shaken Friedman profoundly. He later admitted to considering suicide at this time. If anyone had wholly ingested the glorification of show business stars, it was Philburn Friedman. "Everyone in the business was calling me to find out how Bobby is. It was," he added with some pride, "like he was God."

Chief among the tests that Edwin Ettinger gave Fosse was an angiogram to see how damaged the coronary arteries really were. When he read the results, the cardiologist recommended immediate surgery. Bob asked whether he could have a smoke and think that one over. Ettinger thought it was just a joke. "In hindsight," he said, "I'm not sure Bobby wasn't unfolding a movie at the time. He was fascinated by all the things that were going on."

Of course Fosse shouldn't smoke, Ettinger replied, but at the same time he didn't think that cigarettes had caused the heart attack. He was concerned about the cardiological dangers of smoking, of unchecked cholesterol levels, of high blood pressure, stress, and overweight, but it was his opinion that "no matter how much you smoke or don't smoke, no matter what your cholesterol level or your diet, no matter how much you weigh or your life-style, if your genes call for this to happen, then that's what occurs. It is genetic." And the fact was that the Fosse family was a study in heart disease. Cy and Sadie were dead of it, and all four of the Fosse boys were in its early stages. "Considering your genetic background for cardiovascular accidents," Ettinger told Bob, "you were in line for it" (although not necessarily at the age of forty-seven).

Sitting beside his patient in the private room to which Fosse had been moved, the cardiologist explained the operation he was suggesting. It was relatively new at the time and would later be called bypass surgery. The idea, Ettinger explained, was to "mobilize" a vein or artery from another part of the body and "put it into the heart muscle to bypass around the area of artery narrowing." The graft would be a vein taken from the patient's leg.

"Oh, no!" Bob cried.

Ettinger assumed the protest to be cosmetic, that as a dancer Fosse feared such surgery would leave a scar, but it wasn't that at all since he never danced bare-legged. *His legs were his dancing*, that was his objection. He didn't want them tampered with in any way. When Ettinger consulted with Dr. William Gay, the surgeon who would be performing the operation, an internal mammary artery was proposed as an alternative. It was easier to take a vein from a leg "but this wasn't so unusual," the cardiologist told Fosse. "It's an artery underneath the chest cage, and we'll put it into the heart muscle so that it'll do the bypassing."

Bob's was going to be a single bypass. As Ettinger recalled, "That was the early side of coronary bypass surgery, and we were trying to do less rather than more. Later," the cardiologist said, "the surgeons would try and do more."

On November 14, 1974, the night before the operation, on the eve of Bob's possible death (there was a 2 percent mortality rate during bypass operations) Herb and Paddy were summoned by a Fosse who, as Gwen said, "has always been in the business of dying." He had grown fond of saying, "I've already lived to be older than my parents" but it was not true, Cyril had died at seventy and Sadie at sixty-five. Still, it sounded as if he wanted it to be true, or at least was trying to give that impression. Even now, he was talking to Paddy about dying being "the first honest event in my life." He considered himself almost entirely full of shit, doing routines all the time. As Paddy put it, "Everything he does he thinks it comes out of bullshit. It's a game, a phony, a performance." One thing that wasn't a phony to Fosse was the spectre of aftereffects and, in particular, the loss of sexual potency. That infuriated Chayefsky. "A guy is going up for open-heart surgery," he said. "I don't think the major concern in life is whether you can get a hard-on." Perhaps not to him.

It was not the surgery itself that posed the threat to potency but the aftereffects and medication. Aside from frightening heart rushes and spasms during sex, Enderol, which is commonly prescribed for bypass patients, has been known to cause impotence. Fosse's concerns, then, were by no means unfounded, especially considering the major role that sexuality played in his life.

When Kim St. Leon stopped by the room for a good-luck kiss, Paddy and Herb invited her to dinner and told Bob they would return afterward. The three found a little restaurant near the hospital and "we talked about Bob," Kim remembered. "What was lovely was that it was really just dinner." She expected every man to try and nail her.

Tony Walton and his Genevieve came by to wish Bob luck, and as she leaned over to kiss Bobby, he said to Tony, "Watch my heartbeat on the monitor when I get turned on," but Gen's kiss didn't turn him on. He dozed off. The television set was playing for nobody, and Walton remembered, "Bob looked very vulnerable, weaker than he would allow himself to look." They left a note on his stomach and tiptoed out of the room.

Earlier in the evening, the lawyer Leonard Strauss had stopped by to take changes in Bob's will and then went off to draft them. At midnight, Paddy and Herb were back at bedside to witness the signing, and the attorney was not amused by their frivolousness, nor by Bob's urging them to find him a bottle of wine. He felt that Bob was putting on an act, while actually being scared to death. Fosse dozed off again under the heavy sedation, but when Gardner signed the will, he abruptly awoke with a laugh. Herb and Paddy hurried to join in. "There is now a general low level of giggling," Gardner recalled, and then the surgeon, Dr. William Gay, tall and skinny, loped in to show the patient exactly what the operation was going to entail.

"Oh, God," Bob said to Paddy, "so young," and indeed, Gay was so young that the other doctors called him "Billy."

"He takes out a small pad of Xeroxed heart drawings and a pen," Gardner remembered, "and proceeds to sketch for Bobby the general route his bypass operation will take. Bobby leans forward, attempting straight-faced interest."

At that moment the surgeon dropped his pen on the floor.

"Whoops!" Gay exclaimed. It was not reassuring, a butterfingered heart surgeon.

Bob turned to Paddy and Herb and whispered, "Operation canceled."

They roared. "Paddy is clapping his hands like he always does when he laughs," Gardner remembered. "The three of us are laughing. It's like we left that midnight room and are now at a back table in the Carnegie, laughing at the surgeon, laughing at the will."

The will. Leonard Strauss was still waiting for Chayefsky to sign it as he disapprovingly watched the hijinks. Paddy said that this was a very serious matter, that he could not possibly bear witness to a last will and testament unless he read the document first, and so he sat down with it. Bob had dozed off once more when Chayefsky suddenly blurted, "Hey! I'm not in here!"

A somewhat abashed Fosse said faintly, "Well, you're in good shape, Paddy. You can take care of yourself." He was taking his friend seriously. "I've got Gwen and Nicole to plan for."

"I'm your oldest and best friend," Chayefsky protested, sustaining the routine, "and I'm not in your will?"

"Paddy," Bob pleaded, "there are people who really need taking care of. This has nothing to do with my love for you."

"*You left me out of your will?*" Chayefsky repeated.

"Yes, Paddy," Bob said helplessly. "I did."

"Fuck you!" Chayefsky concluded in disgust. "Live!"

It was as close as he could come to telling Fosse he loved him. "Being amusing is an easy way to visit," he later said to Bob Aurthur. "I couldn't commiserate."

Bobby said good night to Herby and Sidney, and after they left, he telephoned Ann Reinking, hospital to hospital. Joey Harris had been keeping her informed about his condition. Otherwise it was frustrating for her to try and get information from the staff. "Nobody would tell me anything," she complained. "I couldn't make them understand how important this was to me, because I wasn't a relative—I couldn't say I was his mother or father. I could just say I was his girlfriend, and girlfriends aren't important."

Gwen had been filling her in on what was happening, which was extraordinary and generous. "I was grateful, I was frightened, I was real scared," Ann would later recall, "scared that he might have too much pain. I was more interested in the pain than in the outcome."

The first time Bob had called her, "He blamed me for his being in the hospital," she remembered with continuing amazement, but now he sounded drugged. He groaned into the telephone. He had rung for a shot, he told her, but the nurse was down the hall flirting with an orderly and paid no attention to his alarm. "I can't take this pain anymore," he said. "Wish me luck."

"It was very show biz," Ann remembered. "Like an opening night. I felt like breaking out the champagne."

In the early morning of the operation day, a half hour before show time, Bob Aurthur called. The patient sounded spunky. "After the operation," he said, "I won't be able to talk for twenty-four hours. There's going to be one tube up my nose and another up my cock."

Aurthur tried bringing up a more cheerful subject only to realize that their movie project, which was the subject he brought up, was itself morbid. "We sure picked the right subject, didn't we?" Fosse said. "I'm getting a lot of material here."

"Maybe you'd rather do a comedy."

"Don't think I haven't given it a lot of thought."

Then Fosse told his friend about the clause in his will that so pleased him. "Ten thousand dollars," he said, "for a big party to be arranged by Stu Ostrow." Aurthur replied that some years ago he had put a similar provision in his own will.

"Well, guess what?" Fosse said. "You're not the first one either. I thought I was doing something innovative, and then I learned everyone's doing it. Maybe I should cut down the budget anyhow. With Ostrow in charge he can do it for a thousand."

"That's right," Aurthur said. "Stu will give everyone two drinks and then throw them out."

Bob had in fact long since changed the whole concept of his death party. He never could stand being like anyone else and so he added a rider to the will:

> I give and bequest the sum of $25,000 to be distributed to the friends of mine listed . . . so that when my friends receive this bequest they will go out and have dinner on me. They have all at one time or another during my life been very kind to me. I thank them.

He didn't say anything to Bob Aurthur about the revision. Probably didn't want to take a chance on being copied. He only asked a half hour before the heart surgery, "Are you okay? Did you get your contract yet?"

"Don't worry," Aurthur assured him. "Everything's fine."

"I'm going to be out of action for four or five days afterward. They'll have me downstairs in some kind of ward."

"Good luck, Bobby."

"Thanks. I'll be talking to you."

The nurses had arrived.

He had a running bet with Neil Simon on "who is going to be the youngest forever," because they were almost exactly the same age. Phil Friedman was called at ten o'clock that night and was told "they weren't sure if Bobby was going to make it through the night. We all had to pray a lot." If he didn't make it, he would be the youngest forever at a permanent forty-seven which was not the desirable way to win that bet.

They put him on an ice mattress after the operation to reduce his body temperature. It was an unusual procedure but not unheard of in the case of a postoperative fever. He was in convulsion, trembling involuntarily ("shakes and tremors," Gwen said). The tubes made him look incapable of ever making it out of there, and when he was able to call Ann, all he could say was that he was "in a lot of pain and can't talk."

The eighty-three-year-old man in the next bed was also having a difficult time talking. To do it he had to cover his trachea by sticking a finger into a hole in his throat, and on the other side of Bob a nurse was bathing "a twenty-two-year-old baby," as Gwen described it, "and splashing water all over us."

As she stood before the sight of him with the tube in his nose and the wires and the heart monitor with the white dot blipping across the screen, two young women came up to the bed, and one of them said, "Excuse me, Mr. Fosse, but we love your shows, and we were wondering whether we could have your autograph?"

Gwen shouted at them to get the hell out and ran into the hall for help, but by then they were gone. Later, Nicole came, claiming to be less frightened about her father's circumstances than she was by the two exams she was having in school that day. "She kept testing his love," Gwen remembered, "because if he really loved her, he wouldn't die," and when the daughter went home, the mother remained to sleep on a sofa in the lounge at the end of the hall, the lounge with the cathedral windows. "There I was again," she said, "being a wife after five years," and so wishes could come true.

Despite (or as part of) her "assumption of the role of wife," as Bob Aurthur put it, Gwen Verdon was treating Bob's girlfriends with downright warmth, as if they were all members of the same family, with herself the brood hen. She told Bob Aurthur, "I think the real reason I was never jealous of the other women is that I knew his real affair was with death."

She fretted over the hospital forms. "They won't let him out of here if the bill isn't paid," she said nervously, and when Ethel Martin came to visit, Gwen told this old friend from the Jack Cole Dancers, "I think we're going to get back together. Bobby's so happy I'm with him—in his corner."

She brought Kim St. Leon in to see him the day he was moved into a private room on the fifteenth floor. Gwen probably assumed that after the operation visiting restrictions would be relaxed, but nodding toward Kim the floor nurse told her, "Only the immediate family is allowed to see Mr. Fosse, you and your daughter."

"And my other daughter," Gwen smiled, "Nicole," who was standing behind her and chattering with Kim about horses.

As Bob embarked on his recovery, the merriment began. Dr. Ettinger would see his star patient every morning and, he said, "I would get a daily rundown on what was going on in his room. It was a party atmosphere."

Stu Ostrow didn't think that such festivities were appropriate to serious illness or conducive to rest and recovery. He and Bob Fryer would stand in a corner of the room, wedged in by the noisy crowd, and they would shake their heads in disapproval. It certainly looked like a party, filling up with balloons, and Fryer said, "These people were laughing and joking."

"God," Fosse said, "what I wouldn't do for a cigarette," and everyone laughed some more.

"The monitor," Fryer remembered, "kept going up and up, and it shouldn't have gone up, and I was scared to death. I really thought he was going to die."

Sam Cohn and Joey Harris were frequent visitors, of course, and Bob and Jane Aurthur. Tony Walton brought a cassette machine with half a dozen tapes. "He wasn't really responsive to the things I had presumed he would like—Mozart and Brahms. Instead, he said, 'Bring me anything of Mahler's.'" The designer went out and bought several typically sardonic and mordant symphonies by the twentieth century Viennese composer, one of the great musical pessimists. "I can't tell you," Fosse telephoned to say, "what it's meant to me, listening to that music."

Jules Fisher and Graciela Daniele came to visit (Chicago had already made them a couple), and Graciela saw Bob as "a little imp sitting cross-legged on the bed in his chemise." Kathy Doby was there, and Chita Rivera came with Fred Ebb and John Kander. She wouldn't even say "damn" on stage, but off she could be rather colorful. Herb and Paddy practically moved in, and Phil Friedman sneaked over a turkey sandwich from the Carnegie Delicatessen and stashed it under the pillow, and after they were all gone, after midnight, Bob called Ann to dwell on his sexual dreads.

Released from Roosevelt Hospital, she came straight to visit him, and Gwen was there when she arrived. If Reinking was nervous about seeing the wife, Verdon put her at ease. "She knows how things should be," Ann would remember, "and she does the right thing."

That was going to be put to an extraordinary test as Kim arrived. Now there were two girlfriends for the wife to cope with, but it wasn't Gwen who couldn't cope. Her natural dignity and her formidable powers of self-control were equal to this test, and besides, she was still the wife and in the position of power. When Kim stepped into the room, it was Ann Reinking who shouted, "Get out of here!"

The girl was understandably startled. "I just want to know he's okay," she pleaded.

"You don't belong in here!" Ann cried. Gwen tried to calm her. "Kim should stay," she said in her soft and husky voice. "She cares for Bob, and he cares for her."

While Bob slept, Gwen sent the quarrel into the corridor where it belonged and there it raged. "It was a mess," she later said, and it was also a mismatch. Kim St. Leon was young, provincial, and inexperienced, while Ann Reinking was a successful, smart, worldly, poised, confident, and relatively older woman. "Kim was crumbling," Gwen later recalled. "I felt like a lady gangster. It was like *Bonnie and Clyde*, laying down the law to those girls."

When they were pacified enough to return to the room, their edge and spark remained hot. Beneath the calm the dogs snapped and glared. "*Those* men," Ann snarled, correcting Kim's English. "It's 'those men,' not 'them guys,' " but Gwen managed to keep the peace.

Ann Reinking's relationship with Gwen Verdon was of a wary calm. "I was afraid there might be some competition," she said reasonably enough, but instead she found a reserved graciousness. "It was careful," she said, "friendly-careful." Kim's observation was more deferential. "Gwen transcended lover," she said. "Gwen was always the one for Bob, she was his alter ego. He just happened to have this need for physicality with other women that would make any marriage break."

At the moment his need for physicality was cloaked in a fear that no reassurance seemed to allay. Reinking remembered, "He didn't look himself, he didn't act like himself. He was considering having to live differently. It was like his spirit was gone."

She was in the hospital room the evening that Stanley Donen and his then wife, the actress Yvette Mimieux, came to visit. Bob Aurthur was there too and *Chicago* coproducer Marty Richards and Pat Zipprodt, who had brought a present of cut-out paper dolls, sexy paper nurses. Bob sat propped up in bed, wearing his pale blue hospital gown.

"There's going to be a review of *The Little Prince* on the six o'clock news," he said to Stanley. "Do you want to watch it?"

The movie had just opened at Radio City Music Hall.

"No," Donen said in his California suntan and Southern drawl. "We'll see it another time," but Bob insisted and then the news program came on, and in due course the critic appeared. "She chewed the picture up," Donen remembered, "and me. She didn't say anything about Bob, but she gave me the worst review I've ever gotten in my whole life."

Although *Lenny* had opened in New York the previous week to reviews that were decidedly qualified, Bob had not reacted to them as intensely as he did to this rejection of his friend's work. The television critic, Donen remembered, "just went on about what a terrible picture it was and what lousy work I had done, and Bob was watching and listening with me standing there with these other people in the room, and then it happened."

He had another heart attack. He reached for the emergency button, and in moments the room filled up as nurses, residents, floor attendants, and finally a doctor rushed in, to slide Bob onto a rolling stretcher and wheel him out and down the long corridor, back into Intensive Care.

"It was not uncommon," the unflappable Dr. Ettinger said, a heart attack following bypass surgery. "Whether it involved the bypass, we don't know. Whether it involved a different [blood] vessel, we don't know. Nothing necessarily went wrong," he said, but it certainly seemed that way.

The second attack threw a greater scare into Fosse than the first. The second was the one he really thought would do him in, and it was then, he said, that he discovered, "I wanted to live. I don't know what reasons I gave myself. Nicole, mostly. I guess you always find reasons. Even if it's just that you have to take two seconds out of a movie."

Yet after the second heart attack, Bob resumed the hospital partying with even greater abandon. His only concession to conventional values was not playing the Truth Game. "What would you say if it was the last day of your life?" It wasn't a question to be asked at this particular time.

But, Dr. Ettinger remembered, "he didn't change his style at all. It drove me crazy, and still, I don't think any of that hurt him. He continued to smoke, he was doing what he was doing in his room, and I didn't even pretend to know," but the doctor could have guessed because the reports were coming back to him daily. Performers would even audition in the room, and one morning Bob actually climbed out of bed to follow Kim down the corridor and grope her in an alcove.

"Get out of here!" she giggled. "Get back into bed."

But he just smiled and followed her all the way to the elevator in his bathrobe and slippers.

Was it dangerous? Were Herb and Paddy bringing a misguided cheer from its more appropriate home in the Carnegie Delicatessen? Dr. Ettinger thought not. "Nothing was going wrong in there," he said, "and when nothing goes wrong in the hospital, it's a good day."

The staff on the floor was not quite so broad-minded. Fearing blame for permitting rowdyism and peril, they made such entries on Bob's chart as "difficult and demanding" and "argumentative, disruptive, and combative." There was no substance to these notations, Ettinger said. "They needed a means of protecting themselves."

When the crowd was gone and when it was quiet and very late at night and only Ann was left, Bob spoke intimately of his demon, "the fear," she remembered, "of whether he was going to be the same person, especially sexually."

She went to his bed. There was only one way to reassure him, and so they made love. "It was very moving," she later said. "I'd never seen him break up and cry before."

Dr. Ettinger had no reason to check Bob's admitting papers, and so when Gwen referred to him as "my husband," the cardiologist did a double take. "Gwen may have arrived at the Emergency Room with him," Ettinger said, "but I thought he was married to Ann Reinking," who was in the room so frequently and for such long and late hours, taking so proprietary an attitude, that he assumed she was in fact the wife. Medical school and a conservative approach to life had not prepared him for such postoperative complications. "I had never met a show business personality close up," he said, "and I was absolutely *amazed* at what was going on." It later seemed to him that Bob had gotten a tremendous kick out of just that.

The doctor sometimes suspected Bob of tweaking his shockability. That wasn't hard to do. Ettinger once strolled in for a morning visit and found a girl in bed with the coronary patient.

"Having this person, Bobby Fosse, talk to me and watch my expression was something I had never experienced before," said the startled physician. Even stranger to him was not which one was the wife, but Gwen and Ann's compatibility. "The hospital staff didn't know who to relate to," he said. "They didn't know who was the person to be given important information. I would make my rounds and see Gwen and Ann—as if they were *sisters*. It was unbelievable. *Unbelievable*. And then

Nicole, she was like a daughter to *both* of them. I couldn't *believe* what was going on."

Gwen even invited Ann to the family Thanksgiving dinner in the hospital room. Nicole was all dolled up, a twelve-year-old wearing eye liner, false eyelashes, mascara, and green eye shadow. She wore Gwen's jazz pants and took off her sneakers to put on her mom's shoes, which she secured to her little feet with rubber bands. She even wore a hat.

Children are fast to spot the reception accorded their parents by the world at large, quick to react with pride, insult, or embarrassment. Gwen and Bob were being given the full celebrity treatment, and Nicole would saunter down the long hospital corridor, greeting the nurses by their first names. "You know, Daddy," she said, upon making her grand entrance into the room that Thanksgiving, "you can get anything you want in this hospital if you're a celebrity."

Somebody had given Bob a joke glove from a novelty shop, and he grabbed at the nurses like a baggy pants clown while, over the laughter, Gwen set out the tablecloth on the bed, the silver, and the dishes. She poured "wine"—crushed fruit punch with Seven-Up—from a carafe and set out a complete (organic) Thanksgiving dinner. The only wrinkle in her plan was the chief nurse's refusal to admit the violinist she'd engaged.

Preparing for Bob's release from the hospital, Dr. Ettinger talked to him about the future. He described the gradual strengthening, the need for regular medication, the importance of changing his habits. Most beneficiaries of heart bypass operations take this advice. They concentrate on healthy living after "the discipline of the surgery," as it was termed by Dr. John Hutchinson, the chief of cardiac surgery at St. Luke's–Roosevelt Hospital and the surgeon who would perform the bypass operation in Fosse's autobiographical movie, *All That Jazz*.

Some patients, however, look upon the relief from pain and the rescue from a threat of death as a gift of extra life, something to be celebrated and exploited. In resuming excessive habits, they are sometimes accused of being suicidal, but that is not necessarily the case. In fact an argument could be made for their loving life too much to give it up for mere existence.

A patient once came to Dr. Hutchinson with so much damaged heart muscle that he was turned down for a bypass operation. The pain was so great, however, that he pleaded to take the risk. If he lived, he said, he would be happy, and if he didn't survive the operation, then he was willing to go to the grave immediately.

When Hutchinson came to the man's hospital room after the successful operation, he found cartons of cigarettes lined up on a table, along with several bottles of whiskey.

"My God!" the surgeon said. "What's going on here?"

"Well, I told all my friends," the patient said, "if I survive, this is what I want. This is my life. This is what I enjoy."

The man lived for seven more years, Hutchinson remembered, and when he died, his wife wrote to express her appreciation for what the surgeon had done. "She said that I had given her husband a great seven years and that he lived them fully. And he'd never suffered another pain.

" 'It was true,' she wrote, 'that he died because he would not change; however, his attitude was that these were his bonus years."

Everyone who loved Bob Fosse was pleading with him to take the heart attack as a warning about his reckless, self-destructive habits, which, if continued, might be tantamount to suicide. He asked his daughter what she would wish for him—other than giving up smoking. She couldn't think of anything else. "You're physically and psychologically dependent," the precocious twelve-year-old said.

"I don't give a shit," the shaky forty-seven-year-old replied.

"That's dumb," said his darling daughter.

Dr. Ettinger concluded, "He took the heart attack not as a warning but as a challenge. He wasn't able to do anything to change who he was, or didn't want to."

20

Herb Schlein was standing in the hall carrying a large cardboard box when Fosse answered the doorbell. He looked "gaunt and frail," Schlein thought, in a thin cotton bathrobe, and shuffled through the apartment in his scuff slippers as Schlein followed behind.

Jewish delicatessen food was "too spicy for a man in Bob's condition," Herb had decided, and so he'd cooked a chicken and a roast beef "so he could put them in the refrigerator and have food for a couple of days, and I made him peach pie, apple pie, and blueberry pie. He loved my pies. I put in almost no salt. He wasn't supposed to have salt."

Schlein limped into the living room, his gout having worsened with his obesity. "You've got to exercise, you must learn to discipline yourself," Fosse said, which only made Schlein laugh. ("All that drinking and smoking and now the heart attack, and he's telling *me* about self-discipline.")

"So how's it going at the Carnegie?"

"How's it going? It's miserable, that's how it's going," Schlein replied. "They treat me terribly, they pay me nothing. I have to stand on my feet all day, and it's killing me with my foot."

"Why don't you look for something else to do?" Fosse asked.

"*What do?* What else could I do?"

"You could tap-dance," Bob said.

"What are you talking about, tap-dance? I can hardly walk. Only God could make a tap-dancer out of me."

"Well?" Bob asked brightly, his elbows tucked in and his hands outspread. "Here I am."

It was there in the apartment that he celebrated his second round of Academy Award nominations with his secretary, Vicki Stein. He was a candidate for Best Director, Dustin Hoffman for Best Actor, Julian Barry for Best (Adaptation) Screenplay, Bruce Surtees for cinematography, and *Lenny* was itself nominated for the Best Picture of 1974. Two sets of

Academy Award nominations for three pictures, not bad for the brief film career of Bob Fosse.

When the *Chicago* team had been told that the show was postponed, Gwen promptly invited everyone to a cast party. In the middle of that group of actors and writers huddled and stunned at the Broadway Arts rehearsal studios, Fred Ebb raged, "Fosse didn't take care of himself, and now he's done it," but he too offered to host a party to sustain company morale and maintain the sense of an ongoing project. Associate producer Marty Richards reminded the actors that he was still in the casting business and would be in touch with them about work in commercials and bit parts in movies. Few took consolation in that. Pep talks count for little among Broadway actors, who spend most of their lives occupationally frustrated, training for work they never get. As Graciela Daniele put it, "We moved out like zombies."

At Christmas, Gwen gave a second party, and that time she had something to celebrate—Bob's release from the hospital. The whole *Chicago* company showed up at the penthouse apartment where she and Bob had spent most of their married life. As Marty Richards arrived, Chita Rivera was leaving. "You're not going anywhere," he said. He was still new to producing and unsure of his own importance. He was also feeling guilty about the insurance policy on Bob's health, guilty, too, about the discussions he'd had with other directors to take the show over. Jerome Robbins and Harold Prince had been approached with a discretion befitting high-level diplomacy. (Robbins had told them, "If Bob Fosse wants me to direct *Chicago*, I'll do it, but *he* has to ask me.")

"You're walking me into this party," Richards commanded Chita, and he took her by the arm and turned her around. It was noisy inside, and Gwen stepped out from the crowd to kiss him on the cheek.

"How's Bobby?" he asked.

"I'll bring him to you," she replied, her famous husky voice cheerful for the first time in a long time, and she walked off to return with her pale and subdued husband.

"Merry Christmas, Marty," Bob whispered, shaking hands weakly and smiling. "Thanks for helping the kids."

Richards' casting agency had come through for at least some of the actors. The rest were holding their own, or trying to, hoping for an early resumption of rehearsals. At the moment, however, "Bob was working very hard on taking care of himself," Ann Reinking remembered. Why, he had even quit smoking.

But he had not gone so far as to move back with Gwen in their big Central Park West apartment, once the home of William Randolph

Hearst. If she had thought that after the surgery he would need her again, she was mistaken and now knew so. He was back on West 58th Street, he was not coming home, he was not coming back, he was not going to need her.

Chita Rivera was one cast member who had not been able to sit out the postponement. Having brought her daughter east from Los Angeles, she had enrolled the girl in a private school and now needed the money to pay for it. She asked dancer-choreographer Tony Stevens to help her put together a nightclub act. He did it in the mornings and late at night, while performing in the workshop production of a new Michael Bennett show, *A Chorus Line*. A "workshop" was a new way of making a musical, developing it with a company of performers while having the luxury of months to create, rather than the eight weeks of rehearsal allowed a conventional Broadway musical. It was an expensive development, paying performers and using rehearsal space for such a long period. Neither Bob Fosse nor any other director had ever enjoyed so lengthy a working period.

Bennett's *Chorus Line* workshop was being financed by the Public Theater of Joseph Papp, Bob's old Navy chief. When Papp had telephoned to ask for permission to use some old Fosse choreography for a mobile production to be performed in New York's ghettos, Bob granted it without even getting on the telephone to say hello. Had he relaxed and simply been cordial, he might have been able to have a three-month workshop too.

Tony Stevens was a handsome, muscular, high-spirited young man with long, curly black hair and the gossipy humor of a stage gypsy. He had theatrical style—thick sweaters, tight pants, boots, a stage look—and he had the respect of most dancers. He put Chita Rivera's act together in two weeks, danced behind her with Christopher Chadman, and early in January they opened at a small West Side cabaret called the Grand Finale. Bob, Gwen, and Nicole came to see her of course, and afterward Fosse went backstage to congratulate her. "He looked real small," Stevens remembered, "but still impish, and the eyes were going with his head tilted down. It was as if he was looking at you through a director's lens."

Peering upward, Bob asked Tony to work on *Chicago* as an assistant choreographer, because he needed somebody who understood Chita's dance style, and Stevens quit *A Chorus Line* to do it.

Rivera performed her act for two months, taking it to a Los Angeles club (her friend Liza Minnelli staked her to the trip), and by the time she came back to New York for a return engagement, Bob was putting

Chicago into rehearsal. It was exactly three months since he had lain shivering on an ice mattress, a tube running out of his nose. He was now smoking cigarillos.

When he strolled into the rehearsal studio to resume work, the *Chicago* cast and the production team burst into applause, stomping and cheering and whistling. It was Bob's first appearance at Broadway Arts since the truck had rumbled across his chest. "We had to change his work habits," Phil Friedman said. "He couldn't have all those lunch break meetings—sound, costume design, and all that. He had to nap instead, and we stopped night rehearsals." He didn't have trouble napping at those lunch breaks. He usually had to be roused from them. But the show was back in business, and the dances began to re-form. Bob continued to demonstrate steps, but he wouldn't do any of the big lifts. He asked Stevens to "help me with Chita's chair number." Rivera was a "big, energetic dancer," as Stevens described her, "and she needed big moves." Fosse's dancing tended to be small and tight like him, and she had whispered to Stevens, "Get me off the chair, *get me off the chair.*" Once Tony took the dance over, he had her moving off the chair and all over the stage—or as much of it as the set was going to allow.

> "What's A Chorus Line *like?*" Bob asked Tony. "Is it better than this?"
> "It's totally different," Stevens answered. "You can't even compare them."

Working with the girl dancers and his assistant, Kathy Doby, Bob began by teaching three movement combinations, each continuing for four measures of music. The dancers learned all three combinations, and then they were spread across the rehearsal floor.

"You and you," Bob said, "you start combination A. And the two of you, you do combination B. The rest of you do C."

Then, with all three combinations going at the same time, he said, "Okay, now you doing combination A start it on the third measure, and you start combination B on the first measure, and you start combination C on the second measure." And, as Kathy Doby put it, "the overlap made it look like a moving organism." So the *Chicago* dance movement began.

Bob was working alone with Gwen, and "there were times," Stevens remembered, "when I was surprised that she would do some of the things he wanted her to do because they were so unattractive and nasty." As always, Gwen and Bob were being watched not only as stars but as players in a backstage drama. "They were like old friends," composer John

Kander remembered, "until something got tense and then she would say something bitter to him."

Fred Ebb said, "As an artist and performer, Bob was Gwen's number one fan," and Tony Stevens thought "their love affair was their talent— you make me, and I'll make you, but," he agreed with Kander, "there would be personal things that were going on underneath like a little machete, cutting each other down. All that hurt and pain was there."

A week after dance rehearsal, work began with the full company, and Kander found the atmosphere "quite different" from the way it had been three months earlier. It was as if the innocent Bob Fosse had died during that postoperative heart attack. The psychological changes that had been predicted as a result of the operation were beginning to be reflected in the show, a cruelty and morbidness of spirit. "The show got much darker," it seemed to Kander. "Even though it had been acerbic, there was originally a certain joyous quality. After the heart bypass, he was going for something else than what we had started to do."

Jerry Orbach noticed much the same thing. "There was no room in Bobby's concept of the show for real sentiment. He wanted something with an undertone of corruption." In a way, Orbach stood apart from the show. He was not a member of Bob's gypsy entourage like Chita or the dancers or the assistant choreographers. He was not quasi-family like Bob Fryer, Joey Harris, Jules Fisher, or Tony Walton. But Orbach did have one quality in common with Bob Fosse, and it was not so common in the musical theatre. He was a heterosexual male. When Bob asked him, "Which of the girls have you lined up?" the actor replied, "I'm not interested." His marriage was in trouble, and he was not in the mood.

"Oh, yeah?" Fosse grinned, and nodding toward one of the dancers, he said, "I know which one you're after."

"He couldn't believe me," Orbach said, "but I'd already got into enough trouble with that kind of thing. A lot of dancers," he added, "because they were dancers, went overboard to be masculine. They fuck everybody in sight, and they have to talk about all the girls they've nailed, whether it's Baryshnikov, Gower Champion, or Bobby."

Orbach himself hardly seemed even to be in show business. A Depression-era childhood had made him a lifelong realist. He vividly remembered walking along the railroad tracks near his home in Wilkes-Barre, Pennsylvania, "picking up coal that had dropped off the cars and throwing it into a bag. When we got a bagful, we'd go someplace and get a nickel for it."

It was this quality of dirt real that audiences found appealing in him. He had been starring on Broadway for twenty years, but he did not seem like an actor; he treated acting as a job and went home to a private life. He didn't go partying. He preferred sports and poker. When Fosse cast him in *Chicago* as the lawyer Billy Flynn, Orbach's friend Harold Prince said, "I'm going to tell you something that's going to happen. I'm going to make a prediction, Jerry. There is going to come a point in this production— during rehearsals or out of town but sometime—when you are going to be looked at as 'the grown-up.' "

"Me?" Orbach asked incredulously.

"Yes," said Prince, "because you're in there with Bob Fosse and Gwen Verdon and Chita Rivera—you're in with some Peter Pans, and there's going to be a day when all hell breaks loose, and you're going to have to take charge."

"That's crazy," the actor said.

"Remember that I told you," Prince said with a knowing smile.

Fred Ebb had stopped smiling the morning he walked into rehearsal to find the actors working on a scene they had written themselves. "I didn't write a word of it," the coauthor said.

"Hey!" he obliged cheerfully. "What if I write a new speech here?"

"Shut up!" Bob snapped, yet only a moment later he turned to Ebb and "did all this big brother stuff, protector stuff. Everything was going to be okay as long as Bobby was around. He would take care of me and wouldn't let anyone hurt me, insult me.

"He'd insult me himself," Ebb said, "but he wouldn't let anyone else."

Fosse's meanness wasn't limited to the vulnerable. "I'd like Cy Coleman to hear this score," he baited John Kander one morning, with bitchy awareness of how competitive composers were. Another time he suggested, "You only wrote that because you thought you could get an Ella Fitzgerald record." It didn't matter that the time had long passed since show tunes were recorded by popular artists. Ebb took to calling him the Prince of Darkness, and Tony Stevens picked it up.

Paddy Chayefsky was at rehearsal regularly and watched this behavior with disapproval. "Bob's a bully," he told Fred over lunch at the Carnegie, but he also sensed Ebb's willingness to be bullied. "Don't let him push you around. The only problems you'll have with him is when you think he's that much more talented than you that you just can't open your mouth. So open your fucking mouth!"

He looked hard at Fred as if to say, "You hear?" Chayefsky knew about the dance that was done between the strong and the meek.

"And if he ever picks on you again, let me know about it."

Bob could even be sadistic with his favorites. "I've seen him paralyze dancers," John Kander said, "so that they could not move until they had loosened themselves from that kind of tension."

"You're not doing it," he said to one of them at rehearsal. "Do it again."

"What? What aren't I doing?"

"Just do it! Do it again!"

That was "the creative monster" Gwen talked about. "His face changes," she said. "He gets ropey looking. His eyes sink into his head, and it looks like a death mask. . . . He's driven, jumpy, crazed, and psyched up. Raw. He's like those safecrackers in old movies who file their fingertips down to keep them sensitive."

The actors were by no means improvising all the dialogue that Bob was "writing." John Kander believed that "some of the best writing in *Chicago* was really Fosse's, especially a very nasty little speech that he wrote for Roxie." Stripped of specific plot references, it seems like tough talk straight from Fosse's heart.

> Look, I'm gonna tell you the truth. Not that the truth really matters but I'm gonna tell you anyway. The thing is, see . . . I'm older than I ever intended to be. All my life I wanted to be a dancer in vaudeville. Oh yeah. Have my own act. But no. No. No. No. They always turned me down. It was one big world full of "No." Life. I gave up the vaudeville idea because after all those years . . . well, you sort of figure opportunity just passed you by.

According to Tony Walton, however, Fosse never wrote that speech. Herb Gardner did. Fosse just didn't happen to mention that when he handed it to the actors, and there are two drawable conclusions. One is that Fosse would take credit for Gardner's material, and the other is that Gardner wrote it from Bob's improvisation. Both conclusions are probably valid.

One day Buddy Hackett dropped down from the sky, as he liked to do, and the two old pals picked up as usual. Bob had to cut the visit short to leave for rehearsal, and Buddy offered to walk along. It was just a stroll across town from the apartment off Sixth Avenue to the studio on Broadway, but of course everyone in the streets recognized the comedian, and the truth was, he never tired of his public.

"I couldn't walk ten steps," he said, "without somebody saying hello or asking me for an autograph, and that day wasn't any different." As he strolled with Bob, taxi drivers waved from their cabs, pulling alongside the curb and calling out to him. Truck drivers yelled and honked their horns.

He complained to Fosse, "If I had one wish," he said, "I'd have another face."

"You don't mean to tell me you don't love it?" Bob said. "I'd give anything to be recognized like that."

"But you're so much better known than I am in the industry," Hackett said. "Jesus Christ, you're a Broadway director, a movie director. You're a major figure," but he knew exactly what Bob meant. Performers got special attention.

Rehearsals were moved into the 46th Street Theatre, where *Chicago* would ultimately play. Bob occasionally nudged Tony Stevens and whispered, "Watch this," as he sadistically told one of the girls to move to the side or to the back, "just to diddle them," Stevens said. "He was like the emcee in *Cabaret*, the observer, the manipulator, the entertainer, and totally amoral." And, Stevens added, "when he staged Gwen singing 'Funny Honey,' it was so tawdry. She would raise the style, and he would lower it, making her do gross things. Mind you, Gwen has a dark side too, and she thought some of it was funny but not all of it."

She had her own slant on her husband in the cruel mode. "Bob inflicts pain," she told Bob Aurthur, "not for the sake of pain but to call for a response that will advance the creative process." This was a rationalization of cruelty from deep within her dancer self, and she extended the connection between pain and art to Bob's dangerous habits. "His self-destructive things," she said, "put him in touch with his talent. It was the way he could be creative."

No pain, no gain. It was a chilling reminder of lessons Gwen had learned at the feet of Jack Cole. Taking a more mundane approach, Fred Ebb said, "Bob understood his own meanness. But I don't think he should be forgiven it just because he understood it."

He started work on a sexual number that was going to make the Whorehouse Ballet of *New Girl in Town* and the orgy in *Pippin* seem like hopscotch and curtsy. The new piece was set to a Kander and Ebb song that opened with finger snaps and proceeded to sum up a lifetime of Fosse/Riff:

> Give 'em the old razzle-dazzle
> Razzle-dazzle 'em
> Give 'em an act with lots of flash in it
> And the reaction will be passionate

That was lawyer Billy Flynn's advice to Roxie Hart as he stood beneath the scales of justice and began the defense against her murder charge. He sang it standing on a flight of stairs with the judge seated at the top, and Bob was staging the number orgiastically ("pornographically" was producer Bob Fryer's word for it) with dancers writhing and coupling on the stairs in assorted sexual combinations. Fosse said it was to symbolize the corruption of justice, but it seemed like a peep show, plain and simple.

Looking in on the rehearsal, the producers exchanged looks of alarm. Fryer, the only one who had the credentials to give Bob opinions, said, "Well, there goes the matinee audience," and added, after a nervous chuckle, "Listen, Bobby, nobody will pay attention to the scene with all that screwing around going on," but he made no impression.

On the night that John Rubinstein played his last performance in *Pippin*, the actor took over a small French restaurant on 52nd Street and hosted a party for everyone connected with the show. Bob had barely spoken to him since the dawn telephone call about *Lenny*. Now he raised a glass of champagne to toast the actor.

"I was already blushing," Rubinstein remembered, "anticipating some florid praise," but instead, Bob proclaimed, "To John Rubinstein, the most opaque person I have ever met in my life."

The actor was hurt and bewildered by the remark but later conceded, "There was a certain truth in it. I had a history of being accused of not caring about people." Perhaps Bob had spotted a kindred spirit, but the friendship that John had always hoped would develop was now dashed forever.

His replacement in *Pippin* was twenty-two-year-old Michael Rupert, and Fosse used the brief rehearsal as an opportunity to spruce up the two-and-a-half-year-old show. As the new young man was eased into the routine of eight performances a week, "it became difficult to do," Rupert said. "It was sending me bad vibes. Every time you turned around on stage, there were these people looking at you with those eyes and those hands and those poses that Bob did, that body language he used for these people who were trying to get you to kill yourself, even though it was just a play."

The actor began to have a recurring dream about being at the edge of a black lake with a high fence around it. "And there was a huge white house on the other side of the lake, and the only way I could get to the white house—which I had to do in this dream—was to swim through this black water."

After discussing the dream with a psychoanalyst, he realized that "the black lake was my *Pippin* contract. It was like the darkness of the show because the show was very darkly lighted anyhow, and it became a very black experience for me until I worked it out with the shrink."

□   □

It was painfully cold the night that *Chicago* opened in Philadelphia. The audience response had been "terrific," Tony Walton remembered, "and so there was a certain buoyancy about us" as he and Bob slogged back to the hotel through the snow to watch the Academy Awards on television. Although Fosse had been nominated for Best Director and Walton for Best Set Design (for *Murder on the Orient Express*), they hadn't gone to Los Angeles because they had the *Chicago* tryout, and anyway, neither considered himself a likely winner. "As each of us lost," Walton would later say, "it was almost more jokey than sad." *Lenny* didn't win any of the awards for which it had been nominated. Francis Ford Coppola made up for the previous encounter with Fosse by taking the directing Oscar for *The Godfather II*. As a result, *Lenny*, which could have used the box office boost, would need eight years to recover its cost.

They could not be jokey about the reviews for *Chicago* the next morning. The reviews were savage, and Fosse, moving slowly and looking wan, summoned the company for a pep talk. With them all gathered on stage, he sat down in the front row and was about to start when the stage-door watchman stepped out from the wings to say that there was a telephone call for him. He went off to take it while the usual gloomy wisecracks were passed around. "That was about the Harvard Hasty Pudding Club," Bob said on his return. "They just voted *Lenny* the Worst Film of the Year, and *Time* magazine wanted to know my reaction to it."

He laughed, and as he did, Tony Walton's two little girls rushed on stage, his daughter Emma and stepdaughter Bridget. They had suffered through the Academy Award losses the night before and had stayed up making mock Oscars to atone for those that Bob and their dad had lost. The girls had cooked up the statuettes "out of dough and God knows what," Walton said, baking them and painting them gold. While he was opening his award, Bridget presented the other to Bob, but as he pulled away the wrapping, it fell apart in his hands. The little girl had tripped on her dash to the theatre and had dropped the statuette on the sidewalk. Now, as she watched it crumble, she was on the verge of tears but controlled herself, and somehow it was this display of childish bravery that lifted Bob's and the cast's spirits. They went to work. There was plenty of time. There was still Philadelphia.

If there was one thing that everyone agreed on—everyone but Fosse—it was that "Razzle-Dazzle" on the courtroom steps needed fixing. "There were a couple of lines in it," John Kander said, "that were so vulgar they made you forget about the show. Fred and I went backstage before the first preview for one last try, and we pleaded with him to take them out. He began to retaliate by criticizing something of ours in a very nasty way."

"But, Bobby," Fred began to say, only to have John grasp him by the elbow and, remembering Liza Minnelli's advice about "leaving the room," walk him away.

As coauthor, Ebb could not always walk away from a disagreement, and Kander wasn't always there to pull him away. Ever more frequently now, he was hearing dialogue that he had not written or hearing about rehearsals that he had not been invited to. "Bob was treating him as a nonentity," the dance pianist Peter Howard remembered. Fred would leave to fix a lyric, and when he came back an hour later, he would find an entire scene improvised. Bob liked scenes that were played in the midst of songs. They made a show continuously musical. Ebb liked that too, but he didn't like the dialogue being made up by the actors, and he didn't like Fosse unilaterally cutting what he had written—"a lot of funny dialogue," Marty Richards said. "Gee, Bobby," Ebb started to say after sitting through an improvised scene, but Bob cut him short, and when the lyricist finally asked Fosse to give him a break, he was frostily told, "The people I tend to attack are the ones I think most vulnerable."

Ebb later added, "And he thought I was eminently vulnerable."

The blackness of spirit that had been flowing from Fosse was actually expressed in a literal way as Bob pressed Walton and Fisher to darken the scenery and the lighting. "The atmospheric pressure that he imposed on *Chicago* was just too much for it to sustain," Ebb insisted. "Basically, it was just an entertainment. It had something to say about celebrity, about our celebrating killers. I mean, there was Squeaky Fromm [of the Manson family] on the cover of *Time* magazine, and that was what the show was about, but you didn't need people screwing on the stairs under the scales of justice to make that clear. The fact that Roxie and Velma were now starring in vaudeville was quite enough."

His partner agreed. "If Bob was saying the world is a corrupt and shitty place," Kander said, "I don't understand why. Maybe I never knew him well enough to understand what demons he was exorcising."

Tony Stevens was also feeling the grimness. "The fun was going out of the show. Bob wanted it to be dirty and mean. That's not a good feeling for me, five hours a day of that."

"Razzle-Dazzle" with its orgy on the stairs came to symbolize the mean-spirited and dark feeling that Bob was bringing to the project, on and off stage.

"I guess you think it's vulgar too," a martyred Fosse said to Ebb on one of the rare occasions that he said anything to Ebb.

"Yes, I do," the soft-spoken lyricist replied, realizing that "the fact was Bob had thought up the number in the first place," and so nothing was going to be changed. "We all love dirty jokes," he would later reflect, "but we don't put them on stage."

As previews began in Philadelphia, Jerry Orbach, who had to *sing* "Razzle-Dazzle" in the thick of the sex show, approached Kander and Ebb and said, "Listen, guys. This number is crazy. The audience doesn't know where to look or what's happening."

They had to laugh. No fooling. "I know," Kander said. "It's a disaster, but we can't tell Bobby." They had complained to the producer Fryer, but he was also intimidated. Orbach himself knew perfectly well that "Bob was in a black rage, and nobody could or would talk to him," but by now he had decided that "this show was a little in the crack" and that the moment Hal Prince had forecast was at hand.

He approached Fosse.

"When you get a chance, can I have five minutes?"

"Yeah," Bob snapped, flashing Orbach an icy stare, "but I don't know when," and he walked off.

Stu Ostrow had arrived, making for a still stranger situation, another producer on the scene. Fosse asked Fryer if he would mind. "I need someone who's tougher on me than you are," he said. Fryer certainly did mind, but all he said was, "It depends on what capacity he's coming in on."

"My assistant," Bob said. "Not as a producer," but it was as if he was hiring his personal, unthreatening authority figure, a moneyman without purse strings and an intermediary. If the money people had anything to say now, they would have to say it through Stuart. Whatever Ostrow's capacity, John Kander was glad to have someone around who could communicate with Fosse. "I'm really glad you've come," he said, "because Bob isn't having a good time, and Fred isn't, and the show isn't."

"Don't worry," Ostrow said, probably thinking it was a simple collaboration problem. "We'll just fight and fight and fight, and we'll end up with something."

That wasn't quite what the composer had in mind. "If it's going to be a big fight, then I'm going back to New York," he said, and it was no idle threat. He was ready to do just that, whenever Fred Ebb was.

Fred didn't know what to do. "The show was having a terrible, terrible time," he said, "and Bobby was in a terrible, terrible mood, and now he brought Stuart to come and assist him. I was being ganged up on. It was the two of them against me."

Fosse finally got back to Orbach, a half day after the actor had asked for five minutes.

"What do you want?" he snarled.

The actor had used the four hours to work out "this line of bullshit, and now I laid it on him."

He began modestly: "I think I know what you're going for in that whole 'Razzle-Dazzle' sequence. It's like Brecht, isn't it?"

Orbach had gone to college, and his career had been launched off-Broadway in the Bertolt Brecht–Kurt Weill musical, *The Threepenny Opera*. He could lay claim (with Fosse anyway) to being a Brecht authority.

"Yeah?" Bob said uncertainly.

The actor plunged onward: "I see that you're looking to get the [Brechtian] Alienation Effect at the end of it, but, ah, what I think you've forgotten, Bobby, is that the story has to actually carry the audience and get them emotionally involved, so that at the end we can cut off and say, 'Okay, there's the message.' Then they'll alienate."

He could be intimidated by big words—Fred Ebb.

"With all this stuff going on," Orbach continued, "they have no focus to the scene of 'Razzle-Dazzle' and the trial. You know, with all the stuff on the stairs. You're not carrying them into the story enough to"—and he clapped his hands smartly—"*alienate* them at the end."

"Well," said a plainly confused Fosse, "I thank you for your interest."

Remembering the exchange, Orbach said, "I could only do this by appealing to him through Brechtian stuff, because that's where he was so shaky. He hadn't been to college, he hadn't studied Brecht, he didn't know what it all meant, but I'm sure it sounded right to him."

It must have because at next day's rehearsal, Bob told the company, "You know, let's cut all that crap on the stairs and all the fucking. Get rid of that shit. We need to pay more attention to the story."

Nights, almost everyone in the show (except Gwen) went to the Variety Club in the Bellevue–Stratford Hotel. It was an after-hours bar that catered to show people. At one time there had been Variety Clubs all over the country, in the days of touring shows and nightclubs. One of the few remaining, this one had tables, a jukebox, and a small dance floor. The ticket of admission was a job in a local show or a membership card in a performer's union. "It was like the Knights of Columbus for actors," Tony Stevens said, "your own place where you could be with your own people and be loud and show bizzy, and nobody complained."

Bob was there after every preview. He had given up on cigarillos and gone back to Camels. "You're going to kill yourself," Bob Fryer said to him. "You're going to go right back into the hospital," but Bob replied, "No, no. I don't smoke that much. I just need an occasional drag."

He was drinking too. Sometimes he had to be helped off the dance floor and led wobbly to his table. One night, drunk out of the Variety Club, he tumbled down a flight of stairs. Tony Stevens hurried after him and, throwing Bob over his shoulder like a bath towel, carried him back to his room.

"He was hitting on most of the girls in the show too," Tony remembered. "Sometimes it would make him just nastier." They were stunning, those dancers in *Chicago*, "tall and gorgeous," Patricia Zipprodt said, "with legs up to their waists." At rehearsal in front of everyone including Gwen, Fosse said aloud to one of them, "Don't think that you're going to have special treatment just because of last night."

He actually seemed nicer to the ones who refused him, as if a girl became cheap just by sleeping with him. He told John Kander that one of the dancers was "holding out for a fur coat. I know it. She's waiting for a fur coat."

"Yet," Tony Stevens felt, "the stronger he got and the more debauched he got, the better his work got."

When a Broadway show is out of town and trying out, the critics serve a function different from those reviewing on Broadway. Most of them accept this role and treat the show as a work-in-progress. They try to point out where changes and improvements might be made. The Philadelphia critics praised the individual parts of *Chicago*—the music and lyrics, the performances, and Gwen still had her doting press—but they came down hard on the director.

"The reviews had primarily to do with focus," was John Kander's interpretation, "and the darkness that Bob had put on the show." The day they appeared, he called the company together and told them he "sort of expected these reviews." He still had confidence in the show. He didn't specify how he was going to fix it, but he did say, "You know, critics are not much different from regular audiences, and like regular audiences they go through fads. It's very common, not just in the theatre but in all things."

He was turning reflective, pensive.

"People build up an idol," he mused, "and they put him on a pedestal. They give him everything he deserves and then some. And there is no next step up. The next step up is to bring him down. It's a game and a very human game.

"This show," he said, "is paying for my triple crown."

Bob told Jules Fisher, "Never do a show for the wrong reasons," meaning Gwen, and the changes he began to make were "violent," John Kander recalled. The fixer was fixing.

Meantime, Gardner and Chayefsky arrived like troops coming ashore armed with jokes. Nothing imperishable was gained. "If Jesus Christ was alive and living in Chicago today and had two hundred dollars," Chayefsky wrote, "things might have come out different." Sharper in conversation, he told the smoking, boozing Fosse, "You want to kill yourself so that other people will take you seriously."

Gardner could at least get a laugh. "I fired two warning shots," he wrote for one of the murderesses, "right into his head."

Such contributions were only making Fred Ebb more miserable, and he would return from meetings with Fosse and Ostrow ("Gloom and Doom," Chita Rivera called them) in despair, those meetings he was invited to. His partner again told him, "There's no show worth dying for, let's go home," but they didn't.

They weren't the only ones who were upset. Chita was frustrated and wanted to dance more and could dance more because she was young enough to, but she was not going to get that chance. Bob was not going to let Gwen be shown up. Gwen herself "broke down," Stevens remembered, and wailed, "I don't have the 'moment' in the show that I want," meaning a star turn near the end. If she could not dance a big closing number, then she meant at least to sing one. The powerful "Nowadays" was supposed to be a final duet for Gwen and Chita. As Chita described it to Bob Aurthur, "Gwen demanded that she sing the verse of our number alone. It was the first time I'd ever seen her stand up to Bob. She couldn't do it without tears. Her body started to convulse."

Then she began to sing the song. Upset, she could not get through it.

"I don't think so," Bob said icily, but Chita joined in to sing the duet part, as if she hadn't heard him. He began darkening in rage.

"I don't care what you think of me," Chita said to him, "or how you feel about her. We're going to do it this way," and they did, and it was the closest Gwen ever came to standing up to a choreographer.

The show moved on to New York, where all of Broadway was talking about just one thing, and that was A Chorus Line.

"My heart sank," Robert Fryer said, after he saw for himself the brilliant musical downtown at Joseph Papp's Public Theatre. Still in previews, its premiere was scheduled for May 21, just eleven days before Chicago opened. "This is our competition," Fryer knew, and he said so to Fosse.

"What's going to happen to it?" Bob asked.

"I think they're going to move it uptown. It's going to be a big, big hit."

As previews of *Chicago* were about to get under way at the 46th Street Theatre, Bob sat in the darkened auditorium and stared at the set while the stagehand mopped up, a ritual as old as greasepaint. Unexpectedly, Graciela Daniele appeared from the wings. It was an hour and a half before curtain time, long before most of the actors showed up at the theatre. Graciela, however, had a ballet background, and she was accustomed to warm-up exercises. She already had her makeup on. She looked for something to grab onto, anything that would serve as a brace for her barre exercises. "It was good for me," she said. "It prepared me for the show mentally as well as physically, because it was a moment of quiet."

Since there was nothing in the *Chicago* set that she could use for support, she stepped back into the wings and took hold of the handrail on the stairs. As she began to do her warm-up exercises, Bob appeared. He sat down on the steps alongside her and watched, his face cupped in his hands. Then he said quietly, "I admire that about dancers," and after a while he asked, "What is that you're doing? What do you call that, Graciela?" She explained the importance of "contracting the muscles in the backside and hips, opening the thighs and keeping the pelvis down."

"Why are you doing that? What does it do for you?"

After she told him, he said, "You know, I never studied any of that." He said it without regret, merely as a statement of fact. She continued her warm-up exercises. She had studied with Boris Kniasev as a girl in her native Argentina and had then danced with a company in Paris. "I think Bob liked the fact that I was so dedicated," she said.

"I admire that about dancers," Bob said, "the hard work."

Joe Papp's production of *A Chorus Line* opened to sensational reviews, and Michael Bennett was proclaimed the reigning choreographer-director on Broadway on the basis of his first musical as a director. Tony Walton felt "pretty sure that Bob envied Bennett's having made that show out of the very same experiences that he'd had and not thought of using. Now," Walton added, "*A Chorus Line* had stolen whatever potential thunder *Chicago* might have had."

Jules Fisher thought Bob was jealous of the way the executives of the Shubert Organization were "fawning" over Bennett. Nevertheless the fixing of *Chicago* continued. Gwen was getting more confident. Bob was chain-smoking and giving so many notes that Chita Rivera finally screamed, "No more notes!" when Tony Stevens handed her yet another page. Then she burst out laughing when she noticed he'd put on full clown makeup and blacked out his teeth.

The day the critics were to come, Fosse had the company run through the show in the afternoon while he sat and watched it by himself, an audience of one. When they were through, Stevens remembered, "After all the detail and the repetition and the endless, endless notes, he did this incredible thing. Finally, there was no bullshit. He just said, 'You're all wonderful.' "

Climbing on stage, the cigarette hanging from the corner of his mouth, he asked Gwen to do one of the dances a last time. He took off the derby that he was wearing, the derby Stevens had seen before and knew for the gypsy legend it was. "Specially Made for Mr. Fosse," the London hatmaker had embossed in gold on the leather hatband. Bob took off the derby and handed it to Stevens. "Here," he said. "Do the number with her."

The dancers stared. "They gasped," Stevens said, and when he danced with Gwen, "It was the best I ever danced, because I finally got the hat. I had to be good with the hat."

People used to tell him that he was closed in. They said he was cold and unfeeling. People told him that he ought to be more demonstrative and *caring*. More *giving*. The question was whether he was unable to love or just couldn't show it.

"I'm not supposed to love anybody," he said. "People don't think I love anybody."

A postcard that he scribbled to Kim St. Leon was forwarded to her in Los Angeles, where she had moved after getting married. "How could you ignore me like this?" he wrote. "You know I know Frank Sinatra."

The opening night party for *Chicago* was held in the Rainbow Room of the RCA Building high above Rockefeller Center, and while everyone was dancing, associate producer Marty Richards was being given the name of a *New York Times* apprentice who, for a small bribe, would read critic Clive Barnes's review over the telephone. Otherwise it would be another hour before the newspaper hit the streets, and Richards could hardly wait. He made the call from a telephone booth. "The kid read the review to me," he remembered. "When it wasn't good [*Chicago* Disappoints], I started explaining the show to him, to this kid, this apprentice I didn't even know."

Some of the reviews were better, but as an uncompromising depressive, Fosse was no happier with the good notices than the bad. "We really razzle-dazzled those bastards, didn't we?" he told Richards, as if *Chicago*, like *Pippin*, had been a silly show with a flashy front. He could not accept the possibility that he had actually done something worthwhile even after creating what would prove to be the greatest achievement of his stage career. For in the process of eliminating gaiety, a grim honesty had emerged in this show. Fosse's uncovered and eruptive darkness had made *Chicago* one of the most powerful and original of musicals, a snarling entertainment that used vaudeville as a metaphor even if the sense of the metaphor was ambiguous. Perhaps the only meaning was the blackness of its chromium. Perhaps that was Fosse's only statement. If so, it certainly discouraged the kind of good-natured cheer associated with rave notices. One was not, after all, supposed to ask for an encore at a funeral.

Paramount Pictures had already signed Keith Carradine to star in *Ending*, the movie Bob Aurthur was writing for Fosse to direct. As producer Stuart Ostrow described it, the movie "explores the most intimate and universal emotions in dying and, equally, in survival, with an artistic understanding and compassion that few have been able to project."

Perhaps, but Fosse was having second thoughts about it. "The closer we got to shooting, the more depressed I became. I thought there must be some way of making death lighter, more interesting, and sharing it in terms I could handle. I didn't know if I could live with that kind of pain for a year and a half. . . . I wanted music and dancing in it. I wanted to try and move people in different directions. I wanted to show the fear and anxiety a person goes through in the hospital and the stress of someone under business pressure. Many people are under this stress. They are trying to do something with their lives, but instead become destructive with pills and alcohol in psychological ways."

He also knew instinctively that a song and dance about death would be more potent than a heartfelt drama on the subject. And, finally, it did make sense, after all, for the sardonic song and dance man to sashay his way through the graveyard.

Fosse was supposed to be looking for an actress to play Keith Carradine's wife. Instead, Bob Aurthur got a telephone call in East Hampton, summoning him to New York for a meeting with Sam Cohn, and when Cohn called, people came. Aurthur walked into the agent's office, and Fosse announced, "*Ending* is off," quickly adding, "Don't worry, I have a better idea. It's going to be called *All That Jazz* [which had been *Chicago*'s original title]. We'll write it together, and you'll produce it, and it's going to be about everything that happened to me in the hospital."

He was evidently more concerned about Bob Aurthur's not losing the work he needed desperately than he was for his other friend, Stu Ostrow, whose project and original idea had just gone down the drain. But the studio would repay Ostrow for his outlays, and he was still profiting from *Pippin*. His feelings would mend.

Chicago was by no means triumphantly launched. Although it would emerge as Bob Fosse's most artistic work for the theatre, and although it would be particularly respected in England, it was not yet a success on Broadway. And when Gwen fell ill, there was a real chance of its only achievement being a Broadway record for flops—$800,000.

Behind Gwen Verdon lay a history of illness, from *New Girl in Town* to *Redhead* and the famous inhaled feather of *Sweet Charity*. Now, again, she had a problem with her vocal chords, polyps this time, and surgery was going to keep her out of *Chicago* for nine weeks. When Fred Ebb mentioned the crisis to Liza Minnelli, she immediately said, "Why don't I do it?" She had already seen the show in Philadelphia, bringing Goldie Hawn with her, because they were interested in costarring in a movie version. The notion of her being a replacement posed no ego problem. A star's magnitude could in fact be measured by how *little* ego had to be massaged. Richard Burton had just completed a stint spelling Anthony Perkins in *Equus*. In Liza's case she was never even going to be advertised in *Chicago*, billed, named on a marquee, or listed in the program. She would be announced at the start of every performance as substituting for Gwen Verdon. Audiences, which ordinarily groan when such announcements are made, would not quite react in the same way when Liza Minnelli was announced as the substitute. They probably would have groaned had just the reverse been announced—that Gwen Verdon *would* be appearing. Indeed, the situation might have offended *Gwen's* ego. John Kander said, "I'm sure there was some twinge. Gwen knew and liked Liza, but here was a girl many years younger who could do it all—sing, dance, act." However, he conceded, "Gwen had a serious investment in the show."

While Minnelli learned the part, the regular understudy (Lenora Nemetz) played Roxie, and business weakened precipitously. During that week, Bob worked with Liza twelve hours a day, and then she went on, and for the next eight weeks there was not a ticket available. Jerry Orbach loved working with her. "She's the most outgoing, the most sensitive, the most loving person," he said. "You just want to put your arm around her and protect her from all the bad things."

When Gwen returned, *Chicago* was an established hit. Bob had given her a tremendous gift, much more than the money. He had given her one last Broadway show, one last chance to star. But now for sure her dancing days were over.

Ultimately, *A Chorus Line* swept the Tony Awards and probably would have won the Kentucky Derby had it been entered. On the night the Tonys were handed out, Bob sat in the audience like a good sport, the second time (after *Lenny*) that he had been nominated for a prize and not won. He didn't want to get into that habit. Joe Papp, the producer of A

Chorus Line, remembered, "I passed him a couple of times that night. He was very unresponsive," and the Award competition notwithstanding, Papp felt it strange for Fosse not even to acknowledge their youthful Navy past. "It was a real coincidence," he said, "but Bob was very cold and aloof, so I kept my distance."

Fosse smiled in his aisle seat and applauded when Michael Bennett was called up as the best director and choreographer. What would later seem to rankle him the most was not losing the prize but the artistic glow that suddenly surrounded Bennett. A *Chorus Line* didn't deserve all that, Fosse thought. In public he would say, "I find a bit of soap in it. It's a very good show, but I don't think it's a great show." In private he said, "It's a classy 'Dynasty.' Bennett does great glitz," and who knew glitz better than Bob Fosse?

The series of commercials that Ogilvy and Mather was producing for American Express was known around the advertising agency as the "Do You Know Me?" campaign. The phrase had particular resonance for Fosse, who had spent a lifetime needing to be known. Wearing his basic black, a velvet jacket, and turtleneck sweater, he stood in a crowded theatre lobby and smiled into the camera, speaking the campaign's key phrase, "Do you know me?" Then he explained, "I directed the shows *Pippin* and *Chicago* and the films *Cabaret* and *Lenny*. But still people don't know my face. That's why I carry the American Express card."

Afterward he told a friend, "I've been trudging my ass off for years, working, and nobody knew me, and then I made an American Express commercial, and everybody in the world was stopping me in the street. Of course sometimes they got me wrong. 'We know you,' they'd say. 'You're the guy who does the Muppets, right?' '*Right*,' I'd say. 'That's right.'"

What kind of movie was *All That Jazz* anyway, and why was he making it? A movie about his own heart attack, a movie that had death, his own death, as the major deviation from the way things had really happened. *All That Jazz* seems to have been intended as the star vehicle that Bob Fosse had been craving all his life; people would know who he was. It would be his version of his life.

Working on *Lenny* with documented materials must have been satisfying. Its interviewing technique surely fed the ham in him, the interrogator of the Truth Game in him, the listener through the wall, the suspicious paranoid. He decided that as research for *All That Jazz*, he and

Bob Aurthur were going to interview everyone who knew him or had been working or dealing with him at the time of his heart attack. As Jane Aurthur said, "The two Bobs were just nutty, going around with tape recorders asking everyone, 'What were you doing while Bobby was in the hospital?' 'What did you think?' "

They talked to Herb and Paddy, to Sam Cohn and Joey Harris, to Tony Walton, Stu Ostrow, John Kander, Fred Ebb, and the musical director of *Chicago*, Stanley Lebowsky. They interviewed the lawyer Leonard Strauss, Dr. Ettinger, and Bob's psychiatrist, Dr. Clifford Sager. They talked to Ann Reinking, Dustin Hoffman, Chita Rivera, Phil Friedman, Jules Fisher, and of course Gwen and Nicole. This was the ultimate eavesdrop, using the subterfuge of research to run a lie detector test on suspected betrayers. It was a paranoid's paradise.

Fred Ebb remembered his interview in astonishing detail. Bob's call reached him in Los Angeles.

"Can I interview you? Are you busy?"

"No, I'm not doing anything."

"Well, I need you for about an hour."

"Oh, well, that's okay."

"You're sure you aren't doing anything?"

He was being what Ebb described as "very solicitous."

"No, Bobby. It's fine."

"Okay. Hold the telephone. I'm going in the other room and putting on the tape recorder."

As Ebb recalled the questions that followed, "They were absolutely terrifying."

"Were you angry with me when you found out that I was ill?"

"No."

"Did you want me to die so that somebody else could take over and go on with the show?"

"No, Bobby. I never wanted you to die."

"You mean you weren't angry with me *at all*? You didn't feel *any-thing*? What *did* you feel?"

"Well . . . disappointment . . . concern. I worried about you."

"Well, why would you worry about me? We weren't that close."

Ebb remembered Bob as becoming "very abrasive and provocative with this question, trying to get me to say I'd been angry with him for holding up the show."

"After all," Bob said, "you had worked two years on the project, and there I was with a heart attack, unable to go ahead. Did you want another director to come in? That's what I heard."

"No."

"Did you know they solicited another director?"

"After the fact I did."

"Did you know beforehand that they were going to ask anyone?"

"I never did, Bob."

"What would you have said if you knew?"

"I would have asked them not to."

"Did you know? Did it ever come up?"

"Yes."

"What did you say?"

"I said I didn't want to do it without you."

"You actually said that," Bob said sarcastically. "Do you think the cast hated me?"

"No, Bobby."

"Were you at the meeting the cast held? The rah-rah meeting? The 'Bobby's Going to Be All Right' meeting? You spoke, didn't you?"

"Yes."

"What did you say?"

"I told the cast we thought they were all terrific, and I hoped they'd stick with us while we waited for you to recover. I even gave a party at my house with Gwen and Chita cohosting—for the whole company. To keep them all feeling together."

"Oh . . . I guess I've gotten some wrong information," Bob concluded.

He was hardly this accusatory when he interviewed Herb Gardner. He allowed his friend ample time for philosophizing. "You list your crimes at the slightest provocation," was Herb's opening line in Bob Aurthur's transcription of the tape. "I think you do it to absolve yourself. You go on record with your sins. It's the final play, the biggest con of all."

Gardner knew how to talk to Fosse.

Tony Walton talked to Fosse's tape recorder about Bob's regret over having no deep relationships with lovers. Stanley Lebowsky remembered Bob telling him that, after the second heart attack, he was convinced that he wanted to live "because I came so close to death." This was to become the center of *All That Jazz*.

Bob Fryer was especially candid, telling Fosse that his acclaim had hardened him, made him remote and inaccessible. After some fifteen years of knowing Bob, he now felt "in the way, intruding. You became unfriendly. I'm terrified of you at times," the producer told him. "I take a long time to pick up a phone and call you. I'm afraid I'll interrupt you."

Bob brought all the tapes to the house in Quogue, and as he listened with Bob Aurthur to this strange review of his life and his crisis, they began to write the screenplay. As Julian Barry and Fred Ebb had found earlier, Aurthur now discovered that collaborating with Bob Fosse meant nightly writing and daily readings. Each morning he would drive from East Hampton to Quogue, bringing the pages he had written, and the two would go over the work, playing the scenes and talking them out. Aurthur's first draft of the screenplay used the real names. Fosse kept that one under lock and key.

Her back healed, Ann Reinking had returned to work, and out of all the musicals on Broadway she joined A Chorus Line. Fosse didn't complain about that. He even asked Michael Bennett to give Mary-Ann Niles a job in his next production (which Bennett did). He only complained about Michael not bothering to redesign the choreography for Ann so as to capitalize on her ballet training.

Weekends, she came to Quogue. A limousine would wait at the stage door of the Shubert Theatre after the Saturday evening performance. She could doze for the ninety-minute ride, arriving by one o'clock in the morning. Then she could stay until late Monday afternoon, a nice stretch. One Saturday that summer, though, just before the evening show, she called to say that she wasn't going to be able to make it for the weekend. That was how Fosse recounted it to Aurthur. There was just "too much going on in town," she said, but before she had a chance to explain, Bob told her that he had to get off the telephone because he was having terrible chest pains. She tried to telephone him later, but there was no answer. She called into the night. "At two or three in the morning," Jane Aurthur recalled, a panicky Ann telephoned saying that she was terribly worried about Bobby. When she explained why, Bob Aurthur began dialing the Quogue number. He too got no answer. He turned to Jane beside him in bed and said, "There's no way I'm going to drive all the way to Quogue at three o'clock in the morning to check on him." Instead he telephoned the police and asked them to do it, and when they arrived at Fosse's house, they found him sitting in the living room smoking a cigarette, sipping a glass of wine, and listening to music. When Bob Aurthur called the following morning to ask why he had done that, Fosse replied, "She shouldn't have broken the date."

By summer's end the two Bobs had completed a first draft of the screenplay, and they all moved back to New York. Jane was already anticipating friction. "That was going to be a troublesome situation," she knew, when her husband assumed the role of Fosse's on-the-spot (or "line") producer. "Bobby was going to have trouble with whoever was going to say, 'You can't do that.' He was a cop hater, he had to have someone to blame, and it was always the one who said, 'You can't spend the money,' or 'You can't have extra rehearsal,' or 'You can't have that costume change.' "

The movie's executive producer would be less troublesome. Dan Melnick, a tall, swarthy, athletic, handsome man some seven years younger than Fosse, was a type he liked, and their rapport was instant, a couple of cynics with a shared sense of lust.

Melnick was a smart Jewish New Yorker, a serious laugher who was familiar with the Los Angeles movie world but not obsessed with it. He had been head of production at MGM before making a deal with David Begelman who, as he had promised Bob when leaving as agent, had gone on to produce movies. Begelman was now president of Columbia Pictures, and his deal with Dan Melnick was for independent production of movies under the Columbia banner. *All That Jazz* was going to be one of Melnick's first projects for Begelman at Columbia.

David was apprehensive about working with Fosse. "Having been Bob's agent," Melnick said, "David knew how difficult he could be. He was also nervous about the movie, because it defied conventional wisdom. He wasn't sure it was commercially viable," but Begelman did believe in Fosse's talent and, considering the record of three movies and two sets of Academy Award nominations, it was hard not to.

As a gift at the start, when Bob flew out to clinch the *All That Jazz* deal, Melnick introduced him to Jessica Lange. The actress had a bimbo image. As Bob himself said, "After she made *King Kong*, they said she was just the usual dumb blond. Well, I wish I was dumb like Jessica Lange." And in fact she was tough and smart as well as beautiful. For the next half year Bob pursued her while Bob Aurthur rewrote *All That Jazz*, and Dan Melnick went looking for leading men to play Bob Fosse—although nobody was admitting that the movie was actually about him. It was merely about a prominent Broadway choreographer-director who has a heart attack and bypass surgery in the midst of editing a movie about a comedian while simultaneously directing a musical starring his estranged wife, a famous dancer. Otherwise it had nothing to do with Bob Fosse.

Robert De Niro was unavailable. The actor wanted to take a year off because he wanted to "regain his perspective." Warren Beatty already had commitments, he said, for the next 175 years, but he wanted to be asked. Fosse, as an excuse to come out and see Jessica Lange, said he would try to talk Jack Nicholson into playing the part, even if it meant tagging along with the actor to a Los Angeles Lakers basketball game. When Fosse found himself part of an entourage, he turned to Nicholson at halftime and said, "I really don't want to sit through this basketball game," and left. He didn't see Jessica either. Melnick had planted a prankish note at the hotel, ostensibly from the actress, apologizing for menstrual cramps that were going to make it impossible for her to see him.

The good thing about a movie is that when it is done, it is done, and nobody has to keep it in shape from one performance to the next. Life was different on old Broadway. *Chicago* kept grinding out its eight weekly performances, and that was just too much for Gwen Verdon. She had recovered from the throat surgery, but the show was exhausting for even a game fifty-two-year-old, and so Ann Reinking, whose complaisance seems the stuff of legend, stepped out of *A Chorus Line* to—how else to say it?—replace Gwen.

Tony Stevens, the dance assistant who kept on top of the show, looked on with fascination as Bob, growing stronger daily, himself directed Ann, making slight adjustments to tailor the role to her style. "He put tambourines into the song 'Roxie,' and fitted the movement to her. It was obvious," Stevens said, "that Annie could do more physically. She was twenty-three years younger than Gwen. She had a different talent, and Bobby used it."

Stevens' fascination turned to wonder as Bob would pick Ann up after a performance and take her to dinner, sometimes with Nicole and sometimes even with Gwen. Stevens could not have been more show biz. He had seen quite a bit in his young life, and yet he responded to this peculiarly extended family with an ingenuous awe, not unlike that of Bob's endlessly amazed cardiologist, Dr. Ettinger. "They all seemed to be very sophisticated about it," Stevens said. "It was very New York. Gwen became very friendly with Annie. Whether or not she was happy with it, she lived with it."

Bob's sister Patricia, who was the same age as Gwen, died that year, May 1977, which gave his sense of mortality yet another shake. Not only was Patsy the first to go in his generation of the family and not only was she his favorite sibling, but he felt that she was the reason he had become a dancer in the first place. Had Patsy Fosse not been so shy as a child, Bobby would never have gone to dance school at Frederic Weaver's Chicago Academy of Theatre Arts. He thought he owed his career to his sister and said so.

Patsy didn't die of heart disease as had her parents. Women generally have a lower frequency of heart disease than men, at least in their childbearing years. Prevailing medical opinion is that they are protected by female hormones. Patsy Fosse had enjoyed this protection despite her four-pack-a-day smoking habit. However the estrogens did not protect her from lung cancer. The cigarettes were free to do a job on her there.

By the time she died, she had been divorced from George Lane. She left four daughters—Ginger, Judy, Candy, and Lorelei (Laurie). Bob came home for the funeral, and as he sat in the roomful of visitors, he told his brother Buddy he was sure that he was not going to live to be an old man. "Do me a favor, will you?" he asked, glancing around the room of drinking and eating relatives. "Don't do any of this for me."

He sat sunk in the living room armchair ("Swallowed up in it," it seemed to his niece Cindy), and they all thought he was wearing black because of the occasion, his black velvet blazer, black trousers, black boots. He stayed up all night, sitting and smoking in that chair in Cindy's living room on Ramona Street in Lincolnwood, just outside Chicago.

You want to see dancing? I'll show you dancing.

If the success of A *Chorus Line* annoyed him and if he resented the adulation being heaped upon Michael Bennett, nothing could have been more psychologically predictable than his throwing down this challenge before Broadway's most ferocious father figure. Bernard B. Jacobs was the scowling president of the Shubert Organization. He provided the power foundation of A *Chorus Line* and would perform the same role for Bob's next show, *Dancin'*, which seemed to have come in response to A *Chorus Line*.

The sixtyish, white-haired Jacobs had eyes that seemed to glower in a bed of flesh even in the cheeriest of circumstances, and he was conceded to be the most powerful man in the Broadway theatre, controlling enormous funds as well as the country's biggest chain of theatres. Jacobs was assisted by Gerald Schoenfeld, the conservative and lawyerly board chairman of the Shubert Organization, but Jacobs was the lion before whom all theatre folk seemed to cower. And Bernie Jacobs' pride was A *Chorus Line*, the indefinite occupant of his flagship Shubert Theatre; to Jacobs, Michael Bennett was a triumphant son, and Bennett seemed to play that role with a certain wile. The Shubert Organization president, then, was an authority figure to contend with and almost archetypal. Fosse, in competing with Bennett for his respect, was wading into a realm of mixed mythology, a Greek tragedy featuring a wrathful Jewish God/father and a Broadway song and dance man.

Coping with Bernie Jacobs and responding to A *Chorus Line* leaped to the top of his priority list. Fosse postponed movie production. "My dream," he said (as if he had waited a lifetime to admit this), "my hope has been to do an all song and dance show with only minimum dialogue. But this won't be straight dance. If it were, I'd do it at the [92nd Street] 'Y.'

This will be oriented to Broadway and entertainment . . . tap, acrobatics, classical ballet, modern ballet, jazz, rock. Everything I can think of. Soft shoe. If I could think of anything else, I'd put it in."

That was his public statement. In private, the thought of two hours of choreography scared him, and he called Graciela Daniele, asking her to stop by at the rehearsal studio, where he was already working alone.

"How about you doing something on this show, Graciela?"

"What do you mean?"

"I mean choreograph some of the numbers for *Dancin'*."

"What? Why?"

"I'm not sure I can come up with a whole show's worth of dances. If you do some and Tony Stevens does some and Chris Chadman does some, I think I can manage."

"Okay," said this wise young woman. "When you are out of ideas, call me. I have the feeling that once you get into it, you're going to want to do it all." And she left him to his records, his drum machine, and his Magic Trunk. He never had to ask her again and would choreograph all of *Dancin'* himself, with the exception only of the closing number, which Chadman would do.

His assistants on the show, besides Chadman, were Tony Stevens and Kathy Doby, and now they began to work. Stevens found him alone with the records, "bringing in his memories of musical styles and arrangements, his knowledge of vaudeville shtick and old acts." Fosse's notion for the show was to use classical and show music, popular music, rock and roll, Mozart, Bach, George M. Cohan, and contemporary music by Neil Diamond and Melissa Manchester, anything but a new score written by a collaborator. He was going to have no partners. "When you have collaborators, you have all those midnight meetings," he said. "I'm tired of those. And the egos. So I just decided to meet myself at midnight."

The company consisted of eight boy and eight girl dancers, and the evening was to be "a musical entertainment" with virtually no dialogue and little singing. It was dancin' all right, and on the first day of rehearsal Bob told the ensemble, "This is a show about dancing. You have to love to dance, or you should not be in this show. If you do not love it, get out, please. It's going to be hard work for the next three months. You're going to be exhausted, but that's what this show is about."

Three months was quite an improvement on the traditional eight weeks of rehearsal, and it was something he had Michael Bennett and *A Chorus Line* to thank for.

He invited Jessica Lange to come up to the studio at night after everyone was gone—to come and see what he had done so far, to see him dance. They were with each other several nights a week now, and Ann Reinking was being pushed aside to make room, but he was not yet sure of Lange. "I always had the feeling," he said, "that there was, you know, Someone Else. I certainly didn't feel I was her number one guy. And, see, I got this idea. I thought, if I could just get her to see me dance—I'm a really good dancer, really am. One night, if I could just get her into the studio. Get on my little dance shoes. Strut around. Then she'd just, y'know, fall."

So he told Lange, "I don't know whether you'd be interested, but I'm trying to work on an all-dance show. I'm rehearsing a little bit every day. It couldn't be more boring, but if you'd like to—I'm just in my black stuff, it's just me and the mirror."

"Oh!" she replied. "It sounds wonderful! I'd love to see it."

"Well, if you're interested—I'm just getting into some of the dances, and I'd be happy to have you come and watch."

"Oh, that's my favorite thing to do in the world."

"You've done this before?" he asked, his ears pricking up. Later, recalling the conversation, he remembered, "I just couldn't figure out who . . . she was seeing, and then one day I put it together, and sure enough I found out it was Baryshnikov.

"Here I'd had been inviting her to see *me* dance! She finally called up and said, 'You at the studio? How about tonight?' I yelled, 'Forget it!' And I had really been thinking, 'Once she sees me move and all that, oh then, oh then . . .

"Little did I know, right?"

It was a charming story, a self-effacing story, but a sad one because he could not believe that he might have been compared with Baryshnikov, might even have been better in his own way. The truth was that Mikhail Baryshnikov, great ballet dancer though he was, could not have compared to Bob Fosse either, couldn't do his moves, his steps.

Just past New Year's Day of 1978, Kathy Doby leaned against a wall at Broadway Arts as Bob approached his famous trunk. She was still bewitched by this collection of vaudeville props and the way he would reach into it when a song inspired him. It gave him a little extra to work with, something to extend the body. He would take a hat, a cane, and then gesture for Kathy to join him, and they worked together from the music. His weight was up to an amazing (for him) 137 pounds, and he was feeling strong enough to demonstrate most of the steps himself as he began to work with the company. Kathy Doby described one of the girls, Sandahl Bergman, as "a blond Amazon, and we were working on the Melissa Manchester number ['Let it Ride'], and there were quite a few lifts in it, and he was lifting her, all five feet ten inches and a hundred forty pounds of her, more than his own weight."

At the same moment, David Begelman was in "deep, deep trouble," as he put it himself. His forgery of Cliff Robertson's name on a $10,000 check had been discovered, and with further irregularities about to be disclosed, he had no choice but to resign the presidency of Columbia Pictures. Dan Melnick assumed most of those responsibilities. "David is a sick man," Melnick said, at a loss to explain the relatively trivial theft and the tremendous risk taken by a man in so powerful and well-paid a position. "The thing he needs and deserves most from all of us is compassion." But Dan Melnick seemed to be one of the few with time for compassion. Begelman's former client, Bob Fosse, was busy in Boston anticipating the *Dancin'* tryout, and Begelman's former protégé, Sam Cohn, was going there to lend his client psychological support. Not many were offering support to David Begelman.

Just before Fosse left for the tryout, he finally got around to taking the medical examination for the insurance people. He had been delaying the date with the doctor. He hadn't the time for it, that was his excuse; he was too busy creating *Dancin'.* And when he found the time, he found it at midnight. That was when he had Bernie Jacobs arrange the examination, and the Shubert Organization president felt the behavior was perverse.

Fosse walked into the doctor's office after a fourteen-hour rehearsal day, thoroughly exhausted. Uncovering the splendid scar that drove down the center of his skinny chest, he smiled as the physician asked whether he still smoked.

"Yeah, I suppose I do."

Jacobs cringed.

"How much?"

"Oh, about four packs a day."

The insurance was denied, and Jacobs felt that Fosse was just being malicious. A policy was finally acquired from Lloyd's of London, but it was at a considerably higher premium and for a limited time, the coverage ending on the New York opening night.

In Boston, Bob was having a hard time with the sets and giving a hard time to their designer, Peter Larkin, who had been recommended by Tony Walton. Between *Chicago* and *All That Jazz*, Walton needed a respite from Fosse. So would Larkin, and at any moment now, for although he looked like a weight lifter, there was an emotional meat grinder inside. Jules Fisher tried to be protective, and since he was a coproducer of *Dancin'* (with Fosse and the Shubert Organization), that was possible to some extent, but Bob was also upset about a malfunctioning motor for the scenery, and his out-of-town anxieties were fueling the upset to a fury.

"It's going to be fixed," Jules assured him.

"When?" Fosse snapped.

"It's coming from New York."

"No it isn't! You and Larkin have ruined my show!"

"Bob," Fisher said, taking him by the shoulders and shaking him calm. "I care about this show as much as you do, and damn it, I'm fixing it!"

Fosse stared in disbelief. *"You do?"* he gasped.

He was trembling. The lighting designer (as well as coproducer) impulsively embraced him, taking a risk with the ordinarily unhuggable Fosse, but the gesture was accepted. "Bobby couldn't believe that anyone cared as much as he did about the show," Fisher said.

The three of them had scouted Boston ahead of the company, checking the depth and width of the Colonial Theatre stage, each from his own point of view. Now Bob tested the bounciness of the floor, and *Dancin'* was ready for opening. It was in the mixed condition that could only be expected at the start of tryouts. As a program of show dancing, it had an unavoidable sameness, and it lacked a structure, having no story, but many of the dances were smashing. For one of them, Bob put a stageful of Fred Astaires into the true giant soft shoe, "I Wanna Be a Dancing Man" (a song that Astaire had sung). He paid another dancing debt too, using the music of the big band classic, "Sing, Sing, Sing" to toast (or confront) Jack Cole. The music had been the basis of one of Cole's major works, and in the *Dancin'* program Bob dedicated the number "To Gwen and Jack, the latter would have hated it."

Whatever Cole represented to him was wrapped up in that enigmatic reference. Ethel Martin, who had danced with Gwen in Cole's "Sing, Sing, Sing, the Wedding of a Solid Sender," described it as "the ultimate nightclub dance number. Why should Bobby do it? He had already become Bob Fosse with his own style so why do 'Sing, Sing, Sing'?"

Harvey Evans, the longtime Fosse dancer, wondered too. "Bob's dancing is usually tight and little," he said. "You seldom see it going out across the stage. You never see Fosse people doing big stuff like that, and it was so strange seeing it dedicated like that."

Why indeed had Bob done "Sing, Sing, Sing?" He had Cole as inspiration enough for his smutty dances, a trail of questionable value that Jack Cole had blazed—if one can be a pornographic pioneer. Perhaps Fosse saw in Jack Cole some higher dance authority to justify those crude tastes of his. Or perhaps there was something in what he had said to Paddy Chayefsky about Cole: "That's the only guy I was ever afraid of."

By now sleazy numbers seemed compulsive for Bob, and there were two of them in *Dancin'*. The more offensive, "Coming to the City," depicted the sexual bombardment that the average person presumably receives on a visit to New York. It was an old-fashioned literal-minded Broadway ballet, except that its narrative depicted a tourist coping with prostitutes, massage parlors, and dance halls.

The other questionable dance was concocted for Ann Reinking on the occasion of the end of the affair. Bob's pursuit of Jessica Lange had jolted it, and now a burgeoning romance with a beautiful model named Julie Hagerty was finishing it off. But he got it into his head that Ann had taken a lover and felt free to rebuke her for doing so. He gave her a last dance, so to speak, with this piece about a ballet class, in which she acts out a sexual fantasy with the dance master. Bob cast Charles Ward, the man he thought Ann was involved with, as the dance master.

Curiously, and for apparently psychological reasons, in designing the choreography for "The Dream Barre," as the piece was called, Bob was suddenly confounded by his left-handedness. In the past, he'd always had to compensate for his reflexive movements to the left and the resulting counterclockwise turns, but that had long since become as second nature. Now, all of a sudden, he was again doing everything leftways—literally *perversely* to the left. As Kathy Doby watched rehearsal, "Bob worked out his choreography for Charles Ward, and when he was finished, we had to fix it all for right-handed."

The Boston reviews only confirmed what he had already begun to hear about the tourist number, "Welcome to the City"—that it was tawdry. He stood alone against the rising chorus of disapproval. Sam Cohn assumed the role of intermediary, but he would say, "I don't have to criticize my client. Everyone else is doing that."

Bob wasn't listening to anyone else. He was certainly paying no attention to the most vociferous protestors, the Shubert executives Gerald Schoenfeld and Bernard Jacobs (who referred to "Ballet Barre," the less offensive dance, as "the cunnilingus number"). Even Herb Gardner, who had come up from New York, was brushed aside when he criticized "Welcome to the City" for its crudeness. Fosse said to Jules Fisher, "When was the last big successful musical Herb had?"

Perhaps the doting stage manager, Phil Friedman, put it most succinctly: "As soon as you pressured him to get rid of something, you'd get his back up, and he'd resist. You couldn't get anything out of a Fosse show by going up to him and saying, 'That's a terrible number, take it out.'

That'd only make sure he kept it in. He rehearsed that tourist number every day."

Jules Fisher felt, "Bob didn't know where the line was. He liked low comedy, and he liked sex. That combination makes for tacky." He told Bob as much. "I don't think it's in good taste, and worse, I don't think it works. But," he concluded, "you're the boss."

After the Boston critics gave the show mixed reviews, Fosse went into his highest gear, the fixing ratio. He pushed the tempo to a blurring speed. He whittled the evening down to a crisp three acts and thirteen numbers. He gave up on the tourist number, but stood firm on "Ballet Barre." When Alan Heim, his film editor, arrived to work on the television commercial, Bob asked what he thought of the show. "I thought most of it was terrific," Heim said, "but I have to tell you—I really didn't like the dance class."

He not only didn't like it; he thought Bob had put it in just to embarrass Ann. "Maybe," Heim said, diplomatically, "the dance class is hurting the 'Bojangles' number," of which he knew Fosse was especially proud.

With predictable frigidity, Bob said, "Other people have said that to me."

Heim mentioned the conversation to the musical director, Gordon Harrell, who told him, "Bob already cut one number because of criticism. It's not likely he'll cut another."

Heim also mentioned the dance class to Sam Cohn but expected little help from that quarter. "Sam loved Bob, but I never trusted his opinion," the editor said. "He liked everything a little *too* much."

As *Dancin'* was moved into the Broadhurst Theatre for the start of New York previews, Kander and Ebb's latest show, *The Act*, was playing next door at the Majestic Theatre. Bob stopped by one day after a preview to visit Liza Minnelli, the star of the show. He found Fred Ebb in her dressing room.

"How's the show going?" Fred asked about *Dancin'*.

"Maybe it's okay, maybe it isn't. One of these days they're going to find me out," said the triple prize winner, and the remark made Ebb shudder, not just for Bob but for himself. "The worst thing about it," the lyricist later mused, "was being reminded of how I shared that fear and of how I had that same low self-esteem."

Just before the Sunday matinee preview of *Dancin'*, when all the critics were coming, Fosse walked onto his show's set, a stage left bare except for a striking series of vertical louvres that could change angles and colors. The dancers were on stage, flexing and stretching, and Fosse crouched, watching them. One of the dancers approached him, and as if drawn by her boldness, the others converged, forming a circle around him.

"If you could choose anything you wanted to come out of the show," she asked in Truth Game-style, "what would you want most of all?"

What would he want most of all? He looked from one dancer to the next and then to the next. He played to each of them. "If I could get anything out of this?" he repeated. He was pensive and paused before replying: "I'd want hair."

There were hesitant smiles, but he betrayed only the start of a grin. "Yeah," he said, "I'd like hair." He turned to a second dancer. "Like yours," and, to another, "Like yours," and to yet a third, "Like yours."

He was of course yanking his dancers back to reality, to the difference between show business and life. He really did, most of all, want hair and he was telling them that a solid grip on basic truths—perspective—was the one defense a performer could have against the audience rejection that was always threatening, just over the footlights.

Earlier in the day, Bernard Jacobs, the Shubert Organization president, had telephoned to wish him good luck with the critics, and Bob said he was still fixing the show. Now, as he strolled offstage, leaving his dancers to their stretching, he ran into the other moneyman, Gerald Schoenfeld, the Shubert board chairman.

"I spoke to Bernie," Schoenfeld began. He was a white-haired, rosy-cheeked, cherubic-looking man and a tough lawyer. "I'm delighted that you're still working on the show." With that he placed a paternal hand on the shoulder of a Bob Fosse who disliked physical demonstrations of affection.

"Yes, I am," he replied.

"Terrific," Schoenfeld said. "What are you doing about that dream barre number?"

"The matinee ladies are going to love it," Bob said.

"Well, I hope you're right," the executive said, "but I have to tell you, yours is a minority opinion."

Schoenfeld's hand was still on Fosse's shoulder but not for long. Bob angrily shoved it away and snapped, "That's a goddamned lousy thing to say to me at this time."

It was just ten minutes before the start of the critics' performance. For a moment Schoenfeld feared that there might be a fistfight ("If he had taken a swing at me I would have punched him right there"), but Fosse only wheeled and stalked away.

Dancin' was not rejected, but neither did it receive wonderful reviews, because it was not a wonderful show. Some critics gave it high marks. Clive Barnes, who had moved to the New York *Post* from the *Times*, even showed up at the opening night party. Bob was sitting at a table with Jessica Lange ("He was thrilled about her coming with him," Jane Aurthur said. "She was like a trophy"). Barnes leaned down and offered quotable praise from his not yet printed review ("tremendous," "fantastic"). However, Richard Eder, his successor at the *Times*, was not as impressed. The next week Bob Aurthur asked his friend Arthur Gelb, the managing editor of the *Times*, to consider special treatment for *Dancin'*. In turn, Gelb suggested that dance critic Anna Kisselgoff write an additional review of the show. When hers also turned out to be negative, it was not printed. "That was a rare instance of a kind of censorship at the *Times*," said one member of the newspaper's cultural staff.

Dancin' did not suffer from the lack of a good review in *The New York Times*. Audiences flocked to the show, and because he was himself one of the producers, it was to become the greatest financial success of Bob's stage career. He had never worried about money before, and now he would never have to worry about it at all. But the only thing that Bernie Jacobs would say to him about the show was "You call that dancing?"

Fosse was having dinner with the writer Peter Maas at Wally's Restaurant when David Begelman came in, "accompanied by a big entourage," Maas remembered. Begelman stopped at their table to say hello. It was at this self-same restaurant that he had eaten so often with Bob. Now he was up to his throat in scandal. Even the world beyond show business was reading about his possible criminal prosecution.

"After Bobby and I finished eating and got outside," Maas said, "it was pouring rain. We were huddled under that little canopy Wally's had, getting drenched, trying vainly to hail a cab for maybe half an hour when suddenly, there was [Begelman] again, sweeping by us with his entourage and stepping into a stretch limousine and roaring off into the night.

" 'You know,' Bobby said, 'there's something wrong here. We should be in that limo, and he should be in jail.' "

Then he went home to the apartment that David had once given to him while Begelman went home to Los Angeles to turn himself in to the Burbank police on four felony counts.

22

Many of Fosse's friendships carried hints of the entourage. Bob Aurthur's relationship with him was one of those. There was a touch of the devotee in it, and so, not by chance, when the first draft of *All That Jazz* earned Aurthur enough money to move back to New York City, he and Jane found a place only steps away from Fosse. They were on Central Park South, which is actually East 59th Street, and their block-through building had a back entrance on 58th Street, across the street from Bobby's place. Aurthur could just walk his rewrites over, and the only difference between this and working in Quogue was that some of the time Nicole was there, for she had moved out from Gwen and in with her father.

Fifteen is an age of biological and psychological turmoil, especially for girls, and it is almost as exhausting for their parents. The 1970s seemed only to exacerbate the experience. Nicole was part of the era's radical atmosphere—what was called the Dalton Rebellion at the innovative and artistic Dalton School in Manhattan. Gwen was as protective with the teenager as she had been with the child. When the girl was put in a taxi, for instance, her mother would take down the name and hack number of the driver, and when someone sent her home in a taxi, Gwen insisted that they do the same. It was the kind of babying that could make life exasperating for a teenager, and inevitably, as Bob said, "They were at each other's throats." Nicole escaped to her dad's place.

He tried the casual approach. "I don't have time to watch you," he told her. "I don't have a lot of dope in the house or anything like that, that's the rules of the house, and I gotta trust you. You can lie to me, and I'm sure if you're anything like your father, you're a pretty good liar. I just have to trust you're going to be okay and do the right thing."

He would take her to the Aurthurs' for dinner and even take her along on dates. "She had a great relationship with Ann Reinking," Jane Aurthur recalled, "but less so with Jessica Lange, who is a cool type." She had occasional conflicts with some of the younger girlfriends. One evening, Bob brought a young date to see Nicole in a school show, and it was plain that the boys backstage were ogling the girl for themselves. Afterward, Bob took the two young ladies to Trader Vic's for dinner, around the corner from his place, "and Nicole cut this girl up" (he thought, "for no reason"). Finally he said to his daughter, "I don't understand what you're doing."

"I know a lot about you," Nicole said, glaring across the table at the girl.

"Well, Nicole," said Bob the peacemaker, "you owe it to her, if you know a lot about her—what do you know about her?"

"I can tell you all about her," Nicole said in a mean, vague, belligerent, classically adolescent way.

"And then," Bob remembered, "she went after her—'and this and this and this'—real cruel. I never understood why."

They resumed their taped interviews, Fosse and Aurthur, now closing in on the major figures in the story—Ann, Gwen, Nicole, and Bob's psychiatrist, Dr. Clifford Sager. Reinking pondered his dangerous habits, telling Bob Aurthur, "I don't like it. I often take a cigarette out of his mouth," she said, "but the other things [presumably drinking and drugs], it's really wrong, it's an avoidance. It's a way of dealing with his own self-anger. He is so angry," Reinking said.

But what was he so angry about?

"He doesn't like himself," she said, "and if someone else puts him down, he'll say, 'Fuck you, you're wrong,' but believe it."

Gwen, during her interview, told Bob Aurthur, "I was a magnificent tool for Bob because I absolutely trusted him. He told me, 'When I get angry, I know I get deranged.' "

On the subject of marital infidelity she said, "I was faithful when I didn't know *why* I was being faithful, and Bobby didn't take advantage of a double standard—he's the *victim* of a double standard."

Nicole, in her interview with Bob Aurthur, said she believed that her parents still cared for each other. Asked about her father's heart attack, the youngster remembered saying to him, "If your main goal is to kill yourself, then why don't you do it fast?" When Fosse himself interviewed her, he asked her (of all people) what she would say if he died. His fifteen-year-old smartie replied, "The first thing I'd say is, 'I told you so!' " She paused before soberly adding, "I'd be upset and very angry at the same time."

During that interview, Nicole also talked about the unfairness of her dad's double standard. It was a particularly hot topic in those days of burgeoning feminism. She wondered how he could possibly have been angry with Ann Reinking when Fosse thought she was having an affair with Charles Ward after they broke up.

"You mean that, when you were going with her, you were going with other girls?"

"Yes."

"And you got mad at *her?*"

Nicole also talked about dealing with Gwen's boyfriend, Jerry Lanning.

"Sometimes he tries to act like a father."

"Tell him," Bob said, "you've got a father."

Finally, Nicole allowed as that the hot new word at Dalton was "shitsorelli."

Fosse had Aurthur sit in on the interview with his psychiatrist, Dr. Clifford Sager, who told his patient, "You're very cynical about women. Starting with your experiences in burlesque, you had to prove that every woman is a whore. You cut yourself off from letting yourself be loved. You'd let yourself be adored but not loved."

Turning to Bob Aurthur, the psychiatrist added, "Fosse reaches for love but he doesn't allow himself to find it. You see, Bobby," he said, "it all goes back to the disappointment you had about your ability as a performer and the constant need to keep proving yourself. What you haven't proved is your lovability. Applause isn't a substitute for being loved."

Fosse's circle of writer friends had widened into something resembling a literary salon cum fan club. Although Neil Simon and Paddy Chayefsky stood apart as special intimates, the circle included, besides Herb Gardner and Peter Maas, such diverse writers as E. L. Doctorow, Pete Hamill, Noel Behn, Peter Stone, and occasionally Bruce Jay Friedman. Most of them had houses in the Hamptons, and at one time or another Fosse whimsically offered them a class he planned to give in Dancing for Writers. Doctorow remembered receiving a birthday present from Bob of "a pair of Capezios with taps, white gloves, a white scarf and an enameled walking stick, and a sweatshirt that said *Broadway.*"

Among these writers, Noel Behn seemed the most devoted. A successful novelist (*The Kremlin Letter, The Big Stick-Up at Brinks*), he was also affectionately known as the King of 57th Street. On occasions when he joined Bob and the group of the day for lunch at the Carnegie Delicatessen, he would lead the postprandial parade, greeting friends, acquaintances, and the world as they strolled northward, wide across the sidewalk as if a river armada, up Seventh Avenue and east to Carnegie Hall at the corner of 57th Street before the expedition peeled off for Sixth Avenue.

On such a fine afternoon, Behn joined Bob, Paddy, and their sturdy ex-prizefighting pal, Eddie White. The King of 57th Street was feeling particularly regal that day and suggested a friendly bet of one dollar from each stroller on the matter, he said, of "which of our group would be greeted first." They set out from the Carnegie Delicatessen.

White felt confident about the bet. "Some people who might know Bob Fosse or Paddy Chayefsky might recognize them but would not dare to speak to them, but I knew every storekeeper and bag lady by their first names."

Not on this day. "From 55th to 57th Streets," Behn remembered, "Paddy had a decided edge. That day no one said hello to him." They turned at 57th Street and approached Carnegie Hall, which Behn called "Fosse Country. Nothing. My advantage lay next door at the Russian Tea Room. I went as unnoticed as they did. Our walk was near at end with no one having been recognized. Bobby wasn't taking it too well [and in relating this anecdote, Behn didn't seem aware of the significance that being recognized had in the Fosse life]. Then she came into view. Ponytail and swayback and turned-out feet. A dancer talking to another dancer."

Bob tilted his hat to a jaunty angle and fluffed out his shirt. He grinned at the girl and "slid his hands into his pockets," Behn remembered, "and circled her, tilting backward. She couldn't place him. So he danced. Right there on 57th Street, Bob Fosse danced for her."

With this, of course, she knew him. She had not recognized his face, but she did recognize his dance.

"And," Behn said, "she did an answer step."

"Why, you're Bob Fosse," the girl said, and Bob turned to his friends and stuck out a palm for the payoff. He always paid his bets promptly and expected the same in return. They each slapped a dollar bill into his hand, and the dancer said to him, "Discover me," a kindred spirit indeed.

Chayefsky and White were looking on but were not partaking of the cheer. Paddy wasn't feeling well, and Eddie knew it. They worked out in the same gym, and just days earlier they had, as usual, changed into their shorts, T-shirts, and sneakers in the locker room. As Eddie started toward the running track, Paddy said, "I don't think I have the energy today. I can't run with you."

He had long since broken his three-pack-a-day smoking habit and seemed dedicated to physical fitness, and so White was particularly concerned.

"Come on, Paddy," he said, throwing an arm around his pal's shoulder. "It'll do you good," but after one lap Chayefsky quit, and since then, Eddie noticed a descendant gloom. Paddy was stopping by at his apartment almost every weekend but didn't want to talk and didn't want to see anyone. He just wanted to do his crossword puzzle and watch sports on television, and his arguing had taken a strange turn. His movie *Network* had suffered from a vagueness of harangue, and now Paddy was emerging as a knee-jerk-liberal turncoat, what some called a New Conservative. He was devoting a curiously large amount of time to writing an article about the guilt of Alger Hiss during the postwar era of Communist witch-hunts. At one dinner with Fosse and Elia Kazan, he presented his opinions. "Most people disagreed with me about the testimony I gave in the Hiss case," Kazan remembered, "but Paddy supported me, and Fosse agreed with him." Eddie White was sure that *Altered States* was the underlying reason for such unlikely behavior as well as Chayefsky's depressed and darkening spirits.

Paddy's novel was being made into a movie as planned, but the filming was definitely not going as planned. Chayefsky had himself agreed to the discharge of Arthur Penn, an old friend, as the director. The choice of replacement was strange indeed: Ken Russell, a specialist in the fantastic and even bizarre. Paddy had protested so strongly about Russell, once work resumed, that he was barred from the set. Now the daily rushes were being shipped to him from the Texas location on videotape. It was enough, White thought, to depress anyone.

Fosse had his own movie to worry about. Six days after *Dancin'* opened on Broadway, he began preproduction work on *All That Jazz*. Richard Dreyfuss was going to play the lead, that much was settled. The actor had agreed to work for the Screen Actors Guild minimum salary of $785 a week. It was before he won the Academy Award for *The Goodbye Girl* and before he appeared in *Close Encounters of the Third Kind*. While Bob felt, "Rick wasn't built for it physically, he had such energy, such drive, such recklessness, I thought, well, I'll somehow fake around the dancing. There are choreographers that sit on chairs. That's the kind I'll make him."

In the movie, the name of this Fosse alter ego was Joe Gideon, presumably inspired by Paddy Chayefsky's 1961 play, *Gideon*, although it is hard to find a connection between Bob Fosse and Chayefsky's farmer who comes to save the Hebrews.

He engaged Alan Heim, Jules Fisher, and Phil Friedman to play themselves. Leland Palmer, who had more or less played Gwen in *Pippin*, would play her again (Audrey Paris) in the movie. Jessica Lange was going to be the Angel of Death. Bob couldn't get Dr. Billy Gay to perform the on-screen surgery, and so he hired Dr. John Hutchinson to do it (Hutchinson's hobby was medical cinematography). Then he put Nancy Bird, Hutchinson's chief nurse, in the movie. She became the medical consultant on the picture when Dr. Hutchinson convinced Dan Melnick that the studio truly could not afford him. For a time it was incomprehensible to the Hollywood people that *anyone* might consider himself beyond the financial reach of a movie studio. Dr. Hutchinson knew better. The then surgical fee for a bypass operation was $3,000, and he performed four of them a day. In 1979, $12,000 a day was a fair income. When it became clear that there was indeed someone beyond the studio's pocketbook (and therefore something conceivably more important than moviemaking), they settled for Nancy Bird.

Melnick's balancing act as executive producer was going to involve doing right by the studio while looking out for the best interests of his personal projects, *Altered States* and *All That Jazz*. To him, the repeated auditions that Bob put Ann Reinking through were deliberately nasty. "Bobby," Dan said, "you are torturing the girl. You know and I know that she is going to end up doing the part. Stop doing this, because it is very destructive to the character."

"But I've got to be sure," Bob said.

"Sure of what? That she can play herself?"

In fact, Bob's entire relationship with Ann seems to have been punishing, just like the relationship with Gwen. When Reinking was hired at last, and casting was complete, the work began—four weeks of script rehearsal to be followed by four weeks of dance rehearsal while the sets were being built on the Astoria, Queens, sound stages. Dreyfuss arrived to, as Melnick said, "hang out with Bob at dance rehearsals."

The actor was already feeling uncomfortable with the dancer aspect of his role. Bob told him, "I promise I will make this work for you. I know how to protect you. I'm not out to embarrass you." And ultimately Dreyfuss would find it more difficult coping with the emotional aspect of choreography, and its factor of cruelty, than with actual movement. One day, as the actor watched Bob give dancers screen tests and the occasional hard time, Fosse turned to him and said, "I'm having a problem getting the performances I want. I don't think they can give me the performances I want."

"I think they can," Dreyfuss said.

"How?"

"By seducing them, stroking them, liking them, and getting them on your side. Then they'll do anything you want."

Bob's reaction was defensive. "I think you're saying," he said, "that I don't know how to direct this picture."

Dreyfuss was startled by "the leap in his mind. I couldn't figure it out."

"Look," he said, "let's put you and me down to oil and water."

Bob simply repeated what he'd just said: "You don't think I can direct this film."

"Okay, Bobby," Dreyfuss wearily said. "If that's what you want me to say, I'll say it. 'I don't think you can direct this picture.' " And he walked out, went to his hotel, and called Dan Melnick in California.

"I have a problem," he said. "What I am about to tell you is unprecedented. I can't do the movie."

"For God's sake, why?"

"I lack the life experience to play the part," Dreyfuss said evasively. "I'm concerned about going to work every day with a Bob Fosse who is speaking Greek, and I'm speaking Turkish. I just can't find a way to do it. Much as I respect him and *like* him, his method of working is different from my internal method of working. I told Bob, I need a warm, caring environment."

"And what did he say?"

"He said I would have it."

"So?"

"I just can't convince myself that I could ever have been a choreographer or a tap dancer."

Dreyfuss knew that breaking the contract "was going to cost me a shitload of money," but he was unnerved by Bob's icy temper and confused by the paranoia. Melnick at least appreciated the actor's candor. "There was no bullshit about Rick," he said, "and you can't get a great performance from an actor you have to drag to the set," but he wasn't giving up yet. The first to hear the news was Bob Aurthur, who wrote in his journal, "It made me physically ill and very angry." For him, of course, the movie about Bob Fosse's heart crisis was critical to his career. He was being given one last chance with this picture. Clutching at hope, he suggested to Melnick that Dreyfuss probably just wanted to renegotiate his contract ("He keeps telling us that Dusty Hoffman is getting two million dollars for this picture, Marlon three million for that. It's like he knows every deal going down"). Sam Cohn tried to pacify the writer. "Don't tell Bob yet," the agent said. "This too shall pass. Dreyfuss has a signed deal and cannot get out." But Aurthur was unnerved, and he called Melnick again. "Look, Dan," he said, "we're spending nine thousand dollars a day in preproduction. At no time did Rick indicate that he had serious problems with the script. In fact, quite the opposite."

Melnick again reassured him, saying that as they had been considering a short postponement of filming anyhow, there was time to straighten out the problem. This did not allay his anxieties as Aurthur watched Fosse dance alone in front of the rehearsal studio mirror, working out steps for the movie's big opening number. It was going to be the dance auditions for a Broadway musical. It was going to be the Fosse Combinations, filmed with a horde of dancers. It was going to be Bob Fosse's answer to A *Chorus Line*.

Aurthur blurted out the Dreyfuss development. To his amazement, Bobby was not angry, in fact he was pleased. Then he said something that was positively startling:

"I want to play the part."

"What?"

Dreyfuss had himself wondered whether that had been behind Fosse's behavior. When Aurthur grasped the seriousness of Bob's suggestion, he said evenly, "If I propose this to Melnick, he will say I'm crazy and four men in white suits are coming."

"You must support me in this," Bob said urgently. "We'll fly to L.A., I'll read for the role, I'll test for Melnick."

Aurthur shrugged and said fine, but it was hardly fine. It was *Damn Yankees* and *The Conquering Hero*. It was *Pal Joey*. The performer in Fosse had never died, he had only been buried.

Melnick, after meeting with Dreyfuss, called Bob Aurthur to tell him that the actor was not angling for more money. At the New York end of the call, Fosse listened in. He covered his mouthpiece and whispered to Aurthur, "Tell him about me." The writer dived in. Why even bother with Dreyfuss, he said to the executive producer, when Fosse himself can play Joe Gideon? After a long pause, Melnick said, "Aside from the fact that he's too old, it would result in a critical bloodbath. Look, without Dreyfuss we don't have a picture. He's talking to us again tomorrow morning." That was the end of the telephone call, but Fosse was not about to let this acting chance slip away. He was also aware that Bob Aurthur was worried about more mundane things.

"Listen, how about me lending you fifty thousand dollars?"

"What?"

"I know you're broke." There was no denying that. "You can pay me back in ten years. Twenty. Whenever you want."

"Bobby," a moved Aurthur said, "you are probably the most generous man I have ever met."

"I know," Fosse grinned, and he opened the script to change the subject and read out some comments that Paddy had scrawled in it. Then they auditioned bit players through the afternoon. They were pretending that the picture was going to proceed without complications. Toward evening, Melnick called to say that Dreyfuss felt strongly about his decision but had agreed to come to New York and would talk to Bobby "one on one," which meant minus Bob Aurthur. "Rick assures me," Dan said to Bob Aurthur, "that he has great respect and regard for you."

"Fuck him too," the writer said. "If I never see the putz again, I'll be a better man for it."

But after the telephone call, Fosse not only showed little interest in mollifying Dreyfuss, he accused Aurthur of not backing up his campaign to play himself.

"I don't call that supporting my playing the part," he said. "A dancer is absolutely needed to play Gideon. Twenty years ago it would've been Astaire or Kelly."

Well, well.

"Neither Kelly nor Astaire on their best day," Aurthur said, "could act the part we've written." But he later remembered, "It was a totally fruitless discussion." Fosse was committed to portraying himself in the movie.

Dreyfuss ultimately did ask Aurthur to come to the meeting, which was held in an office at the William Morris Agency, and when they arrived, the actor was already seated behind his agent's desk, "looking very contrite," Aurthur recalled. "He has chosen to play pain, that this hurts him more than us."

As Dreyfuss launched into the agony of his decision, Fosse interrupted to make a dramatic plea that he reconsider ("So sincere," Aurthur wrote in his journal, "I almost believed it"). Dreyfuss let Fosse have this scene, and when it was over, he said, "It just comes down to an inability to work together. It's oil and water," he repeated. "It's not the script. It's not that I consider the part too much of a stretch. I still think the movie will be phenomenal. I just feel that at this time in my life, I don't think that I can handle the pain necessary to achieve the results."

"Richard," Aurthur said softly, "is there *any* possibility of an accommodation?"

The actor shook his head with a tremendous and overwhelming sadness, and then it was Fosse's turn ("time to begin *his* little acting number," as Aurthur put it).

He began with an unforgivably low device, saying how, only last night "my daughter, Nicole, had said, 'What a shame, Dad. You're such a great director, and Richard Dreyfuss is such a great actor. It would be tragic if you couldn't resolve this and work together." ("Tears came to my eyes like they were supposed to," Aurthur remembered, "but Dreyfuss was singularly unmoved.")

Fosse urged the actor, "Don't make the decision now. Please, Rick. Sleep on it. Think about it overnight. Call me in the morning."

Dreyfuss nodded as if he were already pondering the matter. Aurthur took his turn, this time playing the tough cop.

"You do understand the consequences of such a decision," he said. "I do."

"You have a signed deal. Based on your commitment, we're deep into this picture."

Dreyfuss nodded again.

"There are dancers who have sublet apartments in Los Angeles to come to New York. People have given up their jobs."

Dreyfuss's head "sinks lower and lower onto the desk," Aurthur remembered, and when the lecture ended, Fosse picked up his cue as the nice cop. "I don't think you should have said that," he chided Aurthur. "You shouldn't make Rick feel guilty. As it happens, I've seen a side to him today that I'd never seen before—softness, contriteness, not the guy who is 'on' all the time. These are qualities that would work for Joe Gideon. I feel stronger about you playing him than ever before."

"I appreciate that, Bobby," Dreyfuss said, rising from his chair, and with that signal, everyone got up to think about it overnight.

In the elevator going downstairs, Aurthur said to Fosse, "You didn't have to knock my producer's pitch, with all the sublets and the actors' jobs."

"You noticed I waited till you were all finished," Bobby laughed.

But Dreyfuss would not be convinced. Soon the entire staff, from the dancers to the Teamster drivers, was being told that there was going to be a delay and that they would be on half salaries while the producers looked for a new star. Bob Aurthur put on his producer's hat and went to work on the cost of the delay, which, at an anticipated eleven weeks, he estimated was going to be more than $350,000. Fosse went to work on his beard, dying it dark for the Tony Awards (he would win as Best Choreographer for *Dancin'*). Richard Dreyfuss would later say, "For a few years I told myself that I was well out of it, and then I finally faced up to it—I'd given up a chance to work with Bob Fosse, and it was stupid of me. I told him so myself."

The search for a new Joe Gideon took on the intensity of a manhunt. Dan Melnick suggested Paul Newman ("who is in New York," Aurthur wrote in his journal, "at, God help us, the UN disarmament meeting"). Sidney Lumet suggested Alan Alda or Gene Hackman. (Lumet had himself agreed to play Paddy Chayefsky in the picture, although the part was later cut.) Sam Cohn repeatedly recommended Roy Scheider, who was not his personal client but was represented by his agency. He arranged for Aurthur and Fosse to meet the actor in his office, and they liked him on sight ("a *very* nice man," Aurthur felt). Scheider was eagerly and earnestly agreeable to whatever Fosse suggested, whether it was about the part or his working methods, although he was no more of a dancer than Richard Dreyfuss.

"How old are you, Roy?" Bob Aurthur asked.

"Do you want to know how old I really am," the actor said, "or how old I tell people?"

"Either one is okay with me."

"The truth is I'm forty-five. I tell people I'm forty-two. Also," he said, touching his hair ("obviously darkened," Aurthur said), "if I let this grow, it comes in gray."

The writer felt "sad and sorry for him," he wrote in his journal. "Here is an almost superstar edging toward a million dollars a picture, and he feels he has to strip himself for us like an actor going for his first job. No wonder these guys get to be monsters once they have the power. Years of being demeaned, of humbling themselves, all that *bullshit* an actor has to go through. Once they get the power, they have to pay everyone back."

When Dan Melnick arrived from California for the grand casting conference with Fosse, Aurthur, and Cohn, they went over the long list of candidates. Newman had not taken the offer seriously ("Hasn't read the script but Joanne did"). Melnick felt that Roy Scheider "is not charming enough." Then Robert Alan Aurthur again suggested that Bob Fosse play Joe Gideon.

The silence was embarrassing, until everyone attacked him for even lending words to such an idea. Fosse attacked him too. Melnick, refusing to allow the suggestion to lie seriously on the table, asked, "Why are you doing this to me? Bobby would die in the middle of shooting, and I don't want to be responsible." Then he suggested George Segal. Agents had called offering Elliot Gould and Robert Blake. In the midst of the meeting, Warren Beatty himself telephoned. He had been teasing them for a year through an agent. Apparently now that there was competition, he wanted the part.

"Just do me a favor," he said to Aurthur, "and don't tell anyone I called," meaning Melnick. Beatty had his pride.

"Okay."

"You'll ask Bobby to keep it quiet?"

"I'll ask him."

They tossed more names into the hopper. Alan Bates (too British), Jack Lemmon (too old). Dan Melnick privately told Bob Aurthur, "Don't let Sam Cohn stampede you into Scheider. Jon Voight is reading it now." But after Fosse watched a special screening of *Coming Home* (for which Voight won an Academy Award), he decided that he would go with Scheider. Probably.

"Let's talk to Warren Beatty some more," Melnick pleaded, hoping for at least some box office attraction to make this death musical potentially profitable. He was very concerned about Scheider's ability to communicate "lovability."

"I forgot to tell you," Aurthur replied. "Warren said he would play the part only if Gideon doesn't die."

"Well, then," Melnick said, "fuck that idea. I mean," he said, sardonic but cheerful, "God forbid we should make a commercial picture."

With the idling expense mounting at an alarming rate, the pressure rose to make an immediate decision. Cohn urged Melnick to accept Roy Scheider, and Fosse offered to work alone with the actor for a week before making a final decision. They met with him at what Aurthur called "a charm session where Roy was supposed to prove that he could be lovable." What none of them seemed to realize in the lovability department was that they were already confusing Scheider with Fosse, mistaking the actor for the lines he was reading from the script—lines Fosse shared in writing. They were wondering about warmth and lovability in Scheider when the script had come to grasp and present the separate, sometimes unrecognizable, and sometimes chilly and unloving/unlovable parts of Robert Louis Fosse himself.

It was almost too much to believe. After all the months of delay, filming was to start in two weeks. The only thing they needed was a leading man.

Meantime, Sam Cohn took the two Bobs and Tony Walton to lunch at his version of the Carnegie Delicatessen, the Russian Tea Room on West 57th Street. He wanted them to meet Giuseppe Rotunno, a man who had worked for one of Fosse's idols, Federico Fellini. A cameraman finally had to be chosen and Rotunno would have been the choice except that while his comprehension was good, his spoken English was halting. He had filmed American movies before, *Carnal Knowledge* among them. That was the Sam Cohn connection. Its director, Mike Nichols, was his client, but Fosse was a more visually oriented director than Nichols, and he was worried about the language problem. "For a while," Tony Walton remembered, "he was moving away from Rotunno, but I argued that with so many levels of reality in the movie—hallucinatory, fantasy, memory, naturalism—the one essential that would help clarify the finished film for an audience was a strong and confident visual sense. That was why I was so strongly for Rotunno." And ultimately, Fosse agreed.

Then he went off to spend the week he had promised to work with Scheider. Even now he wasn't sure about the actor coming across as a dancer. "I think Roy can do it," he told Melnick, "but I'm not sure. I can't even take the responsibility for telling you that I know he can do it, but I have a hunch he can."

Melnick wryly remembered that "we anguished about it in a Talmudic way, but I finally gave in." Bob Aurthur was touched by the moment when Melnick finally sighed and said, "Okay, make the deal." As Aurthur noted in his journal, "Dan is going with Fosse's impulse, betting millions of dollars that Fosse is right, and he is wrong."

The legendary Palace Theatre on Broadway was the setting for the opening sequence, "On Broadway." There were hundreds of dancers on stage, including such Fosse veterans as Sandahl Bergman, Kathy Doby, and Jennifer Nairn-Smith. Seated a few rows back, Bob watched Roy Scheider crouch at the center of the stage in his Fosse costume of black shirt, black pants, and black boots. The actor looked a little taller, a little sleeker, a little more stylish, a little more like an actor than the original, but the original had his eye on the dancers, and turning to his editor, Alan Heim, he said, "I can't believe how many of these auditions I've been through. How cruel and terrible they are."

Several rows behind him, Bob Aurthur clutched at his side, ashen with pain, his brow awash in perspiration. He had hardly been able to drive in from East Hampton, it hurt so badly, but he hadn't let his wife take the wheel. He just kept saying, "Bobby doesn't believe me. He thinks I'm faking."

During a rehearsal break, Aurthur's pain was so obvious to Scheider that the actor gave him the name of a chiropractor, but when he saw the man, he was referred to a physician, who told him, "You are in this great pain, my friend, because you have two broken ribs, and I'm reserving a room for you in New York Hospital."

Even with Aurthur in the hospital, Fosse would not believe that anything was really wrong with him. ("What's broken ribs?" he scoffed. "I danced on Broadway with broken ribs.") However, he agreed with Melnick to keep the hospitalization secret from the studio. Nobody wanted another delay or to cost Bob Aurthur his desperately needed job. They agreed that the movie would be produced from the hospital. A secretary was assigned to the room, and Aurthur was delivered daily reports on the filming, which was already behind schedule. "California was calling," his wife recalled. "The studio was getting upset."

Fosse refused to visit Bob in the hospital even though Sam Cohn kept urging him to do so as a matter of simple decency. Cohn, despite a reputation for toughness, was perhaps Bob Aurthur's most frequent visitor except for Jane. Fosse stayed away because he was truly mortified by hospitals, but that wasn't his only reason. As might have been anticipated, the producer relationship had fractured their friendship. Dan Melnick didn't even think that Aurthur and Fosse would have been able to work together for the rest of the movie. "If Bob [Aurthur] had not gone into the hospital," he said, "they would not have gone the distance together." It was the same old problem with authority. Melnick laughed, saying, "Bobby had a resistance to authority combined with a need for the approval of authority figures." And it was probably that simple.

During an interview a few months later, it was suggested that he "say something nice about Bob Aurthur because *Jazz* is supposed to be a comeback movie for him." Fosse's response was "What happened to Bob Aurthur is as follows, and I hope you never print this. [She didn't.] Bob Aurthur was a swell fellow while he was retired. He became a total prick once I gave him a job. He went to East Hampton, married, had the kid, became a swell guy . . . a wonderful, warm person, and as soon as I gave him this job, he turned into this—he just played producer. Fake. I can't stand fakes. Either you do your job, or you don't do it. If that's cold," he told an astonished Chris Chase, "yeah, then I guess I'm cold."

And Aurthur had positively adored him.

Bob Aurthur's room was on the same floor of New York Hospital that Fosse's had been on. Aurthur even walked down the hall in his bathrobe to smoke a cigarette in the same lounge that Fosse had used when he'd had his bypass surgery. He coughed his way down that hall just as Bobby had, but of course the coughing was doubly painful for Aurthur, with his broken ribs. In fact, the ribs were not the real problem; in fact, the ribs had been *broken* by the coughing. "The terrible cough," Jane said, "was from the fluid in his lungs." The real problem he was dealing with was lung cancer. It was with lung cancer that he coughed his way down the hall to the lounge for his cigarette.

The diagnosis was not made until he had been in the hospital for ten days. By then his wife had the medical education that is the unwanted side benefit of a husband's illness. "He had the kind of cancer," she said, "that throws off cells in liquid, so it's not a tumor you can operate on. He had adenocarcinoma in one lung," and she shook her head in disgust. "Ten days it took them to find out."

Only when Fosse learned that Bob Aurthur had cancer and only at Sam Cohn's insistence did he finally agree to visit his sometime, long-time, one-time friend in the hospital. He had been telling Dan Melnick to "keep that little prick honest," but he was probably alienated only in part by Aurthur's role as the producer of *All That Jazz*. The fact of his dying, not a movie about dying but real dying, *that* repelled him. He was not drawn to the hospital, the cancer, or the wash of death.

Julie Hagerty was waiting for him at home. They'd met when she had tried out for a small part in the movie. Aurthur had urged him to hire this "adorable, cute little girl."

"No, no," Bob had replied. "She's a model. She can't act, but I'm going to see that girl," and he made a date with her. Then he introduced her to Nicole. Julie was wonderful with children. When she was at the Aurthurs', she would stroll into their daughter's room and ask the ten-year-old, "Hey, would you like to play cards with me?" as if she was just another kid. Bob was tired of running around, tired of looking for last-minute dates. He had hung up the telephone in the rehearsal studio just the other night after trying vainly to rustle up a last-minute companion and plaintively said to one of the guys, "You're married. You're lucky. You don't have to do this kind of thing anymore." He was beginning to find it silly at his age and would say so—silly and pathetic. He liked Julie Hagerty. "She doesn't seem interested in acting at all," he told Jane Aurthur. "She's a model, that's fine. Let her go model."

It was easier to visit Aurthur when he went home for a long weekend, something that the hospital seemed to arrange for its own convenience. "They were on a skeleton crew," Jane said, "and nothing could be done there anyhow." She had been given a prescription along with her husband, and her pharmacist was reading it with a perplexed expression on his face.

"What's wrong?" she asked. "It's only Demerol, isn't it?"

"I never saw a prescription like this," he said.

She looked over his shoulder. "Why? Is there anything peculiar?"

"Well, it's for seven hundred fifty tablets," he said, "and that's my whole month's supply."

"What can I tell you?" she said. "That's a New York Hospital prescription paper. That's what they gave me."

Now, as her husband slept and as she sat and talked with Bob, she brought it up again.

"They gave him a prescription for seven hundred fifty Demerols. Bob's only taking twelve a day. He's only home for the weekend."

"Listen, Jane," Fosse said, leaning forward in his chair, "I've never taken Demerol. Joan Simon told me she had one of her babies on it, and it was the greatest trip she ever took."

It gave Jane Aurthur a needed laugh. "Okay," she chuckled. "I'll save some for you, but you can't have them while you're shooting the movie."

That night she suddenly thought about why the prescription might have called for so much Demerol. "Maybe the doctor gave them to me to kill him if I needed to."

She didn't need to. Robert Alan Aurthur died without their assistance on November 22, 1978, at the age of fifty-six, five weeks after he'd entered the hospital. As he had told Fosse, there was a provision in his will for a party "at a Sardi's type of restaurant." It wasn't as elaborate as the Fosse provision, because he wasn't leaving that kind of estate. "It was just a matter of inviting his friends," his widow said. "To have a drink on him and no eulogy."

She asked Sam Cohn to help. "I have to arrange this party," she said. "Bob wanted it. This thing has got to be."

"Why don't we do it at Wally's?" the agent suggested, and it was a good idea. He even persuaded the management to open the restaurant on a Sunday evening for the party's sake. But Jane had to do the inviting. She found that "people didn't want to deal with me—the new widow." Too, there were show business acquaintants who treated it as a purely social event. The restaurant placed a 150 person limit on her invitation list, but people actually called up asking to be invited, and "there were even people," Jane remembered, "who crashed. I mean names."

At the party she told Fosse, "You know, you guys dream up this little gem in your wills, and you don't realize that someone has to *give* the party . . . I mean someone has to make a list, and someone has to do the inviting."

"You're right."

"Who's going to do yours?"

"I don't know," Bob said, knowing that his provision was not for a party but just for friends to go out and have dinner on him. "Maybe Gwen," he said, and then he paused and added quietly, "I'd better make up my list."

23

If *All That Jazz* is Bob Fosse's movie version of his own life—his life the way he saw it—why does he die in it? Was that merely an artistic decision, made for the sake of a story, or did he think he should have died or in some way actually *did* die during his heart crisis? Was this a paranoid's fantasy, punishing the world with his death in hope of watching the guilt-struck grieving at the funeral?

In the movie, Fosse's alter ego, Joe Gideon, in fact directs his own death, and so the movie presents a Fosse masterminding a Fosse figure masterminding a Fosse figure. Gideon, perched atop a camera boom, photographs and even gives acting notes to his dying self, which may well be Fosse's view of himself, an outsider at his own life.

Julie Hagerty moved out, not that she had ever really moved in. She had moved in just enough to push Ann Reinking out. Bob never allowed anyone to move in entirely, not even Ann ("We were together five years," he said, "but we only lived together about six months"). He wouldn't or couldn't let anybody near. The question of whether he was unloving or simply undemonstrative remained. He said he loved Julie as much as he loved anyone, but how much was that? Dan Melnick thought, "He didn't seem able to grow beyond the first part of love. His love would change when the first passion went."

"I miss her," he said about Julie. "I miss her a lot, but I don't have that same feeling about girls anymore. Something's happened. [Maybe it's] a function of age."

Nicole started college at the North Carolina School of Fine Arts. She had her first affair "and it changed her," Bob said. "She's going to be a dancer." He linked the two remarks as if there was a relationship between sex and dancing. "Maybe she'll be lucky," he added, "and not meet anyone like me."

Almost everyone who had been in Bob's recent life was part of the making of *All That Jazz*. Jessica Lange was in it, and so were Ann Reinking, Jennifer Nairn-Smith, Kathy Doby, Phil Friedman, Alan Heim, and Jules Fisher. Nicole danced in it. Julie Hagerty lost the part she had tested for, but she did visit the set. The only one who wasn't there was Gwen. After *Cabaret* she was never involved in any Bob Fosse movie.

All That Jazz begins with sound. Sound was going to be even more of a factor in this picture than it had been in *Lenny*. After the opening measures of brassy show music, a close-up of a tape player is accompanied by the mechanical crunch and click of a cassette being snapped into a player. The full-bodied energy of Vivaldi's *Concerto for Strings and Continuo* instigates an urgent and nervous series of intercut sounds and images: awful coughing, a great open eye, and Roy Scheider squeezing drops of Visine into the bloodshot whites; an Alka-Seltzer tablet resoundingly plopped into a glass of water to begin its antihangover fizz. Then the information turns visual as a cigarette is smoked unawares in the shower and is soaked. A pharmaceutical vial contains prescribed Dexedrine and has the name "Joseph Gideon" on the label. The address is Bob Fosse's own, 58 West 58th Street.

This is an overture, a brief rundown on Joe Gideon's approach to health. "To be on the wire," he says in a voiceover, "is life." With that quote from one of the Flying Wallendas, a circus aerialist is seen falling from high. It is the *Pippin* alternative, risk and excitement in exchange for a flashy and fatal finish. "The rest," Gideon says, "is waiting." Gideon admits to stealing the line; he is a frank fraud. He is making this admission in a ghostly dressing room, visiting with Jessica Lange, "Angelique," the Angel of Death in a wide-brimmed hat with a veil as big as an oxygen tent. Their visit is overdecorated with meaning. It is a flirtation with death and presents Fosse at his worst, thinking very deep thoughts and spelling them out in capital letters.

All at once he is grinning with grim brightness into his bathroom mirror, tucking in his elbows, spreading his hands and opening his fingers in the lifelong Fosse gesture. "It's showtime, folks," he beams to his image, dragging forth the energy to entertain yet again, and then he is kneeling onstage, wearing a black shirt, black pants, black boots, and watching hundreds of dancers auditioning. All of this has taken just under sixty seconds.

All That Jazz is a rhythmic collage that evolves logically from *Lenny*, *Cabaret*, and even *Sweet Charity*. It is difficult to think of an American director other than Orson Welles or Charles Chaplin who has made movies with so consistently and intensely personal a stamp, whose

386 □ THE BIG FINISH

work is so very much *his*. This film of Fosse's interpolates elements of documentary with fiction and fantasy, using musical language as in *Cabaret*, with the intercutting and time phasing of *Lenny*. As E. L. Doctorow, himself a literary time master, put it, "There is real time, there's flashback time, and then there is Fosse time."

Full and leisurely time is expended on the dance audition, a giant version of the Fosse Combinations that, just as in *Cabaret*, avoids being a musical number by being related to the dramatic action. Yet in its photography, in its sense of muscle and leap, the sequence captures Broadway dancing as it was never caught on film, including, ironically enough, the movie version of *A Chorus Line* to come in 1986. The irony is double because this opening scene, already imitative of *A Chorus Line*, becomes even more so when Joe Gideon personally interviews the dancers, which is of course exactly what happens in that show. Fosse seemed to have been the only person on earth not to notice the similarity.

Returning to Angelique as he puts on the makeup of a circus clown, he shakes his head wearily at the sight of Audrey Gideon. "Oh, I really screwed up that marriage," he says, "because I cheated. I cheated every chance I could get."

"Work?" the Angel asks.

"All there is."

As *Lenny* and *Chicago* had been worked on at the same time, so Joe Gideon is editing a movie while starting on a Broadway show. Alan Heim, the real-life editor of *Lenny* (as well as of *All That Jazz*), plays the editor of the movie-in-the-movie, and in that, Cliff Gorman, who had played Lenny Bruce on stage, is cast as the stand-up comedian ("Bob's debt to Gorman," Heim said, "for not having hired him to play Bruce").

The movie sequence that will be edited throughout is a comedy monologue about death. (*All That Jazz*, after all, is about death, and so the routine pertains to it—by now it was second nature for Fosse to relate numbers to the story). In *All That Jazz*, the stand-up comedian's monologue deals with the five stages of dying that Dr. Elisabeth Kübler-Ross had propounded in her book, *On Death and Dying*—Anger, Denial, Bargaining, Depression, and Acceptance. In the "bargaining" aspect of the comedy routine, the stand-up offers to let his mother die in his stead. Angelique takes her cue from that and asks Gideon about his own mother. "Chubby," he replies, "and jolly and sexy." And his father? "A liar, a cheat, a womanizer," none of which is substantiated in Cy Fosse's history. Joe Gideon seems to be saying this on behalf of a Bob Fosse who does not even give his father the courtesy of a bit part in the movie.

Abruptly, as if in a time collage, Gideon's girlfriend makes her first appearance. Kate Jagger is Ann Reinking playing Ann Reinking, devoted to her faithless lover and doomed to perpetual betrayal. He is distractedly clenching and unclenching his left hand, massaging that forearm, trying to shake off the tingly feeling of its being numb or asleep. It is a common symptom of an impending heart attack. Gideon and Angelique look on as Kate Jagger pleads yet again for permission to love him, and then they turn to his adolescence in the strip joints. The club they look in on is called by the name of a Chicago club young Fosse had actually performed in, the Silver Cloud, on Milwaukee Avenue near Pulaski. Sadie Fosse is there too, her kitchen at stageside.

"I'm Joey's mother," she announces with the strippers in the background. "Ever since he was so high, he had a crush on you."

"I've always been fond of Joey too," Death replies all too meaningfully.

"Of all the children," Sadie continues, "he was the least worry. He worked in all those cheap burlesque clubs. Always around stark naked girls, but did it bother him? No. He never paid any attention. Never even looked at them."

As in real life, Sadie never grasps his confusion between her churchgoing Methodism and the stirrings of lust, nor does she explain why she allowed a fifteen-year-old boy to work in all those cheap clubs. Yet, throughout his life, Fosse seemed to feel that he had betrayed his mother by hungrily responding to these strippers.

A cheap comedian is on stage, opening the floor show with the ritual banalities of his trade. Fosse, a professor of show business, could endlessly mimic such material:

> I don't have to do this for a living. I have four chinchillas at home in heat. No, I make a lot of money. I just have trouble passing it. (The comic taps the microphone.) I just have trouble passing it. (He taps it again.) Is this on?

The routine is double-edged, as it would be in a Fosse picture.

> The other day I went to see my psychiatrist. I told him I had suicidal tendencies. He said, "From now on you pay in advance."

Backstage, and photographed through filters, the heavy-breasted strippers tease young Joey until he ejaculates, staining his trousers, and when he goes on (billed, exactly as Bob had once been described by *The*

Chicago Tribune, as "Tops in Taps"), he is humiliated by the crowd of jeering gorillas, as in fact he had once been because of an erection.

Following the pattern of a Bob Fosse musical, dance rehearsals for Gideon's show begin a couple of weeks before full-cast rehearsal. These take place on familiar ground, the Broadway Arts studios. A replica of the old place had to be built in Queens, because the real one had no room for the giant Panaflex cameras, especially considering the extremely high and low angles that Fosse wanted. So only the rehearsals for the "rehearsals" were held in the real Broadway Arts. This movie autobiography, then, was leading life through a funhouse. Which was real, life or the movie? Too, instead of the actor being dressed to look like his character, Fosse was beginning to wear *Scheider's* costumes—Joe Gideon's black shirt, Gideon's black pants, Gideon's black boots.

Broadway Arts got to Fosse as it did to most Broadway gypsies. "The root of my life and my work," he told Tony Walton, "is in the nature of this place," and with that he starting rehearsing "Airotica."

If any number belonged in an autobiography of Bob Fosse, it was a sex dance to sum up and represent and justify all the sex dances in all the shows that had created all the headaches and crises and anger, from the whorehouse ballet in *New Girl in Town* to "Razzle-Dazzle" in *Chicago* and "Welcome to the City" in *Dancin'.*

"I once tried living together with two girls at once," Gideon abruptly tells Angelique, and two women and a man pop up as if in a burlesque sketch. There is even a slide whistle to accent the slapstick comedy. "We lived together, laughed together, drank together, smoked together. Woke up one morning," says the male dancer in this little comedy act, "one of them was gone. On the bureau she left a note." One of the girls recites this note. "I'm sorry. I cannot share you anymore. I want you all to myself . . . or not at all. Please. Try and understand."

It wasn't exactly what Jennifer Nairn-Smith had scrawled in lipstick on the bureau mirror, but it was close, and so was she, just off camera, watching the number. She was dancing in the movie but not eager to play herself.

While the "Airotica" ballet is tirelessly, repeatedly, and relentlessly rehearsed, Gideon's wife Audrey works on her dance solo, and when he comes to watch, the Fosse–Verdon relationship is briefly recounted.

"You know," he says, "I'm only doing this show because you wanted to play that twenty-four-year-old girl."

"Oh, no," Gwen's alter ego replies. "Don't kid yourself that you're doing this show for any other reason except you're guilty about me."

"What guilt?"

"For never going one day when you weren't unfaithful to me."

"What's so great about being faithful? Why do you think so small?"

"It's a great deal better than those affairs you keep tap-dancing through. All the Bonnies, the Wendies, the Debbies, the Donnas."

He can only shrug and resume his routine of Dexedrine, cigarettes, Visine, girlfriends, and hangovers. "It's show time, folks," he beams yet again, the repeating litany creating punctuation and a rhythm, setting a momentum not only for the pull on his system as he jolts himself through the brutal work schedule but for the movie itself.

"Welcome aboard Airotica," one of the dancers solemnly intones, "flying not only coast-to-coast but anywhere your desires and fantasies take you." The first section of the dance number is not without choreographic quality, but it is presumably conceived for the theatre while photographed in such an arty way that its stage look cannot be grasped. Then, at the halfway point, the ensemble strips into briefs, and the rehearsal studio is sprayed with stage fog. An onlooking producer gasps, "They're taking off their clothes," which they aren't—one of the girls merely goes topless. Even so, it is not nudity that makes for vulgarity but a failure of taste, values, perspective, and humor. Fosse's weakness for smut, gleaned from youthful burlesque and polished (if that is the word) by the perverse influence of Jack Cole, is grimly preserved in this number. The vulgar "Airotica" is an essential entry in his dossier.

"Now Sinatra will never record it," mewls the Fred Ebb-inspired co-composer of "Take Off with Us," the song to which "Airotica" is set (it is a shabby imitation of the Kander and Ebb hit, "New York, New York").

As had "Razzle-Dazzle" in *Chicago*, "Airotica" presents assorted sexual combinations, male and female homosexuals, threesomes and miscellaneous mini-orgies. "Oh, oh," one of the producers mutters, paraphrasing one of *Chicago*'s producers, "I think we've just lost the family audience," and the dance ends.

Gathering that his producers are not thrilled with "Airotica," Gideon asks his wife, "What do *you* think?"

He has discovered the miracle of cosmetic autobiography.

"I think it's the best thing you've ever done," Audrey/Gwen tells him and the world, but "nothing I ever do is good enough," Gideon whines to Angelique. "It's not beautiful enough, it's not funny enough, it's not anything enough," and yet what Fosse does next is all of those things, a charming duet for Ann Reinking and Erzsebet Foldi (Michele/Nicole). It is a leggy vaudeville, "Everything Old Is New Again," danced up and down a flight of stairs in his apartment to cheer him up after the "El Stinko, El Floppo screening of Joe Gideon's latest movie." There is more invention and artistry in this easy little number (which was inspired by dances that Reinking used to concoct for Fosse in cahoots with Nicole and Neil Simon's two daughters) than in all the foggy copulation of "Airotica," but of course Bob would never admit to such values. He told Tony Walton that the only reason he did the duet was because "the L.A. people are scared I'm doing a death and dance musical. This'll keep us going for another couple of weeks."

In the show-within-the-movie, the actors read the script aloud on the first day of company rehearsals, while Fosse again paints with sound. He detaches the actors' voices and floats them in the background while amplifying Gideon's loud ticking wristwatch, his scraped stubbing out of a cigarette, his snapping of a pencil (based on the stick doll that had broken when the real heart attack had begun), and in this way he communicates the terror and self-absorption that come with the stab and crunch of a heart attack.

While the actors are reading their lines in a faraway undertone, the truck is rumbling across Gideon's chest. His skin tone is a sickly, grayish, deathly green from a lack of oxygen and a falling body temperature. Fosse determined the precise shade of this green makeup and even the density of Scheider's forehead perspiration through constant conferences with Nancy Bird, the cardiological nurse who had been hired as medical consultant.

The stage manager Philburn Friedman, playing himself, calls a lunch break, and the Angel of Death removes her veil and smiles invitingly at Joe while he watches himself go off to the hospital.

There the cardiologist is named Ballinger (for Ettinger), and in a dazzling series of intercuts, Gideon complains about the diagnosis ("I wasn't sick until I got here") while the producers give the cast the news of the show's postponement. He slips into fear, pain, and an oxygen mask; they sing and dance at booster parties. The producers, in Fosse's movie-made realization of his most paranoid suspicions, sound out another director about taking over the show. In real life Harold Prince took it personally. "John Lithgow is wearing his glasses the way I do," Prince noticed (propped above his brow), "and he is rehearsing on a set like ours for *Pacific Overtures*. But the truth was that I had called Fred and John to say how sorry I was about what had happened. They said, 'We're going to wait for Bobby,' and I told them that was wonderful." Ebb had told Fosse the same thing, but this was one suspicion that Bob had to play out.

When Gideon is moved out of the Intensive Care Unit and into a private room, his partying begins—smoking, groping the nurses, drinking wine, even having sex in his hospital bed. On the television screen, his movie is being reviewed just as *The Little Prince* had been when Stanley Donen had been watching. With Chris Chase playing the critic, Fosse uses the opportunity to write his own critique of *Lenny* (in *All That Jazz* it is called *The Stand-Up*), and while there is so much conversation going on during the review that most of it is obscured, it reveals the severity of his self-criticism and the acuity of his self-knowledge:

> Following Joe Gideon's triumphant directorial achievement with *50 Beautiful Girls 50*, when he won every possible award, it would be nice to report that his latest effort, *The Stand-Up*, was a better film. *The Stand-Up*, however, does not stand up. Leaning toward the frenetic, Gideon falls into his characteristic weakness of trying too hard to please, to entertain. Slickness obscures reality, the old razzle-dazzle sometimes obliterates drama. Had Gideon trusted the truth of his story, the trials and tribulations of an alcoholic night-club comic, we might have had a film to equal the best. As an example, there is one spectacular scene where the has-been comic, played impeccably by Davis Newman, demonstrates his former brilliance in a monologue where clearly director Gideon gave Mr. Newman free rein. Rising above rather commonplace material, the actor creates a classic comic art. But Joe Gideon, in his effort to keep *The Stand-Up* upright, has resorted to the use of crutches: frantic cutting, an earsplitting soundtrack, chopping off the ends of scenes before the drama has played out, left this reviewer with bewilderment and a four-aspirin headache.

Fosse, his own worst critic, knew that some of his strongest cinematic devices, such as intercutting, the use of sound, and abrupt scene changes, could easily become self-parodic, even destructive. He was on to his need to please by entertaining, his weakness for the slick.

The hijinks in the hospital room make the cardiologist in *All That Jazz* angrier than Edwin Ettinger had ever been. Michael Tolan, who played the role, remembered:

> Bobby would never leave the set. While they were lighting it—which usually took a couple of hours—he'd stay there, and because he stayed there so did everyone else. We all got caught up in his intensity and it was so quiet, so totally quiet, that you never needed an assistant director to yell, "Quiet!" when they were ready. We even would rehearse among ourselves, right there on the set, while waiting for the lights, and most of the time he'd be there. I was ready to do the scene where I told the Fosse character off, told him

that if he didn't cut out the smoking and everything, that'd be it. Bobby came over and whispered in my ear, "Look, Mike. This doctor was the star of the hospital. It's his show. He called all the shots. He had never even heard of me, I was just another patient to him." I never knew a movie director to be so intense. I nodded like a prizefighter in a corner.

"If you don't give a damn," the cardiologist says to Gideon, "it's hard to expect us to," and so the movie opens the subject of Bob's interest in living. Then in an inspired number, the kind that only Bob Fosse would have conceived, the cardiologist teams up with the internist and the surgeon for a vaudeville routine on the subject of bypass operations. It sets pratfalls and drum rim shots to the surgical facts. "He had total block in two"—whoosh! pop!—"arteries"—Toot!

What neither Michael Tolan nor any of the actors knew (but Nurse Nancy Bird did) was that throughout the filming, Bob was suffering spasms of the very chest pains the movie was about.

Fosse's problems with betrayal and moneymen surface once more as he counterpoints Joe Gideon's heart bypass operation with the producers' insurance-company negotiations. While there was indeed an irony in the actual producers of *Chicago* possibly making a profit on his death by simply not producing the show, the truth was that they produced the show, they did *not* hire another director, they waited for his recovery, and there is no basis for thinking that they wished him to die for the sake of a profit. The truth in the movie lies, rather, in Fosse's suspiciousness and his inability to trust anyone. That is the autobiography.

The heart surgery in *All That Jazz* is real. This triple bypass (Fosse's was a single) was filmed under the camera and scalpel of Dr. John Hutchinson, and when it was done, the movie was complete except for Gideon's second and fatal heart attack and the death musical fantasy to go with it. Before these could be filmed, Columbia Pictures closed the picture down.

"We were way over budget," editor Alan Heim remembered. "They had a right to pull the plug and chuck the movie. Columbia felt Fosse was never going to finish. You know, it's a little unusual to stop filming for a week to rehearse dancers for a number ['Airotica']."

Shocking as this was, with the end of shooting only eight days away, neither Fosse nor Melnick panicked. Bob functioned best under pressure, and Dan knew what he had to do. He asked Alan Heim to go to work with Bob and not stop until they had patched together a rough cut of whatever there was so far. He had no idea what the movie was looking like, he had kept out of it completely. "We took the opening dance audition," Heim said, "and used it with some of the stronger dramatic scenes." At six o'clock on a Sunday morning, Federal Express delivered the seven reels of film to Melnick's Los Angeles home. The producer showered, dressed, piled up the heavy load, and trundled it to his car. Then he drove to Sherry Lansing's house. She was not only his girlfriend but the production vice-president of Columbia Pictures. The studio's attitude was not unreasonable. As Fosse admitted, the original $6 million budget was already overspent by another $4 million. "Columbia," he said, "wanted us to edit the picture as it stood and then finance whatever extra scenes needed to be shot," so there was nothing irregular about Sherry Lansing accompanying Dan Melnick to the home of Alan Ladd, Jr., who was then the president of 20th Century-Fox.

They walked in on a brunch party. Melnick, "wearing a Meladandri suit and carrying seven reels of film," apologized to the guests for barging in and promptly excluded them from the private screening. He, Lansing, and Ladd watched the seventy-minute hastily assembled picture, and at the end 20th Century-Fox was committed to adding the several million dollars needed to finish it. The two studios would divide domestic and foreign receipts, and the movie would be presented jointly.

In the meantime, Tony Walton was scrambling to create the setting for the final musical fantasy (Philip Rosenberg designed the other parts of the movie). "When I realized that I had to do this final sequence for zero dollars," he said, "I went to Cy Feuer."

Feuer and his partner, Ernest Martin, had produced the Liza Minnelli musical, *The Act*, which Walton had also designed. "Do you happen to have the elevator I designed for the show?" Walton asked.

"Yes," Feuer said. "I've got it in storage. Why?"

"I know there's been a little trouble between you and Bob," the designer said mischievously, "and probably a certain amount of guilt being carried. I just wondered whether I could take advantage of that guilt and borrow the elevator for this Bob Fosse picture."

"No, you can't borrow it," Feuer snapped. It did not surprise even the eternally genial Walton. "But," the producer added, "I'll rent it to you for a dollar a day."

Fosse never did know about that. He was too busy to ask Tony how the elevator had materialized as they rushed to finish the fantasy sequence. "He loved pulling something out of the fire like that," Walton said.

They came, then, to the death musical that would send Joe Gideon dancing down in flames. Here was Bob Fosse choreographing his own flash finish, and it would be dramatic musical making on a level unlikely ever to be surpassed. With four related numbers performed in a hospital amphitheatre while the surgeons work on Gideon's operating table, he was summing up his own death in the language of his beloved/detested show business, using the vernacular of his fluency, the steps of vaudeville, and the lyrics of old songs. They always did deal with fundamentals.

In the first number, Gideon's wife Audrey (Gwen) sings "After You've Gone" with Kate (Ann) and Michele (Nicole) as her backup dancers. Then Kate dances "There'll Be Some Changes Made" as Audrey and Michele back her up. This number is "Steam Heat" danced in limbo, a quirky trio with snapping derbies, popping elbows, and angles at every joint. The lofty camera angles set the Fosse choreography at an oblique remove, raising the prancing figures beyond this life. The leaps and stomps, once merely playful, now seem echoed, distanced.

The third piece in the death fantasy is set to Fosse's recurring favorite, Erik Satie's "Gymnopédies No. 1." This time, however, the music is choreographed for an ensemble of show girls, stately, beautiful, and ghostly. It is a dreamy fan dance, the final version of "That Old Black Magic" which he had choreographed at the age of fifteen for *Hold Everything! A Streamlined Extravaganza in Two Parts*, presented in 1942 by Frederic Weaver's Chicago Academy of Theatre Arts. It is Bob Fosse's final polish on his first dance.

And at last, if there was ever to be an answer to the question of his ability to love, his beloved daughter appears, masquerading in grown-up clothes just as Nicole had at the hospital, breaking her dad's repaired heart at Thanksgiving Dinner:

> Some of these days
> You're gonna miss me, Daddy

Sophie Tucker could sing that song, work that act a lifetime, Fred Weaver had said.

Nicole's accompanying tambourines are played by the cardiologist, the internist, and the surgeon. The images and the power have accumulating momentum. Even Fosse had to admit, "I don't think I've ever seen a picture quite like this. Good or bad, if you like it or you don't like it, it is not a copy of anything. That I'm very proud of," and he had a right to say that because it was so.

Throughout the fantasy, the operating team has been at work on Gideon, vaguely discernible behind a screen, and his words at their conclusion are simply, "Am I alive?" for his lifelong death wish had no truth when put to the test. That too was bullshit. He learned it by filming this autobiography. "Please leave," he begs the Angel of Death, and he wanders into a strange, echoing, watery hospital underground where, in his medical gown, he at last becomes Gene Kelly, sloshing through the water in an eerie, deathly variation on "Singin' in the Rain."

"Don't take me now," he begs Angelique. "What's the matter? Don't you like musical comedy?" he asks, but she *is* taking him. Ben Vereen appears on television doing a Sammy Davis-like routine, which had been cropping up on several screens in the movie, but now appears on the screen of Gideon's heart monitor. Vereen introduces Joe Gideon for his "final appearance." The introduction itself is Bob Fosse's summary of his life in the language of his realm.

> Folks—what can I say about my next guest? This cat allowed himself to be adored but not loved. And his success in show business was matched by a failure in his personal relationship bag. Now that's where he really bombed. And he came to believe that work, show business, love, his whole life, even himself and all that jazz was bullshit. He became the numero uno game player. To the point where he didn't know where the games ended and the reality began. Like, to this cat, the only reality is death. Ladies and gentlemen, let me lay on you a so-so entertainer, not much of a humanitarian, and this cat was never nobody's friend. In his final appearance on the great stage of life (you can applaud if you want to) Mr. Joe Gideon.

Gideon makes his entrance in glittering blue sequins and black pants, and Roy Scheider for once manages to look like a dancer, perched on his hospital bed.

> Bye, bye life
> Bye, bye happiness
> So long loneliness
> I think I'm gonna die

The hospital amphitheatre erupts into whistles and cheers. Gideon plunges from the stage, off the bed, into the audience's midst, shaking hands as he dashes up the aisle, embracing the people of his life, saying good-bye to the strippers of his adolescence, the producers who plagued him, the wife who put up with him, the daughter he adored. The cheers are tumultuous, and then he rematerializes on a hospital table, zipped into a plastic bag.

As the scene was being rehearsed, as Bob was timing it, he looked up at Scheider and said, "You know, that must be kind of exhilarating, running into the house like that."

"Well, why don't you try it?" the actor suggested with a grin.

"Okay, I will," Fosse said, and with that he climbed onto the stage of the hospital amphitheatre, and onto the bed. He looked out, paused a moment, and then dashed into the audience, shaking all the hands and getting all the hugs and hearing all the good-byes, and when it was over, he went to Scheider.

"Jesus Christ," he said, "that was terrific, and you know, Roy? The best part of it is, they forgave *me* too."

24

The wrap party for *All That Jazz* was held on March 10, 1979, and a glamorous party it was, all dressed up at the Tavern on the Green, the sprawling and beautiful Central Park restaurant that was owned by Bob's friend, Warner Leroy.

Outside, all around the restaurant, the trees were lighted with electric bulbs. Leroy had made the place into a Manhattan wonderland that belied the terrifying reality of Central Park at night. The Tavern on the Green suggested instead a safe and magical Gotham of the past. This glittering restaurant was an apparition, then, and although it was a tremendous tourist attraction, New Yorkers knew better than to believe it.

Three big rooms were set aside for dinner and dancing to celebrate the end of photography. Dan Melnick brought Sherry Lansing. Jessica Lange came with Mikhail Baryshnikov, the great ballet dancer who was now openly her number one, just as Bob had suspected. The cheerfully star-struck Chris Chase gazed into the thick of the milling glamour and asked Bob, "Is that Jessica Lange?" She was looking at a blond girl with frizzy hair—"very pretty," Chris remembered, "with white skin and small features."

"No," he replied, as if to add, "silly." It was Julie Hagerty.

"I thought Jessica Lange was your girlfriend."

"Last summer," he said. He was back with Julie but had made the mistake of getting Sam Cohn to come downtown and see her little play. "I think she's going to be a movie star," he said morosely, and although her success would not be spectacular, she was certainly going to make a smashing debut in the spoof *Airplane!*

It was a giant affair, the wrap party, crowded and noisy with hundreds of actors, technicians, executives, and secretaries. Columbia Pictures and 20th Century-Fox had invited staff from both coasts, and there were liquor bars and table loads of hors d'oeuvres, and one of the rooms had been made over into a discothèque.

When Bob walked into the cutting room to begin to edit *All That Jazz*, he told Alan Heim that he had forgotten how nice it was to be alone with just a movie. The rest, he said, was so grueling. "I don't think I have that many left in me," he said, and then they set to work. The first scene that Alan ran was of Joe Gideon shaving while Kate Jagger watched from the bed. The editor winced as Ann Reinking read the line, "It's not fair. You know I can't use words very well. I need a taxi to get to the end of a sentence." Heim switched off the Moviola. "That is so arch," he said, "and it's not only arch, it isn't believable dialogue. Nobody would say that, especially this character."

"Why do you say that?"

"Come on, Bob, it's contradictory. Anyone who doesn't use words very well isn't going to say, 'I need a taxi to get to the end of a sentence.' "

Heim paused before adding, "You didn't write this, did you? Herb Gardner wrote it, right?"

"That's right," Bob admitted, and out it went.

He was adamant, however, about keeping all the open-heart surgery. Dr. John Hutchinson, preparing to film the operation, had wondered whether there would be any trouble getting a patient to agree to commercial filming, but ultimately every one of his four scheduled patients on that day signed a release, so Bob Fosse wasn't the only one who wanted to be in the movies.

As Hutchinson described the surgery, "We prepared the chest by putting on the 'drapes'—the paper and Saran Wrap to cut down the bacteria content. Then," he said, "the operative field was outlined, painted with the Betadine-iodine solution, and I made the first incision. The patient's sternum was cut through with an electric sternal saw. As the saw buzzed through the bone," he said, "there was no flying debris. Just a little blood splashing."

Dan Melnick was worried about such gory details. "In some loony way," Heim said, "we had been saving a shot from that surgery. We kept it out until Dan started complaining." The shot was of a retractor being clamped in and spreading the sternum apart to reveal the heart. "When Dan Melnick told Bob he thought the operation was a little too bloody, we decided to put the spreader in. And that's the place where most people who walked out walked out."

Ethel Schlein died in May. "When my mother passed away," Herb remembered, "I never heard from Bob. Not a phone call. He never said a thing until a few months passed. I knew he knew because Paddy told me, but Paddy also said, 'You know, Bob cannot deal with death.' " Except in the movies.

During lunch breaks Fosse often walked over to Paddy's office to watch the videotapes of the daily rushes that were being sent back from the shooting of *Altered States*. Chayefsky was heartsick over what was being made of his script, and "Bob would come back with his eyes bugged out," Heim remembered.

"Paddy's so depressed over it," Fosse said, "he wants to throw himself out the window. I don't see why. His hero only turns into a fucking gorilla ballet dancer." And Bob danced his ballet dance all over the little editing room, demonstrating the style of the movie's experiment-obsessed drug doctor—the one loosely based on the late Dr. Richard Ariola of rational chemical therapy. There was something of an irony in that gorilla man and this dance. Fosse had a lifetime of experiences with dancing gorillas, from *Damn Yankees* to *Cabaret*.

While he fussed with *Jazz* through the summer of 1979, Gwen tended to *Dancin'*. She was the mistress of his theatre life, a kind of stage wife. In his movie life, she was nowhere to be seen, and many of his closest filmmaking associates never even met her. She certainly was not part of his private life. The couple had arrived at a compromise that seemed to work—at least it worked for Bob, and Gwen didn't complain, which in a way was what the relationship had always been. As her share of the bargain (and in fact) she was still Mrs. Bob Fosse. They would always refer to each other as best friends and would *be* best friends. Acquaintances of the star couple would beam about the wonder of that, the richness and wisdom of such love and respect. Perhaps it was all that he could manage, a love unrelated to sex.

Gwen was being billed as "Assistant to Mr. Fosse" in the Broadway program for *Dancin'*, and when subsequent companies of the show were formed, she staged them and was credited as "Production Supervisor." To her old friend and fellow Jack Cole Dancer, Ethel Martin, this was a painful development, sad and astonishing. "She became his dance captain after being Gwen Verdon," Ethel said.

But if age had taken Gwen out of the frame, at least she had this new and quasi-wifely career. Traveling for *Dancin'*, she would pack the pictures of the family—pictures of Nicole and Bob at the East Hampton house—and whatever else she needed into her old red-and-black checkerboard trunk. Bob would look at that trunk and tell her, "You look like someone in an all-girl band."

When she went to Los Angeles to audition dancers for the national company of *Dancin'*, Jennifer Nairn-Smith showed up at the call. Jennifer had had a baby with the movie director William Friedkin, and she hadn't been working. She wanted to work and needed to, but there was little demand for dancers in California. "Gwen let me dance for five hours out here, trying to get a job with the national company of *Dancin'*," she remembered. "She let me dance my heart out. I was sweating and grunting, and at the end she said, 'Thank you, Jennifer,' with that real mean glint in her eye, like, 'Fuck you, bitch.'

"And I needed that job."

For the national company, "Dream Barre" was cut from the show. Perhaps there was no excuse for it, now that Ann Reinking was out of the company. Bob was feeling secure. As a coproducer of *Dancin'*, he was earning a great deal of money. "I don't think you ever have all the money you need," he said, "but I think that now that I've hung around so long, I suppose I could afford a flop." It was hard to tell whether he meant that financially or emotionally. He said it to Chris Chase, this time for a *Life* magazine interview. He had agreed to the interview only on condition that the magazine assign her to write it, but he knew that *All That Jazz* was going to need whatever publicity it could get.

They met in his apartment, and she absorbed the show business decor, the big "Oh, Wow!" poster, the dancer dolls with feather boas, a pillow with big red lips and another one that Nicole had made (with a patched heart) after Bob's operation. There was a blowup of the sixteen-year-old daughter in leotards and the "Tango Palace" neon sign from *Sweet Charity*. Bob asked Chris if she would like coffee or a glass of wine. "I'm not a good person to interview," he said. "There's a governor on me, always a governor on me," which wasn't quite accurate. Usually he would either weave some filligree of bullshit with an interviewer, or else he would talk too much about his personal life. He asked Chris if she would care to dance, right there in the apartment, and she remembered, "A lot of good dancers hate social dancing, but Bob liked it, and he was good at it." It was also one of his standard seduction ploys.

As they danced, she reminded herself, This is a famous dancer you're dancing with, but all she said was, "Tell me about Ann Reinking."

He grinned and sat down. "She turned out great in the movie. Terrific. She's grown a lot. I'm very proud of her."

"Ex-girlfriends don't get mad at you?"

"Oh, they get mad at me sometimes, but we somehow manage to stay friends."

"Well, what *Life* magazine wants in this piece," she began, "is you."

"You could do that in two words," he said. " 'Fucked up.' That's what my life is like. At home I sit like some brainless thing watching game shows. It makes me sad, lately, that they're so happy, people winning prizes, jumping on each other, kissing, and I get so weepy. I don't know what the hell's going on. Maybe I should be in a contest."

He said he was ready to show a rough cut of *All That Jazz* to the studio people in California, and it was making him nervous. "I can't walk into one of those offices without feeling twelve years old," he said, which was charming enough for her to quote in the article. "But the movie is too long," he said off the record. "That's my problem at the moment. The thing is too long, and my behind gets restless." He had already watched it twice through with Alan Heim and Dan Melnick. They ran a screening for Sam Cohn and his assistant, Arlene Donovan, for Gwen, Nicole, Paddy, and Herb. They didn't all love it, he told Chase. "They've never been stingy with criticism, that's why I like them. They're tough on me."

But they weren't.

"And Herbie helped on the script, you know."

"What did Nicole think?" Chris asked.

"She was the most reluctant of all. She told me, 'I'll have to think about it and tell you later.' "

Nicole had walked home from the screening of *All That Jazz* in silence, all twenty blocks from Times Square to the apartment at 91 Central Park West.

"You know," she finally said to her mother, "the daughter was the only one who cared whether he lived or died."

At least that was the way Bob had made it seem in the picture.

In the printed interview, Chris Chase began, "Bob Fosse says the movie *All That Jazz* is not autobiographical." She then pointed out the obvious similarities between him and Joe Gideon. She let Fosse explain, "On the surface, he looks like me, but he's not." He denied that he ever wanted to play the part ("I'm too old, and I was never a very good movie actor"), and at the end she summed up the film with plain affection for the Bob Fosse she knew and liked so long and well:

> The script isn't sentimental, the eye observing the rake's progress is cold, the hand which dispatches him is ruthless. Yet the story also deals with immortal longings, the longing for love of a man who can't be faithful to anyone but wishes he could, the longing for meaning of a man to whom work is the only answer, but who has a sneaking suspicion that even the work may be meaningless.

When *Life* printed the interview, she was irritated by the headline, "Fosse's Ego Trip," and complained about it, but of course by then it was too late.

□   □

Bob fidgeted with *All That Jazz* until Dan Melnick got him to stop. "If I had left Bobby alone in the cutting room," he said, "we would have had a twenty-minute film, because he was so terrified of boring people." The movie was released early in 1980, and Fosse traveled across the country to promote it. "I'm touring because I believe the movie needs help," he told Glenna Syse of the Chicago *Sun-Times*. "It's not a shoo-in, and I know some people get angry and walk out, particularly during the heart surgery scene, but I'm proud of the picture."

As usual, in interviews, he couldn't stick to business. He told Syse about Nicole dancing at school in North Carolina and playing a snowflake and a flower and Coffee in "The Nutcracker," and then he concluded, "People have always told me how much they liked *Hello, Dolly!* or A *Chorus Line,* and I was always telling them, 'No, that was Gower Champion, that was Michael Bennett.' Now I just say, 'Thank you very much.'"

He wouldn't be confused with Gower Champion for much longer. As if in a *42nd Street* kind of movie, Champion died on August 25, 1980, the day that his musical, *42nd Street,* opened on Broadway. It was a very theatrical way to go. Producer David Merrick halted the curtain calls to announce the death to the opening night audience, and some cynics accused him of deliberately disclosing Champion's death at that time so as to milk it for publicity value. The front-page headlines without a doubt made for added business.

Champion and Fosse never had been friends, but they were certainly linked, first of all as reigning Broadway choreographer-directors and secondly by their past at MGM. Champion died at sixty, and Fosse was only seven years younger. He had reached the age of finding contemporaries on the obituary pages, or as he might have put it, he had at least managed to reach that age.

The critical reception accorded *All That Jazz* was mixed, uncertain about how to treat the film. Was it a musical or a tragedy? Were they supposed to concede it to be Fosse's autobiography or pretend it was fiction? In *The New York Times*, Vincent Canby wrote, "Not even Fellini, Ingmar Bergman, or Woody Allen—all of whom are similarly guilt-ridden—has ever celebrated himself quite so cruelly," which at least kept Fosse in class company. At the box office, Dan Melnick said, "It wasn't a *Rambo*, but both studios got their money back with some left over for the principals," meaning that there was profit enough for Fosse and Jane Aurthur to share in.

□   □

Fosse was spending the summer in his beloved Quogue, using the garage as a dance studio to work on what he told some was a ballet for the Robert Joffrey Company and (perhaps in defense should he prove inadequate to the task) told others was a sequel to be called *Dancin' Too*. He had always received offers to do ballets, and a couple of them were on the table now. One indeed was from Joffrey, and the other from Jerome Robbins at the New York City Ballet. Bob went so far as to ask Ralph Burns to work on a musical score drawn from popular songs of the 1940s, and then he brought his dance notebooks to New York to work with assistants in a rehearsal hall, but just as he had told Jennifer Nairn-Smith years earlier, the thought of fifteen minutes of pure dance was frightening to him.

He turned to the immediate reward of Academy Award nominations. Quite remarkably, *All That Jazz*, for the third Bob Fosse movie in a row, was up for Best Picture, and once again he was nominated for Best Director—three movies so honored out of a total of four.

Nominated, too, from *All That Jazz* were Roy Scheider for Best Actor, Fosse and Bob Aurthur for Best Original Screenplay, Giuseppe Rotunno for Cinematography, Albert Wolsky for Costume Design, Tony Walton and Philip Rosenberg for Art Direction, Alan Heim for Editing, and Ralph Burns for Musical Score. That made nine nominations, quite an achievement for a film that had been greeted with mixed reviews and had been doing only moderate business.

Far from the world of Academy Awards was the Chicago of the other Fosse boys ("a collection of stupid, doltish brothers like you've never seen," Gwen called them), and when Donald died at sixty-four of heart disease, Bob went home for the funeral. The wake was held at Buddy and Margaret's house, and the family stayed the night, Eddie Fosse and his wife Dorothy, and Bob's sister Marianne and her husband John Demos. As they reminisced and exchanged memories of Don, John Demos said, "You know, the next time we do this—get together at another wake—it's going to be one of us right here." That was enough for a Bob Fosse who regularly said that he never went a day without thinking about death. He turned to his favorite sister-in-law and said to Margie, "Listen, I don't want a three-ring circus when I die, and I'm going to make sure of that. I just want one person there, and that's Gwen."

Asked by Marilyn Beck of the New York *Daily News* about the Academy Award, he replied, "It's going to be mostly *Kramer vs. Kramer*. I'm such a long shot that I think anyone who bet on me should get a toaster, like they give out at the bank for having made an investment." On

Oscar night his date was Julie Hagerty; they were on again for a while. Dan Melnick brought Sherry Lansing. The foursome sat in a row, and Melnick was no more optimistic than Fosse. As a veteran player in the movie game, he was aware of the importance of Hollywood politics, and "what stood in the way," he later said, "was that Bob was outside this community entirely. The Academy is quite a conservative and parochial group." But he did tell Bob, "There's one way to guarantee you winning."

"What's that?"

"Die."

Expecting *All That Jazz* to win nothing (Bob used his old line about "practicing my good sportsmanship look"), Fosse and Melnick prepared no acceptance speeches, and then the first three Oscars went to their picture. Ralph Burns won for his music, Albert Wolsky for his costumes, and both Tony Walton and Philip Rosenberg took prizes for their art direction. Melnick leaned across Sherry Lansing and whispered to Fosse, "You'd better figure out what you're going to say in your acceptance speech."

When Alan Heim rose in his seat to stroll down the aisle and accept the award for Film Editing, Bob leaned across Sherry and said to Dan, "You better figure out what *you're* going to say. You'll probably want to go first and use Bob Aurthur, and that'll leave me nothing," but that was all that their movie was going to get. Bob had been right. *Kramer vs. Kramer* won the Best Picture award, bringing with it Oscars for Dustin Hoffman, Meryl Streep, and director Bob Benton. Steve Tesich won the award for writing *Breaking Away*, the movie Fosse had wanted to make ten years earlier. The big winner of the 1980 Academy Awards, then, was Sam Cohn. He had nine Oscars to show for three movies, involving such clients as Bob Benton, Meryl Streep, Steve Tesich, and Fosse. Indeed, those three pictures had all been nominated for Best Movie of the Year.

Paddy was still arguing about ancient Academy Award history, last year's. He'd had a moment's glory, presenting an award and publicly rebuking Vanessa Redgrave for having defended the Palestine Liberation Organization in her acceptance speech. If there was a Favorite Anti-Semite Award, Paddy would surely have given it to Redgrave. He usually had a good time just raging about her, but on this particular night a year later, Eddie White did not think that Paddy was having a good time. They were sitting in Elaine's Restaurant on upper Second Avenue, and, as usual, the place was noisy with famous actors and writers and those who came to look at famous actors and writers. Seated with Paddy and Eddie were Dyan Cannon, Darren McGavin, and Ben Gazzara, but Paddy had got involved in a discussion with Pete Hamill's brother Dennis, who was also a journalist, and it was developing into an argument—as happened to most discussions with Chayefsky. The subject was Arthur Miller's television play about the Holocaust, *Playing for Time*. Of all people, Redgrave had been engaged to play the lead, and Chayefsky was livid about it. "That prick Arthur Miller purposely hired her to play a Jew," he yelled at Hamill with hopeless illogic, "just because she's for the PLO."

Only he wasn't yelling. He tried to but hadn't the energy. "He was too weak to argue," White remembered. Chayefsky had been disintegrating ever since the trouble started with *Altered States*, "and he practically stumbled out of there," said White, who took Chayefsky home in a taxi, fearing for his health.

But there was still fun for them to have. There were a lot of big prizefights during that spring of 1981, and Roone Arledge liked to invite a gang of writers, movie people, and general-purpose celebrities to watch the closed-circuit telecasts at the American Broadcasting Company, where he was president of news and sports. Arledge would set out a full bar and a big buffet, and entertain such fight fans as Frank Sinatra and Mia Farrow, George Plimpton, Chayefsky, Fosse, and Henry Kissinger.

Why not?

By summertime, Paddy's health was collapsing on assorted fronts. His woes ranged from pleurisy to lung cancer. Eddie White thought he was too important a person to die, but on August 4, 1981, he did. His system fell apart entirely, and he was dead at the age of fifty-eight.

The crowd that filled Riverside Chapel on West 76th Street near Columbus Avenue on the steamy funeral afternoon offered testimony enough to Chayefsky's sphere of influence. The mourners included Abe Rosenthal of *The New York Times* and the political historian Arthur Schlesinger. Arthur Miller, at whom Chayefsky had so recently railed, was there, and so were Elia Kazan, Kurt Vonnegut, E. L. Doctorow, Roy Scheider, Bruce Jay Friedman, Martin Balsam, Robert Klein, Noel Behn, Robert Altman, Peter Stone, Sidney Lumet, David Picker, Arthur Penn, Charles Grodin, Cy Coleman, Betty Comden, Adolph Green, and Herb Schlein.

Among those who spoke at the service, Arthur Schlesinger praised Chayefsky's humanity, and Herb Gardner paraphrased his line from the movie, *Network* ("Paddy is dead, and when he finds out, he's going to be mad as hell"). Sidney Lumet broke down in the middle of his eulogy and was almost unable to continue. Then it was Fosse's turn, and he seemed to be in a state of shock. Here was the emotion that he had been accused of so lacking. He could not love a woman as he loved Paddy. Could it have been that simple? That he was unable to relate sex to love? His deep feeling for

Gwen seemed to flourish only in the platonic safety of friendship. It was not unlike his profound feeling for Chayefsky. "He thought he'd go the next day," Schlein said, but first Bob had to keep a promise. "It was part of a pact," E. L. Doctorow remembered. "He had promised, if he survived Paddy, to do this kind of silly thing. They used to laugh about it. He hoped it wouldn't offend anyone."

He had promised to dance at the funeral.

Introducing his act, Bob stood at the lectern and whispered, "I had to audition to become a friend of Paddy's." Then he began his shuffle, and it was Chayefsky's favorite, the time step. Fosse gazed upward as he was finishing the thirty-second routine. "I'm doing it for you, Paddy," he said, his voice breaking. "I can't imagine my life without you."

He was barely in control, he was wracked with sobs. It was the only dance he ever stumbled through. The heartless and frigid Norwegian was shuddering with grief.

After the service, Herb Schlein waited on line to pay his respects to Susan Chayefsky. Like most of the others, he had never met her. Eddie White was on the street outside, upset because he had prepared a eulogy only to have Noel Behn, who had organized the service, overlook him, and White suspected that it was because he wasn't a celebrity. Even now, he didn't know where to go. The cortege was waiting, "and people were getting into cars," he remembered. "They knew what they were doing," but nobody had told him how he would get to the Westchester cemetery. As the coffin was being wheeled out of the chapel, he tapped it and whispered, "So long, Paddy," and then suddenly, Fosse was taking him by the arm.

"You're in the second car," Bob said, "with Arthur Schlesinger."

At the cemetery, while the coffin was being lowered into the ground, the rabbi offered the first Kaddish, the Hebrew prayer for the dead. White turned from the open grave to see that "Bobby had become unhinged." He had walked some hundred feet from the group of mourners, and there he began to sob "in an uncontrollable way."

25

Sam Cohn knew that work was the only way to keep Bob's grief from engulfing him. The agent had been struck by an article in *The Village Voice* and sent it along to his client. The front-page spread was dominated by a photograph of a beautiful blond young woman, who looked as if she belonged not in *The Village Voice* of November 5, 1980, but on the cover of a Second World War issue of *Life* magazine. It was the face of a cheerleader, an open, earnest, and untroubled face. If there was a world to be distrusted, she didn't seem to know about it. Her hair dipped down over one brow in lustrous golden Breck shampoo waves, and she looked into the camera, a graduation picture, her features even and her smile perfect. The 1980 headline over this very 1945 face read, "Death of a Playmate."

The accompanying article by Teresa Carpenter was mesmerizing. Dorothy Stratten had been born Dorothy Ruth Hoogstraten in Vancouver, British Columbia, where she grew up and where, had she been left alone, she probably would have become a secretary (which was her ambition), living out the rest of her life in anonymous satisfaction. At eighteen she was tall, bosomy, and very beautiful, although she didn't seem to realize it until she was enlightened by the twenty-seven-year-old Paul Snider, who discovered her working in a Dairy Queen takeout in 1978. He promptly told a friend, "That girl could make me a lot of money."

Dorothy Hoogstraten had finished high school, but Snider, whose education had ended with the seventh grade, seemed the smarter, at least to her. Nine years is a big difference at that age, and he probably was exciting, for he was handsome, beautifully built, and, as Carpenter wrote in what would deservedly be a Pulitzer Prize-winning article, "He wore mink, drove a black Corvette, and flaunted a bejewelled Star of David around his neck. About town he was known as 'The Jewish Pimp.' "

That was unfair. He arranged dates for businessmen. Whatever happened afterward happened, and anyway, he had grander aspirations—

for instance, promoting wet T-shirt contests. None of these elegant notions succeeded, apparently, nor did any of his other fine ideas. As Carpenter wrote, Snider had just returned from a less than successful foray down the Pacific Coast to Los Angeles, where he had "toyed with the idea of becoming a star or perhaps even a director or producer. He tried to pry his way into powerful circles without much success."

Paul Snider romanced Dorothy Hoogstraten into posing for nude photographs, hoping to promote her as a centerfold nude in *Playboy* magazine—a Playmate—and for once his idea worked. Still, his approach remained a pimp's. "It was part of Snider's grand plan," Carpenter wrote, "that Dorothy should support them both."

The *Playboy* people brought her to Los Angeles, shortening her hair and her name. Even before Dorothy Stratten appeared naked in the August 1979 issue of the magazine, she was playing bit parts in minor movies, socializing with the *"Playboy* family" in the Playboy Mansion, and marrying Paul Snider. He was so elated by her impending success that he bought a Mercedes-Benz with a license plate that read, "Star 80." However, the car did not magically make him into a Hollywood hotshot. He was already being snubbed by *Playboy's* publisher, Hugh Hefner, who told Dorothy that her husband had "a pimplike quality about him" and, Carpenter wrote, "he was held at arm's length by the *Playboy* family, he was only rarely invited to the Mansion."

Dorothy's success accelerated when she was chosen Playmate of the Year for the January 1980 issue, and by then she "was attended by a thickening phalanx of photographers, promoters, duennas, coaches, and managers . . . poised for her big break." That break was a featured role in *They All Laughed*, starring Audrey Hepburn and Ben Gazzara and directed by Peter Bogdanovich, who was then a well-known and successful movie director.

Paul Snider was, in effect, ordered to stay behind, while Dorothy went to New York for the filming, and it was there that a romance developed between the forty-one-year-old Bogdanovich and the twenty-year-old Playmate of the Year. For her it was the start of a new life. The director photographed her with such love that, one of his crew told Teresa Carpenter, "People in the screening room rustled when they saw her. She didn't have many lines. She just looked so good."

When Bogdanovich's lawyers informed Snider that he and Dorothy were "separated physically and financially," *The Village Voice* article continued, he considered suing for the loss of her services, "but even as he squared off for a legal fight," Carpenter wrote, "Snider was increasingly despairing. He knew, underneath it all, that he did not have the power or the resources to fight Bogdanovich. 'Maybe this thing is too big for me,' he confided to a friend."

He tried, "a little pathetically, to groom another Dorothy Stratten, a seventeen-year-old checkout . . . Snider taught her to walk like Dorothy, to dress like Dorothy and to wear her hair like Dorothy. Eventually she moved into the house . . . but she was not another Stratten, and when Snider tried to promote her as a playmate, *Playboy* wanted nothing to do with him."

Thus his remaining bravado crumbled with one good shake of his small-time shoulders, and he sank into an emotional abyss, blaming Bogdanovich and Hefner—men he could not compete with—for the calamitous loss of not merely his wife and his show business fantasies but his meal ticket. Dorothy moved into Bogdanovich's Bel-Air home where "she appeared radiant" according to Teresa Carpenter, "apparently reveling in her own success. She had been approached about playing Marilyn Monroe . . . she had been discussed as a candidate for *Charlie's Angels* . . . but until the end she retained a lingering tenderness for Paul Snider and felt bound to see him taken care of after the divorce . . . she gave a call and agreed to meet him for lunch."

Snider was in heaven, but the meeting was disastrous, and its failure apparently deranged him. On Wednesday, August 13, 1980, he bought himself a twelve gauge Mossberg pump shotgun, and early the next day, when Dorothy came to their house to discuss a financial settlement, he blasted her head away, after which he apparently sodomized her, using a "handmade bondage rack" that he had built himself. Then he turned the shotgun on his own head.

The shabby and macabre tale had great appeal to Fosse for the basis of a movie, and he felt secure enough to sidestep the moneymen once and for all, buying the rights to the article with his own money. In effect he would produce his own picture. He would assign his longtime production manager, Kenneth Utt, and his assistant director, Wolfang Glattes (Kathy Doby's husband) to be coproducers. They could attend to such matters as contracts, payroll, and travel arrangements, but he would himself have no higher-up to report to. He had sounded out Dan Melnick about financing the project, but the executive producer of *All That Jazz* considered the material "tawdry and depressing," and although Melnick loved and admired Fosse, he knew "I could not do a movie whose dailies I would dread seeing." However, considering Bob's unparalleled record of success and honor on film, Sam Cohn had no difficulty finding money for the picture.

Alan Ladd, Jr., approved the project for the Ladd Company, which he had organized after leaving 20th Century-Fox, promising (and giving) Fosse absolute autonomy. In fact Laddie would visit the set only once and see nothing of the movie until he was invited to a screening. In turn, *Star 80* (as it was going to be called) would be the first Bob Fosse film to come in under budget.

From a dramatic point of view, the story is almost operatic in its high-flown tragedy and its language of ambition, humiliation, power, and despair. If one can look at it dispassionately and not turn away in distaste, there is an almost Greek dimension to this epic in mediocrity, its lovers archetypal, their bloodshed inevitable. There is also a metaphoric quality about it, something for which Fosse, the unliterary literary groupie, had an uncanny instinct. These characters seem to mean more than their lives. Finally, "Death of a Playmate" is a show business biography, as were both *Lenny* and *All That Jazz*, and that made it comfortable for Fosse. He was at home in the show world, of course, and he liked biographies, because as true stories of people they allowed him to delve into psychological mystery, which fascinated him. So, "Death of a Playmate" had its myriad attractions.

Perhaps most important, it involved sex and death, his twin obsessions, and its setting was not merely show business but Hollywood. He had a long-standing date with that place. He had already dealt with cheap nightclubs, which were part of his youth; with Broadway, which was part of his past. In Hollywood he would be grappling with his lifelong fantasy and dread. It is even possible to view *Star 80* as the final installment in a semiautobiographical trilogy that started with *Lenny* (*The Bob Riff Story*), continued with *All That Jazz* (*Midlife Crisis*), and is now concluding in flames (*The Big Finish*).

He was already approaching the material as the story of Paul Snider, failed star and desperate starmaker, rather than of Dorothy Stratten. He took for the core of his scenario the resentment and violence evoked in Snider by rejection. He would deal with Paul's anger, an anger that bubbled up before he ever met Dorothy Hoogstraten—an anger that came from all the failures at all the cheap and tasteless things he tried to do, and ultimately from a crushing lack of self-respect. Fosse knew this anger for pain.

There can be little doubt that he identified with Paul Snider. This not very talented, not very bright hustler was a self-described master of bullshit, a small-time operator who built his skinny body into muscle, who needed sex to prove a masculinity he perhaps feared he lacked, and who had no other sense of, or feeling for, women. He hardly, in fact, seemed to love Dorothy. As Dan Melnick said, "Bob was projecting the worst part of himself on Snider."

The differences between Snider and Fosse, of course, were greater than the similarities. Bob Fosse was a very bright and sensitive man, immensely intuitive about human psychology. He was also a gifted show-man and a truly brilliant filmmaker. *Star 80* was not about him; it was by him. But it cannot be doubted that he identified with the central character and brought a truthfulness and power to the film that was born of that identification.

Like Paul, who depended on women to support him, Fosse had married strong, older women. Like Snider he turned to young girls, who posed no challenge and could be ignored. Like Snider, he had hoped to be a movie star, and like Snider he failed. Like Snider he was regularly criticized for being tasteless. Unlike Snider, he was not tasteless to his soul.

Paul Snider created a star in Dorothy Stratten, only to be denied credit for it, just as Bob felt he had been denied credit for his part in Gwen Verdon's success. "I was always interested," he said during an interview about *Star 80*, "in the man behind the woman, especially the show woman."

Snider was enraged about being shunted aside at reward time, and Fosse certainly understood such rejection and alienation. "If they would have accepted him into that group," he said compassionately, "then the tragedy would not have happened. What happens to a character like that," he explained, "is that when he's rejected by the inner circle, which in this case means Hefner and the whole Hollywood movie group, he experiences that hurt of rejection that turns to anger and frequently to retaliation."

Just as Paul Snider was excluded from the paradise of the Playboy Mansion, so had Bob been barred from Hollywood's inner circle, where the secret of Gene Kelly lay, and as he began the writing of *Star 80*, this was the area in which he embellished Teresa Carpenter's article, building Paul Snider's depression and raging self-contempt into something that existed long before he ever ran into Dorothy Ruth Hoogstraten in a Vancouver ice cream takeout.

Tony Walton was "very depressed" by the script Bob gave him to read, but he agreed to be the art consultant. Although the script's authorship is credited to Fosse, Herb Gardner was contributing a considerable amount of material, and his own straits were dire enough for him to share in its mood, for he was not only himself still reeling from Paddy's death but had also just suffered his worst professional setback, and that was going some distance for this author of twenty years of flops. His musical, *One Night Stand*, written in collaboration with composer Jule Styne, had closed on Broadway even before it had a chance to open. Yet he remained optimistic and productive, a modern Candide. "Scenes poured in from Herb," Tony Walton said, as he and Fosse began to scout locations.

They cruised Los Angeles in search of Snider hangouts. Bob would scan the sexual lowlife in the shabby strip joints and tell his designer friend, "These are the places where I feel most at home." Walton agreed with Melnick, saying, "A lot of *Star 80* was very autobiographical of Bob." As they drove all over the Los Angeles landscape, Fosse pointed out the sorry places where he had lived in the painful days at MGM. "He had that very strong feeling about his time in Hollywood," Walton recalled, and when placed upon the matrix of the Dorothy Stratten story, it made for a mordant composition.

"I'm going to die in one of these places," Bob said, glancing around a club on Sunset Boulevard that might have been the Silver Cloud in Chicago. "Here's where I was born."

Wolfgang Glattes, the assistant director, was already in Canada doing Vancouver research. Fosse wanted to use as many of the actual settings as possible, and Glattes even located the Dairy Queen where Paul had met Dorothy. He found a service station attendant who had pumped gas for Snider and who could be interviewed about details of cars and clothes. What Glattes could not arrange was the use of Dorothy's home or any interviews with her family, because Peter Bogdanovich had already signed the Hoogstratens to exclusive contracts. He was writing a book about her to be called *The Killing of the Unicorn*. Glattes had to be satisfied then with repeatedly driving past their little house until he knew it so well he could find a similar one on a similar street.

In Los Angeles, Bob was winnowing out his cast choices. At the sixth callback he told Eric Roberts, "Okay, now dance for me," meaning to improvise, and with that the actor had the role, so the last candidate, Richard Gere, was eliminated. Mariel Hemingway had already been chosen over finalist Melanie Griffith to play Dorothy. Bob cast Cliff Robertson in the featured role of Hugh Hefner.

At just about the same time (April 1, 1982) that Bob's big brother Buddy died, rehearsal began in a West Hollywood church at the corner of Highland Avenue and Franklin. The actors were at it six hours a day, working on scenes as if this were a play. "Bobby worked them so intensely in preproduction," Glattes said, "that they outdid themselves. Look at Roy Scheider, Mariel Hemingway, Liza Minnelli. They were never again as good as they were with Fosse."

For a couple of nights, he moved into a house with Eric Roberts—the very site of the Snider–Stratten bloodbath—and he had the actor sleep in Paul's room. "This is too weird for me," Roberts protested, but Fosse snapped, "Shut up and go to bed!" Even after Eric had rented his own house in the hills, there were surprises. Late one night he was awakened by a loud banging out front. "I picked up a hammer," he remembered, "and went to the door." When he snatched it open, Fosse was standing outside carrying a portable typewriter (it was only one o'clock in the morning).

"We've got a problem," he said. "I think this is going to be the Paul Snider story."

He walked inside, put the typewriter on a table, opened the case, pulled up a chair, rolled in a sheet of paper, and poised his index fingers above the keyboard.

"Okay," he said. "You dance, I type."

So the script was being rewritten even as they moved rehearsals to Vancouver in anticipation of the shooting. They still had not worked on the horrific final scene. It was as if they didn't dare.

Eric Roberts kept lifting weights, filling out his body, and with his hair greased, his sideburns grown long, and a pencil-line mustache, he was developing a marked resemblance to Paul Snider. As rehearsals wound down, it seemed to Wolfgang Glattes that the actor almost believed he was Snider, much as Roy Scheider had come to identify with Bob Fosse. ("Long after *All That Jazz* was finished," Glattes remembered, "Roy had Bob's gestures and mannerisms.") But then Eric Roberts lost himself in the character, drawn too deeply into it. "Shit!" he cried to Fosse one day. "I don't know what the fuck I'm doing."

Bob grabbed him by the shoulders and stared into his eyes. The actor was paralyzed by the intensity of the director's focus.

"Look at me," Bob demanded. *"Look at me!"* and he glared at Roberts. "If I weren't successful," he said, and paused. "If I weren't successful—look at me—*that's Paul Snider.* That's what you're playing."

Well, there it was, wasn't it? Bob Riff, the Fosse without ability and achievement, the lowlife he feared was the real self.

"Now show me *me,*" Bob said.

They finally rehearsed the last six minutes of the movie, the slaying and the necrophilic abuse and the suicide, and "it almost seemed for real," Glattes remembered with a shudder. "It was frightening, I tell you."

□   □

Bob had a girlfriend with him, twenty-two-year-old Elizabeth Canney from New York. He had met her while pining for Julie Hagerty. Liz had been waiting on tables in a Westhampton Beach bar, which was one way to meet girls, but Bob took her away from all that and made her an apprentice editor for *Star 80*. Then, when they got to Los Angeles, the casting director received a telephone call from Kim St. Leon. She hadn't seen Bob in almost ten years, except for a lunch where he had suggested sex "just for old times' sake." Kim was married at the time and had turned him down. "Well," he'd said. "I'm not real thrilled about this attitude you're taking. Couldn't you be more fun?" He had said it with a grin, and she'd grinned right back, saying, "No, I'm a stick-in-the-mud," and honestly he hadn't given her a hard time about that. All he'd said was, "Well, I hope I can make love to you one more time before I die."

Now Kim was again trying to break into acting and hoped there might be a part for her in *Star 80*. Bob invited her to audition and gave her "a funny bit," she remembered, "as one of the *Playboy* girls, having her back teeth extracted to create high cheekbones to show how Hollywood works."

She had been divorced, and when Bob took her to lunch this time, he was able to push the old buttons. Just as she had on the first date in Florida, she cried through her meal while he sympathized with her plight, and that signaled the resumption of their affair. Once again, she ended up spliced out of the movie, this time by Liz Canney, although she showed up briefly in two party scenes. Liz, meantime, seemed secure in the delusion that she was the most important woman in Bob Fosse's life. "We'd go to the K-Mart in Vancouver," editor Alan Heim recalled, "and Liz would shop for clothes for him. He didn't care what he wore, as long as it was black."

The shooting schedule called for six weeks in Vancouver and then six more in Los Angeles. The script was finished, and it was largely true to Teresa Carpenter's original article. Like *Lenny* and *All That Jazz*, this was going to be "nonfiction fiction" similar to the popular development in books. It was Fosse's intention to retell the Dorothy Hoogstraten–Paul Snider tragedy using his developed technique of intercut scenes, restless flashbacks, and flash aheads, creating the effect of a documentary. As in *Lenny*, the major characters would be interviewed on camera with the identity of and reason for the interviewer undeclared. The interviewers in *Star 80* would in fact change, and only twice would Bob's own voice be heard among them.

The movie opens with one of these interviews over the credits, a talk with Dorothy during a montage of her centerfold poses while she explains that "*Playboy's* motto is the girl next door. They look for girls that are wholesome and fresh and young and naive." A bloody and demented Paul Snider is then seen against a giant blowup of her nude centerfold that he'd mounted in their bedroom. It is the scene of the final carnage, but then a series of snapshots returns the time to happy beginnings for Paul and Dorothy, and it is 1978 in Vancouver. He is lifting weights in a room plastered over with *Playboy* magazine clippings. "Paul Snider was a guy," Bob would later say, "who seemed a product of the sort of shallowness that comes from buying hook, line, and sinker the slick-magazine philosophy of what the American male should have. That is, if you have the right kind of car or the right kind of clothes, learn people's names, learn how to say hello charmingly, and all that, then the world will be your oyster."

But Snider is already raging at inner demons. Whatever his philosophy, "Fuck you" is what he snarls at the mirror.

Fuck you all, you bastards.

There seems no reason for his fury. He is alone. It is visited upon himself, and then Fosse flings him back to the bloody room with Dorothy's battered corpse (in fact the room where the real Dorothy was actually murdered).

You're not going to forget me. You rotten fuckers, you tried to kill me. I found her, you didn't. I found her.

Flirting with Dorothy in the Dairy Queen, he begins to rush her and then presses her to pose nude for snapshots. "I know all the tricks," he assures her mother. "I know all the con games. Hey, I know all the bullshit. Together," he tells Mrs. Hoogstraten, "we could be somebody. People would know who we are. People would know our names. People would treat us that special way they treat stars."

At the morning rushes, Alan Heim ran the amusement park scene, and Bob got up out of his chair and danced all around the room. "He always danced when he was happy with the work," Heim said, and he had reason to be pleased with this immaculate, musical photo-essay in which Snider entertains Dorothy's sister Eileen (whose real name was Louise) with junk food and carnival rides. Fosse had learned from Wolfgang's research that the Hoogstraten house was just a block from the Vancouver amusement park, and this photography by Sven Nyquist is breathtaking. Against the montage of colorful rides against the sky, Fosse counterpoints a pimp and a pubescent child, setting out the combination of sexuality and innocence that so often characterizes soft core pornography.

Star 80 could not be shot in sequence because it was too expensive to shuttle repeatedly between Vancouver and Los Angeles, but Bob's intense early rehearsals gave the actors a sense of their characters' development, so that later scenes could be played with earlier ones in mind. Nobody gained more from this procedure than Eric Roberts, whose performance in the picture is a towering build toward a ghastly release of psychic agony, all the more affecting because his character is so inarticulate. Roberts's challenge was to develop sympathy for someone so shallow and brutal.

"If I was in trouble with the part," Roberts said, "I would imagine Fosse. What he had said broke my heart as well as opened my eyes. He was much brighter than a man like Paul Snider could ever hope to be, but the frustration and pent-up anger—were he not successful—that was what he wanted me to find.

"The capacity for anger that Bob had, it was amazing."

"In *Star 80*," John Kander said, "Bob was saying the same thing he was saying in *Chicago*. That everything sexual is disgusting, [but] I never knew him well enough to understand what demons he was exorcising."

Perhaps the demon *was* sexual guilt. Perhaps *Star 80* was an exorcism of that demon, or perhaps it was an expression of his anger with Hollywood and its failure to make him a movie star. Perhaps finally, in some way, he was linking both of these major themes of his life as reflections of the qualities that he feared might be discovered within himself: shallowness, fraudulence, a self who, like Paul Snider, he secretly believed was cheap, unmanly, incompetent, and unlovable. *Riff.*

Bob would call Eric just plain "E," and Roberts called him "Fosse" or sometimes "Foss" because he couldn't stand the way everyone else called him "Bobby" (he'd scornfully mimic that). Bob didn't like to be called by his last name, but Roberts was sure "he loved me and I loved him. Even though he cut himself off from being paternal with me, he reminded me of my dad." Roberts's father had been an acting teacher in Atlanta and New Orleans. "My dad and Foss were the only men I ever talked to about love," he said, "and neither of them took shit from anybody." But close as the director and the actor became, Bob continued to press him during filming.

"What the hell is that you said?"

"I don't know," Eric answered. "It just came out of me."

"I didn't write those fucking words," Fosse said, and it wasn't just Eric he harried. Mariel Hemingway was spending a lot of time crying.

"Get your voice out of your face!" he snapped, stopping the camera. "Get it in your goddamned chest for me!"

"He was that direct," Roberts said. "You've got to hold your own with him, but that was when I loved him best, because he didn't ask anyone to work half as hard as he did. All humble bullshit aside, I owe every innuendo of that performance to him."

The company and crew returned to Los Angeles to pick up *Star 80* as *Playboy* brings Dorothy to Los Angeles. While she is being welcomed into "the family" (Hugh Hefner would be unhappy with the movie's treatment of the *Playboy* family and philosophy), Paul stays in Vancouver, promoting his wet T-shirt contests and sleeping with local strippers. He keeps in telephone contact with Dorothy but seems more interested in Hugh Hefner's parties than in her life. When he finally invites himself to join her, he arrives at the Playboy Mansion in sideburns and polyester—pimp drag—trying too hard to please and rejected even before he has a chance not to charm.

On the set, Eric Roberts was growing increasingly obnoxious, "alienating everybody," Fosse said. "Costume people and hairdressers would come to me and complain about how horrendously he was behaving," and Kim St. Leon told Bob, "I was just standing there, and he was behind me, and he just grabbed my hips and pulled me down in his lap." Fosse started to reprimand Roberts until "I realized what he was doing. He was trying to feel what it's like to say the wrong things and have people reject you and what that does to you and how it sours you."

That had occurred to Kim too. "Maybe he was in character," she thought. "He was playing a sleazeball. Or," she considered, "maybe he *was* that character."

Bob advised her to "stay away from Eric. He hates women."

We had everything going for us . . . but you fucks wouldn't let me in.

As Dorothy's assurance grows, Paul's cracks. He changes his style and goes Hollywood in a clothing-store scene, putting together snakeskin boots, gold chains, and an unmistakable Fosse costume of black—black shirts, black pants. He would wear Fosse black for the rest of the film as *Star 80* begins its ascent to climax, and with full rhythmic music Fosse makes this wordless costuming scene into a virtual dance number. Too, a conscious decision had been made to film the Hollywood sequences with a harshness, with "much more glitter and bite," Tony Walton said, than the Vancouver scenes. "They're much colder in coloration—much meaner, the Hollywood scenes. A lot of this had to do with the collision of Paul, this very naive mini-hoodlum, with the big city. In this very bizarre way," Walton felt, "Bob was identifying with Paul's experience. Running up against the big-time Hollywood environment changed Snider radically. It was this collision that caused all those things to happen."

Snider tries to export his brainstorm of male exotic dancers for female audiences, and Fosse films the scene with a disproportionate length and fascination, a sexual sleaziness beyond the taxi dancers of *Sweet Charity*, the female mud wrestlers of *Cabaret*, the strippers in *Lenny* and *All That Jazz*. With so much time devoted to this and other cheap sex shows, what emerges in sharp focus in *Star 80* is Fosse's inclination to blame public sex—as if something had to be blamed—for private lust. The number that had to be cut from *Dancin'*—"Welcome to the City"—made the same point, but there is *so* much shabby sex in *Star 80* that even with the *Playboy* sensibility as a theme, it seems excessive. Yet the brilliance of the movie, its power, probably could never have been achieved without the crass sex. It is as if the exorcism of Bob Riff required an overdose on sleaze.

In a stunning series of intercuts, Snider fails with his male go-go dancers, he fails in his efforts to please Hefner, and he hurtles yet again to the final, terrifying murder scene. "The actors were so emotionally wrapped up," editor Alan Heim remembered, "that Eric Roberts—he was just an animal. You'd meet him in the elevator, and he would snarl."

> *What did I do wrong? I did everything you did. What did I do wrong? You rotten motherfuckers.*

Abruptly Dorothy and a platoon of Playmates in bikinis are roller-skating at an outdoor party for the *Playboy* family, jiggling to the tune of Benny Goodman's "Sing, Sing, Sing"—a reference to the old Jack Cole number. At this party Dorothy meets Aram Nicholas, the Peter Bog-danovich figure. For legal reasons, Bogdanovich's name was not used, but actor Roger Rees passingly resembles him, and Fosse treats the character rather gingerly—more sympathetically for sure than Teresa Carpenter had in her article. The director takes Dorothy to New York for moviemak-ing and romance.

After she asks Paul for a divorce, he invites her to lunch, "begging for crumbs of affection," as Eric Roberts described him. "Directing the scene, Fosse looked so depressed, he looked like he was about to cry all day."

He kept telling Roberts to turn around in his chair so that the camera could pick up his plastic boots. "My whole performance that day came off him," the actor remembered. "I stole from him like crazy, but it all came off of that first thing he'd said—'Just play me if I weren't anything. If nobody cared.' "

Snider buys a shotgun, and when Dorothy comes to their old apartment to discuss a money settlement, he is pathetic. "So nervous . . . must have combed my hair a million times . . . must have had some crazy idea you would come back. A real schmuck . . . I love you *so much*. . . . Let's make it like it was before . . . I don't think I want to go on living without you."

He tells her that he has bought a gun, and she is aghast that he might even consider suicide.

"Oh Paul—things will change for you."

You mean I'll grow up to be a big movie director?

He begs her to stay just a minute and shows her a poster that he has had designed and printed, a blowup that could outsell, he's certain, the posters of Farrah Fawcett-Major. In it, Dorothy is doffing a Fosse fedora.

Is it too small-time for the big movie star? Too tasteless maybe?

Dorothy tells him that she loves him. She tells him that she owes him so much. He goes and gets the shotgun.

Liar! Liar! Liar! Liar!

She is still under the impression that he is contemplating suicide, and perhaps she is right.

You don't think I'll do it, do you? You think I'm a coward.

She embraces him. "Let's not hurt each other anymore," she pleads, but he hits her.

You fucked the big director. Now me.

She weeps, and he hits her again. Once more he tries to make love to her, but is impotent, and so he roams the room, looking at the pictures that he has posted all over the walls, pictures from their past. He picks up the shotgun and places the nozzle against her head. He asks, "Can you hear me?" and she nods.

They did this.

The blast splatters the wall with her blood.

My queen.

He dips his hand in her blood and gets hold of his sodomy rack, a device for anal sex. He fits her corpse onto it and spreads the thigh supports. There is a lingering montage of erotic magazine centerfolds.

You won't forget Paul Snider.

And he blows his own head off. Bob Riff was dead.

26

Bob was tinkering with *Star 80*, but things were not the same without Paddy, and dedicating the movie to him only made the death irrevocable. He moved out of the eleventh-floor office at 850 Seventh Avenue, leaving it to its memories, and he found new space in the Director's Building on West 57th Street. He adopted Paddy's late habit of dropping by unannounced at Eddie White's apartment on West 55th Street. Chayefsky used to stop in on weekend afternoons when he got restless and depressed ("I can't stand to be alone, Eddie, and you're the only one I trust"), but Bob got restless and depressed at midnight, and so that was when he materialized. Another difference was that when Paddy was escaping *Altered States* and the deterioration of his health, he withdrew, and watching sports on television could rationalize his silence. Bob's midnight anxieties required a more dynamic vent, a need dictated, White suspected, by amphetamines. He needed to talk when he was lonely, and Eddie would listen to the gabble about girlfriend problems, sex life, and the old days of show business, as Fosse stretched out on the black recliner that had always been called the Paddy chair. It was saddest when he lay lost in that big black lounger with his eyes closed, asking, "Eddie, tell me about Paddy."

White was in a taxi headed up Eighth Avenue through an early evening downpour when, stopped at a 45th Street traffic light, he was startled by the sight of Fosse, "a huddled figure with a black raincoat pulled over his head, pushing slowly across the street."

"I'd know that figure anywhere," he remembered, "the way you would know your mother even if her face was covered with a shawl." Rolling down the window, he cried, "Hey, Fosse!"

The derelict figure turned, and White called, "Where you going?"

Looking disoriented as he came toward the cab in the teeming rain, Fosse leaned in and whispered, "I'm going to be editing all night."

"Get in," Eddie commanded. ("His face was white, his cheeks were hollow, he looked like Jesus on the cross.")

"No thanks," Bob said. "I just have to go across the street to the cutting room."

"Bob, you're soaking wet. You're walking around as if you don't know where you're going."

"I know where I'm going."

"Is that right?" White mocked. "Let me take you somewhere. A restaurant, and get you warmed up."

"No, no," Fosse said, edging away. "They've got sandwiches up there. Go home, Eddie."

"And," White remembered, "he shuffled off."

Even watching the Sugar Ray Leonard–Thomas Hearns fight at Roone Arledge's television party a month after Paddy's death seemed to serve as a reminder that he wasn't there. Paddy had loved those parties. Bob brought Liz Canney, but he sat with Eddie White, the missing link making them closer.

In Los Angeles to show *Star 80* to Alan Ladd, Jr., Bob ran into Peter Bogdanovich at the studio, and as a professional courtesy invited the director to see the movie that was partly about him (even though most agreed that legal conservatism had watered down the Bogdanovich character to the point of being innocuous). Bogdanovich was still hunching in the debris of Dorothy Stratten's death, telling people, "I'm a widower." It must have been ghastly for him to see the murder so graphically enacted in the movie, but since he and Fosse were alone in the screening room, that is only surmise. Fosse told Wolfgang Glattes, his assistant director, no more than that Bogdanovich saw the movie and didn't complain.

In a bizarre postscript to the already grotesque tragedy, some years later, Bogdanovich would attach himself to Dorothy's teenage sister Louise, put her in one of his movies, arrange for cosmetic surgery so that she began to resemble Dorothy, and then marry her in December of 1988 when she turned twenty.

Eric Roberts sat beside Bob in the last row of the New York screening room and stared into the silent dark audience as *Star 80* faded from the final bloodbath. "E" turned to "Foss" and whispered, "You kicked ass, motherfucker!" and Bob laughed, but not really.

Sitting there, the actor was unrecognizable. He weighed 35 pounds less than when he'd made the movie, and his hair had been curled to look his part in *The Pope of Greenwich Village* ("where I was playing another wackadoo"). Now he lay back in the seat enjoying his anonymity as Bob rose to accept congratulations. People praised Roberts rather than the movie, and Fosse asked, "Would you like to meet him?"

"You bet."

"Will the real Eric Roberts please stand up?" Bob cried, and when Eric rose, he was given a full-sized ovation, but the roomful of friends was having difficulty telling Bob what they thought of the movie. "I have a feeling it's wonderful," John Kander said to him, and that was typical.

"Bob was morose as hell," Eric remembered, and they went out and got drunk. Editor Alan Heim said, "People hated it. We were shocked by the degree of loathing they had for it. They thought it was vile." Later he told Fosse about a screening "for one of those fancy film classes where people pay a lot of money to see a movie early." Heim had been invited for a postscreening discussion, and he recalled, "As the shotgun scene started, a whole row of people fled, holding hands as if pulling the wagon around themselves for protection." Fosse laughed when he heard that and said, "Well, at least we're reaching them on some level."

"Why did you make a movie about such sick people?" Eddie White asked him.

"I guess it interested me."

"You make a movie like *Cabaret,* one of the greatest. What's this? You see something in it that I don't see?"

"I hope so," Fosse answered. Eddie White was a frank and un-affected man. Bob Fosse couldn't very well explain to him what *Star 80* was about. He couldn't explain the compassion he had for this pathetic and crazed murderer, or that there was more than gore and cheapness of spirit to this powerful, rhythmic, and painterly film. Did he have to explain it? Could he? "I'm not sure I believe that an artist has to be articulate about his material," he'd once said, and he was not alone in that thinking. Of course some artists refuse to explain their work, and literary criticism allows for thematic ambiguity, but there was nothing ambiguous about *Star 80's* exploration of commercial sex on assorted cheap land-scapes. It was *too* clear.

"Well, what is it that I don't see?" Eddie asked.

"It's just that I'm doing it from the guy's point of view," Bob said. "It isn't the girl's story."

In Eddie White's plainspoken way, he was delivering a verdict that would be rendered with rare unanimity by the public and the critics, even those who liked *Star 80*. Very few reviews complained about its filmmak-ing or even dealt with its qualities as a movie. Rather, the subject matter was reviewed and the sensibility. Perhaps that was the highest praise, the thing being accepted as having a life of its own, but what did that matter when the response was so disgusted? Even the picture's enthusiasts admitted to revulsion.

Leading the unenthusiastic revolted was Pauline Kael, who wrote in *The New Yorker* that "*Star 80* is about the degradation of everything and everybody." Her review to such an extent resembled Chris Chase's panning of *The Stand-Up* in *All That Jazz* that it is almost a parody of Fosse's self-rejection. "He uses his whole pack of tricks," Kael wrote, "flashbacks, interviews, shock cuts, the works . . . Fosse must believe that he can just take the idea of a pimp murdering a pinup and give it such razzle-dazzle that it will shake us to the marrow. But this razzle-dazzle is like Paul Snider's loud, flashy clothes and the grease in his hair . . . can a movie get by with total disgust as its subject? Fosse piles up such an accumulation of sordid scenes that the movie is nauseated by itself."

Vincent Canby was not quite so personally violated. In fact he was considerably more appreciative in *The New York Times*, but his praise too was tinted with disgust as he described "a dazzling display of cinematic pyrotechnics designed to call up a contemporary world where sleaziness has triumphed."

In *The Village Voice*, where the Stratten story originated, critic Andrew Sarris took a personal approach. He rejected *Star 80* as "one of the most glumly misogynous movies ever produced," calling the gruesome ending "the biggest treat for women-haters this side of the underground circuit." He then ventured a psychoanalysis. "There is a theory," he wrote, "that Fosse was drawn to this project initially because of the emotional resemblance of the Snider–Stratten relationship to his own stormy life and marriage with the dazzling Gwen Verdon. Fosse's subsequent reputation . . . never entirely erased the memories, at least according to this theory, of his own comparatively wimpish persona as an actor-dancer."

London critics were no more enthusiastic. For instance, Philip French wrote in *The Observer* that the movie was "Fosse's most misanthropic statement . . . it left me dispirited, unenlightened and faintly nauseous." Nausea seemed to characterize the critical consensus. Fosse was once again being accused of tastelessness. But Richard Schickel, writing in *Time* magazine, probably handled *Star 80* most thoughtfully. "Fosse," he wrote, "has stripped away his self-indulgences and he emerges as a masterly director in full possession of a terrible vision. Very few people will 'like' this film. But a few, one hopes, will see it for what it is: the year's most challenging and disturbing nightmare."

Too few. By November 13, 1983, "three days after it had opened,"

Wolfgang Glattes said, "Bob knew it for a flop." He thrashed around for an explanation. He believed, "It's the best picture I've ever made," but he also believed that somehow his old enemies in the power circles of movieland were at work rejecting him again and were responsible for the disaster. "People in the industry were angriest," he said. "They thought it was much too dark a picture of Hollywood. Snider's problems probably weren't from his rejection by Hollywood. They could have come from his childhood and his genes and all that, but it was in Hollywood that it manifested itself." In short, Fosse was blaming Hollywood for Snider's downfall as well as his own.

In his mind, at least, *Star 80* was the best he could do, and very possibly it was the best he had done so far, but all he got for it was the rejection he'd always expected would come after a stripping away of his facade. His secretary Vicki Stein said, "He'll never do another movie again. That was too painful." She probably would have been appalled to realize how right she was.

Herb Gardner may have been depressed by association, but his name wasn't on *Star 80*, and he had work to do. He always managed to plug away no matter how really astounding this losing streak of his was, but wasn't that in the nature of optimism? People wanted to help him—he had that effect—and there was no example of it more striking than *The Goodbye People*, a play that had not only been twice produced on Broadway, but after flopping the second time *was bought for a movie*. Moreover, Gardner was going to both write and direct that movie. No question, he had friends in high places.

The friend in this high place was David Picker, who had produced *Lenny* and was now producing the movie of *The Goodbye People*. Judd Hirsch and Martin Balsam were playing the main characters, two old men trying to reopen a long-closed business in Coney Island. It was more of the Gardner whimsy, a pair of wise and cantankerously funny old Jews reclaiming their originality, their innocence, and their past. Audiences would never buy it, that seemed obvious, and critics would always abuse it, one could count on that, but Gardner would keep on writing it and keep getting it produced.

Bob escaped to Quogue and began spending most of his time there. He traded in the big black Lincoln for a little (black) Mustang convertible and finally bought a house of his own instead of renting. In the summer there were pals up and down the Hamptons shore, and in the off-season he had friends who either lived in Quogue, like Budd and Betsy Schulberg, or were among the increasing number of year-round weekenders like Pete Hamill. The old standbys were also nearby; in fact, it was through Tony and Gen Walton that Bob met Phoebe Ungerer, who was to be his last girlfriend. Tony and Gen brought him along to a party on the lawn of her parents' house in Sag Harbor (her mother was the food writer Miriam Ungerer and her stepfather was novelist Wilfrid Sheed). It was there that Bob pounced on the tall and beautiful girl with the golden hair. "He seemed to be Dorian Gray in reverse," was the way designer Patricia Zipprodt put it. "He got older and his girlfriends got younger, and they all looked like Ann Reinking with legs from here to forever and long straight hair parted in the center."

That was Phoebe Ungerer, and she was very young indeed, twenty-three years to Bob's fifty-seven. He told Kim St. Leon, "I think my friends think I'm silly because I date young girls." He could say that to Kim since she was an elderly thirty-one, and she listened with affection for her aging satyr. "And even with young girls," he continued, "I can't just date one," but he was winding down his three-year romance with the older (twenty-five-year-old) Liz Canney, and would be almost faithful to Phoebe. This youthfully experienced, naively worldly girl would be with him in Quogue and would be with him most of the time in New York. He urged her to find some work to do, but although she made vague noises about becoming an actress, she did little about it. However, she was warm, she was agreeable, and by and large she kept quiet in public, which seemed to be what Fosse wanted from her. "Poor Phoebe," Betsy Schulberg would reflect. "She said very little. At dinner she would just sit there or help out like a waitress. She was never part of the conversation." Then again, there was not a great deal that Phoebe Ungerer had in common with the likes of Herb Gardner, E. L. Doctorow, Cy Coleman, Pete Hamill, or Budd Schulberg.

Budd and Betsy were fast becoming Bob's intimates. Betsy was a smart, independent woman with a special sensitivity about unspoken relationships between people, and Bob seemed to gravitate toward her the way he had toward his sister-in-law Margie. Betsy watched him with fascination for she saw in him a person who exercised extraordinary influence on those he knew. He seemed to mean so much, and so many different things, to his friends. It was apparent to her that they behaved with unusual intensity around him. He brought that out in them, and while he watched them, Betsy watched him.

Budd was just the kind of successful and respected writer he was attracted to, the author of a semiclassic Hollywood novel (*What Makes Sammy Run?*), Broadway plays (*The Disenchanted*), and such acclaimed screenplays as *A Face in the Crowd* and *On the Waterfront*. Moreover, from his politics (a liberal-turned-anti-Communist) to his fatherly nature, in Budd Schulberg, Bob Fosse was looking at a Paddy Chayefsky substitute. It only added to the attractiveness of this bright and thoughtful, genial, cherubic, snowy-haired sixty-three-year-old manly man. Bob began to see a great deal of him, and Budd returned the respect and affection. "He made me feel funny," was his first reaction to Bob. "He would get people to be funny. Sometimes when he was really laughing, I would think, 'Oh my God, I'm not really this funny,' but he had a way of making you funny like a very good straight man. So he made you funnier than you were under ordinary circumstances."

Bob became a regular visitor at the Schulbergs'. Like Chayefsky, Budd was a sports fan, and he and Bob watched their share of prizefights, betting seriously and paying seriously, but Budd also talked seriously, frequently about swans, of all things, and that delighted this extremely city boy. To Fosse, Quogue had come to mean not the beach, as it does for most, but the real country, the country of trees and birds, and Budd Schulberg knew about birds, especially swans; he knew enough to have written a book about them, called *Swan Watch*, and that fascinated Fosse. Schulberg would lecture him about the swan's reputation for being mean and dangerous: "But that's only half true. Swans, if they don't know you and feel threatened, can chase and attack you, and if they hit you with their wings, they can hurt you." But Budd and Betsy Schulberg always put out food for the two swans who would waddle onto their property. The birds got so used to being fed that they would tap their beaks on the window pane in the mornings at feeding time.

"What time is that?" Bob asked.

"Exactly seven twenty."

"Can I come and watch?"

Schulberg told Bob about the cartoonist Charles Addams, who used to live just down the road. "When we first came here and told Charles that we had two swans, he said, 'Be awfully careful with them. They actually killed my handyman.'"

Fosse looked horrified.

"He was joking," Schulberg said. "Charles gave me a cartoon of the swan standing on a handyman's chest. Everyone warned us how dangerous they were, and you do have to wear a glove when you feed them. But after a while, like any other animals, when you feed them, they begin to lose fear of you. I took off the glove, and now they eat out of my hand. I can even pet them."

Bob passed along such fancy facts to his city friends. He was becoming a regular birdwatcher and came into the city only a few days each week now, while the garage was being converted into a dance studio. "When you get older," he would say, "you start looking at how many cardinals and blue jays are in your feeder." He seemed to relish equally the Schulbergs' intimate dinners with urbane and stimulating people such as Elia Kazan, who would drive in from his house in Montauk. Kazan had directed Schulberg's movies *A Face in the Crowd* and *On the Waterfront*. "Bob was curious about me," the legendary stage and film director remembered. "I was a new phenomenon in his life. I thought, and still do, that he and Martin Scorsese were the two most important American film directors, and I told him so, but Bobby wanted to hear about my plays."

That was doubtless his shyness, finding compliments unbearable. Fosse also asked what Kazan thought about directing movies as compared to the theatre. "Somehow or other," Kazan replied, "tell your own story." Well, that was something that Fosse already knew. When, inevitably, he asked Kazan about *Star 80*, the director said that he wanted to think about that one. After he got home, he wrote Bob a letter expressing qualified admiration. Plainly, the movie's failure was still troubling him and next dinner at the Schulbergs, Fosse brought it up yet again, this time with Pete Hamill and Bruce Jay Friedman at the table. The conversation had turned to why certain pictures succeeded and others failed. Friedman mentioned *Porky's*, an adolescent movie whose success fascinated him. After all, he had himself made more money as a screenwriter (*Stir Crazy*) than he did as a playwright (*Scuba Duba*) or novelist. "Why," Friedman asked, "would a dumb movie like *Porky's* have such a tremendous success as compared to other dumb movies?"

Fosse lost his temper. "How could someone like you who wrote *A Mother's Kisses*, which everyone says was a great novel, even *see* a movie like *Porky's*?" He grew so angry that Hamill had to intercede, but the next week Friedman received a note from Fosse.

> After thinking about it a while, I understand what you mean about *Porky's*. I think I happened to write a pretty good little movie and it was trampled on. So I was probably sensitive.

Everyone he saw out there seemed to be working on something, and Fosse couldn't hole up, licking his wounds, forever. He tinkered with a screenplay based on Doctorow's *Loon Lake*. He looked in on Gardner's filming of *The Goodbye People*. He listened to a Dan Melnick movie proposal.

"After the failure of *Star 80*," the producer said, "Bob's attitude toward Hollywood earned him some personal animosity out there. He

couldn't get what he wanted done, but he certainly was offered things."
Fosse told TV Guide that he was offered *Saturday Night Fever* and
Flashdance. "I read the scripts, and I thought they were going to be big
hits, but I didn't think they were for me. I don't know. I probably made a
terrible mistake . . . I think the all want the *Rocky* story in some form."
Fosse probably had been offered *Saturday Night Fever* and *Flashdance*,
but if so, it was before, and not after, *Star 80*. As always, he was self-
revealing when hurt. His contempt was laced with respect for the box
office.

Dan Melnick's proposed movie was *Providence,* named for both its
location and its theme. He reminded Fosse that it was also Nicole's middle
name. He thought a nonshow-business movie might be a good idea. This
one had reached the first draft stage. "At that point," Melnick said, "a project is ready for a director to come in and work with the writer, shaping it."

Trying to sell Bob on the idea, he stressed the script's psychological
aspects. "It's about something you care about," he said. "These are relationships you can understand, and we won't have to go anywhere near
California. We can shoot all the interiors in New York and Providence.
And Rhode Island isn't that far away."

Fosse listened. Melnick didn't mention the other aspect of the script
that he thought might appeal to Bob. "There was enough of the tawdry in
it," he thought, "to make him comfortable," but the tawdry in Fosse had
been killed off and would never be heard from again. The question now
remained, What was left? Were one's worst qualities as essential to whole-
ness as one's best?

"I like it," Bob said after a pause. "I don't love it, but I want to be
talked into it."

Dan stared at him. He felt deep affection and certainly respect, but
he finally said, "That isn't good enough. It lets you off the hook. When we
work together again, I want you to be as committed to the project as I am.
Otherwise it leaves you off the hook."

Bob grinned and said, "You sure know me."

Janet Leigh's autobiography, *There Really Was a Hollywood,* came
out in the spring of 1985. Jove, the publisher, gave a party to celebrate the
event at a discothèque called Limelight, located in a former church on
Sixth Avenue at 20th Street. Bob walked the streets outside in the damp
night mist before deciding to go in, and as he strolled along the sidewalk,
he ran into a casual acquaintance, a Broadway drama critic.

"I meant to tell you I thought *Star 80* was a tremendous accomplishment."

"Thanks," Fosse said. "I wish more of the critics agreed with you."

"They seemed to be so angry."

"You might say that."

"I know it sounds trite, but I think the best thing you could do is make another movie right away."

"The only trouble," Fosse said, "is that the only movie I could get made right now would be about a mermaid breakdancing."

(The box office hits of the moment were several breakdancing clones of *Flashdance*, and *Splash!*, which was about a mermaid, a movie conceived by Bruce Jay Friedman.)

"Bob might have said that out of melodrama or self-pity," Dan Melnick said about the breakdancing mermaid, "but he could have got a movie made, and he knew it." David Picker agreed. "Directors feel that way after a movie has not been well received, but Bob could have worked any time after that. Within reasonable parameters, he could have gotten any movie made."

Perhaps it was the reasonable parameters that made him feel constricted. Perhaps he didn't want *any* parameters. *Star 80* had been his first and his only project, movie *or* show, to be done without any authority figure. He certainly couldn't expect that, next time out.

He walked into the discothèque and gave Janet Leigh a big old hug. They talked, but it was too noisy, and she was being introduced and photographed and interviewed, so Bob faded back and sat by himself for quite some time.

He was walking along Eighth Avenue with Nicole on a warm spring afternoon, taking the fair stroll to the Lotos Club on 66th Street at Fifth Avenue, where she was supposed to dance in a private recital choreographed by Neil Simon's daughter Ellen. Bob stopped abruptly in the middle of the sidewalk.

"Hello, Mary-Ann."

Mary-Ann Niles had not seen him for years and remembered him as a clean-shaven, cleft-chinned, beautiful young man of twenty-one with fine blond hair combed up in a pompadour. Now he was this wiry little middle-aged man with a beard and thinned-out hair and a cigarette in the corner of his mouth. Perhaps she really couldn't recognize him or perhaps her drinking was getting out of hand.

"It's me. Bob."

She was flustered. Everybody's cutup, the wisecracking Mary-Ann Niles, was lost for words, and all she could manage was "You're looking fine," but when she walked away, she said to her companion, "See? He's still after young girls."

Suddenly, Bob was there again. He had turned around and come back.

"I'd like you to meet my daughter Nicole. Honey, this is Mary-Ann Niles. She was my first wife."

Marsha Mason was also on her way to the Lotos Club. Although she and Neil Simon were divorced, they remained friendly, and she wanted to see his daughters, the twenty-two-year-old Nancy and twenty-seven-year-old Ellen. Both girls were going to be dancing, so Marsha broke rehearsal at the little theatre where she was directing a play and went over to see the recital—five dance pieces linked by the theme and title "Cocktail Hour." The notion was to depict various characters in various places in New York at drink time. "There were mini-stories going on in corners of the room," Mason remembered, "and the audience laughed as the dancers mingled with them and made them participants."

Bob watched from Neil's side, and Michael Bennett was there too. He was a small but muscular fellow with a faceful of moles—a beaming Italian face, dark with piercing eyes, framed by black closely cropped hair and yet another Broadway beard. He seemed not at all competitive with Fosse, but he had told Bernie Jacobs, "Bob asks me to give work to Mary-Ann Niles, and then he badmouths me all over town."

Ellen Simon's dance recital had drawn some big names, which was inevitable for a Neil Simon daughter, and he was as proud of her now as when she had danced thirteen years earlier in Majorca.

When the dance was done, Michael Bennett told Ellen Simon, "There are a handful of choreographers who could have done what you did."

"I thought it was a wild piece myself," she grinned.

Fosse, being Fosse, was more critical, "just the way he always was," Ellen affectionately remembered. "You need a little more lighting," he said, and she knew it to be his way of expressing respect, because she knew him. "He was my favorite. I grew up with Bob," she said.

Herb Gardner's miracle began exactly three weeks later at the other end of the country, on stage at the Seattle Repertory Theatre. He might have gone out there just to shake free of *The Goodbye People*, which seemed to play over and over like a scratched record, a final and never-ending disaster. After its two Broadway failures, the movie version refused to be finished, as if afraid to venture forth for still another rejection. Gardner had become so cranky about it (perhaps even he had limits of rejection) that its respected editor, Cynthia Scheider—Roy's wife—had quit in exasperation after working on it for over two years. Now Herb himself was doing the editing. He finally brought Bob into the cutting room. Perhaps *he* could end the torture while Gardner was away in Seattle, seeing to the premiere of yet another play. This one, opening June 6, 1985, was called *I'm Not Rappaport* and was a typical sampler of Gardner whimsy about an energetic old man defending the right to be cranky in a setting (New York's Central Park) that was not only inhospitable but downright dangerous. The combination of central characters oozed with sentimentality, an old Jewish socialist befriending an elderly black janitor.

When the play was produced in New York several months later, the critics were predictably contemptuous, but theatregoers were apparently ready for optimism, even for laughter and tears. Sentimentalism was no longer unfashionable—perhaps it was the Ronald Reagan Effect—and *I'm Not Rappaport* was a smash hit, the review in *The New York Times* notwithstanding. In November it was moved to a bigger theatre, where it was not just successful but head-over-heels successful. Herb Gardner was going to win congratulations, money, and, most wonderful of all, vindication for this play. So there he was, at the end of a long, grim rainbow with the pot of gold waiting as promised, in compensation for all the terrible years he had survived.

As for the movie version of *The Goodbye People*, it was finally released after three years in the editing room. It ran a few weeks in an out-of-the-way theatre, and that was the end of it. But psychologically and financially, Herb Gardner could afford to laugh about this eternal flop, only he probably didn't.

While Bob had been fidgeting with *The Goodbye People* in the editing room, and after he concluded that *Loon Lake* was not going to work out for him as a movie—and when he heard himself talking about doing *Pal Joey* again, this time as a movie for Al Pacino—that was when he decided that it was time at last to turn *Big Deal on Madonna Street* into a Broadway musical. It had been some twenty years since he had first taken an option on the Italian movie about a gang of ineffectual burglars. Now he was going to reset it in the early 1930s, writing, directing, and choreographing it to music written by the only kind of songwriters he cared to collaborate with—dead ones. The score would consist of Depression-era standards, the likes of "Life Is Just a Bowl of Cherries," "I've Got a Feelin' You're Foolin,'" and, "Yes, Sir, That's My Baby." He said, "I can pick the perfect songs that will say the right things, and they're known. We'll have the greatest score in the world because they're all hit songs."

The locale, of course, was to be Chicago, his universal city. The story was to be set among blacks. It was going to be a "sweet, funny, and innocuous" show, he told an interviewer, not "hard edged and cynical" like his movies. "I certainly identify with [the central character Charley, a failed prizefighter] a swaggering bumbler who thinks he's a ladies' man and he's not, but he keeps trying and covering up."

It was a very different Broadway that he was heading toward. He thought he understood that. Most producers, he said, "don't know exactly whether to go with revivals or rock shows . . . they're all panicked, because it now costs up to six million dollars to put on a musical, which means the seats have to go for fifty dollars. It's just crazy." That was true, but for the first time he sounded like an old-timer. The Broadway of *Evita* and *Cats* was indeed different from Fosse's Broadway of *The Pajama Game* and even *Chicago*, but it was not merely a matter of revivals or rock music, and some would deny that Andrew Lloyd Webber, who symbolized the new Broadway, even wrote "rock" music. The difference was more fundamental. The new hits were dominated by music and by visual display rather than the traditional blending of story, dance, and song. The composer had superseded the choreographer-director at the creative center. In short, Bob Fosse, the up-to-date filmmaker, had fallen behind Broadway and didn't yet know it.

Tony Walton, fresh from *Star 80* and in need of another respite from Fosse, begged off *Big Deal* (as the new show was to be called), recommending Peter Larkin. "I think you may have been unjust," he said to Fosse, who had been mean to Larkin during *Dancin'*. "He is really first rate," but when Walton saw Larkin, he said, "I may have let you in for something you may not thank me for." Larkin was philosophical as they stood beside their cars in the Mobil service station just inside Sag Harbor and chatted. "You know," he said, "I think I've finally reached a time in my life when I can understand that those things of Bob's are not maliciously intended. They're just out of insecurity and panic and personality problems. I think I can find a way not to let it hurt me."

Walton admired this sagaciousness and hoped he could himself "get to the point in my life when I can think that way" but when, several weeks later, he asked Larkin, "How's it going?" the fellow designer threw his arms in the air and cried, "Aaaargh!"

"You have to remember," Tony laughed, "Bob's his own worst enemy."

"Not while I'm around!" Larkin snarled.

At dance rehearsals, Kathy Doby wasn't happy either. "The dances were good," she recalled, "but the dancers weren't. Something is happening on Broadway. They don't have the kind of training, and also, you can't tell one choreographer from another. And Bob wasn't so involved with dancing in *Big Deal*. He seemed more interested in the technical aspects."

Many were saying that. *Big Deal* seemed to be more about Fosse's relationship with his movie career than it was about making a musical. He was trying to be a movie director in the less threatening world of Broadway.

"*Big Deal* reminded me of *Star 80*," Doby said. "It was trying to be a movie, but in a movie you can cut, and people see whatever you cut to, but on stage when you have dialogue, three lines here downstage with the spotlight there, and then you jump in time and jump in space and go to another part of the stage for another three lines, and keep going back and forth like that, it doesn't work. By the time your focus switches, it's gone."

Tony Walton similarly said, "Bob wanted to try and get an approximation of what you could do by going into close-up. It was hopeless." Fosse talked to Jules Fisher too in film terms, about lighting the show. "That's meant to be a dissolve," he'd say, "and this is supposed to be a cross fade." He wanted to have an actor's face appear in the middle of a black void—a purely motion picture technique—and he talked about "parallel editing and cross cuts." The lighting designer would later point out that "the control in filmmaking is infinite. You can have a car start and turn the sound up or down. Bob was trying to have a movie director's absolute control of a stage situation."

So *Big Deal* was already in trouble even as rehearsal was just beginning in New York, and perhaps sensing that, Bob was meaner with his team than he had ever been. He was already making Patricia Zipprodt repeatedly redesign her costumes.

"I hate that dress," he said to Loretta Devine when the actress first walked on stage in costume.

"Do you want me to get Pat on the phone?" asked the stage manager, Phil Friedman.

"No," Bob replied, and he picked up a microphone so that everybody in the theatre could hear: "I can only deal with one bad designer at a time and I'm dealing with Jules Fisher right now, and, Jules, I don't want any more of that dumb song and dance lighting."

He was spending most of his time a few rows back in the orchestra instead of on stage where he used to be. There, with Phoebe Ungerer watching from some rows behind, he would confer with Herb Gardner or Sam Cohn. Then he would pick up the microphone to sneer, "Oh, that was a nice effect, wasn't it, guys?" Or, if Fisher asked something, "Shut up, Jules," and it was broadcast over the big speakers. As for the producers (headed by Jacobs and Schoenfeld of the Shubert Organization), Sam Cohn kept them at arm's length, but Bob managed to ridicule them anyway.

"He treated us all like children," Peter Larkin remembered, and kept asking for darker sets. When Fisher tried to bring in a little light, Bob smirked into his microphone, "Oh? What's this, Jules? You're putting a little something up here," and out it would go. "Finally," Larkin remembered, "he had me spray the whole set with black paint, even though every designer knows that if a stage is dark or black long enough, the audience loses its concentration."

So this setting, this setting in Chicago, kept getting darker "until," Fisher said, "he made sure nobody could see the sky."

In Boston for the tryout, Fosse sat down for an interview with Kevin Kelly, the drama critic of the Boston *Globe*, and the article was printed in the February 9, 1986, issue of that newspaper. There was a depressing finality about it. "If I had my life to live over again," he said, "I would have gone the route of Jerry Robbins. God, it's too late, too late now to do that."

He rambled far from the subject of *Big Deal* and slid toward a daze. "There are a lot of actors I've discovered," he said, "and helped along, and I'm always getting hurt," and Kelly reported it all.

"Jessica Lange, Ann Reinking, Julie Hagerty. When I don't hear from them for a long time, I get upset." Why was he telling this to a Boston drama critic?

He told Kelly the Baryshnikov story, how he had thought he could impress Jessica Lange with his dancing. He told Kelly about *Star 80* and how it "said something to me about rejection." He viewed the movie, he said, "as a neon concert for all the terrible mental confusion that rejection can stimulate," and he admitted that its failure had thrown him into a profound depression.

Returning at last to the reason for the interview, which was to publicize *Big Deal*, he described the dark show as being "full of my kinda thing, hats and canes and gloves," which it hardly was—"that sort of stuff only more polished. I'm pretty much singing the same song only better."

What whistling in the dark. He seemed confused, and that was what Kelly was communicating in the article. "You see, the thing is . . . the thing is . . . the thing is, *Big Deal* is a strange mixture of my own life and doing show business again. . . . At a certain point I feel I really don't like what's around, so I'll go out and show 'em. Then I think, 'They'll chop my head off, so why should I?' And I think, 'I know what I am, so why do I have to go out there and have them say either the terrible things or the good things? Why?' "

He answered himself, as people do along such sad rambles, usually not expecting to see any of it in print the next day. "I don't know what else to do," he said, as if there was no longer a movie career, Hollywood having excluded him for life. "Y'know? Maybe I have learned something. There's always pain."

Was he simply discouraged by the show's problems? Were the out-of-town travails of *Big Deal* only adding to the weight of *Star 80*'s disappointment? Was he succumbing to one of his cyclic depressions? Were the ups and downs of Dexedrine and Seconol making him emotionally erratic?

Or was he drifting along on slippery and weird cocaine vapors? There were dancers in the *Big Deal* company who were positive that Bob's visits to the men's room were followed by changes in attitude that came only from snorting cocaine. In a 1984 interview with *Rolling Stone* magazine, he had admitted to having been "a heavy coke user. I did cocaine and a lot of Dexedrine. I love cocaine. I really have to stay away from it."

Yet, in a few weeks he would tell the New York *Sunday News*, "I don't like cocaine." He had always talked too much to interviewers, perhaps overly eager to ingratiate himself, and perhaps on these two occasions he was only trying to prove himself hip for the rock and roll *Rolling Stone*, and moral to the conservative *Sunday News*.

The interview with the Boston drama critic Kevin Kelly came through not as ingratiating, only worrisome. "The thing is," he concluded, "if *Big Deal* doesn't turn out successful, I really don't think I'll be as hurt as I used to be. . . . Maybe."

He leaned over to tie a sneaker and then looked up at Kelly from the crouch. "Waddya say?" he said mockingly. Then he laughed. "He laughed blackly," Kelly wrote.

27

On the New York opening night of *Big Deal*, April 10, 1986, Bob finally spoke to Bernie Jacobs. He said, "I'm going to prove tonight who's really the best choreographer on Broadway." The Shubert Organization president was in no mood to modify his preference for Michael Bennett. "You've already proved it," he replied.

The show got terrible reviews, and audiences turned away from it. Fosse said, "You know what? I liked it a lot. It was some of the best work I've ever done. I was really proud of it." But if he liked *Big Deal*, he was probably the only one who did except for his personal fan club ("A folk opera in operatic time"—E. L. Doctorow).

Responsible for the biggest share of the $5 million investment, Jacobs and Gerald Schoenfeld (the Shubert chairman) approved the purchase of air time to broadcast the show's television commercial, whose production they had also financed. Bob directed it himself, although he looked so exhausted at the all-night (eight until five in the morning) editing sessions that Alan Heim finally made him go home and declare the thing done. The Shubert executives had neither their heads nor their hearts in it, because they didn't think that *Big Deal* had a chance and it hadn't. Jacobs felt it might have been fixed out of town, but even though some seventeen minutes had been cut, "essentially," he said, "it was the same show that had opened in Boston."

Bob had not been helped there by friends supporting his attitude of entrenched artistry. Whether or not he accepted knowledgeable disagreement, he needed that, rather than blind adulation and reinforcement of the delusion that he was inspired, ingenious, and infallible. But whenever someone actually dared venture an opinion—some reckless junior producer who slipped past the inner guard, or a member of the disregarded creative team, or a Boston critic in a review—he ignored them. "Bob thought the show was exactly what he wanted," designer Peter Larkin remembered, "and everyone else was dense."

Pete Hamill, Steve Tesich, and Herb Gardner had all gone up to Boston to help with rewriting, and they were wonderful, except that the first had no experience in the theatre, the second had no experience in the musical theatre, and whenever Gardner made any suggestions, Fosse would tell Larkin, "I don't know what Herb was talking about," or would repeat to Jules Fisher, "When was the last big successful musical *he* had?" From the outside, Tony Walton saw the *Big Deal* situation as similar to the way Bob had handled Gardner's contributions to *Star 80*. "Bob drew this cooperation out," Walton said, "and then found ways not to use it. Or to slightly ridicule it in an offhand way. He could be very mean." Then he would go and beam about some dialogue of his own. "Here," he'd say to Jules Fisher, "listen to this." He was a writer.

The producers came to resent his arrogance so strongly that they lost all inclination to help. He flatly refused to talk to Jacobs. The Shubert president had to route all communication through Sam Cohn. And "Sam," Bernie Jacobs said, "always took the position, 'Don't listen to those idiots. They don't know what they're talking about. You've got real art on the stage, and they don't understand art.'"

A mere two weeks after *Big Deal* was off and struggling, a revival of *Sweet Charity* was due at the Minskoff Theatre. Fosse had been working on both shows at the same time and looked tired and weak. He was coughing and suffering cardiac pain. Dr. Ettinger increased his medication, but Bob said, "There's only one situation that I can foresee, and that's in the ground for me." By then, his morbid remarks were so familiar they went unnoticed.

He hadn't wanted *Sweet Charity* revived in the first place ("Let's leave it as a pleasant memory"). But when his old friend Joey Harris boldly announced that the show was being produced and would be New York–bound after beginning in California—with or without him—he sent Gwen to Los Angeles to supervise the choreography and to coach Debbie Allen as Charity. In the same way, she had helped Shirley MacLaine play herself in this, her signature role, some two decades earlier. By opening week, he was flying out to the West Coast to direct technical rehearsals personally—and, not incidentally, to flee the uncertain future of *Big Deal* for a haven in the comfortable past success of *Sweet Charity*.

Instead of escaping the tension, however, he brought it with him. He worked with just the dancers, his first day there, and worked in his old way, with every routine repeated, every step, until it was maddening. They had started at noon, and at eleven at night were still repeating steps. Since this was supposed to be a technical rehearsal, the repetition was even more tedious than usual, because everyone had to stop whenever the lights were being adjusted. The principals, Debbie Allen and Michael Rupert, were especially slaphappy because most of the day they had only waited and watched. Now while the whole company stood by, the two actors "goofed around," as Rupert put it. They were just kids, but Fosse was not amused. "Boys and girls," he said into his microphone, "we are not as good as we think we are."

That shut them up.

When the revival opened in New York, his name was on the program as director and choreographer, and he was beginning to sound like an old-timer. "It is of some satisfaction to me," he said, "that my work can last twenty years."

Sweet Charity was enthusiastically received, and in June it won the Tony Award as the year's best revival. Those 1986 Tony Awards were ironic. Herb Gardner, the professional loser with the eternal midlife crisis, was now the man with the best new play in town, while Bob Fosse, prince of prizes, was officially crowned has-been of the year by winning the award for the best revival during a season when his newest show had flopped. As far as orchestrator Ralph Burns could see, "He felt he was washed up in the movies and washed up in the theatre." All his nightmares were coming true. Soon, for sure, as he had occasionally joked, Sam Cohn would not be returning his calls.

He ran into Michael Rupert backstage at the Tony Awards. The young actor who had succeeded John Rubinstein in *Pippin* had just taken the prize for the leading role in *Sweet Charity*, and he was clutching the wood base for the silver medallion with its masks of tragedy and comedy. He had an incandescent grin on his lovely young face, and Fosse shook his head at the silly smile.

"You know, Michael," he said, "you should see your face."

"Come on, Bob," Rupert said. "This is my first Tony. I'm having a great time."

Bob wasn't. "He was incredibly depressed about *Big Deal*," Rupert recalled. "He couldn't understand how it could be totally misunderstood and dismissed, and he felt betrayed by the Shubert Organization." Bernie Jacobs had begun questioning the advertising budget when ticket sales went nowhere. "Bobby also knew," Jacobs said, "that I had a much higher regard for Michael Bennett than I had for him, and I guess he resented me for that reason." Jacobs was particularly sensitive regarding Bennett, because the choreographer, about whom he felt paternal as well as proud, had for more than a year been suffering from AIDS. Now he was in the final struggle, seeking out with increasing desperation every experimental drug and treatment. With Bennett in Arizona undergoing radical therapy,

Bernie Jacobs was hardly responsive, at this time, to Bob Fosse's career needs.

Being outdated, though, is a kind of death too. It is not mortal, but in some ways it is worse, for it is a living death, and Bob's fear of it was being noticed. When a show that Michael Rupert wrote was opening off-Broadway, he refused to see it. "It was almost as if he was threatened by it," the actor said. "He almost seemed envious." Even Cy Coleman, who loved Bob as much as anyone, thought "he really feels threatened by the younger generation coming along and taking his place."

He was drunk when he showed up with Phoebe Ungerer to accept the Fred Astaire Award for the year's best dances on Broadway. As it was, the judges had by no means agreed on his merits. During the voting, Howard Kissel, the *Daily News* drama critic, argued that "much of Fosse's movement reminds me of things that crawl under a rock." Clive Barnes, the dance as well as drama critic for the New York *Post*, voted for Peter Martins, a ballet choreographer who had staged half of Andrew Lloyd Webber's *Song and Dance*. Douglas Watt, the *Sunday News* critic, supported Fosse, whom he respected as well as befriended, and so the Fred Astaire Award for 1986 was being cobestowed on Peter Martins and Bob Fosse.

The ceremony was held in a ballroom at the Plaza Hotel. Ginger Rogers was the presenter, which should have stirred Bob's youthful dreams of Astairehood, but instead of being gracious, he took the occasion to castigate the critics of *Big Deal* upon its closing after a pathetic sixty-two performances. He talked as if the show had been just a television commercial away from running as long as *A Chorus Line*. Sam Cohn had tried his best to persuade Jacobs to extend the television advertising, but the Shubert executive finally gave up on the show, with no love for it and even less for its director. Bob, in the bitterness of these circumstances, wove his way back from a slurred and sarcastic acceptance diatribe, stopping to berate Doug Watt's wife and his daughter Patty for what their husband and father had written about his show. Ethel Watt, in fact, was in tears when her husband appeared, and then Fosse launched into him while Phoebe Ungerer stood by, playing her usual passive role. The ordinarily unflappable Watt was understandably angry, but seeing that Fosse was drunk, he took his wife and daughter in tow and only said, "Bob, why don't you admit it? You had a flop."

As the family started away, Phoebe suddenly spoke, and when she did, it was as though a lifetime of inhibition had come uncorked.

"You fucking shit!" she cried to the critic's back.

Douglas Watt was a tall, patrician man in his sixties who, when he chose, could have a beautiful bright smile. He turned to the golden young woman, flashed that smile, and said, "That's not very ladylike." Then he continued away with his family, but Phoebe, having had a taste of self-expression, could not contain herself, and when she saw Patty Watt whisper something to her father, she shrieked, "And I'm no bimbo!"

That was when Cy Coleman rushed toward the little group in an attempt to get Fosse out of there, but by then Ethel Watt was weeping again, and Bob was expressing remorse, and Watt was saying, "Poor Cy, you look so embarrassed. Too bad Bob didn't pick on you."

"I wish he had," the composer said with his nervous, barking laugh. "I could have handled that."

Naturally, Cy and Neil Simon were the first to be invited to the party in Quogue that Bob was throwing for the *Sweet Charity* company. Those were the happiest of his working relationships, collaborating with Cy and Neil. They suffered the occasional professional disagreements that might have shattered ordinary friendships, but smart show people understand the humanness of their vanity and try not to take it seriously. Just as Neil and Bob had overcome the issue of credit for *Sweet Charity*, so they had dealt with a 1982 revival of Coleman's *Little Me*, for which Simon revised his script and from which he tried to exclude Fosse. His reason seemed to be a need to prove that the show was a triumph of writing, not choreography, but eventually Bob was asked to come in and re-create the show's wonderful dances, and in such ways had the Fosse–Simon–Coleman friendship survived. Professional quarrels were recognized as such and were not visited upon the palship.

At the peak of Bob's *Sweet Charity* party, he teased both friends. "When are you going to throw a party?" he asked one of the producers while playing to the crowd, "because I won't bother asking Doc. He's too cheap, and Coleman, you can forget about him. Cy's got the first dime he ever made."

Almost everyone had come early, and now they were laughing, all suntanned and hearty after the big outdoor buffet lunch and the afternoon of Ping-Pong, volley ball, and water polo, played to the usual blatant Fosse cheating. In and out of the games, he moved from one pocket of guests to the next, sitting on the lawn and talking with his big stage family, for it was show people, dancers especially, that he felt closest to, rather than movie people. Marty Richards took the occasion to discuss a movie version of *Chicago*, but ever since the *Sweet Charity* picture, Bob had sworn off any screen versions of his musicals.

For all the mermaid-breakdancing remarks, the side of him that was healthy and productive was already considering film projects. It was probably true, as Stanley Donen said, that he was not as hot as he had been. "He was in the same boat as Francis Ford Coppola, Peter Bog-danovich, and me," all of whom had suffered box office disasters. "Bob could direct someone else's movie," Donen said, but ever since *Cabaret*, he had been conceiving his own pictures and, more problematically, had begun writing them. "Now," as editor Alan Heim put it, "he considered himself a writer and was not interested in other writers' work. People would approach him with scripts, but he did not want to consider doing anything but his own." And the studios did not want to consider doing anything that was his.

Heim believed, "Bob was convinced he was a writer by these pals—Gardner, Doctorow, and the rest—and I wish they hadn't done it."

In a way the situation was comparable to Lenny Bruce's, a natural talent for show business being undermined by sincere but misguided intellectual admirers.

One idea on Bob's mind was a movie about the gossip columnist Walter Winchell. He was also considering a screen biography of Rebekah Harkness, the ballet philanthropist. The book that would be its basis was a show-business biography involving lots of drugs and lots of strange sex. It was a project, then, born in Riffland, but at the *Sweet Charity* party Bob told Marty Richards that he had settled on *Chicago*, even though it had been a stage musical. After all, he had remade the stage musical *Cabaret* into a splendid movie. "I think I can do it—I've got about eight years left. But I don't want it to be an ordinary picture." The star he had in mind was Madonna, the rock singer.

"What do you mean," Richards interrupted, "you 'only have eight years left'?"

"Well," Bob replied, "in eight years I'll be the age my father died, and I'll never outlive that." Morbid or no, at least he had moved Cy Fosse's age up to its true point, as if, by doing so, he was extending his own life.

Abruptly changing the subject, he turned to some of his dancers and asked, "If you were stranded on a desert island, what three movies would you take with you?" The Truth Game always took on a benign form when played with his beloved dancers. (When one of them turned the question on him, he answered, "Something of Chaplin's for sure," but never finished his list.)

Oh, he was in high spirits, and in the evening the party turned gala, with the guests dressed in various versions of show-business-outrageous (and the help in black tie). Bob had arranged for dinner to be served outdoors. There were bottles of champagne and wine on every one of some twenty tables with candles glowing over snowy crisp linen and gaily colored flowers setting off the shining china, with settings for eight at each table.

Then at midnight, after the dining and dancing, he hustled everyone into the converted garage that served as his studio and improvised a big dance number. In the morning they were all invited back for breakfast. It was lucky weather, a warm and sunny day, and the volleyball and water polo resumed. Bob himself stood in the kitchen, wearing an apron and making strawberry pancakes. He had learned how to make them on the Sundays of 1938 Chicago, when Annette and Dorothy Schroeder used to invite him to walk over from Paulina Street and have brunch with them. Mrs. Schroeder had taught them all how to make those strawberry pancakes and now he made them for these people who loved him, and for Gwen too, who was being as warm and friendly with Phoebe Ungerer as she had been toward Ann Reinking.

A special benefit that accrued from the successful revival of *Sweet Charity* was that its theatre, the Minskoff, was only steps away from the Booth Theatre, where Herb Gardner's *I'm Not Rappaport* was playing. The playwright had outlasted his quarter century of rejection without rancor, and there was only a trace of bitterness in his Tony Award acceptance speech. "So there is life after Frank Rich," he had grinned, meaning that a play could, after all, survive a bad review from *The New York Times* critic. Herb was bigger and cuddlier than ever, as tender and loving and funny as his play. One would never sense any inner turmoil except for an occasional tantrum in the *Goodbye People* editing room or several unexplained fainting spells.

Now, with tremendous and deserved joy, he strolled between his hit and Bobby's, an arm around his friend's shoulder. "They just loved visiting back and forth between their shows," according to Craig Jacobs, who had been stage-managing *Sweet Charity* since Phil Friedman was assigned to *Big Deal*. There were, however, strange goings-on backstage at *Sweet Charity*. When Debbie Allen had to leave the show, Bob got (who else?) Ann Reinking to replace her. In life after Fosse, Ann had married into one of the richest families in the country. Her handsome husband, Herbert Allen, Jr., was the scion of a prestigious Wall Street investment banking house, Allen and Company. She lived in astonishing wealth, but when she returned to the theatre, Bob treated her like a stage gypsy. What mattered to him was her rustiness. "He was very tough on her," Michael Rupert remembered. "She was a vulnerable girl and needed reinforcement. He pushed her to the verge of tears, and when he showed his frustration, she would collapse." But it wasn't just the same old perfectionism. "When Annie was put into the show," Rupert remembered, "Bobby suddenly aged. He had always been a boy, with a boyish face and boyish energy. Suddenly he looked old." Then, mysterious accidents began to occur. One night Ann's costumes disappeared from the backstage wardrobe rack, and on another, she took a swig of the prop champagne during the show and screamed, running offstage and into the wings, coughing violently. Someone had replaced the ginger ale with the hydrochloric acid solution that was used to clean the bottle, or had unintentionally confused them. The curtain was dropped while her understudy hurried into costume, and Reinking was rushed to the hospital with burns in her throat. It wasn't disastrous, and she only missed five performances, but it was frightening, and it was never explained. She didn't drink the stage champagne after that.

Even elfin cynics look old when the next birthday is the sixtieth, and as Michael Rupert noticed, a certain weariness began to cloud over Bob's face. He might wink with conspiratorial approval at a friend with a very young date, but he himself seemed to have little enthusiasm left for the chase ("I'm too old," he said, "I can't do that anymore"). Rather, he appeared content with Phoebe. Even when Ilse Schwarzwald called from Germany to say that she was coming to New York and hoped to see him after so many years, he waffled on making a plan.

Of course Gwen was still his wife. "After *Star 80*," his longtime orchestrator Ralph Burns said, "Bob ran back to her womb," and Eddie White agreed. "She would always be there. She was the mother lode, always doing good for him." Perhaps it was that maternalism and a steady passion with Phoebe Ungerer that was the combination to satisfy him finally. Perhaps that was what he was referring to when he chatted with Jan Solomon on the corner of Eighth Avenue and 57th Street in front of the Pottery Barn. He hadn't recognized her when she stopped him on the street, but he hardly could have been expected to, a summer stock apprentice he'd met thirty-five years earlier. Jan Solomon had been an apprentice at the Boston Summer Theatre when Bob had seemed a rising star, playing *Pal Joey* on tour and traveling with Joan McCracken.

"Mr. Fosse!" she cried, and he looked up with a quizzical smile. "I was in the chorus for your *Pal Joey* in Boston."

"Were you?"

"In 1951," she said, "and we went for a walk on the Common. I was very young, and you said to me, 'I want to be a star, but what's more important is loving someone who is right for you.' "

"Did I say that?"

"Yes, you did," Jan bubbled, "and then you said, 'The important thing is loving someone and working at a career that involves something you love to do. If that makes you a star, that's wonderful, but the important thing is doing it.' "

"You sure remember your lines," he said.

"Who could forget a conversation," she replied, "with Bob Fosse?"

"Well, you know what?" he said. "That was my philosophy then, and it's been my philosophy ever since."

Perhaps so, and perhaps Gwen—Phoebe was the someone he loved, but in the fall of 1986 he knew that he had never gotten to be a performing star, never would, and wasn't even so sure he was working on a career.

The entire block was being ripped away, alongside and back of the Broadway Theatre, where the marquee still announced *Big Deal*, even though the show was closed and dead. It might almost have been buried in a cemetery, for there was something morbid and wasted about the stretch of rubble waiting for yet another office building to rise in Times Square. Then again the whole area was being transformed. The crisp and formal night place of turn-of-the-century elegance had long since disappeared. Now the neon excitement and even the grime of a later Times Square were being replaced by the smooth, bland, concrete-and-glass face fronts of city motels with Minneapolis names like Marriott and Holiday Inn instead of such New York signatures as the Astor Hotel, the Paramount and Rivoli, the Morosco and the Helen Hayes theatres, Hansen's Drugstore, and the Maiden Lane Dance Hall.

Walking past the big excavation and the Broadway Theatre with its *Big Deal* marquee, Michael Rupert ran into a Bob Fosse lost in reverie.

"Bobby!"

Fosse glanced up, smiled, and said, "I was just thinking. Look at this," and he nodded toward the flattened city block alongside the theatre. "I'm writing this movie about Walter Winchell. Where am I going to shoot it?"

He looked southward down a Times Square already in transition. "They're tearing everything down," he said gloomily. "It's all changing. This isn't Broadway anymore."

He didn't look well. The summer of 1987 was not his healthiest. He was sick all through it with colds and the flu, and his cigarette cough was constant. After one frightful siege, he finally got his throat clear enough to say, "You know, when I die and they put me in a coffin, as they're closing the lid, I'm going to reach out and ask for one more cigarette."

Michael Bennett died of AIDS on July 2 at the age of forty-four. With Gower Champion already dead and Jerome Robbins long since retired to the ballet, Bob Fosse alone remained from Broadway's great era of choreographer-directors. Some of his assistants with *Sweet Charity*, as if sensing the end of that era, suggested that on a Sunday night when there was no show, they get together with all the old dance captains to put on a special performance of Bob Fosse classics, but when they approached him, he said that it sounded "too much like a funeral."

Hugh Wheeler also died that July. The writer had a long history with Bob, from the abortive musical *Breakfast at Tiffany's* to the screenplay for *Cabaret*, and of course Bob showed up at the champagne memorial that Hal Prince was hosting on the fourth floor of the Sardi's Restaurant building on West 44th Street. A lot of his past was at that party: George Martin, who had danced in the chorus of *Pal Joey* on Broadway when Bob had been the understudy; his wife Ethel, who had worked with Gwen in the Jack Cole Dancers; of course, the host, Harold Prince, who went back to *The Pajama Game* and *Damn Yankees*. Marty Richards was there too, of more recent vintage in Bob's life, and the producer whispered as they shook hands, "You know, there are only two people I've ever worked with that I was so in awe of I couldn't speak to them. You were the first of them that I was able to break that barrier with."

"Who's the other guy?"

Richards nodded across the room. "Steve Sondheim," he said. "I still can't talk to him without feeling nervous."

"Neither can I," Bob grinned, but it was his only smile of the afternoon. He looked "very upset," it seemed to Prince, "about Hugh Wheeler's death."

Ethel and George Martin stood by to reminisce about the *Pal Joey* of a lifetime past. "Bobby always had a bug about that production," Ethel remembered. "I think he felt it was the one that got away."

It was the one that was supposed to make him Gene Kelly. Now he said to the Martins, "Let's do it again."

"*Pal Joey*?" George asked. Blond and trim with his California suntan, he looked no more than a healthy fifty and radiant in comparison with Fosse, who, he thought, surely was not imagining himself playing Joey. "Alexis Smith can be our Mrs. Simpson," Bob suggested.

"Okay," George said, musing along. "And for Joey?" He paused. "What about John Travolta?"

"I don't think he can cut the dancing," Bob said. "Let's think about it." Then he walked over to ask Marty Richards for a favor. "You know, Nicole is up for *Phantom of the Opera*. She thinks she's got the part, but she doesn't know. She's been waiting to hear from them. They told her yes, but she hasn't heard for a long time."

"Them" was Harold Prince, who was directing the Andrew Lloyd Webber musical that was already a London sensation. Bob didn't mention what favor he wanted, but Richards could figure that out.

"They're having problems with Actors Equity," he replied. "They don't know whether Webber's wife can stay here and play the lead. The last thing on their mind right now is final casting. I'm sure if they say Nicole's got it, she's got it."

"But she doesn't *know* it," Bob said. "I remember what it's like. I've been a performer. You know what it is to wait."

So Marty Richards said, as he was supposed to, "I'll ask Hal."

"Don't you dare!" Fosse gasped, but Richards overcame the protest to wind through the crowd to Prince. "I shouldn't do this," he said. "Bobby would kill me. He says that Nicole thinks she's got a job in *Phantom*, but no one's called her, and he's too embarrassed to put you on the spot."

Prince sympathetically shook his head and smiled as he walked over to Fosse and said, "Bobby, Nicole is in *Phantom of the Opera*. It's [the general manager's] fault they haven't called her to give her a contract or tell her, and I'm embarrassed."

"Oh, my God," Bob blushed. "Why did he ask you?"

"Don't be silly," Prince said. "We're both fathers. This is ridiculous. She should know. I love her, and she's going to have quite a prominent little role as a dancer in the show." When Marty Richards was leaving, Bob caught him and threw an arm around his shoulder, saying, "Thanks for that, Marty. It was really sweet of you." Then he paused before adding, "I wish I could show people how much I love them, but the truth is, I'm afraid of loving anyone."

Prince glanced over at Bob talking to Richards, and as he recalled, "I ended up feeling lovely. Circles close. You have a lot of ambition going for both of you, you get on with your lives, you don't stay close. It's somebody you see across a room and wave to, and then you grow older—and Bobby and I were virtually the same age—and you end up in the same room, and you're still here. In the theatre."

Bob talked briefly to Richards about the movie version of *Chicago*. He'd already had lunch with Madonna and given her his synopsis of the script. "Why don't you go ahead and set up a production meeting?" he told the producer. "Call Kander and Ebb and Herbie." That was the notion, to have Ebb and Gardner collaborate with Fosse on the writing of the screenplay.

"For when?"

"Oh, right away," Bob said. "Make it the day after *Charity* opens in Washington," and so Marty Richards scheduled the first production meeting of the *Chicago* movie for Thursday morning, September 24, 1987, but by then Bob would be in a coffin on his way back to New York.

He had told the cast of the *Sweet Charity* touring company that he would do anything to make sure they were a hit in Washington, and dying was what he did. It was front-page news across the country, and "business skyrocketed," according to the stage manager, Craig Jacobs. The coroner cited "cardiopulmonary arrest" as the cause of death, "due to cardiac arrhythmia and Ischemic Cardiac Disease"—in other words, a heart attack. It is fair to say that Bob Fosse also died of a tendency toward depression, of which death is a natural extension, of the postoperation psychology of heart surgery, of the general personality makeup of an epileptic, of rather unhealthy living habits, of a dismaying condition in his career. In short, he was undone by generally unfavorable conditions of the heart.

Ilse Schwarzwald was brushing her teeth in the bathroom of a New York hotel room when she heard the news on the television set inside. "Believe it or not," she had told Bob on the telephone just days before, "I am here legally at last. I have a work permit. The company got it for me." He had replied, "Oh, we've got to get together when I get back from Washington. I'll call you first thing, and we'll have dinner."

Shocked as Ilse was, she thought, "It was the best thing that could have happened. He always had this death wish, and this was just the way he wanted to die—in the midst of a show. He didn't want to become old and feeble and not be able to work anymore."

Nobody does, but then nobody can imagine himself being old and feeble, and Fosse died whether he wanted to or not. The next day, September 24, 1987, the day of the first production meeting for the *Chicago* movie, he was cremated under the supervision of Dr. Carol McMahon at the Trinity Church Crematory on Riverside Drive at 154th Street on the West Side of Manhattan.

That night, the lights of Broadway were dimmed for a minute, and *The New York Times* assigned Jeremy Gerard to write a Broadway reaction article. Harold Prince was, as usual, adult and articulate, calling Bob "an original and irreplaceable." Fred Ebb managed to express his honest fears of Fosse, setting them in a diplomatic framework by saying, "You always wanted to be a fly on the wall when he was working." But Bernie Jacobs' remarks were the ones that had show people talking the next day. He told Gerard of the *Times*, "Really, I'm not the right person to ask for a quote. I didn't get along with him that well, and I didn't think he was a particularly nice person, but if you need a quote just don't put me in a position that makes me sound nasty." Gerard promptly printed Jacobs' remarks in their entirety, making him sound unkind to the dead: "Bobby could be the nicest, most decent, politest, most considerate man you could ever hope to meet. He was thorough and he was hardworking, but he was not a very nice man. He was not just nasty to other people. He was nasty to himself."

Gwen was enraged, especially since she was already blaming Jacobs for aggravating Bob's ill-health by scuttling *Big Deal*.

Of greater interest to the world beyond show business was the rider that was attached to the Fosse will. This was the stuff of gossip columns, the cash bequests to be spent on personal dinners for well-known people who "at one time or another during my life have been very kind to me." It was a theatrical gesture for the general public to enjoy, a flamboyant gift of $25,000 to celebrate his own death.

Among those cited in the will and due for $378.79 apiece, which was more than enough for dinner at a nice restaurant, were such known names as Cy Coleman, E. L. Doctorow, Ben Gazzara, Buddy Hackett, Stanley Donen, Dustin Hoffman, Saul Chaplin, Janet Leigh, Warner Leroy, Chris Chase, Pete Hamill, Elaine Kaufman (of Elaine's Restaurant), Ann Reinking, Neil Simon, John Rubinstein, Gene Shalit, Jerome Robbins, Peter Stone, Ben Vereen, David Picker, Daniel Melnick, Liza Minnelli, Peter Maas, Roy Scheider, Julie Haggerty, Melanie Griffith, Ralph Burns, Elia Kazan, Jessica Lange, Tony Walton, and Stuart Ostrow.

It was left to the public to figure out what these people had in common and how they fit into Bob Fosse's life.

As for the rest of his will, in addition to the house in Quogue, he left an estate of nearly $4 million, including over a million dollars in cash. Virtually all of it was to be divided between Gwen and Nicole. The largest cash bequest was of $100,000 for a Bob Fosse Theatre Scholarship "for education and training in the theatrical arts." (Fosse actually disliked trained actors. "Bob's major advice to actors," editor Alan Heim said, "would be to stop acting. I think that school should be called the Stop Acting School.")

He left Sam Cohn his small interest in the Laundry, an East Hampton restaurant that the agent co-owned, and the remaining bequests were insignificant, even parsimonious. For instance he gave his sister Marianne a mere $20,000, little more than the $15,000 apiece he bequeathed to his housekeeper Millie Hogan and his last secretary, Cathy Nicholas. He left Herb Gardner $7,500, which was a nice gesture since *I'm Not Rappaport* had made the playwright a rich man, but leaving the same amount to Phoebe Ungerer was not generous, considering that they had more or less been living together during his last four years. He left twice as much, $15,000, to Mary-Ann Niles.

The will was put into probate as soon as Gwen returned from Washington, and then she took the urn with Bob's ashes and drove to Quogue with Nicole. They parked the car at the beach, got out, and walked along the sand toward the chilly Atlantic Ocean of late September, and there they released the remains of Bob Fosse, which hardly seemed to weigh more than he had, and then they turned around, got back into the car, and, Gwen told a friend, drove to Bob's house.

It was not a house that Gwen knew or was familiar with. She had never been part of his life in Quogue. It was really the house that Bob and Phoebe had shared; in fact Budd and Betsy Schulberg had been so used to the tall, beautiful blond young woman being there that, if she answered the telephone, they would invite Bob through her. Budd had not seen Gwen Verdon in many years. Betsy had never met her at all.

Gwen walked into that house in Quogue and came upon Phoebe and the cat Bob had named Macho. The girl was devastated. She had learned of Bob's death as a stranger would have—through the television news. Then, as she later told Kathy Doby, after four years of warmth and friendliness, Gwen gave her until Sunday to get her cat, her things, and herself out of there.

While Bob was alive, Phoebe's mother said, "Gwen pretended to be chummy with Phoebe, or pleasant at least. When he died, she turned on her with a vengeance."

As the lawyers began taking inventory of the household possessions, Gwen called Budd and Betsy Schulberg and asked them over. "She told me," Betsy remembered, "that there was a box of Havana cigars that she thought Bob would have wanted Budd to have," and so the Schulbergs came around. "It was a strange feeling for us," Betsy said, "because we were so used to seeing Phoebe there. Bob and Phoebe were the couple."

Handing Budd the cigars, Gwen began to reminisce about Bob and the marriage and the wonderful life that they'd had together. She remembered the parties, she talked about family fun and barbecues. "She talked about it," Betsy Schulberg recalled, "as if it was a conventional marriage. It was one of the strangest things I've ever experienced."

"Bizarre" was Budd's word for it.

"We have too many houses now," Gwen was saying, "we" being the Fosse family. She still owned the places in Bridgehampton and East Hampton, which were to be sold. "She wanted to keep Bob's house," Phil Friedman said, "exactly as it was. The furniture was to stay just where he had it, and of course the dance studio."

"I know," Nicole whispered to the Schulbergs, "that my father would want me to go into that studio and dance. I've got to do that for him."

"It was," Budd said, "as if they were having people in after the death of a husband and a father, except they weren't there when he was alive."

"Now Gwen was the widow," Betsy said.

"Suddenly," as Phoebe's mother Miriam Ungerer put it, "after fifteen years of separation and seeming to accept it, she was the widder Fosse."

28

"Well, what do you know?" Mary-Ann Niles cackled when she heard the news. "I outlasted him." At sixty-four she had lost only a little of her sass and just one of her lungs. The eternal comedienne, her latest line was that her new audition piece was going to be "Poor Mary One Lung," after Rodgers and Hart's "Poor Johnny One Note."

She never would get to spend the $15,000 that Bob left her. A week after he collapsed and died in Washington, Mary-Ann herself slipped away while sitting at her little bar in apartment 2B at 347 West 55th Street. She had always insisted that her friends call it "Mary's Bar" and that was where she was found on October 3, 1987, sitting dead, still upright on the barstool, her head resting down on an arm. She had never taken off her wedding band.

Five nights later, *Star 80* was televised on the ABC network. It had been sharply edited by Fosse himself, stripped of its fury and pain. He had felt an obligation to repay Alan Ladd, Jr. for having had faith in the movie. The least he could do, he said, was help get back some of the lost money, and besides, if he didn't edit it for television, someone else might butcher it. It was a sensible and decent thing for him to do, for a last thing.

Gwen's editing of Bob's life began almost immediately. Having never been divorced, she could now abandon the pose of "best friend." She was indisputably the widow. Stanley Donen called it "a whole Jacqueline Susann, taking over his life after death. It reeked of melodrama."

It might have been more than melodrama, even more than the resurrection of a marriage. Gwen Verdon was a dancer; that was the first and central fact of her life. That, perhaps, was why Bob's choreography now became her first concern and why his life after death was going to be recast in dance terms. Perhaps that was her reward for keeping her love to herself and suffering a dancer's pain during all the years of humiliating infidelity and painful separation. Albert Hague, the composer of *Redhead*, had noticed from the very start of their marriage that she "was totally, irrevocably in love with him. It was a love story." Now Herb Gardner, whose first career had been as a cartoonist, drew a picture of a woman leaning against a clock and gave it to Gwen. The caption read, "Don't tell me the time unless I ask you."

Bob's friends and sycophants closed ranks behind her. It was as if there had been no other life, no other women, and the fantasy that probably had sustained Gwen Verdon through the past fifteen years finally became the reality. It was as if, in a movie fan magazine from Bob's old Hollywood, where she had actually grown up, this celebrated couple was now perfect, the dancer and her choreographer, happy at work and at home.

Death is for the living. Sacrificed to Gwen's reinvented marriage and to her official status as the widow was the mean beauty of Bob Fosse's life: his drive from innocent talent to seek after an ingenuous dream of screen stardom; the heartsore depression that nearly undid him, darkening his spirit so that he might develop complexity as a man and maturity as an artist. Sacrificed was what he had become, a creative being of consequence and a modern man of shadow, texture, and energy to contribute to the human pool. He had exploited his life, which was why he had been so appalled by the notion of death. A man not always certain of his manliness, and in that, manly, he was representative of his time in both the healthiest and the most neurotic of ways—on the one hand, productive and, on the other, convinced of his own fraudulence.

Even sacrificed to Gwen's fantasy was the real relationship between herself and Bob, a mutually respectful bond that paradoxically was severed and yet never broken, a powerful human relationship between a man and a woman who were artistic and emotional mirror images. Her need for privacy reflected his for publicity, her warmth reflected his coolness. But she had waited a lifetime for this transcendence, to justify the breach. No longer limited now to being a man-made star, a chief concubine, or a dance mistress, she was free to serve her choreographer. She could fulfill the role for which she might have been destined from the first step taken in her mother's Denishawn dance school in Culver City. Now she could become the keeper of the flame, the dancer spread-eagled on the choreographer's grave.

Bob's bequest of "dinner on me" was an original idea that would make him a sport not just to the end but beyond it. He had a bone dread of unoriginality but just now he was unavailable for comment while that idea was being subverted and his individual dinner treats were being turned into an ordinary death party.

There was at least one on his bequest list—Stuart Ostrow—who felt that the reason Gwen and Sam disobeyed the provision was because they wanted to add more people to the list (the real beneficiaries were sent copies of the rider with a complete roster of names). It was possible, too, that Gwen and Sam wanted to create a memorial event in which they could play a part. Cathy Nicholas, Bob's last secretary, was enlisted to telephone everyone named in the provision and to ask whether their bequests might be applied to a dinner party at the Tavern on the Green, to which they were urgently invited on October 30, 1987, following a memorial program that was to be held in the afternoon in a Broadway theatre. In some cases, Gwen made the calls herself, describing "a party the way Bobby would have wanted," which was not quite accurate. Some, perhaps the ones she felt less comfortable with—Saul Chaplin for instance—were notified by letter. The usually easygoing Hollywood composer interpreted Gwen's note to mean, "She's taking over."

Among the many who were not invited to the dinner was Charles Grass. The former Riff Brother still lived in Chicago, in the same house on West Warner Avenue where he had lived when he and Bob first teamed up under the management of Frederic Weaver. It was dawn, and everyone in that house was asleep as Charles inserted a blank tape cassette into a recording machine. He pressed the red button and began to whisper, so as not to disturb anyone, "It's been a month since Bob passed away, and maybe it'd be a good idea to record some of the interesting anecdotes that we went through, Bob and I, many years—oh, gosh, fifty years—ago when I was eight and he was nine, and my mom and I used to pick him up to go on club dates. . . ."

At fifty-nine, Charles Grass was a pipe fitter for a construction company. He sometimes wondered what might have been had he quit high school and turned professional as Bob had urged, but even now he feared that his fellow workers at the construction company would think him less of a man if they ever found out that he had once *danced*. "Possibly," he whispered into his cassette tape recorder, "in this day and age, if we were teenagers in high school, our peers would think nothing of what we were doing in the professional field of show business. But whether it was a charade or just protecting ourselves, I guess the charade is over."

A number of the people named in Bob's will were not well enough known to have been mentioned in the newspapers (which of course had got hold of the provision, wills being matters of public record). Liz Canney, for instance, was on the list, and Bob's dance assistant, Christopher Chadman, and Paddy's widow Susan and Sam Cohn's wife Julia Miles, and his assistant Arlene Donovan, and Kathy Doby, Dr. Edwin

Ettinger, Phil Friedman, producer Robert Fryer, film editor Alan Heim, drama teacher Sanford Meisner, cinematographers Sven Nykvist (*Star 80*) and Giuseppe Rotunno (*All That Jazz*), actress Leland Palmer, Bob's psychiatrist, Dr. Clifford Sager, and Herbert Schlein of the Carnegie Delicatessen.

Now Gwen stood at the entrance to the Palace, the theatre where she had met Schlein on the opening night of *Sweet Charity*, and there she greeted her husband's mourners as the bereaved widow. Dressed darkly, her hair as red as legend had it, she smiled graciously and personally welcomed the fifteen hundred or so filing into the theatre. Neither Bernie Jacobs nor Gerald Schoenfeld were among them. Herb Gardner had telephoned the offices of the Shubert Organization at Gwen's behest to leave a message that neither the two executives nor anyone else from the office would be welcome.

She was exercising other prerogatives, such as asking Gardner to alter a short film that Stanley Donen had painstakingly prepared for the memorial. Although Donen was a major Hollywood director, Gardner cut his film without asking permission. Donen was furious when he learned about it upon arriving to take his place among the eulogizers.

"No actors were onstage," Bob's stage manager Phil Friedman noticed disapprovingly. "No dancers either and no dancing." The dancers in *Sweet Charity* had volunteered to perform the Fosse Combinations, which would have been appropriate and even thrilling, but Gwen mysteriously declined. It was her decision too that only men speak for a Bob Fosse whose life had been so involved with women. The speakers were to include E. L. Doctorow, Steve Tesich, Peter Stone, Noel Behn, Peter Maas, Pete Hamill, Herb Gardner, and Neil Simon. Other than Donen and Cy Coleman and several musical performers, the only nonwriter appearing would be Roy Scheider.

"It was curious," Joel Grey felt, "that there were no other actors." And of course even Scheider was not really there as an actor. He was there as Bob Fosse.

When Kim St. Leon arrived at the theatre, Gwen introduced her to Bob's sister, Marianne Dimos, the only member of the immediate family who was present. His brother Ed was too ill to come and, a few months later, would be the last of the Fosse boys to die of heart disease. Kim and Marianne walked down the aisle and sat together, the matron from Evanston, Illinois, and the movie bit player from Dade County, Florida. As they took their seats in the filling theatre, Marianne reminisced about Amundsen High and the swimming team, the track team, the variety shows, Bob's election as class president, and his graduation speech. It was probably the only conversation in the entire theatre about Bob's life before he became Bob Fosse, and it startled Kim, who told Marianne, "Bob led me to believe that he had this awful childhood as a loner, and here he'd been the all-American boy."

Stanley Donen's truncated film opened with snapshots of Bob's career as Bob Riff and then moved to clips from *Sweet Charity*, *Cabaret*, *Lenny*, *All That Jazz*, and the "Snake in the Grass" dance from *The Little Prince*. Missing were Bob's early MGM movies that Donen had directed. John Kander sat down at the piano, and Fred Ebb told the hushed audience about Fosse's love for percussive sound effects. Ebb said nothing of the agony he'd been put through by a moody Bob Fosse fresh from a heart bypass operation.

> What if your hinges all are rusting?
> What if, in fact, you're just disgusting?
> Razzle-dazzle 'em
> And they'll never catch wise

Noel Behn remembered the stroll along 57th Street when all the guys bet on who would be recognized first. He called Fosse "Bobby," as would most of the speakers, as Cy Coleman did while remembering "Bobby's love of vamps, drum catches, especially the rim shots and eccentric rhythms." But, Coleman added, "he hated ballads, especially the ones he thought to be long and drawn out." To the melody of his own "Real Live Girl," from *Little Me*, Coleman then played and sang a parody lyric (by David Zippel) that he said Fosse had enjoyed.

> Pardon me Cy
> But we've just said good-bye
> To your fav'rite song

Stanley Donen talked about filming *Give a Girl a Break* and forcing Bob to learn how to do a back flip although "his dancing was very delicate and small." Even now, Donen didn't realize how much Bob had loved doing that back flip and how many times he had done it before growing too old and trying it once too late and falling on his face.

E. L. Doctorow remembered the Dancing for Writers class and the "Broadway" sweatshirt that had been given for a birthday present along with a pair of dance shoes. The novelist seemed to be trying to sound very show biz, but his literariness transcended that as he recounted a story that Anatole France wrote about a Fosselike juggler named Barnabas who became a monk. Among the writers on stage, Doctorow alone sounded writerly.

> This was an order devoted to the celebration of the Holy Virgin and at Christmas . . . out of desperation . . . [Barnabas] proceeded to juggle his plate on the tip of his nose and catch his six copper balls with his feet and throw his twelve knives in the shape of a wheel. . . . Some of the brothers thought he was committing a sacrilege . . . but . . . the Holy Virgin came down from her pedestal and with her mantle wiped the sweat from the juggler's brow.

Herb Gardner reminisced about how he, Paddy, and Bobby used to call themselves 'Whimsy,' 'Boredom,' and 'Flash.' He remembered Fosse's heart surgeon dropping the pen in the hospital room and the private demonstration of the Snake number from *The Little Prince*. He talked about "Gwen Verdon—the miraculous Gwen, Bobby's very best friend."

Neil Simon was the last speaker, evoking a Fosse dancing "Real Live Girl." He laughed again about Bob "fainting" when Sid Caesar blew his punch lines in *Little Me*, and he remembered the long-running Ping-Pong contest to determine which of them, born just eleven days apart, "was to be designated the youngest forever. He and I finally sat down over a glass of wine," Simon concluded, "and reminisced about our lives. . . . He looked at me with a big smile on his face and said to me so sweetly and sincerely, 'It was great wasn't it?' And Bob won the game. He'll be the youngest forever," for Simon was already older.

"It was as if Bob was orchestrating it," Roy Scheider said of the party at the Tavern on the Green. The setting could not have been more spectacular, and Gwen stood at the doorway to the sprawling restaurant's biggest and best dining room, the Crystal Room. Once again as at the Palace Theatre, she greeted the guests, shaking hands with everyone and kissing the people she knew. It was a diverse group, diversely dressed, some wearing evening clothes, others in jeans or dance tights. Ben Vereen wore his black vaudevillian outfit from *Pippin* and *All That Jazz*. John Rubinstein showed up in a turtleneck, Phoebe Ungerer in a black mini-dress, and Sam Cohn, as usual, wore an old sweater. Chris Chase was spiffy in a long black skirt with a white silk blouse, and just behind her, the tuxedoed Buddy Hackett was sniffing for the cigarette smoke that he found all but intolerable.

Warner Leroy, Bob's friend and the owner of the Tavern on the Green, was smoothly enforcing Gwen's request to keep the press out, but someone always managed to slip through, and Hackett already had a remark prepared. "I don't think Dustin Hoffman should get the same share of the will as me," he said. "I eat a lot more than he does," but Hoffman wasn't there.

When Kim St. Leon arrived, she kissed Gwen on the cheek and whispered, "You did something wonderful for me at the hospital [interceding in the battle with Ann Reinking], and I never had the chance to thank you." Gwen smiled and closed her eyes for a moment as if she had just heard a touching reminiscence.

The ten-man Jerry Kravat band was playing for dancing, and in the garden outside, a magician and a juggler could be seen through the French windows, skinny apparitions in black Fosse costumes with white gloves and dark derbies.

Derbies were the decorative motif. At each place setting there was a miniature gift derby tilted against a wineglass as well as a Lucite magic wand and a battery-operated metal box that, when opened, resounded with whistles, cheers, and applause. Later, the dessert would be chocolate cake made in the shape of a derby.

There were no place cards, and none of the fifteen tables was reserved. Silver candelabra were lifting the candles to glow over bouquets of yellow, blue, and pink flowers, and it was into this setting of elegant candlelight reflected in the crystal chandeliers and the thousand windowpanes of the glassed-in restaurant that the guests began to arrive shortly after eight o'clock.

Coming as the guests did from different parts of Bob's life, many knew nobody, and some scanned the room to stare at the famous performers, the costumes, the whole idea of this party, perhaps a little awed at being there themselves. As Neil Simon would say, "It was such a glamorous party that I was the only person there I never heard of."

Fosse's various girlfriends gossiped like sorority sisters: Jennifer Nairn-Smith, Ann Reinking, Kim St. Leon, Liz Canney, Phoebe Ungerer. "When Phoebe showed up at the party," Kathy Doby remembered, "neither Gwen nor Nicole would talk to her the whole night, and she was in tears."

Dr. Edwin Ettinger came with his wife and sat down to watch with his customary disbelief. "I've never seen anything *like* it," he said. "To have choreographed your own funeral party. Those *people*, that *party*, it was *amazing*."

As the crowd of some 150 was finally seated, they were served the first of the courses, the first of the wines. There were to be no formal speeches, but inevitably the conversations turned to Fosse. At Chris Chase's table, for instance, Kim was saying, "The most amazing thing about Bobby was that, even after you weren't his girlfriend anymore, he was always your friend. He would call from time to time just to see how I was doing."

Herb Schlein was also remembering telephone calls as, with his usual courtliness, he engaged his table companions in conversation. Schlein was sitting with Elia Kazan and Sanford Meisner. "Bob would call me early in the morning," he told the fabled director. The wizened acting teacher had grown hard of hearing and kept asking Schlein to repeat himself. Herb shouted, "*Bob would just say, 'Hello, this is Bob Fosse'!*"

Stuart and Annie Ostrow were seated with Alan and Alison Heim. Stuart and Alan had *All That Jazz* in common, the movie that had begun as Ostrow's *Ending*. "You know," the producer said, "Bob always said that you edited his life," which touched Heim because "Bob had never conceded," he said, "that the movie was about him."

Across the room, as Sanford Meisner leaned over and tried to hear, Herb Schlein told Elia Kazan, "MGM never gave Bobby a chance." At the moment, however, Schlein was thinking, "He was the only human being that I did have a little bit of friendship with. A *little* bit. And who was never mean to me. His body is gone, but the meaning he brought to my life is still there. That is alive."

John Rubinstein also had Bob in mind. "Ours was a very deep relationship that was never played out," he thought. "And it saddened me that he couldn't give me a fucking phone call while he was still on earth."

Chris Chase was telling Kim St. Leon that she too had known Bob to keep in touch. She had once received flowers with the note, "These are for no special reason. Just thinking of you." The signature was "Bob Fosse," in case she didn't know which "Bob" it was. And one of his dancers remarked, "He gave you the feeling he wouldn't turn against you even if you refused to be his lover. If he liked you, he liked you."

Abruptly, Ben Vereen rose in his seat and, borrowing the line from *All That Jazz*, announced, "It's show time!" He strode to the dance floor and began to slither the way Bob used to, and as he did, other dancers rose and made their ways to join him, Gwen, Nicole, Ann Reinking, Jennifer Nairn-Smith, Kathy Doby, Graciela Daniele—but women only. They formed a circle around Vereen, and then Gwen urged Bob's writer friends onto the floor so that they might enter the circle of women and with clumsy good cheer demonstrate the few steps they'd learned at Bob's Dancing for Writers class.

Stanley Donen got up and, leaving Sidney Lumet at the table with Tony and Gen Walton, walked to the edge of the dance floor to watch the dancers taking solo turns. Then, it was just Gwen, Nicole, and Ann Reinking within the circle, the three women closest to Fosse—"Bob's girls," John Rubinstein called them.

The bandleader, Jerry Kravat, took the cue and intensified the beat into a disco rhythm. Gwen, Nicole, and Ann naturally slipped into grind dancing, their eyes closed, their hips rolling, their arms snaking upward. They moved inward and closer to each other. "They were hugging each other," Rubinstein remembered. "Three dancers, and each in her own generation. They weren't just dancing and giggling, being sexy and girlish; they were all being *hot performers*, they were doing that, swiveling their hips. They were being *hot with each other*, an ex-wife and a girlfriend and a daughter—in a complex, almost demented relationship."

Buddy Hackett got up and left, more annoyed by the celebration of death than by the cigarette smoke. He wasn't the only one to be disturbed by a sense of inappropriateness. Budd Schulberg considered it "strange to celebrate death at a social event" and hadn't even come.

Bob's orchestrator Ralph Burns watched mesmerized as the beat grew still lustier, luring all the dancers onto the floor to work themselves into what he called a "ritual dance." Rubinstein thought, "When dancers dance for fun, they tend to dance more fully than the rest of us, and Bob was allowing that to happen in a sexual kind of way." Like many at the party, he talked as if Fosse were actually there.

"And then," Ralph Burns remembered, "*everyone* joined in, the whole crowd. It was flip-out time. Till then everyone was well behaved. Now they just let go. It was like Bobby was directing the whole scene."

Donen thought much the same as he stared transfixed at the crowd of gyrating dancers, and with the room throbbing, seemingly entranced, and with the music pulsating and the thump of feet and the sway, Roy Scheider appeared almost magically beside him, and Donen thought, "My God! I'm watching this with Fosse's ghost."

Turning to the actor, he said, "Now this should be the end of the movie."

MARTIN GOTTFRIED has been the chief drama critic for *Women's Wear Daily*, the New York *Post*, and *Saturday Review*. *Time* magazine said, "He brings to his reviews a vital knowledge of the theater's past and an alertness to the world around him. In any ranking, Martin Gottfried belongs with the best." His first book, A *Theater Divided*, won the prestigious George Jean Nathan Award for Dramatic Criticism. His *Broadway Musicals* is now in its eighth printing with a sequel (*More Broadway Musicals*) forthcoming. His biography, *Jed Harris: The Curse of Genius*, was hailed by *The New York Times* Book Review as one of the Most Notable Books of 1984 and is scheduled to be made into a feature film. He lives in New York City and Amagansett, New York, with his daughter, Maya.

INDEX